After Parsons

After Parsons

A Theory of Social Action for the Twenty-First Century

Renée C. Fox
Victor M. Lidz
Harold J. Bershady
Editors

Russell Sage Foundation
New York

The Russell Sage Foundation

The Russell Sage Foundation, one of the oldest of America's general purpose foundations, was established in 1907 by Mrs. Margaret Olivia Sage for "the improvement of social and living conditions in the United States." The Foundation seeks to fulfill this mandate by fostering the development and dissemination of knowledge about the country's political, social, and economic problems. While the Foundation endeavors to assure the accuracy and objectivity of each book it publishes, the conclusions and interpretations in Russell Sage Foundation publications are those of the authors and not of the Foundation, its Trustees, or its staff. Publication by Russell Sage, therefore, does not imply Foundation endorsement.

Library of Congress Cataloging-in-Publication Data

After Parsons—a theory of social action for the 21st century / edited by Renée C. Fox, Victor Lidz, and Harold J. Bershady.
p. cm.
Includes bibliographical references and index.
ISBN 0-87154-269-2
1. Social action—Congresses. 2. Sociology—Congresses. 3. Parsons, Talcott, 1902—Congresses. I. Fox, Renée C. (Renée Claire), 1928- II. Lidz, Victor M. III. Bershady, Harold J.

HM585.A45 2005
302'.14—dc22

2005042898

The paper used in this publication meets the minimum requirements of American National Standard for Information Sciences—Permanence of Paper for Printed Library Materials. ANSI Z39.48-1992.

Text design by Genna Patacsil.

RUSSELL SAGE FOUNDATION
112 East 64th Street, New York, New York 10021
10 9 8 7 6 5 4 3 2 1

The editors dedicate this book to the memory of two beloved members of the Human Condition Seminar, Talcott Parsons and Willy De Craemer

Contents

Contributors

RENÉE C. FOX is the Annenberg Professor Emerita of the Social Sciences and senior fellow at the Center for Bioethics at the University of Pennsylvania, and research associate at Queen Elizabeth House at the University of Oxford.

VICTOR M. LIDZ is assistant professor in the Department of Psychiatry at Drexel University College of Medicine.

HAROLD J. BERSHADY is professor emeritus of sociology at the University of Pennsylvania.

JEFFREY C. ALEXANDER is the Lillian Chavenson Professor of Sociology at Yale University and co-director of the Center for Cultural Sociology.

ROBERT N. BELLAH is Elliott Professor of Sociology, Emeritus, at the University of California, Berkeley.

CHARLES CAMIC is Martindale-Bascom Professor of Sociology at the University of Wisconsin, Madison.

UTA GERHARDT is professor of sociology at the University of Heidelberg, Germany.

MARK GOULD is professor of sociology at Haverford College.

DONALD N. LEVINE is the Peter B. Ritzma Professor of Sociology at the University of Chicago.

GIUSEPPE SCIORTINO is associate professor of sociology at the Università degli studi di Trento, Italy.

NEIL J. SMELSER is University Professor Emeritus of Sociology at the University of California, Berkeley, and director emeritus of the Center for Advanced Study in the Behavioral Sciences at Stanford University.

HELMUT STAUBMANN is associate professor in the Department of Sociology at the University of Innsbruck.

JEREMY TANNER is lecturer in Greek and Roman art and archaeology and coordinator of the Graduate Programme in Comparative Art at the Institute of Archaeology, University College London.

EDWARD A. TIRYAKIAN is professor emeritus of sociology at Duke University.

HARALD WENZEL is professor of sociology at the John F. Kennedy-Institute for North American Studies of the Free University, Berlin.

Preface

The chapters in this volume were written for a conference held on December 6 to 7, 2002, at the Russell Sage Foundation in New York City, to mark the hundredth anniversary of the birth of the eminent twentieth-century American sociologist Talcott Parsons.

When we approached the president of the Russell Sage Foundation, Eric Wanner, about the possibility of holding a centennial conference in Parsons's honor under the Foundation's auspices, we encountered no hesitancy. He found it entirely fitting that such an intellectual event should take place, and that the principal foundation devoted exclusively to research in the social sciences should help to support it. We are grateful for the funding, the meeting place, and the logistical help that the Russell Sage Foundation provided. Above all, we value the testimonial significance of its assistance and collaboration.

Our organization of the centennial conference was not primarily an act of nostalgia, sentimentality, or filial piety. To be sure, most of the conference participants felt connected to Parsons as a teacher, mentor, colleague, associate, interlocutor, or friend. Those who had not experienced such a professional or personal relationship nevertheless viewed Parsons as a major intellectual figure with whom they felt strongly linked through his prolific published work, which they had studied intensively over many years. Yet this gathering was not intended to be merely a celebration of his scholarship or a review and ratification of his opus. Rather, in the spirit of Parsons himself, who throughout his lifetime continually rethought and reformulated his theoretical ideas in order to place them on more solid foundations, extend their scope, and strengthen their empirical insights, our goal was a critical reconsideration. We sought to make a fresh examination of his theoretical undertaking, its significance for social scientific thought, and its implications for present-day empirical research in the light of current scholarship and historical events. In the proposal we sent to invited participants, we suggested that in this spirit of reexamination, the conference might focus on the emphasis Parsons placed on the normative basis of social institutions throughout his writings. In all other respects we encouraged the contributors to choose their own topics and set their own agendas.

The authors of the chapters assembled in this volume span several generations and nationalities. There were American, Austrian, English, German, and Italian participants. All possess detailed knowledge of the corpus of Parsons's work, and of the key analytic movements through which his theoretical system passed as his thought evolved. Although the issues and phenomena on which the contributors' own work has centered are heterogeneous, together they constitute a cross-section of some of Parsons's foremost conceptual and empirical interests and concerns.

In drawing up a list of prospective participants, we were mindful of the circles of foreign sociologists, particularly in Germany and Japan, who are serious and appreciative scholars of Parsons's theory. Several Germans and Austrians accepted our invitation to attend and write papers for the conference. However, it was not possible for the Japanese sociologists to whom we extended invitations to do so, because they were already involved in organizing and taking part in two conferences in honor of Talcott Parsons's centennial that were held in Japan in December 2002, In Tokyo and Kobe. The Tokyo conference took place on the same days as the Russell Sage conference, and the one in Kobe, on December 14 and 15. (Harold Bershady, Victor

Lidz, Helmut Staubmann, and Harald Wenzel attended the Kobe conference as American and European representatives.) What these conferences indicate is that despite the ostensible waning of Parsons's influence in recent decades, a vibrant international circle of sociologists has emerged whose members maintain a keen and creative connection with his ideas and writings, and with each other.

Talcott Parsons's pragmatic openness to new ideas, his curiosity and sense of wonder; his astute observations of everyday life, social interaction, social institutions, and culture patterns; his concern about important social and political issues of his own times; and the ways that he wove scholarly knowledge together with empirical facts were qualities that infused all the papers presented at the Russell Sage conference, and the vigorous discussion of them. The conference was also pervaded by the sort of intellectual commentary and criticism that Parsons encouraged in his relations with students and colleagues. For the participants it was, as Parsons once described another occasion, "the kind of memorable experience of intellectual effervescence" to which he attached great value.

One of the most striking characteristics of the conference was the degree to which the papers drafted for it and the discussion they evoked coalesced around certain grand themes in Parsons's thought that emerged spontaneously as the central preoccupations of those attending: his concepts and treatment of the "societal community," the "human condition," societal evolution, and modernization and modernity. Branching out from these topics were several subthemes, including social differentiation and cultural diversity, social solidarity, universalism and particularism, and the dimensions of trust and affect in social life. They were explored in the context of a wide range of social institutions—family and kinship, the economy, polity, and the law, medicine, art, and religion—within the historical, comparative, cultural, and cross-cultural analytic perspective that Parsons's work exemplified and fostered.

Although Robert Bellah, Samuel N. Eisenstadt, and Neil Smelser were unable to attend the conference, their papers had been read and pondered by the participants before the meeting occurred, and were discussed extensively. Several papers excited great interest, but we were unable to include them in this volume. They were Eisenstadt's "Parsons' Vision of Social Change and Evolution," on Parsons's comparative and evolutionary analysis (accepted for publication in *Society*); "Some Remarks on Talcott Parsons's Family," a presentation made by Parsons's son, the philosopher Charles Parsons, based on his original research on the family's lineage, heritage, and ethos (to be published in a forthcoming issue of *The American Sociologist*); "The Resilience of Modernity: Parsons and the Problem of Islamism," Frank J. Lechner's speculative treatment of the bearing that Parsons's thought on "the resilience of modernity" as an "evolving global reality" might have on the challenge and "threat" to Western conceptions of modernizing change posed by the spread of violent forms of Islamism; and Jonathan Shay's "Action Systems in Nature," in which he presents his thinking about human action systems as evolving parts of nature, in part an outgrowth of his work with psychologically injured combat veterans.

We would be inexcusably remiss if we failed to include in these prefatory comments our great appreciation for the role that Eric Wanner and the staff of the Russell Sage Foundation played in making the Foundation's handsome conference room available to us; helping us to manage the logistics of convening the participants in the conference; maintaining a flow of communication between them; assembling, reproducing, and dispatching their papers; and surrounding us with the tasteful, warmly hospitable atmosphere in which our meeting unfolded. We are especially grateful for the meticulous and intelligent assistance that we received from Program Associate Bindu Chadaga. We also want to thank the two anonymous reviewers of the manuscripts on which the chapters in this volume are based for their astute comments and suggestions. Finally, this book owes much to Suzanne Nichols, director of publications of the

Russell Sage Foundation, whose candor and insights about individual chapters and the volume as a whole contributed immeasurably to the volume's quality, and also to Genna Patacsil, who directed the production of the book with skill, taste, and an uncommon ability to influence its editors and authors to meet deadlines.

We acknowledge the help of our esteemed late colleague Willy De Craemer, S.J., Ph.D., who suggested our title.

Renée C. Fox
Victor M. Lidz
Harold J. Bershady

Introduction

Renée C. Fox, Victor M. Lidz, and Harold J. Bershady

From the 1930s to the mid-1960s, Talcott Parsons was the leading contributor to the development of sociological theory, in the United States and internationally. More than any other contemporary figure, he shaped the conceptual schemes used in research, the bodies of theory taught to students, and thinking about the issues requiring investigation at the frontiers of sociological knowledge. In some dozen books and hundreds of essays, he elaborated an unfolding theoretical system that not only had a far-reaching, formative influence on sociological thought and research but also extended to other social sciences, including economics, political science, anthropology, psychology, and psychoanalysis. His writings were studied, discussed, critiqued, and applied in empirical research throughout the world. Parsons also had a pervasive influence as the teacher of several generations of students from an array of countries and disciplines, many of whom became notable in fields not confined to sociology or the social sciences. As Leon Mayhew wrote in his introduction to a volume of Parsons's selected writings, "Talcott Parsons is regarded, by admirers and critics alike, as a major creator of the sociological thought of our time" (Mayhew 1982, 1). In the view of Jürgen Habermas, the German philosopher and social theorist, Parsons's work is "without parallel in its level of abstraction and differentiation, its social theoretical scope and systematic quality. . . . [N]o theory of society can be taken seriously today if it does not at least situate itself with respect to Parsons" (Habermas 1987, 199).

During the past four decades, interest in and acknowledgment of Parsons's enormous contributions to the framework of social-scientific thought and to programs of social inquiry has greatly diminished. In part, this development has been a consequence of ideological confrontations between radical and liberal thinkers that affected the social sciences during the 1960s and 1970s, and the polemical spin-offs from them in which Parsons has frequently been labeled, contrary to his own self-understanding, a conservative thinker, an apologist for American culture, institutions, and national power, and a defender of gender relationships as they existed before the emergence of the feminist movement in the 1970s. It has also been associated with the resurgence of positivistic or scientistic conceptions of sociological research, with the emergence of increasing numbers of topically defined areas of specialization as the foci of sociologists' interests and efforts, and with the fragmentation of the discipline into competing schools of thought that have been preoccupied more with what separates them than with what might bridge their conceptual and empirical differences, or integrate their understandings. The sheer complexity and abstract quality of Parsons's thought as well as the density of his writing are without doubt off-putting to many sociologists, especially now that he is no longer a personal presence in the leadership of the profession. As a result of these converging forces, sociology has largely turned away from the conviction, basic to Parsons's theoretical efforts, that the development of a shared conceptual framework is not only a viable endeavor, but one essential to progress in sociology as in other intellectual disciplines.

Even before these developments, but more frequently in recent decades, Parsons has been labeled a "grand theorist" and compared to such methodologically outdated builders of comprehensive theories as Auguste Comte and Herbert Spencer. However, such an interpretation mischaracterizes his undertaking as a theorist. He consistently sought to develop conceptual schemes or frames of reference to facilitate empirical investigation. Following the philosopher Alfred North Whitehead (1925), he viewed the establishment of frames of reference as a logically preliminary task for orienting empirical research, including the phase of empirical research that involves generating hypotheses to be tested (Parsons 1937). He saw his own distinctive contribution as clarifying frames of reference and explicating their implications for generating hypotheses and propositional theories to guide research, as well as interpreting empirical findings of research. Although he participated directly in only a small number of empirical studies himself, many of his most creative essays involved theory-based reinterpretations of the empirical studies of other social scientists, ranging from Max Weber to Paul Lazarsfeld (Parsons 1949, 1953, 1967, 1969, 1977, 1978). Moreover, many of his students and protégés, including authors of chapters in this volume, conducted important empirical studies framed by his concepts and propositions—studies that he read, acknowledged, and drew on.

Throughout his career, Parsons's central concern was to develop a comprehensive and coherent conceptual scheme for sociology that could be applied to every society and historical epoch, and address every aspect of human social organization. This concern provides unity to his extraordinarily diverse theoretical and empirical writings. Writings on specific empirical situations were also, for Parsons, means of applying, testing, and refining basic concepts. Whatever his substantive topic, his underlying interest was in the basic conceptual scheme that he called the "theory of social action."

Parsons's conceptual scheme was designed to be open and supple—to be progressively refined in response to advancing empirical knowledge. Parsons revised many of his formulations on the basis of insights gained from the empirical and theoretical reports of others. Even his most abstract theorizing was basically related to empirical situations and empirical studies. Parsons was also uniquely committed to technical elaboration of his conceptual scheme and to precision in formulating his ideas. However, this commitment to progressive development of theory has created difficulties for scholars who wish to understand, interpret, and critique his theories. The changes he made in major formulations at certain points in his career and the frequency with which he altered subordinate concepts have made mastery of his large body of work difficult.

Before introducing the chapters, written by social scientists who gathered to mark the centennial of Parsons's birth, we want to provide intellectual context for them by presenting an overview of Parsons's chief theoretical ideas and the major metamorphoses they underwent. Our focus is on ideas that we believe carry enduring importance for sociology and thus remain fundamental to the discipline, with a special emphasis on concepts that were utilized by the authors of the chapters in this volume.[1]

AN OVERVIEW OF THE THEORY OF ACTION

Parsons's expansive understanding of the mandate for theory in the development of a "scientific" sociology was based on sophisticated methodological views. These were rooted in seminars on Kant that he had taken during his undergraduate and graduate studies, and came to fruition under the influence of Alfred North Whitehead (1925), whose philosophy of science he encountered during his early years on the Harvard faculty.

Calling his methodology "analytical realism," he attributed its key ideas to Whitehead. In analytical realism, the frame of reference is the crucial theoretical element for the creation of knowledge. A frame of reference is the set of master categories, or concepts, that define the characteristics of a field of objects to be studied. In Parsons's theory, the "action frame of reference" is a set of concepts that defines meaningful human behavior (or action) as a domain for methodical investigation and accumulation of knowledge (Parsons 1937). Parsons emphasized the logical priority of a frame of reference to empirical observation and procedures for validating factual knowledge, because the frame of reference sets the terms for integrating an understanding of objects and events. Without a well-defined conceptual scheme, empirical knowledge cannot integrate the reality it seeks to represent, but leaves that reality fragmented. The progress of a science toward more penetrating and comprehensive empirical understanding thus depends on methodical elaboration of a central frame of reference.

Parsons first proposed a general conceptual scheme for the analysis of social action in an early masterwork, *The Structure of Social Action* (Parsons 1937), which presented a comprehensive, well-integrated, and yet elementary frame of reference that departed radically from the empiricist and positivist approaches that predominated in American sociology. He introduced his conceptual scheme by a critique of leading European economists and sociologists of the generation that bridged the late nineteenth and early twentieth centuries: Max Weber, Émile Durkheim, Vilfredo Pareto, and Alfred Marshall. The "action frame of reference" was proposed as a synthesis of core premises and categories that, Parsons argued, are fundamental to all sociological understanding. He did not suggest that the frame of reference was complete or that it constituted a precise theory. Rather, he justified it as a well-balanced framework of basic concepts essential to the future development of more technical theory. His bold claims for the action frame of reference and each of its categories were supported empirically by a methodical review of the evidence amassed in Weber's studies in comparative civilization and religion, and in Durkheim's major works.

The action frame of reference centered on the idea of the "unit act" as a hypothetical entity representing any and all instances of meaningful human social behavior. Parsons defined the essential elements of the unit act as ends, means, norms, and conditions. In his view, these four categories of elements (and in some statements a less clearly explained fifth element, a "principle" of effort) are essential to all social action, regardless of time, place, or socio-cultural context (Parsons 1937). Every instance of social action contains exemplars of each element.

In developing the notion of the unit act, Parsons emphasized treating the normative element (meaning the rules of conduct and underlying values that regulate human behavior) of social action with the same conceptual weight as the more familiar elements of ends and means. An emphasis on studying the normative elements of social action, and on understanding the ways in which values and norms, when institutionalized, become structural to society, characterized Parsons's work throughout his career. Among the theorists of his own time, Parsons is distinctive in the degree to which he placed normative elements at the center of sociological phenomena.

Parsons limited the scheme of *The Structure of Social Action* to fundamental concepts in order to concentrate on justifying its underlying premises and each of its elements. The justification involved detailed critiques of the complete works, as then available, of Marshall, Pareto, Durkheim, and Weber, with a focus on implications for social-scientific premises and concepts. Parsons (1937) argued that his discussions of the four turn-of-the-century figures demonstrated that though each had written from a different intellectual background, they had "converged" on common concepts—concepts that coincide with the action frame of reference.

In particular, he demonstrated that each had emphasized normative elements as well as means, ends, and conditions.

Parsons's treatments of these four figures became touchstones for critical literature in the social sciences. Nearly seventy years later, they remain starting points for assessment of these theorists. The lengthy discussions of Weber and Durkheim remain particularly influential because of their analytical depth and rigor, even though much more is known today than was then about the two men's biographies, connections with other scholars, and ideological outlooks. The critical discussions of *The Structure of Social Action* have also played a major role in defining the core of the sociological tradition. The pairing of Weber and Durkheim as the predominant figures in the founding of modern sociological thought derives from the influence of *The Structure of Social Action* more than any other source.

Parsons argued that normative elements made it possible for ongoing social relationships to achieve a degree of social order. Social values (ideals for relationships and institutions) and norms (rules of conduct), insofar as they are shared by actors in specific institutions, serve to regulate their selections of goals and means to pursue goals. Values and norms thus constrain actors in their conduct in a sense not true of ends or means. His focus on shared elements of normative order enabled Parsons to probe the integration of social institutions in a manner not open to utilitarians, behaviorists, and other positivists who emphasize ends, means, and conditioning factors as the sole determinants of human behavior.

In 1951, Parsons published two major works, the essay "Values, Motives, and the Theory of Action," with Edward A. Shils (Parsons and Shils 1951), and *The Social System* (Parsons 1951) which together were revolutionary developments in his theory of action. The revolution began with a shift in the principal focus of the frame of reference from the unit act to interactive social relationships among actors and to the institutions that stabilize such relationships over space and time. With this conceptual shift, Parsons centered his sociological thought on the idea of social systems, where a social system is defined, simply, as a set of connected relationships maintained by social actors. At the same time Parsons sharpened his focus on the connections between social systems and other elements of human action. He placed the concept of social system in a broader context of two cross-cutting dimensions for analyzing patterns of differentiation among processes of action. The first dimension pertains to the tendency of ongoing systems of social action to differentiate into three independent but interdependent subsystems: culture, social systems, and personality. The idea of a threefold differentiation of action systems (later changed to a fourfold differentiation) became one of the most influential elements of Parsons's theory. The second dimension concerns a differentiation of elements of action among moral-normative, affective or cathectic, and cognitive gradients. Parsons proposed that cultural, social, and personality systems all differentiate along these three gradients (Parsons and Shils 1951; Parsons 1951). Moreover, they connect with each other along each of the three gradients, so that study of those connections is essential to understanding the general organization of action systems. Tracing out the two dimensions of differentiation and the relationships between them produced a far more detailed analytical scheme than Parsons had put forward in *The Structure of Social Action*. The new analytical scheme approached more closely a level of detail that would be practical for use in empirical studies.

The Social System was a major theoretical monograph that clarified basic issues of defining the concept of social system, introduced a general approach to functional analysis of social systems, and, in chapters that proved highly influential, discussed processes of socialization and personality development, the classic problems of deviance and social control, and the relations between social systems and cultural belief systems. Parsons illustrated the empirical significance of his theoretical arguments with a wide range of brief analyses that drew on his own prior writings as well as studies reported by other social scientists.

Analysis of differences between "traditional" and "modern" institutions and of the tensions involved in transitions from traditional to modern societies was a major empirical concern of *The Social System.* To help in relating his system concepts to this empirical interest, Parsons proposed what he called pattern variables. The pattern variables were a set of five dichotomies that are best understood as, together, breaking down the dichotomy between Gesellschaft and Gemeinschaft, familiar from the works of Ferdinand Tönnies, Georg Simmel, and Max Weber, into distinct analytical dimensions. The five pairs are universalism versus particularism, affective neutrality versus affectivity, achievement versus ascription (later stated as performance versus quality), specificity versus diffuseness, and self-orientation versus collectivity orientation. In each of these pairs, the first item characterizes Gesellschaft-type institutions, the second, Gemeinschaft-type institutions. In the 1950s and '60s, the pattern variables were used in many empirical studies and were among the most widely discussed of Parsons's concepts. Now they are less often used in a formal way, but several of the component terms have become deeply engrained in social-scientific terminology.

With the changes in theory of 1951, Parsons's conceptual scheme for sociology came to focus on abstracting the dynamics of interaction from the more comprehensive processes of meaningful human action or conduct. Sociology became the study of factors of interaction that maintain relationships in stable states (equilibria) or force relationships to change. Parsons again identified shared normative standards as a principal basis of stability and continuity in social relationships, but he cast the normative emphasis in more dynamic terms than previously, emphasizing the importance of normative expectations for specific role relationships and conditions of interaction. As they interact, individuals hold expectations of each other that are based on the specific social roles—employer or employee, doctor or patient, parent or child—that each of them occupies. Actors also support the expectations they hold of one another by employing a variety of sanctioning tactics. The sanctioning tactics typically include, implicitly and explicitly, offering rewards for compliance with expectations and threatening punishments for noncompliance—as well as actually providing rewards or imposing punishments in response to the conduct of the other after it has occurred. Parsons emphasized that concrete sequences of interaction are outcomes of the expectations and sanctions introduced by each party. He argued that a "double contingency" applies to even the most elementary relationships due to the independence of decisionmaking by each party.

In his conceptual scheme, the personalities of individual social actors are not parts of social systems, but rather another type or class of system of action. He thus had to address himself to the question of how social systems and personality systems relate to each other in the ongoing processes of social action. His characteristic emphasis on normative elements led him to focus on a linkage between the institutional norms of a society and the superegos of personalities (Parsons 1951, 1964a). He argued that the normative structures of a society and the superegos of its individual actors are made up of the same cultural content, but incorporated by different mechanisms in the two types of system. The content is internalized in the personality and institutionalized in the society. This formulation drew on dynamic ideas from psychological and psychoanalytic as well as sociological studies and applied them to an understanding of the relationships between "social structure" and "personality." Yet it avoided the temptation, to which others of the period had succumbed, to confound social dynamics with personality dynamics. By contrast, Parsons highlighted the notion of the "institutional integration of motivation," maintaining that the motivational systems of individual personalities can be coherent and directed to specific goals only insofar as they are supported by specific social institutions and relationships (Parsons 1951).

He also emphasized a reciprocal and more dynamic consideration shaping the relations between social systems and personalities. Social institutions can be sustained over time only if the individuals who take part in them are affectively invested in the social role relationships of which they are constituted. In brief, actors must be motivated to fulfill role expectations, or the underlying social institutions will be changed by "inadequate" role performances. Parsons's writings on socialization and on deviance and social control dealt with a wide range of the conditions that strengthen or weaken individuals' affective investments in the institutions in which they take part (Parsons 1951). Analysis of the flows of affect involved in interaction, role relationships, and institutions became one of his continuing theoretical and empirical concerns (Parsons 1964a; Parsons and Platt 1973; Parsons 1978).

The Social System also introduced Parsons's initial formulations in functional analysis. Parsons proposed that all social systems, whether simple dyads, complex institutions, or whole societies, must manage the two problems of resource allocation and social integration. Resource allocation involves establishing processes to help actors in various roles to command the means for attaining the ends expected of them. The nature of the resources in question varies according to the types of roles in question. Specific kinds of tools, personnel trained in various skills, and financial means are among the types of resources that are crucial. Parsons noted that economic markets are the most generalized and efficient mechanisms for allocating resources across the diverse needs of the many units of a society. The need for social integration is in the long run as urgent for social systems as the need for appropriate resources. Mechanisms of social control are necessary to ensure that actors respond to one another's expectations and fulfill role obligations in reciprocal, mutually reinforcing ways. Large-scale social systems require formal, in addition to informal, means of social control and dispute resolution, including courts, legal procedures, and modes of law enforcement.

Parsons recognized that processes of resource allocation and processes of social integration often operate in tension or conflict with each other. Resource allocations that advance industrial efficiency in the early stages of "modernization" have often engendered conflicts among social classes that threaten societal solidarity. In many historical settings, the solidarity of traditional family, kin, and community groupings has led to distributions of financial resources that disperse business capital and precipitate decline in family enterprises.

In the particularly noteworthy chapter 10 of *The Social System,* Parsons applied his new conception of the social system to "the case of modern medical practice." One of his major intentions was to demonstrate the "empirical relevance of the abstract analysis" he had developed (428). To accomplish this he drew on an unpublished field study of medical practice that he had conducted (mainly in Boston) a decade earlier, and on the training in psychoanalysis that he had undertaken. Chapter 10 became a founding document in the emergence of the subfield of medical sociology. It illuminated the importance of health, illness, and medicine in the functioning of a society, their cultural meanings, and their relationships to the human life cycle and the human condition, including suffering and death. It set forth the path-making notion that being sick was not simply "a state of fact" but was also an institutionalized role. Moreover, this "sick role," which exempted an ill person from normal social obligations, was a conditionally legitimized form of deviance that carried with it social control—relevant obligations to try to get well and to seek professionally competent help to do so. It framed the roles of the patient and the physician in relationship to one another. Noting that "it was in connection with [his] earlier study of medical practice that the beginnings of the pattern-variables scheme were first worked out" (429n.), Parsons invoked the pattern-variable pair of "affectivity" and "affective neutrality" to analyze the emotional evocativeness of the physician's role, emphasizing the existential significance of illness and the physical and psychic-emotional intimacies of medical work. This chapter also laid a groundwork for treating "medical uncertainty" as a sociological phenomenon. Parsons argued that uncertainty and limitations are inherent to medical knowledge and practice, no matter what their stage of development, reflecting the frustrations and strains that they entail for both physicians and patients. Parsons identified "ritualized optimism," which he viewed as a form of scientific magic, as a patterned way that doctors and patients mutually cope with situations of uncertainty and frustration, at least in American medical contexts.

The concepts of allocation and integration represented only a start in Parsons's functional thinking. In the years after publication of *The Social System,* he worked to refine the idea of function in social systems, seeking to develop a more abstract, generalized, and multidimensional scheme. The outcome was a set of concepts that Parsons called the four-function paradigm, which evolved, over twenty-five years, into a scheme for integrating ever more diverse theoretical and empirical materials.

The four-function paradigm originated in Parsons's collaboration with his Harvard colleague Robert F. Bales, who had conducted laboratory studies of interaction in small groups that had been assigned tasks that were to be carried out through open-ended discussion (Parsons, Bales, and Shils 1953). For these studies, Bales had devised sixteen coordinate categories to examine different types of contribution to group processes in relation to issues concerning leadership, authority, conflict, maintenance or loss of task focus, and coherence or solidarity of the group (Bales 1950). With these categories, Bales had shown that he could observe groups, rapidly record the predominant category of contribution made by each act of a group member, and later analyze shifting abstract patterns (which he called "phase movements") in the group interaction. Bales argued that over time, phase movements enabled the interaction of group members to address a range of the varied "needs" of the groups—for example, the need for clear coordination to attain specific goals, or the need for mutual positive feelings among members to sustain group solidarity. In their collaboration, Parsons and Bales grouped the sixteen categories of interaction process into four categories that appeared to represent fundamental and enduring "needs," or "functions," of the groups.

In the initial discussion, the four "functional" categories were presented as results of empirical generalization—as an outcome of a series of empirical studies of groups, although groups that, by their design, were possibly representative of social systems generally (Parsons, Bales, and Shils 1953, chapter 3). The four categories were said to demarcate the dimensions of social "space" within which phase movements occur. The phase movements were conceived as responses to enduring needs of the groups as social systems.

A bolder claim soon emerged. This was that any and every social system needs to manage the same four general "system problems" in order to function. Parsons began to argue that social relationships and institutions—or, more precisely, *aspects* of them—could be classified by the ways in which they contribute to managing one or more of the four system problems, which Parsons soon called "functions" (Parsons, Bales, and Shils 1953, chapter 5). In his mature formulations of the 1960s and after, Parsons presented the notion of function less as a "system problem" than as an abstract dimension of social organization (Parsons 1969). The "four-function paradigm" became an explicit or implicit conceptual frame for virtually everything Parsons wrote after the mid-1950s. It approached more closely than earlier concepts, including the pattern variables, Parsons's long-standing goal of developing an abstract, formal, and universal ground of analysis and explanation for sociology and related disciplines.

The four system problems or functions are:

1. Adaptation: The processes of gaining generalized control over conditions in the environment or situation of the acting unit. Typically, adaptive processes involve generating new resources for, or allocating available resources more efficiently among, individual or collective actors in order to secure new capabilities for the system.

2. Goal attainment: The processes of organizing the activities of social units into concerted efforts to achieve a desired change in a shared or collective relationship to the environment. For a given social unit, other social units, including collectivities or whole societies, may be major factors in the environment, and predominating over their interests may be a chief goal.

3. Integration: The processes of mutual adjustment among social units to encourage long-term interdependence, loyalty, and attachment. Typically, these processes involve setting priorities among units, as in systems of stratification, as well as institutionalizing common normative orders and means of social control.

4. Pattern maintenance: The processes of ensuring long-term attachment to the basic principles of action, including shared values, that distinguish the system of reference from other systems. Socialization and acculturation in the most inclusive and flexible senses are among the key processes involved here.

Because the four-function paradigm was so highly abstract, years of work were needed before Parsons's earlier formulations were thoroughly assimilated to it. In fact, Parsons never completed the task of recasting earlier ideas. However, the advantages of the four-function paradigm were fundamental. Earlier "functional" theories, including his own, appealed to indefinite lists of functions and had an essentially ad hoc quality, which limited their appeal as explanatory strategies. The theory of four system problems, however, constituted a closed a priori list of functions. Moreover, even its first statements included a richly heuristic set of hypotheses about how social relationships are differently organized in relation to the social functions they serve. These hypotheses became increasingly clarified as Parsons used the four-function idea in ever wider ranges of empirical analyses while treating their conceptual basis as one integral paradigm.

As early as 1953, Parsons tentatively suggested that the four functions might be used to represent major dimensions of structural differentiation in society as a whole. This speculation became a sort of charter for the next decade of his work (Parsons and Smelser 1956; Parsons 1966, 1969). During the 1950s and 1960s, he gradually produced a theory of four functionally specialized subsystems of society. Each of the four subsystems was treated as a complex set of dynamically interdependent institutions that, as itself a system, could in turn be analyzed by another application of the same four-function paradigm. The resulting theory of societal subsystems, although never completely worked out, remains a more comprehensive, clearly formatted, and analytically precise approach to macrosocial analysis than any alternative.

In outline, the four subsystems of society are:

1. Adaptive subsystem: The economy is the adaptive subsystem, structured around the development and allocation of basic resources for use by individual and collective units of a society. It consists of such institutions as markets for labor and capital, entrepreneurial roles, the legal complexes of ownership, contract, credit, and employment, and the organizational structure of business firms.

2. Goal-attainment subsystem: The "polity" is the subsystem of society that coordinates the attainment of collective goals. Governmental agencies at all levels, including the administrative, executive, legislative, and judicial arms of public authority, are the primary institutional components of the polity. Parsons also emphasized the role of the citizen in analyzing the dynamic relationships between the polity and the other three subsystems of a society, especially the integrative subsystem.

3. Integrative subsystem: The "societal community" is the subsystem that serves the integration of society. Social classes, status groups, ethnic groups, groups that share elements of

"life style," and other groups that maintain enduring ties of solidarity mold a society's pattern of social integration. Shared frameworks of law and informal normative orders, custom, and mores delimit the scope of action and influence of particular groups, establishing bases of trust, confidence, and solidarity among groups. Yet institutions of social control, class structure, status order, and structures of "primordial" solidarity such as kinship and ethnicity also shape and are shaped by phenomena of cleavage and conflict.

4. Pattern-maintenance subsystem: The "fiduciary system" is the subsystem serving the pattern-maintenance function. It is organized around the transmission (or reproduction), maintenance, and development of a society's enduring values and shared culture. Institutions of religion, family and household, and socialization and education are its major constituents. Following Max Weber, Parsons emphasized that change in fiduciary systems, notably in religious ethics and forms of association, have historically been the most profound forces of social change.

Parsons retained his emphasis on normative order in formulating the functional theory of societal subsystems. Indeed, he extended it to a new level in analyzing the many forms that normative structures assume in functionally distinct settings, including economic exchange (Parsons and Smelser 1956), relationships of political authority (Parsons 1969), the solidary ties of status groups (Parsons 1953, 1969), and processes of socialization in family life (Parsons and Bales 1955). This analysis opened a new approach to understanding the many modes of articulation between normative orders and the practical institutions of societal functioning—for example, economic markets, political bureaucracies, class structures, or religious associations. The resulting synthesis transcended old conceptual dichotomies between normative and interest-driven, or ideal and material, factors in social causation. Parsons argued that every effective social institution is an integration of normative and interest-driven, ideal and material, factors. To be sure, the two dimensions can be divided, so that relationships are motivated solely by ideal or by material grounds, by the pursuit of self-interest without regard to normative rules, or by adherence to norms without regard to self-interest. Such circumstances emerge more often during periods of rapid change and intense conflict. Stable social institutions, however, depend upon both normative regulation and practical interests' driving goal setting.

In striving to clarify his idea of four functionally defined subsystems of analysis, Parsons soon found it necessary to treat the subsystems in dynamic relationship with one another. His initial insight was that economists' modeling of the twofold exchanges between the aggregate of business firms and the aggregate of households (wages for labor; goods and services for consumer spending) could be viewed as a boundary relationship between the adaptive and pattern-maintenance subsystems of society (Parsons and Smelser 1956).

Parsons then proposed that each of the four classic factors of economic production—labor, capital, entrepreneurship or organization, and land—might be treated as a form of input to the economy from an exogenous source. Just as labor (meaning a socialized ability to perform work of economic value) is an input from the pattern-maintenance system, so capital (financial means of controlling and allocating "real" economic resources) is an input from the polity, and organization (an ability to develop and sustain innovative relations of production) is an input from the system of social integration. All three of these factors—not only labor—enter the economy as parts of pairs of interdependent exchange relationships, which Parsons began to call "double interchanges." When viewed as exchanges between specific units of the society, double interchanges involving labor, capital, and organization are mediated by highly differentiated market institutions. Parsons treated the factor of land as a special case, using the term to refer to the commitment of resources to economic production rather than to other possible uses—for example, for consumption or political purposes. Land thus represents a factor generated within the economy, but also involves the position of economic values within more general cultural values that transcend the economy and concern allocations of resources to all kinds of social action.

Working out the economy's double interchanges with the other subsystems of society entailed an analysis of differences in function among economic institutions. Parsons again employed the four-function paradigm in this analysis—its first use at more than one level. In analyzing the economy into subsystems (and then sub-subsystems), Parsons also aligned each double interchange with a specific subsystem: the labor-wages, goods-and-services-consumer-spending interchange with the economy's goal-attainment subsystem; the capital-markets interchange with the adaptive subsystem; and the organization interchange with the integrative subsystem (Parsons and Smelser 1956). Markets involving "land" were discussed as a special boundary relation, not a double interchange, between the economy's pattern-maintenance function and the pattern-maintenance structures, principally value systems, of the whole society.

A further implication of Parsons's treatment of the economy's boundary relationships with the polity, societal community, and fiduciary system was that double interchanges constitute the flexible means by which all four subsystems of society adjust their respective internal homeostatic processes to one another. Parsons proposed that the general homeostatic processes of a society as a system could be analyzed in terms of six double interchanges—that is, one double interchange between each pair of societal subsystems. Each of the double interchanges was treated as a flexible, highly differentiated mechanism by which two subsystems adjust to one another's needs for resources (Parsons 1963). Each subsystem was hypothesized to be involved in three double interchanges—one with each of the other societal subsystems—and to obtain different kinds of essential resources through each of these boundary relationships. In addition, each subsystem was understood to regulate its internal operations with a factor that, like "land" in the economy, is a values-based commitment of resources to a general type of social process—economic, political, communal, or fiduciary. Thus, by combining four-function analysis of subsystems with the process-related concept of double interchange, adapted from economic theory, Parsons developed a general model for analyzing the ways in which specific social processes may be "mapped" within the functionally defined "space" of a whole society.

After his work on economic institutions, Parsons wrote several essays that together conceptualize the polity in terms parallel to his four-function analysis of the economy. One essay (Parsons 1969, chapter 9) reinterpreted the conclusions of *Voting* (Berelson, Lazarsfeld, and McPhee 1954)—then the most sophisticated empirical study of the American electoral system—in terms of the part of electoral institutions and processes in the double interchange between the polity and societal community. Another included a four-function analysis of the primary subsystems of the polity (Parsons 1969, chapter 13). Parsons's essay "On the Concept of Political Power" (Parsons 1963) revised the double interchange between the polity and the societal community on the basis of a radically new concept of power. He proposed that in modern democracies, the polity receives a factor of "interest demands"—expressions of opinion about needed public policies—from the organized citizenry as a sector of the societal community, while producing "policy decisions" as a factor for adjusting the lives of the citizenry to contemporary circumstances. The polity then receives "political support" in the form of electoral votes that, when aggregated under election laws, determine holders of offices. In return, the societal community receives "leadership responsibility," assuring that the political process will address the well-being of citizens. Parsons's discussion of this double interchange drew parallels with the double interchange between business firms and households. As a homeostatic process, it contains capabilities to absorb and adjust to social change.

Like modern economies, the polity in this analysis is open to growth, as when new kinds of interest demands (often from newly included groups) enter the political arena and lead to new courses of political action. Yet Parsons also noted that polities experience contractions and downward spirals that reduce the levels of effective political activity and the public's well-being. Contractions in public trust may restrict the scope of interest demands acceptable in the polity and in leadership responsibility acceptable to the citizenry, thereby precipitating "political depressions" (Parsons 1963; Parsons 1969, chapter 13). He cited the McCarthyism of the 1950s and, later, consequences of the "Watergate" events as examples of deflationary events, or depressions, in American politics (Parsons and Gerstein 1977).

In recognizing phenomena of both expansion and contraction in the polity, Parsons raised a question of whether political processes include an analogue of money's role in economic processes. The economist John Maynard Keynes had shown imbalances in the circulation of money as wages and as consumer spending to be sources of depression. Parsons hypothesized that imbalances in the boundary processes of the polity might also involve a symbolic medium. He proposed that political power is a medium that circulates in political relationships and provides a measure of political efficacy parallel to money's role in economic relationships. Power in this view represents capacity to make decisions that formally bind a political entity and is expended with every political decision, just as money is expended with every purchase. If public authorities expend power, then they need ways of gaining "incomes" of power. Parsons proposed that binding decisions issued by public authorities are a kind of calculated investment intended to bring renewed power in the form of support in future elections (Parsons 1963; Parsons 1969, chapter 13).

Parsons knew that this conception of power differs from the conventional view among political scientists. The conventional view emphasizes two basic qualities of power. First, authorities with power exercise it *over* others to frustrate their pursuit of conflicting goals. Power in this perspective is essentially a zero-sum game: if used by one actor, it comes at the cost of others. Second, power is a diffuse capability; the Hobbesian idea is that any means of attaining ends over the will of another becomes power. Parsons argued that both of these ideas are misleading. In his understanding, power is a specialized resource that enables duly authorized officials to make binding decisions for a collectivity, whether a nation, state, city, bureau, agency, business firm, or association. Power consists in the binding quality of the decision. The binding quality distinguishes power from other means of pursuing ends, such as expenditures of money or use of personal influence. Parsons acknowledged that power is often exercised over others: a binding court decision frustrates the aims of one party to a suit or a guilty defendant who goes to prison; a military order sends thousands of soldiers into the risks of battle. But, Parsons also noted, important forms of power are binding only through aggregate acts of many individuals, as when the votes of a majority elect one candidate rather than competitors to office. Properly regulated, power can also serve shared interests of the public and benefit an entire citizenry. Power is not intrinsically zero-sum, but zero-sum only in certain situations, especially in times of political contraction.

Parsons's key insight was that power, like money, is essentially symbolic. The literature has linked power closely with force, but Parsons argued that force is generally used when authorities lack the power to command or their power has been challenged (Parsons 1964b). As a quality of commands that renders them properly authorized and likely to be obeyed, power is linked to the procedures by which commands are issued. Power's symbolic form—as in court orders, legislative enactments, executive regulations, or military commands—is intrinsic to its efficacy, just as legitimate currency takes its value from its precise printed form or a check gains value from a particular authorized signature. Force is typically used when power on the symbolic level has proved ineffective. However, the use of force may be necessary, as in the suppressing of civil disturbances, to secure institutions of power by demonstrating that duly authorized commands cannot be violated with impunity.

With his discussion of power, Parsons concluded that money is not the only circulating symbolic medium, just an obvious member of a class of media. His general model of social process suggested that each subsystem of society must have its own specialized medium. He soon designated influence (or the capacity to persuade, typically by activating a solidary relationship) as the circulating medium of the societal community (Parsons 1969, chapter 15). His formulation built on the research on personal influence, mass media, and reference groups conducted by Paul Lazarsfeld, Robert K. Merton, and colleagues at Columbia University. It also linked the mechanisms of interpersonal influence uncovered by the Columbia studies to macrosocial processes of generating solidarity across the societal community—to be sure, in tension with cleavages, conflicts, and differences of social class, status, race, ethnicity, region, and occupational groupings. Parsons's discussion of influence as a symbolic medium added dynamic qualities to the understanding of how political leaders mobilize ties of solidarity in seeking support from electorates.

Parsons suggested that value commitments constitute a circulating medium for the fiduciary subsystem. By value commitments he meant the generalized promises that actors make to one another to carry out significant projects cooperatively. Actors rely upon others to implement all manner of activities that involve divisions of labor. Although cooperative relations are often coordinated at multiple levels and involve uses of money, power, and influence as well, they depend most basically on the commitments of participants that each will do his or her part. The commitments circulate in the sense that one actor's promise to cooperate with another becomes a condition of participation by third parties. Parsons noted that commitments are often highly generalized: an individual's commitment to perform labor for a business firm, made at the time of employment, may leave open to future decisions just what work he or she will do, in cooperation with whom, through what procedures, and when and where. Yet, the giving and accepting of the commitment reflects the employer's and employee's shared valuation of a kind of production and the skills for executing it (Parsons 1969, chapter 16; see Parsons and Smelser 1956).

One source of confusion about Parsons's writings on power, influence, and value commitments has been that these media do not circulate in clear and palpable quantities as money does. The quantities of money in our wallets and bank accounts, or needed for a specific purchase, can be calculated precisely, even if their "real" value, or purchasing power, changes over time. Power, influence, and value commitments cannot be so precisely quantified: public policies are not promulgated through use of specific amounts of "power chits," nor are there definite "power prices" for making particular policy decisions. Yet we commonly view power, influence, and commitments in quantitative terms. We speak of White House officials as exercising a great deal of power, of leaders in a profession as highly influential, or of a person who has taken on too many responsibilities as overcommitted. We know that structures of authority entail methodical allocations of power, with high officials having greater power than their subordinates.

Although power, influence, and commitments have quantitative aspects, their uses would likely be compromised if they circulated in definite quantities. We can understand this point easily with respect to commitments. Commitments circulate in the form of promises to make efforts that others can rely upon in planning cooperative action. Because the difficulty of fulfilling a commitment often changes with circumstances, actors may know that they have made large commitments, but not know the actual level of effort needed to fulfill them. Nevertheless, a commitment would be valueless if others could not count upon its fulfillment, even if and when circumstances change. A commitment is not measured by a specific quantity of effort to be made, but by its relative priority among an actor's set of value-based undertakings.

Parsons's writings on money, power, influence, and commitments completed a general model of how processes are mediated within each of the four subsystems of society and, in ways that are too technical to review here, how the subsystems relate to each other homeostatically through double interchanges. As some of the chapters in this volume indicate, the model suggested as many new problems as it resolved, and Parsons did not deal with even some of the most important ones. Yet the model does unify structural and dynamic analysis, identifies six double-interchange systems as essential centers of a society's homeostatic mechanisms, and with the four-function paradigm it presents a format for analyzing systems into subsystems, and those systems into still more specific functionally defined sub-subsystems, while retaining a methodical overview of how the parts fit into the societal whole. No other social theory has achieved a comparable level of refinement in formatting macrosocial analysis. For this reason, Parsons's formulations remain a fundamental resource for sociological theory forty years after his first discussions of the symbolic media, and fifty years after the first presentations of the four-function paradigm and its application to the subsystems of society. Essays in this volume that take up problems of the analysis of subsystems of society, the symbolic media, and the major societal interchanges treat theoretical problems of immense importance to the sociology of today.

During the late 1950s and early 1960s, Parsons wrote a number of essays on the modernization of so-called underdeveloped societies and social change more generally (Parsons 1960). These writings revitalized his long-standing interest in comparative institutional analysis and led him to write two short books presenting a theory of social evolution: *Societies: Evolutionary and Comparative Perspectives* (Parsons 1966) and *The System of Modern Societies* (Parsons 1971).

The first book presented a broad typology of "primitive," archaic, historic, and "seed-bed" societies. It drew on a wide range of works in anthropology, ancient history, and civilizational studies to analyze the major institutions characteristic of societies at each "stage" of social evolution, and to demonstrate the range of variation in basic institutional patterns observed among societies at each stage. For example, Parsons discussed archaic societies by comparing the radically different institutions of the Egyptian and Mesopotamian civilizations of antiquity. The book also provided sharp definitions for each of the evolutionary types, listing a number of the cultural and institutional criteria that distinguish each type from the others. Thus, the presence of developed craft literacy, or literacy known only to special status groups of scribes and priests, central cults where priests monopolize the rituals and interpretation of religious beliefs and mythology, written codes of law, a class system secured by legally codified discriminations among aristocrats, commoners, and slaves, a central administrative apparatus, consolidation of authority around an institution of kingship, intensive agriculture, storehouses for essential goods, local markets for craft and agricultural produce, the concentration of the nonagricultural population in towns sets "archaic" societies apart from "primitive" societies, which do not possess these features.

The discussion of historic civilizations covered the classical Chinese, Indian, Islamic, and Roman empires, all of which, as examples of a type, extended over vast domains, included many ethnic groups, and had cultural and institutional systems, including law and status orders based on religio-philosophical belief systems with transcendental conceptions of sources of value and legitimacy. Their social hierarchies included specially honored status groups that were the main proponents and interpreters of their respective religio-philosophical traditions. Following Weber, Parsons focused his analysis on the social makeup and privileged ways of life of these key status groups—for example, the Confucian literati and mandarins in China and the Brahmin priesthood in the Indian "caste" system. He used the four-function paradigm to compare the major institutional complexes developed within each of the historic civilizations.

Parsons gave special attention to ancient Greece and Israel, which he termed "seedbed" societies because their importance to the comparative study of societies derives not from their wealth or power but from the effects of their cultural heritages on the religious and philosophical frameworks of later civilizations. Greek philosophy was the ultimate source of ideals of objective reason that became essential to early Christian theology, medieval theology, Renaissance philosophy, and Enlightenment rationalism, and Greek ideals of the autonomous politically organized city-state, mediated by the Roman republican tradition, became the source since the early Renaissance of modern republican traditions. The Hebraic idea of a transcendent but personal and jealous God who enters history to reward and punish peoples for their achievements and failings became the primary source of Christian theodicy and religious ethics.

The System of Modern Societies discussed modern societies as a distinctive evolutionary type that first emerged in Western civilization but has grown to have worldwide impact. As a starting point in the analysis, Parsons sought to systematize our understanding of why modern society originated in Western civilization. He emphasized the dynamic quality of the civilization that had emerged several centuries before modern institutions in the West, beginning with the emergence of many small, overlapping, yet competing societies after the fragmentation of Western Roman authority. Medieval civilization then developed through a number of consolidating forces: the Christian church with its partly universalistic priesthood and hierarchy; the heritage of Roman ideals of effective law and authority; a class system centering on a pan-European feudal-military nobility based on unstable, ever-changing feudal ties; agricultural production rooted in peasant villages; and active commerce and craft production centered in towns and cities. It was this distinctive European civilization that became transformed by the cultural movements of the Renaissance, with its elaboration of secular culture in the arts, technology, and moral belief, and the Reformation, with its redirection of fundamental religious beliefs.

Generalizing Weber's analysis, Parsons argued that the Calvinist ethic of inner-worldly asceticism provided, against a background of other Reformation movements, a special impetus to break with traditional social arrangements and devise new institutions. The two centuries following the Reformation were a period of intense social conflict and repeated efforts to create new social foundations. Societies in which ascetic Protestant movements predominated, especially England and its American colonies, established stringently disciplined religious ethics and social orders. In the eighteenth century, ascetic Protestantism began to accommodate secular as well as religious ethical reasoning and gave rise to elements of the modern "spirit of capitalism," with its emphasis on creative entrepreneurship and efficient use of secular talents and resources. The economic forces that created the Industrial Revolution spread from England to the Low Countries and the United States, then all of the north and west of Europe, including predominantly Catholic nations. The Industrial Revolution produced a growing, self-confident "middle class," which generated pressures toward democratizing political change. Electoral institutions emerged that enfranchised common citizens and promoted competition among political parties, undermining privileged groups and aristocracies and empowering elected representatives of the citizenry at large.

The United States institutionalized a combination of the Industrial and democratic revolutions more rapidly than any other society. It also went the farthest in placing a middle class without ascriptive privileges in a central position in the class system. The American legal system firmly but flexibly protected new forms of property, contract, and employment. By the early twentieth century, American society had developed the largest and most efficient industrial institutions, with the most highly differentiated occupational structure, in the world. Parsons argued that these changes were complemented by an educational revolution that upgraded popular education well in advance of other nations. As part of this revolution, university-based research and advanced training of personnel in the sciences, professions, and other technical fields transformed the work force and the economy's capacity for innovation.

Parsons suggested that the institutionalization of the Industrial, democratic, and educational revolutions in the United States created a new, "advanced modern" type of society by the late twentieth century. He then discussed the prospects for the spread, in partial or complete forms, of this type of modernity in Europe, the Soviet Union, and Japan. Early in the Brezhnev era, he predicted that the Soviet Union could not sustain its authoritarian political system in a world where democracies predominate (Parsons 1971).

In 1970, Parsons extended four-function analysis to relations between social systems and other subsystems of action, which he began to call the general action system. He replaced the classification of culture, social system, and personality with a scheme of four primary subsystems (Parsons 1970). For the adaptive function, Parsons introduced the concept of the behavioral organism, constituted of aspects of the individual organism that provide resources for physical behavior. The senses, ability to speak and to understand speech, capacities for coordinated motion of the body, and the intelligent capabilities of the brain are primary resources of the behavioral organism. The personality was aligned with the goal-attainment function because of the importance of psychological patterns of motivation to purposeful agency for implementing action and achieving ends. The social system was treated as integrative in its functioning because its normative structures bind actors into common relationships and situations. Culture was linked with the pattern-maintenance function because of the importance of core beliefs, values, and symbols in establishing basic principles and direction for entire action systems. Having identified these functional subsystems, Parsons tentatively designated the symbolic media that regulate their internal operations and interchanges with one another (Parsons 1970; Parsons and Platt 1973, chapter 3). His treatment of affect in a broadly Freudian sense as one of the media of the general action system is discussed in one of the chapters in this volume.

In the mid-1970s Parsons, by then retired from Harvard, led an informal faculty seminar at the University of Pennsylvania (in which the editors of this volume collaborated) to discuss new developments in the theory of action. One issue was an objection that had been raised to the conception of behavioral organism as the adaptive subsystem of action (Lidz and Lidz 1976). The criticism held that the notion of behavioral organism violates the idea of a system constituted entirely of meaningful action, as it consists of physical elements of the human organism. To correct this violation of the action frame of reference, it was suggested that the adaptive subsystem of action should be seen as a system of cognitive schemas in Jean Piaget's sense. Such a system would also correspond to "mind," in George Herbert Mead's usage. Parsons accepted the new proposal, but argued more broadly for a fresh examination of how systems of social action relate to their environing systems, including organisms, the broader biosphere, and the physical cosmos. Discussion of the boundary relations of action systems continued in the faculty seminar for several years.

The major outcome of the discussions was a long essay, "A Paradigm of the Human Condition" (Parsons 1978, chapter 15). Using the four-function paradigm, Parsons here argued that the human condition as experienced by actors involves the action system's relationships with three other systems. Systems of action serve the integrative function of the human condition as system. They exist in three orders of environment, the physico-chemical environment (adaptive), the human organic and ecological environment (goal-attaining), and a telic, or transcendental, environment (pattern-maintaining). To complement these system identifications, Parsons tentatively suggested terms for subsystems, media, and interchange categories.

The idea of a telic system has been especially controversial. In fact, Parsons was not positing that a god or divine principle sets a general direction for human action, but only that all systems of action are intrinsically open with respect to ultimate principles. Any given system of action—even an entire civilization—follows specific ultimate principles. Those principles establish the terms in which people living in the system of action confront ultimate questions of meaning, including the injustices of social life, poverty, illness, suffering, death and other losses, and hopes for "salvation" or other transcendental conceptions of the significance of life. The characteristic principles with which an action system addresses ultimate issues, however, are not the only possible ones. We know that in times of great stress in civilizations, pressures arise to change the principles, as in the Roman Empire during the epoch of Christ, or during the Reformation. Parsons argued that ultimate principles are formulated by social actors, but within a limited set of possibilities. Weber's concepts of inner-worldly and other-worldly, mysticism and asceticism, Parsons proposed, demarcate the dimensions of transcendental possibilities for principles of action. As civilizations struggle to develop and maintain ultimate principles, they confront these essential alternatives for basic orientations of action. The telic order stands for the limited set of possibilities for ultimate principles of action that constitute an inherent environment of all action systems.

Parsons treated action systems as integrative to the human condition because they interrelate elements of all three environments (physico-chemical, organic-ecological, and telic) in terms of their own meaning patterns. A system of action provides the anthropocentric basis of the integration of the human condition, which is different, as Parsons wrote, from the fish condition (or horse, or rat, or paramecia conditions). Moreover, given the importance to humans of meaningful orientations, the human condition has different experiential significance for Americans, ancient Greeks, premodern Chinese, and medieval Muslims, and for various status groups within any of these societies.

The essay on the human condition has attracted attention in part because it was Parsons's last major publication. Not only is it representative of his work in opening large issues, proposing insightful and suggestive answers, and yet leaving significant problems unresolved and awaiting future contributions. It also made manifest an important, albeit often implicit, metatheme that tied together many aspects of his work. Several of the contributing authors to this volume select Parsons's essay on the human condition as a starting point for their own efforts to address the corpus of his action theory. In its broad scope and reflective, philosophic quality, some commentators have noted, the essay has attributes of a final testamentary statement.

THIS VOLUME

All of the chapters in this volume clarify and critique aspects of action theory and strive to extend its reach. Although they take up ideas that are abstract and in many cases macrotheoretical, they are not removed from empirical reality. Quite to the contrary, all of the authors demonstrate a lively interest in considering how Parsons's action theory might be applied to important events in our present-day world and the contemporary condition of sociological thought and how certain elements of his theoretical system might need to be altered in light of them. The contemporary developments to which most frequent reference is made are the complex phenomenon of "globalization"; the historically unprecedented economic, political, military, and cultural power that the United States has attained as an "empire-less empire," and the changes in American institutions associated with those expansions; the emergence of various forms of fundamentalism; the upsurge of "primordial," clanic, tribal, and ethnic conflicts; and the florescence of several types of deterministic or positivistic thought that have assumed (or reassumed) importance in the last several decades, including biological determinism, economic utilitarianism, and rational-choice theory.

The chapters are grouped in four parts: "Social Institutions and Social Processes"; "Societal Community and Modernization"; "Sociology and Culture"; and "The Human Condition." Since several of the chapters—not surprisingly—address more than one topic in the theory of social action, the grouping is, unavoidably, somewhat arbitrary.

Part I: Social Institutions and Social Processes

The first group of chapters takes up issues in Parsons's conceptions of social institutions and social processes, basic material in any sociological theory and an area of analysis with many implications for contemporary work. The first two chapters concentrate on economic institutions and their relationships to broader institutional frameworks, including especially family and household, political institutions, and legal frameworks.

Neil Smelser begins his chapter, "Parsons's Economic Sociology and the Development of Economic Sociology," by reviewing considerations that went into the writing of his and Talcott Parsons's collaborative work, *Economy and Society,* published in 1956. They placed the economy squarely within the larger society, treated the economy analytically as an adaptive subsystem, and analyzed its relations with the pattern-maintenance, integrative, and goal-attaining subsystems, each of which receives vital resources from the others. A conception of double interchanges between pairs of the four subsystems was one of the achievements of the book. Parsons and Smelser's analysis consolidated several strands of sociological and economic thought into a single coherent theory. Nevertheless, the book was not well received by economists whose rationalistic paradigms led them to dismiss nonrational cultural and sociological ideas as irrelevant. Sociologists also paid scant attention to the book because in the mid-fifties they had little interest in treating relationships between sociology and economics at this level of abstraction and rigor. Despite this rejection, the book heralded the beginnings of the mature version of action theory—the four-function scheme and the theory of the generalized symbolic media of interchange.

Over the last twenty years, Smelser notes, independent work in economic sociology has become a burgeoning subdiscipline. Analyses of economic activity affected by population ecology, cultural constraints, embedded networks, organizations, and political institutions have been conducted with disparate but rigorous technical means and have yielded valuable insights. But these many studies and approaches remain an unordered aggregate, and in this respect they are of uncertain theoretical value. Smelser suggests that, given the advances made in sociology and economics in the past forty-five years, the time may be more favorable to attempt a synthesis along the lines of, but not necessarily identical to the one Parsons and he proposed almost fifty years ago.

In his chapter "Looming Catastrophe: How and Why 'Law and Economics' Undermines Fiduciary Duties in Corporate Law," Mark Gould continues his program of developing a sociology of law from the perspective of action theory. Gould's analysis draws in part on insights of Durkheim and Weber and also on implications of Parsons's early work, *The Structure of Social Action,* that have hardly been noted by sociologists and American legal scholars. At issue are the understandings of managerial responsibilities of loyalty to the firm and fiduciary obligations to shareholders as they are codified in corporate law. In discussing several leading legal texts and court decisions, Gould observes that contemporary law regulating the contractual obligations of managers of business firms is based exclusively on utilitarian and rationalist premises. These premises give primacy to the balancing of individual interests, limited only by situational opportunities and constraints, a primacy in accord with individualistic and pragmatic values that Americans prize. This emphasis tacitly puts concerns for the collective entity, the firm, in a distant second place. The firm becomes a zone primarily to negotiate and fulfill individual interests. Given these emphases, loyalty to the firm and care for its shareholders are eroded, and the firm veers toward becoming an atomistic aggregate and loses inner coherence and solidarity. Gould warns that as these processes, supported by contemporary contract law, continue, investor trust and confidence will decline and the viability of firms will be endangered. What is needed, he argues, is a clear legal understanding of the fiduciary responsibilities of managers that are central to the regulation of their contractual obligations.

Gould's analysis of the practical limitations of individualistic and utilitarian understandings of contract law closely parallels Parsons's classic critique of reductionistic utilitarian social theories. However, Gould adds an emphasis on the deleterious consequences for corporate law of institutionalization of reductionistic understandings, whether through judicial decisions, legislation, or regulatory processes. In this way he importantly extends Parsons's analytic argument into an area of policy of immense practical significance for contemporary American society.

Harald Wenzel argues in "Social Order as Communication: Parsons's Theory on the Move from Moral Consensus to Trust" that the solution Parsons developed to the problem of social order in his earlier and middle periods shifted radically in his later work. In the earlier work, Parsons relied primarily on the idea of shared normative order held in common by the members of a society and thus constraining and stabilizing their conduct as the foundation of social relationships. But the centrality of normative order in Parsons's thinking slowly gave way as his appreciation grew of the enormous complexity and variability, indeed the often fleeting quality, of modern social relationships. The idea of a normative order was perhaps adequate to understand social relationships in earlier, more stable, less socially differentiated historical periods. In the modern era, however, normative order alone is insufficient.

Wenzel draws on the work of several other scholars, in particular Erving Goffman and Alvin W. Gouldner, to amplify this point. Wenzel sees in the tacit negotiations, the subtle parrying, the thrusts and counterthrusts that precede a relationship a hallmark of modernity. Judgments of trust are developed in such anticipatory communications and are necessary before constraining norms can be brought into play. Wenzel believes that Parsons's implicit understanding of the importance of such communications of trust begins to appear in his later idea of the symbolic media of interchange. The normative order remains important in Parsons's thinking, but it no longer holds the precedence it had in the earlier work. Parsons began to see that in the modern, highly fluid and differentiated social world, the communication of trust at the very outset of relationships permits the normative order to function.

Harold Bershady's chapter, "Affect in Social Life," examines the kinds and combinations of affective involvement in social life. This is a matter about which Parsons wrote a great deal over the course of many years but which he never fully developed. The binary opposition Parsons drew in earlier formulations between affectivity and affective neutrality—one of the "pattern variables"—is, in Bershady's view, too extreme. Bershady argues that there is always some affective, or emotional, involvement in everything that people do. He agrees in part with Parsons's later view that affect is one of the symbolic media of interchange that circulates through every sector of society, and functions in a way analogous to money, with which it shares many properties. However, Bershady also identifies unique properties of affect that are quite unlike those of money. Affect requires its own analysis.

Bershady cleaves to the insights of Freud and Parsons in considering affect to be a sign of motivation to act, or to continue acting. Affect first appears in bodily manifestations and is a possession of the person, but with few notable exceptions it is shaped in its genre, expression, and appropriateness by many different kinds of norms. Affective expression can thus be communicated independently of the body, and through a variety of representations shared by people physically distant from one another. Bershady discusses a few kinds of poorly regulated or unregulated affect, such as in situations of anomie, effervescence, and panic, and closes with a brief discussion of the anxiety generated by 9/11 and its aftermath. He concludes that affect in general, and anxiety in particular, is an ongoing feature of the human condition.

Part II: Societal Community and Modernization

The first two chapters in this part, by Jeffrey Alexander and Giuseppe Sciortino, focus specifically on evaluation of the concept of societal community. Essays by Robert N. Bellah and Donald N. Levine discuss issues of the understanding of contemporary American society (Bellah) and modern societies (Levine) more generally, but in ways that in both cases relate directly to qualities of community institutions and feeling. The Alexander and Sciortino chapters evaluate the concept of societal community by different methods and reach contrasting conclusions. Alexander's approach in "Contradictions in the Societal Community: The Promise and Disappointment of Parsons's Concept" is based on a close reading of Parsons's definitions of the term "societal community," which he then subjects to an abstract and general critique. Sciortino treats societal community as a second-order concept integrating a wide variety of materials that Parsons drew from nearly all aspects and phases of his writings.

Alexander notes that earlier in his own career he viewed the concept of societal community very favorably. In recent years, however, in part under the influence of Jürgen Habermas's reformulation of critical theory, he has sought a theory that combines a concern for justice with analysis of social integration. This theoretical interest has led him to join the interdisciplinary discussions over the concept of civil society, its dimensions, and its potential that emerged in the 1990s. Alexander reviews key sources of Parsons's concept of societal community in Durkheim's analysis of societal solidarity, Weber's treatment of the city and urban institutions from antiquity through the Renaissance, and T. H. Marshall's analysis of the elements of citizenship. He acknowledges that many of Parsons's essays exhibit an interest in democracy and justice, but suggests that a concern for order emerged as a stronger conceptual interest. Thus, by the time the concept of societal community was formulated, it emphasized the importance of order and tended to place issues of democratic relations, fairness, and justice in the background.

Alexander's close reading of the definitions Parsons provided for the term "societal community" is presented as documentation of this tendency. He then argues, citing mainly *The System of Modern Societies,* that Parsons moved to an overly "buoyant" and "optimistic" analysis of the condition and historical promise of the American societal community. If Parsons did not totally overlook "uncomfortable facts," he tended to recognize them only in the form of qualifications—framed by "buts, despites, howevers, of courses, and althoughs"—that diminished his acknowledgment of them. Alexander proposes that an analysis of social integration that entails a more critical and dynamic vision of the civil sphere and eschews idealizing specific institutions would be a more fitting complement to democratic theory.

In "How Different Can We Be? Parsons's Societal Community, Pluralism, and the Multicultural Debate," Sciortino calls for reconstruction and elaboration of Parsons's notion of the societal community as an integrative subsystem of society. Like Alexander, Sciortino views the concept of societal community as a bold but unfulfilled theoretical vision, but where Alexander sees an overly "optimistic" perspective, Sciortino perceives an insightful, "non-nostalgic" or "anti-nostalgic" understanding of modern pluralistic solidarity—a "sustained criticism of pseudo-Gemeinschaft illusions." He proposes that the concept of societal community should be understood as a "second order phenomenon" that coordinates "several kinds of coordinating systems" that are of recognized importance in sociology, yet not often perceived to be integrated with one another. Thus, societal community involves an integration of mechanisms of formal and informal social control; social classes, strata formation, and lifestyles; the civil institutions of deliberation on public policies; and the more diffuse solidary ties of family, kinship, ethnicity, and religion that support personal identity. He notes that Parsons had written on all of these primary coordinating mechanisms, with emphasis on the "specific social strains" that each entails, before proposing his conception of societal community. Parsons's analysis of the societal community emphasized that societal solidarity can be achieved only through successful combination of several independent factors that are always contingent, fallible inputs from the other subsystems of society: economy, polity, and fiduciary system.

Sciortino argues that Parsons's non-nostalgic perspective led him to stress the pluralism, based on segmentation as well as differentiation, involved in the inputs of factors across each of the societal community's boundaries as well as in its internal institutional structures. Cross-cutting networks of pluralistic solidary relationships thus make up the structural principle that renders modern societal communities possible. Sciortino observes that Parsons emphasized the stabilizing effects of multiple cross-cutting memberships in practically all of his writings on modern societies, and especially those in which he propounded the concept of societal community.

Against the background of this framework, Sciortino suggests several analytical topics and themes that contemporary sociologists should explore more intensively than Parsons did. Among them are the creative variations in value and norms that may evolve from competition and conflict among groups; the continuing importance of diffuse and quality-based solidarities in modern life; the importance of social segmentation in pluralistic structures; and the emergence of mass media, educational systems, and juridical institutions as what Parsons called "storm centers" of contemporary societal communities. Sciortino also proposes a focused but general proposition that deserves empirical evaluation as a corollary to Parsons's hypotheses about pluralism: pluralism is stabilizing in its effects where there is more variance in values and culture within specific groups than across groups.

Robert Bellah's evocative "God, Nation, and Self in America" unfolds around a narrative analysis of how and why he has concentrated so much of his intellectual attention on the study of American society and of the evolution that his perspective on this society has undergone since 1967. That is the year when, at the urging of his teacher and colleague Talcott Parsons, he wrote and published the essay "Civil Religion in America," which, he avers, "changed my life." Threaded through his account is a running comparison of the "points of intersection" between Parsons's view of American society and his own, and of some of the "divergences" between them that developed over time.

As a consequence of his scholarly study of American society, the first-hand research he has conducted in certain American milieux, and his experience and interpretation of the cardinal events of the past five decades of this country's history, Bellah has become increasingly convinced that the Protestant Reformation, which underlies the deepest level of American "self-understanding," was "a mistake"—albeit a "necessary mistake." In his view, this mistake, or its consequences, "needs to be rectified if we are to solve the crises of modernity." What Bellah considers mistaken is that from its inception, the American nation was religiously conceived in a way that "contained destructive as well as creative possibilities" and "cultural consequences." At its core lay the "Protestant temptation" to "confuse religion and nation," and "church and nation"—"to imagine that America had become a realized eschatology." In turn, this dangerous elevation of the nation to transcendent "messiah" status, "unleavened by . . . strong consciousness of divine judgment," opened the door to "the confusion of God and self." Most recently, Bellah claims, "Self seems to have replaced, or . . . subordinated, God and Nation as the predominant idea of our culture." The simultaneously theological and sociological "mistake" involved here is that "the sacred" has become "available only in the fragile consciences of individuals."

Bellah reports that Parsons reacted with strong reservations and ambivalence to these ideas about the flaws and perils of American civil religion, which Bellah first elaborated in *The Broken Covenant*. He attributes this to the fact that although Parsons, too, regarded Protestant Christianity as the primary source of the American value system, he took a more positive view of it.

Indeed, the concepts through which he expressed what he considered to be the essence of Protestant Christianity, which, he believed, provided context for "instrumental activism," "institutionalized individualism," and the "societal community"—brought him, says Bellah, to the edge of viewing the United States as "a version of the Kingdom of God on earth," adding, "a tendency to which Parsons did not entirely succumb, but by which he was sorely tempted."

Bellah is certain that Parsons would not have subscribed to the crux of his argument that the Protestant Reformation was a mistake. And yet, somewhat wistfully, he ends up wondering whether the divergences between his understanding of the development and problems of American society and Parsons's might stem primarily from "generational differences": "I have lived through years very different from those of Parsons's lifetime," he concludes, "but if he could have experienced those years perhaps he would have been more open to the possibility that my argument is valid."

In "Modernity and Its Endless Discontents," Donald Levine reviews and analyzes several features of modernity considered to be troubling, even dangerous, by many prominent scholars of the past one hundred fifty years. Among the chief sources of these discontents with modern life are processes such as equalization leading to an inevitable breakdown of traditional authority and roles in family and workplace; inclusion whereby the dominance once enjoyed by particularistically defined groups is steadily eroded; and differentiation whereby many aspects of social life (governmental, religious, educational, artistic) attain a degree of independence from each other that seems to threaten the unity of society. These processes continue to generate considerable disquiet for many today. Levine discusses Parsons's deep appreciation of the dislocations and disequilibria created by these processes, many of which are of global reach.

But he argues that Parsons did not consider the dilemmas precipitated by these processes to be insuperable, although they were formidable and in many places seemingly intractable. Parsons believed that new ways of resolving many of these dilemmas would be developed, and social unification and synthesis achieved in keeping with the tenor of modernity. However, Levine states, modernity is not one thing, but many things. New, unanticipated dilemmas, some intrinsic to social life, some pertaining to relations of human social life with its environments, are constantly emerging. The various modernities are themselves in process and the dilemmas and discontents they generate have not yet been fully exhibited. As long as modernity continues to develop and change, perhaps they never will be. Our understanding of problems of modernity and our ability to resolve them, Levine implies, remain fragmentary, uncertain, and, much like modernity itself, ongoing.

Part III: Sociology and Culture

The third group of chapters discusses the important concept of culture. Helmut Staubmann begins "Culture as a Subsystem of Action: Autonomous and Heteronomous Functions" by noting that sociological understanding was riven during the nineteenth and early twentieth centuries by the opposition between idealist (cultural) and materialist (economic, political) frameworks, the two alternating in becoming dominant. He points out that whereas Max Weber initially bridged this polarity—as did Georg Simmel in some ways—it was only in Talcott Parsons's *Structure of Social Action* that a systematic synthesis of the two standpoints was achieved.

In Parsons's view, culture is a system in its own right, with its own integrity and autonomy, but it is also a subsystem of the larger action system. In its autonomous functions culture *influences,* but does not determine, processes in the social system, the personality system, and the behavioral system. Culture as a subsystem is also influenced but not determined by each of the other subsystems. In their heteronomous functions, however, cultural elements such as artworks, literature, and knowledge of musical compositions or performers are put to the *use* of political or economic ends, and in this respect such elements are not evaluated by cultural standards but by other considerations such as their monetary value, or as indicators of taste, status, or class position. Staubmann argues that it is largely these heteronomous functions of culture that preoccupy most contemporary sociologists of culture, to the exclusion of its autonomous functions. Staubmann stresses that the actions of snobs, poseurs, and parvenus who use cultural elements in these heteronomous ways are not cultural in meaning but rather have social or economic or political significance.

Although many contemporary sociologists of culture disparage Parsons's functionalism as "idealist," their own equally functionalist but much simpler approach is a reversion in modern dress to the materialist-positivist standpoint of the nineteenth century. Staubmann concludes that the contemporary emphasis in the sociology of culture not only reduces the understanding of culture but also shrinks the understanding of our lives and our social world.

Jeremy Tanner's "Rationalists, Fetishists, and Art Lovers: Action Theory and the Comparative Analysis of High Cultural Institutions" is the first fully articulated analysis of artistic culture based on an action-theoretic framework. It is also one of the two chapters in this volume (the other is Renée Fox's) that integrates empirical materials—here, archival records and museum holdings—deeply in the analysis.

Tanner's organizing concept is "expressive symbolism," the aesthetic-affective representation of normative attitudes and forms as these have been shaped through evolutionary processes originating in Judeo-Christian and ancient Greek societies. His methodology is correspondingly comparative-historical.

Tanner traces differences in conceptions of the sacred on the one hand and political and social life on the other, between ancient Greek and later Western Christian societies, and relates them to corresponding shifts in the role of the artist and the substance of artistic representation. The Greek emphasis on logos and form fostered a rationalized approach to visual representation in which proportion, measurement, calculation of foreshortening, and perspective became established formal aesthetic principles. The artist in ancient Greece was, however, primarily a citizen of the polis and only secondarily an artist, and worked at the behest of the state and state-religious bodies for whom his primary obligation was to defend and provide for the welfare of the state. The aesthetic principles developed by Greek artists were committed to treatises that were then passed on over the generations, and came to serve as the core of later artistic developments. For centuries, artists worked under the patronage of kings, aristocrats, and the church; in later periods, their products were sought after in the market by the rising bourgeoisie. Competition among artists, the emergence of "schools" of art, and then the creation of academies devoted to artistic training became common and even a necessity. The Christian subject matter of art sought to portray the wisdom and will of the divinity in all its beauty, and the artist became linked to the divine as a creator and a genius in his own right. The autonomous role of the creative artistic genius, established firmly in the Renaissance, has been continually developing and becoming more institutionalized. Much of ancient Greek art consisted of a repetition of forms. Modern art, though its representational skills are deeply informed by ancient Greek principles, is embedded in a highly differentiated society. Modern artists abide by a cult of creativity, relying on buyers who are for the most part anonymous. They follow the injunction "Make it new."

Tanner's chapter shows how particular strands of Greek and Judeo-Christian culture, adapting to different political and social environments, yielded a radical differentiation of art and artist from other cultural and social spheres and imparted a cultural pattern distinctive to Western high culture. In a long concluding section he notes that the expressive symbolism of Western high culture is intimately engaged in exchanges with other spheres of Western life—

economic, social, political as well as cultural—and thus profoundly affects our perceptions, our motivations, and our understanding.

Staubmann's and Tanner's chapters are complementary, together indicating the way forward for a new and powerful action-theoretic analysis of art that is both congenial to the art object and illuminating of it.

Uta Gerhardt's and Charles Camic's chapters explore historical roots of Parsons's conception of culture and its role in the body of his theory and in his empirical interests and concerns. Both Gerhardt and Camic make extensive use of primary documents in the Parsons Papers at the Harvard University Archives, but they approach the topic of culture and its role in social action in different ways. Gerhardt's "The Weberian Talcott Parsons: Sociological Theory in Three Decades of American History" covers much of Parsons's career and discusses his contributions to many areas within sociology. Camic's chapter, "From Amherst to Heidelberg: On the Origins of Parsons's Conception of Culture," focuses on a decade in Parsons's early career in which his understanding of the concept of culture changed.

Gerhardt suggests that a unifying theme of Parsons's corpus is his adherence to both substantive and methodological ideas derived from Max Weber's writings. In making this argument she is closely in line with Parsons's own autobiographical writings. She emphasizes commitment to the independence of academic thought and research from religious and political ideologies and commitment to the objectivity of scientific or scholarly concepts as methodological continuities between Weber and Parsons.

She interprets Parsons's efforts to use sociological understanding and insight to contribute effectively to public political discourse as following a Weberian model. To support this view she discusses Parsons's writings on a long list of politically controversial matters: Nazi Germany, planning social change for postwar Germany, the importance of the social sciences as a national resource in the United States, the McCarthyism of the 1950s, the distribution of power in American society, the Cold War, economic development and modernization of underdeveloped societies, civil rights, and university institutions and academic freedom. These essays not only make up a large portion of his work but also are organically related to some of his most creative thought. For example, his writings on social science as a national resource were amplifications of his earlier understanding of the potential of theory-centered research for advancing empirical analysis. His critique of C. Wright Mills's discussion of the power structure of American society led to his innovative conception of political power; and his analysis of the civil rights movement amplified his understanding of societal community in modern societies. Gerhardt also notes that Parsons made frequent use of specific Weberian concepts—the Protestant ethic, modern capitalism, rational-legal authority, and charisma—in these practical or applied writings, thus indicating the extent to which he remained under Max Weber's influence throughout his career.

Camic's chapter examines Parsons's understanding of the concept of culture in the context of the different usages he encountered in the course of his studies at Amherst College, in Bronislaw Malinowski's anthropology seminar at the London School of Economics, and at the University of Heidelberg. At Amherst Parsons was taught—and adopted, if his extant undergraduate papers are a fair indication—a conception of culture as "omnibus," or patterning many domains of human life, and as "loose-knit," or permitting much independence among the different domains. The Franz Boas school of anthropology was the primary source of this conception, but Camic argues that it became an overlay to broad intellectual concerns that American culture of the 1920s, divided between rural or small-town and urban, between fundamentalist and sophisticated versions, was in crisis. William F. Ogburn's theory of cultural lag, which emphasized differences between industrial or technical culture, and moral or customary culture, captured this sense of crisis, and Parsons seems to have adopted a similar view in his undergraduate essays.

In Malinowski's seminar, however, he learned a conception of culture that underscored the ways in which a culture is strongly integrated and functions as a unitary whole. This perspective was strengthened during Parsons's period at Heidelberg, where, he later wrote, the "ghost" of the several-years-deceased Max Weber was the predominant influence in the social sciences. Here Parsons was exposed to the Germanic conception that emphasized Kultur as a unitary, organic expression of the inner spirit of a people or nation. His later writings on culture entail this understanding, notwithstanding his introduction in 1951 of a basic distinction between cultural and social systems. Camic also underscores the fact that Parsons, however much he took from Weber, did not adopt the German sensitivity to the ways that contemporary culture is tragically under attack and vulnerable, a theme highly developed in Weber's writings on modern civilization.

Part IV: The Human Condition

The chapters in the last section of the book take up issues that moved to the foreground of Parsons's thought in the last decade of his life, although, as the essays make clear in various ways, they had been leitmotifs of his work throughout his career.

Edward Tiryakian's contribution centers on one of Parsons's major essays, "A Paradigm of the Human Condition." For Tiryakian, this essay is not just a "capstone" piece that "retraces [the] major steps" Parsons took over the course of his seven decades of "theorizing about action systems." Rather, it breaks new ground in that here Parsons moved beyond the orbit of the social and behavioral sciences, even the most general system of action, into metatheory, and some of the largest and deepest questions about the meaning of human existence.

Tiryakian begins by providing an overview of some of the core components of Parsons's general theory of action, particularly its four function categories and their bearing on his longstanding "motivation to integrate knowledge while advancing sociological theorizing." His general paradigm of the human condition, Tiryakian states, extends the reach of the four-function schema to include the interrelationships of the action system with what Parsons termed the human-organic, the physico-chemical, and the telic systems. For Tiryakian, the most significant feature of the paradigm is the inclusion of the telic dimension, which he attributes in part to the influence of Robert Bellah, and which is the component of Parsons's perspective on the human condition that pertains to the "reality of the nonempirical world," transcendent aspects of human existence, and the ponderably imponderable domain of ultimate meaning. Tiryakian quotes Parsons as stating that the telic has "especially to do with religion," that he recognizes "the philosophical difficulties of defining the nature of that reality," and that he "shar[es] the age-old belief in its existence."

Tiryakian goes on to compare Parsons's approach to the human condition with those of a "peer group" of other intellectuals "drawn mainly from the ranks of social scientists." These include Émile Durkheim, Georges Gurvitch, Edward O. Wilson, Hannah Arendt, and Margaret Archer.

Tiryakian moves on to discuss evidence that, directly and indirectly, Parsons "received an important philosophical justification" for bringing the telic into his conceptual framework from the modern, post-Kantian, existential-phenomenological outlook of the German philosopher Karl Jaspers, who was a member of Parsons's doctoral dissertation committee at Heidelberg. (In later life Parsons wrote a laudatory essay in which he called Jaspers a "social scientist's philosopher.")

Tiryakian enjoins us not to treat the human condition paradigm as a "museum-piece," but to "utilize, elaborate, and update" it. He attempts to do this by placing it in a contemporaneous historical framework, reflecting on how it illuminates the impact of several phenomena: the collapse of the Soviet Union and empire, the current domination of international agendas by the United States, the attack of 9/11, the confrontations occurring between world religion-based civilizations, and the relationship of these developments to the process of globalization, terrorism, and the "antinomy of war and peace."

Renée Fox's chapter is the only one in the volume based on firsthand ethnographic research and as such illustrates the two-way interchange between theory and research that Parsons espoused. It grew out of her studies of Médecins Sans Frontières (MSF—Doctors Without Borders), the international organization devoted to medical humanitarian and human rights witnessing action, and of the emergence and ramifications of bioethics in American society. Both are medically centered developments with roots in the value-oriented social protest movements of the 1960s, MSF in France and continental Europe, and bioethics in the United States. Fox's immersion in Parsons's theoretical perspective on the importance of health, illness, and medicine to the functioning of a society and on their cultural and human condition significance contributed to her recognition of the sociological import of MSF and bioethics, her motivation to study them, and her conceptual approach. Conversely, some of her data and insights suggest ways in which certain Parsonian ideas might be enriched or modified.

Fox focuses on the complex relationship within both MSF and American bioethics between "universalism" and "particularism"—the components of one pair of Parsons's "pattern variables." Intellectually and morally, in their ethos and practice, MSF and U.S. bioethics are strongly committed to universalism: in the case of MSF, in their dedication to responding to the suffering of people urgently in need of medical care, regardless of their nationality, ethnic group, location, and the cause of their suffering; in bioethics, through its adherence to a notion of a "common morality" that it considers authoritative for all persons in all places. Their allegiance to universalism creates strains for both MSF and bioethics in dealing with social and cultural differences, and also results in tendencies for them to universalize some of the particularities of their underlying worldviews.

Fox's chapter opens with a discussion of the connections between universalism and particularism and the evolutionary unfolding of modern society that Parsons delineated in many of his works, and the way that they are experientially encountered by members of MSF and by American bioethicists. Both MSF and American bioethicists exhibit a belief in the worthiness of modern society, shaped by Western cultural tradition. But Fox's research highlights the tenacity of ascriptive particularism and, beyond that, of internecine conflicts between particularistic groups in the face of modernizing global forces. These conditions that MSF confronts in its field missions represent a development that Parsons may have underestimated. Furthermore, at the beginning of the twenty-first century U.S. bioethics and MSF confront new, politicized forms of particularism that constitute serious challenges to their universalism.

Fox concludes with the suppositions that Parsons would have recognized how his theory might need to be altered to account for these developments, and that he would also have been perturbed by the societal and global implications of the threats to universalism that U.S. bioethics and MSF presently encounter.

In the final chapter, " 'Social Evolution' in the Light of the Human-Condition Paradigm," Victor Lidz finds that the comprehensive analysis of the human condition that Parsons developed in 1970s undermines the conceptual status of the theory of social evolution that he had developed in the 1960s. Lidz shows that Parsons's writings on social evolution had deep roots in the development of his thought. They are connected with his studies of Max Weber's writings on religion and comparative civilizational analysis and to his early teaching on comparative social institutions, and also draw on his use of biological models in theory construction, including concepts of equilibrium, function, and cybernetic control. Lidz traces the complex typology of societies that Parsons developed as part of his evolutionary theory, and suggests that it continues to be valid and useful as an important starting point for contemporary comparative sociology. However, relying on theoretical writings of the evolutionary biologist Ernst Mayr, Lidz argues that the logical form of Parsons's typology actually departs fundamentally from that of neo-Darwinian taxonomy. It is not actually an evolutionary theory. In Lidz's view, the paradigm of the human condition suggests that the concept of evolution, strictly construed, should be limited to the domain of living systems or biology. Human action systems have evolved out of biological systems, but the dynamics of their change are different from those of living systems subject to natural selection. Theories of social change can be developed around Parsons's typology of stages of societal development, but they should not be constrained by an effort to make them fit the dynamics of evolutionary biology.

CONCLUSION

This collection of essays constitutes the work in progress of a loosely knit yet strongly allied group of colleagues who find Parsons's theory of action a valuable resource for understanding contemporary issues in sociological theory. All of the chapters select elements of the theory and critique, adapt, refine, or extend them to gain fresh purchase on problems that confront sociologists today. None of the chapters presents simply an "application" of the theory of action as Parsons formulated it, and we are hopeful that readers will appreciate that a fixed or static theory that can be applied to particular problems in a mechanical fashion was not Parsons's legacy to us. Parsons himself strove constantly for extension, tighter codification, and refinement of his theory, and above all for fresh insight, empirical as well as theoretical. We believe that the chapters in this volume demonstrate the continuing vitality of this heritage in the social sciences.

NOTE

1. The following section draws on materials previously presented in Victor Lidz (2000) and Lidz and Harold J. Bershady (2000).

REFERENCES

Bales, Robert F. 1950. *Interaction Process Analysis: A Method for the Study of Small Groups.* Cambridge, Mass.: Addison-Wesley.

Berelson, Bernard R., Paul F. Lazarsfeld, and William N. McPhee. 1954. *Voting.* Chicago: University of Chicago Press.

Habermas, Jürgen. 1987. *Theory of Communicative Action.* Boston: Beacon Press.

Lidz, Victor. 2000. "Talcott Parsons." In *The Blackwell Companion to Major Social Theorists,* edited by George Ritzer. Oxford: Blackwell.

Lidz, Victor, and Harold J. Bershady. 2000. "Convergence as Method in Theory Construction." *Österreichische Zeitschrift für Soziologie,* special issue 6, edited by Helmut Staubmann and Harald Wenzel. Wiesbaden: Westdeutscher Verlag.

Lidz, Victor, and Charles W. Lidz. 1976. "Piaget's Psychology of Intelligence and the Theory of Action." In *Explorations in General Theory in Social Science,* edited by Jan Loubser, Rainer C. Baum, Andrew Effrat, and Victor M. Lidz. Volume 1. New York: Free Press.

Mayhew, Leon H. 1982. "Introduction." In *Talcott Parsons on Institutions and Social Evolution: Selected Writings,* edited by Leon H. Mayhew. Chicago: University of Chicago Press.

Parsons, Talcott. 1937. *The Structure of Social Action.* New York: McGraw-Hill.

———. 1949. *Essays in Sociological Theory, Pure and Applied.* Glencoe, Ill.: Free Press.

———. 1951. *The Social System.* Glencoe, Ill.: Free Press.
———. 1953. *Essays in Sociological Theory.* Revised edition. Glencoe, Ill.: Free Press.
———. 1960. *Structure and Process in Modern Societies.* Glencoe, Ill.: Free Press.
———. 1963. "On the Concept of Political Power." *Proceedings of the American Philosophical Society* 107(3): 232–62.
———. 1964a. *Social Structure and Personality.* New York: Free Press.
———. 1964b. "Some Reflections on the Place of Force in Social Process." In *Internal War: Basic Problems and Approaches,* edited by Harry Eckstein. New York: Free Press.
———. 1966. *Societies: Evolutionary and Comparative Perspectives.* Englewood Cliffs, N.J.: Prentice-Hall.
———. 1967. *Sociological Theory and Modern Society.* New York: Free Press.
———. 1969. *Politics and Social Structure.* New York: Free Press.
———. 1970. "Some Problems of General Theory in Sociology." In *Theoretical Sociology: Perspectives and Developments,* edited by J. C. McKinney and Edward A. Tiryakian. New York: Appleton-Century-Crofts.
———. 1971. *The System of Modern Societies.* Englewood Cliffs, N.J.: Prentice-Hall.
———. 1977. *Social Systems and the Evolution of Action Theory.* New York: Free Press.
———. 1978. *Action Theory and the Human Condition.* New York: Free Press.
Parsons, Talcott, and Robert F. Bales. 1955. *Family, Socialization and Interaction Process.* Glencoe, Ill.: Free Press.
Parsons, Talcott, Robert F. Bales, and E. A. Shils. 1953. *Working Papers in the Theory of Action.* Glencoe, Ill.: Free Press.
Parsons, Talcott, and Dean R. Gerstein. 1977. "Two Cases of Social Deviance: Addiction to Heroin, Addiction to Power." In *Deviance and Social Change,* edited by Edwin Sagarin. Beverly Hills, Calif.: Sage Publications.
Parsons, Talcott, and Gerald M. Platt. 1973. *The American University.* Cambridge, Mass.: Harvard University Press.
Parsons, Talcott, and Edward A. Shils, eds. 1951. "Values, Motives, and the Theory of Action." In *Toward a General Theory of Action,* edited by Talcott Parsons and Edward A. Shils. Cambridge, Mass.: Harvard University Press.
Parsons, Talcott, and Neil J. Smelser. 1956. *Economy and Society.* Glencoe, Ill.: Free Press.
Whitehead, Alfred North. 1925. *Science and the Modern World.* New York: Macmillan.

Part I

Social Institutions and Social Processes

Chapter 1

Parsons's Economic Sociology and the Development of Economic Sociology

Neil J. Smelser

In this chapter I will say a few words about the intellectual origins in Talcott Parsons's development of the ingredients that were synthesized into a culmination of his most mature theoretical statement in *Economy and Society* and outline the essential features of that statement. I will comment on that book's subsequent "fate" in light of developments within sociology and to some extent economics, and sketch the reinvigoration of economic sociology in the past two decades, and present a critical assessment of work in those decades, partly from a "Parsonian" point of view—an assessment that will yield, finally, a programmatic statement of needed developments in economic sociology in general.

INTELLECTUAL THREADS IN PARSONS'S EARLY ECONOMIC SOCIOLOGY

As one reads Parsons's early work, it is possible to discover many of the ingredients of the intellectual perspectives—many of them still nascent, programmatic, and theoretically indeterminate—that were combined and reached their full development in the writing and publication of *Economy and Society* in the period from 1954 to 1956.

- From his undergraduate and graduate days he absorbed much of the institutional economics and anthropological critique of economics and adopted the view that formal economics could be criticized for its individualism, rationalism, abstractness, and assertions of generality if not universalism. At the same time he came to reject the positivistic, antitheoretical implications of institutional economics.
- In his doctoral dissertation he rejected both one-sided economic (Karl Marx) and "Geist" (Werner Sombart) explanations of capitalism in particular and economic life in general in favor of the multisided Weberian view of the explanation of economic activity (1928–29). In fact, Max Weber's work dominated Parsons's thinking about the origins of capitalism and economic sociology in general in his early career.
- He more or less rejected economic rationality as a psychological postulate, both in his thoroughgoing attack on utilitarian theory in *The Structure of Social Action* (1937) and in pressing for its reinterpretation as an institutional or normatively regulated orientation in his essays on professions and the social structure (1939) and the motivation of economic activities (1940).

- He argued for the infusion of economic life with value elements (especially in his focus on Weber's religious factor and Alfred Marshall's writing on the moral dimensions of "wants"), and with normative elements (especially in his focus on Émile Durkheim's insistence on both the formal-legal and informal regulation and integration of economic activities [1937]).
- While not questioning the fundamental legitimacy of analytic economics, Parsons insisted, with Vilfredo Pareto, that it was only one "aspect" or analytic "factor" along with others (1936). We were to modify this particular version of the relations between the economic and noneconomic in *Economy and Society*.
- In his early Harvard years he solidified his antipositivist position regarding the necessity for and independent significance of theory and the importance of the concept of system (mainly under the influence of Frank Taussig, Alfred North Whitehead, and Lawrence J. Henderson).

ECONOMY AND SOCIETY

This combination of discrete elements of Parsons's early economic sociology was made possible by the independent development of his general theory of action. This was a chain of developments beginning with the early formulation of most of the pattern variables in his famous disaggregation of Ferdinand Tönnies's famous dichotomy as set forth in "Note on *Gemeinschaft* and *Gesellschaft*" in *The Structure of Social Action* (Parsons 1937, 686–96); his consolidation of the pattern variables in his empirical essays several years later; his elevation (with Edward Shils) of these pattern variables to a general theoretical status and their incorporation into a general theory of action (Parsons and Shils 1951); and, finally, principally in his work with Robert F. Bales, the transformation and consolidation of the pattern-variable scheme into the four-functional-problem scheme, composed of adaptive, goal-attainment, integrative, and latent (AGIL) pattern-maintenance and tension-management dimensions (Parsons, Bales, and Shils 1953). Whatever may be said about the ultimate formal theoretical status of these formulations—and I have recorded some reservations along these lines—taken together they provided Parsons and me with a framework that, when combined with many of Parsons's accumulated writings and insights on economic sociology, produced a much more substantial theoretical statement of the nature of economics and of the nature of the relationships between economic and sociological theory than had heretofore existed.

To illustrate, Parsons's earlier views represented economic factors as one of a larger set of analytic factors (or aspects, or variables), which combine to produce empirical outcomes. These factors were never fully categorized, and the ways in which they might interact were never adequately formulated. The residue was a valuable and valid perspective, but one that nevertheless remained quite indeterminate. The AGIL schema provided us with an instrument where the "factors" involved in economic and noneconomic life could now be formulated as "subsystems of the larger social system" (Parsons and Smelser 1956, 6). These subsystems (of which the economy is one) are determinate in number, one subsystem corresponding to each of the four functional problems. Furthermore, in identifying these analytic subsystems as such, it became easier to conceive of the kinds of relations that might obtain among them. And since each of the subsystems could be analyzed into further subsystems, doing this brought us closer to appreciating the structures and processes appropriate to each of the subsystems and the relations among these. I regard this shift from "factors" to "systems" identified within a definite theoretical framework as a major step in the direction of greater theoretical determinacy.

The theoretical ramifications of this shift were many. We were able to formulate the relations among subsystems in terms of an exchange among them, in which the typical products or outputs from the standpoint of one of them would prove to be resources for the others, and vice versa. This permitted us to reexamine the famous economic "factors of production" (land, labor, capital, and organization) and to identify their sources from other specific systems in society, and also to identify the outputs of the economy in terms of their origins in the polity, the integrative system, and the latency system.

In considering the boundary exchanges further, we developed the idea of mediated double interchanges among the economy and other societal subsystems. For example, the exchange between labor on the one hand and consumer goods and services (the exchange between the economy and the latency system) was not a direct exchange in a differentiated society but was, rather, facilitated by an intermediate mechanism—in this case, money—which permitted the move away from barter exchanges to more flexible exchanges (money wages for labor, money payments for items of consumption). We treated money as a generalized resource and examined its significance at all the boundaries of the economy.

The idea of double interchanges led us in two additional directions. First, we were able to reinterpret the work of John Maynard Keynes and Joseph Schumpeter as consisting in large part of variations and modifications of parametric assumptions at the boundaries of social subsystems exchanging with the economy and the analysis of the ramifications of these modifications. Second, we were able to take a general, independent theoretical look at the intermediate mechanisms, which we called the generalized media of exchange, and develop both a classification of the major types of media (money, power, influence, and value commitments, corresponding to each subsystem), and to develop a seven-level scheme of generality of commitment of these resources. Each of the generalized media were to become subjects of independent statements by Parsons in the years after the publication of *Economy and Society* (Parsons 1969a, 1969b, 1969c).

I mention briefly three further avenues of theoretical development in *Economy and Society*. The first had to do with specifying the ways in which the boundary exchange between the economy and other subsystems are regulated normatively. We used the AGIL scheme to organize this analysis as well and revisited the elements of the major institutional complexes of contract, occupation, and property as regulating mechanisms. Second, we broke down the economy itself into further subsystems according to the AGIL scheme, and attempted to reanalyze issues such as the trade cycle, the consumption function, and the investment function. Third, we developed a model of structural differentiation of the economy, building on the models of learning and personality change developed by Parsons and Bales (1955). This model once again utilized the AGIL model of the economy as a way of systemizing the deficits and opportunities that triggered processes of structural change in the economy; we used the famous separation of ownership and control in the corporation as a running empirical example.

THE RECEPTION AND INFLUENCE OF *ECONOMY AND SOCIETY*

It is generally appreciated that the impact and enduring influence of *Economy and Society* has been less than one might have expected, given the depth and implications of the theoretical innovations I have sketched. To give an account of the reasons for this requires a complex mental experiment involving considerable speculation, because the initial expectations may have been wrong; the data regarding impact are necessarily incomplete; and one has to imagine what the impact might have been if the "reasons" cited had not been present. Undaunted by these difficulties, I will now undertake such an experiment.

Most economists reacted either negatively or with indifference to *Economy and Society*. Parsons's Marshall Lectures, delivered in 1953 at Cambridge University, were received rudely by the Cambridge economists, with the exception of one scholar, and the reviews of the book by economists were cold. I believe there are two reasons for this. First, economics was at that time very self-contained as a theoretical enterprise, certainly more so than now; and the range of theoretical issues raised in our book did not resonate with technical issues in economics; most regarded it as not relevant to their preoccupations. Furthermore, no discipline, especially a proud one, wants to be labeled a special case of something more encompassing, but that is precisely what Parsons did in his Marshall Lectures and what we did in *Economy and Society.*

As for sociologists, although Parsons's influence was at its height in the 1950s, most sociologists did not interest themselves in his abstract theory, and almost none had training in formal economics. Most of the economic sociology of the day focused on concrete issues, dominated by "industrial sociology" as fashioned by the Hawthorne studies and their ramifications, interest in labor relations, interest in class and consumption, interest in the economic domination of politics, and the early development of modernization theory. All these factors contributed to a low level of receptivity to *Economy and Society* in the mid-1950s.

Fifteen years later the prospects for the influence of the book and the approach it represented were much darker. By 1970, functionalism in general and Parsonian thought in particular were under attack on multiple fronts. The siege comprised a political assault from the left, associated with the general political turmoil throughout the society and in sociology as well. On the macroscopic side, there was a resurgence of radical sociology, Marxist sociology, and the "domination" side of Weberian sociology, not including his economic sociology. Modernization and development theory (including Parsons's contributions, such as Parsons 1960) was attacked as functionalist-inspired and West-centric, and was challenged also from the left by the dependency theory and world-systems theory alternatives. In the field of economic sociology itself, one of its main pillars, industrial sociology, came under attack from the left as "management sociology." The research available on the rest of economic sociology was not notable in amount or quality. During the decade between 1962, when I published my synthetic volume, *The Sociology of Economic Life,* and 1973, when I prepared the second edition (Smelser 1973), I encountered only very modest ongoing empirical research.

Dealing as it did with societal systems, subsystems, and system-processes, the main impulse of *Economy and Society* was macrosociological. The so-called "microsociological revolution" of the late 1960s and 1970s also took sociological concerns away from the macro level. In this development I include the social behaviorism of George Homans (1974), the exchange theory of Peter Blau (1964), the revitalization of symbolic interactionism (Blumer 1969), the ethnomethodology of Harold Garfinkel (1967) and others, the micro-conflict theory of Randall Collins (1975), and "collective action" theory inspired by the economist Mancur Olson (1971), which also had ramifications for sociology. Guy Swanson once asked me why the boundary-exchange paradigm of *Economy and Society,* which he found valuable, did not generate very much sustained interest and research in sociology. I was never able to find a satisfactory answer to that question, but I think a partial answer is that the idea of exchange was captured by the microsociological revolution, and as a result the focus came to be primarily on inter-individual exchange processes.

The radical and Marxist impulses themselves turned out to be temporary and collapsed as intellectual forces first in Eastern, then Western Europe, and then in the United States—partly preceding and partly coinciding with the demise of international Communism in general. Yet the approaches that dominated in the 1950s and early 1960s and were the victims of events of the late 1960s and 1970s did not return. In the late 1970s, then, there was a kind of double void in economic sociology caused by the widespread discrediting of two sets of traditions in relatively rapid succession. It was in this context that the field soon began to experience a multisided renaissance, to which I now turn.

THE NEW ECONOMIC SOCIOLOGY AND OTHER DEVELOPMENTS

Beginning in the late 1970s and the early 1980s, economic sociology experienced a great rejuvenation, a substantial impulse that has continued to accelerate to the present time. The movement, drawing in significant numbers of very talented researchers, was multisided and somewhat eclectic from a theoretical point of view, even though it was consistently characterized by a preoccupation with and polemic against the limitations of neoclassical economics. The signs of institutional vitality in the subfield are evident:

- A proliferation of courses in economic sociology in college and graduate school curricula, as well as a substantial interest in schools of business, especially in organization studies.
- The high quality of contributing scholars and their formation into critical masses in a number of prestigious universities—Princeton University, the University of Pennsylvania, Cornell University, Stanford University, and the University of California, Berkeley.
- The appearance of a number of journals, collections of essays, textbooks, and handbooks on economic sociology.
- The successful formation and crystallization of a sizable and vital section on economic sociology in the American Sociological Association.

In regarding the movement as a whole, it is possible to identify major strands of development.

Embeddedness and the Focus on Networks

The development of the concept of the "embeddedness" of economic actions and the focus on the significance of networks to economic activity is associated mainly with the work of Mark Granovetter. A decade after the publication of his influential work on interpersonal ties in the labor market (Granovetter 1974) he published a theoretical essay (Granovetter 1985) in which he identified a "new economic sociology," which he contrasted with the "old economic sociology" of Parsons, Smelser, and Wilbert Moore, which he saw as vital in an earlier period but then as "suddenly died[ing] out." He regarded the Parsonian effort to negotiate a truce between sociology and economics as futile, and called for a more fundamental and militant critique of neoclassical economics. His more positive formulations focused on what he called "embeddedness," a term taken from the work of Karl Polanyi that he defined for himself by saying that economic actions are "embedded in concrete, ongoing systems of social relations" (Granovetter 1985, 487). Networks among economic agents are an essential ingredient of embeddedness, and subsequently he linked networks to institutions, which he termed "congealed networks" (Granovetter 1992, 7). Economic institutions in particular involve "the mobilization of resources for collective action" (Granovetter 1992, 6).

This idea of embeddedness, modified in specific meaning from time to time, has been influential in the recent literature and has come to stand as something of an identifying symbol for the "new economic sociology." In fact, the term is sometimes used more or less synonymously with the idea of structure.

Applications of Organization Theory

Three theoretical approaches in organization theory have developed as part of the revival of economic sociology. The first is resource-dependency theory, which, as the name suggests, means that organizations are dependent on their environments to survive. Ronald Burt (1983) suggests that the three principal sources of profit are the number of suppliers, competitors, and customers. The more "structural autonomy" a firm has—that is, if there are more suppliers, few competitors, and many customers—the better position a firm will be in to buy cheaply and sell expensively. Burt's formulation is in one aspect an extension of the theory of imperfectly competitive markets.

The second application is population ecology, in which the main driving force of organizations is adaptation in the interests of survival (the influence of the Darwinian tradition is evident). Studies have indicated that the diffusion of an organizational form typically passes through several distinct stages: a very slow beginning, then explosive growth, and finally a slow settling down (the influence of Marx and Schumpeter is evident; see Hannan and Freeman 1988). Individual studies of this dynamic have focused on railroads, banks, and telephone companies.

The third broad perspective is called "new institutionalism," which focuses on the cultural and cognitive aspects of organizations (see Powell and DiMaggio 1991). DiMaggio has argued that the contribution of the new institutionalism is that it explores "factors that make actors unlikely to recognize or to act on their interests" and that it also focuses on "circumstances that cause actors who do recognize and try to act on their interests unable to do so" (DiMaggio 1988, 4–5). In a study of the large corporation in the United States, Neil Fligstein (1990) notes that the multidimensional form of organization spread not only because it was seen as a model but also because this organization form made it easier for firms to take advantage of new technology and the emerging national market.

Cultural Economic Sociology

There is a group of sociologists who are committed to focusing on the symbols and meaning structures in the economy. At the forefront of this group are Viviana Zelizer and Paul DiMaggio, who have carved out the main directions of this "cultural economic sociology." In a programmatic statement, Zelizer criticized contemporary economic sociology for its tendency to reduce everything to social relations and networks, which she labeled "social structural absolutism" (1988, 629), though she was careful to avoid an equally unwelcome reduction, "cultural absolutism," in taking cultural factors into account. In DiMaggio's account (1994), culture's role in economic relations can be either "constitutive" or "regulative": "constitutive" refers to categories, scripts, and conceptions of agency, and "regulative" refers to norms, values, and routines. DiMaggio's position is fully compatible substantively if not terminologically with Parsons's view of the significance of culture; in particular, Parsons formulated culture as analogous to genetic codes and programs in his later writings. One main difference in emphasis is that Parsons gave more salience to cosmological aspects of culture, in which both values and normative systems are grounded.

Three studies by Zelizer are informative of the cultural impulse. Her first major work was a study of life insurance in the United States, with special emphasis on the clash between sacred values and economic values (Zelizer 1979). Later she published a study entitled *Pricing the Priceless Child* (1985), where she described a similar movement, but this time in reverse: children, who in the nineteenth century had an economic value, would in the twentieth century be seen increasingly in emotional terms and be regarded as "priceless." In her most recent study (1994), she argues that money does not constitute a neutral, nonsocial substance but appears in a variety of culturally influenced shapes ("multiple monies").

Strengthening a Historical and Comparative Tradition

A number of comparative-historical studies that echo Weber's monumental tradition have been an ingredient of the revival of economic sociology. Among these are Bruce Carruthers's study of finance in seventeenth- and eighteenth-century England (1996), and several other recent attempts to challenge Alfred Chandler's (1977) account of the rise of the large industrial corporation in the United States. In particular, Carruthers is interested in establishing the influence of politics on economic action, as well as economic influence on politics. Using primary materials on the trade in shares of the East India Company in the early 1700s, he demonstrates that political ambitions clearly influenced the choices of buyers and sellers. The critique of Chandler has similarly emphasized the state's role in the emergence of the large industrial corporation. Chandler has also been criticized because his key idea—that recent advances in technology made it necessary around the turn of the century to reorganize the large multidivisional unit—does not account for political and social considerations (Fligstein 1990; Roy 1988).

There have been fewer explicitly comparative studies than comparative-historical ones. One notable study is Frank Dobbin's (1994) study of industrial policy toward railways in the United States, Britain, and France in the nineteenth century. Dobbin shows that in the case of the United States, local self-rule and a weak federal state translated into antimonopoly policy and attempts to safeguard private initiatives in the area of railway regulation. The tradition of a centralized state in France inspired an approach assuming strong interference from the authorities in the planning and running of the railroads. And the tradition of safeguarding elite individuals in Britain helped to bring about an industrial policy that shielded the small entrepreneurial firm.

James Coleman and Interest-Based Sociology

The most radical attempt during the past few decades to develop a sociological interest deriving from the utilitarian and classical economic tradition is that of James Coleman. His efforts, begun in the 1960s, culminated in the publication of *Foundations of Social Theory* (1990). Though his work was not in economic sociology as such, he attempted to lay a basis for all of sociology using principles derived from economic theory (it might be said that Coleman was attempting to generalize Gary Becker's (1976) effort to do economic analyses of particular topics such as family life, crime, racial discrimination, and addiction).

Although the creation of a social theory was Coleman's primary agenda, *Foundations of Social Theory* and some of his other works contain a number of analyses that are relevant to economic sociology. Three of particular importance are trust, social capital, and the modern corporation. Coleman characterized trust as a conscious bet: one calculates what one can win and lose in trusting someone. Social capital is defined by Coleman as any social relation that can be of help to an individual in fulfilling an interest; notably, social capital is usually the unintended result of some action, undertaken for a different purpose. "The function identified by the concept 'social capital' is the value of those aspects of social structure to actors, as resources that can be used by the actors to realize their interests" (Coleman 1990, 305). For example, a firm represents a form of social capital. Coleman was, further, interested in the fact that once people have created a firm to realize their interests, the firm can develop interests of its own. To Coleman, the firm is basically a social invention, and agency theory is particularly useful for analyzing it.

Two Special Substantive Foci

To round out the picture, I should mention two substantive foci of recent economic sociology, both reflecting recent developments in the world's economic organization. The first is the rising significance of the global economy. Although neither the phenomenon nor scholarly interest in it is entirely new one (see the work of Vladimir I. Lenin [1939] on imperialism a century ago), its magnitude as a world phenomenon accelerated dramatically in the twentieth century. Renewed interest in the international dimension emerged more than three decades ago with the crystallization of dependency theory (Cardoso and Faletto 1969; mainly relating to Latin America) and world-systems theory (Wallerstein 1974). Both those approaches are still with us, but have lost their salience, both because of accumulating criticisms of them and because of the dispersion of interest in the global economy to more particular aspects. Recent work has focused on the fate of the state in the context of global economic trends and the development of multinational firms, international capital markets, new forms of production such as commodity chains, the international division of labor and international migration, global cities, and the internationalization of culture through the mass media.

The second focus of economic sociology has been the economic aspects of the transition to various forms of capitalism resulting from the demise of command economies associated with communism and socialism in many parts of the world. A considerable literature on this transition is accumulating. Lawrence P. King and Ivan Szelenyi (2005) have identified three ideal types of transition: capitalism from above (exemplified by post-Soviet Russia); capitalism from below (exemplified by China), and capitalism from without (exemplified by Eastern European countries such as Hungary and Poland). King and Szelenyi trace the differences to inherited variations in the class and political structures of the countries involved, as well as to their distinctive cultural traditions. The larger context of efforts such as King and Szelenyi's is the burgeoning literature on "varieties of capitalism."

Developments Within Economics

In the meantime, the past decades have not been inactive ones in economics, and that statement applies to aspects of special interest to economic sociologists. The label "mainstream" still refers primarily to the neoclassical tradition, which still maintains a certain centrality, if not dominance, in the field. Its version of economic rationality is definitely the negative polemical target of those economic sociologists who include a critique of economics in their work. Yet over time this line of criticism has come to lose some its edge because of internal developments in economics that have diversified the field and weakened the neoclassical dominance.

Among the areas of internal criticism and diversification, neoclassical assumptions concerning risk and information are crucial. Economics has developed traditions of analysis based on assumptions of risk and uncertainty (for example, Sandmo 1971; Weber 2001) and information as a cost (for example, Stigler 1961; Lippman and McCall 2001). In addition, numerous alternative versions of economic rationality—for example, Herbert Simon's (1982) emphasis on "satisficing" and "bounded rationality"—have appeared and been consolidated into definite traditions. Still other variations on rational behavior have been developed in behavioral economics, which incorporates many psychological assumptions that are at variance with the mainstream (Mullainathan and Thaler 2001) and which attends more to experimental and other empirical data than has been the case in the past. Theoretical developments in game theory have pushed conceptualizations of rationality in interactional—as contrasted with individualistic—directions. New preoccupations with economic change and evolution (such as path dependency) have appeared, along with new literatures on topics such as agency theory and transaction costs. The latter have commanded the attention of a group known as "new institutional economists," who regard the development of institutions such as contract and property as rational adaptations that facilitate market interchange.

In principle, all this dynamism increases the probability of openness at the boundaries of economics and the prospect of interdisciplinary penetration and collaboration, including that between economics and sociology. In practice, however, such new relationships have been slow to develop, and economic sociology and economics remain relatively isolated from each other. There are many reasons for this state of affairs, but in my estimation the main barrier is a product of the persistent methodological individualism of the economic perspective and economists' insistence on *some* kind of rationality and choice (however modified) and sociologists' stress on relational factors and their focus on nonrational constraints on economic choice and behavior. Those differences remain so profound as to constitute a continuing paradigmatic chasm between the two disciplines.

"PARSONIAN" REFLECTIONS ON DEVELOPMENTS IN ECONOMIC SOCIOLOGY

At this point I would like to develop a series of critical reflections on the developments traced in the preceding section, whereby I have no intention of suggesting that theory is absent in contemporary developments in economic sociology, particularly with reference to micro- and meso-levels of analysis (where micro refers to the individual actor and meso to organizations and relations among them). One need only mention the rational-choice theory of Coleman, the structuralism of Harrison White (1992), the evolutionary underpinnings of organizational ecology, and neo-Marxist elements in some of the work on the international economy. My observations are selective and are aimed at certain threads of economic sociology, not the whole. My comments will be consistent with the Parsonian perspective as found both in his earlier works and in *Economy and Society,* but they should not be construed as insisting on a return to the specific substance of Parsons's work. Rather, I mean to identify some important gaps and voids and thus some potential avenues for productive inquiry.

Structure and Pattern

Perhaps the most notable recent line of development has been the stress on networks as social conditioners of economic processes, decisions, and outcomes. This perspective has dominated work on labor-market outcomes, the ethnic economy, and in large degree relations among organizations. As corollaries, the main sustaining mechanism in networks is inter-individual and inter-organizational trust, and the main "medium" that makes networks viable is mutual influence among them. Insofar as networks are represented as social structure—the terms "network" and "structure" are often used more or less interchangeably—a rather micro and barren notion of social structure emerges from the "network" model. A number of elements are missing:

- The interplay of a variety of sanctions other than influence.
- The normative constraints, both informal and institutional, that invariably are a part of social structure.
- The value and other cultural ingredients by which both the interplay of sanctions and normative invocations are justified.
- The processes of strain, breakdown, reequilibration, and change of the structure.

Of course, all of these ingredients are conspicuous in Parsons's own understandings of "structure," and stand in contrast with a network conception of structure. (By way of qualification, in other strands of contemporary economic sociology, legal and political structures are invoked as influences on economic action; my remarks apply less well to these lines of analysis.) Zelizer (2005) asserts that too much of contemporary economic sociology is limited to discussions of structure; to this she might add that the notion of structure is itself limited in scope and nuance.

Meanwhile, a related but distinct limitation can be found in the formulations of those who explicitly include cultural dimensions as elements of the fabric of economic life. Zelizer herself is foremost among these scholars. She develops a sharp critique of the cultural barrenness of economists' abstract and universal formulations of the "meaning" of economic transactions in general and consumption in particular. At the same time she is opposed to "reductionism" of all sorts—economic, structural, and cultural (Zelizer 2005). Her particular analytic formulation is that it is necessary to "build bridges connecting continuously negotiated, meaning-drenched social relations with the whole range of economic processes" (349). In her own work she has brilliantly illustrated this penetration of cultural ingredients into economic areas such as life insurance, the economic significance of children, money, and consumption in general.

The key question—and limitation—resides in the terms "continuously negotiated" and "meaning-drenched." The importance of these cultural elements and processes is not in doubt. In my estimation, however, these concepts constitute the beginning step of scientific cultural analysis, and the main question is how and where to carry her insight further. The terms have a nongeneral quality that invites particularistic empirical descriptions of cultural intrusion into markets and processes—and this is the main line of cultural analysis that has been carried out. Still to be undertaken is an effort to seek and identify typical patterns and processes, for example, types of cultural modification of economic activities, typical tensions between the particularities of cultural meaning and standardization of economic meanings, processes of change in cultural meanings such as synthesis, syncretism, and secularization. These general elements are very much in the Parsonian repertoire, and are necessary if we are to move beyond the limits of case-specific and particularistic descriptions, however instructive these might be.

System and Theory

We can generalize that most of the inquiry in the revitalized economic sociology has been at the micro (individual) and meso (organizational) levels, with rather little attention to the macro level, that of the economy as a whole and its interactions with other sectors or systems of society. (The analysis of the state and economic activity would be an exception to this generalization. The continuing work in world-systems theory, such as it is, would also be an exception.) The general picture is one of middle-range thinking. Furthermore, because most of the recent lines of development in economic sociology tend to stress the importance of one or two variables or frameworks such as culture, gender, networks, or organizational evolution, inquiry has tended to limit itself to "factors" rather than looking at larger "systems" of combined variables and forces (this distinction is discussed on p. 32 of this chapter). This stress on discrete factors sometimes generates a certain amount of side-play and polemical interchange as to which factors are primary and what each neglects. This phenomenon of explanatory fragmentation at the cost of synthetic explanation is widespread in the social sciences, and not a feature of economic sociology in particular.

Although this pluralistic factor-based approach has given economic sociology its current richness and vitality, efforts at creative synthesis of the classics (especially Weber, Schumpeter, and Parsons) are notably missing. Without that complementary line of theorizing, the field of economic sociology—like any area of inquiry with areas of specialization and subspecialization—tends toward sprawl. Sharpening the theoretical focus of economic sociology and working toward synthetic interpretations of its findings seems essential at this time of the field's development.

To put the matter in Parsonian language, one might invoke the model of pulsating tendencies between processes of differentiation and those of integration—rooted in the theoretical framework that informed Durkheim's *Division of Labor in Society,* later analyzed by Parsons and Bales in the small-group context but then generalized. As a subfield, economic sociology has experienced a very vigorous season of differentiation, and now it would profit from the development of more general models and theories that systematically relate societies, institutional structures, and systems to one another; generate models of systematic interaction among global, national, and local levels; and integrate the range of middle-range findings that continue to accumulate in economic research.

A comment on interdisciplinary work, especially with economics, is also in order. Economic sociology as a subfield has a special problem in that it sits on the perimeter of a well-established, distinguished, proud, and territorially conscious body of scientific inquiry by economists. As a result, those "doing" economic sociology can hardly avoid the ever-present framing by, if not overwhelming shadow of, economists and their work. (The same generalization can be made of political sociology vis-à-vis political science, though political sociology has meshed with political science research far more readily than has economic sociology with economics.)

The implications of this circumstance for interdisciplinary inquiry are considerable. On the side of economics the "interdisciplinary impulse" has tended to take three forms: first, ignoring sociological and other factors because of their long tradition of "assuming" social context as parameters of their models and theories; second, when acknowledging them, "converting" them into such parameters as a way of preserving the formal structure of their models and theories; and third, undertaking some kind of imperialistic extension of economic models to explain nonmarket and noneconomic phenomena. On the side of sociology, the tendency has been to take an ambivalent and hostile attitude toward economics (especially its commitment to rationality and choice) and let "interdisciplinary" take the form of polemical criticism or of a sociological form of imperialism, in other words, invoking sociological interpretations of economic phenomena. None of these strategies has proved especially fruitful, and the main picture is one of an abiding separation of the disciplines.

One line of interdisciplinary work that I have urged over the years has been that of "complementary articulation," an acknowledgment that any explanation will have to avoid treating everything as a causal determinant, and will have to focus on certain operative variables and determinants, and "freeze" others into parametric assumptions. Often the territory that is "frozen" is the very territory that is problematical from the standpoint of some other line of social-science inquiry. For example, some version of "rationality" is assumed in most economic analysis, but it is problematical for psychologists; as a rule, political stability is assumed as a parameter in economics, but it is problematical in political science and sociology. The kind of articulation that I have in mind is that on both sides of disciplinary lines investigators acknowledge the need for this kind of structuring of explanation and modeling, but explicitly rely on the substantive theory and empirical findings to inform the "freezing" process and to remain prepared to be flexible in changing the parametric assumptions of models and theories in accordance with substantive knowledge in neighboring fields. My suggestion is not especially radical. This kind of articulation is not altogether unknown in contemporary work. For example, the work of behavioral economics consists largely of systematically modifying psychological assumptions and proceeding from there to build explanations and models. If such a method were to be consciously attempted, however, it would introduce a more positive and potentially productive interdisciplinary mode into the picture, and certainly would constitute a better mode of interdisciplinary work than those we now practice.

Science

Except for the dearth of self-conscious and systematic theorizing noted, most lines of contemporary work in economic sociology that continue to give attention to the norms and procedures of social-scientific inquiry remain intact—identification of empirical variables, attention to issues of representativeness of samples, sensitivity to issues of measurement and design, and an appropriate concern with causal priority.

In certain areas, however, a "constructivist" perspective giving little attention to those ingredients has entered the scene, as it has in other disciplines and in selected areas of sociology. In a review of the tradition of the interplay between economic and religious forces—a tradition that includes the great names of Marx, Weber, and Ernst Troeltsch—Robert Wuthnow (2005) discovered in recent research a preponderance of case studies relying on the language of particularized and complex discourse analysis. Wuthnow concluded that "much of the recent work seems to have abandoned claiming to be scientific" and went on to observe that "having established that social life is messy, scholars now face the more difficult task of imposing some order on that messiness." (622). Wuthnow's diagnosis coincides precisely with mine.

CONCLUSION

It is appropriate to offer the warmest of welcomes to the vital resurgence of economic sociology that has occurred in the past quarter century. The hoped-for next step is to revisit the economic sociologies of Marx, Weber, Durkheim, Polanyi, Schumpeter, and Parsons. I do not advocate a literal embrace of their theories, but certainly a recognition and pursuit of the scope of their pioneering analyses is in order.

REFERENCES

Becker, Gary S. 1976. *The Economic Approach to Human Behavior.* Chicago: University of Chicago Press.

Blau, Peter. 1964. *Exchange and Power in Social Life.* New York: Wiley.

Blumer, Herbert. 1969. *Symbolic Interactionism: Perspective and Method.* Englewood Cliffs, N.J.: Prentice-Hall.

Burt, Ronald. 1983. *Corporate Profits and Cooptation: Networks of Market Constraints and Directorate Ties in the American Economy.* New York: Academic Press.

Cardoso, Fernando H., and Enzo Faletto. 1969. *Dependency and Development in Latin America.* Berkeley: University of California Press.

Carruthers, Bruce. 1996. *City of Capital: Politics and Markets in the English Financial Revolution.* Princeton, N.J.: Princeton University Press.

Chandler, Alfred. 1977. *The Visible Hand: The Managerial Revolution in the United States.* Cambridge, Mass.: Harvard University Press.

Coleman, James S. 1990. *Foundations of Social Theory.* Cambridge, Mass.: Harvard University Press.

Collins, Randall. 1975. *Conflict Sociology.* New York: Academic.

DiMaggio, Paul. 1988. "Interest and Agency in Institutional Theory." In *Institutional Patterns and Organizations,* edited by Lynn Zucker. Cambridge: Cambridge University Press.

———. 1994. "Culture and Economy." In *The Handbook of Economic Sociology,* edited by Neil J. Smelser and Richard Swedberg. New York and Princeton, N.J.: Russell Sage Foundation and Princeton University Press.

Dobbin, Frank. 1994. *Forging Industrial Policy: The United States, Britain and France in the Railroad Age.* Cambridge: Cambridge University Press.

Fligstein, Neil. 1990. *The Transformation of Corporate Control.* Cambridge, Mass.: Harvard University Press.

Garfinkel, Harold. 1967. *Studies in Ethomethodology.* Englewood Cliffs, N.J.: Prentice-Hall.

Granovetter, Mark. 1974. *Getting a Job: A Study of Contacts and Careers.* Cambridge, Mass.: Harvard University Press.

———. 1985. "Economic Action and Social Structure: The Problem of Embeddedness." *American Journal of Sociology* 91(3): 481–510

———. 1992. "Economic Institutions as Social Constructions: A Framework for Analysis." *Acta Sociologica* 35(1): 3–11.

Hannan, Michael, and John Freeman. 1988. *Organizational Ecology.* Cambridge: Cambridge University Press.

Homans, George. 1974. *Social Behavior: Its Elementary Forms.* New York: Harcourt, Brace, Jovanovitch.

King, Lawrence P., and Ivan Szelenyi. 2005. "Varieties of Post-Socialist Economies." In *Handbook of Economic Sociology,* edited by Neil J. Smelser and Richard Swedberg. 2nd edition. Princeton: Princeton University Press.

Lenin, Vladimir I. 1939. *Imperialism: The Highest Form of Capitalism.* New York: International Publishers.

Lippman, Steven A., and John J. McCall. 2001. "Information Economics." In *International Encyclopedia of the Social and Behavioral Sciences,* edited by Neil J. Smelser and Paul B. Baltes. Vol. 11. Oxford: Elsevier.

Mullainathan, Sendhil, and Richard H. Thaler. 2001. "Behavioral Economics." In *International Encyclopedia of the Social and Behavioral Sciences,* edited by Neil J. Smelser and Paul B. Baltes. Vol. 2. Oxford: Elsevier.

Olson, Mancur. 1971. *The Logic of Collective Action: Public Goods and the Theory of Groups.* New York: Schocken.

Parsons, Talcott. 1928–29. " 'Capitalism' in Recent German Literature: Sombart and Weber." Parts 1 and 2. *Journal of Political Economy* 36(6): 641–62; 37(1): 31–51.

———. 1936. "Pareto's Central Analytic Scheme." *Journal of Social Philosophy* 1(3): 244–62.

———. 1937. *The Structure of Social Action.* New York: Macmillan.

———. 1939. "The Professions and Social Structure." *Social Forces* 17(4): 457–67.

———. 1940. "Motivation of Economic Activities." *Canadian Journal of Economics and Political Science* 6(2): 187–203.

———. 1960. "Some Reflections on the Institutional Framework of Economic Development." In *Structure and Process in Modern Societies.* New York: Free Press.

———. 1969a. "On the Concept of Political Power." In *Politics and Social Structure.* New York: Free Press.

———. 1969b. "On the Concept of Influence." In *Politics and Social Structure.* New York: Free Press.

———. 1969c. "On the Concept of Value-Commitments." In *Politics and Social Structure.* New York: Free Press.

Parsons, Talcott, and Robert F. Bales. 1955. *Family, Socialization and Interaction Process.* Glencoe, Ill.: Free Press.

Parsons, Talcott, Robert F. Bales, and Edward A. Shils. 1953. *Working Papers in the Theory of Action.* Glencoe, Ill.: Free Press.

Parsons, Talcott, and Edward A. Shils, eds. 1951. *Toward a General Theory of Action.* Cambridge, Mass.: Harvard University Press.

Parsons, Talcott, and Neil J. Smelser. 1956. *Economy and Society.* Glencoe, Ill.: Free Press.

Powell, Walter, and Paul DiMaggio, eds. 1991. *The New Institutionalism in Organizational Analysis.* Chicago: University of Chicago Press.

Roy, William. 1988. "Functional and Historical Logic in Explaining the Rise of the American Industrial Corporation." *Comparative Social Research* 12(1): 19–44.

Sandmo, Agnar. 1971. "On The Theory of the Competitive Firm Under Price Uncertainty." *American Economic Review* 61(1): 65–73.

Simon, Herbert. 1982. *Models of Bounded Rationality.* Cambridge, Mass.: MIT Press.

———. 1973. *The Sociology of Economic Life.* 2nd ed. Englewood Cliffs, N.J.: Prentice-Hall.

Smelser, Neil. 1973. *The Sociology of Economic Life.* 2nd ed. Englewood Cliffs, N.J.: Prentice-Hall.

Stigler, George. 1961. "The Economics of Information." *Journal of Political Economy* 69(3): 213–25.

Wallerstein, Immanuel. 1974. *The Modern World Systems.* Vol. 1. *Capitalist Agriculture and the Origins of the European World Economy in the Sixteenth Century.* New York: Academic.

Weber, M. 2001. "Risk: Theories of Decision and Choice." In *International Encyclopedia of the Social and Behavioral Sciences,* edited by Neil J. Smelser and Paul B. Baltes. Vol. 20. Oxford: Elsevier.

White, Harrison. 1992. *Identity and Control: A Structured Theory of Social Action.* Princeton, N.J.: Princeton University Press.

Wuthnow, Robert. 2005. "New Directions in the Study of Religion and Economic Life." In *Handbook of Economic Sociology,* edited by Neil J. Smelser and Richard Swedberg. 2nd edition. Princeton: Princeton University Press.

Zelizer, Viviana. 1979. *Morals and Markets: The Development of Life Insurance in the United States.* New York: Columbia University Press.

———. 1985. *Pricing the Priceless Child: The Changing Social Value of Children.* New York: Basic Books.

———. 1988. "Beyond the Polemics of the Market: Establishing a Theoretical and Empirical Agenda." *Sociological Forum* 3(4): 614–34.

———. 1994. *The Social Meaning of Money.* New York: Basic Books.

———. 2005. "Culture and Consumption." In *Handbook of Economic Sociology,* edited by Neil J. Smelser and Richard Swedberg. 2nd ed. Princeton: Princeton University Press.

Chapter 2

Looming Catastrophe: How and Why "Law and Economics" Undermines Fiduciary Duties in Corporate Law

Mark Gould

The inability of scholars and practitioners in the field of law and economics to conceptualize the value commitments that characterize professional responsibility, their expectation that all actors will act opportunistically in situations of imperfect information, and their commitment to private ordering and the undermining of legal rules have weakened severely the duties of care and loyalty that ground corporate law. Should we be surprised that corporate officers fail to put shareholder and firm interests above their own (the duty of loyalty) and that they fail to adhere to transparent processes providing shareholders and other stakeholders sufficient information to make independent judgments (the duty of care) when they are tutored by economists and when their legal obligations are more and more interpreted through the filter of a naïve economic theory? The paradox is that market economists may lead us into a situation where the trust necessary to sustain a market economy is undermined by their focus on the interests of discrete actors.

In this chapter, drawing on the work of Talcott Parsons, I explain why neoclassical economic theory is incapable of conceptualizing norms of fiduciary responsibility. I start by outlining the logic of neoclassical theory and explaining why a consistent neoclassical model must reduce normative orientations other than the norm of instrumental rationality to either the situational sanctions that support social norms or to individual preferences. I then explain why perfect-information neoclassical models have no need to conceptualize norms of fiduciary responsibility, and why the imperfect-information models that dominate contemporary law and economics thinking must do so, even though they cannot do so successfully. Finally, drawing on the work of Émile Durkheim and Max Weber in addition to that of Parsons, I provide the resources necessary for a theoretically viable conceptualization of corporate fiduciary duties, indicating why both the duty of loyalty and the duty of care must be defended if corporate relationships are to be treated as valid, and if corporate relationships are to be reproduced successfully.[1]

THE LOGIC OF NEOCLASSICAL ECONOMIC THEORY

We may characterize the logic of neoclassical economic theory in terms of four attributes:[2] atomism, a single positively stated normative orientation, exogenous ends, and methodological empiricism.

Atomism is akin to methodological individualism. It restricts conceptualizations to individual unit acts and to systems of interaction between unit acts. The simplest system is the agent, understood as the aggregation of unit acts attributable to individuals or to corporate actors. The relationships between unit acts may be complex, but in an atomistic theory, they must be reducible to the attributes of the unit acts that make up the system. One act affects another only insofar as it modifies the situation in which the second takes place.

In neoclassical economic theory, there is a single positively stated conceptualization of each and every actor's normative orientation. This is usually a form of instrumental rationality, where actors are seen as selecting means from among those available to them that are most efficient to attain their goals. In the jargon of economics, this is "maximization against constraints," where goals, arguments in a utility function, are maximized within the actor's situation. This means that there are three active mechanisms: the ends, which are maximized, the situation (the constraints), and the single positively stated normative orientation (maximization, the norm of instrumental rationality). Neoclassical theories address themselves to the nature of social "constraints" primarily when they are constituted by other unit acts in the system under analysis. Although ends are usually conceptualized as selfish, logically they may also be altruistic.

When actions are found to be inefficient or irrational, they are attributed to either error or ignorance (the absence of perfect knowledge, uncertainty). Alternatively, it is possible to suggest that the theorists' attribution of the actor's end was erroneous; the agent may be seen to have been maximizing a want different from the one the analyst previously imputed to her; this goal may be said to be revealed by the agent's actions.

Ends are treated as given; tastes are "unanalyzable" (or at any rate unanalyzed).[3] Ends are, therefore, theoretically exogenous. They are independent of the actor's situation (we often cannot state a functional relationship between the situation and an actor's tastes) and the theory says nothing about their selection, other than that they must be consistent, transitive, and obtainable within the relevant situation. The only postulated relationship between individual ends is dependent on the consequences of each for the other; the selection of one end in the first action may constitute part of the environment for future actions by others. As indicated above, one act may alter the situation within which another occurs; this may make a particular end of the second actor attainable or unattainable, or it may make one act more or less desired than another.

In this context empiricism may be characterized as the methodological position that allows the introduction of concepts only when they are reducible to directly observable "phenomena." Empiricists reject the introduction of "constructs," conceptualizations like the Freudian unconscious, Durkheim's collective conscience, or, more generally in the social sciences, social structures irreducible to the actions of atomistically conceptualized actors.

Neoclassical Perfect-Information Models

Perfect-information models are one variant of neoclassical theory. They are characterized by the four attributes enunciated in the previous section (atomism, a single positively stated normative orientation, exogenous ends, and methodological empiricism); they are differentiated from imperfect-information models by a particularly stringent application of the notion of instrumental rationality. As in all neoclassical models, in perfect-information models instrumental rationality is the sole positively stated normative orientation; actors in these models select the means most efficient to attain transitively ordered ends and all selected ends are attainable. Unlike other consistent neoclassical models, perfect-information models assume perfect knowledge for all actors. Error and ignorance as deviations from instrumental rationality are not present; information costs are zero and there is no uncertainty.

In perfect-information models, perfect competition prevails;[4] no buyer or seller has an effect on prices, as each atomistic unit is a price taker. These models are "frictionless." For example, fired employees are able to move to another comparable job immediately and without transaction costs and the costs of enforcing contracts.

In this model, in equilibrium each factor of production receives the value of its marginal product as its price. All factor markets are of the same type; labor is sold as a commodity and within the model functions like any other commodity. If the disjunction between consummate and perfunctory cooperation is recognized (Williamson 1985),[5] it has no significance, as the assumption of perfect information allows labor to be treated like any other input. Costless information allows for a simple translation between the capacity to work and the work actually accomplished. There is no problem in motivating employees as the nature and the amount of their work is manifest transparently to the employer; in consequence, in equilibrium workers are paid the value of their actual marginal product. No employer will pay any worker more and no employer will be able to pay any worker less than the value of her marginal product.

There can be no involuntary unemployment in this model. Given that there is no "friction," information is perfect and transactions are instantaneous, an unemployed worker is one who chooses not to work for the value of her marginal product. Labor markets, like all other markets, clear.

Although I have focused on labor, the same arguments apply to any physical input into the production process. In equilibrium, all inputs are paid the value of their marginal product. Since the equilibrium in this model is Pareto optimum, it represents a rational adaptation of all actors to the extant technology matrix, their own personal endowments, and their property holdings. It makes no difference whether capital hires labor or labor, capital. In either case, competitive pressures require that the most efficient technologies available, as defined by physics, be utilized.

The only caveat to this nirvana of efficient social order grounded in the instrumentally rational action of atomistically conceptualized actors is that a particular Pareto optimum is dependent on each individual's starting position, on her alienable and inalienable endowments. Thus, economic theorists generally granted the state the right and the obligation to utilize situational sanctions to protect property rights and to enforce contracts.

Contrary to Parsons's argument in *The Structure of Social Action,* there is no problem of order in perfect-information neoclassical models. Order is not created in these models through the anomalous assumption of a "natural identity of interests," which violates the logic of neoclassical theory. Instead it is created by the assumption of perfect information, which may be arbitrary but is consistent with the logic of the theory. The state may supplement this order by protecting property and person, but this, too, is consistent with a neoclassical (and Hobbesian) theory.

Next we will see that there is an alternative neoclassical way of looking at this set of issues; it entails challenging the assumptions on which orthodox perfect-information models are grounded.

IMPERFECT-INFORMATION MODELS

In perfect-information models, social norms, even social norms mandating rationality, are redundant. In situations of perfect information, an individually conceptualized notion of instrumental rationality suffices to explain social order. In equilibrium, each actor reaches an optimal state given her original endowments of alienable property and inalienable traits (a Pareto optimum). Social norms are unnecessary, would not emerge empirically, and are not conceptualized theoretically.[6]

While imperfect-information theorists accept instrumental rationality as the sole positively stated normative orientation, in their theories the status of error and ignorance differs from the one postulated in an assumption of perfect information. In imperfect-information models, uncertainty is manifest; information is not perfect, is likely to be asymmetrical, and is costly to obtain. Thus, rationality is limited and an actor's understanding of complex environments, incomplete.

In Oliver Williamson's version of transaction-cost economics, the existence of error and ignorance is manifest in two behavioral assumptions: bounded rationality and opportunism. In situations of bounded rationality, actors intend to act rationally but cannot do so because of the complexity of their environments. The fact that actors are subject to bounded rationality entails uncertainty as a constituent element within economic activities and forces recognition of the cost of information to reduce uncertainty. With perfect information, a comprehensive bargain can be struck at the onset of the employer-employee relationship and competition between employers eliminates any possible quasi-rent due to variations in work by employees. Bounded rationality forces the theorist to pay attention to the nature of governance structures within the firm and to the logic of the relationships whereby employers control and motivate their employees.

Actors, both employers and employees, are liable to act opportunistically, "which is a condition of self-interest seeking with guile" (Williamson 1985, 30, 47–49).[7] In the absence of opportunism, parties to a contract would "extract all such advantages as their endowments entitle them to when the initial bargain is struck" (31). Assuming bounded rationality and opportunism, Williamson presents "the following compact statement of the problem of economic organization: devise contract and governance structures that have the purpose and effect of economizing on bounded rationality while simultaneously safeguarding transactions against the hazards of opportunism" (xiii).

More generally, the situation constituted by the absence of perfect information may be thought of as a principal-agent problem. John W. Pratt and Richard Zeckhauser (1985) state, "The challenge in the agency relationship arises whenever—which is almost always—the principal cannot perfectly and costlessly monitor the agent's action and information. The problems of inducement and enforcement then come to the fore" (2–3). Agency relationships seek to bring order out of Hobbesian chaos.

The fact that men act rationally means that they will select the most efficient means to their ends and the most efficient means may well be force and fraud. In a world of asymmetrical information, actors will act opportunistically unless there are proximate situational sanctions that delimit "honest" activities as more efficient means to their ends, or unless situational incentives result in their selection of ends that do not rationally require the utilization of deceitful means. For Hobbes, an absolute sovereign wielded constraining sanctions. In much transaction-cost literature, they are to be wielded by a hierarchical authority, by fiat.[8]

Imperfect information and the consequent possibility of opportunistic action raise the problem of order. The social order that is a direct consequence of the assumptions of perfect-information models must be explained in models where the assumption of perfect knowledge is called into question. In neoclassical imperfect-information analyses the mechanisms of control and order are proximate positive and negative situational sanctions, which ensure or fail to ensure the maintenance of control and stability.

In their more enlightened forms, principal-agent theories recognize that a mutuality of "trust" facilitates order in social relationships and further recognize that trust is socially constructed. Pratt and Zeckhauser note that Kenneth Arrow "suggests that we must move beyond the usual boundaries of economic analysis—for example, looking at social values that might be internalized during an education process, not just monetary incentives—if we are to achieve adequate explanatory and prescriptive formulations" (Pratt and Zeckhauser 1985, 26; see also Arrow 1985). No doubt, but if the analysis remains consistently neoclassical, these "social values" must be reduced to the goals themselves or to the rewards, the situational sanctions, maximized in meeting individual goals.

In the next section, I explore these limitations of imperfect-information models when they remain within the neoclassical paradigm.

Motivating Employees to Work Effectively In perfect-information neoclassical models labor may be treated as a commodity; assuming perfect information allows the neoclassical theorist to ignore the distinction between the worker and her work (in Marxian terms, between labor power and labor), as work may be monitored costlessly. In these models, labor is merely one among many inputs to the firm, and like every other commodity used in production, the employee will receive the value of her marginal product in compensation. In equilibrium, no change would be manifest if labor hired capital instead of capital hiring labor; thus the logic of the economy may be portrayed as a set of input-output relationships where the firm is depicted as a black box. All choices are free and uncoerced; in equilibrium their outcome must result in the selection of that extant mode of production found most efficient by physicists. It is not necessary to examine the internal governance structure of a firm.

When the assumption of perfect information is dropped and opportunistic action becomes a possibility, the distinction between consummate and perfunctory work must be introduced. Employees must be motivated to work effectively and a variable amount and quality of labor may be forthcoming for any given wage; in consequence, crucial conclusions of perfect-information models are called into question.[9] Here questions of power and control must be raised at the level of employer-employee relationships within the firm.

This analysis may be put in terms of the principal-agent literature. Each employee may be treated as an agent motivated to work through situational sanctions (Akerlof and Yellen 1986; Bulow and Summers 1986; Shapiro and Stiglitz 1984/1986). Given the workers' presumed opportunism (ceteris paribus, it is in their interest to do as little work as possible within capitalist relationships) and the employers' imperfect knowledge, the extraction of work must be viewed as a variable subject to only partial control by the employer. In consequence, the extraction of work is always dependent on a recurring process of negotiation and bargaining between employers and their various employees. It is only in circumstances where the employers have absolute control that the distinction between consummate and perfunctory labor disappears and labor truly becomes a commodity like any other commodity.

Once bounded rationality and opportunism enter the picture, principal-agent problems of all sorts arise. Principal-agent problems are those where the principal attempts to induce the agent to act in the principal's interest. Within the firm, these quandaries raise questions of governance and control.

The reader will remember that neoclassical theory, whether in its perfect- or imperfect-information form, allows for the conceptualization of only one positively stated normative orientation, usually the norm of instrumental rationality. The actor is seen as selecting those means most efficient to attain her end and the theory says nothing about the selection of ends, other than requiring their transitive ordering and their situational attainability. Additional "norms" are reduced to the actors' ends or else they loose their normative nature and are conceptualized as situational sanctions that enforce the "norms," reducing those "norms" to the situational sanctions; in consequence, the mechanisms of control in a principal-agent theory are generally limited to situational rewards and punishments.

The problem with this formulation is that it is easy to see that it does not allow for the adequate explanation of when and why agents may act in their principal's interest even when those principals cannot monitor their efforts effectively. Even extreme contractarians such as Armen

Alchian and Harold Demsetz are forced to allude to the effects of normative orientations, in their case to "loyalty and team spirit," when explaining why workers sometimes cooperate consummately in situations of imperfect, asymmetrical information (Alchian and Demsetz 1972, 790–91). Such insights are, however, wasted, because their adequate implementation would violate the logic of neoclassical theory. A few examples show how theorists retreat from them.

Joseph E. Stiglitz comes close to and then retreats from the insight that action may be at least in part motivated by nonrational value commitments, moral obligations. In his discussion, these obligations entail a managerial commitment to corporate rationality, to rational action as traditionally understood in neoclassical economics and not to the manager's own self-interest (Stiglitz 1985). He retreats from this insight by suggesting that "Akerlof has provided an insightful 'rational' explanation for such seemingly irrational [that is, nonrational] behavior" (136, n.10). Alternatively, he might have claimed, tautologously, that these corporate officials seek to maximize an other-regarding preference, the corporation's interest.

Williamson tells us, "Transaction cost economics characterizes human nature as we know it by reference to bounded rationality and opportunism." At this point he adds a footnote stating, "I originally intended also to include a discussion of dignitarian values and how these influence economic organization. The effort was not successful, however. I regard this as a regrettable shortfall and hope that it will be remedied" (Williamson 1985, 44, n.3). In fact, Williamson has retreated from this task, now arguing that trust and, a fortiori, other normative orientations may be explained in light of the alignment of incentives (Williamson 1993).

These tentative steps (and this list of examples could be extended ad infinitum) were bound to be aborted because the inclusion of normative obligations (value commitments, dignitarian values, and so forth) within economic theory requires the transformation of its neoclassical paradigm through the inclusion of more than one positively stated normative orientation.[10] In neoclassical theory, any normative orientation—moral values, normative expectations, situational goals—is reduced to the sanctions that support the social norm or to a revealed preference. In the first, the sanction inhibits or motivates activity. In contrast, as Jan Elster puts it, normative orientations may motivate action even without the fear of punishment or the anticipation of reward (Elster 1989, 14 n.3). Although the second always allows for an ad hoc reconceptualization of socially structured actions, it does not allow for their successful explanation. Here, where norms constitute intrinsic incentives for acting in a certain way, preferences will often be ill-behaved, nontransitive, and contradictory.

Elster gives a wonderful example of the problem of poorly ordered preferences:

> Consider a suburban community where all houses have small lawns of the same size. Suppose a house-owner is willing to pay his neighbor's son ten dollars to mow his lawn, but not more. . . . Imagine now that . . . [this house owner] is offered twenty dollars to mow the lawn of another neighbor. It is easy to imagine that he would refuse, probably with some indignation. But this has the appearance of irrationality. By turning down the offer of having his neighbor's son mow his lawn for eleven dollars, he implies that half an hour of his time is worth at most eleven dollars. By turning down the offer to mow the other neighbor's lawn for twenty dollars, he implies that it is worth at least twenty dollars. But it cannot both be worth less than eleven and be worth more than twenty dollars. (115)

In this situation, where norms regulate desires, preferences are not transitively ordered and the theoretical apparatus of neoclassical theory crumbles, as its arguments become indeterminate. One cannot explain actions by desires and opportunities when the desires are inconsistently ordered. Ill-ordered preferences are routine in situations where social norms are conceptualized as regulating the selection of both ends and means; what is desirable and obligatory (normative) often conflicts with what is desired (wanted, preferred). Yet the necessity for the inclusion of normative orientations into imperfect information models is manifest even within the brief discussion I have provided of simple principal-agent problems.

SOCIAL NORMS: THEORY AND ILLUSTRATIONS

Neoclassical theorists must reduce normative orientations either to individual preferences or to the sanctions that support the normative orientations. When a rational actor orients herself to a normative orientation from within this theoretical perspective, it is either as a preference to be maximized or a situational sanction, a constraint, partially constitutive of the situation she confronts. Often such analyses focus on the reputation effects of conforming to or deviating from such "norms." In either case, social norms are not treated as binding, as constitutive of obligations for actors. In some instances it is recognized that this type of discussion of social norms reduces them to behavioral regularities, to descriptive statements of factual norms with no normative content, with no independent capacity to regulate social activities (Posner 2000).[11] These conclusions hold for both the more general economics and rational-choice literatures and for the law and economics literature, where "norms" almost always refer to extralegal, informal, expectations.

These characterizations are not foolish, but they are incomplete, and they cannot stand on their own. Actors do bring different orientations to social norms, including calculating orientations, where the norm is taken into account only if it is accompanied by some probability of situational sanctions. However, actors may be committed to a norm. Sometimes law and economics scholars recognize this commitment, but when they do so they must, if they are to be consistent theoretically, reduce it to an individual preference. As Robert Cooter and Melvin Eisenberg (2001) write, "Internalizing a normative standard incorporates it into preferences" (1725). This conceptualization, in addition to falling prey to the genesis of nontransitively ordered preferences, fails to acknowledge the distinction between what is desired (preferred) and what is desirable and obligatory. Though the two may be related, they sometimes contradict one another.[12]

If norms are reduced to preferences or situational sanctions and perhaps are viewed as mere behavioral regularities, they can make no independent contribution to the explanation of social action. They may be convenient summary statements of activities otherwise explicable, but they can have no role in the explanation of legal activities (Posner 2000). The problem with this conclusion is that the attempt to conceptualize social norms is responding to a genuine anomaly within imperfect-information neoclassical theories. Above I typified that anomaly in a brief discussion of principal-agent theories; the onslaught of discussions of social norms from within the economics and "law and economics" literatures is in response to substantive variants of the same theoretical problem. Social order, cooperation, and much conflict (Coser 1956; Simmel 1955) are inexplicable without a satisfactory conceptualization of social norms, without the inclusion of normative expectations within social theory.

Institutions and Sanctions

Crucial to an understanding of social norms is their institutionalization, which emphasizes both their autonomous effects and their theoretical and empirical integration with situational sanctions. Crudely, we may say that a normative orientation is institutionalized when it is subsumed under, legitimated by, a social value, when conformity to the expectations it delimits is rewarded and deviance punished, and when the facilities necessary to conform to it are available to the relevant actors.[13] Positive and negative sanctions, situational rewards and punishments, are mobilized from within social groups and collectivities. Situational facilities are the instrumentalities required to implement social goals and may include actors in roles.

It is important to note that the same concrete object may be a facility or a reward. For example, role performances are the normatively regulated participation of actors in social interactions with specifiable role partners. Depending on the level of analysis, they may be considered to be either the limiting case of a collectivity or to be instrumentalities in the pursuit of some social goal.

Any concrete unit in a social system is always a combination, albeit not necessarily institutionalized, of all four components. We often allude to social norms as if they were concrete entities, but strictly speaking this is incorrect. There are no social norms without collectivities and role relationships. There is no social role that is not regulated by social norms and values within some collectivity or set of collectivities. Even so, the four components of social action, while interdependent, may vary independently. We may, for example, speak of social norms as varying independently of social groups in that the content of the norm may not be deduced directly from the nature of the collectivity (see Parsons 1966, 19).

Social norms are inextricably linked to the sanctions that support them, but an adequate understanding of this relationship requires the recognition that sanctions are more than incentives that must be aligned with the normative expectations. The reduction of a norm to sanctions, for example, by reducing it to a reputation effect, eliminates the autonomous effect of the normative orientation and precludes the resolution of the anomalies I have pointed to in imperfect-information models. Even so, one of the crucial functions of sanctions is to induce conformity with social norms. It might be rational for an actor to violate a social norm in a situation where no negative sanction is attached to that violation. If deviance is met with severe sanctions, it may no longer be possible to attain the first-order goal, and a second-order goal entailing conformity to the norm may be the rational outcome of "maximizing against constraints."

If the first function of sanctions is easily conceptualized within a neoclassical theory, the second escapes its confines. For Durkheim, the primary function of punishment is to characterize the boundaries of acceptable activity, to aid in constituting the normative. If an actor violates a legitimate norm, he must be punished to reinforce the binding nature of the norm among those already committed to it (Durkheim 1893/1984, 63). If known violations of social norms are allowed to pass unpunished, the sense of normative obligation will be undermined (240). When the punishment is vested in an organized body representative of the social group, the institutionalized status of the norm for members of that group is manifest (52). The consequence of this punishment is the maintenance of social cohesion, by way of a reinforcement of the vitality of normative expectations.[14]

Lastly, the application of negative sanctions in the face of deviance protects the righteous from being treated as suckers. If conformity to a social norm puts one at a disadvantage in comparison to opportunistic violators of that norm, knowing that deviance is likely to be punished enables those committed to the norm to conform to it without feeling like chumps, without feeling that they function at a comparative disadvantage to their more opportunistic compatriots (Hart 1961/1965, 193). Normative obligations may mandate conformity to certain expectations, but actual conformity is more likely when interest and obligation are well aligned, when desire and desirable are congruent.

Legitimation and Justification

Many recent economic analyses attempt to explicate the necessity of including autonomous normative expectations within a theory of social order. Many of these arguments confuse the conditions that necessitate the emergence of normative expectations (to explain social order) with their validity.[15] Although it may be true that the emergence of norms is grounded in the impossibility of creating order in situations of complexity and double contingency solely in terms of cognitive expectations (Luhmann 1972/1985, 31), the necessity of generalizing experience (25) does not explain why norms are treated as binding when it would be in the interest of an actor to violate them. Luhmann's analysis, the most sophisticated of these attempts, seems to suggest the reason: cognitive expectations lead actors to understand that in the long run order is superior to chaos, and thus normative expectations are accepted as valid. This reduces norms to rational—or, maybe better, reasonable—choices and comes close to recreating Locke's assumption of a natural identity of interests, an anomalous assumption within a neoclassical theory (Parsons 1937/1949, chapter 3).

To explain normative validity—the binding nature of normative obligations—two forms of normative orientation must be distinguished: legitimation, the subsuming of norms and activities under a set of morally constituted value commitments, and justification, procedural due process, where a constituted norm or activity is justified as the outcome of some set of procedural, constitutive norms.[16] Many discussions implicitly see procedures as the source of legitimation in modern societies; others, like Luhmann's analysis, make this point explicitly (Luhmann 1969/1983). Luhmann misses the continued importance of value legitimation in modern societies and forgets that procedural norms must themselves be legitimated; it is only legitimate procedures that justify successfully.[17] In consequence, he, like his counterparts in economics, fails to provide a convincing explanation of the binding nature of the normative expectations that emerge from within the social accommodation to uncertainty.

Values and Procedural Norms

Values are constitutive of binding moral obligations; at the same time, they characterize what is desirable within the context of a particular system. Moral values or principles appear "to us under a double aspect: on the one hand, as imperative law, which demands complete obedience of us; on the other hand, as a splendid ideal, to which we . . . aspire" (Durkheim 1925/1961, 96). They are defined with sufficient generality to be, in the ideal case, internalized by all members of the system of reference. In a college classroom, for example, both students and faculty should be committed to the principles of cognitive rationality.

For Weber, an "order" is regarded as legitimate when actors view the expectations it entails as binding obligations. While expectations may be fulfilled as a consequence of a rational cost-benefit analysis or because obedience has become habitual, such expectations constitute a legitimate order only when they are obeyed out of a sense of duty, because they are regarded as obligations. Obedience to a legitimate expectation entails conformity to the content of the expectation as the basis of action for its own sake. "Furthermore, the fact that it is so taken is referable only to the formal obligation, without regard to the actor's own attitude to the value or lack of value of the content of the command as such" (Weber 1926/1968, 215), that is, without regard to the actor's desires in regard to the obligation.[18] In Weber's view, the stability of an "order" is greatly enhanced when it is viewed as legitimate (31).

Weber is not discussing the existence of objective constraints that entail the necessity of conformity to some set of expectations. While a competitive machine-capitalist economy "forces the individual, in so far as he is involved in the system of market relationships, to conform to capitalistic rules of action," it does not constitute a legitimate order on these grounds (Weber 1904–5/1958), 54; see also 72, 181–82, 282 n.108). He is discussing a set of obligations akin to the Protestant ethic that are supported by a set of psychologically effective sanctions (Weber 1926/1968, 326–27). This ethic gave "direction to practical conduct and held the individual to it" (Weber 1904–5/1958, 97–98; see also 197 n.12, 217 n.3). It was constituted not as a dogma, but as a set of binding value-commitments, and as such it had the consequence of facilitating the construction of a valid economic order (Gould 1981a; 1986; 1987, chapter 4).

In Durkheim's terms, Weber is suggesting that an order is legitimated in terms of the system's moral obligations. For Durkheim, the collective conscience is constituted as a set of shared value-orientations. These values entail the possible subordination of private utility to the collective interest. As noted above, they constitute beliefs as obligatory and, at the same time, desirable (but not necessarily as desired).

When viewed as obligations, rules are withdrawn from individual discretion. In consequence, an institutional structure is stabilized when obedience to its rules is treated as a duty. What is crucial for Durkheim is the combination of the individual internalization of moral obligations and their external control over individual discretion. He distinguished habits, which dominate us from within, from moral values, which are *internalized* yet which "act upon us from the outside" (Durkheim 1925/1961; 1895/1982, 44). These values provide the solidarity "which, deriving from resemblances, binds the individual directly to society." It is this solidarity that Durkheim labels "mechanical" (Durkheim 1893/1984, 61).

In contrast, habitual actions are activities of long standing; they are customary "rules devoid of external sanction" (Weber 1926/1968, 29). They are very different from obligations. A habitual course of action may be changed with impunity. In contrast, for Weber, an order is recognized as valid (legitimate) only when an open violation of it is punished (32). This is, of course, the way that Durkheim defines crime, as actions "contrary to strong, well-defined states of the [collective conscience]," where the societal reaction to this violation is the punishment of the offender.

Social norms are universalistic rules that are defined at a lower level of generality than values; they constitute expectations that are differentiated across units within a system. They may be specified in terms of the category of unit to which they apply and according to the consequences of their violation. Procedural norms are the constitutive rules that characterize the process whereby norms are justified. If the constitutive rules are followed, the constituted outcome is justified. In positivistic conceptions of the law, any rule justified in terms of procedural, constitutive, rules is valid.[19] As I suggested above, however, this conclusion is fallacious; only those procedures that are legitimate, subsumed under accepted social values, justify.

In sum, norms and activities are legitimate when subsumed under and treated as specifications of accepted social values. Norms and activities are justified when the duly constituted outcome of legitimate procedures.[20] The importance of maintaining the analytical autonomy of legitimation and justification is manifest in the fact that they may be empirically independent. A norm may be viewed as procedurally justified and simultaneously be seen to violate institutionalized societal values. Judicial review embodies this principle, recognizing that procedurally valid outcomes may be illegitimate. In other words, there is a range of activity beyond which procedurally acceptable constituted norms will not be treated as binding. The clearest manifestation of this is found in acts of civil disobedience, where a moral commitment leads persons into public violations of a law (including procedurally valid laws), even though they expect to suffer a negative sanction for their violation.

With the differentiation of social and cultural norms, the process of subsuming norms and activities under social values is subject to the strictures of a culturally constituted and thus variable logic. This logic delimits the range of activities subsumable under a particular set of value orientations and constitutes what is consonant and dissonant with the values.

As I suggested above, persons may adopt a calculating or a noncalculating attitude toward valid, institutionalized social norms (including legal norms). Those for whom a legal norm is illegitimate or neutral, even if justified, will adopt a calculating orientation toward it. For them the law is reduced to the severity of the sanction attached to it and to the probability of its implementation in the face of a violation. When a violation of the law is perceived to be in the agent's interest, the probability of deviance is increased substantially.[21] In the absence of this variegated conceptualization of normative expectations, neoclassical theorists can characterize deviance, and perhaps they can characterize civil disobedience, but they cannot provide adequate explanations for them. Nor can they provide a satisfactory explanation for the binding nature of legal norms.

The Duties of Loyalty and Care

Corporate law grounds the fiduciary responsibilities of corporate officers. Conventionally, these responsibilities are conceptualized as the duties of loyalty and care. The duty of loyalty requires corporate officers to act in the interest of corporate shareholders (and perhaps in the interest of other corporate stakeholders) and to forgo their own interests when they contradict shareholder interests. The duty of care delimits procedures to which corporate officers must adhere when making significant corporate decisions. Both are mitigated and in some instances effaced within contemporary law and economics discussions of corporate law. I will here focus on the logic of nexus-of-contracts arguments, the law and economics arguments that reduce corporations to a set of contractual relationships, arguments that understand the notion of contract within a naïve free contract model. Such arguments necessarily undermine the nature of the duty of loyalty, which makes substantive demands on corporate officials; often they undermine the duty of care by restricting due process to its narrowest limits while recognizing that contracting agents must be guaranteed procedurally the autonomy necessary to make a free contract. I argue that the fallaciousness of this perspective may be made manifest in an analysis of contract law, emphasizing that a valid contract is both legitimate in terms of legal values and justified in terms of the procedures that Durkheim labeled the noncontractual aspects of contract. While this perspective on corporate law is unusual, it will, I hope, enable me to convince the reader of the veracity of my argument, that law and economics undermines the fiduciary elements in corporate law, and it will set the stage for a fuller elaboration in future work of how corporate law is being undermined.[22]

THE CORPORATION AS A NEXUS OF CONTRACTS

The locus classicus of nexus-of-contract theory in corporate law is Frank H. Easterbrook and Daniel R. Fischel's *The Economic Structure of Corporate Law,* but the theoretical foundation for their legal argument is provided by Alchian and Demsetz's 1972 article, "Production, Information Costs, and Economic Organization."

Alchian and Demsetz

In their 1972 article, Alchian and Demsetz assert: "To speak of managing, directing, or assigning workers to various tasks is a deceptive way of noting that the employer continually is involved in renegotiation of contracts on terms that must be acceptable to both parties" (Alchian and Demsetz 1972, 777). In this model, the firm entails "a *team* use of inputs and a centralized position of some party in the contractual arrangements of *all* other inputs. It is the *centralized contractual agent in a team productive process*—not some superior authoritarian directive or disciplinary power" (778) that constitutes the contractual form Alchian and Demsetz call a firm.

For Alchian and Demsetz, firms emerge because of team production where it is difficult or impossible to determine individual marginal products. If four workers are moving a piano, the employer may not be able to determine each individual's marginal product and thus shirking emerges as a possibility. Firms emerge when it is possible to increase productivity using team production and it is economical to estimate marginal productivity by observing input behavior. "The simultaneous occurrence of both these preconditions leads to the contractual organization of inputs, known as the *classical capitalist firms* [sic] with (a) joint input production, (b) several input owners, (c) one party who is common to all the contracts of the joint inputs, (d) who has rights to renegotiate any input's contract independently of contracts with other input owners, (e) who holds the residual claim, and (f) who has the right to sell his central contractual residual status" (783).

One method to reduce shirking is to have someone specialize as a monitor. One way to monitor the monitor is to give her the residual, "the net earnings of the team, net of payments to other inputs" (782). The monitor earns her residual through the reduction of shirking. In Alchian and Demsetz's argument, the monitor has no power over workers. Instead, the residual claimant enters into spot contracts with workers (and other suppliers); these contracts are voluntary and necessarily benefit all parties that enter into them.[23]

Corporations emerge, Alchian and Demsetz argue, because "for the most part, capital can be acquired more cheaply if many (risk-averse) investors contribute small portions to a large investment. The economies of raising large sums of equity capital in this way suggest that modifications in the relationship among corporate inputs are required to cope with the shirking problem that arises with profit sharing among large numbers of corporate stockholders. One modification is limited liability" (787–88). More effective control over corporations is found when management is shifted to a small body of managers, centralized negotiators, away from many shareholders, owners; this results in each shareholder having the ability to sell her shares in the business without the approval of others. If they disapprove of how managers are running the corporation, shareholders can exit from the firm (788). Also decisive is the possibility of shareholders ousting management (788).

Easterbrook and Fischel

In Easterbrook and Fischel (1991) the emphasis shifts from one principal-agent problem, how managers motivate workers to work in the manager's interest, to another, how shareholders motivate managers to work in the shareholders' interest. Here I am not interested in the complexities of their argument, but only in its rudimentary logic. For them, as for Alchian and Demsetz (1972), firms are a cluster of spot contracts. Their conceptualization of these contracts emerges from the parallel traditions of free contract doctrine and neoclassical economics.[24] Thus they can contend the following: "The normative thesis of the book is that corporate law should contain the terms people would have negotiated, were the costs of negotiating at arm's length for every contingency sufficiently low. The positive thesis is that corporate law almost always conforms to this model" (Easterbrook and Fischel 1991, 15).

These arm's-length negotiations are contracts, "voluntary and unanimous agreement[s] among affected parties" (Easterbrook and Fischel 1991, 15). According to Easterbrook and Fischel, firms are nexuses of contracts, and corporate law is simply a substitute for decisions people would have made contractually and in fact do make contractually. Consequently, corporate law is efficient. As this suggests, corporate law is contractual in setting the fallback terms for corporate relationships. "These terms become part of the set of contracts just as provisions of the Uniform Commercial Code become part of commercial contracts when not addressed explicitly" (16). These fallback conditions are the terms "that the parties would have selected with full information and costless contracting" (22). When courts fill gaps in the explicit corporate contracts that constitute firms, they "duplicate the terms the parties would have selected, in their joint interest, if they had contracted explicitly" (22).[25]

For Easterbrook and Fischel, "Corporate law—and in particular the fiduciary principle enforced by the courts—fills in the blanks and oversights with the terms that people would have bargained for had they anticipated the problems and been able to transact costlessly in advance. On this view corporate law supplements but never displaces actual bargains, save in situations of third-party effects or latecomer terms" (34), and third-party effects are insubstantial (21). The law completes open-ended contracts, but they contend that there is no reason why it should impose a term that defeats actual bargains (35).

Their clearest statement of the role of fiduciary principles in corporate law begins by their noting that such principles are uncommon in contractual relations. Why, then, if corporations are a complex set of contracts, do fiduciary duties "sneak into these contracts"? Their answer presumes imperfect-information over time. The corporate contract locates these uncertainties in the equity investors, the holders of residual claims. They receive few promises; instead, they get the protection of fiduciary principles, the duty of loyalty and the duty of care. "The only promise that makes sense in such an open-ended relation is to work hard and honestly. In other words, the corporate contract makes managers the agents of the equity investors but does not specify the agents' duties. To make such an arrangement palatable to investors, managers must pledge their careful and honest services" (91). These fiduciary duties protect, or so Easterbrook and Fischel imply, the equity holders' interests. The need for such protection is manifest because "When one person exercises authority that affects another's wealth, interests may diverge. The smaller the managers' share in the enterprise, the more the managers' interests diverge from the interests of those who contributed capital. This phenomenon exists in any agency relation" (91).[26]

It should be obvious, however, that this argument is self-contradictory. If all actors are understood within neoclassical theory to be individual maximizers, it makes sense to suggest that a "pledge of careful and honest services" is effective only under one of two conditions. The preferences maximized by corporate managers must be those of their shareholders or the interests of managers and shareholders are aligned with situational sanctions. Easterbrook and Fischel ignore the former (except in noting that corporate ownership by managers serves to better align their interests with those of shareholders), and while acknowledging (even within their implicitly perfect-information competitive model) that monitoring mechanisms may be inadequate to deal with one-time defalcations (92), they nonetheless reduce fiduciary principles to the sanctions that support them.

For them, the two fiduciary principles are alternatives to elaborate promises; they replace prior supervision, whatever that means, with deterrence. They contend that "socially optimal fiduciary rules approximate the bargain that investors and managers would have reached if they could have bargained (and enforced their agreements) at no cost" (92). Although this is in accord with their contention that courts treat firms as nexuses of contracts, there is no reason to assume that managers will adhere to these rules unless they align with their own interests. Further, in the agency relationship between equity holders and managers, even under the best circumstances, there is little reason to believe that managers' and shareholders' interests and preferences will be aligned in the absence of monitoring and situational sanctions. In effect, the fiduciary rules are reduced to the sanctions that support them.

Given their argument, it also makes little sense to draw a sharp distinction between the duty of loyalty and the duty of care. Both are reduced to agency costs due to conflicts of interest between managers and shareholders (103); neither is understood as regulating managers' performance in the absence of sanctions. This enables Easterbrook and Fischel to reduce the duty of loyalty to a market test, that any transaction with a possible conflict of interest yields the firm "a deal at least as good as it could have obtained in an arm's length transaction with a stranger" (104). Although they sometimes suggest that the procedural guarantees of the duty of care are insufficient (compare 105 to 104), the logic of their argument reduces the duty of loyalty to the duty of care. Their model of the firm as a nexus of contracts does not allow for the substantive regulation of contracts. As long as fiduciary principles complete incomplete bargains in contracts, "it makes little sense to say that 'fiduciary duties' trump actual contracts" (93), that they trump contracts that are procedurally justified. Easterbrook and Fischel implicitly reduce fiduciary duties to the consent of the parties in situations where the proper procedures are followed.

In situations of imperfect information, a neoclassical theorist should expect managers to act opportunistically, not in the interest of their shareholders and not in the interest of their firms: "Such behavior is privately rational but wealth reducing" (101). The question is how to regulate and constrain managers to act in the interest of their shareholders. Fiduciary regulation seeks to construct a quasi-professional ethos, a set of commitments that result in managers' acting in their firms', not their individual, interest.

The legal sanctions that support fiduciary obligations serve the three functions of sanctions. They constitute, as Easterbrook and Fischel recognize, incentives; in addition, they reinforce the commitments of the already committed; and they reduce the penalty suffered by those committed to them in a world where not everyone shares this commitment (the sucker effect). Neither fiduciary principles nor the sanctions that support them may be evaluated successfully solely in terms of the first function, the sanctions that support the performance of contracts. In what follows I problematize the notion of contract implicit in Easterbrook and Fischel's analysis; in so doing, I constitute a place for both the duty of care and the duty of loyalty in corporate law.

THE LEGITIMATION AND JUSTIFICATION OF CONTRACTS: THE DUTIES OF LOYALTY AND CARE

The theory of freedom of contract presumed by Alchian and Demsetz and Easterbrook and Fischel argues for the enforcement of private transactions. Contracts are based on mutual agreement. Within a very wide range of activities, parties are free to make whatever contracts they wish. No one can be compelled to make any particular contract, and only rarely will the law void a contract on substantive grounds. The role of the law is twofold: to police the rules of the game and ensuring that the autonomy of contracting parties is respected, and to enforce the contract in case of its violation. Violations are understood as possible, even in the face of agreement, because contracts are usually projected into the future. Over time, preferences may change, and what looked like a good agreement may end up looking like a bad one. Also, situations may change and transform what looked like a rational agreement for attaining one's goals into an irrational one.

Classical contract doctrine specifies a set of constitutive rules that must be followed if an agreement is to count as a contract. Constituted agreements within these rules are legally binding. Agreements in contravention of these rules do not result in legally enforceable covenants. For example, agreements made under conditions of duress, fraud, incapacity, or mistake are not considered to be freely agreed to and do not count as contractual agreements. They are in violation of the rules of the game and they are not enforceable at law.

Classical contract theory is procedural. Adherence to a stipulated set of guidelines validates agreements as legally enforceable contracts, and substantive considerations that could invalidate a contract are raised only within a very narrow range of activities. For example, one may not be able to sell oneself into slavery. Even substantive constraints of this sort are usually legitimated in procedural terms: namely, slavery abrogates the autonomy necessary to make a contract. In classical contract doctrine it is contended that there is no reason for courts to abrogate a consensual agreement between competent adults.

A brief discussion of the notion of unconscionability will serve to illuminate the logic of this argument and its relevance to Easterbrook and Fischel's understanding of fiduciary principles.[27] Contractual unconscionability is usually divided into two categories, procedural and substantive. Procedural unconscionability concerns the justifiability of a contract; contracts are justified when they are articulated in terms of the noncontractual elements of contract, the constitutive rules that Durkheim analyzed (Durkheim 1893/1984, 149–75). Substantive unconscionability concerns the legitimacy of a contract; contracts are legitimate when consistent with social values, the collective moral obligations that Durkheim analyzed under the rubric of the collective conscience (31–66). Procedural and substantive unconscionability represent two differentiable aspects of the social regulation of private agreements. Although this neat separation is analytically clear and sometimes empirically manifest, it presents complications: First, the constitutive rules that justify contracts are themselves in need of legitimation. Not every procedure justifies a contract, as may be seen by the fact that we reject Hobbes's contention that a contract made under duress is nonetheless voluntary. Second, actual contracts are often deemed procedurally unconscionable and in violation of the rules of the game only when they are deemed to be substantively illegitimate. This is because in most cases contracts are adjudicated only when one party to them feels unfairly treated in a way that relates to a substantive issue.

In a theory that limits unconscionability to its procedural forms, those entering a contract have only to comply with the noncontractual elements of contract, the constitutive rules that determine whether a contract is binding, to enter into an agreement enforceable at law. The law is said to be neutral regarding the distributional effects and moral status of the agreement (Atiyah 1986/1990, 329–30). As Richard A. Epstein put it (1975, 294–95),

> The doctrine [of unconscionability] should not, in my view, allow courts to act as roving commissions to set aside those agreements whose substantive terms they find objectionable. Instead, it should be used only to allow courts to police the process whereby private agreements are formed, and in that connection, only to facilitate the setting aside of agreements that are as a matter of probabilities likely to be vitiated by the classical defenses of duress, fraud, or incompetence.

In Easterbrook and Fischel's model, courts determine what counts as a fair contract by asking about the market outcome of a relationship in a situation of perfect information. But this contention is vitiated by the fact that, as Easterbrook and Fischel note, contracts extend over time and the situation in which they are formed may have changed by the time they are adjudicated. Even if one claims that the law should enunciate provisions that the actors would have agreed on in a perfect-information situation, this contention is invalidated by the recognition that in the real world what they would have agreed to at one time may differ from what they would have agreed to at another.

What should a court do when a contract is voided as procedurally unfair? When courts are forced to read clauses into a contract, some standard must be used to decide what is reasonable. Durkheim's sociological analysis of substantive unconscionability helps us to come to grips with what this means.

Durkheim wrote from within the context of the French civil law tradition, where notions akin to substantive unconscionability have a longer heritage than in the Anglo-American common law. Perhaps this is the reason why, within the context of a discussion tracing the emergence of the consensual contract and emphasizing that a contract is binding only on the condition that consent has been given freely (Durkheim 1922/1958, 203–4), he argued that "an unjust act could not be sanctioned by law without inconsistency. This is why any contract in which pressure has a part, becomes invalid. It is not at all because the determining cause of the obligation is exterior to the individual who binds himself. It is because he has suffered some unjustified injury, in a word, such a contract is unjust" (207). According to Durkheim, this condition, that a contract must be objectively just, is superimposed on the free consent of autonomous parties as a necessary condition for the validity of a contract (208).

Durkheim assesses the validity of a contract in terms of its consequences for the parties. "It is because the consent has been grievous in its effect that the society considers it null and void: that the individual has not, in a true sense, been the cause of the consent he has given is not the reason. And thus the validity of the contract becomes subordinate to the consequences it may have for the contracting party" (209). It is not (only) a question of consent; it is (in addition) a question of whether the contract diverges too greatly from our moral standards: "It hardly matters that he does not resist the indirect constraint put upon him and that he may even voluntarily accept it. There is something about this exploitation of one man by another that offends us and rouses our indignation, even if it is agreed to by the one who suffers it and has not been imposed by actual constraint" (210–11). Contracts in which fair value is not given "must seem to us immoral: no one will deny it. For contracts to be accepted as morally binding, we have come to require not only that they should be by consent, but also that they respect the rights of the contracting parties. The very first of these rights is that things and services should not be given except at the fair price. We disapprove any contract with a 'lion's share' in it, that is, one that favours one party unduly at the expense of the other; therefore we hold that the society is not bound to enforce it or, at least, ought not to enforce it as fully as one that is equitable, since it does not call for an equal respect" (211).

Whereas equity sometimes drew on principle to cancel unconscionable transactions, common law, to overcome the dualism between law and equity, made inventive and sometimes covert use of the techniques at its disposal to at least sometimes cancel unconscionable transactions. This situation persisted even after the merger of common law and equity courts in the United States. It was to remedy this situation and to develop a general standard of fairness that section 2-302 of the Uniform Commercial Code, the section that deals with the definition of unconscionability, was written. Courts were given the power to strike down contracts or clauses of contracts deemed to be unconscionable at the time they were made. In such a case, the court is required to allow the parties to provide evidence about the commercial setting, purpose, and effect of the contract, thus highlighting the court's concern both with consequences and with the situation in which the contract was formulated. The first comment to section 2-302 is: "The basic test is whether, in the light of the general commercial background and the commercial needs of the particular trade or case, the clauses involved are so one-sided as to be unconscionable under circumstances existing at the time of the making of the contract." Further: The distributional consequences of inequalities of bargaining power are not the focus of the section.

Karl Llewellyn, the dominant force in the formulating of section 2-302, recognized that it was not the business of the courts to draft contracts; nevertheless, a contract that shocks the conscience (Llewellyn 1960, 370), is "oppressive or overly harsh," is substantively unconscionable.

Another way of putting this same point is to draw on the analogy of contracts as private laws; the application of the doctrine of unconscionability then becomes akin to the constitutional regulation of such "laws." The "constitutional" standard is conscience; its legal meaning is specified in the application of legal values by the courts, where successive courts must be sensitive to the consequences their forebears have wrought. Laws in violation of constitutional principles are void.

The constitutional analogy is, I think, applicable to corporate governance, where the courts hold managers to principled standards, to their fiduciary obligations. These standards are both procedural, the duty of care, and substantive, the duty of loyalty. Drawing on Easterbrook and

Fischel's insistence that corporations are no more than a nexus of contracts, we might suggest that if this is indeed the case, then these contracts must be regulated by both procedural norms (they must be justified) and substantive principles (they must be legitimate). Put differently, a more sophisticated understanding of contract than the one implicit in Easterbrook and Fischel's (not to mention Alchian and Demsetz's) discussion enables us to better understand the independent role of fiduciary duties in corporate law.

This same analytical point has been stated (Kahn 2000, 513–14) in slightly different terms:

> Corporate fiduciary law has focused on supporting the integrity of corporate managers as it affects their official behavior. Indeed, corporate fiduciary law has historically had the preeminent role in defining *professional standards of conduct* for corporate directors and officers vis-à-vis corporate shareholders. And in applying corporate fiduciary law to individual cases, courts have not shied away from constructing such *standards in terms of expressly personal and moral commitments* on the directors' parts. . . . Although it operates in the adjudication of individual, civil suits, corporate fiduciary law expressly acknowledges the value and fragility of trust as a form of social capital requisite to economic transacting. Thus, it has been the special role, the unique nature and function of corporate fiduciary law to speak expressly to the importance of supporting *norms of managerial trustworthiness,* and thus shareholders' ability to trust in such trustworthiness. (Emphasis added)

The dominant law and economics perspective in corporate law must, in contrast, treat managers as maximizing their individual utility against situational constraints. From this point of view, the role of corporate law is to minimize agency costs, to facilitate an alignment of interests between managers and equity holders. From within the perspective of a neoclassical theory, this task can be conceptualized only in terms of situational sanctions. If corporate law is reduced to the situational sanctions that support it, it provides no grounding for the commitment that managers must manifest and that the courts must enforce if professional standards of conduct and the norms of managerial trustworthiness are to be maintained. Paradoxically, only when the courts' decisions serve to reinforce conviction among the already committed will they be able to provide incentives and punishments that serve to reinforce this commitment as they guide the uncommitted (Holmes's [1896] "bad men").

In contrast to the perspective on fiduciary law that Faith Kahn highlights in the long quotation reproduced in the previous paragraph, the implementation of a law and economics perspective on corporate law will foster managerial opportunism. Normatively constructed trust, moral obligations, and professional ethics are all vehicles to regulate opportunism, to foster social relationships that construct and reinforce managerial commitments to the appropriate values of fiduciary responsibility. Although procedures mandating disclosure can impose reputation effects to help control managerial malfeasance (a bad reputation may lead to negative situational sanctions), such processes cannot constrain corporate actors successfully in situations of imperfect information. Needless to say, such situations are pervasive. In situations of imperfect information, morally unregulated managers will act opportunistically in their own, not in their corporation's, interest. A reconstituted set of moral standards is necessary to promote effective managerial performance.[28]

To sum up, effective corporate performance is dependent on both its procedural justification in terms of effective shareholder control and its legitimation in terms of the appropriate societal values.[29] Law and economics arguments are incapable of conceptualizing the values that tacitly legitimate corporate activity and in consequence of their exclusive focus on a single positively stated normative orientation (instrumental rationality), preferences and situational sanctions, are incapable of specifying a legal regime capable of regulating effectively managerial opportunism and malfeasance. The pervasiveness of law and economics perspectives, suggesting to corporate officials that it is acceptable for them to maximize their own individual interests while implying that such maximization is in the social interest, has undermined the fiduciary standards of corporate law and with them the commitment to principle among corporate officers. If this trend continues, it will undermine the trust necessary to sustain our corporate system, as investors become wary of turning over their money to actors presumed to be maximizing their own, and not their shareholders', interests.

NOTES

1. It is perhaps worth noting that this exercise is a specification of a general theory that I have discussed in other contexts to this specific case. See Gould (1990a, 1990b), where I revisit the Parsons-Merton controversy concerning the benefits of general and middle-range theory. The current essay derives from and takes considerable text from Gould (2001b), which is itself grounded in previous theoretical work.
2. This characterization is derived from the one Parsons provides in chapter 2 of *The Structure of Social Action*. I have discussed and modified Parsons's discussion in several places (see Gould 1981b, 1989, 1991a, 1991c, 1992, 1996b).
3. The implication of these two points—the attribution of inefficient action to error or ignorance, and viewing ends as revealed—is that neoclassical theory is inherently tautologous.
4. There are, of course, many models of imperfect competition. In this essay I assume the existence of competitive constraints, although this means very different things in perfect- and imperfect-information models. The constraints are a mathematical consequence in Arrow-Debreu general equilibrium models. They have to be situationally manifest within nonorthodox theories (Granovetter 1985, 504).
5. This is similar to Marx's distinction between labor, the capacity to work, and labor-power, the actual work undertaken. Marx emphasized that employers hire labor-power and then have to motivate their employees to work.
6. Niklas Luhmann (1972/1985) provides a discerning analysis of the association between uncertainty and the emergence of social norms.
7. Opportunism is the natural consequence of rational action within a situation of imperfect information.
8. For a penetrating critique of the efficacy of "fiat," see Robert F. Freeland (2001).
9. In imperfect-information models economically homogeneous workers no longer need receive the same wage, involuntary unemployment becomes a virtual necessity, and labor-market discrimination may be a stable equilibrium outcome (Bowles 1985; Bowles and Gintis 1985; Gould 1991b; Shapiro and Stiglitz 1986; Stiglitz 1987; 1991).
10. It also requires the inclusion of nonatomistic concepts (social structures), the normative regulation of ends (making them endogenous within the theory), and a nonempiricist methodological orientation (Gould 1989, 1991a, 1991c; Parsons 1937/1949).
11. The classical discussion of the distinction between factual social regularities and the normative orders that are sometimes crucial in explaining them is Parsons (1937/1949).
12. This disjunction does not mean that what is desired is untouched by what is viewed as desirable. Most persons have erotic desires that, Freud tells us, were originally polymorphous perverse. Most persons come to believe that it is wrong to engage in sexual relations with sheep; yet most persons, we may presume, have no desire to engage in sexual relations with sheep. A moral prohibition may affect what actors desire. Nonetheless, what we desire is autonomous from what is desirable. The same person who has no desire to have sexual relations with a sheep may well want to sleep with the person in the next office, even though she views the consummation of that desire to be morally wrong. Desires are independent of, yet interdependent with, the structure of moral obligation. On independence, dependence, and interdependence, see Parsons (1937/1949, 25 n. 2).
13. Legitimation is discussed in the section titled "Legitimation and Justification of Contracts."
14. It may appear that Posner's signaling theory (2000) is capable of explaining this consequence of punishment, but this is an illusion. For Posner, a signal is a costly action indicative of an individual's low discount rate, and thus her willingness to cooperate into the future. At other times, however, it is no more than an indication of

group membership and loyalty. An actor may discriminate against members of an out-group while conforming to the norms of her in-group. Posner suggests that the former action signals a high discount rate in regard to out-group members and the latter action, a low discount rate in regard to in-group members. Thus, unlike in standard economic arguments, where a discount rate is a stable preference for an actor, one that holds across situations, in Posner's book signals are context-dependent (and not only in the sense of what counts as a signal), often indicating no more than group affiliation. Quite apart from the fact that Posner gives no explanation of how actors might distinguish between a genuine and a false signal—a special problem if the discount rate for an individual is variable across situation—he presumes what requires explanation, the constitution of the relevant groups and an individual's loyalty to one group instead of another.

15. For two recent sets of discussions where this confusion is sometimes manifest, see Michael Hechter, Lynn Nadel, and Richard E. Michod (1993; Hechter and Karl-Dieter Opp (2001).
16. This distinction emerges from Parsons's discussion in his analysis of Durkheim's *Division of Labor in Society;* see (Parsons 1967, chapter 1).
17. Imagine a situation where blacks are excluded from a jury that convicts an actually guilty black man of a crime. That outcome is not justified because the procedures used in reaching it are (now deemed to be) illegitimate.
18. In the social sciences, the term "value" may refer to either what is desired, a preference, or what is desirable and obligatory.
19. The most sophisticated discussions are Hart 1961/1965; Luhmann 1972/1985.
20. I have argued elsewhere that the validity of social relationships depends on their being both legitimate and justified (Gould 1996a; 2001a).
21. The adoption of a calculating attitude to the law is one of several necessary and sufficient conditions for the occurrence of deviant action. I have proposed a theory of deviance in Gould (1987, chapter 3).
22. In this paper I have not attempted to ground my argument in either the case law nor in a comprehensive examination of the law and economics literature. In this forum it seemed wise to present my argument schematically, emphasizing the critique of the mode of reasoning entailed in neoclassical arguments about the law.
23. This is not the place to explain the fallacies of this argument in detail. I will restrict myself to two points. While it is correct that no actor in an Arrow-Debreu model of the economy has power over any other actor, it is easy to demonstrate that this is not the case in an imperfect-information model of the economy (Gould 1994). Second, it is just as easy to demonstrate that Alchian and Demsetz introduce power into their model. Their discussion of power ignores two things: first, employers do not negotiate each time they give employees an order. They give orders by fiat. Their contracts with workers, and their expectations of workers, are open-ended (albeit within certain limits); worker expectations of employers are more closed-ended; thus they have to negotiate with employers when they want things done. They cannot order employers by fiat. Second, employees cannot move costlessly to a new job of comparable quality if they do not like an order. In general there is an asymmetry between the walk-away costs of employers and employees, and this creates a power disparity between them. This is recognized implicitly by Alchian and Demsetz when they write of employers "disciplining" members of the team (780, 782), when they note that employers have the "authority to terminate or revise contracts" (782), and, more generally, when they suggest that "to discipline team members and reduce shirking, the residual claimant must have power to revise the contract terms and incentives of *individual* members without having to terminate or alter every other input's contract. Hence, team members who seek to increase their productivity will assign to the monitor not only the residual claimant right but also the right to alter individual membership and performance on the team . . . only the monitor may unilaterally terminate the membership of any of the other members" (782–83). The reader might want to compare this comment to ones found in Hobbes's *Leviathan* and to Parsons's critique of Hobbes in chapter 3 of *The Structure of Social Action.*
24. Easterbrook and Fischel assume repeatedly, and falsely (Stiglitz 1985, 1987, 1991), that conclusions derived from perfect-information Arrow-Debreu models are robust for the imperfect-information model they presume, but do not specify with any precision, in their discussion. The mechanism that justifies their conclusions is competition, which in their discussion constrains firms to produce efficiently, which includes selecting efficient modes of governance. Competition functions as a deus ex machina in perfect-information models but not in imperfect-information models. Consequently their argument boils down to the contention that whatever is, is optimal and right.

In perfect-information Arrow-Debreu models, where capital (the residual interest) and labor would be constrained to make the same decision in a competitive economy, and where that decision would be efficient, Easterbrook and Fischel are correct, the individual interests of the residual claimants are isomorphic with the social interest (at least if we accept the starting positions of all actors). Competitive constraints would force whomever controls the firm to act in the same way, efficiently. In an imperfect information model, where capital and labor might make different decisions, and where power matters, their conclusions are no longer robust. Here, however, I ignore most of the problems that emerge in their analysis because of the conflation of perfect- and imperfect-information models.

25. Another indication that Easterbrook and Fischel assume that conclusions from perfect-information models are robust in imperfect-information models is their contention that "questions of distribution among investors are unimportant; allocating gains to one rather than another changes relative prices but not social wealth" (24). One of Stiglitz's primary conclusions is that, in imperfect-information models, it is not possible to separate efficiency from distribution issues. See, for example, Stiglitz (1991).
26. There is no clearer indication of the lack of rigor in Easterbrook and Fischel's argument than their repeated tendency to equate the firm with its managers. For the most overt example, see p. 95. This equivalence is manifest only in perfect-information models and it eliminates the principal-agent problem.
27. This discussion is taken from and sometimes refers to my more comprehensive analysis, with the appropriate legal references, in a very different context, in Gould (1996b).
28. Mark Gould, Charles Heckscher and Frank Domurad (1996) demonstrate the importance of loyalty and the commitment to professional standards of conduct in explaining, albeit in different circumstances, effective managerial performance.
29. For my statement of this position in the context of policies regulating consensual sexual relations at colleges and universities, see Gould (1996a, 2001a).

REFERENCES

Akerlof, George A., and Janet L. Yellen, eds. 1986. *Efficiency Wage Models of the Labor Market.* Cambridge: Cambridge University Press.

Alchian, Armen, and Harold Demsetz. 1972. "Production, Information Costs, and Economic Organization." *American Economic Review* 62(5): 777–95.

Arrow, Kenneth J. 1985. "The Economics of Agency." In *Principals and Agents: The Structure of Business,* edited by John W. Pratt and Richard Zeckhauser. Boston: Harvard Business School Press.

Atiyah, P. S. 1986/1990. *Essays on Contract.* Oxford: Oxford University Press.

Bowles, Samuel. 1985. "The Production Process in a Competitive Economy: Walrasian, Neo-Hobbesian and Marxian Models." *American Economic Review* 75(1): 16–36.

Bowles, Samuel, and Herbert Gintis. 1985. "The Labor Theory of Value and the Specificity of Marxian Economics." In *Rethinking Marxism,* edited by Stephen Resnick and Richard Wolff. New York: Autonomedia.

Bulow, Jeremy, and Lawrence H. Summers. 1986. "A Theory of Dual Labor Markets with Application to Industrial Policy, Discrimination, and Keynesian Unemployment." *Journal of Labor Economics* 4(3, part 1): 376–414.

Cooter, Robert, and Melvin Eisenberg. 2001. "Fairness, Character, and Efficiency in Firms." *University of Pennsylvania Law Review* 149 (June): 1717–1733.

Coser, Lewis. 1956. *The Functions of Social Conflict.* Glencoe, Ill.: Free Press.

Durkheim, Émile. 1922/1958. *Professional Ethics and Civic Morals.* Translated by Cornelia Brookfield. New York: Free Press.

———. 1925/1961. *Moral Education.* Translated by Everett K. Wilson and Herman Schnurer. New York: Free Press.

———. 1895/1982. *The Rules of the Sociological Method and Selected Texts on Sociology and Its Method.* Translated by W. D. Halls. New York: Free Press.

———. 1893/1984. *The Division of Labor in Society.* Translated by W. D. Halls. New York: Free Press.

Easterbrook, Frank H., and Daniel R. Fischel. 1991. *The Economic Structure of Corporate Law.* Cambridge, Mass.: Harvard University Press.

Elster, Jan. 1989. *Nuts and Bolts for the Social Sciences.* Cambridge: Cambridge University Press.

Epstein, Richard A. 1975. "Unconscionability: A Critical Reappraisal." *Journal of Law and Economics* 18(2): 293–316.

Freeland, Robert F. 2001. *The Struggle for Control of the Modern Corporation: Organizational Change at General Motors, 1924–1970.* Cambridge: Cambridge University Press.

Gould, Mark. 1981a. "Marx $\stackrel{?}{=}$ Weber: The Role of Ideas in History." Paper presented at the Annual Meeting of the American Sociological Association. Toronto, Canada (August 24–28).

———. 1981b. "Parsons Versus Marx: 'An Earnest Warning . . .' " *Sociological Inquiry* 51(3/4): 197–218.

———. 1986. "Puritanism and the English Revolution." Paper presented at the Princeton University Mellon Colloquium. Princeton.

———. 1987. *Revolution in the Development of Capitalism: The Coming of the English Revolution.* Berkeley: University of California Press.

———. 1989. "Voluntarism Versus Utilitarianism: A Critique of Camic's History of Ideas." *Theory, Culture and Society* 6(4): 637–54.

———. 1990a. "Gould Replies to Blalock." In *Robert K. Merton: Consensus and Controversy,* edited by Jon Clark, Celia Modgil, and Sohan Modgil. London: Falmer.

———. 1990b. "The Interplay of General Sociological Theory and Empirical Research." In *Robert K. Merton: Consensus and Controversy,* edited by Jon Clark, Celia Modgil, and Sohan Modgil. London: Falmer.

———. 1991a. "Parsons's Economic Sociology: A Failure of Will." *Sociological Inquiry* 61(1): 89–101.

———. 1991b. "The Reproduction of Labour Market Discrimination in Competitive Capitalism." In *Exploitation and Exclusion: Race and Class in Contemporary U.S. Society,* edited by Abebe Zegeye, Leonard Harris, and Julia Maxted. London: Hans Zell.

———. 1991c. "*The Structure of Social Action:* At Least Sixty Years Ahead of Its Time." In *Talcott Parsons: Theorist of Modernity,* edited by Roland Robertson and Bryan S. Turner. London: Sage.

———. 1992. "Law and Sociology: Some Consequences for the Law of Employment Discrimination Deriving from the Sociological Reconstruction of Economic Theory." *Cardozo Law Review* 13(5): 1517–78.

———. 1994. "Structured Inequality and Power in a Theory of Competitive Markets." Paper presented at the Annual Meeting of the American Sociological Association. Los Angeles (August 5–9).

———. 1996a. "Consent and the Morality of Sexual Relationships: The Regulation of Consensual Sexual Relationships Between Employees and Students in Colleges and Universities." Paper presented at the Annual Meeting of the Law and Society Association. St. Louis, Mo. (May 29–June 1).

———. 1996b. "Law and Philosophy: Some Consequences for the Law Deriving from the Sociological Reconstruction of Philosophical Theory." *Cardozo Law Review* 17(4–5): 3001–24.

———. 2001a. "Empirical Sociological Theory and the Resolution of Normative Dilemmas." In *Talcott Parsons Today: His Theory and Legacy in Contemporary Sociology,* edited by A. Javier Trevino. Lanham, Md.: Rowan & Littlefield.

———. 2001b. "Social Norms: A Critique of Law and Economics Formulations and a Guide to their Correct Conceptualization." Paper presented to the joint meeting of the Law and Society Association and the Research Committee on the Sociology of Law, International Sociological Association. Budapest, Hungary (July 4–7).

Gould, Mark, Charles Heckscher, and Frank Domurad. 1996. "Loyalty, Professionalism, and Rationality in Corporate Downsizing." Paper presented at the annual meeting of the American Sociological Association. New York (August 16–20).

Granovetter, Mark. 1985. "Economic Action, Social Structure, and Embeddedness." *American Journal of Sociology* 91(3): 481–510.

Hart, H. L. A. 1961/1965. *The Concept of Law.* Oxford: Oxford University Press.

Hechter, Michael, Lynn Nadel, and Richard E. Michod, eds. 1993. *The Origin of Values.* New York: Aldine de Gruyter.

Hechter, Michael, and Karl-Dieter Opp, eds. 2001. *Social Norms.* New York: Russell Sage Foundation.

Holmes, Oliver Wendell. 1896. "The Path of the Law." *Harvard Law Review* 10: 457–78.

Kahn, Faith Stevelman. 2000. "Fiduciary Duty, Limited Liability, and the Law of Delaware: Transparency and Accountability: Rethinking Corporate Fiduciary Law's Relevance to Corporate Disclosure." *Georgia Law Review* 34: 505–28.

Llewellyn, Karl N. 1960. *The Common Law Tradition: Deciding Appeals.* Boston: Little, Brown.

Luhmann, Niklas. 1969/1983. *Legitimation durch Verfahren.* Frankfurt am Main: Suhrkamp.

———. 1972/1985. *A Sociological Theory of Law.* London: Routledge & Kegan Paul.

Parsons, Talcott. 1937/1949. *The Structure of Social Action.* New York: Free Press.

———. 1966. *Societies: Evolutionary and Comparative Perspectives.* Englewood Cliffs, N.J.: Prentice-Hall.

———. 1967. *Sociological Theory and Modern Society.* New York: Free Press.

Posner, Eric A. 2000. *Law and Social Norms.* Cambridge, Mass.: Harvard University Press.

Pratt, John W., and Richard Zeckhauser. 1985. "Principals and Agents: An Overview." In *Principals and Agents: The Structure of Business,* edited by John W. Pratt and Richard Zeckhauser. Boston: Harvard Business School Press.

Shapiro, Carl, and Joseph E. Stiglitz. 1984/1986. "Equilibrium Unemployment as a Worker Discipline Device." In *Efficiency Wage Models of the Labor Market,* edited by George A. Akerlof and Janet L. Yellen. Cambridge: Cambridge University Press.

Simmel, Georg. 1955. *Conflict.* In *Conflict* and *The Web of Group-Affiliations.* Translated by Kurt H. Wolff and Reinhard Bendix. New York: Free Press.

Stiglitz, Joseph. 1985. "Credit Markets and the Control of Capital." *Journal of Money, Credit and Banking* 17(2): 133–52.

———. 1987. "The Causes and Consequences of the Dependence of Quality on Price." *Journal of Economic Literature* 25(1): 1–48.

———. 1991. "The Invisible Hand and Modern Welfare Economics." NBER working paper 3541. Cambridge, Mass.: National Bureau of Economic Research.

Weber, Max. 1904–5/1958. *The Protestant Ethic and the Spirit of Capitalism.* Translated by Talcott Parsons. New York: Scribner's.

———. 1926/1968. *Economy and Society.* Translated by Guenther Roth, Claus Wittich, and others. New York: Bedminster Press.

Williamson, Oliver. 1985. *The Economic Institutions of Capitalism.* New York: Free Press.

———. 1993. "Calculativeness, Trust, and Economic Organization." *Journal of Law and Economics* 36(1, part 2): 453–86.

Chapter 3

Social Order as Communication: Parsons's Theory on the Move from Moral Consensus to Trust

Harald Wenzel

Although one might be sceptical of Talcott Parsons's research program for social theory, there is much less doubt in viewing his solution of the so-called Hobbesian problem of social order as a turning point in the development of sociological thought. In providing proof of the thesis that the main representatives of sociological thought in Europe converged on a solution for this problem, Parsons (1937/1968) did two things. First, he built upon the classical phase of sociological theory to bring it to a remarkable completion, and second, he established the foundation for the dominance of a normatively oriented functionalism in American sociology that lasted into the 1960s (Davis 1959; Wenzel 2001a).

After the retreat of functionalism a proliferation of alternative approaches to sociological theory began: interpretative and interactionist theories, theories of rational choice, of conflict, power, and authority, to mention some of the main ones. However, these were only in part new approaches; for the most part they were "comebacks" of older paradigms. The "normal science" (Kuhn 1962/1970) of functionalism gave way to a scientific revolution that still flourishes. There is now a competitive pluralism of theories lacking a dominant paradigm (Alexander 1987, 1990; Eckberg and Hill 1980; Giddens 1977). Although the future of theoretical debate in sociology may at the moment seem very much open, there can be no doubt that Parsons's status as a classic is undisputed. But the question remains: What part do classical contributions to social theory play?

Jeffrey Alexander suggests that classical theories in the social sciences are functional equivalents for successful instances of empirical—in many cases experimental—research. Such instances of research are paradigm-building in the natural sciences, whereas in the social sciences they are extremely rare (Alexander 1987, 19–29). The social science classics provide for the integration of theoretical discourse; they simplify, condense, and unify discourse. Lacking a dominant paradigm, the social sciences grant the classics the status of a virtually dominant ersatz, or substitute, paradigm. Such old dragons can be slain again and again without real risk. And more than that: Without this quasi-dominant ersatz paradigm of the classics no oppositional reading would be possible, no deconstruction of the classical text, no search for the different, the excluded, the absent elements in it (Alexander 1987, 27–28).[1]

If one looks at what has been made of Parsons's convergence thesis, one sees this pattern of interpretation realized almost literally. Originally the convergence thesis likely goes back to a parallel reading by Parsons of Max Weber's studies on the role of the Protestant ethic in the emergence of modern society (Weber 1920/1978) and of Alfred Marshall's theory of economic action—in particular his "Study of Man" (1925). The idea of convergence is extended to the works of Vilfredo Pareto, Émile Durkheim, and, finally, Sigmund Freud. Step by step, the picture was completed: All partial elements of the convergence thesis—the practice of economic virtues in Marshall, the strength of the Protestant faith to motivate economically rational action in Weber, the goal a society pursues in Pareto (Parsons 1937/1968, 249), the system of normative rules establishing a state of solidarity in Durkheim (Parsons 1937/1968, 333–34), the superego in Freud (Parsons 1964)—refer to a common value element with obligatory character, to a *morally binding value consensus.* These values are ends in themselves that cannot be means for further ends, as they would be in, say, the rational calculation of economic action.

This step-by-step discovery of convergence reveals the *simultaneous discovery* of a normative model of social order in European sociology. Although the convergence thesis is based solely on the interpretation of theories, Parsons conceives of it as an empirical statement about the character of modern society (Parsons 1937/1968, 719). It is then against Parsons's interpretation of the classics, against his convergence thesis, against his normative model of social order that new, oppositional readings of the classics have to struggle for acceptance.[2] Although functionalism has lost the battle, we are still fighting the slain dragon—for exercise purposes, for internalizing an ersatz-paradigm of sociological theory whose dominance has already withered away. Without such a *substitute* we would not be able to develop oppositional readings of classical theories and create new, postclassical theories.

In a radical way one can turn this argument against Parsons's theory as well—as the last representative in a series of classical contributions. By way of such an oppositional reading of Parsons, the classic reappears as a leading post-classic: he revises a central assumption of classical sociological theory—the normative character of social order. Parsons himself is part of the scientific revolution that expels normative functionalism from its dominating stance and makes way for a competitive pluralism of theories based on alternative, non-normative conceptions of social order. This oppositional reading also pertains to the debate on continuity or discontinuity in the development of Parsons's theory. By far, the majority of secondary interpretations entertain the thesis of continuity whereas discontinuity is most often diagnosed as a break between the voluntarism of action emphasized in *The Structure of Social Action* (Parsons 1937/1968) and the normative control which is the focus of structural functionalism (Parsons 1951/1959; Parsons and Shils 1951/1959).[3]

At least two discrete evolutionary steps are attributed to Parsons's work: first, the early voluntaristic theory of action, and second, structural functionalism. The existence of a third, most recent, step equal in rank with the first two is not fully acknowledged. Usually only aspects of a third version are taken into account such as the introduction of the four-function paradigm, the hierarchy of cybernetic control, and so forth.

Of course there is such a third version: one can call it *systemic functionalism,* since functional systems gain central importance in the theory. Systemic functionalism represents a complete new approach of the theory, one that is in marked contrast to structural functionalism (Parsons, Bales, and Shils 1953/1981). Systemic functionalism is extended by the reconstruction of the interdependence of functional systems in a scheme of exchange relationships (Parsons 1953/1986; Parsons and Smelser 1956/1984) and later by the theory of symbolic media of interchange (Parsons 1963/1969a, 1963/1969c, 1968/1969d) and the theory of the human condition (Parsons 1978).

There actually are some excellent interpretations that have tried to do justice to Parsons's late work on systemic functionalism. For instance, Jeffrey Alexander (1983) criticizes Parsons's cultural determinism, which—owing to the introduction of cybernetic premises—narrows the originally multidimensional layout of his theory. Richard Münch, in contrast, is a typical representative of the continuity thesis, which he sees as being based on Kantian assumptions. Given this continuity, only smaller revisions had to be made in the step from structural to systemic functionalism (Münch 1982, 1987).

Both Alexander and Münch are heading for a new synthesis in social theory and they try to go beyond the standard of theorizing set by Parsons.[4] In one sense their interpretations remain without consequence. For them, Parsons still is the last classic and a representative of the normative solution of the problem of social order. Instead of escaping this dominant reading of Parsons, they elaborate, criticize, and correct this reading with only minor changes. Even where Parsons's theory is made the object of radical criticism, a similar picture appears: systemic functionalism is either ignored (as in Gouldner 1970) or it is explicitly brought into line with structural functionalism (as in Giddens 1979). Where, on the other hand, systemic functionalism is acknowledged as a discrete and decisive step in the development of theory, the interpretation of the early and middle phases of Parsons usually is biased toward the non-normative model of social order that Parsons developed in his late work; (rare) examples of this reading are the theories of Niklas Luhmann and Jürgen Habermas. Both adapt parts of Parsons's systemic functionalism for their own ends. In particular, the theory of symbolic media of interchange (money, power) turns out to have a crucial importance for their theories (Luhmann 1975, 1976, 1984; Habermas 1980, 1981a, 1981b). However, they also take a distinctively critical attitude toward the older versions of Parsons's theory, or reject them outright.

The topic of the following discussion is the new approach in conceiving social order in Parsons's late work. In an oppositional reading of Parsons's theory, particularly his formulation of the media of symbolic interchange, I will try to show that Parsons turns away from the classical solution to the problem of social order. In this new perspective, the burden of social integration no longer rests on a morally binding value consensus but, rather, occurs through and is based upon processes of communication. The character of morality changes—morality is not interpreted any more as an unconditional obligation to comply with a norm. Morality acquires a post-conventional character, becomes a decision problem of the autonomous personality and can no longer be the central safeguard for social order. In Parsons's late work the question arises: How can social order be established without a morally binding shared culture? What lies beyond value consensus?

Parsons was himself one of the scientific revolutionaries in opening up his theory for considerations that are typical for the postfunctionalist phase of theorizing in the United States—that is, for the proliferation phase of non-normative models of social integration. I will first turn to the normative model of social order as it was understood by Parsons. I am particularly interested in the contrast between this model and its non-normative alternatives. Alvin Gouldner's radical criticism of Parsons's theory turns out to be especially elucidating in this regard. Then I shall present an oppositional reading of social order based on Parsons's systemic functionalism and the symbolic media of interchange. Last, I shall present a sketch of the non-normative approach to order in Parsons's late theory as it is grounded in the symbolic exchange media of value commitments, influence, and trust.

PARSONS'S NORMATIVE CONCEPT OF SOCIAL ORDER AND ITS NON-NORMATIVE CRITIQUE

Parsons uses the category of norms in both a narrower and a wider sense: in the narrower sense, only legal and comparably concrete and unequivocal norms would count. In the wider sense, the category of norms extends to goals, to ends, to all purposive or teleological acts, and to values; roles and need dispositions also have a normative quality deducible from values. The concept of values (including ultimate ends, value attitudes, value orientations, evaluative orientations, and normative orientations) is decisive for the understanding of Parsons's early model of social order. But what is meant by this wider sense of normativity? Which problem is this concept supposed to solve?

Parsons's career as a social theorist starts with a discussion of orthodox economic theory and utilitarianism. The rational orientation of homo economicus to maximize utility and the conflicts resulting from an uneven distribution of wealth and power in modern society based on such rationality are the preconditions for a renewed appeal to the state of war. The so-called Hobbesian problem of social order was: How can the passions of individuals be checked and a permanent state of peace and social order established? In Vilfredo Pareto's sociology, which refers to a "single common system of ultimate ends" in society, Parsons found an explicit normative solution for the resolution of these conflicts. "But all these distributive questions," said Parsons (1937/1968, 249),

> concern only the settlement of potential conflicts of individual claims to wealth and power without indicating the basis of unity on which the structure as a whole rests. This basis of unity Pareto finds in the last analysis to lie in the necessary existence of an "end the society pursues." That is, the ultimate ends of individual action systems are integrated to form a single common system of ultimate ends which is the culminating element of unity holding the whole structure together.

Ultimate ends, or values, are the morally binding part of a shared culture, which make up a value consensus. The normative value orientations that regulate unit acts and action systems acquire an analytical status: they are not merely fragments of traditionally given conceptions of the good life that we cling to; they can no longer be thought of merely as concrete, empirical ends of action. They are, rather, understood as nonempirical, abstract objects, exemplified in actions that are catalysts for linking and interweaving unit acts and for building up elaborate action systems. They function as modes of relationship between actions.

Embedded in utilitarian and rationalist thinking about action, Parsons observes, are three such modes of relationships: technological, economic, and political rationality (Parsons 1937/1968, see especially 233–41). The efficiency of the single unit act, the rational calculation of utility by a single actor in face of scarce means and a multiplicity of ends, and the rational calculation of the coercibility of an alter ego to comply with an order, are the respective analytical normative standards implied here. Two nonutilitarian standards are further added: moral consensus and the internal coherence of values. These value standards are not only tools to describe single acts but are also ways and means to reflect on the buildup of action systems. With the elements of economic and political rationality, consensus, and coherence, Parsons anticipates the intrinsic value standards of functional systems and subsystems—the four-function-paradigm of his later theory.

The next crucial step Parsons takes in elaborating his model of a normative social order is the introduction of the so-called *interpenetration thesis* (Parsons 1951/1959; Parsons and Shils 1951/1959), which constitutes the core of structural functionalism. Cultural values are institutionalized in social systems as roles and they are internalized in personality systems as need dispositions. Culture, society, and personality thereby interpenetrate. A common value system is still central for this conception of order. Crucially important for developing structural functionalism is the notion of affective orientation rooted in a discussion of Freud's concept of cathexis (Parsons 1939).

Freud's concept of cathexis was the basis to extend the idea of a normative value-consensus to the makeup of the personality, its needs, and its desires. Durkheim's lectures titled *L'Éducation morale* (Durkheim 1925/1973) particularly paved the way for the interpenetration thesis. A normative order not only rules over the selection of means for given ends, but also has moral authority over the choice of ends. The normative order constitutes the needs and desires of the personality. No longer is action regulated solely by external coercion; norms are internalized by the actors (Parsons 1937/1968, 382). A morally neutral, rationally calculating orientation to the external situation of action based on the avoidance of negative sanctions, is replaced by the need-constitutive, internalized attitude of respect towards the norm—in other words, by a moral obligation. "Durkheim's thought, . . ." observed Parsons (1937/1968), "provides the basis of a solution . . . of the Hobbesian problem of order. . . . That men have this attitude of respect toward normative rules, rather than the calculating attitude, is, if true, an explanation of the existence of order" (386).

The internalized collective conscience implied in this solution is just another name for the value consensus that pervades society. If one projects this solution back onto Durkheim's study of the social division of labor (Durkheim 1893/1964), the social order of modern society turns out to be still a form of *mechanical solidarity,* a notion Durkheim had reserved for archaic societies whose members all internalize the same set of norms. The organic solidarity of modern society, however, should no longer be dependent on such a mechanical value consensus; instead, such a consensus should arise spontaneously from the social division of labor—that had been Durkheim's original idea.

Although the idea of organic solidarity proves to be rather short-lived in Durkheim's work, the question remains whether the social order of modern society shouldn't be conceptualized on a more recent, complex, and specific foundation than the concept of mechanical solidarity can provide. In the decision to conceive social order as a morally binding value consensus, a predetermined breaking point is built into Parsons's theory. A concept that has been coined for the analysis of premodern society is overextended when used for the analysis of modern society; sooner or later it will come under pressure and break.

Why didn't Parsons react much earlier to this weakness in the construction of his theory? A serious reason for this negligence may have been his orientation to the philosophy of Alfred North Whitehead. Whitehead's philosophy provides an epistemological blueprint for Parsons's methodology, namely, Whitehead's "analytical realism" (Parsons 1937/1968, 34–41; Wenzel 1991, 2003). However, for Whitehead, epistemological and ontological questions are intertwined. Thus Parsons accepts Whitehead's conception that values can be understood as "eternal objects" (Parsons 1937/1968, 441–47, 482, 763; Parsons 1961; Whitehead 1925/1967, 1929/1978; Wenzel 2000, 269–73), as timeless, abstract objects or ideas that are exemplified in the constitution of all events, of all that is becoming real.[5]

But there is more to this concept. Whitehead also provides Parsons with a solution to the problem of a social order! In his philosophy he coins the concept "society" as a terminus technicus for a group of events, or *actual entities,* all of which exemplify the same more or less complex eternal object: value. It is Whitehead's sociomorphic terminology that confirms Parsons's own ideas about the character of the social. In his early work, Parsons was going to develop an empirical application of Whitehead's cosmological scheme (Whitehead 1929/1958). A concept of social order as a mechanical value consensus was in full accord with Whitehead's philosophy.

An exemplary attack on the predetermined breaking point, which is unequaled in its vehemence and strategy, is Alvin W. Gouldner's *The Coming Crisis of Western Sociology* (1970). In this book Gouldner launches a sharp critique of the conservatism and preference for conformity in Parsons's structural functionalism. In Gouldner's view, Parsons's theory is a social technology designed to maintain the existing status quo in society at all costs (1970, 335). Gouldner cannot accept the notion that the internalization of values and norms furnishes social order with a secure base. Although he does not repudiate the notion that the realization of values provides intrinsic gratifications for an actor, he argues that the selfish, rational calculation of the consequences of actions is a basic trait of all actors. Norms and values may still be internalized;

however, the experience of the fulfillment of norms and values is bound to a rational calculation of consequences.

With the increasing significance of bureaucracy, technology, and science, according to Gouldner, the need for morality is decreasing (1976, 274–77). Technology in particular provides ever more nonmoral, non-normative gratifications. The replacement of normative, mechanical solidarity by a non-normative, organic solidarity seems for Gouldner to be obvious: "There has, in consequence, been a growing hiatus between the moral and technological sources of social solidarity in advanced industrial nations. As Durkheim saw—but for different reasons—the solidarity rests increasingly on nonmoral gratifications: the role of the 'collective conscience' has diminished" (Gouldner 1970, 283).

The welfare and the police states are the consequence of this development. With the breakthrough of organic solidarity, conflicts over the distribution of resources are not muted at all. Money and power are clearly extrinsic gratifications, whereas *moral self-affirmation or self-approval* provided by the fulfillment of normative demands and the realization of values describe a still-existing, intrinsic type of gratification. In this case, the gratification is *privatized;* the actor acting in a way that conforms with internalized norms has to gratify him- or herself. The appreciation of ego's norm-conforming behavior by an alter ego characterizes a fourth type taking a middle position between extrinsic and intrinsic gratification and making up the basis for an *order of prestige.* Gouldner regards this order of prestige as essential for the maintenance of social order in modern society, since it can convey an independent form of gratification to the poor and powerless.

The gratifications of the prestige order indirectly support the privatized gratifications of moral conformity, that is, the self-approval of the actor. As Gouldner (1970, 329) puts it:

> Essentially, then, the stability of a moral code within a society having a significant measure of class stratification will depend on the society's ability to mobilize *approval* or prestige for conformity with its prescriptions. This means that approval must be given for things other than wealth or power themselves, and yet things defined as being of great importance. Without this, the poor and the powerless would have only the slimmest chance to achieve the gratifications necessary to sustain their conformity with the moral code, for there would be few important values that they might share with the advantaged. (original emphasis)

The economic, political, prestige, and moral orders must be clearly and unequivocally differentiated from each other to maintain social order—and although Gouldner surprisingly ignores Parsons's systemic functionalism in his 1970 published critique he nevertheless duplicates its paradigm of four functional systems.

Even if the existence of a moral code is admitted, Gouldner nevertheless doubts that intrinsic gratifications are sufficient to maintain social order. He argues against conformity with norms for its own sake; indeed, conformity can even produce effects that are adverse for social integration! In an economic analysis of conformity with norms, he points to the decreasing marginal utility of norm-conforming action: the amount of gratification decreases with every increment of conformity to norms, so that ultimately norm-conforming action will fail and nonconformity will replace it. The more reliably the actor conforms to norms because they have been internalized, the more his gratification will tend to decrease, which in turn makes the problem of the marginal utility of conformity with norms even more incisive. Consequently, moral action is due to a conflict between the duties and desires of the actor. In cases where both are congruent—as is the rule with the internalization of norms and values—no moral appeal is needed, alter is in immediate conformity with ego's demands. Conflicting desires, however, add to the decreasing marginal utility that can be drawn from the fulfillment of duties and so further diminish the probability that alter and ego will conform to norms. Conformity thus becomes even more precarious and uncertain.

Social order, then, is based in part on the fact that certain contributions of actors are still due or are not yet reciprocated; social order is not based on something like a perfect normative order. The most probable scenario is a state in which conformity is intermingled with conformity-still-due and increasing degrees of nonconformity. But the decisive deviation from Parsons's normative model of social order is Gouldner's preference for the model of a single, rationally choosing actor. The intrinsic gratification of conformity with norms is counteracted by the premium awarded to the rational calculation of the utility of nonconforming action. Gouldner says (1970, 239):

> Parsons seems to assume that the scarcity or level of gratification as such will not effect system stability, so long as Ego and Alter share a common moral code. Presumably, the common code will lead to complementary rights and obligations: Ego will want no more gratifications from Alter than Alter willingly provides. But the gratifications that Alter is willing to provide Ego depend not only on Alter's conception of his duty, but also on the costs of his performing it; these costs affect the supply of gratification Alter provides and, in turn, depend upon the supply available to him. Any party's conformity with his moral obligations is a function of the level, the scarcity or abundance, of his own gratifications, and of the cost of producing them.

This model of a cost-calculating actor stands in a peculiar relation to the privatized self-affirmation that the individual can draw from norm conformity. Surprisingly, in both cases Gouldner presupposes a reflecting and anticipating self that is autonomous toward the moral expectations and demands of society or social groups. This is a *morally postconventional self* who is no longer chained to its internalized norms and values, who can actively shape them and follow rational, non-normative strategies of action. Gouldner's model of a rationally calculating and choosing actor, however, implies that there may be a premium on nonconformity with norms. In this non-normative model of social order, Gouldner provides the basis for the specific type of radical sociology with which he identifies. Nevertheless, the picture he paints of the modern social order is still incomplete, as I will show in the next step of my discussion. We have to think again, and seriously, about the increasing autonomy of the modern actor—and about how this is linked to the proliferation of non-normative models of social order.

FROM CONSENSUS TO COMMUNICATION

What are the reasons for the proliferation of non-normative models of social order? In which way are these new approaches related to an increasing autonomy of the personality? To answer these questions one has to point to an internal revision of Parsonian theory that did not eliminate the model of a mechanical value consensus but gave a much more precise interpretation of its role in the genesis of modern society. Here I draw on ideas concerning religious evolution that Robert Bellah developed in a joint seminar with Parsons in the mid-sixties.

In a certain sense Bellah is reconsidering the convergence thesis; his interpretation of the relevance of ascetic Protestantism for the development of modern society at least implies a reevaluation and relativization of Parsons's normative model of social order and the convergence thesis. In the transition from early to high modernity, culture's moral consensus loses its function as a guarantee of the social order of society. In Bellah's words (1964/1991, 44):

> Early modern society, to a considerable degree under religious pressure, developed . . . the notion of a self-revising social system in the form of a democratic society. But at least

> in the early phase of that development social flexibility was balanced against doctrinal (Protestant orthodoxy) and characterological (Puritan personality) rigidities. In a sense, those rigidities were necessary to allow the flexibility to emerge in the social system, but it is the chief characteristic of the more recent modern phase that culture and personality themselves have come to be viewed as endlessly revisable. This has been characterized as a collapse of meaning and failure of moral standards. . . . Yet the very situation that has been characterized as one of the collapse of meaning and the failure of moral standards can also, and I would argue more fruitfully, be viewed as one offering unprecedented opportunities for creative innovation in every sphere of human action.

Parsons's normative model of social order rightly applies to early modern society, where the interpenetration thesis is most adequate: originally, a premodern, orthodox-Protestant value consensus that informed the Puritan personality was the supporting platform upon which modern society as an endlessly revisable system could form. For Bellah, this capacity for self-revision is based on, and is the basis of, the democratic constitution of modern society. This presupposes an enlightened public and differentiation of a functionally autonomous political as well as legal system. An enlightened public and an autonomous legal system are essential components of an integrative societal community in the systemic functionalism of Parsons's scheme. Bellah could also have listed the differentiation of the functionally autonomous economic system as well as other autonomous systems as science and art (Luhmann 1990, 1995). The crucial point is the capacity for endless self-revision based upon the autonomy of functional systems. For my argument, there is no difference whether the internal differentiation of society into functionally autonomous subsystems is conceived deductively from a four-function paradigm, as in Parsons, or inductively, from a theory of autopoietic systems, as in Luhmann.

High-modern society's capacity for endless self-revision implies the radical functional independence of its subsystems. The support postulated by the thesis of the interpenetration of culture and personality now proves to be redundant, for culture and personality themselves become endlessly revisable, separate, and independent systems of action (Parsons 1954, 1959, 1961). Social theory reacts to this high-modern situation with the proliferation of non-normative models of order—social, cultural and personal.

The collapse of meaning and the failure of moral standards are not necessarily the consequence of this transition from early to high modernity. Forms of social action that are not based on norms can support social order quite as well as normative forms can endanger social order. The label of a non-normative, rational choice approach to social order, which can be attached too easily to Gouldner's critique, can as well be seen as the outcome of the increased autonomy of the personality as an endlessly self-revisable system. A rational choice following an egotistic calculus of preferences is an indication of a highly reflexive, autonomous personality, as is the privatized moral self-approval in realizing values and fulfilling normative expectations of others. Moral judgment and moral action can now be based on postconventional, universalistic moral principles; the self develops a "personal morality" (Parsons and Platt 1973, 166). The disintegration of social order is not the necessary outcome of this process of gaining autonomy; on the contrary, new forms of order are created.

So far, one may note the following: a process of increasing autonomy takes place, first, within society, and, second, among the other subsystems of the generalized action system, particularly culture and personality. The first leads to the transition from early to high modernity, the second to a process taking place within high modernity. Non-normative models of order indeed play a much more important role as this transition is completed. What is missing in Parsons's theory is an account of this transition based on concrete historical and comparative data. Parsons's theory of evolution clearly does not give such an account (Parsons 1966, 1971). Neither does his theory of symbolic exchange media (Parsons 1963/1969a, 1963/1969c, 1968/1969d). Yet the symbolic media of interchange do have a crucial importance for the differentiation and reintegration of the functional subsystems of society and the generalized action system. It is primarily in the context of the theory of symbolic interchange media that Parsons develops a new non-normative approach to social order. The societal media *influence* and *value commitments* and the generalized action medium *affect* form the core of a new model of social order. They all invite a reconceptualization in terms of a theory of trust.

It should be noted that Parsons himself was unsure how far the symbolic media can be held responsible for the *functional differentiation* of society and generalized action system. Together with Neil Smelser, he considers the medium money as a catalyst for dissolving segmentary differentiations and prompting the rise of the social division of labor (Parsons and Smelser 1956/1984, 104).[6] The *integrative effect* of the symbolic exchange media, however, cannot be doubted. As Parsons put it, "The need for generalized media of interchange is a function of the differentiatedness of social structures; in this sense they are all partly integrated mechanisms" (Parsons 1968/1977a, 199).

In the absence of substantial comparative historical research, the process of functional differentiation and reintegration of society and the generalized action system can only tentatively be referred back to the causal role of money, power, and other symbolic media. But some observations can be made, if the social division of labor is described in terms of the theory of symbolic media. With the use of symbolic media of interchange, ego reaches an understanding with alter without sharing complex cultural assumptions with him or her. Ego and alter can have a minimal knowledge of each other, can be anonymous, complete strangers to each other and nevertheless cooperate successfully (Baum 1976, 551). In this characterization, the real accomplishment of symbolic media should be obvious. The capacity of the media for (re-)integration certainly is a promising candidate for giving Durkheim's idea of organic solidarity a more precise definition. We have to return to the question: How can the actor withdraw from mechanical solidarity? How does value consensus lose its integrating, coordinating grip on actors in processes of social action?

Parsons is confronted with these non-normative forms of coordination in the process of transforming his structural functionalism into systemic functionalism. In 1953 he was invited to give the Alfred Marshall lectures at Cambridge University (Parsons 1953/1986). On this occasion he returned to the relationship between economic and social theory. Quite some time had passed since he had criticized classical and neoclassical economic theory from the standpoint of sociology as a science of value-oriented action. The primary object of his renewed interest was John Maynard Keynes's *General Theory of Employment, Interest, and Money* (1936/1991). In contrast to classical and neoclassical economic theory, Keynes takes money seriously as a symbolic medium of interchange with a logic of its own—money matters! The continuing evaluation of investments on the stock exchanges that are influenced by this intrinsic logic of money prevents the anticipated perfect equilibrium of supply and demand on the markets from being realized—at least in the short run, and possibly with catastrophic consequences for the level of employment and investment.

The *General Theory of Employment* is Keynes's reply to the crisis of the world economy in the 1930s. The stock exchange uncouples investment decisions from long-term value orientations, as Marshall had described them in his "Study of Man" (Marshall 1925). The speculator at the stock exchange has continually to anticipate the fast-changing, short-term expectations of the participants in the market. It is these higher-grade expectations, particularly the presence or absence of certainty and confidence gained from entertaining them that determine market processes. Those who invest show confidence in the further development of the markets, that is, they contribute to the "state of confidence," a state that radiates and reverberates through the markets and motivates other participants to invest. The state of confidence has to be created anew from moment to moment.

Whereas the grounds of this confidence seemed irrational to Keynes, indeed appeared to be some kind of "animal spirits," Parsons—once again—discovers noneconomic elements at work in the economy and aims to reconstruct these elements in terms of social theory (Parsons 1953/1986, 40). Together with Neil Smelser he developed the so-called interchange paradigm, a comprehensive scheme that lists all the relationships between the functional subsystems of society, including the economy. This was a first version of the sought-for reconstruction; it consisted of an elaborate account of the interdependence of each subsystem in terms of input from and output to other subsystems (Parsons and Smelser 1956/1984, 68). The economy stands in relationships of interchange with the polity, the societal community, and the fiduciary subsystem of society; all these systems perform specific services for each other. The state of confidence is sustained by processes of symbolic interchange (Wenzel 2001b, 273–320).

The interchange paradigm is the starting point for the development of the concept of symbolic media of interchange. These symbolic media give the interchanges between systems a generalized form. Each of the four functional systems has its own medium at its disposal. Parsons's study "On the Concept of Political Power" is usually considered the basis of a theory of symbolic media (1963/1969a). But Parsons had presented the first ideas for a theory of symbolic media earlier, shortly after his collaboration with Smelser. "Money," said Parsons (1959/1960), "is probably the most striking case of an institutionalized medium which is not ordinarily thought of in the context of communication . . . In my opinion, political power is also such a language and medium. . . . In the case of money . . . its societal guarantee, partly by public authority . . . , partly by informal 'confidence,' makes it possible for it to function as a circulating medium" (273).

Parsons here again refers to the "state of confidence." Without supporting informal confidence or trust, the communication of money is just as precarious as without institutional sanctions, that is, without a supporting public authority, such as the central bank, which guards the growth of the money supply and thereby keeps the value of the currency stable and inflation low. The communication of money, on the other hand, contributes to the state of confidence. The societal media of symbolic interchange are specialized languages of trust.

The state of confidence is the new paradigm of Parsons's social theory. This is exactly parallel to the critical procedure he undertook decades before. Again the science of economics has provided the starting point to elaborate on the noneconomic elements of the economy. Whereas the former solution put *values* at the core of social theory, now the *communication of trust* gains central importance for Parsons's systemic functionalism. But we still have to answer the question, how is the transition from a normative social order to a model of social integration resting on symbolic media of interchange accomplished?

Three steps of that transition in the concept of social order can be identified. In the first phase we find forms of social action and cooperation that are based on ascription. Duties and liberties are ascribed to status positions or social categorization. The social division of labor of a caste system may serve as an example. Cooperation and the social division of labor on the basis of ascription are limited in their development by rigid traditions and a fixed value consensus.

In the second phase of the transition, the actors still need a relatively extensive knowledge of each other to cooperate successfully. This knowledge, however, increasingly loses the character of a common, morally binding value system and gradually gains the character of a knowledge about complementary interests. In acts of barter the parties exchange goods and services with each other and thereby break up the limits of ascription. What, when, with whom, and on which terms one can exchange is not fixed beforehand; the actors act on their own, voluntarily. However, they are restricted by the paired complementarity of their needs.

The last step is the introduction of a generalized, symbolic medium of interchange. Since alter has no suitable barter object at hand, he gives ego a promissory note and the execution of the exchange is put off for the time being. If the promissory note is issued by a particularly trustworthy third party (Coleman 1990, 119–29, 186–89) a first form of the money medium has been established. The institutional protection of the promise from corruption by *sanctions* and *informal trust* are both characteristic for all societal exchange media. Cooperation and social order gain additional degrees of freedom if they are coordinated by symbolic media. Ego can then act more flexibly, more freely as far as time, goods, partners, and terms of transaction are concerned. For this type of interchange a value consensus is completely redundant. Values do play a role, though. The social order is subject to the intrinsic logic of the medium. The economy, for example, is the system in which cooperation is subject to an analysis of the rational calculation of utility.

At the beginning of the process of transition, cooperation is nearly exclusively regulated by morally binding norms and values, but by the end of the transition these common value orientations prove to be superfluous. Ego's knowledge of alter, which is necessary for cooperation to be successfully carried out, has shrunk drastically. On the basis of generalized symbolic media we can cooperate with complete strangers. What had been traditional values shared by the members of society now has become intrinsic values of functional systems like utility and solvency in the case of the money-controlled economy.

This transition from a normative social order to a non-normative one by way of introduction of symbolic exchange media can also be seen from a slightly different angle. In this transition, ascription is replaced by achievement as the means to condition social order. The conversion from ascription to achievement sets free the affect that was bound in ascription. If duties and liberties are no longer rigidly fixed, then the cathexis of objects becomes more flexible. The particular (in-)group of people who have diffuse—in principle boundless—expectations toward each other no longer is the only source providing the actor with a partner for cooperation. Such a partner can be every person whose performance satisfies the specific demands of the task to be accomplished. The conversion from the family rule of the captains of industry to professional managers may serve as an example (Wenzel 2001b, 303–8). Traditional mechanical solidarities are breaking up and new voluntary associations are created. High-modern society can be characterized by a pluralism of solidarities that have rid themselves of the particularistic and diffuse character typically associated with a rigid value consensus. Solidarity then is increasingly produced by inclusion (Parsons 1965/1969b, 280). Affect, finally, is conceived of as that generalized symbolic medium of the generalized action system that is related to the society and social system–level of analysis (Parsons 1970; Parsons and Platt 1973).

VALUE COMMITMENTS, INFLUENCE, AND TRUST

In the last steps of my argument, I will discuss the model of non-normative order that issues from Parsons's systemic functionalism. My focus will be on his theory of symbolic media of interchange. Two media on the societal level are especially relevant for Parsons's new model of social order: value commitments and influence (Parsons 1963/1969c, 1968/1969d).

A prerequisite for the functioning of all symbolic media is the fact that a unitary, morally binding consensus of cultural norms and values shared by all members of society alike no longer guarantees social order. "The very emergence of such a medium . . . ," Parsons (1970/1977b), writes, "depends on the fact that the value-system of a society is highly complex, and not a unitary entity, which as such either is internalized by an individual or a class of them, or is not" (351). Value commitments mobilize a generalized readiness for the selective implementation of values. The fiduciary subsystem is responsible for the *integrity* of society—as the economy is responsible for the utility of its interchanges, its communications. There no longer is a rigid cultural "identity" of society. The fiduciary system prevents disruptions and incoherencies in the self-understanding of society and facilitates the *consistency* of values in the continuing process of society's cultural self-definition. This implies the implementation of new values. New values are "bought" by moral appeals—in other words, value commitments buy readiness to implement, to realize, values without specifying what they imply in detail. The continual interchange of value commitments is the micro aspect of the macro process of value generalization.

Many different markets for value commitment exist. Value commitments for the implementation of cognitive rationality are not interchangeable with value commitments for parental care or technical safety. There are markets where value commitments are almost uniformly distributed. Since nearly everybody has an idea of what justice, human dignity, health, and so forth mean, it is difficult to accumulate generalized motivation to implement such values. This is more easily accomplished where an unequal distribution of value commitments occurs, that is, when an asymmetry between laymen and experts exists. "Moral" authority has greater leverage and moral appeals are more effective when, for example, physicians advise special treatments for rare illnesses.

Solidarity characterizes the intrinsic logic of the communication of influence as a symbolic medium. The social integration of society is the outcome of such communications. The notion of consensus has changed its meaning in this new context. *Consensus* has become the standard to be fulfilled in order to secure the coordination of social actions. Influence is a means to produce a continually revised network of partial consensual solidarities. These solidarities are no longer maintained by a *value* consensus of all members of society, but are shifting coalitions of *interest*. The act of persuasion with which influence is communicated is aimed at the mobilization of a generalized support for interests that are still open to specification. As Parsons's (1966/1969e) puts it, "The essential point is the establishment of solidarity and a contribution to its operation, without immediately specifying just *what* goals or interests are to be actively supported" (336, original emphasis).

Persuasion does not require specifying "good reasons" because such reasons are "intrinsic persuaders" for which no influence is needed. Persuasion, rather, successfully mobilizes support *without* being able to give good reasons. The persuader's prestige, that is, the accumulated influence of a single person or collectivity, must suffice as reason.

Influence is necessary when there is a pluralism of reference groups, voluntary associations, and shifting solidarities (Lidz 1991). The communication of influence is the microprocess of inclusion. New and existing solidarities can be continually (re-)created and extended. The need for influence is caused by the associational pluralism of modern society, which produces an increasing rate of cross pressures from conflicting expectations of different reference groups, group memberships, and solidarities. Influence is the means to eliminate or mitigate these potential conflicts because the interests involved can remain unspecified to a considerable degree.

Although there is no doubt that Parsons did not develop the notion of trust as a central concept in his late theory, in the last step of my argument I will attempt to present trust as a core concept of a revised Parsonian theory of social order. The following sketch forms a link to the newer debates in social theory on the role of trust for the integration of high-modern society.

There are two approaches to a Parsonian theory of trust. The first starts from Parsons's reconstruction of the state of confidence, the second from the notion of affect as the symbolic medium of the generalized action system related to society and social systems. I will concentrate primarily on the first approach here. In building a theory of societal media of symbolic interchange, Parsons indeed did see trust as the groundwork of interchange, cooperation, and social order. As he pointed out (Parsons 1963/1969c), "There is a sense in which all four of the mechanisms [the four societal media of interchange, money, power, influence, and value commitments] under consideration here depend on the institutionalization of attitudes of trust" (415). The societal media of symbolic interchange are special languages of *institutionalized trust.* They rely not only on trust alone, what could be called "raw" or "thin" trust (explained below), but are supported by institutions (the central bank in the case of money) and their sanction mechanisms (the brute physical force applied by the police and the military in the case of power). It is for this reason that Parsons gives a systematic account of the societal media of symbolic exchange in terms of positive and negative, internal and external sanctions (Parsons 1963/1969a, 363; Parsons 1940/1993, 113). Their institutionalization makes the acceptance of a communication from such specialized trust media significantly more probable and thereby expectable and calculable.

To understand trust one has first to explain the phenomenon of "raw" or "thin" trust (Williams 1988). How can an act of cooperation between ego and alter be based on the communication of trust *without* institutional guarantees and sanctions? Usually the communication of trust takes place in a standard sequence. There is a trust giver and a trust receiver. The trust giver initiates the communication by offering a good or a service for which the trust receiver has not asked. The trust giver thereby tries to start off a process of cooperation that is successfully accomplished when the trust receiver will have reciprocated the initially offered gift of trust by his completion of their conjoint act of cooperation. A communication of raw trust is given if and only if the trust receiver is free not to reciprocate the initial offer of trust by the trust giver. There are no sanctions that can bind the potential receiver into compliance with the trust giver's expectation that the initiated act of cooperation will be completed.

Of course, if the trust giver and the trust receiver cooperate on a regular, continual basis and the roles of giver and receiver can in due course be exchanged, then the trust relationship acquires the character of mutuality and an intrinsic sanction potential is prone to develop. In this situation, each party will lose an advantage should he or she quit the relationship. This is, however, a special case in the theory of trust. A theory of trust needs first to explain cooperation in a one-sided and solitary act of trust communication. The most important question then is: What is the basis of such a communication of trust?

The rational-choice approach to trust as developed by Coleman (1990) and Piotr Sztompka (1999) makes the calculation of the subjective probability that a communication of trust will be reciprocated the basis of trust. To trust is to bet. Trusting is a game that has to be won. We behave rationally if we look for information that will permit us to settle the question whether to participate in the game or not. It is assumed that this information, at least in part, is independent of the actions of the potential partner in the game, that it cannot be falsified or manipulated. But this is merely a further assumption. If we look at strategic-interaction games (Goffman 1969/1980), we learn that we never can be certain that we will not be deceived by the other players. Actually, if we could get certainty, we would not need to *trust* any longer, we just would *know* for sure. The self-presentation, the performance of the person to be trusted may be an important factor in the communication of trust. The person has to be trustworthy (Luhmann 1973). Thus trust may be grounded in the trustworthiness of the potential trust receiver. Trust may also be grounded in a convincing definition of the situation, as Harold Garfinkel's experiments of trust have shown. We can trust if we have an interpretation at hand that normalizes a common reality for both trust giver and trust receiver (Garfinkel 1963/1990, McHugh 1968).

Raw trust is a risky business. It exemplifies what can be called an "as-if" characteristic of a transaction. The initiating act of giving trust is a kind of fiction that has yet to be realized. The realization depends solely on the reciprocating, completing act of the trust receiver. Ego, the trust giver, initiates a common project of cooperation with alter, the trust receiver, that must be affirmed by alter in order to lose this fictional character and to become real. There are two reasons why this fiction can become real: performances of personalities as they present themselves, and definitions of the situation that may create a common understanding of reality.

In initiating an act of cooperation by giving trust, ego at the same time initiates what Erving Goffman (1967) calls a *face,* which, to be made real, alter has to affirm. In initiating an act of cooperation by giving trust, ego at the same time initiates a common understanding of reality, a definition of the situation. Alter has to affirm both, ego's face and the definition of the situation, to transform the potential transaction into something actual. In both respects, alter is free not to reciprocate ego's acts; there are no sanctions that can be placed upon alter. The success of this communication is thus precarious. This is the decisive difference as against the societal media of symbolic exchange that make success probable by sanctions and sanction-performing institutions. Trust, performance capacity, and the definition of the situation are, together with intelligence (Lidz and Lidz 1976), the symbolic media of the generalized action system; they are the catalysts of the functional autonomization of society, personality, and culture in high modernity, as Bellah has described it.

Exploring the bases of trust opens a perspective in which to reconceptualize these communications media and their interdependence. It opens a renewed way to ground social order on generalized forms of affect—trust is positive generalized affect; mistrust is negative generalized affect. A common, unitary, morally binding consensus of norms and values is no longer implied here. It opens up Parsonian theory to alternative, non-normative approaches of order such as Goffman's work on the theory of face and the presentation of self and Garfinkel's ethnomethodology stating the conditions for the accomplishment of a common reality. This could also be the first glimpse at the renewal of the convergence thesis—a convergence now based on non-normative notions of order.

NOTES

1. For the concepts of "dominant" and "oppositional reading" see Stuart Hall (1980).
2. The reading of Durkheim and Weber may serve as an example. Explicitly oppositional readings of Weber are, for example, developed by Reinhard Bendix (1960), Jere Cohen, Lawrence Hazelrigg, and Whitney Pope (1975a, 1975b), Schluchter 1980, of Durkheim by Pope 1973. See Parsons's replies: Parsons (1975a, 1975b). Much earlier Alvin Gouldner tried to correct Parsons's reading of Durkheim and to repudiate the convergence thesis in his edition of Durkheim's 1928 posthumously published study *Le Socialisme:* Gouldner (1958).
3. For exemplary arguments on the discontinuity of Parsons's theory see John Finlay Scott (1963), Ken Menzies (1977), and Hans P. M. Adriaansens (1980).
4. An interesting fact is that both authors (and others, too) recapitulate the whole development of sociological theory, as Parsons already had before them—a clear affirmation of the function of classical text as mentioned above.
5. Parsons continued to understand culture on the basis of the concept of "eternal objects," from his early work to systemic functionalism. In the latter version of his theory such objects cover the structural, or code, aspect of culture as against the process aspect of culture. Clifford Geertz (1973) sees in this view of culture a crucial deficiency of Parsons's theory, writing:

   > The workability of the Parsonian concept of culture rests almost entirely . . . on the degree to which the relationship between the development of symbol systems [the structural aspect] and the dynamics of social process can be circumstantially exposed, thereby rendering the depiction of technologies, rituals, myths, and kinship terminologies as man-made information sources for the directive ordering of human conduct more than a metaphor. This problem has haunted Parsons's writings on culture from the earliest days when he regarded it as a set of Whiteheadian "eternal objects" psychologically incorporated into personalities and thus, by extension, institutionalized in social systems, to the most recent where he sees it more in the control-mechanism terms of cybernetics. (250–51, emphasis added)

6. Luhmann clearly opts for the causal role of symbolic media in the process of functional differentiation of society, writing (1976, 518–19):

> Generalized media evolve . . . in close interdependence with social systems. Although stimulated . . . by recurrent problems in interaction, the differentiation of media into distinct institutional mechanisms depends on the social evolution at the level of society. It would not suffice to explain the development of generalized media as a consequence of system differentiation. On the contrary, *system differentiation seems rather to follow the lines of possible media.* (emphasis added)

REFERENCES

Adriaansens, Hans P. M. 1980. *Talcott Parsons and the Conceptual Dilemma.* London: Routledge & Kegan Paul.

Alexander, Jeffrey C. 1983. *Theoretical Logic in Sociology.* Volume 4, *The Modern Reconstruction of Classical Thought: Talcott Parsons.* London: Routledge & Kegan Paul.

———. 1987. "The Centrality of the Classics." In *Social Theory Today,* edited by Anthony Giddens and Jonathan Turner. Cambridge: Polity Press.

———. 1990. "Beyond the Epistemological Dilemma: General Theory in a Postpositivist Mode." *Sociological Forum* 5(4): 531–44.

Baum, Rainer C. 1976 "Communication and Media." In *Explorations in General Theory in Social Science,* edited by Jan Loubser, Rainer C. Baum, Andrew Effrat, and Victor M. Lidz. New York: Free Press.

Bellah, Robert N. 1964/1991. "Religious Evolution." In *Beyond Belief: Essays on Religion in a Post-Traditionalist World.* Berkeley: University of California Press.

Bendix, Reinhard. 1960. *Max Weber. An Intellectual Portrait.* Garden City, N.Y.: Doubleday.

Cohen, Jere, Lawrence Hazelrigg, and Whitney Pope. 1975a. "De-Parsonizing Weber: A Critique of Parsons's Interpretation of Weber's Sociology." *American Sociological Review* 40(2): 229–41.

———. 1975b. "On the Divergence of Weber and Durkheim: A Critique of Parsons's Convergence Thesis." *American Sociological Review* 40(4): 417–27.

Coleman, James S. 1990. *Foundations of Social Theory.* Cambridge, Mass.: Belknap Press/Harvard University Press.

Davis, Kingsley. 1959. "The Myth of Functional Analysis as a Special Method in Sociology and Anthropology." *American Sociological Review* 24(6): 757–72.

Durkheim, Émile. 1893/1964. *The Division of Labor in Society.* New York: Free Press.

———. 1925/1973. *Moral Education: A Study in the Theory and Application of the Sociology of Education.* New York: Free Press.

Eckberg, Douglas Lee, and Lester Hill, Jr. 1980. "The Paradigm Concept and Sociology: A Critical Review." In *Paradigms and Revolutions: Applications and Appraisals of Thomas Kuhn's Philosophy of Science,* edited by Gary Gutting. Notre Dame: University of Notre Dame Press.

Garfinkel, Harold. 1963/1990. "A Conception of, and Experiments with, 'Trust' as a Condition of Stable Concerted Action." In *Ethnomethodological Sociology,* edited by Jeff Coulter. Aldershot, England: Edward Elgar.

Geertz, Clifford. 1973. *The Interpretation of Cultures.* New York: Basic Books.

Giddens, Anthony. 1977. *New Rules of Sociological Method: A Positive Critique of Interpretative Sociologies.* London: Hutchinson.

———. 1979. "Functionalism: Après la lutte." In *Studies in Social and Political Theory.* London: Hutchinson.

Goffman, Erving. 1967. *Interaction Ritual: Essays on Face-to-Face Behavior.* Garden City, N.Y.: Doubleday.

———. 1969/1980. *Strategic Interaction.* Philadelphia: University of Pennsylvania Press.

Gouldner, Alvin W. 1958. Introduction to *Socialism and Saint-Simon,* by Émile Durkheim. Yellow Springs, Ohio: Antioch University Press.

———. 1976. *The Dialectic of Ideology and Technology.* New York: Seabury Press.

———. 1970. *The Coming Crisis of Western Sociology.* New York: Basic Books.

Habermas, Jürgen. 1980. "Handlung und System—Bemerkungen zu Parsons' Medientheorie." In *Verhalten, Handeln und System: Talcott Parsons' Beitrag zur Entwicklung der Sozialwissenschaften,* edited by Wolfgang Schluchter. Frankfurt am Main: Suhrkamp.

———. 1981a. *Theorie des kommunikativen Handelns.* Frankfurt am Main: Suhrkamp.

———. 1981b. "Talcott Parsons—Probleme der Theoriekonstruktion." In *Lebenswelt und soziale Probleme: Verhandlungen des 20. Deutschen Soziologentages,* edited by Joachim Matthes. Franfurt am Main: Campus.

Hall, Stuart. 1980. "Encoding/Decoding." In *Culture, Media, Language: Working Papers in Cultural Studies, 1972–1979,* edited by Stuart Hall, Dorothy Hobson, Andrew Lowe, and Paul Willis. London: Hutchinson.

Keynes, John Maynard. 1936/1991. *The General Theory of Employment, Interest, and Money.* San Diego: Harcourt Brace.

Kuhn, Thomas S. 1962/1970. *The Structure of Scientific Revolutions.* Chicago: University of Chicago Press.

Lidz, Charles W., and Victor M. Lidz. 1976. "Piaget's Psychology of Intelligence and the Theory of Action." In *Explorations in General Theory in Social Science,* edited by Jan Loubser, Rainer C. Baum, Andrew Effrat, and Victor M. Lidz. New York: Free Press.

Lidz, Victor M. 1991. "Influence and Solidarity: Defining a Conceptual Core for Sociology." In *Talcott Parsons: Theorist of Modernity,* edited by Roland Robertson and Bryan S. Turner. London: Sage.

Luhmann, Niklas. 1973. *Vertrauen: Ein Mechanismus der Reduktion sozialer Komplexität.* Stuttgart: Enke.

———. 1975. "Einführende Bemerkungen zu einer Theorie symbolisch generalisierter Kommunikationsmedien." *Soziologische Aufklärung.* Volume 2, *Aufsätze zur Theorie der Gesellschaft.* Opladen: Westdeutscher Verlag.

———. 1976. "Generalized Media and the Problem of Contingency." In *Explorations in General Theory in Social Science,* edited by Jan Loubser, Rainer C. Baum, Andrew Effrat, Victor M. Lidz. New York: Free Press.

———. 1984. *Soziale Systeme: Grundriss einer allgemeinen Theorie,* Frankfurt am Main: Suhrkamp.

———. 1990. *Die Wissenschaft der Gesellschaft.* Frankfurt am Main: Suhrkamp.

———. 1995. *Die Kunst der Gesellschaft.* Frankfurt am Main: Suhrkamp.

Marshall, Alfred. 1925. *Principles of Economics.* London: Macmillan.

McHugh, Peter. 1968. *Defining the Situation: The Organization of Meaning in Social Interaction.* Indianapolis: Bobbs-Merrill.

Menzies, Ken. 1977. *Talcott Parsons and the Social Image of Man.* London: Routledge & Kegan Paul.

Münch, Richard. 1982. *Theorie des Handelns: Zur Rekonstruktion der Beiträge von Talcott Parsons, Émile Durkheim und Max Weber.* Frankfurt am Main: Suhrkamp.

———. 1987. "Parsonian Theory Today: In Search of a New Synthesis." In *Social Theory Today,* edited by Anthony Giddens and Jonathan Turner. Cambridge: Polity Press.

Parsons, Talcott. 1939. "Actor, Situation, and Normative Pattern." Unpublished paper. Talcott Parsons Papers, Harvard University Archives, box 1, HUG(FP)42.45.4.

———. 1954. "Psychology and Sociology." In *For a Science of Social Man,* edited by John Gillin. New York: Macmillan.

———. 1959. "An Approach to Psychological Theory in Terms of the Theory of Action." In *Psychology: A Study of Science.* Volume 3, *Formulation of the Person and the Social Context,* edited by Sigmund Koch. New York: McGraw-Hill.

———. 1951/1959. *The Social System.* Glencoe, Ill.: Free Press.

———. 1959/1960. "The Principal Structures of Community." *Structure and Process in Modern Societies.* New York: Free Press.

———. 1961. "Culture and the Social System—Introduction." In *Theories of Society: Foundations of Modern Sociological Theory,* edited by Talcott Parsons, Edward Shils, Kaspar D. Naegele, and Jesse R. Pitts. New York: Free Press.

———. 1964. *Social Structure and Personality.* Glencoe, Ill.: Free Press.

———. 1966. *Societies: Evolutionary and Comparative Perspectives.* Englewood Cliffs, N.J.: Prentice-Hall.

———. 1937/1968. *The Structure of Social Action.* New York: Free Press.

———. 1963/1969a. "On the Concept of Political Power." In *Politics and Social Structure,* by Talcott Parsons. New York: Free Press.

———. 1965/1969b. "Full Citizenship for the Negro American?" In *Politics and Social Structure.* New York: Free Press.

———. 1963/1969c. "On the Concept of Influence." In *Politics and Social Structure.* New York: Free Press.

———. 1968/1969d. "On the Concept of Value-Commitments." In *Politics and Social Structure.* New York: Free Press.

———. 1966/1969e. "The Political Aspect of Social Structure and Process." In *Politics and Social Structure.* New York: Free Press.

———. 1970. "Some Problems of General Theory in Sociology." In *Theoretical Sociology. Perspectives and Developments,* edited by John C. McKinney and Edward A. Tiryakian. New York: Appleton-Century-Crofts.

———. 1971. *The System of Modern Societies.* Englewood Cliffs, N.J.: Prentice-Hall.

———. 1975a. "On De-Parsonizing Weber." *American Sociological Review* 40(5): 666–70.

———. 1975b. "Comment on 'Parsons's Interpretation of Durkheim' and on 'Moral Freedom through Understanding,' " *American Sociological Review* 40(7): 106–11.

———. 1968/1977a. "Social Systems." In *Social Systems and the Evolution of Action Theory.* New York: Free Press.

———. 1970/1977b. "Equality and Inequality in Modern Society, or Social Stratification Revisited." In *Social Systems and the Evolution of Action Theory.* New York: Free Press.

———. 1978. *Action Theory and the Human Condition.* New York: Free Press.

———. 1953/1986. *The Integration of Economic and Sociological Theory: The Marshall Lectures, University of Cambridge 1953.* Uppsala University Department of Sociology Research Reports. Uppsala, Sweden: Uppsala University.

———. 1940/1993. "Memorandum: The Development of Groups and Organizations Amenable to Use Against American Institutions and Foreign Policy and Possible Measures of Prevention." In *Talcott Parsons on National Socialism,* edited by Uta Gerhardt. New York: Aldine de Gruyter.

Parsons, Talcott, and Robert F. Bales. 1955/1956. *Family. Socialization and Interaction Process.* London: Routledge & Kegan Paul.

Parsons, Talcott, Robert F. Bales, and Edward A. Shils. 1953/1981. *Working Papers in the Theory of Action.* Westport, Conn.: Greenwood Press.

Parsons, Talcott, and Gerald M. Platt. 1973. *The American University.* Cambridge, Mass.: Harvard University Press.

Parsons, Talcott, and Edward A. Shils, eds. 1951/1959. *Toward a General Theory of Action.* Cambridge, Mass.: Harvard University Press.

Parsons, Talcott, and Neil J. Smelser. 1956/1984. *Economy and Society: A Study in the Integration of Economic and Social Theory.* London: Routledge & Kegan Paul.

Pope, Whitney. 1973. "Classic on Classic: Parsons's Interpretation of Durkheim." *American Sociological Review* 38(4): 399–415.

Schluchter, Wolfgang. 1980. "Gesellschaft und Kultur—Überlegung zu einer Theorie institutioneller Differenzierung." In *Verhalten, Handeln und System: Talcott Parsons' Beitrag zur Entwicklung der Sozialwissenschaften,* edited by Wolfgang Schluchter, Frankfurt am Main: Suhrkamp.

Scott, John Finley. 1963. "The Changing Foundations of the Parsonian Action Scheme." *American Sociological Review* 28(5): 716–35.

Sztompka, Piotr. 1999. *Trust: A Sociological Theory.* Cambridge: Cambridge University Press.

Weber, Max. 1920/1978. *Gesammelte Aufsätze zur Religionssoziologie.* Volume 1. Tübingen: J. C. B. Mohr.

Wenzel, Harald. 1991. *Die Ordnung des Handelns: Talcott Parsons' Theorie des allgemeinen Handlungssystems.* Frankfurt am Main: Suhrkamp.

———. 2000. "Dewey, Whitehead und das Problem der Konstruktion in der Sozialtheorie." In *Philosophie der Demokratie: Beiträge zum Werk von John Dewey,* edited by Hans Joas. Frankfurt am Main: Suhrkamp.

———. 2001a. "Functionalism in Sociology." In *International Encyclopedia of the Social and Behavioral Sciences.* Oxford: Elsevier.

———. 2001b. *Die Abenteuer der Kommunikation: Echtzeitmassenmedien und der Handlungsraum der Hochmoderne.* Weilerswist: Velbrück Wissenschaft.

Whitehead, Alfred North. 1929/1958. *The Function of Reason: The Louis Clark Vanuxem Foundation Lectures, 1929.* Boston: Beacon Press.

———. 1925/1967. *Science and the Modern World.* New York: Free Press.

———. 1929/1978. *Process and Reality.* New York: Free Press.

Williams, Bernard. 1988. "Formal Structures and Social Reality." In *Trust: Making and Breaking Cooperative Relations,* edited by Diego Gambetta. New York: Blackwell.

Chapter 4

Affect in Social Life

Harold J. Bershady

Talcott Parsons conceived the idea of the generalized symbolic media of interchange in his later work. The very large question or set of questions this idea was designed to answer is this: What are the contributions each subsystem of society makes to the functioning of each of the other subsystems? A well-developed answer to this question, he believed, would provide action theory with an analysis of dynamic processes more comprehensive and rigorous than had so far been achieved.

Parsons took money as his prototype medium (Parsons and Smelser 1956). The properties of money and variability when it is circulated in exchange for goods and services in all sectors of society had been well analyzed by economists. Drawing analogies to money, Parsons published a set of innovative papers on power, value commitments, and influence, each of which was analyzed as a medium of exchange akin to money in its properties and circulatory course (Parsons 1969). All of the media were, like money, held to have value only in exchange, all could be invested and grow, all could be withdrawn, and none was intrinsically of a zero-sum kind in its distribution. It soon became apparent, however, that these new media shared some of the properties of money, but not all. Moreover, each medium was unlike the others in several respects (Lidz 2002). Although cognizant of these difficulties, Parsons pressed on to conceive the media that operated at the most comprehensive level of the general system of action, namely the media pertaining to and circulating among the cultural system, the social system, the personality system, and the mind, sometimes called the behavioral system (Parsons and Platt 1973).

Parsons left his analysis of the media, and perhaps also their enumeration, uncompleted. This paper is written in the belief that the idea of the media, what they are and how they operate and combine, has great promise for the theoretical understanding of social life. I have chosen only one medium to discuss, namely affect. Although acutely aware of many of the features of affect, Parsons's treatment of affect as a medium of exchange was not well developed, and in certain respects his view of the theoretical placement of affect was misleading and ambiguous. I believe that human affect is fundamental to social relationships, that it reaches into all spheres of social life, and that it can be understood, as Parsons himself understood it, in sociological as well as psychological terms. My analysis will concentrate on sociological aspects of affect, but, with a few exceptions, will leave the question of its circulation for future discussion.

AFFECT IN SOCIAL LIFE

Parsons developed the idea of affect as a symbolic medium of interchange from two main sources. The first was in the pivotal importance Émile Durkheim attributed to moral sentiments in integrating the normative order (1947, 1960, 1961). Although the origins, makeup, prevalence, and kinds of moral sentiments were not well analyzed by Durkheim, he was unequivocal in underlining their significance. And since, in Durkheim's view, the normative order is coextensive with society, in a certain sense is society, and gives to social life whatever coherence it has, moral sentiments are by definition crucial to social life.

The other source was in Sigmund Freud's analysis of the origins and meaning of affect. Affect, in Freud's view, is a kind of energy that is signified in a person's motivations for or attachment to an object, any object—the self, another person, a thing, a pursuit, a mental entity (1930, 1950a, 1955, 1959). Affect is thus a feature of every one of our activities. And, although Freud never quite put it this way (he spoke of the super-ego and conscience), a considerable part of every child's affective growth is taken up with developing normative attachments, including attachments to appropriate ways of expressing affect.

In seeing a convergence between Durkheim's view of moral sentiments and Freud's view of affect, Parsons accomplished several things. First, he provided a dynamic analysis of the conception of moral sentiments, their origins, kinds, and variations, which was missing in Durkheim's treatment. Second, he provided a much fuller, more complex analysis of normative elements in the super-ego that was beyond Freud's technical interests (1960, 1964). And third, because affect is a signifier, he was able to formulate affect as a general symbolic medium of interchange that, since it was now so clearly linked to the normative order, circulates throughout the entire action system (Parsons 1977, chapter 9).

Of the four subsystems that make up the general action system—mind, personality, social system, and culture—the social system functions to integrate all the others. In this respect, the social system is to the general action system what moral sentiments are to the normative order: both are integrative. It is perhaps because of this common function that Parsons was uncertain whether to place affect within the personality, as Freud did, or in the social system (Parsons 1977). Nevertheless, despite this uncertainty, Parsons concentrated a great deal of his discussion of affect on the relation of affect to norms, and I will maintain this distinction.[1]

Over almost three decades Parsons wrote on affective involvements in the family, schools, professions, race relations, politics, leadership, student protests, among many other fields.[2] He underscored the importance of affective attachments in upholding the moral order and in creating solidarities among persons and collectivities of many kinds. He noted the effect of the combination of affect with other normative elements, such as rational standards, in the way particular attachments are chosen and facilitated. He also wrote on perturbations in affective attachments that diminish or compromise collective solidarities. Yet he never wrote on affect specifically as a medium of interchange in terms equivalent to his papers on the other media of interchange: money, power, value commitments, and influence (see in particular Parsons 1969, chapter 14). In his characterization of affective involvements, however, Parsons attributed to affect many of the properties of money (Parsons 1977). Affect, as Freud also thought of it, can be invested, banked, spent; has value only in exchange, not in use; is subject to inflation and deflation; may, like an economy, undergo periods of depression or expansion; and can accumulate, be withheld or withdrawn; among many other seemingly money-like properties. The analogy to money in these respects is striking; indeed, Parsons's usage of the money analogy to describe a variety of affective situations is illuminating (see in particular Parsons and Platt 1973).

However, unlike money, affect cannot be numerically scaled. An amount of affect can be described as more or less, great or little, some or none, but there are no clear, discrete, stable units of affect that can be added, subtracted, divided, or multiplied. This means that although affect can and indeed does circulate, it does not operate quite like money. Affect must have other properties that permit it to circulate in particular ways. In the remainder of this paper I will first discuss some of the properties of affect, including the relation of affect to norms, and then turn to a few of its non-normative manifestations.

AFFECTIVE PROPERTIES

Affect appears first and foremost in the body (Scheler 1954). The cry of pain, the smile of pleasure, the blush of shame, the scowl of disapproval—these and many other clichés of affective gesture, or their equivalents, are found in all languages. To be sure, there is enormous cultural and historical variation in the gestural and vocal expressions of affect, as Marcel Mauss (1979) has shown and as other anthropologists and travelers have also often observed. There must, therefore, be a common affective capacity, a kind of diffuse energy distinguishable from other capacities of the body, which although expressed differently from one society to the next is possessed by all peoples. This general capacity is seized, given affective definition, and shaped through socializing processes in accordance with a society's norms.

All children who are physiologically normal learn the modes approved in their social settings of expressing kinds and degrees of affect. It is true that many of the ways of expressing affect remain linked to and are sublimations of their earliest sources in the body. However, affect can become a signifier only when, in the process of being shaped and defined, affective modes are established as categories of the mind, analytically distinct from other categories, such as space, time, and causality, although operating in association with them. These categories permit one to select affective expressions and to recognize affective expressions in others.

Whenever an affective expression occurs, its particular kind is almost always learned. (Exceptions to this will be discussed below.) As part and parcel of this learning, children also learn to recognize when affect is excessive, insufficient, or inappropriate to a situation. An affective response is thus a matter of judgment, one based on interpretation of the situation, selection from the available affective materials, and adaptation of the affect to the norms of expression considered relevant to the situation. Most adults have an affective repertoire that includes many nuances and shades of potential affective attachment and response. I do not believe it is possible fully to enumerate or count the contents of this repertoire, as one would a cache of coins, although we are able to recognize or decipher the appearance of one or another affective element. Nor is there reliable evidence that members of modern societies have larger, more developed repertoires of affect than members of traditional or so-called less-developed societies.[3] The affective differences between these two kinds of societies more likely lie in the extent to which affect is regulated by norms. In societies with recurring and increasing periods of anomie, such as our own, there will be less affective regulation, but not necessarily less affective expression.

Bodily affective manifestations of the sort mentioned are clearly modes of communicative exchange. Even when there does not appear to be the minimal two parties required for such an exchange, the two parties often exist, if only in the memory of the one who is present. We occasionally observe, for example, a person we know with a smile on his or her face apparently directed to no one in particular. When questioned, we discover this person is smiling in pleasureful and approving remembrance or commendation of some thing, event, or person in the recent or more distant past. We automatically take this as evidence of attachment to what is remembered and also of a tacit interchange in which some approval is given for something received. Affect may at times appear to be free-floating—we have all encountered persons who exude anger or happiness—but if affect is to be part of an exchange, then there are always potential objects, actual or illusional, to which the affect is or is ready to be directed.

Although norms of affective expression inscribe themselves on the body, they are not the body. It is for this reason that affect can also be represented outside the body—in language, drama, painting, music. Affective representation is not affect; one may even consider it, in analogy to money, a kind of counterfeit of affect, although it is perhaps more appropriate to think of it in analogy to forgery in painting. Nevertheless, affective verisimilitudes, whatever their use, have affective consequences. We have all heard or read stories of con men (the grist of many a sociological mill) whose mastery of faking affect has allowed them to bilk the unwary of their goods or money. Yet is there anyone who has not been moved by a story, a novel, a piece of music, a painting, a movie? It is in sharing the communicated meaning of affective representations that some part of the solidarity among people is made possible.

Affective representations have other functions as well. They provide reflective screens in which we recognize and reaffirm our loves and our hates, our commitments to family, friends, community, nation, and the transcendental. In this way our identity is deepened and reinforced. High and popular culture alike repeatedly project a range and intensity of affectively charged objects that embody much of what we care for as well as reject. It has not escaped the attention of governing agencies and other organizations of every contemporary Western, mid-Eastern, Asian, and African society that artistic representations have the power to move people to act. Nor, as we remember, was this power unknown to one of our great philosophers of antiquity, Plato, who, in The Republic, put strict limitations on the artist's social and political participation. Whether considered human frailty or strength, or sometimes both, our capacity to identify with others represented or actual, to be moved by them or to oppose them, has fundamental consequences for the solidarities of social life.

To summarize: The organization and allocation of our motivational energies is resident in our personalities.[4] However, the forms and modes of affective expression are drawn simultaneously from and circulate to all parts of the general action system: from the affective categories of the mind, from the identifications with others that are embedded as parts of the personality, from the intensities of affective investments that integrate us with the objects of our investments, as Parsons so well understood, and, finally, from the cultural and normative meanings that are in the repertoire of our affective responses. Affect is shaped by each sector of the general action system and functions as a complex in which all elements of this system are simultaneously present in varying ways and degrees in everything we do.[5]

POORLY REGULATED AND UNREGULATED AFFECT

Affect always points beyond itself, to what is valued or despised, to things, persons, events, or entities we want to have, be like, care for, participate in, hurt, destroy, or have lost. Although our motivational investments are for the most part regulated by norms, there are a few kinds of affective situations that are not well or perhaps not at all normatively regulated. One such was referred to earlier as occurring, when norms are unclear, unstable, or weakly assimilated. In such anomic conditions, affect tends to run amok, as Durkheim forcefully observed, and there is no clear beginning or end to affective involvement (1961). We have seen spectacular instances of such unbridled pursuit in the scandals of corporate greed and corruption of the past few years. Many other examples can be given.

There are other situations in which affective expression can become unregulated. It would be inaccurate to characterize these situations as anomic because norms do not seem ever to have held in them. I refer to two kinds of such situations, those that produce extreme effervescence, akin to euphoria, and those that produce panic.

Durkheim and his students described effervescent experiences as a buoyancy of mood, thought, and affect associated with celebratory rituals (Durkheim 1947; Hubert and Mauss 1964). As their studies have made abundantly clear, celebratory rituals are part of the makeup of all societies. They mark rhythms of social life—religious, national, local, and familial—and are integral to transitions in the life cycle. The affect expressed varies according to particular culture and is ritually shaped to the occasion. But even though ritualized and thus expected, occasions of effervescence are not for those reasons unmalleable. It is because of their "buoyancy," as Parsons observed, that effervescent experiences contain a potential for creative innovation in expression, thought, and conduct (1949, 437, 450).

Rituals of effervescence serve, for those who participate in them, mainly as a sign of and a medium that strengthens social ties. At the extreme of its expression, effervescence is, for the duration of its occurrence, unbounded. The rush of shouting and jubilant people onto the streets of every city in the United States within seconds of the radio announcements that the Second World War had been won and was ended was an extreme effervescent moment, truly euphoric, in the life of the nation. This was an affirmation not only of the hard-won American victory over dangerous enemies but of the belief that Americans of all kinds—rich, poor, old, young, of all ethnicities—were not strangers, were members of the same community. It hardly needs saying that there were no ritualized precedents for this occasion, yet it was clearly celebratory. Such extreme effervescent experiences occur in communities of varying sizes and kinds—a city whose team wins a contested World Series, or a scientific group whose members achieve a difficult breakthrough.

All occurrences of effervescence, ritualized or spontaneous, are in part expressions of shared feeling on the part of a community and imply a value of things shared by the community of celebrants. As opposed to ritual effervescence, however, the unbounded kind occurs without warning, without the expected repeatability in time and place of the ritualized forms. Unanticipated, unbounded celebrations break into the routines of daily life. They may become established as ritual celebrations of the event that called them forth, or they may fade from memory. The longer-term effects of such eruptions of affect are not predictable.

By contrast, situations that produce intense anxiety and panic are exactly opposite of effervescence in their social consequences. Freud thought of anxiety as an affective response to the loss or threat of loss of a loved object (Freud 1989). When an internal or external danger is greater than the individual has resources to cope with, Freud observed, the individual's reaction is one of helplessness and also sometimes flight (see chapter 11). These reactions, which may be physical or psychological or both, Freud called anxiety.

Freud's view of anxiety was based primarily on his analysis of individual patients, and although he forayed briefly into considerations of group phenomena, his views of anxiety remained at bottom psychological (1950b, 1950c, 1989). Nevertheless, some of his observations can be adapted to sociological ends.

Loved objects are not limited to parents, siblings, spouses, children, and friends, as Freud emphasized. Social entities such as norms and sometimes whole patterns of life that are held dear can also be love objects. Many novels, plays, and movies of immigrant life in the United States depict the anxiety experienced by an older generation as well as by their children at the inexorable loss of the old culture and the consequent distancing of the generations as the children begin to assimilate new American ways.

Cherished objects are heterogeneous and indefinite in number. They may be human, animal, material, and cultural. They may be books, paintings, musical instruments, and houses, as well as things we think of as belonging to us such as certain public buildings, or monuments, neighborhoods, cities, whole countries. Their threatened loss evokes anxious responses. But what is an anxious response? Consider, for example, the anxiety of the wailing child who circles haphazardly in search of a lost pet, or the spectators in the closing seconds of a fiercely played sporting event in which both teams or players are tied, or a student in a very difficult course, or a professor about to enter the classroom for the first time, or the musician and actor who have never been able to give the same performance twice, or the applicant being interviewed for a job—the examples are countless.

Are there in these examples particular norms that regulate the expression of anxiety? Freud does not address the issue sociologically, although he speaks of psychological mechanisms of inhibition and denial that at times mask the appearance of anxiety. There are, however, social norms that regulate anxiety when its appearance might be considered improper, bad form, or a sign of weakness, and there are many serious portraits as well as caricatures of the extremes to which such norms are sometimes taken. Those who hold to such norms initially endeavor to suppress and thus hide the physical signs—perspiration, rapid and shallow breathing, rigidity of body ("frozen with fear" as the expression has it)—commonly associated with anxiety. Such suppression may be transformed into inhibitions that become deeply rooted features of the personality (Freud 1989). There are people who have been so successful at denying anxiety that they are always, or always appear to be, "cool" and show no affect of any kind; we may wonder whether they have attachments to anything other than their appearance.

There are also occasions when unmistakably anxious affect breaks out among many people simultaneously, and in its most intense and extreme form—as panic—it may appear to be uncurbed. This phenomenon occurs in disasters and it may be called a community of anxiety, to adapt Max Scheler's language (1954, 13–15). To this type of anxiety outbreak I now turn.

Studies of disasters such as earthquakes, volcanic eruptions, fires, storms, and floods that destroy lives and property all describe the shock and terror of the survivors and the panic that often ensues (see Havenaar, Cwikel, and Bromet 2002; Hoffman and Smith 2002). When a greatly threatening disaster strikes, when fear is intense and escape routes and help appear to be cut off, then, as Neil J. Smelser observed (1962), people panic and flee outside of "established patterns of social interaction, in order to save life, property or power from that threat" (89–92, 146–47). Collective flight can be subdued only when leadership is quick to emerge, mobilizes resources to deal with the damage, provides reassurances of safety, and by both personal example of courage and the judicious use of restraints is able to restore normative controls (Smelser 1962).

Very much this pattern occurred in New York City and to a lesser extent the nation on September 11, 2001, when the greatest dissipater in the nation's history since the Civil War occurred. The panic and near panic were soon brought under control, and some of the anxiety was replaced by mourning for those who died and for the terrible wound both to the city and to the nation. Despite the cessation of a panic condition, anxiety in the city and in the nation was reported to persist at fairly high levels for several days, even weeks. The enemy was hidden, fanatical, and highly dangerous. No one knew when or where there would be another terrorist attack. For many months afterward New Yorkers continued to ask one another where they had been on 9/11 and to retell and perhaps through retelling attempt to diminish their shock. People who streamed to the city from other parts of the country to help in the rescue work—volunteer firemen, police, first-aid workers, nurses, social workers, owners of guide dogs, and others—continued for almost two years, although with lessening frequency, to send letters and articles to local and community newspapers and magazines describing the horror they felt on 9/11 and the aftermath, and the anxiety they still felt.[6]

Many people in New York City likely remain deeply disturbed by the collective trauma of 9/11. But most people, both in New York City and in the nation, continue to work and live their lives despite an often-expressed mood of general apprehension. A light pall of anxiety has settled on all of us that darkens whenever warning of an imminent terrorist attack is announced. Such warnings will be ongoing in the foreseeable future, and there is considerable likelihood that attacks will occur. The effects of this mood on people's work and lives are not clear and in any case are likely variable. Perhaps some have been spurred to greater efforts to rescue and salvage as much as they can, while others may remain locked in grief and anger over the things they have lost. We read in interviews of New Yorkers and in the accounts of journalists and counselors that many people in New York since 9/11 are easily startled, that there has been an increase in the suicide rate of survivors, and that there is greater incidence of psychological stress among New Yorkers and those who came to aid them. The findings of recent studies support these observations (see Hoffman and Smith 2002).

People want assurances in the presence of elusive and enormous threats. Anxiety persists but is often normatively constrained. It combines with any other affect but if intense enough to burst through its constraints is able to displace any other affect. At such times, anxiety becomes all-pervasive. I do not believe, however, and am not saying, that anxiety is necessarily a negative affect. By negative affect I mean one that closes off or is destructive of relationships. The negative consequences of anxiety depend on its degree. Nor do I think we live in an "age of anxiety," as was said some generations ago in the mid-twentieth century. As is true of any other type of affect, anxiety in varying degrees has been and continues to be potentially present in everything that we do, in each activity in which we have attachments of any kind, which is to say, in all activities of social life. This, too, is part of the human condition.

Affect cannot have social consequences unless it appears either in bodily signs or in representations. Whether such appearances should always be considered part of a communicative interchange or a prelude to an interchange is, I think, not certain. Extreme anxiety seems to put an end to interchange. Any affect can combine with others, effervescent love with anxiety, for example, or love with hate and anxiety. How combinations of affect appear and are manifested, the degree to which affective appearance is constrained, the scope of affective communication, given its various combinations, are features of the circulation of affect as a symbolic medium. In many of these respects, affect is not like money.

I am grateful to Renée C. Fox, Mark Gould, Victor M. Lidz and Ewa Morawska for their very helpful suggestions.

NOTES

1. I have argued in an earlier paper that affect is not to be confused with moral sentiments and is located in the personality. See Bershady (1997).
2. In his early formulation of the pattern variables, Parsons made a sharp distinction between affectivity and affective neutrality, and assumed that affective neutrality is a norm that pertains predominantly in technical and professional roles, such as that of physician (1951, chapter 10). As Renée Fox has shown, however, the dichotomy between affectivity and affective neutrality is not absolute and is bridged in the actual practice of physicians who maintain a "detached concern," as she put it, for their patients (Fox 1979, 484ff.) Detached concern is not an attitude limited to physicians. The same combination of detachment and concern occurs with teachers in relationship to their students, lawyers to their clients, coaches to their charges, psychotherapists to their patients, and so on.
3. Ewa Morawska has suggested to me the highly plausible (and so far as I know unexplored) hypothesis that in a more differentiated society such as our own, there will be many more shades of normatively regulated affective expression than in a less differentiated society.
4. See Bershady (1997).
5. I have endeavored in this paper only to show that affect draws definition from each of the four quadrants of the general action scheme, not to develop the quadripartite structures of affect pertinent to each of the four quadrants.

6. Indeed, an article appeared in a community newspaper published in Philadelphia in November 2002 describing the experiences of a social worker who worked in New York City many weeks after 9/11 (see the *Chestnut Hill Local,* November 14, 2002, p. 2).

REFERENCES

Bershady, Harold J. 1997. "The Production and Distribution of Affect." Paper presented at the national meeting of the American Sociological Association. Toronto (August).

Durkheim, Émile. 1947. *The Elementary Forms of the Religious Life.* Translated by Joseph Ward Swain. Glencoe, Ill.: Free Press.

———. 1960. "The Dualism of Human Nature and Its Social Conditions." In *Essays on Sociology and Philosophy by Emile Durkheim et al.,* edited by Kurt H. Wolff. New York: Harper Torchbooks.

———. 1961. *Moral Education.* Translated by Everett K. Wilson and Herman Schnurer. New York: Crowell-Collier.

Fox, Renée C. 1979. *Essays in Medical Sociology.* New York: John Wiley.

Freud, Sigmund. 1930. *Civilization and Its Discontents.* Translated by Joan Riviere. London: Hogarth Press.

———. 1950a. *The Ego and the Id.* Translated by Joan Riviere. London: Hogarth Press.

———. 1950b. *Group Psychology and the Analysis of the Ego.* Translated by James Strachey. New York: Norton.

———. 1950c. *Totem and Taboo.* Translated by James Strachey. New York: Norton.

———. 1955. *The Interpretation of Dreams.* Translated by James Strachey. New York, Basic Books.

———. 1959. *Inhibitions, Symptoms and Anxiety.* Translated by Alix Strachey, revised and edited by James Strachey, with a biographical introduction by Peter Gay. New York and London: Norton & Co.

———. 1989. *Inhibitions, Symptoms and Anxiety.* Translated by Alix Strachey, revised and edited by James Strachey, with a biographical introduction by Peter Gay. New York: Norton.

Havenaar, Johan M., Julie G. Cwikel, and Evelyn J. Bromet, eds. 2002. *Toxic Turmoil: Psychological and Societal Consequences of Ecological Disasters.* New York: Kluwer Academic Press.

Hoffman, Susanna M., and Anthony Oliver Smith, eds. 2002. "Catastrophe and Culture: The Anthropology of Disaster." *Journal of Urban Health* 79(3): entire issue.

Hubert, Henri, and Marcel Mauss. 1964. *Sacrifice: Its Nature and Function.* Translated by W. D. Halls. Chicago: University of Chicago Press.

Lidz, Victor M. 2002. "Language and the 'Family' of Generalized Symbolic Media." In *Talcott Parsons Today,* edited by A. Javier Treviño. London: Rowman & Littlefield.

Mauss, Marcel. 1979. *Sociology and Psychology: Essays.* Translated by Ben Brewster. Boston: Routledge & Kegan Paul,

Parsons, Talcott. 1949. *The Structure of Social Action.* Glencoe, Ill.: Free Press.

———. 1951. *The Social System.* Glencoe, Ill.: Free Press.

———. 1960. "Durkheim's Contribution to the Theory of Integration of Social Systems." In *Essays on Sociology and Philosophy by Emile Durkheim,* edited by Kurt H. Wolff. New York: Harper Torchbooks.

———. 1964. *Social Structure and Personality.* London, The Free Press. Collier-Macmillan Publishers, Ltd.

———. 1969. *Politics and Social Structure.* New York: The Free Press, Macmillan.

———. 1977. *Social Systems and the Evolution of Action Theory.* New York: Free Press.

Parsons, Talcott, and Gerald Platt. 1973. *The American University.* Cambridge, Mass.: Harvard University Press.

Parsons, Talcott, and Neil J. Smelser. 1956. *Economy and Society.* Glencoe, Ill.: Free Press.

Scheler, Max. 1954. The Nature of Sympathy. Translated by Peter Heath. London: Routledge & Kegan Paul.

Smelser, Neil. 1962. *Theory of Collective Behavior.* New York: Free Press.

Part II

Societal Community and Modernization

Chapter 5

Contradictions in the Societal Community: The Promise and Disappointment of Parsons's Concept

Jeffrey C. Alexander

Within the strongly empiricist framework of American social science, there is very little acknowledgment of the nonempirical, theoretically driven dimension of scientific change. Yet the major developments in social science do not emerge primarily from simple accumulation of empirical knowledge or from proving previous theories false. They grow from confrontations with other, hegemonic theories. These confrontations, which are often intense and highly emotional, may take the form of critical experiments that crystallize and operationalize more general commitments, but they usually also present themselves as more general, less empirical arguments about theoretical logic itself.

Because of the supra-empirical issues involved, it would be tempting to say that challengers to hegemonic theories are motivated simply by nonscientific concerns. It would be more accurate, however, to suggest that their social-scientific concern—their sincere, often fervent sense that the hegemonic theory is cognitively inadequate—is motivated as much by shifting historical experience among the challengers as by any technical inadequacy in the theories they challenge. Changing generational ideals; different class interests and cultural consciousness; ethnic, national, gender, sexual, and religious identities that depart markedly from the identities of those who created the hegemonic theory—these are all critical elements in creating new sensibilities and a sense of urgency about creating social scientific change. Because of this historical experience, social processes will be seen in new ways.[1]

These new sensibilities find intellectual expression at different places along the scientific continuum (Alexander 1982–83). They can be expressed in conflicts over presuppositions about action and order; in divergent feelings about social conflict and equilibrium; in more utopian or more pessimistic orientations to contemporary politics; and in different conceptions of social science itself, for example, in stronger beliefs in the legitimacy of pure positivism or in the contrary belief that normative commitments should become central to the practice of social science.

Such confrontations occur not only between social-scientific traditions but within them. Below the calm surface of the typical scientific community (Hagstrom 1965) that organizes disciplinary practice (Toulmin 1972), internecine disagreements often create whirlpools of discontent. When they remain below the surface, these tensions are the cause of theoretical revisionism. When contentious intellectual politics breaks through to the surface, the roiling results in broad-scale reconstruction and sometimes, when the stars are in the right place, in new theory creation.[2]

Whether these revisions, reconstructions, and recreations are progressive or regressive—whether they result in the creation of genuinely new knowledge or lead to a simplifying reduction of complexity—is difficult for contemporary participants and observers to assess in an objective way. It is not much easier, in fact, for historians looking back from another time. Did intraparadigmatic revision ever lead to *genuine* reconstruction? Did overt efforts at reconstruction at some point lead to *authentic* theory creation? Even if reconstruction and theory did happen, did they actually lead to better theories, or just to new ones? Participants at the time may feel one way, subsequent observers may have very different judgments, and still later intellectual historians may make wholly different assessments.

Although this cognitive status of social scientific change is difficult to assess, its sociological path is pretty straightforward. In the human sciences, the scientific process proceeds in a tension-filled, nonlinear manner. It was not the objective facts of early industrial society that induced Karl Marx to become a materialist focusing on economic and class dynamics. These social circumstances were filtered through his participation in a series of different theory groups, and this group participation was subject to the kinds of experience shifts I have mentioned. Marx first was a Hegelian (elaboration), and then a left-Hegelian (revision and reconstruction), before he became a Marxist (theory creation). These transitions were induced not only by his generational and political experience, which offered Zeitgeists from liberal reform to revolutionary socialism, but by Marx's simultaneous participation in different national theory groups—the movement from Hegelianism to French socialist to English political economy not only was intellectual but represented actual geographical immigration as well.

Each new theory group in which Marx participated and from which he learned involved fundamental internal tensions, conflicts within which he took active part and from which his theory continued to evolve. In a significant manner, for example, the mature Marx could be called a political economist. In critical respects, his political economy differed in only degrees from Ricardo's, and even less so from the more radical, left-Ricardians of his time. Yet to Marx these degrees of difference seemed to be significant departures, and for those who became his followers they seemed to leverage Marx's theory onto a fundamentally different plane than the earlier, equally brilliant and sometimes even equally radical forms of political economy.[3] Each of the stages in Marx's theoretical development, in other words, involved intraparadigmatic conflict, conflict that eventuated in his stepping outside an established community to establish a new one of his own.

Similarly fraught internal relationships have also been critical in less historically exalted realms of theory creation. Harold Garfinkel was an ambivalent Parsonian (reconstruction) before he moved completely to a new theory group, becoming a sociological follower and interpreter of Alfred Schutz. Within the latter frame, he quickly became dissatisfied as well, moving away from reconstruction to a new theory. This new theory, like Marx's later work, responded to an ambition for separation as much as to fundamental differences of ideas. Garfinkel's ethnomethodology differed from the ideas of Schutz, Wittgenstein, and Husserl in relatively small ways and could have been expressed in terms of revision and reconstruction, but, from the perspective of theory creation these small differences became highly significant. In a related tradition, Erving Goffman seemed at first to be brilliantly revising and reconstructing the symbolic-interactionist tradition. Eventually, it became apparent that he was actually creating a new, dramaturgical theory of his own, or at least that is what many of his interpreters have claimed.

Talcott Parsons gained prominence by confronting and displacing earlier forms of American sociological theory. This conflict between what became known as the earlier and the later, Parsonian school of American sociological theory is well known, as is the conflict between Parsonian functionalism and Marxist and critical theory. What is much less well understood is that Parsons also defined himself antagonistically against classical European sociological theory. While claiming (Parsons 1937) that the early versions of his voluntaristic action theory merely crystallized and synthesized the insights of the paragons of the European tradition, Émile Durkheim and Max Weber, Parsons actually revised and reconstructed their ideas. As his intellectual career developed, and despite his continuing formal obeisance to Durkheim and Weber, Parsons not only reconstructed but eventually displaced these classical traditions, creating a new theory of his own. This complex and often ambivalent intellectual development spiraled through processes of critical reinterpretation, incorporation, and secession, the result of which were new phases and forms of Parsonian theory.

What has always been of even less interest to Parsons's interpreters is that his intellectual demarche generated conflicts within his own theory group even as it drew boundaries that challenged others. As Parsons moved from one phase of theory creation to another, the students whom he had earlier trained often became subtle opponents of later versions. From Robert Merton, Kingsley Davis, Robin Williams, and Bernard Barber to Robert Bellah and Neil Smelser and then to Leon Mayhew and Mark Gould, the loyal, intellectually convinced students of one time quietly claimed that the new Parsons had abandoned truth. Parsons was accused of moving backward to the future, and these former students constructed their functionalism not only upon earlier ideas of Parsons but often upon reconstructions of them that combined his theory with elements from those with which he had been in conflict (see Alexander 1979, 1983, 1991, 1992).

My own decade-long effort to create a neofunctionalism challenge to orthodox functionalism (Alexander 1985, 1997a; Alexander and Colomy 1985, 1990) represented a challenge of just such a reconstructionist type. It emerged after an initial phase of my intellectual development that aimed at theoretical elaboration and revision (Alexander 1978, 1979, 1982). After working for some years within the more critical, openly reconstructionist approach to Parsonian theory, I eventually gave up on such efforts entirely. In the last decade, having abandoned neofunctionalism (1997b), I have tried to initiate two new lines of theory creation, one in cultural sociology (Alexander 2003), the other in civil society (for example, Alexander 2001a, 2001b, 2001c).

My efforts to theorize a civil sphere evolved in part from a sympathetic but critical engagement with Parsons's thinking about the societal community. In my earlier career, I understood the concept of the societal community as almost entirely satisfactory, interpreting it as among Parsons's most original ideas and building my own empirical projects upon its creative extension and elaboration (Alexander 1980, 1981, 1982). During my later, reconstructonist, phase, I tried still to work with Parsons's concept, though with such qualifications that a whole series of ad hoc theoretical and empirical adjustments had to be made (see, for example, Alexander 1988). In the last decade, however, as my work moved outside of any direct connection with the Parsonian vocabulary, I have left the concept of societal community for civil society, for reasons that I first presented in "After Neofunctionalism: Action, Culture, and Civil Society" (Alexander 1997b).

Certainly one can trace an internalist logic to this shift, but this movement beyond neofunctionalism was also stimulated by external influences. From the late 1980s, I became increasingly interested in the new forms of critical theory developed by Jürgen Habermas and in the debates within democratic political theory more generally. At the same time, I became much more sympathetic to developments in hermeneutic, semiotic, and poststructuralist thinking. Although I was not convinced of the face validity of either of these broad movements as such—the critical or the cultural—each left an indelible mark. The latter encounter pushed me to my theorizing in cultural sociology, the former, to my work on civil society.

Yet there were also nonintellectual elements pushing me to a new sociological theory of civil society. I had formed my generational sensibility during the late 1960s and early 1970s, during which time I had joined so many others in strenuously objecting to how American national interests led to military interventions despite democratic pressures and other kinds of national opportunities. During Reagan's presidency, in the 1980s, I organized and remonstrated against American state policy in South Africa and in Central America. Throughout these formative decades I remained deeply disturbed, as were so many other members of my postwar cohort, by the yawning gap between the promises of justice that were made by the American political tradition and the continuing realities of inequality, disorganization, and prejudice. I also become increasingly sensitive to an extra-national event that eventually affected my thinking in an even broader way. Along with other North Americans and Europeans in the postwar cohort, and most especially those among this group raised in the Jewish tradition, I felt increasingly compelled to reflect upon the world-historical implications of the Nazi Holocaust. The effect was that I became further distanced from the optimism about modernity that was everywhere reflected in Parsons's later work.

DUAL AMBITIONS AND DIVERSE ORIGINS: INTEGRATION AND JUSTICE

The technical and intellectual origins of the societal-community concept reveal the possibilities for its achievements but also the limits of its understanding. In the most immediate sense, it grew from Parsons's interest in developing a more sophisticated theory of what he called the integrative (I) subsystem of the AGIL interchange model that he and Smelser developed in the later 1950s (Parsons and Smelser 1956). More generally, the societal community emerged from the normative, integration-centered solution to the Hobbesian problem of order that Parsons had much earlier offered in *The Structure of Social Action* (1937).

Underlying these Parsonian theoretical commitments was Durkheim's concern for solidarity as a distinctive dimension of social life. The great French thinker believed that solidarity could exist only when a community's members share the same moral sense, a belief manifest in the fervor with which Durkheim continually evoked his master concept, society. Yet, as Bellah noted on the first page of his still relevant introduction to Durkheim's writings (Bellah 1973), even while Durkheim evoked the term "society" he was never able, or perhaps was never inclined, to move beyond vague metaphorics and conceptualize the notion in a clear and systematic way.

This is what Parsons aimed to do with the societal-community concept. It would systematically articulate for the first time Durkheim's more intuitive interest in solidarity and morality. What Parsons realized was that this Durkheimian focus would be conceived as an institutional, or functional, dimension of society, one that would be separate but equal with the economic (the A subsystem), the values-oriented (L), and the political (G). The societal community would provide a model for talking about the integrative subsystem and the functions it fulfilled.

Integration was not, however, the only interest that informed Parsons's effort to conceptualize the societal community. It is clear that he also had the problem of justice in mind, a problem that had animated Durkheim's concern with solidarity as well. Durkheim was not a conservative, the putative identity for which he was criticized by Lewis A. Coser (1960) and praised by Robert A. Nisbet (1965). He preferred restitutive to repressive law, and he did not fail to insert a third book, on the pathological division of labor, to his 1893 thesis, *The Division of Labor in Society*. Yet book III of this work, and even the discussions of anomie and egoism in *Suicide*, remained residual categories in Durkheim's systematic theory of modernity. To think sociologically about justice and injustice Durkheim provided precious little to go on besides evolutionary clichés and functionalist principles. To find more grist for his concept of the societal community idea, Parsons turned to Weber and to the democratic socialist tradition.

Weber provides a comparative-historical theory of how societies were able to create rules so universalistic as to discipline and morally regulate the various economic, political, and status groups in society. This interest was most visible in his concept of fraternization, which he develops in his chapter on the city in *Economy and Society* (Weber 1978, 1212–1372). In these pages Weber explains that the origins of universal citizenship are to be found in the ethico-religious conception that all men and women were brothers and sisters, a conception he found institutionalized, not only as morality but as law and regulation, in the city states of the European Renaissance. Guided by this liberal spirit in Weber's work—of which the section on the city was only one example—Parsons wanted his societal-community concept to refer not only to communal solidarity as such but also to solidarity of an abstracted and universalizing—that is, Weberian—type.

In those revealing but neglected passages of *Economy and Society,* Weber had emphasized that universal religious ethics provided a framework that enabled the urban working classes to demand such rights as labor protection and wage increases. It seems appropriate, then, that when Parsons wished to further fill out the democratic dimension of societal community he turned to the social democratic theorizing of T. H. Marshall (1964). Building on Weber, Parsons used Marshall to demonstrate that the primordial solidarity of traditional society could be transformed into the moral bindingness of inclusive citizenship. Looking at the effects of war and economic conflict on the emergence of cross-class solidarity in modern capitalist society, Marshall (1964) had suggested that the hopes of reformist democratic socialism were fulfilled by the welfare state, which could provide an antidote to class stratification without the necessary demolition of market society. Although I will suggest below that Parsons's attitude toward democratic solidarity is much more fraught than Marshall's, there seems little doubt that in his later work Parsons did come to equate the modern societal community with the culture and institutions that sustained Marshall's three-level model of citizenship.

As I define the origins of Parsons's societal community concept, then, it emphasized two distinctive dimensions, integration and inclusion. Parsons himself would probably have rejected the idea that such a duality exists. Nevertheless, the relative autonomy of these two concepts—and the sociological forces to which they refer—is central to the argument that I will make about the ambitions and the difficulties of Parsons's work.

My argument can be simply stated. At its best, Parsons's approach to societal community sought to articulate the tense connection between the claims of social integration and the possibilities of justice. A good society needs to have community solidarity. But this community has to be articulated in a manner what allows its symbols and norms to include every group that is functionally involved in, or organizationally subject to, the values and institutions of the social system.[4] If you don't have solidarity, you do not have the subjective dimension of community. Without such subjective community, you cannot have feelings of mutual obligation, and without feelings of obligation there can be no voluntary assumption of responsibility. Yet feelings of moral solidarity are not enough in and of themselves. If the solidary norms of society are not broad and inclusive, the subjectively powerful community operates in a limited and excluding way. It will not, in other words, be just. You can have cultural hegemony without the normative structure of democracy, integration without justice.

Parsons was not sufficiently attentive to this distinction between integration and solidarity, and his theoretical and historical writings on societal community tended to confuse rather than clarify their relation. Obscuring the potential conflict between hierarchy and horizontal integration, these writings sometimes suggested that the functional need for hierarchy is more important, even in moral terms, than the question of whether the members of the wider society feel solidarity with one another. Without intending to, Parsons often sacrificed justice for solidarity.

At the same time, and to the contrary, in his empirical treatments of the contemporary American societal community Parsons actually tended to idealize rather than to neglect the connection between integration and justice. He seemed to assume, without in any way explaining how, that in the United States an almost perfect blend of social integration and social justice had in fact already been achieved.

I will suggest below that Parsons's evolutionary theory of modernity can be seen as an effort to finesse these two ambiguities in his thought—on the one hand the theoretical relation between justice and integration, and on the other the empirical relation between the United States and the rest of world history. That this resolution was not successful, I will demonstrate, is revealed by the train of semantic stuttering, or hesitations, that mark Parsons's exclamations about America's democratic triumph.

The major thrust of this essay is concerned with examining these problems. After bringing them to light, I will draw what I regard as the logical conclusion: something beyond reconstructing the terms of Parsons's societal community is needed. We need a new theory, one that recognizes, from the beginning, the tension between integration and justice. Separating the ideals of community from their uneven institutionalization, acknowledging that the symbolizations of collective identity depend on negative and not only on positive symbols, such a new theory would begin from a recognition that exclusion and inclusion are dialectically related in real existing societal communities.

FOUNDATIONAL AMBIGUITY ABOUT THE PROBLEM OF ORDER

Ambiguity about the relationship between integration and justice was already ensconced at the center of Parsons's theoretical project in *The Structure of Social Action.* While explicitly an effort at pure analytic theory, aiming only at interpretation and explanation, *The Structure of Social Action* implicitly addressed the issues of democracy, order, and justice raised by the social movements and instabilities of the interwar period. As I have suggested elsewhere (Alexander 1983), there are really two solutions to the problem of order in *The Structure of Social Action,* one democratic and critical, the other nondemocratic and potentially conservative. Both solutions derived from Parsons's critique of theories that emphasized instrumental rationality, which he called rationalistic utilitarianism or radical positivism.

Instrumental presuppositions about the nature of action, Parsons believed, made it impossible to understand how social order could be possible. In his democratic solution to the order problem, Parsons insisted that, insofar as a theory assumed purely instrumental action, it could envision only an aggressive, polarizing, and destructive social conflict. Within this framework, the only way to achieve order was to impose it from the outside, as Thomas Hobbes had believed when he argued the necessity for a coercive, antidemocratic Leviathan. As an alternative Parsons recommended that sociological theory step outside of limiting assumptions about instrumental rationality and recognize the centrality to social action of normative and cultural orientations. In this manner a more democratic solution to order would become possible.

This is my wording, not Parsons's. The way he himself put it was that bringing the normative element back in would allow theory to recognize *voluntary, self*-control. Such voluntaristic control creates an institutional and moral basis for an order that differs from antidemocratic power. In this solution to the problem as stated by Hobbes, Parsons followed John Locke's political response to Hobbes's antidemocratic opposition to the English revolution. Parsons himself does acknowledge Locke, but only in an analytical, not a normative, sense. Avoiding an explicitly normative position, Parsons follows Elie Halévy's (1901–1904/1972) criticism of Lockean political economy for emphasizing the natural as compared to the artificial identity of interests.

He goes beyond Halévy by suggesting that a sociological theory of normativity can translate the artificial identity of interest into more realistic (in other words, more institutional) and more democratic terms.

In Parsons's later work—from *The Essays in Sociological Theory* (1954) to *The Social System* (1951), the AGIL model (Parsons and Smelser 1956), and his evolutionary theory (Parsons 1966, 1973)—one can trace a line of theorizing that builds upon this democratic solution to the order problem. Parsons developed a model of the components of social action and social systems that constitutes a continuum from coercive to self-regulating and free (Parsons 1967 and, more generally, Parsons 1966, 1973). This continuum pushed to one side and implicitly criticized the dehumanizing and antidemocratic practices of instrumental rationality and coercion, and pointed to the alternative of cybernetically higher levels of intentional, culturally guided action and meaningful cooperation. Explicitly, Parsons praised cybernetic control for its efficiency. Relying upon information rather than energy, this normative solution evoked for Parsons the logic of the information revolution that so intrigued thinkers in that postwar period. But Parsons's emphasis on these normative forms of action and order allowed him also to achieve a different, more ideological purpose: to outline a social system based on ethical institutions such as law (Parsons 1977) and citizenship (Parsons 1965/1969), one in which the major media of communication were influence (Parsons 1969a) and value commitments (1969b) rather than power and money. It was this line of thinking that informed the democratic potential of Parsons's societal-community idea.[5]

The tragedy of Parsons's theorizing, in my view, is that from the very beginning of his work this democratic line in his thinking was shadowed by a nondemocratic one. This shadowing began with a different kind of solution to the order problem. In *The Structure of Social Action,* it turns out, Parsons was not only concerned with solving the order problem in a voluntaristic manner. He often suggested that the problem with the Hobbesian Leviathan was not its antidemocratic ethics but its empirical weakness. External force could not really solve the order problem. To be effective in curbing chaos and anomie, social order needed an internal reference: it would have to work on subjectivity. This internal order, or consciousness, can be altered only through norms; unlike material organization, norms can be internalized.

From this minimalist perspective, normative order represents an ideal in and of itself. Norms are the solution to the problem of order, and normative order is an alternative to Hobbes. The problem is that normative order per se is not democratic. It is merely cultural. If cultural control is powerful enough, it can achieve integration, inducing internally generated cooperation, consensus, and agreement. Yet such integration will be only hegemony, in Antonio Gramsci's pejorative sense, if it does not also define democratic alternatives, which means normatively emphasizing pluralism, criticism, and universalism. In other words, the minimalist solution to the order problem has the latent effect of substituting integration for justice, a displacement that has always been central to conservative, antidemocratic thought, the animus of which is revolution and disorder. If stability is all that matters, any normative framework will do. It need not be the sort of normative framework that promotes justice.

To make integration and stability so central is to sacrifice justice. If the basic tenets of justice are equality and recognition (Nancy Fraser [1997]), then the search for justice often leads to conflict, increasing rather than decreasing disorder and immediate social strain. Clearly, democratic forms of normative order can produce intense dissatisfaction and conflict, for there is a gap, or an endemic strain, between the idealized implications of a normative order—what might be termed its transcendent reference (Eisenstadt 1982)—and its particular institutionalization in any historically specific social system. If a society's norms are to inspire self-criticism and reflexivity, and to motivate and legitimate demands for justice, they inspire not only consensus but also social conflict, in order to allow social change. The institutionalization of a normative order may lead to trust in the ideals that anchor a system, or even in the system as such, but at the very same time it can delegitimate those who hold authoritative positions or dominant role definitions (Barber 1983).

AMBIGUOUS DEFINITIONS OF SOCIETAL COMMUNITY

This presuppositional and ideological ambivalence about order and normativity is inflected in the foundational definitions that Parsons offers for societal community. These ambiguities are not residual to Parsons's definitions, but deeply embedded in them. They reveal themselves in virtually every definition Parsons offers of societal community. In what follows, I offer close readings of two of Parsons's most fundamental discussions of societal community. I differentiate the key statements in each discussion by number and the key propositions within each statement by letter. Parsons's own statements are in italics. My critical glosses follow after the italics.

It was in *Societies: Evolutionary and Comparative Perspectives* (Parsons 1966) that Parsons introduced the concept of the societal community for the first time.

> 1. [a] *"The core of a society . . . is the patterned normative order through which the life of a population is collectively organized.* [b] *As an order, it contains values and differentiated and particularized norms. . . . As a collectivity, it displays a patterned conception of membership,* [c] *which distinguishes between those individuals who do and do not belong."* (Parsons 1966, 10)
>
> 1a. Parsons introduces here the distinction between the core of a society and the population at large. Whether he means to identify the core with a group per se or the center in a more metaphorical sense, it is clear that Parsons equates this core with both the normative order and the collective, non-normative organization of the life of the population. By the life of the population, Parsons seems clearly to refer to the individuals and groups who are administratively or functionally part of the social system but who are outside the core.
>
> 1b. Whereas the normative dimension refers to values that in principle can be shared across groups, the organizational, or collective, dimension defines the nature of membership and confines the enforcement of normative meanings to members of a particular group.
>
> 1c. Membership defines the distinction between those who are inside and those who are outside the organized collectivity.
>
> 2. [a] *Problems involving the "jurisdiction" of the normative system may make impossible an exact coincidence between the status of "coming under" normative obligations and the status of membership,* [b] *because the enforcement of a normative system seems inherently linked to the control (e.g., through the "police function") of sanctions* [c] *exercised by and against the people actually residing within a territory.* (Parsons 1966, 10)
>
> 2a. Those who are expected to adhere to the normative order may not actually be considered members in the society to which this normative order is considered to apply.
>
> 2b. There is a difference between the symbolic reach of a normative order and its enforcement. Enforcement involves complex organizational sanctions and often coercion, as the nearly universal existence of the policing apparatus suggests. It is the enforcement mechanism that defines effective membership in the sense in which the latter term refers to a social organization.
>
> 2c. People may be part of a society's territory, that is, part of the life of the population, but they may be excluded from membership and be the subjects of coercive sanctions. This repression may be authorized by one segment of the population, gen-

erally the core members, against another segment whose members may or may not accept the dominant normative order.

3. [a] *We will call this one entity of the society . . . the societal community. . . . It is constituted both by a normative system of order and by statuses, rights and obligations pertaining to membership* [b] *which may vary for different sub-groups within the community.* [c] *To survive and develop the social community must maintain the integrity of a common cultural orientation, broadly (though not necessarily uniformly or unanimously) shared by its membership, as the basis of its societal identity.* (Parsons 1966, 10)

3a. The societal community is that part of the normatively defined community that establishes collective membership, though, as we will see below, membership itself actually may be graduated in some manner.

3b. There are many subgroups in a social system that do not have full membership in the societal community.

3c. The normative element of the society that defines the identity of the society is the culture shared by its core group members.[6]

These passages point to the tension between Parsons's explicit interest in integration and his implicit concern for justice. While committed to the possibility that the societal community can reconcile or synthesize these concerns, Parsons encounters rough seas when he confronts the fragmentation that characterizes empirical societies. What is so striking about these foundational passages is that, despite his clear stress on the integrating nature of the societal community, Parsons is compelled to acknowledge not only the existence of subgroups and segmentations that fragment actually existing social systems but also the fact that because of these divisions, it is unlikely that the norms of a binding community can be effectively applied to the population that inhabits a given territory. The reason Parsons offers for this alarming fact is that the normative reach of cultural values exists in tension with the realistic possibility of their enforcement. This is the reason, he suggests, why norms do not only create moral integration but also define membership: who's in and who's out. Taken by themselves, the norms that define the culture of the societal community might refer to everybody in the territory, the life of the population. There are subgroups inside this population, however, who may not actually be members of the community. For them, integration is not voluntary but coerced; the norms apply also to them, whether or not they believe in them. When this is the case, cooperation can be secured only by police power, that is, repression, not by influence or normative control.

This reading of Parsons's initial discussion of societal community suggests that Parsons implicitly acknowledges that it may not be integrative for society in general but only for its core group. This possibility makes manifest that integration and justice are empirically unrelated. In fact, rather than combating exclusion, the societal community might actually produce it. This emphatically is not the way Parsons himself presents the case. He makes it seem as if the integrative impulses would embrace the community, if only it were not for the police function, which somehow has got in the way. If ever there were a residual category, this is it. Policing is not just a functional requisite of society. It develops also in response to the strains between those who are members and those who are not, and the efforts of the former to protect themselves, in terms of both identity and interest, from the latter.

The same systematic ambiguity about integration and justice affects the definitions for societal community that Parsons offered in his companion volume, *The System of Modern Societies* (1973). The purpose of this later discussion is to bring societal community from ancient into modern societies. Whereas in the first book societal community was considered in terms of the empirical reference of simple, archaic, and seedbed societies, the later book brings the societal community concept into contact with more recent Western history, from medieval society to the present day. Despite the difference in its empirical material, however, this second treatment repeats and reinforces the problems of the original discussion.

1. [a] *Because we treat the social system as integrative for action systems generally, we must pay special attention to the ways in which it achieves—or fails to achieve—various kinds of levels of internal integration. We will call the integrative subsystem of a society the societal community. Perhaps the most general function of a societal community is to articulate a system of norms with a collective organization that has unity and cohesiveness. . . .* [b] *The collective aspect is the societal community as a single, bounded, collectivity. Social order requires clear and definite integration in the sense, on the one hand, of normative coherence and, on the other hand, of societal "harmony" and "coordination." . . .* [c] *The primary function of this integrative subsystem is to define the obligations of loyalty to the societal collectivity, both for the membership as a whole and for various categories of differentiated status. . . .* [d] *In its hierarchical aspect, the normative ordering of the societal community in terms of memberships comprises its stratification scale, the scale of the accepted . . . prestige of subcollectivities, statuses, and roles and of persons as societal members. It must be coordinated . . . with universal norms governing the status of membership* (Parsons 1973, 11–12).

1a. Societal community is explicitly identified with integration in the sense of stability, unity, and homogeneity.

1b. The scope of normative integration is equated with a bounded and organized collectivity.

1c. This emphasis on loyalty seems to, but may not always, suggest that normative integration is inimical to criticism and that even those who are excluded from the organized collectivity can legitimately be expected to be loyal to the norms of the membership community.

1d. These sentences would appear to suggest that there are degrees of membership even within the societal community itself. Through prestige rankings, normative integration is adapted to the vertical imperative of stratification, allocating the qualities that define the core group to those who are most fully its members. More universal norms of membership might be in conflict with this stratificational dimension of normative order.

2. [a] *A society must constitute a societal community that has an adequate level of integration or solidarity and a distinctive membership status.* [b] *This does not preclude relations of control or symbiosis with population elements only partially integrated into the societal community, such as the Jews in the Diaspora, but there must be a core of fully integrated members.* (Parsons 1973, 17).

2a. The societal community is the core part of the social system that has a distinctive membership and achieves integration and solidarity.

2b. Solidarity and integration of the core group can exist side by side with coercive control exercised by the core group against excluded members. The achievement of solidarity is not mitigated by the existence of this repression, for membership as a category and a fact still exists for some subgroup in the population.

THE MAGICAL SOLUTION TO AMBIGUITY: RETURNING TO THE JEALOUS GOD OF EVOLUTION

Parsons was a liberal, not a conservative (Alexander 2001d). He could not accept in good conscience a societal community that integrates only the minority core group and justifies the exclusion and repression of those who remain outside. Yet this is precisely the situation he has conceptualized in the discussions I have analyzed above. How will he escape this dilemma? One way would be, in effect, to *theorize* the contradictions. How would societal community have to be conceptualized to explain how and why integration in one part of the society can produce exclusion for others? To take this path would involve a critical examination of every actually existing form of societal community. From the perspective of Parsons's personal theoretical development, there would appear to be two problems with this approach. First, it would undermine the upbeat attitude Parsons takes to social integration generally. Second, it would undermine the celebratory quality of his treatment of contemporary American society, an issue to which I will return. If Parsons was to avoid these problems, he would have to find another way of resolving this ambiguity. He locates this path in the approach he had once famously disparaged as the jealous god of social evolution (Parsons 1937, 3).

If Parsons had confronted the ambiguity of societal community head-on, he would have had to enter into the thicket of contradictions that it entails, exploring why and how the societal community becomes embedded in, and disembedded from, the primordial values and powers of a society's core group. Rather than embracing and articulating ambiguity, however, Parsons engages in a kind of splitting. He makes use of evolutionary theory to place the bad, nondemocratic societal community on one side of the evolutionary scale and the good, democratic societal community on the other. In this manner, Parsons makes his societal community discussion linear rather than dialectical: it emphasizes progress and betterment rather than contradictions and negative possibility.

The more democratic the societal community, the more congruence exists between integration, membership, and the population living inside the relevant territory. Parsons puts this possibility into evolutionary terms; it becomes a matter of going from the traditional to the modern period. In the traditional forms of society, Parsons's favorite polemical targets were China and India. In Imperial China, despite the possibilities for integration opened up by social structure and culture, "the Confucian cultural system . . . prevented Imperial China from . . . including the masses of the population in the reorganized system" (Parsons 1966, 77). As for India, the duality which was central to its religious legitimation was never transcended in the direction of the inclusion of the nonprivileged in a more equalized societal community (Parsons 1966 78–79). It is in this manner that the exclusionary dimensions of societal community are confined to earlier forms of society.

Insofar as modernity is achieved, the tension between integration and justice is resolved. Contemporary social structure, Parsons writes (1973, 99) with evident relief, is characterized by a special kind of integration. What has happened is that the subsystems that fused and overlapped in traditional society have undergone a series of "declarations of independence" (1973, 99). Just as the market, the state, and the family have all become independent of one another, so, most important for Parsons's concern, has the societal community. It is no longer connected to core groups or to any particular value, but has become an abstract community of equals, a single societal community with full citizenship for all.

Such differentiated societal community based on transcendental solidarity evidently was not adumbrated but precipitated by what Parsons calls the "evolutionary breakthroughs" of world history. The possibility began with Greek philosophy, which Parsons describes as "the first formal and general conceptualization of the normative framework of human life which clearly abstracted moral obligations" (1966, 106). This first breakthrough was carried further by the European Renaissance and Reformation. These cultural high points contributed singly to the process that Parsons conceptualized as value generalization, the gradual separation of the normative culture that regulated society from the normative values of the core-group values.

More institutional change points in the same direction, involving an ongoing process of structural differentiation. Taken together, value generalization and structural differentiation add up to adaptive upgrading, the optimistic, ameliorating concept that Parsons employs to characterize historical development as such. The wonderful thing about evolutionary theory is that it literally compels integration to take a less primordial, less core-group-centered form.

> Adaptive upgrading . . . *requires* that specialized functional capacities be freed from ascription within more diffuse structural units. . . . Upgrading processes may *require* the inclusion in a status of full membership in the relevant general community system of previously excluded groups which have developed legitimate capacities to "contribute" to the functioning of the system. (1966, 22, emphasis added)

The difficulties of maintaining such a buoyant outlook on the inclusive character of social development in the latter half of one of history's bloodiest centuries are not to be underestimated. One maintenance strategy is to avoid spending too much time on the repressive and violent episodes that have marred the path of modernity. Thus, while Parsons expansively lauds the Reformation and Renaissance, his discussion of the Counter Reformation is terse and condensed (see Alexander 1988). As for the Nazi movement, even with its immense mobilization of power, from the vantage point of two decades Parsons feels safe in concluding that it seems to have been an acute sociopolitical failure and not a source of major future structural patterns (1973, 130). Parsons even finds a way to be optimistic about the uncomfortable link between modernity and war. While acknowledging that certainly the history of modern societal systems has been one of frequent, if not continual, warfare, Parsons observes what he takes to be the reassuring fact that "the *same* system of societies within which the evolutionary process that we have traced has occurred has been subject to a high incident of violence, most conspicuously in war but also internally, including revolutions" (1973, 141, original emphasis).[7] But Parsons's major strategy for maintaining evolutionary optimism is to focus on the United States, which he called the new lead society of contemporary modernity (1973: 86). In the United States, Parsons suggested, "The principle of equality has broken through to a new level of pervasiveness and generality. A societal community as *basically* composed of equals seems to be the 'end of the line' in the long process of undermining the legitimacy of . . . older, more particularistic ascriptive bases of membership" (1973, 118–19, original emphasis).

With the emergence of American society, and its maturation during the civil rights era, the conflict between integration and justice has disappeared. In terms of social evolution, it is the end of the line, or at least the beginning of the end.[8] The jealous god of evolution has been appeased.

Or has it? Despite his declarations that evolution is progressive and that the American societal community is fully evolved, Parsons still cannot entirely avoid certain uncomfortable facts. Although he is not able systematically to discuss or explain the continuing repressiveness and exclusionary qualities of contemporary societies, very much including the United States, neither can he entirely wish them away. What he does instead is to establish a series of lexical exceptions to his semantic rule. The pathologies of modern societal communities are not systematically discussed, but their existence is noted by conjunctive and adverbial qualifiers that denote their absence.

Parsons's evolutionary treatment of contemporary societies is punctuated by a grammar filled with buts, despites, howevers, of courses, and althoughs. It is through this grammatical technique that all the particularistic repressions that restrict actual existing societal communities are magically overcome. Here are some illustrations selected from *The System of Modern Societies* (1973; emphases added):

> "At one extreme, the principal content of the normative order may be considered more or less universal to all men. *However,* this raises acute problems of how far such highly uni-

versalistic norms can be effectively institutionalized in the actual operations of so extensive a community. . . . [Thus,] modern societal communities have generally taken a form based upon nationalism" (20).

"In fully modern societies . . . there can be diversity on each basis, religious, ethnic, and territorial, because the common status of citizenship provides a sufficient foundation for national solidarity. . . . The institutions of citizenship and nationality can *nevertheless* render the societal community vulnerable if the bases of pluralism are exacerbated into sharply structured cleavages. Since the typical modern community unifies a large population over a large territory, for example, its solidarity may be severely strained. . . . This is particularly true where . . . regional cleavages coincided with ethnic and/or religious divisions. Many modern societies have disintegrated before varying combinations of these bases of cleavage" (22).

"*Despite* Ireland, therefore, Britain became relatively united ethnically" (57).

"American territory was *initially* settled mainly by one distinctive group of migrants. . . . The United States was *for a long time* an Anglo-Saxon society, which tolerated and granted legal rights to members of some other ethnic groups *but* did not fully include them" (87–88).

"Negroes are still in the early stages of the inclusion process. . . . It may, *however,* be predicted with considerable confidence that the long-run trend is toward successful inclusion" (89).

"*Although* American society has always been differentiated internally by class, it has never suffered the aftermath of aristocracy and serfdom that persisted so long in Europe" (90).

"The participation of the wealthier and more educated groups . . . has been disproportionate, *but* there has also been a persistent populist strain and relative upward mobility" (90).

"*Although* the franchise was originally restricted, especially by property qualifications, it was extended rapidly, and universal manhood suffrage, *except* for Negroes, was attained relatively early" (91).

"*On the whole,* the structural outline of 'citizenship' in the new societal community is complete, *though not yet* fully institutionalized" (93).

"This movement has thus meant an immense extension of equality of opportunity. . . . At the time, *however,* the educational system is necessarily selective" (95).

"*Although* 'discrimination' by lineage membership, social class, ethnic origin, religion, race, and so on is tenacious (110).

"In our general paradigm of social change, we have stressed the connection between inclusion and adaptive upgrading . . . *but* they are not identical (115).

"There are *of course* important flaws. One surely is war" (115).

"The second mode is focused in the institutionalization of equality of opportunity. . . . This ideal is *of course* very far from full realization" (120).

"There has, *of course,* been a great deal of conflict, 'frontier' primitivism, and lag in some of the older parts of the system relative to the more progressive parts" (140).

"*Certainly* the history of modern societal systems has been one of frequent, if not continual, warfare" (141).

THE IDEOLOGICAL MOMENT AND AMERICAN HUBRIS

In the preceding discussion I have concentrated on the theoretical distortions in Parsons's thinking about societal community. I have demonstrated how the nondemocratic solution to Hobbes marked Parsons's presuppositions, models, and empirical explanations. As I have also suggested, however, there is as well an ideological dimension at play, and I wish to briefly acknowledge it here.

During the Cold War, Parsons wished (rightly in my view) to defend capitalist democracies against Communist dictatorships. For him, this defense entailed (wrongly in my view) reading modernity in an American manner. This complacent liberalism became more pronounced in Parsons's later work, whose polemical intent Parsons just about wears on his sleeve.

Writing during the polarization of the late sixties, Parsons in *The System of Modern Societies* acknowledges (1973, 116) that despite his optimistic declarations about evolution, there is a "general moral malaise in modern society." In the same work he even goes so far as to admit that "current widespread fears of imminent and ultimate nuclear holocaust raise a question that cannot be answered objectively with much confidence" (141). Rather than offering a systematic explanation for such fears and dangers, however, Parsons blames the messenger. Like many antiradical theorists before him (for example, Aron 1957), he accuses intellectuals of overlooking everything that is positive about modern life. "Contrary to the opinion among many intellectuals," he insists, "American society—like most modern societies without dictatorial regimes—has institutionalized a far broader range of freedoms than . . . any previous society" (Parsons 1973, 114). The problem is not in society, but in the intellectuals themselves: "ideological complexes with paranoid themes are very old indeed" (116). Parsons's ambition could not be more clear. It is "to establish sufficient doubt of the validity of such views" (142).

UNDERSTANDING THE DIALECTICS OF MODERNITY

At one point Parsons acknowledges that, while "in our general paradigm of social change we have stressed the connection between inclusion and adaptive upgrading . . . *they are not identical*" (1973, 115, emphasis added). This is an extraordinary admission. That they are identical was the point of Parsons's evolutionary theory. He did not try to explain, except in an ad hoc, residual way, what in fact might constitute the gap between them. What might such an attempt at theoretical explanation entail?

To reconstruct a more satisfactory theory of the societal community, one would have to look closely at how processes of anti-universalism, which have often led to destruction rather than progress, were (and are) built into the processes and definitions of modernity itself. In evolutionary terms, how has the modern societal community remained fused with market, state, and cultural communities, including those defined by class, race, sex, ethnicity, religion, and gender? Does this fusion allow hierarchy and fragmentation to be legitimated in modern societal communities, to the extent that even democratic societies are repressive and exclusionary in significant ways? If the gap between membership categories and populations-in-territory remains wide, is it not the case that core-group integration often proceeds at the expense of justice for stigmatized groups who are outside the centers of modern societies?[9]

If the endemic and dangerous persistence of particularism and exclusion is theorized, then one must dispense with the utopian idea that value consensus will produce social integration, much less justice. The "index of incomplete institutionalization," Parsons (1973, 103) once suggested, "is the insistence by individuals and groups on recognition of their particular and partial 'rights' by means of techniques ranging from simple assertion through organized protest to obstruction." Parsons implies here that protest for rights expansion reflects the failure of modernity to somehow become complete. It would be immensely preferable to acknowledge that rights-oriented conflict actually is evidence of the fullness of modernity, not of its failure but of its success. As Shmuel N. Eisenstadt (Alexander 1992) suggests in his very different theory of institutionalization, the tension between ideal and reality can never be eliminated. The gulf initiated during the axial age will not be overcome, and duality will always mark the modern and postmodern condition.[10]

By understanding the contradictions in Parsons's concept of societal community, one can envision what a more critical, dynamic, and systematic theory might be. For there is, indeed, a sphere of solidarity that needs to be differentiated from the other spheres if justice is to be achieved. In terms of its idealizing aspirations, such a civil sphere envisions a system of culture and institutions that rests upon demanding norms of mutual respect, equality, and autonomy. The degree to which such a differentiated community actually exists can be empirically investigated and theoretically conceived. This investigation would show that the very culture of rationality and universalism creates a shadow discourse of repression and that the continual fragmentation of actually existing civil spheres justifies core-group domination and subjugation—even as it provides the culture and institutions to create justice in turn. It would expose new kinds of boundary relations, between the civil and uncivil spheres, and develop a theory, not only of facilitating inputs, but of destructive intrusions that trigger social movements for civil repair (Alexander 2000).

This new approach to civic solidarity might transform and extend Weber's idea of fraternization. It might make more specific and institutionally grounded Durkheim's concept of society. It might provide a more critical sociological companion for democratic theory.

NOTES

1. In the 1960s, a radical postwar generation issued fundamental challenges to dominant theories. In the three decades since, dominant theories have been challenged by feminist theorists, newly self-conscious race intellectuals, and by those who have spoken on behalf of gay and homosexual rights. These are only the most obvious examples of the experiential basis for intellectual change. For a broader discussion of the social sources of intellectual challenge in the American case, see Andrew Jamison and Ron Eyerman (1994).
2. Alexander and Colomy (1992) have earlier conceptualized scientific change in terms of a continuum stretching from least challenging to most challenging: elaboration and specification, revision, reconstruction, and new theory creation. "When the stars are right" refers to many ideal and material factors of social organization that are independent of the cognitive status of theory creation.
3. Marx often said that his mature work differed from Ricardo's only in the technical sense in which he had been able to conceptualize surplus value, which was dependent upon what he considered the critical insight that workers sold their labor power, not their labor per se, to the capitalists for a wage.
4. Habermas (1996) tries to resolve this problem in two related but unsatisfactory ways. First, he classifies all substantive values as belonging, not to the sphere of Kantian morality, but to the ethical sphere. Yet, no matter what the philosophical justification for such bifurcation, it is meaningless in sociological terms, since both "morality" (in the rationalistic, Kantian sense) and "ethics" must be institutionalized in the social system. Second, Habermas tries to avoid the tension between normative integration and justice by claiming that the normative order regulating the public sphere is, or at least must be, exclusively procedural in nature. This would not be a good idea even if it were possible, but it is not.
5. Jean Cohen and Andrew Arato, following Habermas's stress on the importance of Parsons's work but showing more sympathy and insight about the sociological power of Parsonian sociology for democratic social theory, make (1995) a sophisticated and intriguing connection between civil-society theory and Parsons's theory of influence. They argue that a democratic civil society, one dominated by procedurally oriented discourse ethics, grows out of the preconditions that allow influence to replace money and power as the central medium of exchange. This discussion points to the same democratic line in Parsons that I reference here and makes some of the same fundamental criticisms I will level below.

The force of Cohen and Arato's argument is to some degree vitiated, however, by their insistence that the democratically appropriate form of influence can only be "the achievement of solidarity through discussion and deliberation of individuals who choose to participate in an association" (Cohen and Arato 1995, 131), a position they contrast with a conception of value-based, diffused influence. This distinction, from a sociological perspective, is untenable, since every free and rational discussion must be based upon the presuppositions of a language game, or set of value commitments, that is itself, at the time of argument, not open to question. That is one of the fundamental points in Parsons's analytical model of the generalized media of exchange. Although I no longer find this work satisfactory in many ways, this point remains entirely valid, pointing to the empirical-sociological as compared to the normative-philosophical point of view. Leon Mayhew's *The New Public: Professional Communication and the Means of Social Influence* (1997) presents a more institutionally oriented critique of societal-community theory from a Habermasian perspective.

6. This critical reading differs rather fundamentally from Uta Gerhardt's, which in other respects contributes a helpful scholarly reconstruction of the history of the societal-community concept:

> Parsons wrote the slim volume *Societies: Evolutionary and Comparative Perspectives* (1966). In the second chapter, the core of the book, he used the notion of societal community for the first time. He ventures [to answer the question of] what were the integrative forces that held a society together to the effect that social relations would not disintegrate in the face of institutional differentiation in the course of the history of modernization. His answer contained the concept of societal community, explained tentatively as that forum for moral commitment which rendered more or less diverse populations identifiable members united in their identification with their cultural and/or national common heritage. (Gerhardt 2001, 180)

7. Parsons hardly wrote about Stalinism at all, perhaps a legacy of his earlier, 1930s "progressivism" and his continuing antagonism, during the postwar period, to the rigidly anti-communist foreign policy of American conservatives. When Parsons wrote about the USSR in the postwar period, he tended to emphasize its modernizing tendencies and its capacities for evolutionary progress, implicitly opposing the more radical-right elements of America's Cold War foreign policy.
8. I am aware that one can locate references in Parsons's writing that illuminate future developmental challenges for social evolution, such as his references to the affective revolution in his later work. In Giuseppe Sciortino's chapter of the current volume (chapter 6), he builds from such discussions to present an alternative to the critically oriented reading of societal-community theory I offer here, transforming such ad hoc references into a coherent and pluralistic theory of contemporary solidarity. This is an impressive interpretive achievement. Still, in my view Sciortino gives the original Parsonian project too much sympathy, downplaying the conservative and quiescent, nondemocratic lines I am pointing to here. Sciortino engages in both revision and reconstruction, in my terms, his goal being to present what a "complete theory" of the societal community would look like. Because I see more fundamental contradictions in Parsons's theory, I do not find the conceptual resources within the theory to complete it. So I believe the only viable option is theory creation.

   The inadequacies that Sciortino himself finds in the societal-community theory point beyond it. He criticizes Parsons for his difficulty in articulating the "relational nexus between the normative definitions of membership . . . and the actual pattern of social solidarities and groupings existing in any given society," his "lack of a structural theory of solidary groups," and his focus in modern society on differentiation rather than on segmentary groups—"segmental categories are often mentioned but seldom placed at the center of inquiry." Despite this disagreement, Sciortino's hermeneutical reinterpretation of Parsons which aims at finding the resources to explain such phenomena is impressive and useful.
9. In a different and earlier Parsonian language, this is exactly the point that Mayhew (1968) quietly made in perhaps the most acute criticism ever penned by a card-carrying Parsonian. Mayhew argued against seeing ascription as traditional and achievement as modern. He demonstrated how achievement carries strong imperatives that sustain ascription, such that ascription is functionally efficient.
10. This is similar to the argument Cohen and Arato (1995, 125 n.6) make in their "immanent criticism" of Parsons's societal-community theory, with which in other respects I have disagreed. They suggest that it "both elaborates the normative achievements of modernity and represents these as if they were already institutionalized." The job of critical theory, by contrast, is to "throw much doubt on the claims of successful institutionalization."

REFERENCES

Alexander, Jeffrey. 1978. "Formal and Substantive Voluntarism in the Work of Talcott Parsons: A Theoretical and Ideological Reinterpretation." *American Sociological Review* 43(2): 177–98.

———. 1979. "Paradigm Revision and Parsonianism." *Canadian Journal of Sociology* 4(4): 1–24.

———. 1980. "Core Solidarity, Ethnic Outgroup, and Social Differentiation: A Multidimensional Model of Inclusion in Modern Societies." In *National and Ethnic Movements,* edited by J. Dofny and A. Akiwowo. Beverly Hills: Sage.

———. 1981. "The Mass News Media in Systemic, Historical and Comparative Perspective." In *Mass Media and Social Change,* edited by E. Katz and T. Szecsko. Beverly Hills: Sage.

———. 1982. "Revolution, Reaction, and Reform: The Change Theory of Parsons' Middle Period." *Sociological Inquiry* 51(3–4): 267–80.

———. 1982–83. *Theoretical Logic in Sociology.* Berkeley: University of California Press.

———. 1983. *The Modern Reconstruction of Classical Thought: Talcott Parsons.* Volume 4. *Theoretical Logic in Sociology,* by Jeffrey C. Alexander. Berkeley: University of California Press.

———. 1985. "Neofunctionalism: An Introduction." In *Neofunctionalism.* Beverly Hills: Sage.

———. 1988. "Durkheim's Problem and Differentiation Theory Today." In *Action and Its Environments.* Berkeley: University of California Press.

———. 1991. "Must We Choose Between Criticism and Faith? Reflections on the Later Work of Bernard Barber." *Sociological Theory* 9(1): 124–30.

———. 1992. "The Fragility of Progress: An Interpretation of the Turn Toward Meaning in Eisenstadt's Later Work." *Acta Sociologica* 35(2): 85–94.

———. 1997a. "From Functionalism to Neofunctionalism: Creating a Position in the Field of Social Theory." In *Neofunctionalism and After.* Oxford: Basil Blackwell.

———. 1997b. "After Neofunctionalism: Action, Culture, and Civil Society." In *Neofunctionalism and After.* Oxford: Basil Blackwell.

———. 2000. "Contradictions: The Uncivilizing Pressures of Space, Time, and Function." *Soundings* 16(Autumn): 96–112.

———. 2001a. "The Long and Winding Road: Civil Repair of Intimate Injustice." *Sociological Theory* 19(3): 371–400.

———. 2001b. "Theorizing the 'Modes of Incorporation': Assimilation, Hyphenation, and Multiculturalism as Varieties of Civil Participation." *Sociological Theory* 19(3): 237–49.

———. 2001c. "Robust Utopias and Civil Repairs." *International Journal of Sociology* 16(4): 579–91.

———. 2001d. "Parsons as a Republican Critic of Industrial Society: A New Understanding of the Early Writings." In *Parsons' "The Structure of Social Action" and Contemporary Debates,* edited by G. Pollini and G. Sciortino. Milan: FrancoAngeli.

———. 2003. *The Meanings of Social Life: A Cultural Sociology.* New York: Oxford University Press.

Alexander, Jeffrey, and Paul Colomy. 1985. "Towards Neofunctionalism: Eisenstadt's Change Theory and Symbolic Interaction." *Sociological Theory* 3(2): 11–23.

———. 1990. "Neofunctionalism Today: Reconstructing a Theoretical Tradition." In *Frontiers of Sociological Theory,* edited by George Ritzer. New York: Columbia University Press.

———. 1992. "Traditions and Competition: Preface to a Postpositivist Approach to Knowledge Accumulation." In *Metatheorizing,* edited by George Ritzer. Beverly Hills: Sage.

Aron, Raymond. 1957. *The Opium of the Intellectuals.* New York: Doubleday.

Barber, Bernard. 1983. *The Logic and Limits of Trust.* New Brunswick, N.J.: Rutgers University Press.

Bellah, Robert. 1973. *Emile Durkheim on Morality and Society.* Chicago: University of Chicago Press.

Cohen, Jean, and Andrew Arato. 1995. *Civil Society and Political Theory.* Cambridge, Mass.: MIT Press.

Coser, Lewis A. 1960. "Durkheim's Conservatism and Its Implications for His Sociological Theory." In *Essays on Sociology and Philosophy by Emile Durkheim,* edited by Kurt H. Wolff. New York: Harper Torchbooks.

Eisenstadt, Shmuel N. 1982. "The Axial Age: The Emergence of Transcendental Visions and the Rise of Clerics." *European Journal of Sociology* 23: 294–314.

Fraser, Nancy. 1997. "From Redistribution to Recognition?" In *Justice Interruptus,* by Nancy Fraser. London: Routledge.

Gerhardt, Uta. 2001. "Parsons' Analysis of the Societal Community." In *Talcott Parsons Today,* edited by A. Javier Treviño. New York: Rowman & Littlefield.

Habermas, Jürgen. 1996. *Between Facts and Norms.* Cambridge, Mass.: MIT Press.
Hagstrom, Warren. 1965. *The Scientific Community.* New York: Free Press.
Halévy, Elie. 1901–04/1972. *The Growth of Philosophic Radicalism.* Clifton, N.J.: Augustus M. Kelley.
Jamison, Andrew, and Ron Eyerman. 1994. *Seeds of the Sixties.* Berkeley: University of California Press.
Marshall, T. H. 1964. *Class, Citizenship, and Social Development.* Garden City, N.Y.: Doubleday.
Mayhew, Leon. 1968. "Ascription in Modern Society." *Sociological Inquiry* 38: 105–20.
———. 1997. *The New Public.* New York: Cambridge University Press.
Nisbet, Robert A. 1965. "Emile Durkheim." In *Emile Durkheim.* Englewood Cliffs, N.J.: Prentice-Hall.
Parsons, Talcott. 1937. *The Structure of Social Action.* New York: Free Press.
———. 1951. *The Social System.* New York: Free Press.
———. 1954. *Essays in Sociological Theory.* New York: Free Press.
———. 1965/1969. "Full Citizenship for the Negro American?" In *Politics and Social Structure.* New York: Free Press.
———. 1966. *Societies: Evolutionary and Comparative Perspectives.* Englewood Cliffs, N.J.: Prentice-Hall.
———. 1967. "Some Reflections on the Place of Force in Social Process." In *Sociological Theory and Modern Society.* New York: Free Press.
———. 1969a. "On the Concept of Influence." In *Politics and Social Structures.* New York: Free Press.
———. 1969b. "On the Concept of Value Commitments." In *Politics and Social Structures.* New York: Free Press.
———. 1973. *The System of Modern Societies.* Englewood Cliffs, N.J.: Prentice-Hall.
———. 1977. "Law as an Intellectual Stepchild." *Sociological Inquiry* 47(3–4): 11–57.
Parsons, Talcott, and Neil J. Smelser. 1956. *Economy and Society: A Study in the Integration of Economic and Social Theory.* New York: Free Press.
Toulmin, Stephen. 1972. *Human Understanding.* Princeton: Princeton University Press.
Weber, Max. 1978. *Economy and Society.* Berkeley: University of California Press.

Chapter 6

How Different Can We Be? Parsons's Societal Community, Pluralism, and the Multicultural Debate

Giuseppe Sciortino

The notion of societal community is a focus of the theoretical work carried out by Talcott Parsons in his last decades. As with most of his ideas, any attempt to identify the evolution of the notion of societal community reveals both the strong continuity of his intellectual project and the frequent restructuring of his intellectual tools and vocabulary.

There are few doubts about the importance of the notion of societal community to Parsons's work. His analysis of the societal community is a cornerstone of his attempt to analyze the structure of contemporary societies, and of his interpretation of historical evolution. The concept is crucial for his theory of social integration, a topic Parsons had identified as part of sociology's turf since *The Structure of Social Action*. His later efforts to develop the notion of societal community can also be seen as a way to synthesize—and improve upon—the strands of empirical research he had been pursuing since the late 1930s on the significance of religious and ethnic pluralism, the structural features of associational bodies, the polarizing tendencies involved in modernization processes (and the kinds of mechanisms that can prevent the escalation of their destructive externalities), and the scope and impact of the educational revolution. On a more biographical note, Parsons's recurring attempts to write a book on American society—his last effort was a manuscript entitled "American Societal Community"—can be interpreted as a way to vindicate the analytical power of his action theory. This project, as it is documented in surviving manuscripts, was clearly intended to demonstrate that his abstract endeavors could produce a much more adequate analysis of contemporary societies than the more popular, and apparently "empirical," critical and "humanist" works.

Notwithstanding its centrality, Parsons's work on societal community is one of the less recognized components of his intellectual heritage. The history of this project is still scarcely known (Lidz 1989b; Gerhardt 2001), and relatively few contributions in the secondary literature pay adequate attention to its relevance and novelty. Only recently have we witnessed attempts to develop this component of the Parsonian legacy in the way Parsons himself would have approved: increasing its analytical sharpness and testing its usefulness to understand crucial social phenomena (Lidz 1989b; Habermas 1990/1998; Alexander 1998, 2001; Münch 1999; Gerhardt 2001; Bortolini 2002).

Moreover, this strand of Parsons's work is largely absent from the life of the discipline at large. It is hard to identify in current debates over social theory (besides those of Parsons scholars) any acknowledgment, even a polemical one, of the existence and availability of a theory of the societal community. Some of the most interesting debates in current social science are taking place as if this aspect of Parsons's work did not exist. This is hardly surprising. Most of Parsons's work that is explicitly focused on the societal community was published when he had already ceased to be a dominant figure in the discipline. Many conceptual innovations introduced by Parsons after the mid-1960s have not been noticed or adequately discussed (Parsons 1976). Furthermore, during his lifetime Parsons did not produce a full, systematic statement of his analysis of societal community, worked out at the necessary level of detail. We know he attempted such an endeavor, devoting a significant portion of his activities in the last years of his life to writing a large manuscript, currently available in the Parsons Papers in Harvard University Archives (Parsons 1979a). To explore the meaning and implications of the notion of societal community in his published work, however, involves searching for passages and arguments scattered in a variety of contexts, as well as a fairly large amount of speculation. Not many sociologists have considered such a task necessary for their work.

In this paper I will argue that this is unfortunate, because an adequate appreciation of the notion of societal community could significantly contribute to our understanding of Talcott Parsons's heritage and of some current intellectual debates. In particular, I will stress how such a notion could add to the development of a better analytical frame for discussing some key phenomena of contemporary social life by deepening the debate on the implications of increasing social heterogeneity, the outcome of difference-based conflict, and the evolution of the culture and institutions associated with the citizenship complex.

At the same time, I do not wish to argue that the basic ignorance about this aspect of Parsons's legacy should be attributed wholly to its neglect by contemporary theorists. Most of Parsons's analyses of this concept are far from being the full-fledged statements that we would like. For the concept of societal community to be used effectively beyond the boundaries of Parsons's scholars, we need a serious and focused work of critical reconstruction, a task that has only recently begun (Lidz 1989a; Sciortino 1994; Bortolini 1999; Gerhardt 2001). Understanding this work entails facing the challenging fact that, as Rainer C. Baum (1975, 306) observed nearly thirty years ago, "The integrative subsystem of society has remained one of the least charted of the four functional boxes" in Parsons's work. In other words, to prepare the notion of societal community for contemporary use requires the kind of creative and disciplined elaboration of missing links and conceptual bridges that Parsons adopted in his treatment of his own intellectual forebears.[1]

In the first section of this paper, I shall provide a short sketch of the conceptual evolution of the notion of societal community and an analysis of its relations to Parsons's theory of social evolution and social pluralism. I will then focus on two conceptual imbalances that may be currently identified in Parsons's work on the concept of societal community. Drawing upon his intellectual corpus, I will try to identify some ways to redress such unbalances, thus generating a more adequate conceptual framework. Finally I will provide a short example of such potential usefulness, documenting how the Parsonian notion of societal community may help to elaborate and clarify some issues in the current debate over multiculturalist claims and practices in Western societies. I do not contend that if Parsons had lived longer he would have arrived at the same conclusions that I outline in this paper. I think, however, that the solutions I propose are consistent with his overall framework and with many strands of his work.

SOCIETAL COMMUNITY: A BRIEF HISTORY OF THE CONCEPT IN PARSONS'S WORK

Parsons has always stressed the importance of focusing on the integrative structures of social systems. Early in his work he identified social integration as the key topic for sociology and he repeatedly expressed dissatisfaction with available theories in this regard (Parsons 1942a).

According to Parsons, contemporary theories of social integration had failed to distinguish adequately between the analytically different issues of integration and loyalty, and were rooted in a simplified vision of social life. What Parsons was seeking was a complex theory of social integration that would be able to define societal integration as a second-order phenomenon, as a coordination among several kinds of coordinating structures, each of them entailing specific social strains and producing significant effects on the others. As he spelled out in his rethinking of Durkheim's categories (Parsons 1960), societies have to manage the coordination of both mechanical solidarity, which relates to the units of society as equally included, and organic solidarity, which relates to the same units in terms as differentiated identities.

Parsons stressed that in Western society, mechanical solidarity is rooted in the institutions of citizenship, which apply equally to all included individuals, whereas organic solidarity is typified most clearly in the institution of the contract, which formalizes cooperation among differentiated interests and roles. An adequate theory of social integration must focus on how the solidary structures produced along both dimensions can be regulated and made compatible. Parsons held that such a theory could not rely on a single factor, because the integrative outcomes of markets, hierarchies, networks, and communities require a theory that could explain how they were combined and regulated. As Parsons rightly stresses in most of his works, social integration requires economic resources, cultural values, and political decisions; yet these factors do not automatically produce solidarity.

A similar concern is to be found in his treatment of the generalized media, particularly influence (Parsons 1963a; 1963b; 1969; 1979a). Parsons regarded the ability to identify and conceptualize a specific generalized medium anchored in the integrative system to be important both for explaining the linkages between integrative processes and structures (including between integration and loyalty as separate but connected problems) and between (analytically independent, but empirically interpenetrating) integrative subsystems and other societal structures. The analysis of influence as a generalized medium remained at the core of Parsons's later research, although the outcomes were mixed, fascinating yet unsatisfactory (Lidz 1989b; Gould 2001).

The first major presentation of the term "societal community" came in *Societies: Evolutionary and Comparative Perspectives,* Parsons's 1966 book on the theory of social evolution. Having defined the core of a society as "a patterned normative order through which the life of a population is collectively organized," Parsons added a second dimension, the societal community, defined as a collectivity displaying "a patterned conception of membership which distinguishes between those individuals who do and do not belong." Further down on the same page, he added a second condition for the existence of such kind of collectivity: "It must maintain the integrity of a common cultural orientation, broadly (through not necessarily uniformly or unanimously) shared by its membership, as the basis of its societal identity" (Parsons 1966a, 10). He also stressed that such a collectivity is plural and differentiated.[2] Already in this early formulation, the notion of societal community is elaborated in two directions. First, the relationship between the normative order and the structural organization of such a collectivity has to be defined in a way that allows for variance and changes. Second, the relationship between the societal community and the various subcollectivities existing within it has to be explored in a way that allows for a conceptually adequate treatment of a system of social solidarities. Parsons's subsequent treatment of societal community shows how conscious he was of these conceptual constraints, and that he was willing to enlarge and clarify the notion on both counts. From 1966 on, he displayed a growing tendency to include in the notion of societal community an increasing variety of relationships among solidary structures, and to search for an adequate framework for the analysis of its normative definition and regulation. For example, in *Politics and Social Structure* he stated (1969, 3) that there was a need to specify that "the comparable structural focus of the societal community is the normative system, as embodied above all in law, but extending well beyond that. Such a community must, however, also have an underpinning which directly articulates with the motivational orientations of individuals. It is this underpinning which is the focus of the sociological conception of solidarity." He went on to clarify that although all collectivities are primarily "political" in function, they are grounded in the "solidarities of various kinds and levels of associational 'communities' which, with their institutionally normative 'definition of the situation,' function in ways which are at least to a considerable degree independent of collective decision-making and enforcement mechanism."

Elsewhere in the same book he observed how his previous treatment of influence as a generalized medium failed to adequately address

> the relation of the influence mechanism to the functioning of plural systems of interpenetrating solidary groupings, as distinguished from its operation within a single such collective system . . . influence, like other media, should be conceived as to be *transferable* from one solidary grouping to another. . . . Here the unit, individual or collective, with common membership acts as a "node" through which influence may flow from one group to other. (1969, 431, 434, emphasis in original)

The system of solidarities is identified as the mediating variable between the normative system and the motivational orientations of individuals.[3] On the one hand, such a normative system must be compatible with the functioning of a differentiated set of solidary structures. On the other, such structures must be able to command the loyalty of their members in ways compatible with the loyalty to the system of which they are part (Mayhew 1971; Baum 1975). It is in its relation to such structural pluralism—to what Parsons considered the "extent of the market" for influence—that he identifies a main area for integration research (Parsons 1969).

A further layer of meaning was added in 1970, when Parsons reflected on the role of the societal community within the context of the analysis of equality and inequality in modern society.

> Diffuse solidarities constitute the structure of modern "communities." It is important to our general argument to be clear that there is no one community in a sociologically relevant sense but that a modern society is a very complex composite of differentiated and articulating—sometimes conflicting—units of community. This is one of the two primary respects in which such societies are "pluralistic." . . . Even at the level of the societal community as a whole there is major variation, e.g., as to the degrees to which people have transnational affiliations, on the basis of kinship, occupation or other grounds. . . . The other primary respect in which modern societies are pluralistic has to do with the functionally specific roles of which occupation is prototypical." (Parsons 1970/1977, 333)

Such description pays full attention to the existence, within the system of solidarities, both of vertical inequalities and horizontal differences. This implies again a second-order integration problem. In the mechanical-solidarity dimension, there are strains related to the existence of a plurality of collective identities, the differences that are assumed to attach to membership in the various groups, and the complex expectations associated with each membership. In the organic-solidarity dimension, there are strains over the allocation of resources among competing ends and over the externalities among the various clusters of relationship. Parsons further elaborated such complexity in his subsequent book, *The System of Modern Societies* (1971a). Here he stressed quite explicitly how the societal community is

> a complex network of interpenetrating collectivities and collective loyalties, a system characterized *both by functional differentiation and segmentation.* Thus, kinship-household

> units, business firms, churches, governmental units, educational collectivities, and the like are differentiated from each other. Moreover, *there are a number of each type* of collective unit. . . . The system of norms governing loyalties then must integrate the rights and obligations of various collectivities and their members not only with each other but also with the bases of legitimating of the order as a whole." (13, emphasis added)

Parsons did not take this complexity for granted, nor did he think it could be managed easily. On the contrary, he recognized a strong potential for conflict and strain in this configuration:

> The salient foci of tension and conflict, and thus of creative innovation, in the current situation does not seem to be mainly economic in the sense of nineteenth-century controversy over capitalism and socialism, nor do they seem political in the sense of the "justice" of the distribution of power, though both these conflicts are present. A cultural focus, especially in the wake of the educational revolution, is nearer the mark. The strong indications are, however, that the storm center is the societal community. . . . The most acute problems will presumably be in two areas. First is the development of the cultural system as such in relation to society . . . Second is the problem of the motivational bases of social solidarity within a large-scale and extensive society that has grown to be highly pluralistic in structure. . . . [N]either set of problems will be "solved" without a great deal of conflict. (Parsons 1971a, 121, 143)

This line of development in this analysis brought Parsons to question further the existence of a difference in kind between the societal community and a variety of other solidary forms. In his study of *The American University* (Parsons and Platt 1973) and particularly in his essay on ethnicity (Parsons 1975), he defined the societal community—together with kinship, religious, and educational-cultural associations—as a form of fiduciary association entrusted with a responsibility for the maintenance and development of a tradition (Parsons 1975, 61). As was the case with other fiduciary forms, he said (Parsons 1975, 58), the societal community was characterized by a dual reference to ascriptive and contractual elements.

> A diffusely defined collectivity which has the property of solidarity and is a major point of reference for defining the identity of its members [has] two primary aspects: first that of a common distinctive cultural tradition applying to a "population" of members; and, second, something of the equivalent of a social contract, that is, a component of membership status which is in some essential respect voluntary.

Parsons established a connection between his conception of the societal community and a large number of issues. The societal community became a key concept under which he clustered many societal features that were at the center of his intellectual interests: the relationship between ascribed and achieved roles and orientations and between specific and diffuse forms of solidary relationships, the deep transformations—and yet continuity—of cultural traditions, the emergence of collegial forms of coordination, the social basis of the liberal order, and the role of normative elements in shaping both individual action and the integration of the social system. The task of systematically working out the connections among these phenomena is a large one. Moreover, no single presentation of the idea of societal community in Parsons's texts conveys the whole range of meaning and research problems that he identified with it.

It is not surprising, then, that during the seventies Parsons developed the ambitious project of writing a full-fledged study of the societal community in the United States. "American Societal Community" (1979a), an unpublished manuscript, followed on his previous attempts to write a book on American society (Lidz 1989a). In it Parsons shows how class, ethnicity, and religion, as well as local and regional residence, can provide bases for structurally significant solidary groupings. Considerably in advance of other streams of social theory, he places quality-based solidary networks on an equal footing with class-based actors as significant actors in the modern social scene (Parsons 1979a, chapters 6 to 8). The manuscript also includes a careful description of the internal differentiation of the normative order, as it pertains to such a system of solidarity.

Partly refining the argument he developed earlier (Parsons 1970/1977), Parsons saw such a normative system as developing in relation to two conceptual pairs: freedom versus constraints, and equality versus inequality. He proceeded on this ground to further elaborate the charting of the basic components of this normative system.[4] The result is a strong combination of liberal and progressive normative elements matched with a fully pluralistic vision of membership in contemporary American society. The manuscript pays a great deal of attention to the structural pluralism of the societal community. This pluralism is described in emancipatory terms, as an introduction of important degrees of freedom in relation to the cultural tradition and to the culture—maintaining institutions of the fiduciary complex (Parsons 1979a, chapter 5). Thus, the references to cultural tradition that characterized Parsons's description of the societal community since the seminal account of 1966 are qualified by the identification—side by side with the three components of the citizenship complex identified by Thomas H. Marshall—of a specialized cultural complex, concerning precisely the ideals that envision the form of solidarity to be institutionalized in the societal community. With reference to American society, Parsons writes (1979a, chap. 4, 21):

> I have suggested that [the cultural component of citizenship] stood at the level of values, precisely the values special to the societal community, under the more general pattern of instrumental activism, and which define the conditions of the mode of solidarity which should be institutionalized in the societal community. This is, I suggest, none other than the pattern of institutionalized individualism.

Thus the relationship between the societal community and the broader cultural tradition should be viewed as a transformation rather than simple reproduction.

THE SOCIETAL COMMUNITY AS AN EVOLUTIONARY ACHIEVEMENT

The foregoing indicates how Parsons revised and qualified the concept of societal community to an extent such that it could represent the integrative subsystem of structurally pluralist societies. This is hardly surprising. Although it is rarely acknowledged, Talcott Parsons is a major theorist of contemporary societal pluralism (Sciortino 1994; Kivisto 2004). As documented in dozens of essays, for most of his career he worked to develop a conceptual framework that would satisfactorily analyze social pluralism in differentiated societies (Parsons 1961a; 1968c).

In his approach, the fact that modern societies are characterized by a plurality of solidary structures is not a historical accident but rather a functional necessity. Parsons, moreover, stresses how such pluralism is produced both by the increase in organic solidarity and by variation across segmental units or components of the society (Parsons 1968c; 1975). There is a well-known pluralism born out of the differentiation of economic and political interests and subcultures. But there is also a pluralism born of religious and ethnic diversity as well as intellectual and professional specialization.[5]

Parsons's essays on pluralism are among the best examples of his antinostalgic outlook and of his sustained criticism of pseudo-Gemeinschaft illusions (Holton and Turner 1986). His assessment of contemporary pluralism can be sharply distinguished both from the nostalgic vision of conservative thought and from the jeremiads of critical theory. Where others see the breakdown of a common cultural tradition into fragments of highly specialized, narrowly developed tastes, Parsons stresses the development of a sophisticated normative order in which the requirements of common membership are distinguished from conformity pressures exercised by particularistic traditions. Where others identify in the existence of segmental loyalties a danger to the unity of the "national" societal community, Parsons stresses how such networks—once embedded in universalistic individual rights—are a source of strength and flexibility in a democratic society. Where others lament the "end of the common good," Parsons identifies the highly institutional premises of the "freedom from ascription and from compulsory allegiance" (Parsons 1979a, 11). Where others see the eventual corruption of the moral order, Parsons sees the emergence of a pluralist societal community existing in relation with, but analytically independent of, economic control, political power, and cultural imposition (Parsons 1971a; 1971c; Mayhew 1990).

It is within this evaluative context that Parsons develops his theory of the evolution of human societies. This strand of Parsons's work may be criticized on several grounds. The role attributed to increase in adaptive capacity as a master trend of evolution is problematic (Granovetter 1979). The development of an evolutionary model that starts from the most "developed" unit, according to what Parsons calls the principle of "the special significance of the most highly developed case" (1979b, 53), can also be criticized (Bortolini 2002). There is consequently ground to question the adequacy of his analysis as a general evolutionary theory (Luhmann 1984). However, such criticism is not applicable to his more specific analysis of the transformation of the integrative spheres. This analysis addresses the structural consequences of the detachment of ascriptive categories (ethnicity, kinship, religion, and so forth) from the normatively prescribed hierarchy of higher and lower social statuses; and the breaking of normatively sanctioned connections between membership in such diffuse categories and opportunities to perform in other social roles, especially economic, political, cultural, and educational. The lasting achievement of Parsons's work on evolution may well turn out to be his inquiry into the highly unlikely structural preconditions for the institutionalization of an inclusive "single societal community with full citizenship for all" (1965, 740), able to sustain and nurture a fully pluralistic large-scale system of social solidarities.

Social inclusion is not considered by Parsons to be a "natural trend of history."[6] It is triggered, not caused, by differentiation. At any stage, societies face very different alternatives. A hierarchical right or a political difference among groups may be reestablished. Fundamentalist reactions may repress the very structural basis of such challenge. Even if differentiation alters the structure of ascriptive loyalties, the outcome may still vary from subordinate incorporation to structural polarization (Parsons 1968b, 1971a). The specific solution of "a single societal community with equal citizenship for all" becomes conceivable and feasible only in very special cases, and only after a long series of conflicts (Parsons 1965, 740). The assumption by a society of the normative goal of the elimination of "*any* category defined as inferior in itself" (Parsons 1965, 739, emphasis in original) is a highly unlikely occurrence. To explain how such a goal becomes an inherent part of the normative project of modern societies is a major aim of most of Parsons's evolutionary analysis. In other words, Parsons's works on evolution may be read more along the lines of Max Weber's attempt to understand the preconditions for the rise of capitalism in Western Europe rather than as an aspiration to replicate Herbert Spencer's ambitions.

Although the notion of societal-community development is sometimes presented by Parsons as matter of changing the normative definition of societal membership (sustained and protected mostly by juridical means and welfare-state provisions), his reformulation of the societal and juridical definition of membership is only part of the story. As we have already seen, Parsons defines modernization as a set of "inclusive *and* pluralizing" forces (1968b, 367, emphasis added). The normative redefinition of membership is matched by a structural change in the constellation of social solidarities.[7] Pluralism is not a structural outcome of the cumulative processes of inclusion. It is also a key element of further inclusion and of societal resistance to polarizing strains (Parsons 1968b; 1971a).[8]

In isolation, each of these processes would fail to trigger the development Parsons is defining. Redefining membership without making a structural change in the societal configuration would end up producing only expectational strains and a polarizing backlash inspired by fears of a debasement of the value of membership (Parsons 1945a, 1965). Yet the increase in societal heterogeneity that has characterized many city-states and empires of the past may be easily managed within a stable ascriptive hierarchy of social ranks. One of the most unlikely attributes of the modern societal community is the extent to which it entails the simultaneous institutionalization of social pluralism and democratic individualism.

In Parsons's analysis the modern societal community is both a generalized normative system wherein all actors are linked by common rules and are legitimized, no matter how different their specific identities, by a common membership, and a pluralist structure of social solidarities. This societal community has emerged through a restructuring of the juridical bases of social membership—the citizenship complex—as well as the establishment of institutions focused on the interpretation and adjudication of social conflicts pertaining to the consequences of such common membership. In other words, it requires the detachment of the public sphere both from ascription-based allocation processes and from particularistic cultural traditions. The definition of membership in a modern pluralist society, according to Parsons, is characterized by the fact that the duties of the public sphere are *not* identified with the "protection" of particular cultural traditions or with the rights of any collectivity over its members. Rather, it entails the protection of the pluralism of social collectivities—a kind of societal "antitrust legislation," so to speak—as well as the right of the individual to choose his or her solidary networks. As Parsons writes (Parsons 1979a, 11):

> The institutionalization of pluralism with reference to criteria which are clearly ascriptive, requires norms with a double reference. One is the refusal to lend special "public" legitimation to any one among the plural units. . . . On the other hand, unless pluralization is to be prevented by suppression, as is approximately the case with organized religion in some communist countries, there must also be, as in our case with religion, protection of the "free exercise thereof." This combination may be called the "privatization" of a pattern of solidarity, in which either the individual is protected in the activities of the subgroups of his choice or, where the ascriptive element remains, he and the others of his group are protected from discrimination because of membership in it—the case just mentioned of the irrelevance of the subgroup membership for other contexts.

A generalized normative order does allow societal pluralism to develop. At the same time, such pluralism stabilizes a normative order, as the differences among categories and groups impedes the success of fundamentalist reactions trying to recouple societal-community membership to particular group identities. Societal pluralism, in other words, plays a selective role in the evolution of normative systems. When combined with common membership, moreover, societal pluralism also has a much more important integrative function. From an action theory perspective, the main integrative problem for a complex social system is not social conflict, but rather social polarization (Parsons 1942a, 1964, 1968b). Any social system has to avoid breakdowns in structural interdependencies as well as in the motivations of members (Parsons 1971a). We also know that Parsons discerned polarizing tendencies in the development of all social systems. In many strands of his work, social pluralism is viewed as a strong counterforce to polarizing tendencies. Embedded in a generalized societal community, Parsons argues, social pluralism implies multiple memberships spanning any single cleavage. Far from being an atomized mass of lonely individuals, Parsons and Winston White, writing in a critique of David Riesman's works, argued that in such a pluralistic American society, "an increasingly ramified network of crisscrossing solidarities has been developing" (Parsons and White 1960/1969, 251). Membership in multiple groupings are the best check for polarizing tendencies even under conditions of heavy strain:

> The very looseness of the relation between structural solidarities other than the political party and the party structure itself can be said to constitute an important protection against the divisive potentialities of cleavage. The essential fact here is that the most important groupings in the society will contain considerable proportions of adherents of both parties [groups]. . . . The pressure of political cleavage—by activating ties of solidarity at the more differentiated structural levels that cut across the line of cleavage—tends automatically to bring countervailing forces into play." (Parsons 1969, 223–24).

SOME PROBLEMS WITH PARSONS'S ANALYSIS OF THE SOCIETAL COMMUNITY

Parsons's work provides a fascinating glimpse into what a complete theory of the societal community would look alike. And his notion of societal community has provided fertile ground for thinking about societal integration in contemporary terms (Lidz 1989b; Münch 1999; Alexander 2001; Gerhardt 2001, Bortolini 2002).

At a theoretical level, however, such a sensitizing function is not enough. Parsons imbued the notion with the more rigorous requirement of serving as the starting point for an adequate theory of social membership and solidarity. The concept of the societal community is rooted in the theoretical prerequisites of action theory and in Parsons's lifelong search for a theory of social solidarity (Mayhew 1984). Viewed in this perspective, Parsons's analysis is inadequate, failing to articulate the analysis of the complexes of integrative mechanisms and institutions in a systematic and convincing way.[9] These limits may derive in part from the fact that this aspect of Parsons's legacy is the outcome of work spanning several years, during which time Parsons's thought continued to evolve but did not undergo a final systematic revision (Lidz 1989a, 34). Other problems, however, may be the result of long-standing difficulties in Parsons's treatments of solidarity structures. I will concentrate here on two of them that are particularly relevant for the development of an adequate theory of the integration of a pluralistic society.

The first concerns the idea of the societal community as a relational nexus between normative definitions of membership and their associated duties and rights and the actual pattern of social solidarities and groupings existing in any given society. We find here a serious imbalance in Parsons's corpus. The attention paid by Parsons to the normative dimension is not matched by an equally sophisticated analysis of the actual system of solidarities, and the ways categories and groups in this system are distinguished, structured, evolving, and interacting.[10] Although the relationships among social classes, status groups, and diffuse solidarities are considered to be a major focus of the analysis of social integration (Parsons 1961a), their actual analysis is often derived from detailed discussion of their normative regulation or treated in a marginal way.[11] Although Parsons's analyses of normative regulation are very sophisticated, it cannot be assumed that they encompass all aspects of the integrative subsystem.[12]

Because of this imbalance, Parsons has not sufficiently exploited his approach to the societal community. We have already seen how Parsons's notion of the societal community includes the basic elements of an analysis of social pluralism as an integrative mechanism per se. This analysis, with its emphasis on the importance of the mix between "bridging" and "bonding" connections, has anticipated much of the current debate on social capital (Burt 1992; Putnam 2000). However, Parsons has not systematically developed this line of thought. The same thing might be said about how he dealt with his insight that, from the point of view of any single unit, the societal community, given its pluralism, may be considered a reference group system (Parsons 1969, 435). In developing analysis of influence as a generalized medium, moreover, Parsons pointed out that individual members are exposed to influence through the mediation of primary groups and settings, and suggested that mechanisms of generalized, society-wide influence may face problems of penetrating to all segments of the community that are analogous to "extent of the market" problems in the economy. These ideas could have led to the development of a research program on the structure of such networks of solidary ties, the particular social conditions in which they are formed, and the ways in which they mediate the flows of influence. But Parsons did not pursue these lines of inquiry further; he simply asserted that many features of the solidary groups exist without systematically examining them.

The lack of a structural theory of solidary groups also places a limit on the general analysis of the relationship between the system of social solidarities and the normative order. Parsons forcefully points out that structural differentiation allows for the increased autonomy of the integrative system over the cultural one. He also stresses that the same process allows for the increased autonomy of solidary groupings over the specific normative content of the definition of societal membership. However, he does not explore the "space" of these two forms of autonomy. For example, in several instances Parsons writes about the selectivity function embedded in the process of institutionalization: in other words, about the fact that which part or which version of the value system becomes part of the institutionalized pattern is not only contingent on the internal value constellation but also on the structural configuration of the social system. The very fact that continuity at the level of value system may go hand in hand with variations in the criteria of legitimate membership is a proof of such autonomy. Although more specific, the normative definitions of membership and of what follow from such memberships still leave ample room for interpretation and negotiation in everyday interaction that takes place in a more general context of normative regulation (Parsons 1961a, 1968a). As Parsons argues in his well-known paper on the American Negro (1965), change in the structure of interactions may take place before the exigencies leading to re-definition of normative standards of conduct have reached a critical level. This has two theoretical implications. First, it should be possible to assume the existence of an interactional citizenship partly independent of the normative definition of citizenship.[13] Second, it opens up a need to include in the analysis of a system of social solidarities an aspect of ongoing struggle for the recognition of capacity to name and represent collective identities, including the rhetorics associated with such struggle. In turn, this requires an investigation of the social creativity of competitive struggles and negotiations, as well as of the possibility that the understanding of cultural variations should be grounded in an interactional framework (Mayhew 1984, 1997). It raises questions of the structural contexts in which interpretations of normative standards and group identities may gain influence or fail to do so (Sciortino 2003). In addition, it opens up the interesting possibility that cultural and social norms, although institutionalized in a social system, may be interpreted in the light of widely different expectations, thus reinforcing oppositional subcultures even in presence of a shared commitment to the normative system (Gould 1997). This would in turn help to clarify the mix of ascriptive and contractual elements that Parsons identified as specific constituents of modern diffuse solidarities. With the major exception of Parsons's analysis of the civil rights movement (Parsons 1965, 1966c), this line of argument is scarcely pursued in his writings.

A second imbalance is visible in Parsons's treatment of the different kinds of solidary structures. As we have seen, in this definition of the societal community Parsons insists that its units are based both on differentiation *and* segmentation. In several passages he also defines the system of solidarity as including both performance-based and quality-based solidarities. What is more, Parsons recognized, earlier than any other contemporary theorist, the enduring relevance of diffuse solidarities, including those based on ascriptive features.

Nevertheless, in his treatment of the societal community he focused his theoretical attention nearly exclusively on differentiated, rather than segmented, units at least in connection with modern society. Such imbalance is particularly evident in his treatment of the system of social solidarities, where with the partial exception of the household, quality-based formulations are seen mainly as a legacy of the earlier structures.[14] His analysis of structural change exemplifies this. Parsons acknowledges as a broad generalization that social differentiation increases both performance-based and quality-based pluralism. In his specific analyses, however, while interest-based solidarities are linked propositionally with the increase in adaptive capacities, identity-based solidarities are only associated with it in a descriptive way through the analysis of integrative consequences of modernization.[15] Even though Parsons was quite innovative in showing how diffuse solidarities of the segmental kind are transformed, rather than eliminated, by societal modernization (Sciortino 2005), he never proceeded to an analysis of their enduring structural relevance in contemporary achievement-oriented settings (Mayhew 1968) and processes of production.

These two sets of conceptual imbalances may have several origins. In part, they may result from the fact that Parsons's interest in developing an analysis of quality-based solidarities in modern society was not as strong as his involvement in defending modernized forms of social relationship, and in proving, against the dominant trends of social thought, that they could be a source of genuine solidarity. It is also possible that these imbalances are related to more general features of Parsons's thought, such as his idealistic tendency and genuine commitment to the vision of the United States as "the city on the hill" (Alexander 1983). In any case, to redress such imbalances is a necessary step for the development of a theory of the integrative sphere based on action-theory premises.

A way to contribute to redressing such imbalance can be found within Parsons's own corpus of work. Some ideas developed in a number of his essays can in fact be used as starting points for the development of a more complete and satisfactory theory of social categories and solidary groups in modern society.

A "PARSONIAN" APPROACH TO QUALITY-BASED SOLIDARY STRUCTURES

Over the course of his life, Parsons wrote about a variety of empirical problems, with the double aim of advancing sociological theory and dealing with certain features of modern society that he regarded as insufficiently or erroneously understood in the existing literature. Many of these essays are focused on detailed analyses of solidary structures. Parsons applied his framework to the analysis of interaction among ethnic and racial groups at many points during his intellectual career (Parsons 1942b, 1945b, 1946, 1965, 1966c, 1968b, 1975, 1980, 1975/1994). The meaning and forms of religious pluralism were always at the center of his empirical interests (Parsons 1958, 1962, 1966b, 1971b, 1974). He also developed analyses of other quality-based groups with emphasis on their associational processes (Parsons 1967, 1971d; Parsons and Platt 1973).[16] In number and significance, these essays are comparable to his better-known works concerned with the professions and with health (Sciortino 1994). I wish to argue that if they are read systematically and hermeneutically it is possible to identify in them some strong conceptual continuities that contain the elements necessary for developing a general theory of quality-based groups in modern society, their interaction, and change. The conceptual continuities provide an outline of a processual analysis of the integrative, often group-specific, strains in modern societies. They also deal in depth with the ways in which such strains are related to the normative system.[17]

The first strong conceptual continuity concerns the definition of difference-based categories and groups. As early as the 1930s, following Weber, Parsons did not take their "existence" for granted, or attribute to them any "natural" or primordial status.[18] On the contrary, he recognized that the membership criteria of ascriptive categories are often quite arbitrary and that the sharing of ethnic or racial markers does not necessarily imply ethnic identity (Parsons 1945b). This stance allowed him to show that the social significance of ascriptive identities may not be accompanied by any substantial behavioral requirements. In other words, Parsons accepted the idea that categorical symbolism may include what David Schneider called "empty symbols," markers that are socially recognized yet void of social content (Parsons 1975).

Parsons defined such categories in fully sociological terms. He argued against any attempt to see both loyalty and opposition to ethnic, gender, or religious categories as the outcome of psychological prejudice or irrationality. While he recognized that some psychological processes, such as categorization, stereotyping, and projection, often played a crucial role, he regarded their actual content as socially selected (1945b, 185). He saw presence of ascriptive markers as socially significant only within the process of interaction between in-groups and out-groups (Parsons 1942b; 1945b). In his view, even racial markers could be shown to be the result of a long history of shifting semantics (Parsons 1968b). He argued that to a significant degree the stereotypical features of ascriptive groups might be the product of the reaction of their members to how they were regarded and treated by other groups. In any case, Parsons never considered such processes in isolation, as self-sustaining and self-explanatory ones; nor did he define ascriptive categories as atomic concepts; rather he saw them rather as complex combinations of ascriptive and voluntary elements—of both "contract" and "blood." He was among the first theorists to stress the optional elements of contemporary ethnic identity and group membership and the sociological relevance of processed "passing" from one socially accepted identity to another (Parsons 1975, 1975/1994).

It should also be stressed that Parsons's perspective does not allow diffuse or ascriptive categories and grounds of solidarity to be treated as intrinsic or natural. In his view, an adequate theory of their existence and mobilization must take the form of a general theory of quality-based solidarities. For example:

> A racial group acquires the kind of solidarity which can make it an important factor in group antagonism only in so far as it develops many of the characteristics of religious groups. Conversely, religion is a factor in group antagonism in so far as, among other things, it generates a type of group structure often characteristic of racial groups. (Parsons 1945b, 184)

The refusal to grant a "natural" status to ascriptive categories does not imply that Parsons relegated them to the status of mere ideological decoys or psychological illusions. On the contrary, he stressed how such categories nearly always shared with kinship the highly significant feature of common descent, with its associated rich symbolism. Ascriptive categories' subcultural traits, he postulated, tend to be implicitly transmitted through early socialization rather than learned in explicit ideological formulations. For this very reason, such distinctive and esoteric socialized features are particularly apt both as a basis for collective identity construction and for exclusionary standards. The latter are also facilitated when, as in "race," there are physical or institutional markers that cannot be readily altered or concealed (Parsons 1945b, 186).

Reading what he wrote with contemporary glasses, we could say that Parsons's action theory challenges both primordialism and naïve constructionism. The structure of collective interaction may definitely deny members of some categories access to key resources or, less directly, discourage them from trying to access other resources. Such discriminations typically create "distinct" and "objective" social statuses for them. Groups may also adopt quite effective boundary-maintaining mechanisms to ensure the survival of their distinctive identities across space and time.

As a consequence, Parsons does not deny as a matter of principle that there may be correlations between quality-based membership and behavioral traits nor that such correlations may cause interactional strains with other groups. Rather, what he says is that the transformation of quality-based *categories* into quality-based *groups* is a social, not a psychological or cultural, process.

An illuminating example of his reasoning in this regard can be found in his controversial 1942 essay, "The Sociology of Modern Antisemitism." Parsons went to great length to show how, historically, the specific social organization of Judaism has played a significant role in defining the identity of the group as well as in maintaining its boundaries in relation to other groups. In this essay he seemed to accept that the working of such mechanisms might activate emotional strains in some instances both among Gentiles and among Jews themselves. Yet, he stressed that the emotional dynamics between Jews and Gentiles are not the outcome of a clash between specific "personality types" deriving from the "imprinting" of their respective cultural traditions, but rather of structural effects related to the discrepancy between the normative complex of equality of opportunity and the structural reality of discrimination (Parsons 1942b).[19]

One implication of this is that the social patterning of the system of ascriptive categories does not derive sic et simpliciter from the existence of cultural differences. Parsons pays strong attention to the symbolism associated with solidary groups and to their cleavages. In this sense, he could even be considered a precursor of the current "cultural turn" in sociology. In the case of ethnicity, Parsons stresses how both "blood" and "contract" are culturally constructed and enacted. Racial markers are to be understood not only as visible factors but also as symbols (Parsons 1945b, 185–86; Parsons 1968b).

In the case of religion, Parsons stresses that an impressive array of references to descent, kinship, and transgenerational loyalty may be found even in faiths that emphasize individual commitment and personal calling. Eschewing naïve constructionism, Parsons draws upon action theory to show how such symbolism is analytically independent from social structure, yet hardly an uneven set of randomly assembled or ad hoc symbols, modifiable at will. Such symbolism has a logic and a structure of its own, deeply connected with basic patterns of human culture (Parsons 1975/1994). Consequently, the rhetorics of such "imagined communities" may draw upon rich and complex symbolic repertoires connected to kinship and transgenerational solidarities. Parsons is quick to point out, however, that such symbolism does not "determine" the solidary reality or it operates in isolation. Such symbolism, he states, is shared by a variety of communitarian forms, including many not based on ascriptive features (Parsons 1975). Both inclusion and exclusion processes may draw on the very same symbolic complexes, utilizing the same texts, rituals, and keywords (Parsons 1968b).[20]

Parsons fails to explore in full the consequences of this theoretical stance. He does not deal with the fact that the structure of such symbolism may operate in one and the same society to support a plurality of contrasting claims. Nor does he explore how the same normative system may be shared throughout a community, but still produce sharp group differences when matched by different assessments of the social realities associated with various categories of membership.[21]

A final conceptual continuity is to be found in Parsons's assessment of the "causes" of difference-based conflicts. Parsons has done more than any other theorist of his period to dispel the myth of an ideally solidary communitarian past.[22] A key dimension of his critique of the "historical understanding" of the discipline centers on the absurdity of any notion of the existence of a totally homogeneous society, even in the most remote past. In his evolutionary analysis, he stresses the empirical rarity of linguistically, ethnically, or religiously homogeneous societies. He also asserts that pluralism is increasingly characteristic of modern societies, and he accords this transformation a crucial role in his analysis of modernity (Parsons 1971a). At the same time, Parsons does not ignore the potential strains, tensions, and conflicts that are embedded in social heterogeneity. Any categorical difference to which subcultural features have become attached is a potential cause of strains. Any subcultural difference may in turn involve differences in the definition of the situation and hence create expectational strains and conflicts between groups (Parsons 1942b). Moreover, some dimensions of conflict in the interaction among different categories and groups may involve "real" factors of political and economic resources. Quality-based identities are often linked with "culturally patterned conflicts in *claims* to status, power, resources, etc." (Parsons 1945b, 191). Finally, any categorical difference is a fertile ground for scapegoating, distortion, and overreaction. Parsons emphasizes the absence of a political "quick fix" for most of such strains (Parsons 1945a; 1946).

We find here evidence that Parsons was anything but a social "harmonist"; on the contrary, he recognized that societies are filled with strains, tensions, and conflicts, and derived from this recognition the theoretical centrality that he accorded to the mechanisms of social integration. His acknowledgment of the potential for conflict, however, does not imply that Parsons regarded heterogeneity as a "social problem." Rather, he identified the causes of conflict as structural in nature, associated both with sources of free-floating aggression and the lack of countervailing controlling forces (Parsons 1945b, 190–93).

In his writings in the early 1940s, about the presence and structural significance of racial and religious hate, Parsons denied that racial prejudice was the outcome of a flawed socialization process or particular forms of psychopathology. He argued that the configuration of some key structures of Western society—particularly the family and the occupational system—made frustration and anxiety an endemic feature of modern settings. Such feelings were often channeled toward a social scapegoat (Parsons 1942b). The precipitating events emanate mainly from the paradoxes of achievement, the channeling of affect that takes place tends to identify the scapegoat according to a quality-based symbolism.

The existence of a racially defined minority functions as a safety net for the lower strata of the majority population. As a consequence, an escape from the role of scapegoat is often possible only when a new category of outsiders may absorb the same function (Parsons 1946). Parsons takes a similar position in his later work, where he repeatedly stresses the importance of taking into account the strength and structural basis of "resistances to inclusion" as a piece of the puzzle, rather than attributing racial prejudice solely to the existence of die-hard racists (Parsons 1965, 1966c). He highlighted the importance of how the tensions underlying racism are managed within the social system. In his view, although the development of structural strains may be endemic, the emergence of polarized subcultures and the subsequent cumulative segmental differentiation are not necessary outcomes but rather are products of the failure of the control mechanisms operating in all of the societal subsystems. In this connection it is interesting to note that the allegedly "idealist" Parsons is skeptical about any attempt to modify the situation through cultural reform and normative appeals. He identifies the reform of the occupational system and an active stance toward social mobility as needed political actions (Parsons 1946, 1965).

Taken together, these several elements of conceptual continuity may provide a workable framework for analyzing the configurations of difference-based ties of social solidarity in modern societies. The framework provides orientation on how to investigate the formation of quality-based cleavages. It also sensitizes us to the fact that the crystallization of polarized subcultures tends to follow the structural coupling of categorical cleavages with the distribution of so-called "real" societal resources. Given the potential for free-floating aggression in modernizing contexts, there is some ground to think that contemporary societies may be particularly prone to this kind of polarizing that may unleash even deadly conflict. Parsons's early analysis addresses the "darker side" of the modernization process that, when linked with his later treatment of the cumulative effect of normative re-definitions of societal membership and increased social pluralism provides a framework for the analysis of structural change in terms of a balancing of polarizing and depolarizing processes.

A need also exists for a theoretical account of the dynamics of change within a system of solidarities. According to Parsons, such an account involves two separate issues: the dynamics of process within an established structure of a system and change in the structure of a system.[23] He deals with the first mainly in his analyses of influence as a generalized medium. The use of influence, as Parsons made increasingly clear, is bounded by established reference-group structures, including those of social stratification. It is rooted in the activation of obligations that are embedded in the underlying established relationships of solidarity (Parsons 1963a, 1969, 1979a; Parsons and Platt 1973).

The activation of influence—and its inflationary and deflationary fluctuations—defines the domain for analysis of changes in the constellation of solidary networks and in their reciprocal interchanges with other subsystems of society. What interests Parsons more, however, is the structural change in the configuration of the system of social solidarities. As we have seen, this is a main focus of his theory of societal evolution. The problem here is that although his evolutionary approach delineates the highly unlikely structural preconditions of change in the normative definition of membership, it cannot explain how such structural preconditions are activated or acted upon. Defining the functional requirements for inclusion does not explain how it takes place. Moreover, this level of analysis cannot explain how comparatively high levels of structural differentiation and value generalization coexist over the long term with ascriptive discrimination at institutional and social levels.

To develop an adequate theory of social inclusion, an interactional scheme able to account for the internal structure of inclusion processes is needed along with a group-specific evolutionary analysis. The lack of the group-specific level of analysis is often cited as a main weakness of Parsons's work on social change (Gouldner 1970; Gouldsblom 1987). Yet Parsons's empirical analyses of inclusion processes offer precisely the kind of processual, group-oriented scheme that can be integrated into the analysis of evolutionary tendencies (Alexander 1981; Sciortino 2005).

The main example here is the scheme of "demand" for and "supply" of inclusion that Parsons developed in his analysis of the civil rights movement in the United States. (Parsons 1965, 1966c). On the "supply" side, Parsons lists the "qualifications for membership" of the excluded group that make its participation viable within the broader structural conditions and the framework of the basic citizenship complex. In other words, the "supply" side consists of factors that foster the organic solidarity between the included and the excluded as well as the elements that make a normatively prescribed solidarity feasible: the degree of value generalization, the opportunities for political mobilization, the structure of the normative system, and the arena for seeking influence.

Nevertheless, Parsons stresses that inclusion processes will not advance without a "demand" for inclusion, collective action to exploit the opportunities for and to manage the consequences of inclusion. For inclusion to result, sectors of both the excluded and the included groups must be persuaded that inclusion is normatively desirable and be willing to work toward this goal.[24] In some cases, mobilization of groups toward inclusion may happen in a decentralized, barely visible way. Where the gap between normative definitions and reality is highly entrenched, however, the inclusion process requires the emergence of a public movement able to challenge established structures of social identity.

In his analysis of the civil rights movements in the United States, Parsons elaborates the conceptual foundations for a voluntaristic theory of social movements (Parsons 1965, 1966c). He argues that, on the supply side, the success of such movements depends on the historically specific relational composition of resources in the other subsystem (Parsons 1966c). These resources are necessary but not sufficient factors of inclusion processes. Once available, they must be exploited on the demand side, by a social movement able to establish solidary ties among groups across established divisions, which is the essential character of the inclusion process—thus, a pluralistic associational base is necessary for generating an adequate support. A pluralistic base is also important for responding to anxieties over possible debasement of the value of membership. When he writes about the civil rights movement, Parsons stresses that the demand for inclusion would have been much more difficult to develop without the existence of segmental, quality-based institutions in the excluded community such as the African American churches. The existence of strong quality-based groups and institutions does not necessarily constitute an obstacle to the development of generalized concepts of common membership. On the contrary, it may well be a prerequisite.[25]

Movements for inclusion, according to Parsons, will show a structural tendency to generalize their grievances, as a way to broaden their coalition base and acquire additional resources. The same is true of countermovements. Parsons argues that both such generalizing and polarizing tendencies are made possible and delimited by the structural pluralism of differentiated societies:

> If continued indefinitely, such a process [of generalization of grievances] would result in the polarization of society between the "radicals" and their opponents. American society, however, seems to have reached a level of pluralization which makes it unlikely that any polarization process can get so far. After a point, generalization is likely to be checked on both sides of the issue by the involvement of the relevant population elements in other issues which cannot be identified too directly with the initial point of reference. (Parsons 1966c, xxvii)

The conceptual scheme that Parsons developed to analyze the civil rights movement may be generalized to a theory accounting not only for the change of diffuse, quality-based solidarities but also for the emergence of new ones. Such a scheme would again require the presence of a supply of resources from other societal subsystems that—directly or indirectly—create specific clusters of societal conditions. As Leon Mayhew (1971) convincingly argued, even highly differentiated societies produce distributions of societal resources that selectively tailor certain quality-based groups and institutions. Quality-based criteria enter into the decision making of actors as secondary selection devices and as ways to reduce the complexity of the decisions to be made (Mayhew 1968).[26] Most if not all of such biased distributions of resources tend to follow established patterns of exclusion, thereby reinforcing previous symbolic definitions of membership (Alexander 1990).

At the same time, reactions to this situation may take creative forms. New quality-based identities and solidarities may emerge as members of different categories combine with one another and reformulate their prior quality-based symbolism. Leadership entails a capacity of social "entrepreneurs" to combine diverse and even distant sources of influence to promote common interests across the cleavages separating social groups (Lidz 1989b). Yet such leadership may produce exclusionary outcomes, as when political leaders reject the interests and claims of certain groups or categories in order to avoid alienating opposing groups and networks whose influence is well established. Another possible outcome is that social entrepreneurs will promote new quality-based categories, challenging the established system of social identities with the claims that new "identities" deserve the community's attention.

The increased autonomy of the symbolism, and the availability of empty symbols in modern cultures, make outcomes of this kind more rather than less likely. When such social movements are successful, a variety of bridging social relationships may be established and over time become the base of differentiated solidary networks. Some of these movements—such as the European nationalist movements of the 1840s—developed entirely new identities yet presented them as ancient (Anderson 1983). Others have stressed their own novelty (Sciortino 1999).

To be sure, processes of creation of new segmental categories and social networks show no sign of diminishing in scale in modern society. Contemporary societies exhibit constant attempts to institutionalize new quality-based categories, as was shown in the recent case of the "struggle" in England and Australia to have the Jedi religion, based on the Star Wars movies, recognized in the census. Nor are such possibilities restricted to movements acting within the established "types" of quality-based categories. Lifestyle and sexual-preference groups are other examples. Parsons's scheme of the demand for and supply of inclusion, if properly reconstructed, may play a significant role in helping theorists identify and study the social conditions under which such processes occur and come to be stabilized. His later notion of institutionalization as the equivalent of natural selection in the evolution of social systems may be also useful in this regard.

TESTING THE PARSONIAN FRAMEWORK: SOCIETAL COMMUNITY AND THE MULTICULTURALIST DEBATE

I have argued that the notion of the societal community is a key theoretical resource in the Parsonian legacy that is still largely unappreciated, and that some of its shortcomings may be alleviated when it is read hermeneutically against a background of important strands of Parsons's specific analysis of modern societies. The main argument of this paper is that this Parsonian approach should be used as a conceptual resource in contemporary debates. It is also important to document how it can contribute to a satisfactory conceptual framework for defining research issues. In the following pages, I will try to provide an example of the fruitfulness of the Parsonian approach, using as a test its capacity to provide a satisfactory view of the current debate on multiculturalism and multicultural issues in modern society.

Currently there is a broad intellectual and social interest in the social and political consequences of cultural heterogeneity. Multiculturalism is invoked in many contexts of political and intellectual debate. A search conducted at Amazon.com reveals that 777 books in English about multiculturalism have been published, including theoretical treatises, self-help manuals, undergraduate texts and biographical novels. The search engine Google lists 276,000 Internet pages linked to multiculturalism.[27] This is all the more striking in the light of the fact that, at least in the United States, the term "multiculturalism" was hardly used before 1989 (Glazer 1997, 7).

For the purposes of this chapter, it may be useful to start by stressing that the very existence and significance of such debates is an interesting example of the capacity of the notion of societal community, as developed by Parsons, to sensitize the reader to significant and innovative features of contemporary society. The claims and practices that are currently considered under the concept of multiculturalism are quite consistent with the overall framework of Parsons's analysis of the societal community. As early as the 1970s, when an emphasis on class conflict dominated the sociological literature, Parsons already stressed that a major set of issues in contemporary society centered on the motivational basis of social solidarity in highly pluralistic settings, along with the related issues of social recognition, diversity, and normative compliance. He emphasized that pluralist societies were continuously involved in "normative work" over the production and institutionalization of new situational norms as well as in the revision and rejustification of established ones. He argued that this process was necessarily accompanied by a variety of contingent and situational accommodations (Parsons 1961a; 1979a).

A second, equally interesting, feature of such social phenomena is that the main location of multicultural claims and conflicts have been centered in the educational, the juridical, and the mass media institutions, rather than in the political system in the strict sense.[28] This pattern is consistent with Parsons's analysis of the societal community and with his prediction that such institutions would be at the center of conflict and controversies—the "storm centers," to use his own words—in the current phase of societal development (Parsons 1971a).

A third feature of the multicultural debate is that it is being argued over social categories that in the previous two decades have seen structural gains in their social standing, namely women and ethnic minorities. Such gains have been uneven, slow, and often inadequate, but they are documented by most statistical sources. This, too, is consistent with Parsons's analysis of inclusion processes, especially his argument that the demand for inclusion is not strictly a function of a previous rigid exclusion but follows a blurring of the boundaries of established performance-oriented solidarities. As we have seen, inclusion is triggered by processes that shift the existence of a status consistency (between ascriptive and achieved roles) from the state of moral normality to the status of moral anomaly—to quote Parsons, in an instance such as when "it is no longer safe to infer that a person has a working class background from knowing that he is a Catholic of Irish descent" (Parsons 1966c, xxi).

A final significant feature is the rapid spread of such inclusion movements across democratic societies, with the forging of a variety of robust transnational links among the engaged forces. Again, this is consistent with Parsons's emphasis on the existence of a "system" of modern societies.

Thus, many current "multicultural" practices may be described within action theory as "normal" features of advanced and differentiated societal communities. It is likely that Parsons himself would have seen many such claims as evidence for the need of further processes of value generalization as he did with the new forms of religious activity in the 1970s (Parsons 1971b, 1974).[29] It is unlikely, however, that he would have been sympathetic to the kind of conceptual framework often adopted for invoking and comparing multicultural movements and ideologies. It is more likely that he would have reacted very critically to many current conceptual approaches, trying as in many cases before to show that a sophisticated social-science framework built on voluntaristic premises could provide a more adequate understanding of their meaning and a less pessimistic vision of their impact on democratic societies.

From an analytical viewpoint, a major problem with the current debate on multicultural issues refers to the meaning of the term "culture." According to many spokespersons for multicultural policies (as well as many of its opponents and critics), the main justification for their claims is the existence, within the same Western nation-states, of different "societal cultures."[30] The existence of segmental cleavages and difference-based categories, in other words, is linked by many multicultural theorists directly and mechanically to the existence of different cultural groups, said to be kept in line by a set of power relations.[31] Given such a situation, it is implied that the existence of a common membership derived from a unified normative system should be considered as a sort of false consciousness serving the interests and ideology of the dominant groups. If such statements were true, most of the Parsonian notion of societal community would be radically shattered. There are however several reasons for assuming the matter is not so simple.

Empirically, the evidence for the existence of sharply distinguished cultural groups within each Western society is shaky. Once structural variables are controlled for, the variance in values across quality-based cleavages is usually less than the variance within difference-based groups and categories. Most national surveys and comparative studies show the existence in the large majority of each population of variations in a set of common values.[32] As far as Europe is concerned, empirical research has shown that even foreign residents' assertions of interests, claims, and outlook increasingly take shape within the established framework of national political cultures (Koopmans and Statham 2001). Though there are frequent cases of strains and conflicts over the scope, meaning, and implementation of social norms, even the most heated conflicts to seem take place within a network of shared beliefs, and the respective claims are nearly always framed in terms of the same generalized set of values and normative discourses.[33] The contention about such norms is usually grounded in the assertion of a discrepancy between the structural reality and the normative ideals. There is also evidence that civil membership is discernibly being freed from ascriptive bases as far as the definition of citizenship is concerned in the set of liberal states (Joppke and Lukes 1999). The dynamics of multicultural claim making, in other words, can be much better clarified and analyzed within a conceptual framework that distinguishes analytically between values and norms and between norms and factual constellations.

A second, equally important, problem in the current multicultural framework resides in the assumption that claims and conflict are rooted in the existence of distinct groups, each one endowed with its specific cultural forms, practices, and ways of life, its solidarity rooted in a common experience of oppression (Young 1990; Stimpson 1992). Again, the empirical evidence available as evidence of the strength of such features is shaky. No doubt a certain number of members of quality-based categories display particular behavioral propensities and identity markers. When other variables are considered, however, research generally reveals that such behavioral propensities and identity markers are far from being homogeneous within the groups. The available evidence suggests that, when not backed by legal regulation or by forms of exclusionary social control, relationships among members of different categories tend to be multilayered and not consistently congruent across institutional domains. Most of the observed behavioral propensities tend to be limited to specific domains, where subcultural scripts are enacted and exposed according to contextual logics. When "bridging" social capital is available, it is likely that it will be activated in case of need for advancing interests of diverse groups and their members (Lin 2001, 165–83).

Such elements are quite consistent with the view of the societal community as a system of differentiated and segmented networks, where the adoption of different scripts—and the cultural understanding to distinguish where and how certain scripts should be used—is one of the basic competencies of actors. As Parsons himself noted, even ascriptive identities have a voluntary, "contractual" element (Parsons 1975). An emphasis on contextuality and optionality do not presuppose an absence of shared identities, nor the possibility that such identities become a ground for collective action. But neither does this emphasis presuppose (as does the model of the Marxian "Klasse für sich"/"Klasse an sich" [class in itself/class for itself]) that the individual sharing membership in a social category automatically shares also a similar set of experiences and actions. Even less does this emphasis assume that such commonality will inevitably result in similar symbolic constructs and sensibilities. A framework such as that developed by Parsons allows both for situations where such quality-based membership works as an empty symbol (Parsons 1975) and for situations where shared collective experience is elaborated into a collective identity and social movement (Parsons 1966c).

A final frequently made assumption is that quality-based claims are radically different and somewhat antithetical to interest-based solidarities and political action. Recognition of one's status in a community is seen by many as a sharply different goal than redistribution of economic or political resources. A claim is made that community politics is substituting, displacing, or at least gaining greater significance than class politics (Fraser 1995; Martin 1998; Young 1997; Melucci 1996). Yet there is a lack of reliable comparative assessments of the relative frequency and structural significance of the two clusters of inclusion-related types of conflict. Conceptually, however, the distinction between interests and identities, redistribution and recognition, is far from adequate. Many researchers still regard "interests" as derived from socio-structural positions, and easily discernible from subjective, discursively mediated identities. But at closer range, "interests" turns out to be as discursively constructed and culturally mediated as quality-based claims. After all, class conflicts may still produce, and very often do produce, culturally constructed identities. For example, working-class movements in Europe have reacted both to exploitation and to cultural degradation and they have produced in the process new identities, subcultures, and lifestyles (Zincone 1992). Identity claims, on the other hand, are usually developed linking the aspirations for collective recognition with assertions that such recognition is necessary for protecting the material interests of the group (Bell 1975).

Even if it were possible to distinguish sharply between the two kinds of conflicts, however, displacement would still be unlikely to take place. The idea of an earlier societal structure characterized by overarching class-based vertical conflict is a myth. All known societies have operated within a set of vertical *and* horizontal tensions, triggering distributive *and* recognition strains. Nowhere is this more evident than in the development of modern Western society, with the joint and entwined development of classes and nations as main forms of collective power structures, and with their ensuing messy interactions. Neither classes nor nations have in a previous historical era been overdetermining realities. Since their beginning, sectional and segmental actors have coexisted with classes, and local-regional and transnational groupings have coexisted with nations (Mann 1993). In this respect, the Parsonian analyses reconstructed earlier seem to offer a definite advantage for understanding the structure of social contentions and conflicts in contemporary societies. They sensitized researchers to see any social setting as characterized by both redistributional and recognitional strains as well as solidarities. More deeply, Parsons's notion of social stratification is rooted in the idea that redistribution and recognition are not independent fields of social competition, but are reciprocally interacting (Parsons 1984). As we have seen, the upgrading of the criteria for membership toward greater inclusion is a process that Parsons treats as contingent upon both a redistribution of structural resources and a restructuring of prestige criteria.[34] Parsons insists, moreover, on the necessity of treating both performance-based and quality-based solidarities within the same conceptual framework, without giving a conceptual priority to any of these forms.

To summarize, there is room to argue that the conceptual framework developed by Parsons may prove quite useful for understanding the current field of social contentions. Parsons's vision of the emergence of a differentiated system of social solidarity supported by a universalistic definition of membership is a highly fertile ground for developing an adequate and non-nostalgic theory of social solidarity. His theory offers a strong argument in favor of the capacity of contemporary societies to include and accommodate a bewildering array of social identities and diversified lifestyles along with the kinds of institutions more involved in the societal processes relevant to the regulation of the consequences of such shared membership. It conceptualizes relationships of domination and exploitation without assuming that they are the only possible structural realities and processual outcomes. It identifies the claims and conflicts as part of an ongoing process of social negotiation and value generalization.

Such a perspective does not deny that modernity is an incomplete and rather unfinished business, or ignore the endemic presence of structural conflations between access to societal resources and ascriptive privilege. As Parsons himself wrote, "Anything like a "culminating" phase of modern development is a good way off—very likely a century or more. Talk of 'postmodern' society is thus decidedly premature" (Parsons 1971a, 143). The same can be said for a theory of social solidarity: its "culminating phase" is surely a good way off, but many elements of Parsons's legacy can be quite useful as starting points.

NOTES

1. Such a program obviously has to confront an alternative possibility: that the current state of Parsons's notion of the society community is contingent upon some intrinsic conceptual limitations. If this is the case, the effort placed in the proposed theoretical reconstruction would be much better spent starting a new theoretical project or (at best) interpreting reconstruction only as a preliminary step toward such a goal. In his paper published in this volume, Alexander argues precisely and consistently in favor of such an alternative.

   Our two chapters embody quite different strategies and aims. I believe only the future will tell which of the strategies has turned out to be more fertile; here I would like to stress two points. The first is that Alexander and I appear to be in broad agreement on most factual textual points, as well as on the overall intellectual respect in which we hold Parsons's work. The second is that both strategies are equally legitimate: as Parsons himself stressed, "I also take as a tribute . . . that I have not made 'disciples.' A scientific theory is not something one [can] 'subscribe to' but which one uses, develops, tries out, modif[ies]. I hope it is possible to keep the distinction clear between competent understanding of what has been done, which after all is the indispensable basis for good criticism positive or negative, and commitment to doctrines, the latter being inevitably grounded in noncognitive motives" (Parsons 1961b, 349).
2. The societal community "is constituted both as a normative system or order *and* by statuses, rights, and obligations pertaining to membership which may vary for different sub-groups within the community" and "the societal collectivity can act effectively as a unit when required, and so can various of its sub-collectivities" (Parsons 1966a, 10, original emphasis).
3. See the definition of solidarity adopted later in Parsons and Gerald M. Platt (1973, 83–85). In other sections of Parsons's work, this role is apparently entrusted to the "political" subsystem.
4. To my knowledge, the first such attempt may be found in the technical appendix to Parsons (1970/1977, 370).
5. At a certain point Parsons even suggests that contemporary society may also be characterized by a noticeable degree of ethical pluralism (Parsons 1968c).
6. For a contrary opinion, see Stanford Lyman (1972, 169).
7. There is also the need to further develop the same notion of law in this respect. In Parsons's analyses of the societal community, the model he has in mind is clearly the common-law one. It would be interesting to understand how such a model can account for the European "continental" juridical tradition.
8. Parsons has developed this idea in a quite interesting correspondence with Eric Voegelin during World War II. A main topic of their correspondence was the reasons why some European countries had been more able than others to resist the "totalitarian solution" to the rise of anxiety and free-floating aggression caused by modernization processes. Already in such early texts, Parsons focused on the history of previous inclusions as a key variable. The correspondence may be consulted in the Talcott Parsons Papers, Harvard University Archives, box 27, HUG(FP)15.2.
9. The same may be seen in his analysis of influence as the generalized medium of the integrative subsystem. Compare Victor Lidz (1989b).
10. Although the surviving pages are still pretty rudimentary, there is evidence that in writing the manuscript of "American Societal Community," Parsons was also trying to elaborate his treatment of influence as a generalized medium, and analyze the modes of articulation between normative and non-normative aspects of the integration of action systems. Within the same folder in the Talcott Parsons Papers is a section of the manuscript dealing with the institutionalization and operation of solidary communities (chapter 5). The manuscript has many sections dealing with solidarity at the level of the general action system, including an analysis of the loyalty

dimension. It is possible that such an imbalance was acknowledged by Parsons himself. I believe, however, that the criticism developed here also holds true for the analysis contained in the manuscript.

11. Similar, and most likely related, criticisms of other sections of Parsons's works have been made on the basis of his analysis of social interaction (Levine 1980; Habermas 1981), and of his treatment of differentiation processes (Alexander 1990).
12. It is likely that such imbalance is related to the more general idealist tendency identified in Parsons's work by Jeffrey C. Alexander (1983).
13. I read a similar idea in the early nineties in a paper written by Paul Colomy. However, I have been unable to identify the exact reference, locate the text, and verify that the argument was really similar to mine.
14. To cite several examples: "My inclination is to treat [the ethnic group] as a kind of 'fusion' of the community and kinship ties. This would mean that the two have *not yet* come to be clearly differentiated from each other where ethnicity is involved" (Parsons 1975, 62–63, emphasis added) or, "[Kinship] is then articulated with the other principal bases of diffuse solidarity, which include the massive *historic* ones of ethnicity and religion" (Parsons 1970/1977, 332).
15. And we may detect such imbalance even in the analysis of the societal community as a whole, given that issues of variation across segmental categories are often mentioned but seldom placed at the center of inquiry (compare Parsons 1968c, 1971a). Such imbalance may extend as well to the analysis of values and cultural pattern.

    In an earlier attempt to provide an account of U.S. society, Parsons and White prepared a rather long chapter, currently kept among the Parsons Papers in the Harvard University Archives, concerning the "American value system." In their analysis they paid considerable attention to the establishment of variation in terms of endorsement and interpretation of such a system of values across different territorial, ethnic, and religious categories. This analysis, however, seldom entered into discussion of the value system. Both authors were more concerned with issues of institutional differentiation and specialization.
16. None of these listings is meant to be exhaustive.
17. The procedure I advocate is hardly original. It has been previously shown how Parsons's theory of social change may be improved by infusing his evolutionary scheme with the processual, group-specific analyses of social change that Parsons himself had produced in the forties (Alexander 1981).
18. This has also be noted for gender (Johnson 1989).
19. This stance moreover is consistent with Parsons's sustained criticism of any attempt to proceed directly from culture to personality (Parsons 1961a).
20. Since most of the literature describes Parsons as becoming more idealistic with age, it may be worth noting that his interactional view of solidary symbolism is stronger in his later works. For example, in the 1950s Parsons seemed only marginally to accept the idea of a "very general, though perhaps not universal, association between whiteness and purity" that would place dark-skinned people in a peculiarly vulnerable position as scapegoats (Parsons 1945b). In his later criticism of the works of Roger Bastide and Edward Shils, however, Parsons argues forcefully that this "natural" (in other words, psychological) symbolism of color, if it exists, has little explanatory power for the ethnic and racial hierarchies of modern Western societies. He writes, "Although its primordial status makes the color line in some sense 'intrinsic,' this does not determine how it will be interpreted or what consequences it is likely to have for the development of the world system. These problems must be seen in the context of the whole development of Western society in its relations to the rest of the world" (Parsons 1968b, 367). In another context he writes, "Color is a symbol and, if the context of its historic meanings is sufficiently changed, the prospect is that it will cease to be the basis of a stigma" (Parsons 1965, 465).
21. An interesting analysis along these premises may be found in Mark Gould (1997).
22. Parsons has recently been criticized for his theory of modernity, precisely along the line that his theory does not set any intrinsic limit for inclusion and value generalization. According to this argument, Parsons's theory of modernity is basically a denial of the authenticity of cultural values (Nielsen 2001).
23. There is room to argue that such a clear-cut distinction is more problematic than it appears. Parsons may have been unduly bound by the structuralist assumption that structural boundary changes cannot be caused by factors operating at the same level in the hierarchy of control. As matter of fact, it seems plausible that the use of influence may in the long run result in a growing pressure toward structural change. Moreover, the amount of negotiation allowed within a solidary structure may, under social conditions to be further investigated, lead to a renegotiation of the same boundaries. For useful steps in such a direction, see Leon Mayhew (1984) and Victor Lidz (1989b).

24. This connects the analysis of inclusion with issues of cross-cutting influence and structural pluralism.
25. There is a strong conceptual affinity between Parsons's analysis and the argument developed by Donald N. Jacobs (2000) in favor of ethnic news media.
26. A similar argument is developed, along strictly systems-theoretical lines, by Niklas Luhmann (1995).
27. Both searches were performed in November 2002. A similar search conducted in February 2001 showed the existence at the time of 727 books and 198,000 webpages.
28. At least this is true in the United States. A different analysis would apply to Canada and most countries in Western Europe (Sciortino 2005).
29. For a sharp criticism of Parsons precisely for such an open stance, see Jens Nielsen (2001).
30. See, for example, Charles Taylor (1992) and Will Kymlicka (1995). It may be worth stressing that this assumption is formulated in a sharply distinguishable way by the various strands of multiculturalist theorizing. As a matter of fact, Kymlicka openly excluded from this notion nearly all the categories that would be included in it within the U.S. debate. In the same vein, most of the Western European debates are centered on religious pluralism, an issue conspicuously absent in the U.S. debate.
31. For an analysis along this line, see the collection of papers edited by Cynthia Willett (1998). In a decidedly different context, Charles Camic (1989) has cited the existence of widely divergent subcultures that are rarely reconciled through higher values as empirical disproof of Parsons's assumptions about the significance of common values as determinants of order within society. There are theoretical grounds to claim that Camic's assertion is wrong, as it applies an empirical statement to an analytical argument over the consequences for social order of the presence (and degree) of a system of common values. However, it may also be argued, as it will be done here, that there is much empirical evidence about the existence in modern Western societies of a remarkable degree of subscription to the same *values* system.
32. We follow Parsons here in defining social values as normative conceptions of desirable social states, not necessarily of the desired ones.
33. A set of interesting analyses along these lines may be found in the collection edited by Neil Smelser and Alexander (1999).
34. On these bases, Parsons stressed how the civil rights movement could be considered the "American style 'socialist' movement" (Parsons 1966a, 740).

REFERENCES

Alexander, Jeffrey C. 1981. "Revolution, Reaction and Reform: The Change Theory of Parsons's Middle Period." *Sociological Inquiry* 51: 267–80.

———. 1983. *The Modern Reconstruction of Classical Thought: Talcott Parsons.* Berkeley: University of California Press.

———. 1990. "Core Solidarity, Ethnic Outgroups and Structural Differentiation: Toward a Multidimensional Model of Inclusion in Modern Societies." In *Differentiation Theory and Social Change,* edited by Jeffrey C. Alexander and Paul Colomy. Los Angeles: Sage.

———. 1998. "Citizen and Enemy as Symbolic Classification." In *Real Civil Societies,* edited by Jeffrey C. Alexander. New York: Sage.

———. 2001. "Theorizing the 'Modes of Incorporation': Assimilation, Hyphenation and Multiculturalism As Varieties of Civil Participation." *Sociological Theory* 19(3): 237–49.

Anderson, Benedict. 1983. *Imagined Communities: Reflections on the Origins and Spread of Nationalism.* London: Verso.

Baum, Rainer C. 1975. "The System of Solidarities." *Indian Journal of Social Research* 16(1–2): 306–53.

Bell, Daniel. 1975. "Ethnicity and Social Change." In *Ethnicity: Theory and Experience,* edited by Nathan Glazer. Cambridge, Mass.: Harvard University Press.

Bortolini, Matteo. 1999. "Inclusione politica, inclusione sociale: La democrazia come differenziazione in Talcott Parsons." *Sociologia e Politiche Sociali* 2(3): 93–116.

———. 2002. "I limiti della pluralità: Categorie della politica in Talcott Parsons." *Quaderni di teoria sociale* 2(1): 33–60.

Burt, Robert. 1992. *Structural Holes.* Cambridge, Mass.: Harvard University Press.

Camic, Charles. 1989. "Structure After 50 Years: The Anatomy of a Charter." *American Journal of Sociology* 95(1): 38–107.

Fraser, Nancy. 1995. “From Redistribution to Recognition? Dilemma of Justice in a ‘Post-Socialist’ Age.” *New Left Review* (212, July/August): 68–93.

Gerhardt, Uta. 2001. “Parsons’ Analysis of the Societal Community.” In *Talcott Parsons Today,* edited by A. Javier Treviño. Lanham, Md.: Rowman & Littlefield.

Glazer, Nathan. 1997. *We Are All Multiculturalist Now.* Cambridge, Mass.: Harvard University Press.

Gould, Mark. 1992. “The New Racism in United States Society.” *The Dynamics of Social Systems,* edited by Paul Colomy. Newbury Park, Calif.: Sage.

———. 1997. “Race and Politics: Normative Orders and the Explanation of Political Difference.” *Social Identities* 3(1): 33–46.

———. 2001. “The Generalized Media of Communication and the Logic of Cultural Intelligibility: Micro and Macro Analyses in Luhmann, Habermas and Parsons.” In *Parsons: The Structure of Social Action and Contemporary Debates,* edited by Gabriele Pollini and Giuseppe Sciortino. Milan: FrancoAngeli.

Gouldner, Alvin W. 1970. *The Coming Crisis of Western Sociology.* New York: Basic Books.

Gouldsblom, John. 1987. “The Sociology of Norbert Elias.” *Theory, Culture and Society* 4(2): 323–38.

Granovetter, Mark. 1979. “The Idea of ‘Advancement’ in Theories of Social Evolution and Development.” *American Journal of Sociology* 85(3): 489–515.

Habermas, Jürgen. 1981. “Talcott Parsons: Problems of Theory Construction.” *Sociological Inquiry* 51(3): 173–96.

———. 1990/1998. *Between Facts and Norms.* Cambridge, Mass.: MIT Press.

Holton, Robert J., and Bryan S. Turner. 1986. *Talcott Parsons on Economy and Society.* London: Routledge.

Jacobs, Donald N. 2000. *Race, Media and the Crisis of Civil Society: From Watts to Rodney King.* Cambridge: Cambridge University Press.

Johnson, Miriam. 1989. “Feminism and the Theories of Talcott Parsons.” In *Feminism and Social Thought,* edited by Ruth Wallace. Newbury Park, Calif.: Sage.

Joppke, Christian, and Stephen Lukes. 1999. *Multicultural Questions.* Oxford: Oxford University Press.

Kivisto, Peter. 2004 “Inclusion: Parsons and Beyond.” *Acta Sociologica* 47(3): 291–97.

Koopmans, Ruud, and Paul Statham. 2001. “How National Citizenship Shapes Transnationalism: A Comparative Analysis of Migrant Claim-Making in Germany, Great Britain and the Netherlands.” *Revue européenne des migrations internationales* 17(2): 63–100.

Kymlicka, Will. 1995. *Multicultural Citizenship.* Oxford: Oxford University Press.

Levine, Donald N. 1980. *Simmel and Parsons: Two Approaches to the Study of Society.* New York: Arno Press.

Lidz, Victor. 1979. “The Law as Index, Phenomenon and Element—Conceptual Steps Toward a General Sociology of Law.” *Sociological Inquiry* 49(1): 5–25.

———. 1989a. “The American Values System: A Commentary on Talcott Parsons’s Perspective and Understanding.” *Theory, Culture and Society* 6(4): 559–75.

———. 1989b. “Influence et solidarité, définir un fondement théoretique à la sociologie.” *Sociologie et sociétés* 21(1): 117–42.

Lin, Nan. 2001. *Social Capital: A Theory of Social Structure and Action.* Cambridge: Cambridge University Press.

Luhmann, Niklas 1984. *Soziale Systeme: Grundriss einer allgemeinen Theorie.* Frankfurt am Main: Suhrkamp Verlag.

———. 1995. “Inklusion und Exclusion.” *Soziologische Aufklärung.* Volume 6. Opladen: Westdeutscher Verlag.

Lyman, Stanford M. 1972. *The Black American in Sociological Thought.* New York: Capricorn.

Mann, Michael. 1993. *The Sources of Social Power II: The Rise of Classes and Nation-States, 1760–1914.* Cambridge: Cambridge University Press.

Martin, Bill. 1998. “Multiculturalism: Consumerist or Transformational?” In *Theorizing Multiculturalism. A Guide to the Current Debate,* edited by Cynthia Willett. Malden, Mass.: Blackwell.

Mayhew, Leon. 1968. “Ascription in Modern Society.” *Sociological Inquiry* 38(2): 105–20.

———. 1971. *Society—Institutions and Activity.* Glenview, Ill.: Scott, Foresman.

———. 1984. “In Defence of Modernity: Talcott Parsons and the Utilitarian Tradition.” *American Journal of Sociology* 89(6): 1273–1305.

———. 1990. “The Differentiation of the Solidary Public.” In *Differentiation Theory and Social Change,* edited by Jeffrey C. Alexander and Paul Colomy. New York: Columbia University Press.

———. 1997. *The New Public: Professional Communication and the Means of Social Influence.* Cambridge: Cambridge University Press.

Melucci, Alberto. 1996. *Challenging Codes: Collective Action in the Information Age.* Cambridge: Cambridge University Press.

Münch, Richard. 1999. "The Problem of Social Order, Sixty Years After *The Structure of Social Action.*" In *Agenda for Sociology,* edited by Bernard Barber and Uta Gerhardt. Baden-Baden, Germany: Nomos.

Nielsen, Jens. 2001. "Are There Cultural Limits to Inclusion?" In *Parsons: The Structure of Social Action and Contemporary Debates,* edited by Gabriele Pollini and Giuseppe Sciortino. Milan: FrancoAngeli.

Parsons, Talcott. 1942a. "Review of 'The Integration of American Society,' by R. C. Angell." *American Journal of Sociology* 48(2): 251–54.

———. 1942b. "The Sociology of Modern Antisemitism." In *Jews in a Gentile World,* edited by Isaac Graeber and Stuart Henderson Britt. New York: Macmillan.

———. 1942c. "Some Sociological Aspects of the Fascist Movements." *Social Forces* 21(2): 138–47.

———. 1945a. "The Problem of Controlled Institutional Change." *Psychiatry* 8(1): 79–101.

———. 1945b. "Racial and Religious Differences as Factors in Group Tensions." In *Approaches to National Unity,* edited by Louis Bryson. New York: Conference on Science, Technology and Religion in their Contribution to the Democratic Way of Life, Inc.

———. 1946. "Certain Primary Sources and Patterns of Aggression in the Social Structure of the Western World." *Psychiatry* 10: 167–81.

———. 1958. "The Pattern of Religious Organization in the United States." *Daedalus* 87(3): 65–85.

———. 1959. " 'Voting' and the Equilibrium of the American Political System." In *American Voting Behavior,* edited by Eugene Burdick and Arthur Brodbeck. New York: Free Press.

———. 1960. "Durkheim's Contribution to the Theory of Integration of Social Systems." In *Emile Durkheim, 1858–1917,* edited by Kurt H. Wolff. Columbus: Ohio State University Press.

———. 1961a. "An Outline of the Social System." In *Theories of Societies,* edited by Talcott Parsons, Edward Shils, Kaspar D. Naegele, and Jesse R. Pitts. New York: Free Press.

———. 1961b. "The Point of View of the Author." In *The Social Theories of Talcott Parsons,* edited by Max Black. Englewood Cliffs, N.J.: Prentice-Hall.

———. 1962. "The Cultural Background of American Religious Associations." In *Ethics and Bigness,* edited by Harold Cleveland and Harold. D. Lasswell. New York: Conference on Science, Technology and Religion in their Contribution to the Democratic Way of Life, Inc.

———. 1963a. "On the Concept of Influence." *Public Opinion Quarterly* 27(1): 232–62.

———. 1963b. "Rejoinder to Bauer and Coleman." *Public Opinion Quarterly* 27(1): 83–92.

———. 1964. "Communism and the West: The Sociology of Conflict." In *Social Change,* edited by Amitai Etzioni. New York: Basic Books.

———. 1965. "Full Citizenship for the Negro American? A Sociological Problem." *Daedalus* 94(4): 1009–54.

———. 1966a. *Societies: Evolutionary and Comparative Perspectives.* Englewood Cliffs, N.J.: Prentice-Hall.

———. 1966b. "Religion in a Modern Pluralistic Society." *Review of Religion Research* 7(1): 125–46.

———. 1966c. "Why 'Freedom Now,' Not Yesterday?" In *The Negro American,* edited by Talcott Parsons and Kenneth B. Clark. Boston: Beacon Press.

———. 1967. "The Nature of American Pluralism." In *Religion and Public Education,* edited by Theodore R. Sizer. Boston: Houghton Mifflin.

———. 1968a. "Interaction: Social Interaction." In *International Encyclopedia of the Social Sciences,* edited by David L. Sills. Volume 7. New York: Free Press.

———. 1968b. "The Problem of Polarization on the Axis of Color." In *Color and Race,* edited by John H. Franklin. Boston: Houghton Mifflin.

———. 1960/1968c. "Social Systems." In *International Encyclopedia of the Social Sciences,* edited by David L. Sills. Volume 15. New York: Free Press.

———. 1969. *Politics and Social Structure.* New York: Free Press.

———. 1971a. *The System of Modern Societies.* Englewood Cliffs, N.J.: Prentice-Hall.

———. 1971b. "Belief, Unbelief and Disbelief." In *The Culture of Unbelief,* edited by Rocco Caporale and Antonio Grumelli. Berkeley: University of California Press.

———. 1971c. "Comparative Studies and Evolutionary Change." In *Comparative Methods in Sociology,* edited by Ivan Vallier. Berkeley: University of California Press.

———. 1971d. "Kinship and the Associational Aspects of Social Structure." In *Kinship and Culture,* edited by Frank L. Hsu. Chicago: Aldine de Gruyter.

———. 1974. "Religion in Postindustrial America: The Problem of Secularization." *Social Research* 41(2): 193–225.

———. 1975. "Some Theoretical Considerations on the Nature and Trends of Change of Ethnicity." In *Ethnicity. Theory and Experience,* edited by Nathan Glazer. Cambridge, Mass.: Harvard University Press.

———. 1976. Afterword to *The Social Theories of Talcott Parsons,* edited by Max Black. London: Feffer & Simons.

———. 1970/1977. "Equality and Inequality in Modern Society, or Social Stratification Revisited." In *Social System and the Evolution of Action Theory,* by Talcott Parsons. New York: Free Press.

———. 1979a. "The American Societal Community." Talcott Parsons Papers, Harvard University Archives, HUG(FP)42.45.2.

———. 1979b. "Chapter 8. The American Polity." *Parsons Papers.* Harvard University Archives. HUG (FP) 42.45.2.

———. 1980. "Postscript to 'A Sociology of Modern Antisemitism.' " *Contemporary Jewry* 5(1): 31–38.

———. 1984. "Stratificazioni sociali." In *Enciclopedia del novecento.* Volume 7. Rome: Istituto dell'enciclopedia Italiana.

———. 1994. "The Unpublished Section of 'Some Theoretical Considerations on the Nature and Trends of Ethnicity.' " *Comunità Societaria e Pluralismo: Le differenze etniche e religiose nel complesso della cittadinanza.* Milan: FrancoAngeli.

Parsons, Talcott, and Gerald M. Platt. 1973. *The American University.* Cambridge, Mass.: Harvard University Press.

Parsons, Talcott, and Winston White. 1960/1969. "The Mass Media and the Structure of American Societies." *Politics and Social Structure,* by Talcott Parsons. New York: Free Press.

Putnam, Robert D. 2000. *Bowling Alone.* New York: Simon & Schuster.

Sciortino, Giuseppe. 1994. "Introduzione." In *Comunità societaria e pluralismo: Le differenze etniche e religiose nel complesso della cittadinanza,* by Talcott Parsons. Milan: FrancoAngeli.

———. 1999. " 'Just Before the Fall': The Northern League and the Cultural Construction of a Secessionist Claim." *International Sociology* 14(3): 321–36.

———. 2003. "From Homogeneity to Difference? Comparing Multiculturalism as a Description and as a Field for Claim-Making." *Comparative Social Research* 22: 263–85.

———. 2005. "Toward a Structural Theory of Social Pluralism: Talcott Parsons, Ethnicity and Ascriptive Inequalities." In *Action Theory: Methodological Studies,* edited by Helmut Staubmann. Berlin: LIT-Verlag.

Smelser, Neil J., and Jeffrey C. Alexander. 1999. *Diversity and Its Discontents.* Princeton: Princeton University Press.

Stimpson, Catharine R. 1992. "On Differences: Modern Language Association Presidential Address." In *Debating P.C.: The Controversy over Political Correctness on College Campuses,* edited by Paul A. Berman. New York: Delly.

Taylor, Charles. 1992. *Multiculturalism and "the Politics of Recognition."* Princeton: Princeton University Press.

Willett, Cynthia, ed. 1998. *Theorizing Multiculturalism: A Guide to the Current Debate.* Malden, Mass.: Blackwell.

Young, Iris M. 1990. *Justice and the Politics of Difference.* Princeton: Princeton University Press.

———. 1997. "Unruly Categories: A Critique of Nancy Fraser's Dual System Theory." *New Left Review* (222, March/April): 147–60.

Zincone, Giovanna. 1992. *Da sudditi a cittadini.* Bologna: Il Mulino.

Chapter 7

God, Nation, and Self in America: Some Tensions Between Parsons and Bellah

Robert N. Bellah

Talcott Parsons had a lifelong interest in American society, an interest that was both professional and personal. I, too, have spent much of my life studying American society, though I did not originally intend to do so, and my motivation was as much that of a citizen as a sociologist. In this chapter I can give adequate treatment neither to Parsons's view of American society nor to my own. Rather, I will discuss some key points of intersection and some divergences in our views that developed over time. Under the influence of my undergraduate Marxism, I had a quite critical view of American society and foreign policy, but in my graduate years (1950 to 1955), as I studied with Parsons and read much of his work, I developed a more nuanced view, learning to appreciate many of the achievements of our society, though still believing, as Parsons did, that American society fell short of its ideals.

My year as a Fulbright scholar in Japan (1960 to 1961) gave me critical distance from my own society and an opportunity for close observation of a very different one. Much as I admired Japanese culture, American society never appeared more attractive to me than during that year abroad.[1] It was during that year that I developed in a talk for Japanese audiences the first sketch of what would later become my essay "Civil Religion in America." My positive evaluation of American society continued after my return home and reached its high point with the passage of the civil rights legislation under President Lyndon Johnson in 1964.

At the very moment when I felt proudest of my country, however, the United States embarked on a war in Vietnam, the legitimacy of which became increasingly doubtful in my eyes. It was in this situation that I wrote my essay "Civil Religion in America" (Bellah 1967); Parsons had urged me to write a paper for a *Daedalus* conference on religion in America preparatory to a subsequent issue of the magazine. I had not wanted to participate because I did not feel I knew enough about America. I was, after all, a Japan specialist; but Talcott assured me that a sociologist can write on anything. The germ of what I had to say had already been expressed in my Fulbright lectures in the spring of 1961, soon after the inaugural address of John F. Kennedy, which plays a significant role in that essay. In its initial form it was not an effort to speak to an American audience, but to explain to the Japanese, who had been so sternly lectured to by the occupation on the critical importance of the separation of church and state, why no American president could be inaugurated without mentioning God in his inaugural address. In preparing my *Daedalus* paper, I developed this basic idea in the context of national controversy over involvement in the Vietnam War, and I saw it as an opportunity to use central elements in the American tradition to criticize our military policy at that time. Parsons, who also opposed the

Vietnam War, greatly appreciated my paper, especially when I gave a version of it as a lecture in the course on the sociology of religion that we jointly taught.

In ways neither Talcott nor I expected, the publication of that essay changed my life. The many invitations to speak and write on related subjects that the *Daedalus* article stimulated, and my feeling that turning them down in a period of national crisis would not be responsible, led me to an intensive period of self-education in American studies, as I had no serious scholarly preparation for what was to come. I had made significant progress by the time I was asked to give the Weil Lectures at Hebrew Union College–Jewish Institute of Religion in Cincinnati in the fall of 1971. Published in 1975 as *The Broken Covenant,* it was my most substantial effort to describe what I meant by civil religion in America (Bellah 1975/1992). I argued that the American civil religion was not a competitor to church religion, which it never challenged, but operated at a different level. My focus was on the nation religiously conceived and was marginally, if at all, on the church.

Nonetheless I did argue that the Protestant Reformation was the single most significant archetype underlying American self-understanding, particularly in the colonial and revolutionary periods. I argued for a deep analogy between the Protestant idea of conversion as liberation from the bondage of sin, followed by covenant as the institutional expression of the social life of the converted and revolution as liberation from the bondage of political oppression, followed by constitution as the institutional expression of the social life of the liberated. That is, as conversion was to covenant for the New England colonists, so revolution was to constitution for the new nation. Although I didn't put it that way, I was clearly arguing that the nation, if not replacing the church, was modeled on the (Protestant) church at its deepest level of self-understanding. G. K. Chesterton made this point when he spoke of the United States as "a nation with the soul of a church." The ominous side of this analogy was not overlooked in the book; indeed, it was expressed in the book's very title, *The Broken Covenant.* Chapter 2, "America as a Chosen People," pointed to the fact that Americans were long able to overlook two primal crimes that haunted our country from the beginning, the genocide of the American Indians and the enslavement of Africans, by assuring themselves that they were a chosen people.

The danger inherent in the idea of a messiah nation unleavened by the strong consciousness of divine judgment (as that judgment was expressed in, for example, Lincoln's second inaugural address) was indeed the central message of the book. Parsons's reaction to *The Broken Covenant* was, to say the least, ambivalent. Without rejecting my analysis altogether, he nonetheless felt the book was far too critical. It was one thing to oppose the Vietnam War; it was quite another to argue that the American project was deeply flawed from the very beginning. Quite aside from how critical of the United States the book was, as I look back on it now I find it still far too close to Parsons's own view of American society, a view from which I have moved ever further over the passing years.

Parsons's analysis of American society is complex and is spelled out in many publications. Here I cannot do more than offer a highly abbreviated version of it.[2] I want to focus on two key terms that express the essence of American values in Parsons's mind: "instrumental activism" and "institutionalized individualism." Parsons and Platt explicate (1973, 41) instrumental activism as follows:

> The society as a system tends to be evaluated, not as an end in itself but as *instrumental* to bases of value outside itself. Its desirability is to be judged in terms of its contribution to these *extra*societal grounds of value. The value orientation is *activistic* in the sense that, in the relation between the society and its environments, what is valued is not passive adjustment to the exigencies of the environment but increasing the sphere of freedom of action within the environment and ultimately control over the environment. (original emphasis)

Parsons goes on to say that the activist component of this value system could have come to focus on societal goals, but that the instrumental component, with its stress on extrasocietal references, led to a focus on the goals of groups and individuals within society rather than on those of the society as a whole as the focus of activist achievement. The tendency toward individualism was not, however, atomistic but took place within a strong normative framework, so that Parsons, following Émile Durkheim, came to speak of *institutionalized individualism.* The freedom and dignity of individuals was emphasized, but at the same time their obligation to contribute to the "welfare and values of the society" and standards of justice in the "treatment, rewards, and access to facilities of different individuals and subgroups" were also emphasized (Parsons and Platt 1973, 42).

Parsons saw Protestant Christianity as the primary source of this value system, particularly in its Puritan version. Max Weber's notion of "this-worldly asceticism" as characteristic of Calvinist Protestantism lay very much at the base of Parsons's idea of instrumental activism. And the Protestant emphasis on the direct relation between the individual and God, unmediated by sacrament or church, lay behind the idea of institutionalized individualism.[3] Even though Parsons insisted that American Protestants had left behind the collectivist tendencies of early Calvinism, he did not entirely abandon the idea that a collective purpose continued to be significant, even if individual purposes increasingly took precedence. In several places he speaks of the importance for American Protestants of "building the Kingdom" and the creation of a "holy community" (Parsons 1963/1967, 405, 412; 1968/1978, 202.) In one place he connects the building of the holy community with the development of American nationalism (1968/1978, 203) and elsewhere he connects the Reformation with "the emergence of national communities" (1977, chapter 7). Although Parsons connects Protestantism as a religion with nationalism as an ideology (or a quasi-religion, as implied by "civil religion") and what Durkheim called "the cult of the individual," he never to my knowledge does so systematically and chronologically. I will attempt such a connection briefly below, but first I would like to take a fresh look at the contributions of Protestantism to modern culture.

Among the many contributions of Protestantism, I have only learned recently of the relation of Protestantism and environmentalism. David Vogel, professor of business and political science at Berkeley (who has no intellectual connections to either Parsons or to me), in a paper entitled "The Protestant Ethic and the Spirit of Environmentalism" (2002) has looked at the twenty-one richest nations in today's world. The purpose of his study was to understand why, although all rich nations have embraced the cause of environmentalism, some have done so much more enthusiastically than others. He divides the twenty-one nations into two groups, of which he denominates eleven as light green, concerned mainly with the quality of air and water that directly affect their population, and ten as dark green, concerned with the whole ecosphere: endangered species, rain forests, ozone holes, and all the rest.

Vogel found that all but one of the ten dark-green countries (the exception is Austria) are of Protestant heritage and none of the eleven light-green countries are. The latter include six Catholic countries, one Greek Orthodox country (Greece), one Jewish country (Israel), and three Confucian and Buddhist countries (Japan, Korea, and Taiwan). But the correlations don't stop there. Vogel found that the Protestant countries, in comparison to the non-Protestant countries, are the richest (Japan is an exception here), have been rich the longest, are the most modern and have been modern the longest, are the most democratic and have been democratic the longest, and have the most vibrant civic cultures. Vogel has discovered a range of correlations with Protestantism that would probably have surprised Weber, though perhaps not Parsons, who believed that central value systems often derive from religious roots.[4]

According to Vogel, it is important not to confuse a Protestant-heritage country with a Protestant country. He argues that historically Protestant culture overrides religious pluralism:

"For the purpose of my analysis *all* Americans are Protestants regardless of what particular religion they do or do not practice, just as are all Germans" (2002, 312). Vogel seems to be confirming G. K. Chesterton's famous remark that "in America, even the Catholics are Protestants."

The relation between Protestantism and dark-green ideology is not simple: Vogel found that the religious group least concerned with the environment in America today is Evangelical Protestants, from whose tradition he argues, such ideology derives. Evangelical Protestants are more likely to evince an older Protestant mastery-over-nature orientation. How then does Vogel explain the correlation of Protestantism and dark-green environmentalism? He does so in two ways. Following the historian Donald Worster he shows that the origin of modern American environmentalism was in Evangelical Christianity. Worster has a fine essay on John Muir tracing his development from fervent Evangelical Protestant to pantheistic environmentalist. But even more important to Vogel's point is the structural continuity even when explicit religious connection is disavowed. He asserts (2002, 315): "Contemporary dark green environmentalism should be understood as a secularized version of Protestantism. Without necessarily making or acknowledging any explicit connection to religious beliefs or practices, it draws on the rhetoric and imagery of Protestantism." Vogel points to several structural similarities:

> First, both dark green environmentalists and Protestants share a deeply pessimistic view of the world, one in which man is wicked and has committed multiple sins. For Protestants, the sins are against God, for environmentalists they are against nature. For the former, the "wages" of this sin are eternal damnation; for the latter it is the impending destruction of the eco-sphere. Both share an essentially apocalyptic vision. Thus if we continue in our present behaviors and values we are doomed. It is only by radically changing our ways—which include both our behaviors and our values—that we can possibly be "saved." The notion of Calvin and other Protestant reformers that we live in a depraved world filled with sinners bent on their own destruction echoes in much contemporary "dark green" environmental rhetoric.

Second, Vogel notes the common importance of asceticism, expressed by the environmentalists in a concern for recycling, walking rather than driving, and so forth. Third is moralism: Both Protestants and environmentalists are quick to make strong moral judgments. "By contrast," he writes, "in non-Protestant cultures citizens talk about the environment less, and in less moralistic terms." Fourth, he argues, Protestantism has a strong sense of personal moral responsibility, so that each individual bears some responsibility for the fate of the world. Fifth, he notes, Protestantism is a "relatively egalitarian religion." This is a feature that links Protestantism to democracy. What the environmentalists do is extend the concept of the rights of man to include the rights of nature. "If people are equal in God's eyes, then so are natural objects such as whales, trees, animals, and rivers." Finally, Vogel argues, precisely because Protestantism has a weakened sense of liturgy and sacramentalism it is open to an aesthetic appreciation of nature. Indeed it is largely on Protestant soil that Romanticism as an aesthetic movement evolved. Environmentalism clearly has inherited the nature mysticism that Protestants have been prone to (2002, 317–18).

Ironically, Protestantism and environmentalism are also connected by sharing an ethic of mastery, the very ethic that, Vogel says, "has been associated with the subjugation of nature." But environmentalism gives the notion of mastery a new twist. As Vogel puts it, "If one believes that control or mastery of the world is possible, one can just as readily choose to save or restore nature as dominate or exploit it. In any event, it is people who are ultimately responsible for what happens to nature" (2002, 320).

To sum up what I think the connection is between Protestantism and cultural values, let me quote Donald Worster (1993, 200): "Protestantism, like any religion, lays its hold on people's imagination in diverse, contradictory ways and that hold can be tenacious long after the explicit theology or doctrine has gone dead. Surely it cannot be surprising that in a culture deeply rooted in Protestantism, we should find ourselves speaking its language, expressing its temperament, even when we thought we were free of all that."

Vogel has done two things with which Parsons would have agreed: he has seen Protestantism as the ultimate cultural source of many positive things in our society, and he has shown that the cultural influence of religion can continue independently of the religious impulse itself. Nonetheless, I would argue that the cultural consequences of Protestantism are by no means all benevolent and that the changing forms in which Protestant culture has expressed itself in the United States have more than a few troubling aspects.

Andrew Delbanco, in *The Real American Dream* (1999), vividly describes how our fundamental cultural premises have varied over time. Delbanco organizes this small book into three chapters entitled "God," "Nation," and "Self." These he sees, using Emersonian terminology, as "predominant ideas" by means of which Americans have successively organized their culture and their society, providing a context of meaning that can bring hope and stave off melancholy. In speaking of God as the predominant idea that first organized our culture Delbanco is thinking primarily of the New England Puritans of the seventeenth and eighteenth centuries. Nation became the predominant idea from the time of the Revolutionary War until well into the twentieth century. Most recently, Self seems to have replaced, or if not replaced, subordinated, God and Nation as the predominant idea of our culture. Delbanco does not argue for strict chronological epochs, seeing many overlaps, but I would argue that all three ideas were present at the very beginning, and that, although changing in degree of dominance ever since, some of our deepest problems arise from the form of Protestant Christianity which first put its stamp on colonial culture.[5]

Certainly the Puritans were focused on God; indeed they were God-obsessed. But from the beginning both nation and self were significant subtexts. If one takes even so great a document as John Winthrop's 1630 sermon "A Model of Christian Charity," which was preached on board the *Arbella* in Salem harbor just before the Puritans stepped ashore, we find a fusion of church and nation that leads Winthrop to a conscious identification of the Massachusetts Bay Colony with ancient Israel. If Winthrop took Moses' farewell sermon (Deuteronomy 30) as his basic text, he had copious New Testament allusions to strengthen his case, perhaps the most famous (notorious?) of which is the metaphor in Matthew 5:14 of a city on a hill: "We shall be as a City upon a Hill; the eyes of all people are upon us." It took Ronald Reagan to embellish the city with the adjective "shining," found neither in Matthew nor in Winthrop, but suggestive of the long-lasting tendency to identify the United States with the City of God, a tendency to which Parsons did not entirely succumb but by which he was sorely tempted.

It has often been pointed out that the Protestant Reformation paved the way for modern nationalism by breaking the hold of the international church and replacing it with state churches instead. "The glory of God was replaced by the glory of the nation; by a curious dialectic the Reformation paved the way for this development" (Ramirez and Boli 1987, 194). But the American case was extreme in fusing the glory of God with the glory of the nation in a sense of millennial hopes fulfilled: America as redeemer nation for all the world. A sense of the judgment of God hanging over the nation was evident in the closing lines of Winthrop's sermon where he warned that we will "perish out of this good land" if we do not obey God's commandments. A sense of God's judgment was very evident in Lincoln's second inaugural address, in which he attributed the sufferings caused by the Civil War to the judgment of God against slavery and quotes Psalm 19:9: "The judgments of the Lord, are true and righteous altogether." But, as Roger Williams pointed out in criticism of the views of Winthrop, the basic problem came not from the absence of a sense of judgment (though that would be an often realized temptation), but from the confusion of the nation with the communion of the saints. For Williams the error was to confuse "a *people,* naturally considered," with the millennial ark of Christ, which as a result would be "to pull *God* and *Christ* and *Spirit* out of Heaven, and subject them unto *naturall,* sinful, inconstant men" (Bercovitch 1975, 110). Although Williams had a very problematic view of the church, still he knew it could not be identified with a nation. For Lincoln, as far as we know, the church had lost all significance. It was only the nation that had to bear, unworthy though it was, the burden of the great mission.

The Protestant temptation to confuse church and nation was linked to the very same conception of the church that would open the door to the confusion of God and self. On the face of it nothing could be further from the Puritan mind. The conquest of the self so as to make oneself transparent to God lay at the center of Puritan piety. And yet the very focus on the individual struggle, was, as Sacvan Bercovitch points out in *The Puritan Origins of the American Self* (1975, 20), finally a form of self-assertion:

> . . . the individual affirming his identity by turning against his power of self-affirmation. But to affirm and to turn against are both aspects of self-involvement. We can see in retrospect how the very intensity of that self-involvement—mobilizing as it did the resources of the ego in what amounted to an internal Armageddon—had to break loose into the world at large.

Just as Lincoln represents a critical step toward a nation that has replaced the church, so Emerson represents a critical step toward a self that has replaced the church, one ratified by William James in his *Varieties of Religious Experience,* which is Puritan in its fascination with individual religious experience and yet is not only free from but inimical to any "institutional form" that that religious experience might take. James divides religion into two "branches," the personal and the institutional. He chooses to focus entirely on personal religion, leaving institutional religion aside, for, as he said (James 1987, 34–35), it lives "at second hand upon tradition."[6] Yet in this case, too, the Puritans foreshadowed later developments. Delbanco quotes John Cotton in the seventeenth century as saying: "If . . . the Papists aske, where was the Church visible, before *Luther?* The answer is, it was visible, not in open Congregations . . . but in sundry members of the church" (1999, 27)—that is, individual members who were persecuted by the church in their day.

When John Donne said in a sermon that every believer "hath *a Church* in himself" (Bercovitch 1975, 11) he was certainly not speaking of the natural self but of the converted self. Yet the locus of the church in the individual, with the church as an association only coming into existence through the voluntary action of the already converted, was the very notion that opened the door to the elevation not only of the self but also of the nation to transcendent status. With respect to the fatal notion that the church consists only of the already converted, Roger Williams was if anything even more extreme than John Winthrop, however right he was to reject the conflation of church and nation.

Delbanco sums up his story about the United States in a paragraph near the end of his book (1999, 103):

> The history of hope I have tried to sketch in this book is one of diminution. At first, the self expanded toward (and was sometimes overwhelmed by) the vastness of God. From the early republic to the Great Society, it remained implicated in a national ideal lesser than God but larger and more enduring than any individual citizen. Today, hope has narrowed to the vanishing point of the self alone.

Taking Delbanco's argument as a starting point but moving beyond it, my argument is that the entire story of declension is present in germ, so to speak, in the very form of Protestant Christianity practiced by the first colonists.[7] A critique of the fundamental premises of American society and culture, then, would require not only a critique of ontological individualism and its strange complementarity with the confusion of God and nation, but a critique of the Protestant Reformation itself, at least in its most influential American forms. Such a critique would show that the United States is not the City of God that it claims to be, but only another tired version of the city of man, with all the Augustinian horrors that implies. The great Protestant mistake, one into which also some Catholics have at times fallen, was to confuse religion and nation, to imagine that America had become a realized eschatology. Our participation in the great wars of the twentieth century only confirmed our sense of ourselves as beyond history, uniquely chosen in the world to defend the children of light against the children of darkness. The long twilight struggle of the cold war allowed us to continue in that illusion. For a while in the 1990s, after the fall of the "evil empire," it seemed that we had no mission, no enemy, and no anti-Christ to combat, and that the Protestant individualism that is responsible for so much of the best in our society had left us with almost nothing to hold us together. If what Parsons called the societal community, which he believed provided the institutional context for institutionalized individualism, was essentially the same as what later came to be called civil society, then there was indeed much to worry about, for every aspect of civil society was suffering serious decline, according to Robert Putnam's influential book *Bowling Alone* (2000).

Then came September 11, 2001, a great national catastrophe that appeared to provide us with the enemy and the mission that we had lost with the fall of Communism. September 11 was indeed followed by a strong reassertion of national identity, as the nearly universal display of the flag indicated, but even when the war on terrorism became a war with Iraq (which continues as this chapter is being written), there does not seem to be a significant revival of the societal community or civil society: polls continue to indicate that most Americans believe the nation is headed in the wrong direction. While the catastrophe of 9/11 has led us to an unprecedented assertion of American power of global magnitude, as evidenced in George Bush's *The National Security Strategy of the United States of America,* issued on September 20, 2002, there remain doubts as to whether our ascetic Protestant heritage prepares us adequately for what amounts to managing a global empire.

For many purposes—for example, David Vogel's treatment of the relation between Protestantism and environmentalism—one can treat Protestantism as an undifferentiated tradition. Nonetheless, as Ernst Troeltsch noted, the tradition of an established church survived in some Protestant groups, and within these groups the inherent tendencies of the Reformation were mitigated, at least for a while. It is significant that it was these church Protestant traditions, mainly the Presbyterian and Episcopal churches, from which until recent decades the American elite was largely drawn. The dissenting traditions, mainly Baptists and Methodists, who from early in our history became a numerical majority, were the groups within which the inherent tendencies of Protestantism reached their most logical conclusion. It is, therefore, not insignificant that only in the last several decades have Protestants from the dissenting churches become prominent in the American business and political elite.

Two aspects of dissenting Protestantism have deeply influenced the religious understanding of our nation and of our obligation as citizens today. For one thing, dissenters have an aversion to government. This is natural, since governments with established churches have sought to enforce just the beliefs and practices on dissenters that the dissenters were dissenting from. But the aversion to government went beyond aversion to government interference with religion. It was expressed in a general feeling that people should do things for themselves rather than rely on government, and that the primary instrument for doing things for themselves was the voluntary association, based on the model of the dissenting church itself, which was a voluntary association. "Strong society, weak state" was the model for the United States for much of its early history. Hegel went so far as to say that we had no state at all. Given the enormous power of the federal government today, especially its military power, that would hardly describe us at present. With the decline of every kind of voluntary association in the last forty years, as documented by Robert Putnam (2000), we might even say "weak society, strong state" is a better description of our present reality.

However much the reality has changed, ideology has not. Ideologically, hostility to government is as strong as ever. Even Clinton said in his 1998 State of the Union Address, "The era of big government is over," at a time when government had never been more powerful at home and abroad. Another indication of the strong American hostility to government is our aversion to taxes. When asked whether they want tax cuts, Americans say yes by large majorities. Congress, responding to presidential requests, has legislated several multi-billion-dollar tax cuts at a time when federal expenditures, in particular the expenses of empire, have been rising dramatically. But when Americans are asked if they would like to see cuts in most of the programs funded by the federal government, they say no, because when the programs are named they see that they need them. Of course, dissenting Protestantism is not solely responsible for this disconnect between ideology and reality, but it is a factor that makes this disconnect greater than it is in any other Western nation.

There is another aspect of dissenting Protestantism that contributes to making the United States different from other Western nations with established church traditions. Established churches—Catholic, Lutheran, or Anglican—think of their membership as including everyone, saints and sinners. Some are more pious than others but it is the job of the church to nurture the less pious so that they understand better their religious obligations, and to nurture in the nation those institutions that will contribute to a more ethical society. In contrast to this, dissenting churches are exclusive, not inclusive: they are churches of the saved and they exclude the reprobate. Rather than seeing the church as a moral hierarchy in which some are more morally exemplary than others, they tend to see society and the world as split between the righteous and the unrighteous. The dissenting churches have been and are still today ardent missionaries, but their aim is not to include the converted in their difference, but to transform them as much as possible into the image of the saved, not only religiously but culturally as well.

Thus we have the paradox that a nation with a powerful aversion to "big government" is currently asserting absolute military and cultural domination of the globe. Can our dissenting Protestant tradition help us explain that? Not entirely, but it certainly is part of the explanation. Our tendency toward moralistic splitting, of thinking of the world as divided between the saved and the damned, the good and the evil, can trump our aversion to power. If evil is loose in the world, it is up to us to put a stop to it. Many have noticed how presidential rhetoric after 9/11 has been continuously punctuated by the words "evil" and "evildoer." Perhaps the most extreme use of the word came right after 9/11 in the service in the National Cathedral on September 14, 2001 (and repeated in the National Security document of September 2002), when Mr. Bush declared that it is "our responsibility to history" to "rid the world of evil." Rid the world of evil? It is hard to exaggerate the breathtaking sweep of that assertion. What even God has not done America will do.

Moral splitting is a general human propensity, and the United States has no monopoly of it, but we are more prone to it than other Western nations. Even though dissenting Protestantism is surely one source of it, this tendency is now secularized and pervasive in our popular culture, disseminated by movies, television, and video games. At a deeper level our infatuation with technology plays into this idea: technology, particularly military technology, will give us the equivalent of the supernatural invincibility of superheroes.

In the midst of unprecedented imperial reach, there remain serious questions about the moral and religious resources for sustaining an American empire. Dissenting Protestantism at its most confident is an unlikely candidate for imperial power. But dissenting Protestantism is not at its most vigorous today. Even within apparently vigorous congregations, consumerist attitudes are evident: programs that once were supported by willing volunteers now have to be sold as "adding value" to the participants. Even more problematic is the weakening of the influence of Evangelical Protestantism, in the broadest sense of that term, in the culture as a whole. That influence that was once so pervasive has been undermined by the very individualism that it has helped to unleash. Max Weber argued just 100 years ago that Protestantism, in helping to create capitalism, was unleashing a genie that would come back to haunt it. Capitalism gives rise to a secular version of Protestantism that operates through the culture of mass consumerism and the ideology of privatized self-fulfillment. If Protestantism helped to create capitalism, it also helped to create modern democracy, but consumerism and privatization undermine the very institutional basis of democracy, that is, the structure of voluntary association, the civil society, without which democracy becomes, as Tocqueville warned, democratic despotism or the rule of an economic aristocracy.

It is not my purpose here to do more than suggest some of the ways in which American Protestantism and the secular culture that has grown out of it, in spite of enormous positive contributions in our history, may at the moment be contributing to very destructive consequences. I am not arguing that this is because a creative tradition has recently gone astray. Rather, I am suggesting, as in my discussion of Andrew Delbanco's book, that the Reformation at its very inception contained destructive as well as creative possibilities. I would even go so far as to say that the Reformation was a mistake, though a necessary mistake. If Luther and the pope could have reached a compromise it would have been healthier for the western tradition; a compromise not being possible, Protestantism was an important opening up of potentialities that had been previously limited. But the price was high.

The core of the mistake was the denial of sacramental mediation. Once the sacraments were marginalized, coequal with the Word though they were in the Christian tradition, then the sacred itself was pushed out of nature and society and remained available only in the fragile consciences of individuals. The mistake was at once theological and sociological. The visible church was devalued; the church became "invisible," as Parsons frequently noted. But when the isolated individual could no longer find God, then the world was open to the disenchantment that Weber described. For a while the nation took the place of the visible church, drawing an idolatrous loyalty to whatever imperial cause was at hand. The temptation to view the nation in an idolatrous fashion still exists.

In most of the advanced industrial world, the nation is no longer the bulwark it once was, and one can question the depth of American patriotism, still in some quarters so ostentatiously on display. Ultimately only the sacred individual remains, but the idea of a world composed of autonomous individuals alone is sociologically impossible. Parsons's notion that instrumental activism is premised on making society "*instrumental* to bases of value outside itself" is, for good Durkheimian reasons, also a mistake. Making society instrumental turns out to have been a road to disaster. The idea of a visible church, itself the only sign of the Kingdom of God on this earth, returns us to social realism, the idea that society is an end in itself and not instrumental to anything. Only such social realism makes possible the building of an environmentally and humanly responsible society today.

In conclusion, let me return to the differences between my understanding of the development of American society and Parsons's. The crux of my argument is that the Reformation was a mistake—a necessary mistake, to be sure—but one that needs to be rectified if we are to solve the crises of modernity. That is surely not a view to which Parsons would have subscribed. Yet I believe that the differences between us are not fundamentally theoretical—they derive from different interpretations of history. When I differ with Parsons about the description of basic American values it is not the categories that I challenge, but only the way they are applied.

Perhaps our differences arise from generational differences more than anything else. Parsons grew up in a world in which Protestantism was a de facto established church in America. Most of the Supreme Court decisions that drove (Protestant) religion out of American public life came after World War Two. Parsons experienced this cultural hegemony, came to take it for granted I believe, during his formative years. I came of age in the 1950s, just when Protestantism was making its last stand as the dominant influence in American culture, and experienced much more acutely than Talcott the collapse of that dominance and all that went with it during the 1960s. I was too old to be a member of the sixties generation, yet young enough to be more closely in touch with it than I think Parsons ever was. That Talcott could hold, even metaphorically, that the United States was a version of the Kingdom of God on earth was a possibility that for me had disappeared.

In the decades since Parsons's death, the problems of American society at home and abroad have convinced me ever more strongly that only serious problems at the level of central values could explain our difficulties and that only reform at that deepest of levels could move American society toward a solution. I have lived through years very different from those of Parsons's lifetime, but if he could have experienced those years perhaps he would have become more open to the possibility that my argument is valid.

NOTES

1. This positive view was expressed most clearly in the first of the three lectures delivered as "Values and Social Change in Modern Japan" at International Christian University in the spring of 1961 (Bellah 1963). I included only the second and third lectures in my chapter of that title in *Beyond Belief* (1970/1991).
2. A convenient brief statement of "The General American Value-System," on which I shall rely here can be found in Parsons and Platt (1973, 40–45).
3. Parsons's views of the relation between Protestantism and modern society generally as well as American society in particular are developed in many of his publications. Perhaps the most important of these are "Christianity and Industrial Society" (1963/1967), "Christianity" (1968/1978), and *The Evolution of Societies* (1977).
4. This and the following paragraphs appear in somewhat different form in Robert N. Bellah (2002b).
5. This and the following paragraphs appear in somewhat different form in Robert N. Bellah (2002a).
6. Charles Taylor (1999, 18–20) offers a useful brief commentary on *Varieties*. Taylor stresses the contemporaneity of James's views just in the degree to which the personal is favored over the institutional.
7. Delbanco, who started his scholarly career as a student of New England Puritanism, uses this very Puritan term "declension" to characterize the historical course he is describing (1999, 41–42). His story is not pessimistic, however, as he believes that the hunger for meaning, unappeased by exclusive concentration on the self, will eventually lead Americans to larger concerns.

REFERENCES

Bellah, Robert N. 1963. "Values and Social Change in Modern Japan." *Asian Cultural Studies* (International Christian University, Tokyo) 3: 13–56.

———. 1967. "Civil Religion in America." *Daedalus* 96(1): 1–21.

———. 1970/1991. *Beyond Belief: Essays on Religion in a Post-Traditional World.* New York: Harper & Row. (Second edition, Berkeley: University of California Press.)

———. 1975/1992. *The Broken Covenant: American Civil Religion in Time of Trial.* New York: Seabury Press. (Second edition, University of Chicago Press.)

———. 2002a. "Epilogue. Meaning and Modernity: America and The World." In Richard Madsen, William M. Sullivan, Ann Swidler, and Steven M. Tipton, eds., *Meaning and Modernity: Religion, Polity, and Self.* Berkeley: University of California Press. 255–76.

———. 2002b. "The Protestant Structure of American Culture: Multiculture or Monoculture?" *The Hedgehog Review* 4(1):7–28.

Bercovitch, Sacvan. 1975. *The Puritan Origins of the American Self,* New Haven: Yale University Press.

Delbanco, Andrew. 1999. *The Real American Dream: A Meditation on Hope.* Cambridge, Mass.: Harvard University Press.

James, William. 1902/1987. *The Varieties of Religious Experience. Writings 1902–1910.* New York: Library of America.

National Security Strategy of the United States of America. 2002. Washington: The White House. Available online at whitehouse.gov.

Parsons, Talcott. 1963/1967. "Christianity and Industrial Society." In Talcott Parsons, *Sociological Theory and Modern Society.* New York: Free Press.

———. 1977. *The Evolution of Societies.* Englewood Cliffs, N.J.: Prentice-Hall.

———. 1968/1978. "Christianity." *Action Theory and the Human Condition.* New York: Free Press.

Parsons, Talcott, and Gerald M. Platt. 1973. *The American University.* Cambridge, Mass.: Harvard University Press.

Putnam, Robert D. 2000. *Bowling Alone: The Collapse and Revival of American Community.* New York: Simon & Schuster.

Ramirez, Francisco O., and John Boli. 1987. "On the Union of States and Schools." In George M. Thomas, John W. Meyer et al., *Institutional Structure: Constituting State, Society, and the Individual,* edited by George M. Thomas and John W. Meyer. Newbury Park, Calif.: Sage.

Taylor, Charles. 1999. "Transformations in Religious Experience." The William James Lecture. *Harvard Divinity School Bulletin* 28(4).

Vogel, David. 2002. "The Protestant Ethic and the Spirit of Environmentalism: Exploring the Cultural Roots of Contemporary Green Politics." *Zeitschrift für Umweltpolitik und Umweltrecht* 3: 297–322.

Worster, Donald. 1993. "John Muir and the Roots of American Environmentalism." In *The Wealth of Nature: Environmental History and the Ecological Imagination.* New York: Oxford University Press.

Chapter 8

Modernity and Its Endless Discontents

Donald N. Levine

If there is anything like a great tradition in social theory, it must be the multigenerational effort to come to terms with what has been called "modernity." For well over a century prior to World War I, members of the lineage of classical social theorists posited some inexorable direction of modernization that sooner or later would encompass the human world. Their formulas ranged from Comte's law of ineluctable stages to Alexis de Tocqueville's irresistible trend toward social equality to Karl Marx's dictum of de te fabula narratur to Herbert Spencer's law of evolution to Max Weber's thesis of world-historical rationalization. Although investigations of more limited scope came to eclipse such formulations in the interwar years, the generation of social scientists after World War II came to revitalize that tradition, in the process creating what were arguably some of the finest intellectual productions of social science of the twentieth century.[1]

For the modernization theorists of the latter period, the work of Talcott Parsons offered a constant point of reference. Their investigations occurred at a time when Parsons had returned to the concerns of his first publications, those stimulated by his study of Werner Sombart and Max Weber as analysts of modern capitalism. Although a later generation would reject the "modernization" rubric, thereby dismissing both the literature it stood for and Parsons's intellectual leadership, a glance at Parsons's bibliography during this high point of modernization studies may correct certain one-sided readings of that material. For example, far from restricting attention to the nation-state, in *The System of Modern Societies* (1971) Parsons analyzed the modern societal universe as a global system. Far from projecting convergence of its constituent nations toward a uniform pattern, within the global system he identified significant differences in the roles played by different nations, as well as the different development paths they follow in the course of modernizing. Far from assuming continuous historical progress and a conflict-free staging of modernity, in a span of twelve years Parsons focused on the dynamics of fascism and communism, strains that produced McCarthyism, sources of military aggressiveness in Western nations, structured strains in the lives of women and young people in industrial societies, and problems of integrating African Americans into American society—all in the service of contributing ideas to replace the simpler models of social and cultural evolution of the nineteenth century.

Although the reaction against Parsons and modernization theory may have resulted in the removal of such contributions from the contemporary sociological canon, it cannot do so indefinitely. If modernization has been removed from the curriculum, it has not been removed from historical actualities. And just as Parsons discovered, after posing the unforgettable question "Who now reads Spencer?"—only to write, a quarter-century later, that Spencer had in fact provided "very much of the framework of a satisfactory sociological scheme" (Parsons 1961, x)—so, too, social science must now discover, a quarter-century after asking "Who now reads Parsons?" that in regard to modernization as to much else,[2] the work of Parsons remains a valuable resource. Still, it goes without saying that just as Parsons's thinking underwent continuous evolution—at a pace that often dizzied those who followed him—so what he had to say about societal change and modernity contributes some telling words, not the last word, to the endless task of understanding modernity. Here I shall allude to three of his contributions: the theory of evolutionary universals, the notion of breakthrough revolutions, and the functional differentiation schema.

THE NATURE OF MODERNITY

Participants in the discourse conceive of modernity in three radically different senses: as a historical epoch; an identifiable set of phenomena and processes; or a set of ideas and ideals regarding the future development of society. Björn Wittrock (2000), who proposed this typology of definitions, prefers to consider modernity in the third sense—as a set of ideals often associated with the Enlightenment, such as the progress of knowledge and its rational application, the expansion of freedom, the growth of equality, the extension of community, and the establishment of world peace.[3] In an evocative phrase of Martin Luther King, Jr., he calls these ideals the "promissory notes" of modernity.

Others describe modernity as a contemporary period, one that began in 1920, or 1850, or 1789, or 1640, or some other founding point and extends either to the present or to a point in time at which a different period—postindustrial, postmodern, global, or the something else—was initiated.[4] In this sense, anything that happened in the twentieth century would willy-nilly be a manifestation of modernity. Against this definition, Wittrock argues that in order to demarcate the boundaries of an epoch, one needs substantive criteria. Providing temporal boundaries for modernity simply begs the question of effectively defining it.

At the same time, Wittrock rejects definitions of modernity in terms of identifiable phenomena, on grounds that diagnostic criteria commonly used for that purpose, like unregulated markets and multiparty political democracy, have not characterized most of the societies we would be willing to call "modern." That may be true, but is it decisive? Those particular criteria did not appear in the foundational statements of modern social theory that analyzed the distinctive features of the modern order.

To be sure, there is little consensus about what constitutes these defining forms. Most of these voices identify one or two central features of modernity and examine their causes and numerous ramifications. Some of them have analyzed modernity essentially in terms of the division of labor, specialization, and increased productivity (Adam Smith, Marx, Emile Durkheim); some in terms of political centralization, mobilization, and nation building (Norbert Elias, Tocqueville), and some in terms of increasing equality and extension of rights (Georg Hegel, Tocqueville, Lorenz von Stein). Others have stressed the advancement of objectified knowledge and scientifically educated elites (Comte, Weber, John Dewey) or the creation of world-shaping ideologies (Vilfredo Pareto, Shmuel Eisenstadt); still others, in terms of changes in the condition of persons, for example, as becoming either more disciplined (Weber, Sigmund Freud, Elias) or more individuated (Durkheim, Georg Simmel).

Inasmuch as each of those theorists tends to finger *one* phenomenon as the central defining feature of modernity, each tends to subordinate if not ignore altogether those emphasized by the others. In what follows I shall create a universe of dialogue among them by designating the phenomena they discuss in terms of six major categories (see table 8.1).[5]

TABLE 8.1 *Conceptions of Modernity: Essential Processes as Viewed by Major Contributors*

	Differentiation					
	Social-Functional	Individual	Unification	Equalization	Disciplining	Rationalization
Locus classicus	Smith, *Wealth of Nations*	Simmel, On *Social Differentiation*	Tocqueville, *Ancien Régime*	Tocqueville, *Democracy in America*	Weber, *Protestant Ethic*	Comte, *Positive Philosophy*
Other contributors	Comte Spencer Durkheim Marx	Durkheim Thomas Redfield Eisenstadt	Comte Elias Geertz Bendix Apter	Hegel Durkheim Weber Ortega y Gasset Marshall	Freud Mannheim Elias Bendix Gorski	Hegel, Weber Simmel Mannheim Riesman Black Bell

Source: Author's compilation.

Modernity as Functional Specialization

Theorists of modernity have used the notion of differentiation at least three different ways. Initially it connoted the division of labor in production and exchange. Later it came to signify the separation of different institutional sectors or spheres of action from one another. In addition it came to designate the process whereby individuals become increasingly distinct and unlike one another, called "individuation" (discussed in a later section).

The division of labor figures as perhaps the most frequently defined marker of the modern order. Adam Smith, arguably the founding father of modernity theory, centered it in the characteristics of what he called commercial society. These properties were twofold: a remarkable improvement in the dexterity of productive labor, and the extension of opportunities to exchange the products of that labor through a monetarized market. Behind all this was an extended process of division of labor. Specialization in production was not planned, but evolved spontaneously as individual producers came to see the benefit of exploiting an advantageous position, however it was attained, in a system of exchange.

The idea of the division of labor was developed more or less continuously by the major theorists of modernity. Comte analyzed ways in which the division of labor promotes cooperative endeavors and societal stability, and considered the division of labor in the sciences as well as in industry.[6] Marx advanced the analysis by distinguishing between the division of labor in society at large, which he described as arising spontaneously through a series of historical stages, and division of labor in the industrial workplace, which he saw as centrally planned and forcibly instituted for the sake of competitive advantage. Spencer generalized the concept into a cosmic process of increasing complexification, from incoherent homogeneity to coherent heterogeneity. Standing nimbly on Smith's shoulders, Spencer celebrated the growth of functional specialization in the modern economy and extended its scope to include the differentiation of political and ecclesiastical structures. Durkheim famously focused on the division of labor in his first major monograph, extending Comte's notions about the solidaristic effects of functional specialization. In this century, most theorists of modernization have included some reference to functional specialization as a key principle of the modern socioeconomic order. In our own time, Niklas Luhmann has insisted that *functional* differentiation must serve as the master concept for all those who theorize about modern societies, and contrasts this type of differentiation with forms of differentiation found in premodern societies, segmentation, and stratification.

Modernity as Individuation

Simmel inaugurated his work as a sociologist with a monograph, *On Social Differentiation,* which analyzed a number of respects in which the process of individuation occurs in developments from premodern epochs to the present. These include the transposition of jural responsibility from collectivities to individuals; the enlargement of groups, which creates more space for the expression of individuality; the transition from a condition where mental activity is circumscribed by shared beliefs to one that permits individualized intellectual achievement; and the shift from a pattern of compulsory group affiliations based on birth and propinquity to a pattern of more voluntary associations that create an individuated constellation of affiliations (Simmel 1890/1989).

Durkheim linked his master trend of functional specialization to a process of individuation with its attendant cult of the individual. W. I. Thomas (1923, 70) described the "individualization of behavior" as a process of

> evolution, connected with mechanical inventions, facilitated communication, the diffusion of print, the growth of cities, business organization, the capitalistic system, specialized occupations, scientific research, doctrines of freedom, the evolutionary view of life, etc., [whereby] the family and community influences have been weakened and the world in general has been profoundly changed in content, ideals, and organization.

Robert Redfield (1941) charted the path of modernization across four Yucatecan communities as an ideal type constructed as if a single historic change were involved. He found decreasing isolation and increasing heterogeneity among the four communities, accompanied by progressive individualization, for which he adduced twelve different types of evidence, including increased assignment of individual rights in land and diminished use of collective labor and the extension of primary kinship terms beyond the elementary family (Redfield 1941, 355–57). Shmuel Eisenstadt views the importance of conscious moral choice among members of fundamentalist movements as an indicator of one of their distinctly modern characteristics: the modern emphasis on the autonomy of human will (Eisenstadt 1999, 91).

Modernity as Political Unification

In this view modernity actually combines three processes: political centralization, popular sovereignty, and popular mobilization. They have in common the extension of connections between a political center and peripheries, such that the center becomes more effective in influencing the peripheries and at the same time more accessible to and affected by them. Tocqueville analyzed the linkage between the mobilization of the populace in the French Revolution—their animation on behalf of great duties and common causes—and the increased jurisdiction of a central state authority, and he depicted in unforgettable lines the power of the sovereign populace in the American republic. Comte considered the formation of societies of increasing scale, culminating in a society that encompasses all of humanity, to be the master trend of secular history. G. H. Mead (1929) tied the formation of national-mindedness to growing responsiveness to an emerging international community.

Elias, in his historical sociology of French society, analyzed state formation as a recurrent process of centralization over ever-expanding territories and a devolution of authority from the center to wider peripheries. Reinhard Bendix likewise emphasized the modern process of nation building and extension of citizenship in Western Europe, Russia, India, and Japan. Karl Deutsch investigated the formation of modern nations by examining processes of communication and mobilization. Daniel Lerner's classic highlighted the changed orientation of locals toward a wider social world as a key feature of modernization in Turkey. In a seminal paper of enduring value, Clifford Geertz depicted the simultaneous processes of centralization and centrifugal assertions in the modernizing states of Asia and Africa, showing that the former involved newly awakened popular desires to build an efficient, dynamic modern state: "a demand for progress, for a rising standard of living, more effective political order, greater social justice, and beyond that of 'playing a part in the larger arena of world politics' " (Geertz 1973, 258).

Modernity as Jural Equalization

For Tocqueville (1835–40/1969), the dominant phenomenon of modern society is the secular trend toward equalization of social status in the community. Although he found this phenomenon most pronounced in the United States, he interpreted it as a master trend for all societal orders. (The prospect of its inexorability, he said, filled him with "une sorte de terreur religieuse.") Surveying its progression across the centuries of French history, Tocqueville noted how privileges that distinguished different social orders were one by one dissolving in the face of this awesome process.

For Hegel, too, the extension of rights figured as a master trend over the ages. The movement from states where one is free to those where some are free to those where all are free entailed an expansion of rights guaranteed by formalized law. Incorporating Hegel's notion of law and ideas about the Prussian bureaucracy of Hegel's time, Weber depicted the foundations of rational-legal bureaucracy as a core phenomenon of modern social organization. As Weber observed, this inexorable process of bureaucratization had a leveling effect, in that all persons were to be treated equally by its rational-legal norms.

Another key feature of the modern order that some of the Scottish writers highlighted was its promotion of personal liberty, through the progress of the rule of law and the declining intervention of government in civil society. Thus, Smith hailed the emerging "system of natural liberty" associated with the progress of society, which, as he says in *An Inquiry into the Nature and Causes of The Wealth of Nations,* leaves everyone "perfectly free to pursue his own interest his own way" (1776/1976, volume 2, 208).

Durkheim's treatment of this process was more muted, but he too considered it a necessary part of the work of modernization. Absent the equalization of opportunity in a functionally differentiated society, the forced restriction of occupations to specific social strata would produce pathological conflicts. Durkheim thought that sooner or later inheritance rights would have to be curtailed as part of this leveling. Although Juan Ortega y Gasset had a negative stance regarding this development, he too considered the equalization of opportunities and resources to be unstoppable. T. H. Marshall went on to analyze the array of rights—civil, political, and social—that were progressively enacted and extended to more and more parts of the population.

Modernity as Extension of Discipline

For a small but significant number of authors, modernization is marked by a substantial change in socialization patterns and moral habits. Weber famously put his finger on this change as an essential part of the transformation into capitalist society, regarding the ascetic, methodical organization of daily activities in this world as essential to the operation of the capitalist form of organization. Continuing Weber's thought, Karl Mannheim analyzed the ways in which the functional rationalization of worldly activities requires a heightened level of self-rationalization. Bendix investigated the ways in which industrial managers sought to extend this new kind of discipline to factory workers in Russia and the United States. Approaching the issue with a very different kind of interest, Freud analyzed the discontents of modern civilization in terms of a heightened level of control of natural impulses.

In *The Civilizing Process,* the master analyst of this shift, Norbert Elias, documented the slow and steady increase of control of psychic drives over the past millennium (1936/2000). The major agent of this transformation in recent centuries has been the institution of primary education, where pupils are taught punctuality, orderliness, and other forms of self-control along with basic academic skills. Charles Camic (1983) has illuminated how philosophers of the Scottish Enlightenment came to acquire habits of independence and universalistic values through changes in the socialization processes to which they were exposed. Michel Foucault speaks of the formation of a "disciplinary society" in modern times, one in which specialized institutions (schools, hospitals, penitentiaries) and state apparatuses (public bureaucracies, the police) utilize a variety of techniques of correction and control (Foucault 1975/1979, 215–16). More generally, this phenomenon has been so dramatic that it has been referred to as a "disciplinary revolution" (Gorski 1993).

Modernity as Cultural Rationalization

Some theorists have focused on the progressive accumulation of knowledge as the key phenomenon of the modern epoch. Taking a page from Anne-Robert-Jacques Turgot, Comte laid the groundwork for this view by taking the maturation of biology and the arrival of sociology (called social physics at first) as positive sciences to be markers of the new era. The hallmark of the new age would be the guidance of societal development on the basis of positively grounded social knowledge. Hegel espoused a comparable conception, identifying modernity with the triumph of reason through history. For him, this formed the groundwork of the modern era, albeit in ways that Comte (and Marx) would consider residues of a metaphysical age. Hegel also drew a clear distinction between objective and subjective rationality, the former consisting of the progressive embodiment of a struggle to attain perfected systems of morality in the state and its laws; the latter consisting of the growth of self-consciousness and the articulation of that self-consciousness through art, religion, and philosophy.

Georg Simmel (1971, ch. 16) continued to observe a distinction between objectified forms of knowledge and their appropriation by subjects for the sake of personal growth. The former consisted of such objectified forms as science, ethics, art, philosophy, and the like; the latter took the form of what he called "subjective culture," or personal cultivation. Unlike Hegel, he saw the creation of objective culture in the modern world far outstripping subjective culture. Weber began his work on rationality by investigating the process of subjective rationalization as part of the system of modern Western capitalism, and concluded his comparative studies of the world religions by attending to the objectified forms of Western rationality in all institutional and cultural spheres. Cyril Black dealt with the phenomenal growth of knowledge in recent centuries as the central factor in modernization. Christopher Jencks and David Riesman (1968) connected this growth of knowledge with the ascendance of research criteria in universities as a modernizing process that had revolutionized the academic world. Daniel Bell went on to take the centrality of objectified knowledge as the key identifying feature of late capitalism, which he called postindustrial society, a finding that later theorists have continued to develop.

THE REVOLUTIONS OF MODERNITY

These processes were none of them novel. They evolved over several centuries, as many authors have noted.[7] Each process possesses adaptive advantages. As such, one might interpret them in the mode of what Parsons referred to as evolutionary universals—structures offering such adaptive advantages that any society incorporating them would want to hold on to them and that all societies would sooner or later wish to incorporate them (Parsons 1964).

Despite their long prehistories, the fact that the changes of the past two centuries have struck so many people as creating a radically different sort of life-world must be acknowledged. Another idea from the Parsons repertoire helps us do that, the idea of breakthrough. For what happened in the modern period was an acceleration and intensification of certain processes such that differences of degree became flagrantly qualitative differences.

In addition, what was novel in the modern world was not only the intensity and rapidity with which these processes unfolded, it was also an unprecedented level of enthusiasm for their very novelty. Innovation as such came to be prized, and *that* was a momentous change. Recall that the word "modern" comes from Latin "modo" ("just now"), a term that historically had negative connotations. Even up to the nineteenth century, "modern" was a suspect term, signifying something brash or deviant, in poor taste compared with what was ancient or venerable (Williams 1983, 208).

What is more, the notion that the world could intentionally be remade also figured as a distinctive feature of the modern world. For example, Eisenstadt's characterization of the key features of the civilization of modernity emphasizes a turn toward autonomy in human agency across several dimensions. Such autonomy includes reflexivity and exploration, active reconstruction of nature and society, and free access to the centers of social and political order (Eisenstadt 2000; 2003, volume 2, 494ff.). For some philosophers as well, the element of self-determination constitutes the central defining feature of modernity (Pippin 1999).

Intensification of long-brewing changes, celebration of the new, and intimations of intentionality have led many to refer to the transformations that ushered in the modern order with the trope of revolution—most commonly, the Industrial and the democratic revolutions, at times also the scientific revolution, the managerial revolution, the education revolution, the communications revolution, the social revolution, and others.

In keeping with that usage, I provide in table 8.2 a schema that connects a typology of breakthrough revolutions, using terms coined by the authors named, with the central modernizing processes just surveyed, and indicates some benefits associated with each of these transforming processes.

The Benefits of Modernity

In many accounts of modernization, changes associated with the improvement of production and enhancement of commerce figure prominently. They form the centerpiece of what Adam Smith considered the new type of society, which he described as "commercial" in contrast to the previous "agricultural" type of society. The division of labor was the most important single factor in producing a dramatic rise in the standard of living, such that a frugal peasant in his modern society lived far better than kings who ruled over thousands of savages.[8] Smith's hyperbole was outdone by that of Marx and Friedrich Engels, who proclaimed that the division of labor as instantiated in capitalist society had led to monumental productions, far surpassing Egyptian pyramids, Roman aqueducts, and Gothic cathedrals. Like the Scottish moralists, Durkheim lumped together as "civilization" such consequences of the division of labor as progress in the

TABLE 8.2 *The "Revolutions" and the Benefits of Modernity*

Key Process	Differentiation: Social-Functional	Differentiation: Individual	Unification[a]	Equalization[a]	Disciplining	Cultural Rationalization
Associated revolution	Industrial Revolution		Integrative revolution (Geertz)	Social revolution (Fararo)	Disciplinary revolution (Gorski)	Academic revolution (Jencks and Riesman)
Adaptive benefits	Goods and services	Freedom	Collective efficacy	Justice	Civility	Knowledge

Source: Author's compilation.
[a]What is often called the democratic revolution consists of a combination of both of these processes.

arts, sciences, technology, and standard of living, though he denied that any of these benefits possessed a moral nature.

The benefits of political unification were also hailed by a number of theorists of modernity. These included pacification of territories under the command of a single regime, the ability to mobilize citizenries to combat disasters from nature or attacks from outside powers, and the provision of greater benefits to all within its boundaries. The movement toward hegemony of universalistic norms has had many benefits. Among these benefits Tocqueville included the accessibility of primary education to all, the enhanced productivity that comes from the promise of mobility, the diminution of warlike passions from eliminating stratification based on honor, and the toleration of diverse religions. As Durkheim foresaw, securing the rights of previously disadvantaged groups has promoted social harmony. Equalization under the law led to a more contented populace as well as to a sense of living in a more just society. Despite his misgivings about equalization, Ortega y Gasset observed that extending rights and resources to more of the population was a change that promoted vital energies and vastly increased human possibilities.

The benefits of discipline included the capacity of citizens to live together in a civil manner as well as the ability to perform occupational tasks on a regular and reliable basis. Many authors (Weber, Mannheim, Bendix, Philip Gorski) have found modern industrial labor and bureaucratic work to be dependent on new levels of self-discipline. Elias has found this essential for people to get along in situations of dense interaction, and Freud considered such self-control generically important for the achievements of civilization. Others, however, have found the new levels of self-control to be intrinsically valuable; thus, Weber considered the formation of genuine personality through ethical regulation of daily conduct to be a beneficial outcome of the spirit that ushered in the era of modern capitalism (Hennis 1988).

The benefits of rationalized culture are similarly both instrumental and intrinsically valuable. From the Enlightenment onward, the enlargement of a knowledge base has been hailed as a crucial resource for enhancing human well-being. This includes both the development of bodies of codified knowledge and the spread of techniques for improved cognition. Modern consumers came to expect continuous improvements in commodities of all sorts thanks to new kinds of validated knowledge. Beyond that, the very existence of bodies of works representing an uninhibited quest for truth has been taken as a key feature of civilization (Whitehead 1933).

The Discontents of Modernity

From the onset of the modernizing revolutions, a host of discontents have been associated with the division of labor and its effects in the modern occupational and market systems (see table 8.3).

Intense specialization in industrial production elicited critiques about the dehumanizing consequences of such work. Repetition of simple operations was said to make workers "as stupid and ignorant as it is possible for a human creature to become" and the dexterity thus acquired to come "at the expense of [a person's] intellectual, social, and martial virtues." The hegemony of commerce created a society in which, as Smith further put it, "every man . . . becomes in some measure a merchant"—with the attendant calculating, profit-oriented habits of mind (Smith 1776/1976, volume 2, 303; volume 1, 26).[9] The monetarization of exchange, in Simmel's analysis, has led to the reduction of all personal and aesthetic values to cash values and the conversion of what was original a means into an absolute end. Proliferation of consumable products elevated consumerism to a dominant place in life.

The economic system that lay behind all these developments was faulted by Marx and his followers for a number of noxious effects. These include a base line of chronic unemployment, the instability of cyclical booms and busts in the economy, growing inequality between the top and bottom levels of the income hierarchy, and fragmentation of the community into a plethora of narrow economic interests. Individuation has also been associated with a number of modern ills, including swollen suicide rates (Durkheim), increased loneliness and anxiety (Slater 1976), and reduced public engagement (Sennett 1998) and social capital (Putnam 2000).

Drawing together certain strands of this type of analysis, Fred Weinstein and Gerald Platt (1969) scrutinized common psychological reactions to the individual's emancipation from traditional, hierarchical authority. In particular, they argue, for most of human history "the models for ego endeavor did not include autonomous initiative, and for centuries there were no systematic demands for personal and social autonomy" (Weinstein and Platt 1969, 197). The uniquely modern wish to be free has generated a good deal of guilt and anxiety, leading to regressive solutions that take violent forms; these include the revolutionary imposition of new values in excessive and polarized fashion, and the radical enforcement of a return to traditional values (1969, 38–42).

Transformations associated with political democratization entailed other disadvantages. Enfranchisement of the masses led to less informed policy decisions. It caused vulnerability to

TABLE 8.3 *The Modern Revolutions and their Associated Discontents*

Process	Differentiation: Social-Functional	Differentiation: Individual	Unification	Equalization	Disciplining	Cultural Rationalization
Revolution	Industrial		Integrative	Social	Disciplinary	Academic
Benefits	Commerce		Efficacy	Justice	Civility	Knowledge
Associated discontents	Hyper-specialization; alienation; consumerism	Personal malaise; social deficits	Repressive centralization; violence	Support for mediocrity; erosion of standards	Psychic repression	"Tragedy of culture"; Jacobin barbarities

Source: Author's compilation.

demagogues, with the possibility of introducing despotic regimes. It also entailed the tyranny of the majority, with attendant suppression of minority views. Tocqueville not only warned of these costs, he also regretted the loss of liberties of towns and parishes attendant on centralization. He and others (Edward Sapir) warned about the consequent erosion of local peculiarities and cultures. Still others have emphasized the violence inherent in processes of political modernization, including the revolutionary violence that accompanied the formation of modern states (Barrington Moore), the inflammation of hostilities among primordial groups (Geertz), and a propensity for conflict between more modern and less modern elements of the population (Parsons, Gabriel Almond, Eisenstadt). They also have noted the specifically modern tendencies toward militant nationalism and interstate violence (Parsons, Hans Joas).

The institution of universal rights was viewed with less apprehension than the other features of modernity, except by bigots and those with parochial interests to protect. Even so, the leveling it entailed evoked concerns in some quarters. Tocqueville criticized the lowered quality of those who became political leaders under egalitarian conditions as well as the basement of cultural standards. Ortega y Gasset faulted the new egalitarian regime for producing many fewer people who were willing to assume the burdens of public leadership and maintaining standards for cultural productions. Military violence has also been occasioned or justified by a mission to promulgate the safeguarding of human rights beyond a nation's borders.

Spencer was among the first to call attention to the ill effects of heightened discipline attendant on intensified schooling in modern society. He decried the dangers of excessive demands on students for study, since they make learning distasteful, produce aversion to books, unduly privilege knowledge acquisition over organization of knowledge, weaken mental power for other pursuits, and yield knowledge that is soon forgotten anyway (1861/1911, 148–50).

The psychic malaise attendant on disciplinary revolution was famously analyzed by Sigmund Freud in *Civilization and Its Discontents.* Freud argued that the control of drives needed for the work of civilization exacted pathogenic levels of psychic costs. Weber scored the repressive consequences of discipline in both factories and bureaucracies. Mannheim argued that the rationalized control of drives in modern society was producing persons less capable of independent thought and thereby prey to demagoguery. Foucault goes even further than Weber in arguing that the modern extension of disciplinary processes involves an unprecedented diminution of human freedom.

The rationalization of culture constitutes a highly complex phenomenon, which cannot be explicated here. One discontent was famously articulated by Simmel, with his notion of the tragedy of culture. For Simmel, modernity was marked by the accelerated production of "objective culture," all those forms of symbolic work such as science, art, music, philosophy, and the like. This enormous output took place at the expense of subjective culture, that is, of the capacity of human subjects to engage and digest those objective forms for the sake of their personal growth. As a result, he said, modern man feels himself in a typically problematic situation—his sense of being surrounded by an innumerable number of cultural elements which are neither meaningless to him nor, in the final analysis, meaningful. In their mass they depress him, since he is not capable of assimilating them all, nor can he simply reject them, since after all they do belong *potentially* within the sphere of his cultural development (Simmel 1968, 44).

In some exceptionally insightful and provocative analyses, Eisenstadt (1996) has focused on value rationalization as the central hallmark of modernity. According to this analysis, the attempt to reconstruct society forcibly in accord with articulated ideals has produced a Jacobin mentality responsible for much of the barbarism of totalitarian regimes of the past two centuries, leading to mass annihilations on the basis of adherence to utopian ideologies.

TALCOTT PARSONS AND THE ANATOMY OF MODERNITY

In assessing the work of Talcott Parsons (or any other major thinker), it is important always to hold in mind the distinction that Jeffrey Alexander drew long ago (1983) between what can be done within Parsons's theoretical system and what the author himself has done with it. Although Parsons himself did not identify all of the features and benefits of modernity that we have surveyed thus far, nor did he treat many of its discontents extensively, if at all, his conceptual framework enables us to classify, interpret, and relate a great number, if not all, of them. It does so by employing the master notion of *functional differentiation among action systems.* The Parsonian framework conceives of action as behavior filled with meaning, which is derived from a synthesis of biological and psychological impulses with social expectations and cultural values. Parsons analyzes the universe of action as organized in boundary-maintaining systems that vary independently but that admit mutual interpenetration. In the course of human evolution, these systems become differentiated from one another functionally along two dimensions (see table 8.4).

The first dimension concerns the different levels of action systems. Over time, systems of cultural symbolism became independent of the systems of social roles that bore them (objectification), and personalities became independent of the social roles in which they had been encompassed (individuation). These appear on a cybernetic hierarchy, upward from high energy potentials and downward from high control potentials. From top down, the systems are called cultural, social, psychological, and behavioral, or mind.[10] The differentiation of each of these subsytems of the general universe of action yields a particular evolutionary outcome.

Below the level of mind are the systems that do not partake of action—the biological organism of humans, and the other biological and physical environments. Above culture is what Parsons calls the environment of ultimate meanings.

The second, horizontal dimension refers to subsystems devoted to the performance of particular functions: adaptation, goal attainment, integration, and pattern maintenance. The subsystems of primary interest to theorists of modernity are at the social-system level, consisting of the economy, or adaptive subsystem (A); the polity, or goal-attainment subsystem (G); the societal community, or integrative subsystem (I); and the fiduciary subsystem (latent) pattern-maintenance subsystem (L).

As these levels and subsystems of action came increasingly to separate from one another, they became organized by distinct boundaries, within which homeostatic and self-generating processes were active. In the earliest times, for example, personal identities were encompassed within social roles, which in turn were defined in terms set by the culture. Economic, political,

TABLE 8.4 *The Organization of Action Systems*

Action System (Evolutionary Variable)	Functional Subsystems	
L: Cultural system (value generalization)	Constitutive symbolism Science	Normative codes Art
I: Social system (inclusion)	Fiduciary systems (l) Economy (a)	Societal community (i) Polity (g)
G: Personality system (individuation)	Personal identity (ego ideal) Reality orientation (ego)	Conscience (superego) Motivational resources (id)
A: Behavioral system (mind) (adaptive upgrading)	Genetic base Implementive capacity	Affective capacity Cognitive capacity

Source: Author's compilation.

integrative, and fiduciary functions alike were performed by kinship groups. These groups also knew and transmitted the whole repertoire of cultural symbolism, constituted by the commonsense culture of the group, without specialized subsystems of symbols. Table 8.5 suggests a way to relate the central processes, benefits, and discontents of modernity already noted to concepts from the action theory framework.

Discontents Specific to Each Process of Systemic Differentiation

In an exceptionally creative adaptation of the action-theoretic schema, Frank Lechner (1985) points to the multiple sources of tension that the very process of systemic differentiation itself engenders. He lays out a paradigm of discontents that inhere in the central processes of sociocultural evolution, the processes that Parsons refers to as value generalization, inclusion, individuation, and adaptive upgrading.

The process of value generalization involves the extension of overarching beliefs to include a greater number of constituents by couching values at a higher level of abstraction. This implies that the bounds of any tradition have been loosened and that greater reflexivity is needed to interpret and implement values. As the value framework thereby becomes more distant and less directly meaningful, its utility in directing action becomes attenuated. The main source of compensation for the biological understeering of action becomes weakened and people may come to suffer from "cultural understeering."

The evolutionary variable of *inclusion* involves the extension of solidarity beyond parochial bounds such that those formerly considered strangers are included and a feeling of solidarity stretches beyond the primordial limits. With this loosening of the communal boundaries, the solidarity framework can be experienced as more distant, impersonal, and less binding. With the relativization of old bonds, individuals may suffer from a lack of solidarity, as Comte and Durkheim long ago indicated.

Lechner's treatment of the process of *individuation* focuses on the loosened bounds of personal biographies. This means that much more effort is required to mobilize the resources needed for personal identity and that the attainment of a coherent self becomes problematic.

TABLE 8.5 *The Hallmarks of Modernity in Action-Theoretic Terms*

	Differentiation					
Modernizing Process	Individual	Social-Functional	Unification	Equalization	Disciplining	Cultural Rationalization
System function	Personality different from social systems	Social system (A): economy	Social system (G): polity	Social system (I): jural community	Social system (L): "schooling"	Cultural systems different from social systems
Benefits	Personal freedom	Commerce	Efficacy	Justice	Civility	Knowledge
Associated discontents	Personal malaise; social deficits	Hyper-specialization; alienation; consumerism	Repressive centralization; violence	Support for mediocrity; erosion of standards	Psychic repression	"Tragedy of culture"; Jacobin barbarities

Source: Author's compilation.

Regarding the heightened upgrading of *adaptive* skills and resources, Lechner writes (1985, 162):

> The limits of traditional adaptation to nature have been transcended . . . world-mastery has increased and become more abstract and self-sustaining. . . . Having become more autonomous, intelligent adaptation can be seen as itself out of control, distant from other spheres of action, and no longer oriented to the problems that are meaningful to solve in the first place. With more degrees of freedom for behavioral-system operation . . . [intelligent adaptation] may be perceived as producing more problems than it solves, becoming controlled by its own products, and creating uncertainty by infinite learning.

Given these discontents that stem from radical understeering, overcomplexity, and meaninglessness, Lechner delineates a series of antimodern reactions to them. These take the form of movements that aim at revitalizing aspects of a pattern perceived to be underemphasized and seeking to "radically restore order by dedifferentiation from the highest level down" (163).

The first of these revitalization syndromes emerges in reaction to discontents triggered by value generalization. It upholds the primacy of premodern culture patterns in what has come to be called a fundamentalist mode. Erasing the boundaries that mark off other differentiated action systems, it subordinates them all to ultimate belief.[11] Another type of antiliberal syndrome emerges in reaction against pressures toward great political inclusiveness. These involve efforts to make communal and political organization congruent, as in the various forms of "ethnic nationalism."

Both of these syndromes represent attempts to resolve the discontents of modernity by escape from freedom into new forms of severe, all-pervading constraint. By contrast, revitalization syndromes that work to revitalize the processes of individuation or adaptive upgrading pursue a sort of "super-emancipation" in ways that undermine the bounds of controlling systems.[12] To revitalize individuation, a variety of "expressive-therapeutic" movements have arisen, which subordinate all cultural systems to aesthetic purposes and all solidaristic forms to groups oriented to self-development and self-help. Revitalization in the service of adaptive upgrading gives rise to what Lechner calls a "Promethean" syndrome, in which all other concerns are subordinated to the interest of heightened productivity and world mastery.

Uneven Development of Different Systems

A related set of tensions derives from the uneven development of different sociocultural sectors, a phenomenon thematized by William Graham Sumner (1907/2002) and W. F. Ogburn (1922). In Ogburn's systematic treatment of social change (1922), he listed four factors that account for cultural evolution: invention, accumulation, diffusion, and adjustment. Since all sociocultural elements are interrelated, any pronounced change in one element will provoke changes in other elements. Since these adjustments take a long time to occur, he famously described them with the concept of "cultural lag." In Ogburn's conception, it has been noted, "The lag relationship comes into play when it can be *demonstrated* that, of two hitherto closely related and mutually compatible parts of culture, one changes in such a way as to disrupt the relationship and impair the compatibility" (Duncan 1964, xvi). Although the inventions he had in mind often appeared in the sector of technology—telephones, automobiles, and the like—thereby reflecting a certain resonance with Marxian historical materialism, for Ogburn they could also take the form of changes in ideas.

Pulling such a notion into the Parsonian framework, Paul Colomy employs the concepts of "unequal development" and "uneven differentiation." Colomy points to the structured strains engendered both by processes of uneven development across institutional sectors and by variations in the rates and degrees of differentiation within institutional sectors. These strains can lead to political corruption, breakdowns of modernization, anomie, and cycles of inflation and deflation (Colomy 1985, 133).

Conflicts Between Differentiated Action Systems

Even when subsystems have evolved to comparable levels of development, there are inevitable conflicts and strains owing to the fact that each subsystem is oriented to different goals and regulated by different values:

- The tension between the adaptive interest in efficiency and the jural interest in universalistic procedural norms (Weber [1968], on bureaucracy)
- The tension between the discipline in work needed in modern occupations and the hedonistic emphasis in the consumerism of commercial society (Bell [1976], *The Cultural Contradictions of Capitalism*)
- The tension between the dispositions that make the market system work and those needed for mobilization on behalf of public projects (the famous freeloader dilemma) (Olson 1965)
- The tension between the critical distancing essential to science and the commitments needed for civic action (Simmel [1978] on money, Jeffrey Goldfarb [1991] on the cynical society)
- The tension between rationalized culture and individuation (Simmel [1911/1968] on the tragedy of culture)

Conflicts Between Action Systems and Their Environments

The discontents viewed through the lens of action theory do not exhaust what might be listed in a complete catalogue of the ills of modernity. Two orders of discontents lie outside the framework of that theory. One set of omissions has to do with the extent to which an action-theoretic approach to sociology truncates the range of commonplace social phenomena that get attended to: the substratum of material bodies through which social actions are carried out. By defining the social domain in terms of institutionalized norms and the boundary-maintaining systems that they delineate, action theory cuts sociology off from what Durkheim called social morphology, and what Robert Park (1926/1967) counterposed to the moral order—the ecological order. More concretely, this would have to do with demographic trends such as birth and death rates, morbidity rates, and migration patterns and ecological phenomena such as urbanization, suburbanization, traffic patterns, and the like. Developments in these domains associated with modernity—the demographic revolution and the urban revolution—must surely be included in any thorough inventory of its transformations.

The other set of omissions pertains to changes in the nonhuman environment, changes that have leaped into prominence in the last few decades. Insofar as the general value system of the modern order gives prominence to the pattern that Parsons called instrumental activism, it embodies the disposition toward mastery of the environment. Weber contrasted this with harmonious adaptation to the environment. Instrumental activism has enabled many discontents to germinate and grow without being attended to for generations: pollution of air and water, destruction of species, erosion of soil, ozone depletion in the troposphere, despoliation of landscapes. Such phenomena have resulted from human action, yet they take place across the boundary between action and its environments—a phenomenal universe encompassed by the paradigm of the human condition, but not of the action paradigm by itself. Although these phenomena were largely excluded from consciousness during the previous two centuries, they surely cannot be excluded from attention in a comprehensive list of the problems of the modern order.

The final chapter of this discourse would consist of a search for actual or imaginable responses to these discontents. It might be worthwhile to outline the range of equilibrating and transforming processes that Parsons and others have examined (see Levine, forthcoming).[13]

MODERNITY IN THE GLOBAL ERA

Recent critiques of the modernization literature have focused on the changed realities attendant on our increasingly globalized era. One thesis, represented most vocally by Martin Albrow (1997), urges us to abandon the term "modernity" altogether. Albrow argues that while it was appropriate to use the term "modern" to designate the epoch of the past few centuries, that epoch has now ended, and we have entered a new one, which he calls the global age.

The thesis is arresting and warrants a considered response. My response is twofold. On the one hand, the burden of proof would have to be on whoever argues that the five revolutionary processes described above are no longer significantly operative in the contemporary global world. Clearly, that is not the case. Each of them simply has continued to manifest itself on a wider stage.

On the other hand, globalization began centuries ago, and contemporary globalities simply continue all of the processes identified above. As Marx and Engels observed in the late 1840s, already the expansion of commerce under capitalism had brought about the universal interdependence of nations, and the extension of intellectual creations had produced a world literature. Simmel, late in the First World War (which he initially championed), forecast a supranational European community. Durkheim and G. H. Mead analyzed processes that were promoting international-mindedness. Even so, I see no objection to referring to the contemporary period as a global age, and there are some advantages in doing so. The point is not to prolong usage of the term "modernity" at all costs, but to be clear about what the actual historic processes consist of.

The other thesis affirms the continued aptness of using "modernity" for the contemporary period, but insists that modernity can no longer be taken to signify a unitary complex. Instead, it must be understood to have multiple manifestations—that there are in fact "multiple modernities."

Here, too, it would be instructive to recall a number of earlier analyses, especially from the ill-reputed modernization literature of the 1960s. Most of those writings showed a clear awareness that the core processes of modernization would be realized differently according to the varying cultural and social-structural backgrounds of the nations in question. One thinks of Geertz's classification of a half dozen different configurations of the integrative revolution; Lloyd Fallers's contrast of the ways in which the modernization of stratification-systems would differ among Western societies, India, the Islamic world, and sub-Saharan Africa; or Cyril Black's pronouncement that modernizing societies find themselves "in the process of seeking their own formulas of political modernization" (Weiner 1966, 20).

As noted, Parsons built into his conception of the system of modern societies the assumption that different countries would configure their modernity profile in different ways. Richard Münch (2001) has pursued this line of thought with exceptional fruitfulness, indicating the very different modes of ethical transformation manifested by England, France, Germany, and the United States (although his own forecast is that sooner or later, the American pattern of balanced interpenetration between ethics and world will develop in all modern societies).

Even so robust a proponent of the notion of multiple modernities as Shmuel Eisenstadt must assert a common core of all modernizing societies, even if its contents are colored differently. For Eisenstadt, this core consists of the effort to remake the world in accord with some sort of ideal program. To say this is to say that a core attribute of modernity is the instantiation of a high level of value rationality. This means that fundamentalist movements and societies are eminently "modern," in so far as they are geared to pursue such a program. The problem with a formula like "multiple modernities" is that it systematically neglects to represent the whole range of other processes that are constitutive of modernity besides value rationality, that is, functional specialization, individualization, political mobilization, normative universalism, new forms of discipline, and the rationalization of other cultural systems.

If the ideas put forward here make sense, then perhaps we might reconsider what needs to be said regarding the human condition in the modern era. This era has been marked by revolutions of many kinds, along lines that ushered in enormous benefits but that have also produced a wide range of unanticipated disadvantages. If to use the term "modernity" means to imagine that we inhabit an ever-improving epoch in a self-congratulatory state of mind, then perhaps we should follow the advice of analysts such as Albrow, Nico Stehr (2001), and others who counsel us to stop using the term. But if we link our analyses with those of the past two centuries and more by theorists of modernity who viewed the modernizing revolutions as producing unprecedented problems and challenges, and recast our image of modernity not as a destination but as a complex process of endless growth, problems, and challenges, then perhaps we can secure a more grounded, more inclusive dialogue about its central features and challenges. In such an effort, the pioneering ideas and insights of Talcott Parsons should stand us in good stead.

NOTES

1. Including the following:
   Karl Deutsch (1953), *Nationalism and Social Communication*
   Reinhard Bendix (1956), *Work and Authority in Industry*
   Neil Smelser (1958), *Social Change in the Industrial Revolution*
   Lloyd Fallers (1963), "Equality, Modernity, and Democracy in the New States"
   Clifford Geertz (1963), "The Integrative Revolution"
   Seymour M. Lipset (1963), *The First New Nation*
   Shmuel N. Eisenstadt (1963 to 1968), *Tradition, Change, and Modernity* (essays)
   Reinhard Bendix (1964), *Nation-Building and Citizenship*
   Lucien Pye and Sidney Verba, eds. (1965), *Political Culture and Political Development*
   David Apter (1965), *The Politics of Modernization*
   Edward Shils (1965), *Political Development in the New States*
   Myron Weiner (1966), *Modernization: The Dynamics of Growth*
2. Mark Gould (1991) has notably described *The Structure of Social Action* as being "sixty years ahead of its time."
3. Many philosophers have construed modernity as a set of ideals. See Jürgen Habermas (1987), Robert Pippin (1999), and Charles Larmore (1996).
4. Members of this group maintain that the term "modernity" should no longer be used to describe the current era. Some of them maintain that conditions in the past generation or two have altered so dramatically that we are now living in a postmodern or at least postindustrial society. This view has been rejected by me and others, who argue that the defining features of modernity have simply come to manifest themselves on a wider stage. However, some of those who reject the postmodernist position go on to claim that the current era is separated from a temporally demarcated modern era as a result of our now living de facto in a single world. This point is considered in a subsequent section of this chapter.
5. In so doing, I deliberately avoid other ways of dealing with intellectual differences of this sort, for example, by viewing them as so many alternative theories (what may be called a "pluralist" account); by maintaining the primacy of one to which all others are either subordinated (a "positivist" account); by trying to integrate them into a single conception (a "synthetic" account); or by reducing them to expressions of underlying socioeconomic or cultural interests (a "contextualist" account). See Donald N. Levine (1995).

6. "C'est seulement quand la répartition régulière des travaux humains a pu devenir convenablement étendue que l'état social a pu commencer à acquérir spontanément une consistance et une stabilité superieures à l'essor quelconque des divergences particulières" (Comte 1969, 479).
7. Smith, Marx, and Durkheim described the division of labor as having evolved over millennia. Comte and Elias described the formation of increasingly inclusive societal entities as an age-old process. Tocqueville and Elias represent the evolution of equalizing and civilizing processes, respectively, over many centuries of French history. For Comte and Weber, the processes of cultural rationalization extended across millennia.
8. Smith's account followed that of Adam Ferguson, whom some have called the "first sociologist" and who may be said to have initiated discourse on the social theory of modernity. In his *Essay on the History of Civil Society* (1767/1966), Ferguson offered a theory of the development of society from a "rude" to a "polished" state. The characteristics of polished society include the cultivation of arts and sciences, the attainment of efficient administration, and the refinement of commercial practices. Smith's analysis was carried forward by John Millar, who explored the impact of progress in the arts and manufactures upon the relations of the sexes and the structures of government.
9. Smith's critiques were echoed by his Scottish compatriots Adam Ferguson and John Millar, writers generally known for championing the new commercial order. As one commentator put it, the three of them looked at the other, dark, side of the coin of modern civilization, and saw "the paradox of the progress of commerce and manufactures . . . inevitably producing a second-rate sort of society full of second-rate citizens pursuing comparatively worthless objects" (Ferguson 1767/1966, xii).
10. Victor Lidz has made the interesting suggestion that Parsons's distinction between psychological systems and behavioral systems be viewed as equivalent to G. H. Mead's distinction between self and mind.
11. Lechner (1985, 165, second paragraph).
12. In the language of an earlier version of Parsonian action theory, one might say that the first two reactions represent an alienative response, whereas the latter two represent the type of reaction to ambivalence that takes the form of compulsive performance.
13. Dialogical analysis of initiatives proposed by educators in response to these problems will appear in Levine (forthcoming).

REFERENCES

Albrow, Martin. 1997. *The Global Age: State and Society Beyond Modernity.* Palo Alto: Stanford University Press.

Alexander, Jeffrey, ed. 1983. *The Modern Reconstruction of Classical Thought: Talcott Parsons.* Berkeley: University of California Press.

———. 1985. *Neofunctionalism.* Beverly Hills: Sage.

Bell, Daniel. 1976. *The Cultural Contradictions of Capitalism.* New York: Basic Books.

Camic, Charles. 1983. *Experience and Enlightenment: Socialization for Cultural Change in Eighteenth-Century Scotland.* Chicago: University of Chicago Press.

Colomy, Paul. 1985. "Uneven Structural Differentiation: Toward a Comparative Approach." In *Neofunctionalism,* edited by Jeffrey C. Alexander. Beverly Hills: Sage.

Comte, Auguste. 1839/1969. *Cours de la philosophie positive.* 5th edition. Paris: Éditions Anthropos.

Duncan, Otis Dudley. 1964. Introduction to *William F, Ogburn: On Culture and Social Change.* Chicago: University of Chicago Press.

Eisenstadt, Shmuel N. 1996. "Barbarism and Modernity." *Society* 33(May–June): 31–39.

———. 1999. *Fundamentalism, Sectarianism, and Revolution: The Jacobin Dimension of Modernity.* Cambridge: Cambridge University Press.

———. 2000. "Multiple Modernities." *Daedalus* 129(1): 1–29.

———. 2003. *Comparative Civilizations and Multiple Modernities.* 2 volumes. Leiden, The Netherlands: Koninklijke Brill.

Elias, Norbert. 1936/2000. *The Civilizing Process: Sociogenetic and Psychogenetic Investigations.* Translated by Edmund Jephcott. Malden, Mass.: Blackwell.

Ferguson, Adam. 1767/1966. *An Essay on the History of Civil Society.* Edinburgh: Edinburgh University Press.

Foucault, Michel. 1975/1979. *Discipline and Punish: The Birth of the Prison.* Translated by Alan Sheridan. New York: Vintage Books.

Geertz, Clifford. 1973. *The Interpretation of Cultures.* New York: Basic Books.

Goldfarb, Jeffrey. 1991. *The Cynical Society: The Culture of Politics and the Politics of Culture in American Life.* Chicago: University of Chicago Press.

Gorski, Philip. 1993. "The Protestant Ethic Revisited: Disciplinary Revolution in Holland and Prussia." *American Journal of Sociology* 99(2): 265–316.

Gould, Mark. 1991. "*The Structure of Social Action:* At Least Sixty Years Ahead of Its Time." In *Talcott Parsons: Theorist of Modernity,* edited by Roland Robertson and Bryan S. Turner. London: Sage.

Habermas, Jürgen. 1987. *The Philosophical Discourse of Modernity.* Cambridge, Mass.: MIT Press.

Hennis, Wilhelm. 1988. *Max Weber: Essays in Reconstruction.* Translated by Keith Tribe. London: Allen & Unwin.

Jencks, Christopher, and David Riesman. 1968. *The Academic Revolution.* Garden City, N.Y.: Doubleday.

Larmore, Charles. 1996. *The Morals of Modernity.* Cambridge: Cambridge University Press.

Lechner, Frank. 1985. "Modernity and Its Discontents." In *Neofunctionalism,* edited by Jeffrey C. Alexander. Beverly Hills: Sage.

Levine, Donald N. 1995. *Visions of the Sociological Tradition.* Chicago: University of Chicago Press.

———. Forthcoming. *Powers of the Mind: The Reinvention of Liberal Learning.* Chicago: University of Chicago Press.

Mead, G. H. 1929. "National-Mindedness and International-Mindedness." *International Journal of Ethics* 39(4): 385–407.

Münch, Richard. 2001. *The Ethics of Modernity.* New York: Rowman & Littlefeld.

Ogburn, W. F. 1922. *Social Change with Respect to Culture and Original Nature.* New York: B. W. Huebsch Inc.

Olson, Mancur. 1965. *The Logic of Collective Action.* New York: Schocken Books.

Park, Robert E. 1926/1967. "The Urban Community as a Spatial Pattern and Moral Order." In *Robert E. Park on Social Control and Collective Behavior,* edited by Ralph H. Turner. Chicago: University of Chicago Press.

Parsons, Talcott. 1961. Introduction to *The Study of Society,* by Herbert Spencer. Ann Arbor: University of Michigan Press.

———. 1964. "Evolutionary Universals in Society." *American Sociological Review* 29(3): 339–57.

———. 1971. *The System of Modern Societies.* Englewood Cliffs, N.J.: Prentice-Hall.

Pippin, Robert B. 1999. *Modernism as a Philosophical Problem.* 2nd ed. Maiden, Mass.: Blackwell.

Putnam, Robert D. 2000. *Bowling Alone: The Collapse and Revival of American Community.* New York: Simon & Schuster.

Redfield, Robert. 1941. *The Folk Culture of Yucatan.* Chicago: University of Chicago Press.

Sennett, Richard. 1998. *The Corrosion of Character.* New York: Norton.

Simmel, Georg. 1968. *The Conflict in Modern Culture and Other Essays.* Translated by Peter Etzkorn. New York: Teachers College Press.

———. 1911/1968. "On the Concept and Tragedy of Culture." In *The Conflict of Modern Culture and Other Essays.* Translated by K. Peter Etzkorn. New York: Teachers College.

———. 1971. *On Individuality and Social Forms.* Chicago: University of Chicago Press.

———. 1978. *The Philosophy of Money.* Boston: Routledge & Kegan Paul.

———. 1890/1989. *Über soziale Differenzierung. Georg Simmel: Gesamtausgabe.* Volume 2. Frankfurt am Main: Suhrkamp.

Slater, Philip. 1976. *The Pursuit of Loneliness.* Boston: Beacon Press.

Smith, Adam. 1776/1976. *An Inquiry into the Nature and Causes of The Wealth of Nations.* Chicago: University of Chicago Press.

Spencer, Herbert. 1861/1911. "Physical Education." In *Essays on Education and Kindred Subjects.* New York: E. P. Dutton & Co.

Stehr, Nico. 2001. *The Fragility of Modern Societies.* London: Sage.

Sumner, William Graham. 1907/2002. *Folkways: A Study of Mores, Manners, Customs, and Morals.* Mineola, N.Y.: Dover.

Thomas, W. I. 1923. *The Unadjusted Girl.* Boston: Little, Brown.

Tocqueville, Alexis de. 1835–40/1969. *Democracy in America.* New York: HarperCollins.

Weber, Max. 1968. *Economy and Society,* edited by Günther Roth and Claus Wittich. New York: Bedminster Press.

Weiner, Myron, ed. 1966. *Modernization: The Dynamics of Growth.* New York: Basic Books.

Weinstein, Fred, and Gerald M. Platt. 1969. *The Wish to Be Free.* Berkeley: University of California Press.

Whitehead, Alfred North. 1933. *Adventures of Ideas.* New York: Macmillan.

Williams, Raymond. 1983. *Keywords: A Vocabulary of Culture and Society.* Revised ed. New York: Oxford University Press.

Wittrock, Björn. 2000. "Modernity: One, None, or Many? European Origins and Modernity as a Global Condition." *Daedalus* 129(1): 31–60.

Part III

Sociology and Culture

Chapter 9

Culture as a Subsystem of Action: Autonomous and Heteronomous Functions

Helmut Staubmann

> The purpose of the following statements lies in the discovery that, besides societal life as a basic force and a comprehensive formula of human life, the origin and interpretation of the latter must also be based on the objective meaning of its contents and on the nature and productivity of individuals as such.
>
> —Georg Simmel (1917/1999, 78)[1]

> If human beings developed culture to survive, nevertheless cultural objects, which exist only as a result of the struggle to survive and otherwise would not exist, are no longer necessary to sustain life. Culture's irrevocable attainment of independence vis-à-vis society . . . is itself . . . something societal. . . . If this independence is simply denied, then culture becomes suppressed and serves no less an ideological purpose for the existing order than there where it is ideologically assumed as something absolute.
>
> —Theodor W. Adorno (1959/1972, 121)

The German poet Johann Wolfgang von Goethe once said that all the clever ideas have already been had; it is only a matter of thinking them again. There is hardly any other intellectual field that would provide more evidence for Goethe's dictum than sociology and the history of ideas associated with our discipline. In this sense, the following considerations do not claim to present something really new. Following Goethe's invitation, they are directed toward a reconstruction. It will be a matter of calling to mind an important intellectual tradition that nevertheless became largely submerged in the collective memory—as we now say—of our sociological community. The focus will be on the reconstruction of some of the basic assumptions, implications, and consequences of Talcott Parsons's concept of culture within his general theory of action in order to locate it within a wider tradition of the theory of culture and also to confront and contrast it with issues in the contemporary debate on culture in the social sciences. This debate is dominated by a current of thought labeled "cultural theory," "cultural sociology," or simply "cultural studies."

PARSONS'S TRANSCENDENCE OF A "FALSE DILEMMA"

"In the jungle of certain kinds of communication . . . ," Parsons (1977, 127) wrote in his commentary on Harold Bershady's *Ideology and Social Knowledge* (1973), it would be hard to get rid of some labels associated with his work. But, he continued, "I would still like to be on record as protesting" against their appropriateness. However one assesses the success of his protest, I think that what Parsons formulated in respect to certain interpretations of him as a structural-functionalist might also be valid for his image as a theorist of culture.

The common historiography of the development in the theory of culture locates Parsons on one extreme point of a pendulum swing. The rise of materialistic "profoundly anti-cultural social theories" in the late sixties such as neo-Marxism or conflict theory is seen by some as a "massive reaction against cultural explanation in American sociology" (Smith 1998, 1) that was closely associated with Parsonian functionalism. The "new cultural sociology" in turn is interpreted by others as correcting an overreaction of these materialistic perspectives to the alleged "functional determinism" (Anne Kane [1998, 85], explicitly referring to Robert Bellah [1957] and Neil Smelser [1959]). Thus, a new intellectual generation "embraced culture, swinging with the pendulum into an almost empty field" (Smith 1998, 3). We are now warned against the too far-reaching idealism of cultural sociologists, who, as Kane continues, "often have gone to extremes in their culturally deterministic explanation" (1998, 85, referring to Jeffrey Alexander [1988], for example). The beginning of such pendular oscillations in the views taken of culture might be traced back at least to the nineteenth century and Marx's famous claim to have turned Hegel's dialectics right side up, from standing on its head to standing on its feet. In an ironical rendering one could say that the history of sociocultural ideas appears in such a perspective as a sequence of somersaults or cartwheels, at one moment the head is up, at the next, the feet, but owing to a structural imbalance of the position of one part of the body, sociocultural ideas keep on tumbling.

All such unproductive cyclic movements of thought could have come to an end in 1937 at the latest when Parsons's *The Structure of Social Action* appeared. This work is a lengthy elaboration of the insight that the dichotomy of idealism and materialism or positivism as such is flawed. This is a core idea that Parsons discussed and developed from the very beginning of his first opus magnum and throughout his entire work.

In the very last talk Parsons gave, in May 1979 in Heidelberg, he spoke of three pillars of action theory. All of them are the result of the overcoming of false dilemmas in which diverse intellectual traditions were trapped, an achievement he attributed to Max Weber: the methodological dilemma arising from the distinction between "natural sciences" and "cultural sciences," the sociological dilemma stemming from Ferdinand Tönnies's dichotomy of "community" and "society," and in addition what he called the "philosophical pillar." "It seems to me," he said, "that Weber transcended the dilemma of dichotomizing action-reality in terms of the two categories 'Realfaktoren' and 'Idealfaktoren.' He refused to accept an either-or in this respect, and that either-or had permeated not merely German but much more broadly based thought. It had something to do with the intellectual structure since the philosophical revolution of the seventeenth and eighteenth centuries. It culminated in the dichotomy of idealism and positivism, and positivism in action theory was an extension of the concept of real determinance, from the world of nature to the world of human action, whereas idealism emphasized a different order of concern" (Parsons 1979, 152–53). Parsons's argument may well be rooted in Weberian works, but it is genuinely Parsons's achievement to have elaborated this thought in a systematic way and to have made it an essential feature of his theory of action.

This was *the* guiding idea from the very beginning of what was by then called the voluntaristic theory of action, which is that neither the instrumentality of the utilitarian-positivistic action model nor, to put it simply, the normativity of the idealistic action model is sufficient to describe and explain action. Both paradigms refer to structurally independent action components that have to be given corresponding consideration in all action analyses (see Staubmann 1998, 507). With this elementary idea, Parsons criticized the "basic fallacy of idealistic thought" (Parsons 1982, 57) as well as the concomitant fallacy of positivistic-materialistic thought. Parsons thereby took an important first step in overcoming one of the most persistent "false dilemmas" impeding the development of the social sciences.

The expression "structural independence" implies that action is not a mere addition of action components that would be quantitatively specifiable in percentage terms—for example, the writing of a book is 90 percent cultural and 10 percent economical whereas the printing of the same book is 90 percent economical and 10 percent cultural. As Parsons put it: "In general such a question is meaningless, being of the same order as the old biological argument over heredity versus environment" (Parsons 1977, 50). This makes clear that Parsons's voluntarism is not a compromise between idealism and positivism in the sense of a middle position. Arnold Schönberg's bon mot that all roads lead to Rome with the exception of the middle one would also apply here. The result of what Parsons called convergence meant a genuinely new synthesis.[2] A sociology that tries to reach beyond the mechanistic understanding of social action has to restate the problem as such. This is exactly what Parsons did in a discussion of the relationship of social systems and culture that he wrote with Alfred Kroeber, where they say, "It is no longer a question of how important each is, but of how each works and how they are interwoven with each other" (Parsons and Kroeber 1958, 583). Traditional concepts of action are too simplistic to deal adequately with these questions. Thus, the solution must be sought in a "more differentiated conceptual scheme." The voluntaristic frame of reference outlined in *The Structure of Social Action* is a first version of such a differentiated conceptual scheme that Parsons continued to refine and broaden throughout his life.

The attempt to sketch an answer to the question of how culture works and how it is interwoven with other components of human action is based on two axioms, or premises, implicit in all stages of the development of Parsonian action theory. In its most mature version, the codification of action theory within the AGIL paradigm, these are:

First, the clear differentiation of structurally independent subsystems of the general action system: culture, social system, personality, and behavioral systems. Structural independence means that "neither can be directly reduced to terms of the other; that is to say, the order of relationships within one is independent from that of the other" (Parsons and Kroeber 1958, 582). This includes their subdifferentiation according to what Parsons called the basic modes of orientation: cognitive-instrumental, cathectic-expressive, moral-evaluative, and constitutive-religious.

Second, the description of the interrelations of the subsystems of action. A core intention of Parsons's description of interrelation of culture with the other subsystems of action can be expressed by distinguishing two types of function that the respective subsystems achieve for each other, namely an autonomous function or a heteronomous function. In regard to our question of the status of culture within the general system of action, the term "autonomous function" relates to the fact that culture as such influences the processes and structures of social, personal, and behavioral systems. The term "heteronomous function" describes the "use" of culture for noncultural purposes such as economical or political ones—to anticipate two of the most evident examples of central concern in cultural sociology.

CULTURE AS A STRUCTURALLY INDEPENDENT SUBSYSTEM

Every action requires a form in which it is carried out. Each of these forms can be analytically separated, and in the course of sociocultural evolution can be detached as an objective entity from the interacting subjects. In this sense culture is indeed "accumulated history" (Bourdieu 1983, 83), sedimented in patterns of knowing, feeling, valuing, in forms of religious and artistic experiences, of producing goods, of intimate relationships, and so forth. The crucial point, however, in Parsonian action theory is that the accumulation of action products is not to be understood as a mechanistic piling up of history. This is not even true for the process of economic accumulation. We only can speak of cultural forms when the respective patterns attain a structurally independent status vis-à-vis the historical process. In terms of traditional philosophy, as formulated, for example, by Georg Simmel, culture transcends actions and the respective circumstances by which it is produced. Modern systems theory expresses the same idea with the notion of the emergent quality of culture. Karl Popper kept the term "objectivity" for what he called the "third world," despite the danger of falling within an intellectual cohort labeled by postmodernists as "objectivist fools" (Kenneth Gergen). Adorno insisted that art, as culture in general, is autonomous vis-à-vis social and personal life, and has a sui generis existence.

These examples demonstrate that Parsons's culture concept is thoroughly compatible with a wider tradition of culture theory, even if this tradition is regarded by cultural sociologists as merely "the atavistic legacy of European structuralist rhetorics" (Smith 1998, 8). At any rate, the basic fact of Parsons's view needs to be kept in mind: art and science, like all cultural forms, are not to be interpreted and explained as mere accumulations of action products but as entities that in the course of action and interaction attain meaning and reality in their own right.

To illustrate this thought, take the example of the nearly identically worded critique of materialistic art theories of Talcott Parsons and Georg Simmel. Simmel explicitly posed the question "What do we see in a work of art?" His answer (Simmel 2005, 147–48) contrasted a genuinely artistic experience with that of a naturalistic conception:

> Here lies the most basic error of historicism and psychologism that is repeated in the naturalistic theory of art. . . . all these intellectual tendencies bear a formal resemblance, namely they bind the specific quality and essence of an attained result, a being or work that has come into existence, a realized category to the quality and essence that are specific to the conditions and realizing mediations of those achievements. Those theories are ultimately opposed to [the notion that] there might be contents, categories, and worlds—that are not deducible from each other—within the objective realm; and that there might be a genuine creative act in the subjective realm. For them, an existence or a sense, a value or an arrangement, should be nothing other than that which we are presented with by the various phases undergone by that which has come into being. . . . And to construct . . . a culture out of economic circumstances, an idea out of experiences, a work of art out of impressions from nature, is no more sensible than developing the fully formed bodily figure out of the foodstuffs *without* which it clearly could not have come into being. (emphasis in original)

Parsons formulates (1961, 969) his view of the same subject in the following way:

> The cultural categories which belong here . . . are categories of expressive symbolism, as distinguished from the intrinsic cathectic interest in "real" objects. . . . An example would be the Madonna and child of Renaissance painting as the portrayal of a realistic social relationship type of great importance in the society of the time, but as "meaning" more than a pictorial representation of an actual mother and child. The facilities which are necessary to build up . . . a symbolic representation are the technical devices and procedures utilized by the artist . . . But this technically produced symbol acquires its artistic meaning by virtue of its incorporation in still higher-order meaning or pattern systems.

According to this line of thought, culture clearly is to be understood as the product of action but it constitutes an order in its own right, transcending the social and individual forces by which it is produced. This very thought has frequently been misunderstood and correspondingly criticized, especially by "cultural sociologists." An example is Ann Swidler's specific version (1998, 173) of the well-known attempt to "de-Parsonize" Weber:

> For Weber's interest in the historical role of ideas, Parsons substituted global, a-historical values. Unlike ideas, which in Weber's sociology are complex historical constructions shaped by institutional interests, political vicissitudes, and pragmatic motives, Parsonian values are abstract, general and immanent in social systems. . . . Indeed, Parsons does not treat values as concrete symbolic elements . . . which have histories and can actually be studied. Rather, values are the essences around which societies are constituted. They are the unmoved mover in the theory of action.

Besides some obvious distortions of Parsons's view, such a critique is based on a conflation of the question of the production of culture and its resulting autonomy, a mistake that leads to sociologism or to a sociological reductionistic interpretation of culture to which I shall refer later. Within the broad tradition of culture theory, of which Parsonian action theory is a part, culture indeed reaches beyond the pursuit of particularistic social interests and individual pragmatic motives. However, the conclusion that this implies for the conception of culture as an "unmoved mover" displays ignorance of the many excellent examples provided by Parsons and his collaborators of how culture is produced in the course of action and interaction. Let me remind the reader of Parsons, Robert Bales, and Edward Shils's (1952) study on "phase movement in relation to motivation, symbol formation, and role structure," a study that describes in a theoretically most sophisticated way how cultural orientation patterns are the result of resolving concomitant functional problems on the individual motivational level as well as on the level of social interaction.

THE AUTONOMOUS FUNCTION OF CULTURE FOR SUBSYSTEMS OF ACTION

Parsons's specific solution of the clear distinction of a culture system with its own logic and his subsequent description of the interrelation with other subsystems of action resolves a further "false dilemma" of the common cultural discourse: the, let's say, archetypical dichotomy of relevance versus autonomy. Adorno, in his aesthetic theory, called this alternative the wrong nomenclature of (bourgeois) formalism on one side and (socialist) realism on the other. To escape such a "disjunction of sheep and goats" (Adorno 1970, 380) requires what Adorno called a double reflection of culture, which relates the immanence of the laws of cultural forms to the specific social and psychological conditions. It is exactly in this sense that Parsons replaced the mechanistic pair of opposites by the idea that precisely the autonomous status of culture is a prerequisite of its relevance to the individual as well as to the social world. Personal and social life unfolds and realizes itself within objectified cultural forms. This is the fundamental significance of culture within (sub)systems of action.

To describe this process of accessing exterior cultural patterns on behalf of the more or less successful development of individuals and social systems, Parsons incorporated concepts from a variety of disciplines: general systems theory, cybernetics, psychoanalysis, biology, and others. The most familiar terms are internalization and institutionalization. Neither of these processes is to be understood as a simple input mechanism in the sense of a cultural determinism blurring the clear distinctions between subsystems attained beforehand. Such a determinism degrades humans to mere cultural puppets as expressed by the much acclaimed yet unjustified criticism of the alleged conception of an "oversocialized man." On the contrary, it is a matter of the formation of genuinely personal and social structures and processes. In both cases, however, this is accomplished by giving primacy to culture in the criterion of their forming. Within the AGIL-paradigm Parsons went on to develop a highly complex interchange paradigm and described "zones of interpenetration" that crosscut subsystems on the basis of the respective functions.

The ideal type, as it were, of a "cultural study" based on such indispensable action-theoretical premises is Parsons's last monograph *The American University* (1973, written with Gerald M. Platt). Its main concern is the status and development of rational components of action in a differentiated modern society. On the cultural level the subdivision in question is knowledge structured in cognitive-rational patterns of meaning. In general, the "autonomous function" of this part of culture is to serve as orientation and provide solutions for problems associated with rational-instrumental types of action and, on the social level, the guidance of rational types of interaction and communication. This requires a concomitant capacity of individuals, a rational competence which in turn is dependent on the culturalization of a behavioral prerequisite that Parsons named intelligence.

The central role of universities is to deal with and further enhance the cognitive rational components on all these levels of the general action system. They can only do so in that they are, as social organizations, committed to values of rationality, to "the ethos of science" (Merton 1990, 67) as part of an institutionalized commitment to culture. The respective structures and processes of the social system are described as the "culture fiduciary" subsystem.

Within modern society, this commitment to cultural rationality standards of universities can only be realized insofar as it coincides with the interests of other social forces in precisely its autonomous function.

> In relation to the conception of a cultural pattern, the criterion of institutionalization is the engagement of the interests of acting units, individual and/or collective, in the implementation of normatively defined patterns. The main criterion of institutionalization is that, ideally, the goal-interest of the unit coincides with the functional significance of its contribution from the point of view of the subsystem. (Parsons and Platt 1973, 34)

The relationships between subsystems are in a delicate balance that Parsons analyzed in terms of his theory of generalized media of communication and interchange. Instabilities such as inflation or deflation of trust in rationality and in the diverse features of the cognitive complex, appear as crises based on the extent of the fulfillment or disappointment of expectations concerning the performance of the core functions by universities.

HETERONOMOUS FUNCTIONS OF CULTURE FOR SUBSYSTEMS OF ACTION

The alternatives to the autonomous function of culture for "subsystems of action" as exemplified in Parsons's study of the American university system are twofold. On the one hand, culture can be deprived of its significance for action at all. The expression of the university as an ivory tower suggests this, for which the slogan "l'art pour l'art" is the aesthetic analogue. On the other hand, the connection can be "reduced to an instrumental one" (Parsons 1977, 96), as Parsons formulated it in a critique of Bronislaw Malinowski's *Scientific Theory of Culture.* Cultural sociology in general takes the second path by "deconstructing" culture as a product as well as a means—a "tool-kit"—of the pursuit of political or economical interests.

One of the chapters of Adorno's *Introduction to the Sociology of Music* (*Einleitung in die Musiksoziologie,* 1973) carries the simple title "Function." It is a brilliant explanation and critique of what I call the heteronomous function of culture. He starts with the question of what it means that a quantitatively relevant part of our intellectual and cultural life has a fundamentally different social function than it would have according to its specific meaning. "What does a phenomenon mean for society which as such, what it is, does not even reach society?" A (heteronomous) social function is "the rest of what remains of art, when the moment of art has dissolved in it" such as entertainment, distraction, the demonstration of a superficial musical expertise for status reasons, characteristic of a type of person for whom Adorno used the untranslatable derogatory expression "Bildungsbürger" (culture snob, literally, cultured middle-class person). According to Adorno, the latter devote much time to a subject that remains inaccessible to them (Adorno 1973, 223). Cultural sociology is endangered in face of a similar fate on the theoretical level. It is an irony and logically irresolvable paradox that the same intellectual movement that attacked Parsonian functionalism now stands for a position of cultural functional analysis that is even worse in its reductionistic one-dimensionality than the one they had baselessly ascribed to Parsons.

As an illustration, "I may use an example of special concern to that category of investigators labeled 'cultural (cultural added H. St) sociologists' " (to use Parsons's wording [1977, 105]). There is a unanimous accord that "Pierre Bourdieu . . . offered new ways of thinking about culture's relationship to social stratification and power" (Swidler 1998, 172). In Parsonian terms, however, Bourdieu's probably best-known "monumental study" (Mary Douglas in Bourdieu 1984, back cover), his social critique of the judgment of taste, is thoroughly within a positivistic tradition without displaying any sign of what Parsons called convergence. It reads like a mixture of John B. Watson's behaviorism and Marx's materialism: different objective class situations determine concomitant forms of what Bourdieu calls "habitus." Methodologically, he demands (1984, 101) that

> one must return to the practice-unifying and practice-generating principle i.e., class habitus, the internalized form of class condition and of the conditionings it entails. One must therefore construct the *objective class,* the set of agents who are placed in homogeneous conditions of existence imposing homogenous conditionings and producing homogeneous systems of dispositions capable of generating similar practices.

This passage clearly demonstrates that Bourdieu operates with a theoretical frame, which one could well characterize as the "conception of the over-economized man."

Accordingly, resulting aesthetic judgments are a matter of class distinctions. This conception explicitly claims to "deconstruct" the idea of "pure taste" in the autonomous cultural sense as a disguise of "real" social forces. The randomness of likes and dislikes in fashion are thereby equated with aesthetic judgments within the arts. Someone who has a preference for Bach's Well-Tempered Clavier (see Bourdieu 1984, 19) does not do so because of an aesthetic appreciation of this music per se but to display a bourgeois habitus. Similarly the piano is "the bourgeois instrument par excellence" (Bourdieu 1984, 19), elevating its owner to high class status, and must not be naïvely misunderstood as primarily a means for the creation of music. In short, the social meaning of taste for Bourdieu is its use for nonaesthetic purposes, above all to symbolize status and power.

For Parsons, as he wrote in *The Social System,* this is the special case of the snob or of "the vulgarity of the parvenu. He . . . tends to distort style symbols from their more intrinsic expressive significance in relation to disciplined appreciative norms, into predominately status symbols. . . . His need to symbolize his status is compulsive" (Parsons 1951, 421). A theory of such deplorable creatures cannot simply be taken as a model for cultural sociology in general. This would transfer the amnesia toward the objective content of aesthetics that certain people suffer, as Adorno expressed it, into an analogous conceptual amnesia of action analysis toward the significance of culture. To avoid such a shortcoming it must be acknowledged and taken into account that "concern with knowledge and its advancement is analytically independent of its practical uses. Similarly, art is not primarily concerned with furthering societal interests, nor is religion primarily an instrument of enhancing economic productivity" (Parsons and Platt 1973, 33).

Bourdieu's concept of cultural capital has been well received and has stimulated much research in the field of cultural studies. In the spirit of Parsons's endeavor to unify different intellectual traditions, there has recently been an attempt to establish parallels between what Bourdieu calls cultural, social, political and economical capital with some of Parsons's symbolic media of interchange, particularly money, power, influence, and value-commitment (see Fararo 2001, 291–93).

There may indeed be some terminological similarities. However, in the line of the argument that I have presented up to now we are dealing with totally incompatible concepts. Capital and power are for Bourdieu synonymous concepts. The different forms of capital are a result of a considerable effort to reveal the fact that they are all objectively of economical character (see Bourdieu 1983, 184; 1991, 170). According to him, an economical science of praxis has to grasp capital and profit in all their appearances. Thus, both cultural and social capital are forms of economic capital, which in turn is equated with political power. Cultural capital is by no means a matter of the accumulation of cultural capacities as described by Parsons or of a commitment to cultural standards but a means of the attainment of positions via, for example, academic titles and thus the possibility to convert such cultural capital (back) into that what it "in reality" is anyway: economical capital.

Research based on such a concept of cultural capital, such as Paul DiMaggio's study of the role of cultural capital in school success, clearly shows that cultural capital is reduced to a means of the allocation of positions, mobility strategies, spouse selection, and so forth. His attempt to link Bourdieu's cultural capital with what he describes as "Max Weber's notion of *status culture*" (1998, 260) blatantly illustrates the conceptual ambiguity. For Weber, a certain type of social class (German "Stand") is defined by the positive or negative social assessment of honor connected with shared characteristics of a plurality of persons which finds its expression in a specific common style of life (see Weber 1925, 635). This very specific conception of a connection between a valued lifestyle and a social class turns in DiMaggio's terminological remake into a general concept of status culture. The latter now appears as an arbitrary social construction motivated by matters of prestige. Accordingly, similar patterns of art museum visitation, concert attendance, and literature reading in higher classes are explained by the prestige which these art forms convey. Consequently, cultural behavior is identified as "instruments for the appropriation of symbolic wealth *socially* designated as worthy of being sought and possessed" (Bourdieu, quoted by DiMaggio 1998, 261; emphasis added), which is the definition of cultural capital.

Such a "debunking of culture" (Adorno 1977, 88) is itself an ideological pattern frequently disputed in Parsons's work: "The very ready tendency to derogate such symbolism often takes the form immortalized by Veblen in the phrase 'conspicuous consumption,' with the allegation that people lived in comfortable and tasteful houses, or wore attractive clothes, *in order,* for instrumental motives, to enhance their prestige" (Parsons 1977, 364). Insofar as this occurs it is a special case of a general problem in differentiated societies—namely, the conflation of symbolically generalized media. Sociology needs to work with a conceptual scheme that allows the perception of this problem as an empirical question.

A theory of social stratification and of power that does not take into account the independent status and the content of culture gives up the chance to explore the specific effects of culture on social relationships. Culture, precisely because it is a supra-subjective phenomenon, affects other forms of authority, domination, and subordination than prestige. It would be the primary task of cultural sociology to reveal and explore the respective relationships. To perform this task it is necessary to go beyond Bourdieu's largely accepted monistic theory of capital, where forms of capital are merely different appearances—and thus easily convertible among each other—of one and the same power, which results "in the last instance" from an economically defined praxis.

Simmel, who was often less polite than Parsons in formulating his critique, commented strongly on similar positions of his time: "For the naïve person only the world of . . . praxis is the reality as such; . . . if the world is formed by the categories of art or of religion, of emotional values or of philosophical speculation, this is only of concern as a superstructure above that only real existence or it is thought of as opposed to it. . . . From this there arise uncertainties and confusions in the concepts of world and life" (Simmel 1995, 43).

To avoid such problems, we should take the warning of confusion literally. Instead of taking the path of postmodern dedifferentiation and the regressive fusions of concepts and disciplines as represented in large areas of cultural sociology, we need to further pursue the Parsonian lead and meet his demand for a conceptual differentiation in the theory of action. It is this important legacy of Parsons that Niklas Luhmann, one of his students, called "sociological enlightenment": providing a highly complex theory to help us come to terms with the increasing complexity of our contemporary sociocultural world.

NOTES

1. All quotations from German works are the author's translations.
2. For a profound elaboration of the "obvious relevance to the construction of a genuinely synthetic historical sociology of art" in precisely this sense of synthesis beyond the "continued oscillation between idealism and materialism" (Tanner 2000, 287), which is repeated in the sociology of art, see Jeremy Tanner (2000).

REFERENCES

Adorno, Theodor W. 1970. *Ästhetische Theorie.* Frankfurt am Main: Suhrkamp.

———. 1972. "Theorie der Halbbildung." In *Soziologische Schriften.* Frankfurt am Main: Suhrkamp.

———. 1973. *Einleitung in die Musiksoziologie.* In Volume 14, *Gesammelte Schriften.* Frankfurt am Main: Suhrkamp.

———. 1977. "Veblens Angriff auf die Kultur." In *Prismen: Kulturkritik und Gesellschaft.* Frankfurt am Main: Suhrkamp.

Alexander, Jeffrey C. 1988. "Cultural and Political Crisis: Watergate and Durkheimian Sociology." In *Durkheimian Sociology,* edited by Jeffrey C. Alexander. New York: Columbia University Press.

Bellah, Robert. 1957. *Tokugawa Religion.* Glencoe, Ill.: Free Press.

Bershady, Harold. 1973. *Ideology and Social Knowledge.* Oxford: Blackwell.

Bourdieu, Pierre. 1983. "Ökonomisches Kapital, kulturelles Kapital, soziales Kapital." *Soziale Welt,* special volume 2, 183–98.

———. 1984. *Distinction: A Social Critique of the Judgement of Taste.* London: Routledge.

———. 1991. *Language and Symbolic Power.* Cambridge: Polity Press.

DiMaggio, Paul. 1998. "The Role of Cultural Capital in School Success." In *The New American Cultural Sociology,* edited by Philip Smith. Cambridge: Cambridge University Press.

Fararo, Thomas J. 2001. *Social Action Systems: Foundation and Synthesis in Sociological Theory.* Westport, Conn.: Praeger.

Kane, Anne. 1998. "Analytic and Concrete Forms of the Autonomy of Culture." In *The New American Cultural Sociology,* edited by Philip Smith. Cambridge: Cambridge University Press.

Merton, Robert K. 1990. "The Normative Structure of Science." In *Culture and Society: Contemporary Debates,* edited by Jeffrey C. Alexander and Steven Seidmann. Cambridge: Cambridge University Press.

Parsons, Talcott. 1937. *The Structure of Social Action.* 2 Volumes. New York: Free Press.

———. 1951. *The Social System.* Glencoe, Ill.: Free Press.

———. 1961. "Culture and the Social System—Introduction." In *Theories of Society: Foundations of Modern Sociological Theory,* edited by Talcott Parsons, Edward Shils, Kaspar D. Naegele, and Jesse R. Pitts. New York: Free Press.

———. 1977. *Social Systems and the Evolution of Action Theory.* New York: Free Press.

———. 1979. "On the Relation of the Theory of Action to Max Weber's 'Verstehende Soziologie.' " In *Verhalten, Handeln und System: Talcott Parsons' Beitrag zur Entwicklung der Sozialwissenschaften,* edited by Wolfgang Schluchter. Frankfurt am Main: Suhrkamp.

———. 1982. "Action Symbols and Cybernetic Control." In *Structural Sociology,* edited by Ino Rossi. New York: Columbia University Press.

Parsons, Talcott, Robert F. Bales, and Edward A. Shils. 1952. "Phase Movement in Relation to Motivation, Symbol Formation, and Role Structure." In *Working Papers in the Theory of Action,* edited by Talcott Parsons, Robert F. Bales, and Edward A. Shils. New York: Free Press.

Parsons, Talcott, and A. L. Kroeber. 1958. "The Concepts of Culture and of Social System." *American Sociological Review* 23: 582–83.

Parsons, Talcott, and Gerald M. Platt. 1973. *The American University.* Cambridge, Mass.: Harvard University Press.

Simmel, Georg. 1995. *Die Religion.* In Volume 10, *Georg Simmel: Gesamtausgabe.* Frankfurt am Main: Suhrkamp.

———. 1917/1999. *Grundfragen der Soziologie.* In Volume 16, *Georg Simmel: Gesamtausgabe.* Frankfurt am Main: Suhrkamp.

———. 2005. *Rembrandt: An Essay in the Philosophy of Art.* Translated, edited, and with an introduction by Alan Scott and Helmut Staubmann. New York: Routledge.

Smelser, Neil J. 1959. *Social Change and the Industrial Revolution.* Chicago: University of Chicago Press.

Smith, Philip. 1998. "The New American Cultural Sociology: An Introduction." In *The New American Cultural Sociology,* edited by Philip Smith. Cambridge: Cambridge University Press.

Staubmann, Helmut. 1998. "Overcoming Flawed Dichotomies: The Impact of Georg Simmel on American Sociology." *International Journal of Politics, Culture and Society* 11: 501–15.

Swidler, Ann. 1998. "Culture and Social Action." In *The New American Cultural Sociology,* edited by Philip Smith. Cambridge: Cambridge University Press.

Tanner, Jeremy. 2000. "The Body, Expressive Culture and Social Interaction: Integrating Art History and Action Theory." In *Talcott Parsons: Zur Aktualität eines Theorieprogramms,* edited by Helmut Staubmann and Harald Wenzel. Wiesbaden: Westdeutscher Verlag.

Weber, Max. 1925. *Wirtschaft und Gesellschaft.* Tübingen: J. C. B Mohr.

Chapter 10

Rationalists, Fetishists, and Art Lovers: Action Theory and the Comparative Analysis of High Cultural Institutions

Jeremy Tanner

> I do not think one can be a first rate interpreter of any current social situation without comparative and evolutionary perspective nor, vice versa, that one can be a good comparativist or evolutionist without the deepest concern for one's own society and the "meaning" of its characteristics and trends of change.
>
> —Talcott Parsons, "Comparative Studies and Evolutionary Change" (1971a, 1977, 320)

> Man [after the Fall] pursued many useful occupations differing from each other; and some were and are more theoretical than others; they could not all be alike, since theory is more worthy.
>
> —Cennini, circa 1400 (1960, 1–2)

This chapter deals with two key issues in the sociology of art, the social construction of the role of the artist and the nature of high culture. It poses the question of how they might be approached differently than they are in currently popular approaches, and attempts to answer it by using the comparative and evolutionary perspective advocated by Parsons as part of action theory. I will briefly sketch the state of play in contemporary sociology of the artist and high culture, and the set of concepts and models from within action theory that I will use to approach these issues. The core of the chapter is a comparative analysis of artistic differentiation in ancient Greek and modern Western culture, focusing in particular on the social and cultural construction of aesthetic experience and the broader entailments of variant structurings of such experience.

INTRODUCTION: CONCEPTS AND PROBLEMS

The dominant orientations in recent sociology of art have been characterized by a materialist approach seeking to desacralize the modern institution of art. Their practitioners focus in particular on the concept of the artist as "creator" and the discourse of "art loving" associated with normative etiquette of art consumption. Adherents of the production-of-culture perspective have shown how even apparently the most autonomous of creators, modern painters, are embedded in networks of social relationships—with suppliers of painting materials, dealers, collectors, and critics. These relationships shape both their working life and their professional motivation in ways similar to those of more ordinary workers. Dealers' payments to artists for paintings according to the size and number of paintings per month are perceived as being similar to factory workers' piece rates (Moulin 1967/1987, 117). The avant-garde tradition of the new, demanding constant radical innovation, places artists in a similar position to other workers in late-capitalist societies, a position characterized by overspecialization, rapid obsolescence of skills, and commodification of the self to fit the market (Adler 1975, 362–63).

Scholars such as Howard Becker (1982, 135) argue that the primary significance of the critical discussion of the aesthetic features of art works centers on their use to allocate symbolic, and thus material, rewards. Further, the allocation of such rewards depends less on the coherence of critical discussion and the intrinsic qualities of the works of art to which such discussion refers than to the underlying material interests of critics and dealers seeking to maximize their own prestige and profits on the art market (Mulkay and Chaplin 1982). The concept of the artist as autonomous creator, it is concluded, is a mythical residue of nineteenth-century Romanticism, wholly at odds with the real structure of social relations in the modern art world and the orientations to artistic practice to which they give rise (Wolff 1987; see Zolberg 1990, 116, for the suggestion that the concept of the artist as creator is, from a sociological point of view, "virtually oxymoronic").

Similarly, Paul DiMaggio and Pierre Bourdieu have argued that the cultural significance attributed to art museums, the cult of connoisseurship, and the ideology of the art lover are best understood in terms of the role played by art consumption in marking elite status and reproducing social stratification. Cultural capital acquired in the family, both in terms of an early exposure to art and a favorable attitude toward schooling, permits those of privileged background to capitalize on literary critical skills learned as part of formal education—for example the capacity to classify literature in terms of authors, genres, schools, and dates—by transposing them into the field of art (Bourdieu 1968, 1984). Here, the imperceptible process of familiarization involved in acquiring the abilities of the connoisseur lends itself to the charismatic ideology according to which only the true art lover can unlock the mysteries expressed in the product of the artist's creative genius. The minimalist labeling preferred by art museums, and their morphology, reinforce the division between the art lovers and the philistine barbarians not possessed of the cultural competencies necessary to engage with the artistic legacies of the past or the contemporary avant-garde, thus legitimating as a fact of nature status distinctions created through unequal access to culture (Bourdieu 1968, 610).

DiMaggio's work on the construction of American high-cultural institutions in the nineteenth century has given historical depth to Pierre Bourdieu's theory. Drawing on Durkheim's sociology of religion and a rather instrumentalist version of Weber's account of status group formation, DiMaggio argued (1982) that the classification of painting, sculpture, and classical music as "fine arts" separate from "mass entertainment," their organization by not-for-profit institutions, the cultural framing of art appropriation in terms of an ethic of connoisseurship and an ideology of art loving—informed by professional art criticism and art history—reflected the desire of the social elites of northern East Coast cities (most notably the Boston Brahmins) to segregate themselves from nouveaux riches industrialists and second-generation immigrants who increasingly challenged the old elites' domination of the economic and political life of the late-nineteenth-century United States.

Even today, it is argued, the value to consumers of cultural goods such as museum visits derives from social strategies of identity marking, and the demand for such experiences is a function of "social processes, not aesthetic needs" (DiMaggio 1991, 133). Just as "high culture emerged as the status culture of a class in formation," so now, as local city-based elites are replaced by a more mobile national elite, high culture will be eroded and with it the quasi-religious aura with which it is associated in the attribution of the status of creator to artists and in the construction of aesthetic experience in terms of the discourse of art loving. As one of Bourdieu's epigones argues, democratization will bring the death of the art museum, since there "are no grounds to suppose that their apparent function—to make objectively valuable culture and knowledge equally accessible to all members of society—will have any substance," once their "real but hidden function—to preserve social differentiation—has been removed" (Robbins 1991, 59).

In fact, Parsons himself had—in advance, as it were—taken on board the basic sociological insights of these perspectives and also criticized their shortcomings. Like sociologists in the production-of-culture perspective, he recognized that the existence of a differentiated role of "artist" raised problems of disposal and remuneration parallel to those of other workers, such as scientists (Parsons 1951, 408–10). He was also, however, alert to certain aspects of the artist's role in the modern West that he saw as remarkable: first, the attribution of the characterization of "creative" to artists rather than scientists, which he interpreted in terms of the different constraints of the environments they were concerned to represent; and second, the special difficulties involved in the integration of the artistic role in the modern West, manifested in the phenomenon of Bohemia. Unsure whether to attribute this to the intrinsic character of the artistic role, combining high demands for instrumental technical action with intense expressivity, or to a tension between expressive roles and the emphasis on affective neutrality institutionalized in an especially high degree in modern Western societies and particularly fitting the interests of the scientific role, Parsons concluded that only careful comparative analysis could adequately clarify these issues (Parsons 1951, 409).

Similarly, Parsons was alert to the massive expansion of serious aesthetic and cultural interests, particularly among students but also more broadly in American society in the late 1950s and early 1960s. While recognizing the link between social status and artistic consumption, he criticized those who interpreted these changes solely in such reductionist terms, and argued that this interest in the arts manifested both a general upgrading of aesthetic standards and a compensatory shift in emphasis in the cultural investments made by American society in order to balance a "rise in instrumental demands for achievement" with "heightened expressiveness" (Parsons and White 1961/1964, 229).

These observations of Parsons are characteristic of the penetrating insights into issues of the sociology of art that were thrown up by the logic of his theoretical program but that have been little developed since in empirical research in the sociology of art. In this essay, I seek to sketch what such an action-theoretic sociology of the modern art world might look like by building on three key concepts developed by Parsons: art as expressive symbolism, seedbed societies, and the expressive revolution.

Parsons defined expressive symbolism as any acts or objects that stand for the attitude or feelings of an ego toward an alter and thereby mediate the affective component of interaction. He illustrated the significance of such symbolism with the type case of the mother-infant relationship, in which he showed how the attribution of expressive meaning to certain acts that took place between mother and child at the same time constituted the internalization by the child of the mother as a motivationally significant alter. The mother was then able to control the child's behavior through symbolic means, the expression of approval or disapproval.

Building on this basis, Parsons argued that expressive symbolism played a central part in the institutional integration of motivation in interaction systems more generally, mediating actors' mutual identification with each other and with the shared norms through which collectivities might be constituted, thus stabilizing patterns of interaction beyond what might be possible simply on the basis of short-term instrumental interests. From this concept of expressive symbolism, Parsons logically extrapolated the concept of "art" on the basis of general principles informing the differentiation of action systems. In sufficiently complex systems of interaction, the expressive strands might become differentiated from the instrumental and the evaluative, leading first to the development of actions with purely expressive meaning, then to a specialized concern with the production of objects specifically designed for the communication of expressive meanings. The work of art is simply a highly differentiated expressive symbol—for example, a portrait of a leader that is designed to inculcate feelings of dependence and loyalty on the part of the ruled.

The emergence of the distinct role of "artist" represents an extremely specialized concern with the expressive culture of a highly differentiated social system (Parsons 1951, 399–417, especially 408–14). Understandably, given the focus of *The Social System,* Parsons's primary concern was with cases where expressive culture was fused with religious and, in particular, evaluative culture—notably in his discussion of reward symbolism. He recognized that the structure and functioning of an autonomous system of the arts represented a qualitatively different level of differentiation that that of specialized production of art objects which remained embedded in other social subsystems: performing or responding to a Bach mass in the context of a religious service, he noted, was an act of a different order than doing likewise in a concert hall (Parsons 1951, 411). Nevertheless, he was able neither to deduce analytically exactly how an autonomous system of the arts, "pure art" as he calls it, might be functionally articulated with its wider social environments, nor to intimate how such developments may actually have occurred in the formation of modern Western society. (In large part this was because Parsons lacked studies comparable to those of Weber and Merton that provided the basis for a rather more satisfactory discussion of the corresponding issues concerning belief and science in chapter 8 of *The Social System.*)

Parsons's account of the place of science in modern Western society as one component of rational-intellectual culture more generally was developed to a higher level of theoretical sophistication in *The American University.* As in *The Social System,* Parsons implicitly suggests, although without parallel elaboration, the analysis of an "expressive complex" as the counterpart to his and Gerald Platt's analysis of the cognitive complex in *The American University.* For example he draws a parallel between the revolutionary innovations of Galileo and Michelangelo within their respective cultural fields, and between the research function in the university and creativity in the arts more generally (Parsons and Platt 1973, 140). This parallelism becomes more explicit in his subsequent conceptualization of both heightened interest in the arts and certain strands of the counterculture in terms of an "expressive revolution," parallel to the cognitive and educational revolutions with which he was primarily concerned in *The American University.*[1]

Parallelism, with appropriate adjustments, in the conceptualization and modeling of the functioning of corresponding systems is implicit in the logic of action theory, and a number of analogies with Parsons's analysis of the cognitive complex may be fruitful in developing our understanding of its expressive counterpart. First, I wish to suggest that participation in sophisticated aesthetic culture grounds the affective capacity of actors, in complex modern societies, in a way analogous to higher level learning grounds cognitive capacity or competence (see Parsons and Platt 1973, 26). Second, we should seek to locate the modern system of the arts as a differentiated expressive system, analogous to the university, within a broader expressive complex, having substantial autonomy in relation to other subsystems but interdependent with them in new ways. This autonomy exists on both a cultural and a social level. On a cultural level, art as expressive symbolism maintains boundaries against religious, moral evaluative and cognitive symbolism but is also dependent on them in new ways. For example, criticism, as an output of the cognitive system on the cultural level, is essential to the proper functioning of the expressive system in ways that I will sketch later (see Parsons and Platt 1973, 48).

The social institutions of the art world are a key component of what Parsons and Platt designated the telic system, the goal-attainment sector of the fiduciary system, where cultural system and social system interpenetrate (Parsons and Platt 1973, 18–20). Like universities, we might suggest, the institutions of the art world have a fiduciary character, linked to their trusteeship of the expressive-aesthetic tradition. This involves both special privileges and special responsibilities, resting on the belief that the long-term protected development of a society's artistic tradition confers more benefits than the demand that expressive symbolism should only be produced for more immediate use in more immediately practical contexts. The autonomy of the art world depends on interchanges with more conditional institutions, whereby the art world makes contributions to the functioning of these institutions, which justifies the economic, political, and other subsidies that make an autonomous art world possible. Autonomy is seriously threatened when inputs from other institutional structures are withdrawn, particularly if confidence in the value of autonomous art is called into question, for example as a result of fundamentalist movements of one kind or another wishing to subordinate art to moral or religious purposes.

The American University represents an interesting combination of purely theoretical deduction on the basis of established principles and models within action theory, and inductive research into the history of the cognitive complex in the United States and Western culture more generally. In particular, the nature of the tensions that Parsons detected within the American university system were a result not just of intrinsic tensions between, for example, instrumental and expressive orientations, such as one might deduce theoretically. Rather, in addition to many other more short-term factors (Smelser 1973), they were partly determined by a specific institutional structuring of the relationship between cognitive rationality and other interests rooted in very long-term patterning of the American value system, in particular the emphasis on instrumental activism (Parsons and Platt 1973, 40–45). Like Weber and Merton, Parsons traced these patterns back to classical Greece and, via Protestantism, ancient Israel. These societies Parsons characterized as "seedbed societies," by which he meant that they had developed cultural resources that proved crucial for the particular history of social and cultural evolution in the West but did not in the same degree transform their originating societies, since these did not afford the necessary conditions for the institutionalization of these cultural patterns in their most radical form (Parsons 1966, 96; 1971b, 33).

This provides the rationale for my comparison of ancient Greek with modern Western high culture. On the one hand, as we shall see, the modern high-cultural system is genetically related to its ancient Greek counterpart, which in part explains the insistent ingression of logos, critical rationality, into modern Western processes of aesthetic-expressive rationalization and differentiation (in comparison, for example, with their Chinese counterparts). On the other, the patterns inherited from the Greek world were thoroughly transformed through being integrated within Judeo-Christian cosmology during the Renaissance.[2] The strong sense of transcendence implicit in the Judeo-Christian concept of a creator god facilitated certain breakthroughs to levels of autonomy that Greek artists had been unable to achieve within the Hellenic culture of rationalism. It also underlies the societal commitment to the universalization of the cultural competencies involved in the sophisticated appreciation of high culture in the modern West, which contrasts with the restriction of such capacities to an intellectual elite in the ancient Greek world.[3] That is to say, the institutionalization of the aesthetic ethic of the art lover, characteristic of modern Western high culture, has entailed quite strong value pressures toward the democratization of art and the inclusion of all citizens within the community of art lovers, which in certain respects counter, and have progressively undermined, the socially exclusive aspects of high culture analyzed by Bourdieu and DiMaggio. Comparatively speaking, it is the inclusiveness of modern high culture, not its exclusiveness, which is remarkable and in need of explanation and understanding.

In the rest of this chapter these concepts are used to explore the historical question of why the modern high-cultural system looks the way it does, and what is comparatively distinctive about it in both its cultural and its social dimensions. In particular, I shall suggest that the idea of the artist as creator and the aesthetic ethic of the art lover, rather than being evanescent epiphenomena of the commodification of art and the stratification of arts consumption as they developed in the nineteenth century, are derived from key themes of Judeo-Christian culture that, synthesized with the rationalist art-theoretical legacy of classical Greece, not only provided the cultural foundation for the breakthrough to an autonomous art world in the modern West after the Renaissance but are also built into the structure of the modern art world in ways that are crucial to the continued structuring of the role of the artist as autonomous and to the character of modern aesthetic experience.

Further, I explore the larger systematic question of why it should matter that there be a differentiated autonomous art world that is structured the way it is by analyzing certain aspects of the functional articulation of the modern system of the arts with the broader structures of modern society. Rather than demonstrating the social significance of art and aesthetics by reducing them to supposedly more fundamental dimensions of society, whether economics or social stratification, I suggest that the social significance of art in the modern world depends on characteristically differentiated structuring of both autonomy and interpenetration between the artistic system and its various environments. Many of the key processes and debates in the modern art world can be understood in terms of the fragile but ongoing institutionalization of this differentiatedness in the face of varying threats of, and pressures toward, dedifferentiation.

SOCIAL DIFFERENTIATION AND THE ARTS COMPLEX IN ANCIENT GREECE AND THE MODERN WEST

The processes of the differentiation of art in ancient Greece and the modern West are characterized by a series of remarkable parallels. In both cases, the development of naturalism in art was followed by artists beginning to write theoretical treatises about their art, both in order to articulate the representational problems to which naturalism gave rise and in order to make claims to an enhanced status for themselves as artists by distinguishing theoretically informed art from mere craft. This marked the first step in far-reaching processes of artistic differentiation that in both cases ultimately involved the disembedding of art from the political and religious contexts for which it had originally been created and the development of specifically artistic settings oriented to a set of high-cultural practices, including art history writing and connoisseurship, which conferred social distinction on their bearers.

The parallels are so striking that some art historians have regarded the processes as identical, apparently confirming Bourdieu's assertion that the concept of the creator is the natural occupational ideology of artists seeking autonomy (Bourdieu 1984, 491) and that the love of art is the natural concomitant of connoisseurship and stratification in arts consumption (Bourdieu 1968, 608; see Bourdieu 1984, 3, 66–68).

But there are also striking differences. First, whereas the initiation of processes of artistic differentiation in artists' status claims during the Renaissance provided the basis for a more or less continuous process leading to the role of the modern fine artist as autonomous creator, Greek artists' project to redefine their status and the social function of art was unsuccessful: most art remained embedded, and the kinds of claims to autonomy made by fifth- and fourth-century B.C. artists were not repeated in later periods of classical antiquity. Second, whereas art history and self-reflexive historical awareness became built into the definition of the artist's role in modern Western art, in ancient Greece, only the art of the classical period, the fifth and fourth centuries B.C., ever came to be perceived historically, and that occurred only some centuries after its original production.

Here I seek to explain those differences by comparing, first, the reconstruction of the artist's role in classical Greece and the Renaissance and after and, second, the social and cultural construction of high culture in the ancient Greek world and the modern West. My approach is a neofunctionalist one (Alexander and Colomy 1990). I shall argue that the distinctive outcomes result from the intersection of the two parallel processes of artistic differentiation with variant cultural frames and the varying characteristics of the social bearers of those cultural frames, whether organizations such as states, or social groups such as autonomous cultural elites or ruling elites. The cultural frames in question are those developed in Parsons's seedbed societies. In Greek philosophy the sacred was understood as an intellectually intelligible world-immanent reason ordering a providential world within which salvation could be secured by rational adaptation to that order. In the Judeo-Christian tradition, the sacred was conceptualized as a world-transcending creator god, and evil was conceptualized as the willful pursuit of one's own purposes in defiance of God's will. Salvation was the reward for active mastery and transformation of the creaturely and fallen world in accordance with the will of God, best accomplished in the context of a community of believers bound together by their love of God and of their Christian brothers.[4]

The Role of the Artist

The poleis of late archaic and early classical Greece attributed primacy to the political sphere. Man, as Aristotle stated, was a "politikon zoon," an animal designed by nature to live in a polis. This ideal was represented by the autarkic peasant-farmer and citizen, contributing to the political community as a hoplite in warfare or as an active participant in the periodic assemblies in which major decisions affecting the life of the community were made. The primacy of the political determined the functions of art, artistic patronage, and attitudes towards visual artists.[5] The state dominated artistic patronage and principal art production was in the form of cult statues, civic portraits, and history paintings. Art was consumed in religious and political settings, and was evaluated and responded to in terms of a vocabulary that fused aesthetic with religious and moral-evaluative criteria (Tanner 2000; 2001). Visual artists, like other craftsmen, or technitai, were held in low esteem, since the character of their work neither helped them gain the physique suited to hoplite warfare nor permitted the leisure required for proper political participation.

The development of naturalism in fifth-century B.C. art was a form of substantive rationalization of art, serving to integrate artistic languages originally derived from Egypt and the Near East more closely into the religious and moral evaluative culture of the developing democratic city-states. The representational problems generated by naturalism—for example contrapposto (the distinction between weight-bearing and free leg) in statuary and foreshortening and perspective in painting—also gave rise to more formal aesthetic rationalization. Following the lead of other literate practitioners of rationalizing "technai," visual artists began to write treatises exploring specifically artistic questions of representation: the use of proportional systems in composition, symmetry, and color and so on—all, at least initially, designed as a means for artists to think through representational problems generated by naturalism in order to produce better solutions to the artistic problems generated within civic and religious contexts. In the fourth century, the dominance of patronage by the state was eroded with the relative decline of Athens, but new patrons emerged: kings on the margins of the Greek world, philosophical schools commissioning portraits of their leaders, and private individuals investing in funerary art as state sumptuary laws were increasingly relaxed or ignored. Competition between patrons enhanced artists' freedom of action. The increasing commodification of art that was produced speculatively for private purchasers rather than as bespoke commissions also distanced artists from direct patronal control.

In this context, sculptors and painters began to make claims to a higher level of status and a corresponding autonomy as they sought to redefine both their role and the function of art. In seeking to personify their role in a new way, they modeled themselves in their dress and self-presentation on more autonomous cultural specialists like the Sophists, in whose circles they moved and with whom they seem to have identified. Traditional practical workshop-based training of artists, heretofore done within the family, was supplemented by more professional training purchased from specialists outside the family, like the new style of education the Sophists had initiated. It involved the major branches of contemporary learning with a particular emphasis on mathematics and geometry. The continuing tradition of art writing promoted the development of a secular aesthetic vocabulary in which a term like "charis," referring to divine splendor, was reinterpreted as a specific kind of pictorial charm achieved through mastery of line and simplicity of color and particularly associated with the painter Apelles.

Ultimately a small number of leading artists, seeking to redefine their role as the explorers of aesthetic forms for their own sake or in terms of self-expression, produced works of a self-referential character. Zeuxis painted a family of centaurs: a father and mother and two breast-feeding babies. Centaurs were normally represented in violent narratives in which their function was to articulate Greek conceptions of moral boundaries and the consequences of their transgression. Avoiding a narrative content, which might point to an extra-artistic order of meaning, Zeuxis maximized attention to the formal aspects of the painting, especially his artistic mastery. Even parts of the content of the painting could be interpreted as an allegory of his painterly skills. In an inscription accompanying a statue of Eros, Praxiteles claimed that the model for the image was derived from his own art. The unseen power of Eros' arrows provided an allegory of the autonomous power of the work of a skilled artist to move the viewer merely by being gazed upon (Tanner 1999, 154–56).

The claims to autonomy implied by these works of art were never institutionalized. After the fourth century no further examples were produced, and art production remained largely embedded in political and religious frameworks. The tradition of theoretical art writing also seems to have come to an end, and Hellenistic and Roman-period sculptors and painters made only modest claims to prestige. In large part the failure of artists to bring to fruition their attempts to redefine their role and the function of art in more autonomous ways can be attributed to the unwillingness of the primary bearers of the new culture of rationalism, the philosophers, to endorse their claims and provide the kind of charismatic push on which the development of new institutional orders seems to depend (see Eisenstadt 1990, 21). In the *Republic,* book 10, Plato memorably discounts artists' pretensions to knowledge. True knowledge, he argues, is knowledge of ultimate reality, the world of the transcendent forms, understood in their full significance only by the intellect of philosophers. Even a carpenter's knowledge of couches, for example, concerned not the form of "couch" as such, but merely the skills required to manufacture particular couches. The painter of a couch could make no authentic claims to knowledge, producing "that which is bred at two removes from nature," "far removed from the truth" (Plato, *Republic* 597–98).[6]

Not only was mimetic art distant from Reason, it was corrosive of it. Perspectival painting, creating the appearance that some objects on a flat surface were farther away than others, exploited natural deficiencies of human embodiment and confused the untrained mind. The contents of works of art representing the tragic afflictions of Oedipus or Medea encouraged emotive responses on the part of viewers who identified with those characters, a pathology that perverted viewers' limited capacity for self-control. Aristotle (*Poetics* 6, 26) made similar judgments, regarding Greek tragedy as acceptable only when read as a text and thus disembedded from the dangers of visual spectacle and stagecraft.

Artistic imagination was correspondingly defined in a very limited way. Visual art, like other technai, imitated nature. Forms, "eidea," were conceptualized as substance without matter, the active principle, whether immanent in a seed and determining its pattern of growth into a plant or present in a craftsman and shaping the couch that he, through the agency of the form as the active principle in his soul, "begets out of" the material with which he works (Aristotle, *Metaphysics* 1032b–1033a). The process of production in craft as in nature is one of teleology, guaranteed by the world-immanent reason that is nature (Aristotle, *Physics* 199a). Craft is not set apart from nature as a specifically human cultural activity that masters and transforms nature. Rather, craft is embedded in nature and conforms with it (Vernant 1983).

When, in subsequent generations, a history of Greek art was written, it was informed by the same teleological assumptions: that artists discovered the means of realistic representation through the imitation of nature rather than, as we might think, being valued for creating new aesthetic forms. This history described the discovery of contrapposto and foreshortening and of the sculptural representation of bodies fully in the round. Then, when all the devices of naturalistic representation had been discovered, roughly by the end of the fourth century, art, or at least artistic innovation, "stopped—cessavit" (Pliny, *Natural History* XXXIV.52). The development of painting and sculpture had reached its natural telos. All that remained for subsequent artists was to recombine the relevant representational techniques in appropriate ways in producing further works of art. Correspondingly, postclassical high art constituted a closed tradition in which the art produced for collectors and connoisseurs consisted largely of copies or variants upon works of the more famous artists of the fifth and fourth centuries.

A similar set of factors to those in classical Greece precipitated artistic differentiation in the Italian Renaissance. The development of naturalism in early medieval Italian religious art, like its classical Greek counterpart, was intended to intensify attachment to traditional religious representations of a laity whose status in the Eucharist had been upgraded during the twelfth-century reformation (Kempers 1987/1992, 145–47; Antal 1948, 276; Hawthorn 1991, 128–55). Economic growth and social differentiation enhanced levels of church patronage of the visual arts but also eroded its dominance as the courts of secular princes and individual members of developing urban elites became increasingly important as patrons of art. Competition among various patrons for artists' services enhanced artists' autonomy, to the extent that by the early sixteenth century the most sought after artists might be offered open commissions in which they determined the subject matter and even the medium for themselves (Hauser 1962, 51–52; Baxandall 1972, 1–23).[7] As in Greece, the combination of the representational problems generated by the developing tradition of naturalism and the model of an emerging autonomous cultural elite, the humanists, gave rise to theoretical reflection on art in the form of treatises and the rationalization of artistic pedagogy, in which practical workshop apprenticeships were supplemented by more abstract theoretical education.

The example of Greek artists, preserved in the texts of Pliny and Vitruvius, served as a model both for the claims Renaissance artists made to prestige and autonomy and for the theoretical rationalization of their own artistic practice. Following the example of classical antiquity and the intrinsic problems of artistic rationalization raised by naturalism, science and mathematics were used to elevate the visual arts from the level of craft to that of liberal art, implicitly in Alberti's *De Pictura* and explicitly in the writings of Leonardo da Vinci (Blunt 1940, 48–50). This time, however, the process of theoretical rationalization was not embedded in the metaphysics of reason characteristic of the Greek world. This had two consequences. First, the humanists, who shared visual artists' interest in the revival of antiquity, were, unlike Plato and Aristotle, ultimately broadly supportive of visual artists' aspirations. Second, as the claims and ideas inherited from classical Greece were reiterated they were also gradually transformed in ways that integrated them with the presuppositions of the dominant Christian metaphysics. Greek Stoic ideas of adaptation to nature are gradually changed through an emphasis on the will and world-mastering transformation (Kemp 1991, 7–9, on Stoic elements in Alberti; Blunt 1940, 5, 18–19, on their Christianization).

This served to endow the artist with a specific occupational charisma as "creator," which provided a powerful legitimation to claims for autonomy and distinguished visual artists from other cultural specialists such as humanists and philosophers on the basis of at least equality of prestige. Both the Greek elements of the artist as intellectual and the concept (though not the role definition) of the artist as creator were institutionally secured with the foundation of the Florentine Academy by Vasari in 1563. Sculpture and painting, as arts of "design," were separated from other crafts, and a program of scientific education in design based on geometry and anatomy was implemented as a curriculum of artistic training. This supplemented and replaced the traditional workshop training of the guilds, from whose restrictions artists were now emancipated (Kempers 1987/1992, 288–89; Kristeller 1990, 182). At the funeral of Michelangelo in the following year, Vasari drew an explicit analogy between the creative powers of God and those of the great artist and claimed "the reverence and love" thus due to the charismatic Michelangelo for visual artists in general (Wittkower and Wittkower 1964, 83, 110; Kemp 1989, 45).

The interplay between these two strands of culture, the Christian and the Greek, shaped the continuing development of the concept of the artist as it was articulated in theory and the role of the artist as institutionalized within the changing social contexts in which artistic practice in Europe took place in the following centuries. The spread of the academic system throughout Europe during the seventeenth century owed much to its suitability as an organizational form for newly emergent absolutist states seeking to develop teams of highly trained artists capable of meeting such states' needs for artistic self-projection through highly complex and monumental allegorical narrative paintings (Kempers 1987/1992; Warnke 1985). The academic system also promoted the formation of nationally distinctive and uniform state high cultures, produced in such organizations as the royal porcelain and tapestry workshops (Perry and Cunningham 1999).

The academies institutionalized rational critical aesthetic debate as a central component in the artistic enterprise (even if the final products were oriented to courtly display and, later, under the influence of Enlightenment criticism, to the inculcation of moral norms). Such discussions promoted a sense of the autonomy of aesthetic values and increasing awareness of both personal and regional, emergently national styles (Barasch 1985, 354). They also provided a context in which the nascent concept of the artist as creator and its implications might be further elaborated in appropriately baroque forms. Sixteenth- and seventeenth-century academic writers developed Marsilio Ficino's Christianized Neoplatonic metaphysics to conceive beauty as an emanation from the divine mind, perfectly reflected in angels, less well and variably in human souls, poorly in the materialized forms of the natural world, where ugliness was attributed to the resistance of profane matter to penetration by the divine. The artist—whose artistic capacity is taken as an indication of an exceptional endowment of "that divine light infused in us by special grace, which has made us not only superior to the animal creation but even, if we may say so, like god himself" (Vasari, *Lives,* preface)—becomes a steward of divine grace, bound by virtue of his extraordinary charismatic gift to perform the messianic function of building God's kingdom on earth. This he accomplishes, according to Carlo de Ridolfi's treatise of 1648, *Le Maraviglie dell'arte,* by restoring brute matter through the aesthetic alchemy of beautiful painting to the state of grace which existed before the Fall and the corruption of God's newly created world by evil (Panofksy 1924/1968, 235).

Enlightenment criticism of absolute monarchy, and the development of a sense of a national community that transcended specific governments or monarchs promoted an increasingly abstract or generalized definition of the artist's role as being one of responsibility to "the people" for the preservation and elaboration of artistic tradition (Bürger 1982, 15). This corresponded to the increasingly anonymous character of the relationship between the artist and consumers. In England, the role of the state and the monarchy in artistic patronage had been drastically reduced by the political and cultural revolutions of the seventeenth century.[8] First in England, and increasingly throughout Europe, the large aristocratic household gave way to more restricted and self-contained bourgeois families. This greatly eroded the demand for the major decorative programs within houses and palaces, the services the academic system had originally been designed to provide. This change undermined both the capacity and the motivation of patrons to employ artists on a long-term basis as family servants or dependents. The participation in the arts of the new gentlemanly elite, incorporating newcomers whose wealth was not based on land and inheritance, took the form of purchasing paintings on the market, or making one-off commissions from artists. The artists were increasingly treated as the client's equal, since such commissions did not entail a long-lasting relationship of dependence of the artist on the patron.

During the course of the nineteenth century, as the market more completely displaced state patronage and the art world became increasingly internationalized, the national dimension of the artist's relationship to artistic tradition was eroded. The conception of the genius who created "new forms, ideas and images that exceed all bounds of theoretical or rule governed understanding" was first articulated in secularized form in Romantic and Kantian aesthetics at the point of the transition from an academic-patronal to a market system. It became the dominant institutional definition of the artist and was legally codified in the concept of artists' "moral rights," established in France in the first half of the twentieth century.

The moral rights of artists function to protect the creativity of artists perceived to be a general public good by exempting artists from some of the normal pressures of bureaucratic and market controls or democratic accountability, in a similar way to the protection, for example tenure and academic freedom, given to other fiduciary roles like that of academics.[9] These rights are not property rights; they are personal rights that protect the freedom and integrity of artistic expression. Rights of paternity guarantee the artist's right to be recognized as creator and have been used to void contracts in which artists were expected to use a pseudonym or not sign the work at all (Duboff 1984, 230). Rights of divulgation protect the artist's right to create in both a positive and a negative sense. Contracts for creation are not judicially enforceable: "Lack of inspiration is held a normal risk of contract for creation, which is reasonably foreseen by both parties, and no damages may be had for non-performance on this ground" (Duboff 1984, 226). In their underlying assumptions these measures are clearly pattern-consistent with Vasari's description of the authentic expression of artistic charisma—"an artist's talent can only truly express itself when prompted by his intellect and when he is in a state of inspired rapture: it is then that he demonstrates his divine concetti" (Vasari, *Lives* II.204; Kemp 1989, 54). The moral rights of artists are publicly actionable—the artist in question needn't make the claim—and violators can be assessed for punitive damages rather than merely restitutive compensation, suggesting a profound societal interest in and commitment to the protection of artistic creativity (Duboff 1984, 233–35).

Although it was only in the twentieth century that this idea of the artist as creator became codified in law, that is not to say that it did not profoundly shape artistic practice and the development of the artistic tradition much earlier. The concept of the artist as creator had been internalized much earlier by artists and was available as resource for those seeking to explain and respond to radical innovations beyond accepted aesthetic norms. This in part explains the very different shape of the evolution of the Western art tradition compared to that of the postclassical Greek world.

Michelangelo was perhaps the first artist fully to identify with the emergent conception of the artist as autocratic creator, an identification manifested in his poetry and enacted in his individualistic working practices (Hauser 1962, 48). Profoundly affected in his conception of his own identity, first by the Christianized Neoplatonism of Ficino and the so-called Florentine Academy and second by Savonarola's teaching of justification by faith, Michelangelo, writing in the 1530s, described the artist as divinely inspired by a world-transcending God, through whose gift the artist "subdues and surpasses nature" by mastering the world and shaping it in accordance with the divine beauty of God's will (Blunt 1940, 72–78). Michelangelo's charisma seems to have been broadly recognized, both in the relative freedom he enjoyed in his work and in viewers' responses to his art. "The recorded effect of the creations of Michelangelo's transcendent talent upon spectators was to overcome their minds with wonder. . . . Terms such as *stupendo, stupore* and *meraviglia* began to be used in connection with his works in order to suggest that their effects lay beyond rational comprehension and the descriptive power of language" (Kemp 1989, 45; for a detailed discussion see Summers 1981).

Like God, the creative artist is inscrutable. As with Michelangelo and the Baroque, so with Beethoven and the development of Romantic symphonic music.[10] It is a repeated motif of modern Western art history that both the artist's self-identification as an autocratic creator and the availability of the idea that it was quite in order for the work of a creative genius to surpass rational understanding facilitated paradigmatic revolutions in art in a way that lay outside the capacity of the rationalist tradition within Greek art.[11] What was exceptional in the case of Michelangelo has become conventional expectation in the avant-garde, where art is routinely about changing the rules of the game—the aesthetic principles of art and even the very definition of art itself.

The structure of the modern artist's role exemplifies what Parsons referred to as "institutionalized individualism," where social norms and cultural values provide a framework within which the autonomy of the individual is enhanced and the motivation and performance of the artist, compared with that of his predecessors, is more strongly shaped by internalized than by external constraints. Further, these internalized constraints are formulated at a higher level of cultural generality, thus enhancing autonomy.[12] As Marshall Berman has put it, modern western artists "feel that they are not really alive if they are not transcending themselves" by transcending their predecessors (1992, 37).[13]

The Construction of High Culture

The development of a more culturally differentiated and individualistic order also characterizes the history of regimes of aesthetic reception in the Greek world and the modern West, but in each case the regime was distinctively patterned by its variant cultural tradition and the different social structures within which the new arrangements were institutionalized.

In the classical Greek poleis the dominant modes of aesthetic reception took place in religious and civic space (temples, the agora) and were embedded in religious and moral-evaluative culture. For example, cult statues were interpreted through a religious vocabulary. This facilitated the precipitation of the viewer into a religious experience, as if of a divine epiphany. It involved the viewer in a pattern of engagement and response that was more embedded in the action and empathic reaction of the properly socialized viewer's body than in abstract, distanced, specifically aesthetic contemplation (Tanner 2001).[14] Such cultic and communal settings and the associated modes of aesthetic reception were designed to secure the viewer's passive identification with the contents projected by the image rather than a reflexive, autonomous engagement.

Plato was of course highly critical of what he regarded as the pathologies of identification associated with this institution of art. Aristotle's comments (*Poetics* 26) to the effect that tragedy can be better appreciated when read as a text than when seen in performance mark the beginnings of a rationalist disembedding of the aesthetic-expressive culture of the polis from its social context. This was carried much further in the third and second centuries B.C., when the monarchs of the new kingdoms that replaced the poleis as the highest level of political organization created libraries and cultural institutions, such as the Library at Pergamum and the Museum of Alexandria. Here, literary scholars and philosophers, rather marginal figures within the Greek polis, were employed to collect, codify, and extend the tradition of Greek literary, intellectual, and scientific culture—the disciplines of logos, the word or reason. Although visual arts such as sculpture and painting were not included in these new, more autonomous, cultural institutions, the theoretical texts of earlier generations of artists were collected and edited and thus provided the basis for writing a history of fifth- and fourth century art, knowledge of which came to be a key component of a sophisticated elite culture of viewing. This culture of viewing was applied first to works of art expropriated from their original political contexts by the Hellenistic kings, who initiated the practice of collecting works of art. It was then extended to copies of classical art placed in sculpture gardens or picture galleries of a Mediterranean-wide social and cultural elite in the last centuries before and the early centuries of the Christian Era.[15]

This mode of viewing was one part of a broader "paideia," or culture of self-cultivation. It was characterized by an extensive formal aesthetic vocabulary, a knowledge of artists' names and of the history of fifth- and fourth-century art, and a practice of attentive viewing—all the features that Bourdieu identifies as indicators of specifically artistic competence in modern high culture (Bourdieu 1967, 195; 1968, 594–96, 604). The application of these cultural tools within the framework of a practice of attentive viewing enabled connoisseurs to make explicit the specific artistic bases on which different aesthetic-expressive effects were created, and to explain them in terms of specific artists' contribution within the history of art to the development of the means of representation. Failures in knowledge, or shortcomings in the application of such knowledge, were considered indicators of a lack of humanitas. Alongside this new culture of viewing occurred associated institutional developments that parallel those of modern Western high culture: art collecting and dealing, including the forging of old masters, and artistic tourism.

Notwithstanding these structural parallels, the aesthetic ethos that articulated these practices and styled viewers' expressive relationship to works of art was fundamentally different from that of modern Western high culture as a result of its specification on the basis of the rationalist cosmology characteristic of Greek intellectual culture and of a set of critical practices derived from the rhetorical education enjoyed by most members of the elite. Insofar as there was a discourse of art loving, it served to characterize deviance from accepted norms of cultivated viewing and art collecting. For example, Pliny the Elder describes how Tiberius, a notoriously "bad" emperor, was said to have "fallen in love" (adamatum) with a statue of an athlete by the fourth-century sculptor Lysippos. He had the statue removed from public display and placed in his bedroom until compelled to restore it by popular outcry. By this stage of his reign the emperor was no longer "imperiosus sui," no longer emperor over himself, and "non quivit temperare sibi in eo," could not keep himself within a state of temperate self-control (Pliny, *Natural History,* XXXIV.62).

Rational self-control was a primary qualification for the proper exercise of power by the Greco-Roman elite in general and the emperor in particular. Art and the pleasures of the eye, which were seen to be halfway between intellect and the body, were useful means to distinguish the rational viewer from the irrational one, since they permitted the possibility of a sensuous response in which lower bodily impulses, or affects grounded in embodiment, might escape proper control. Art viewing thus lent itself to helping the observer distinguish the proper members of a ruling elite from upwardly mobile pretenders. In a satirical novel by Petronius, the mock hero, Encolpius, a homosexual of indeterminate status, is wandering through Naples after recently losing his boyfriend and enters a picture gallery. At first he seems to display the cultural competence proper to a member of the elite. He admires the veritas, or truth to nature, of Protogenes, the subtilitas, or fine line, of Apelles. But then he comes to pictures of Zeus and Ganymede and of Hylas the beloved of Herakles being ravished by a nymph, and his aesthetic distance breaks down, to be replaced by an unabashed subjectivism as he takes the gods' passions as an analogue for his own and cries out at his misfortune (Petronius, *Satyricon* 83).

Among the cultivated, a specific style of viewing was developed that permitted a sophisticated aesthetic engagement with art without succumbing to the dangers of the kind of sensuously mediated emotional response that was characteristic of Encolpius and Tiberius and was criticized so heavily by Plato. In a treatise concerning proper ways of reading poetry and viewing art, Plutarch, writing in the early second century A.D., suggests that appropriate pleasure in paintings of mythical themes, such as the story of Oedipus or Medea, lies not in the action represented, nor in identification with the protagonists, but in the rational-technical mastery of the painting. Owing to our natural human endowment with reason and a corresponding fondness for techne or art, when admiring painterly skill, we evaluate the appropriateness of the means the artist has used to represent the subject at hand and the consequent degree of his success in representing it. (Plutarch, *Moralia* 14–37, especially 18).

The mythical content of images, which in the classical city had been internalized as the basis of religious and moral identities, becomes instead a vehicle to address art-critical concerns and to praise the artists' technical skills in the context of a display of the critical viewer's wide-ranging aesthetic and cultural knowledge and intellectual dexterity and wit. Intellect, intellegere, not feeling, was the quality most prized in aesthetic response. A critical poem by the late-second-century B.C. poet Antipater of Sidon analyzes a painting of Aphrodite by Apelles, playing on the story of the judgment of Paris as a paradigm of aesthetic judgment: "Look on the work of Apelles' brush: Cypris just rising from the sea, her mother; how grasping her dripping hair with her hand, she wrings the foam from the wet locks. Athena and Hera themselves will now say, 'No longer do we enter into the contest of beauty [*morphas*] with thee' " (*Palatine Anthology* XVI.178).

This style of viewing was elaborated in critical practices—ekphrasis, or "description," and synkrisis, or "comparison"—that were learned as part of the preparatory exercises in an orator's training and were normally made use of in the context of political or forensic oratory to vividly describe the setting and events of a crime or compare the relative virtues of politicians or emperors. The arrangement of works of art in the new autonomous settings created for their display, sculpture gardens and picture galleries, rewarded viewing in these terms. For example, paintings of different periods or sculptures treating the same theme in slightly different ways might be arranged alongside each other to facilitate for comparison (Brilliant 1984; Bartman 1991). The cultural framing of sophisticated aesthetic experience, the critical techniques through which it was elaborated, and the practices of display all served to construct a very distinctive aesthetic ethos, a rationalist sensibility. The first-century Roman poet Statius describes how one art collector, Pollius, cultivates tranquillity of mind within a picture gallery and sculpture garden in his country villa. Sitting here, enjoying the objects of his collection comprising works of art by such masters as Apelles and Pheidias alongside portraits of the great philosophers, Pollius is able to withdraw and detach himself from worldly engagements, "untroubled and steadfast in thy tranquil virtue, and ever lord of thy own heart" (Statius, *Silvae,* II.ii.63–72).

The construction of modern Western high culture also involved the creation of new reception settings differentiated from the political and religious contexts in which painting and sculpture had hitherto been preponderantly consumed. In England, this was partly conditioned by the relative withdrawal of church and state from artistic patronage after the seventeenth century, and the rise of a market-oriented art production system in the eighteenth century. At the same time members of the English aristocracy were acquiring numerous sculptures and paintings during the course of their travels on the Grand Tour. These works of art were intended in the first place to decorate such aristocrats' country houses, but they also circulated through the art market as collections were formed, extended, and sold off. As in Hellenistic Greece, so in eighteenth-century England and then in Germany, traditions of art writing and criticism originally restricted to practitioners of the arts were taken up and elaborated by intellectuals. Such intellectuals sought to give guidance to an expanding middle class, whose members visited English country houses in emulation of the aristocratic Grand Tour. Their writings instructed middle class tourists in proper ways to look at and respond to works of art, now disembedded from their original functional contexts.

This is the context in which the modern Western tradition of art history writing and aesthetics developed, starting with Jonathan Richardson's *Discourse on the Science of the Connoisseur* (1719) and culminating in the aesthetics of Moritz, Kant, and Schiller via J. J. Winckelmann's *History of Ancient Art* (1764) (Abrams 1989a, 1989b). In this tradition of art writing the concern was not only to ensure that viewers were more critically informed but also to deepen and intensify the viewers' emotional engagement with works of art. Jonathan Richardson argued that a love of art enhanced moral feeling and was a civilizing force (Gibson-Wood 1984). Winckelmann, in addition to writing *Treatise on the Capacity for the Feeling of Beauty,* interspersed his historical exegesis of Greek art with lengthy descriptions of specific works of art. Partly reliant on the erotic tropes of Pietist hymns, these highly emotive essays were designed to intensify viewers' response and augment the levels of aesthetically mediated emotion realized in the viewing experience (Potts 1982, 387; 1994, 167). Winckelmann's art history also provided the model for histories of national traditions of art, which began to be written in the late eighteenth century, and for the creation of the historical character of art museum displays, with which we are familiar today.[16]

Two features sharply distinguish modern Western high culture from its ancient Greek counterpart: first, the value placed on the love of art and the norm of a feelingful response; second, the much greater emphasis placed on the historicization of art, most clearly manifested in the historical character of displays in art museums. The first feature is best interpreted in terms of the continuing shaping role of Christian culture in the development of Western aesthetic thought; the second, in terms of the developing role of the state as the bearer of a national tradition of high culture mediated to the citizen-viewer.

The idea of the love of art and the premium placed on feeling are on one level logical developments of the ideas developed in Renaissance academic circles, notably by Lomazzo and Bellori, to legitimate the special status of the artist as autonomous creator of beauty. However the elaboration of these notions in order to shape not just attitudes toward artists but also the ground of expressive orientation toward works of art depended on their synthesis with certain strands of eighteenth-century religious culture. The role of ascetic Calvinist Protestantism in the development of the instrumental-rational side of modern culture has been well understood since Weber's classic study, *The Protestant Ethic and the Spirit of Capitalism.* An independent development in Protestant culture gave rise to a religious affirmation of sentiment and feeling as a manifestation of divine grace.[17] The austere logic of Calvin's teachings on predestination encountered a reaction embodied first in the Arminian movement and later in Methodism and Pietism, which emphasized the idea of God as a God of love and benevolence as the primary characteristic of the good Christian. Just as, for Puritans, rational world mastery demonstrated in business success served to secure certitude of salvation and in secularized form shaped modern conceptions of professional vocations, so, among Pietists, charitable and sympathetic feelings toward one's fellow men were interpreted as a mark of God's grace, and a premium was set on experiencing and giving expression to such feelings as a manifestation of the workings of the grace of God within the heart. Admission to the community of the faithful involved not only a confession of faith but also an account of how God's grace had manifested itself within one in the form of all the appropriate feelings of Christian love and sympathy. This structure of response survived in a secularized form and was extended as part of the cult of sensibility celebrated and developed in eighteenth-century novel writing; by the time it was satirized in Jane Austen's *Sense and Sensibility* the movement had passed its peak.

These two patterns of culture—the love of art and the artist, and the premium placed on feeling in Pietism—were synthesized to form the cultural basis of a differentiated and secular orientation to art as high culture in eighteenth-century art writing. The most important eighteenth-century art writers no longer wrote within the context of Academy as an art institution; rather, they wrote within the context of the public sphere, seeking to frame people's experience of art at auctions and in country house collections. But they extracted from academic art writing the idea of the beauty produced by an artist in a work of art as a self-sufficient object of disinterested and loving contemplation, like an angel or a ray of divine beauty. They used this idea, shorn of its theological trimmings, as a basis for articulating the newly developed self-sufficiency of paintings and sculptures disembedded from their original political and religious contexts and placed in collections. There was an obvious affinity between this conception of the work of art as an object of love and deeply feelingful responses to art modeled on a by now secularized form of the valuation of deep feeling as a sign of God's love and grace (Abrams 1989a, 1989b). These two strands of thought were gradually fused in a tradition of art writing that extended from the Earl of Shaftesbury in the early eighteenth century through Richardson and Thomas Martyn and achieved codification in the late-eighteenth-century writings of Karl Philipp Moritz, a German Quietist, and Immanuel Kant, who had been educated in a Pietist milieu.

These two cultural patterns reinforced each other and gave an autonomous ground to viewers' expressive-affective orientations that was differentiated from religious or moral evaluative culture. Kant's *Critique of Judgment* characterizes a work of fine art as an object that pleases for its own sake, irrespective of external ends of utility or morality. Its sole function is to be contemplated and responded to with taste and feeling. Alexander Baumgarten characterized poetry and painting in terms of "the perfection of sensuous cognition" and attributed their specific value to their use of the sensate nonlogical capacities of the human mind to expand the parameters of human affective experience in a uniquely pleasurable way (Abrams 1989b, 174–77).[18]

The development of art history writing and aesthetics was parallel to the development of national self-consciousness in the eighteenth century, both being dependent on the increasing autonomy of civil society and the public sphere in relation to the state. The processes also became intertwined in the creation of new spaces for the display and consumption of art, a development that corresponded to the growing awareness of its historical character. Eighteenth-century protocols of display in aristocratic country houses and private collections were organized to provide an effective mise-en-scène for their owners, a gentlemanly equivalent of the more overtly political way in which art framed and projected the power of the ruler in courtly settings (Ernst 1993). Seen as reflections of the taste and projections of the cultivated identity of their owner, such displays balanced uneasily between a valuation of art as such and the appropriation of art to a more specifically social function, as a prestige symbol, notwithstanding the fact that unlike in courts and churches there was not so direct a relationship between the style and contents of the artworks and the identity the collector wished to project. The parallel development of a more generalized orientation toward art and of the concept of a national moral community that was a counterweight to and in certain respects transcended the state promoted a sense of national artistic traditions as symbols of national identity.[19] This paralleled the increasingly abstract orientation of artists within a market system to "the people" and the artistic tradition itself. This gradually supplanted the more concrete and less- differentiated orientation of artists toward their patrons' expressive needs and cultural values, which long-term patronal relationships had promoted.[20] Political criticism and growing interest in the arts led to concern for the protection of national artistic heritage and to criticism of the state if it seemed to be failing to accord to art the love and respect that were now considered its due. The creation of the Louvre (1793) as a museum of art history was in part a response to criticisms of the French crown's failure adequately to display and conserve paintings in the royal collection, which was decaying largely unseen in inadequately lit and poorly ventilated private rooms in various royal palaces (McClellan 1984, 439). A number of projects were developed to counter these criticisms, including conservation of art and the development of new systematically historical modes of display stressing the celebration and continuation of a national tradition in art. These replaced displays that were in some cases simply haphazard, in other cases based on eclectic academic principles mainly intended to allow young artists to imitate and synthesize the different technical accomplishments of individual old masters (McClellan 1984, 454–9). Royal "love of art" and commitment to protect national heritage increasingly replaced the now obsolete divine right of kings, which had hitherto legitimated the absolute monarchy. The new concepts represented part of a wider claim on the part of an increasingly embattled monarchy to represent the nation, and sought to counter the challenges to such claims made by the growingly self-assertive parliaments of the second half of the eighteenth century (McClellan 1984, 451). The creation of a historically oriented display served to project French art as the legitimate heir of the privileged classical tradition and to define it in relationship to the other national traditions of European art. Making the display publicly accessible as a museum demonstrated the state's responsibility toward art as an intrinsic good and consequently made an implicit claim on citizens' regard for and loyalty toward the state as the primary bearer and promoter of national cultural patrimony.

Insofar as the nation transcended the state, it was not difficult for the same ideas and institutional arrangements to be taken over by the revolutionary state in the 1790s, and parallel movements in the nationalization and (relative) democratization of high culture took place in England and Germany during the same period. Thus, from the beginning, there was a strongly inclusive thrust to the institutionalization of high culture. In part, this derived from its Protestant cultural background. In part, it depended on the links between the formation of the new high cultural institutions and the development of modern national states, in which citizens, in principle each other's equals, replaced the old feudal status orders of the absolutist monarchies. Although on one level art continued to perform a political function on behalf of the state, it did so in a much more abstract and generalized way than before. Art was no longer simply an instrument for aesthetic-expressive demonstration of state power and inculcation of political ideologies, as it had been for earlier states, including those of the Greek and Roman worlds. On the contrary, insofar as the state wished to claim to represent the nation, it had obligations to promote and protect art for its own sake and to make it publicly available to the community of citizens whose cultural patrimony that art was now defined as being.

THE MODERN SYSTEM OF THE ARTS

My discussion thus far has concentrated on the differentiation of the role of the artist and the system of artistic production, and also the differentiation of practices of artistic reception from the social contexts in which they are embedded in early societies. My focus has been on the social and cultural conditioning of such processes and in particular on how certain strands of Christian culture promoted a much more radical differentiation of art from other cultural systems and society than had characterized otherwise similar developments in classical Greece and, further, lent a distinctive cultural pattern to Western high culture that cannot be attributed solely to its function as a marker of status.

Now I wish to take a more synchronic approach and explore some dimensions of the functional articulation of the differentiated modern system of the arts with its environments. First, I explore how the distinctive practices of high-cultural viewing effect the way expressive culture shapes the ways in which the bearers of such practices construct their patterns of affective identification in the context of increasingly complex structures of modern societies. Second, I use this analysis as the background to think through some of the major changes and debates characteristic of the contemporary art world in terms of tensions between a deepening institutionalization of an autonomous system of the arts and pressures toward dedifferentiation.

Art Criticism, Art History, and Aesthetic Experience

Parsons's concept of expressive symbolism implies that a proper understanding of high culture must also involve an exploration of the intersections between changes in the organization of art and changes in the organization of the personality, since expressive culture plays a central role in mediating the relationship between the personality and its environments and thus in organizing the motivational structures of the personality. The implication of the institutionalization of high culture and the creation of art museums for the social organization of the cultural production and shaping of affect through expressive culture is perhaps most easily and strikingly indicated negatively. The creation of the great art museums of the European states was accompanied by a massive expropriation of art from the Church, notably in Spain and France, which in some degree emancipated the ascriptive boundedness of the affect produced by art to these particular institutions. Conversely, the institutionalization of high culture may be interpreted as having enhanced processes of generalization in the organization of affect. How does this work?

Art history and art criticism are not as such components of expressive culture but rather aspects of cognitive culture that, when internalized as part of their behavioral system enable actors to handle expressive culture in distinctive ways. The interpretation of all expressive symbolism is perceptually mediated and cognitively organized. On the most simple level, the capacity for the interpretation of expression seems to be a biological endowment: babies are naturally endowed with the capacity to recognize and respond to their mother's smile, just as they are naturally endowed with the capacity to smile. But from a very early stage in the maturation and development of the infant, such biological bases of expression become interwoven with and increasingly overlaid by culturally learned and socially mediated ones. An infant unable to learn on these levels will be unable to generalize from the specific expressive acts of the mother to more generalized attitudes and an underlying affective orientation on the part of the mother (Alexander 1983, 124).

Charles Lidz and Victor Lidz have described how such operations of the "imaginative intelligence" permit an actor to understand the expressive significance both of other persons' actions toward him and of the actor's own projected lines of action (Lidz and Lidz 1976, 219–21). The schemas of imaginative intelligence are what permit the interpretation and formulation of expressive symbols on a relatively simple level within ordinary everyday interactions. Like more cognitive-perceptual and moral schemata, the schemas that constitute imaginative intelligence comprise a staged sequence acquired in the course of child development. Early stages of development are characterized by very simple egocentric structures: for example, Mummy crying is tiresome because it means she is too preoccupied to attend to me. Subsequent stages are characterized by progression to the more open and transformationally complex operational capacities presupposed by empathy and considerateness for others. It is as a result of the development of such capacities that ego's projects and motivational needs can be coordinated with those of others on the basis of an understanding of their motivational expressions and needs.

In relatively simple artistic traditions, those in which art, even if produced by specialists, remains embedded in everyday contexts of social interaction (for example, religious and political contexts), the artistic schemata generated and the schemata required to interpret works of art will be of the same order of complexity as those involved in routine interaction, notwithstanding the possibility that the production of such art might depend on highly specialized technical skills to materialize the expressive schemata and condense dimensions of meaning in a more powerful way than might ordinarily be encountered. In more complex societies, those in which the production of art becomes disembedded from the relatively direct controls of actors within nonartistic institutions such as occurs when a priest commissions an altar piece or a king, a portrait, art acquires greater autonomy and a more reflexive character. Artists are able to explore the fundamental conditions of the production of expressive meaning through formal aesthetic experimentation without immediate regard for the broader social and cultural entailments of such experiments. Such expressive symbols are inevitably structured in ways that are highly complex in a relatively purely artistic way and are not accessible to the kinds of interpretive skills routinely employed in everyday interactions.[21] The social cost of this change is the removal of art from a relatively direct purchase on society and the perception that art is irrelevant to the expressive needs of ordinary people. The benefit is that such "research" or experimentation permits artists to develop new, more complexly structured expressive symbols more adequate to the complexity of the social and cultural milieux with which actors must be motivationally engaged in highly complex differentiated societies.

Correspondingly, I would suggest that connoisseurship and art-historical and art-critical competence do not merely endow the viewer with an increasingly fine set of perceptual discriminations, as empiricist accounts suggest. In addition, they endow viewers with operational schemata that are adequate to the complexity of the organization of the artistic symbolism produced within a historically self-conscious and aesthetically self-reflexive tradition. Drawing on Piaget-Kohlberg's work on cognitive development, Michael Parsons (1987) has outlined a model of the development of capacities for aesthetic judgment. On a purely perceptual level, both young children and sophisticated art critics see the same painting and can discriminate its constituent features, but the way they relate those features to each other and their own experience varies greatly. Although children learn to see pictures as representations by as early as two years of age (Parsons 1987, 33), at first they see the features of paintings in a piecemeal way and relate each element immediately to their own experience. For example, a young child may judge a Renoir painting to be good because it includes a dog, like Fido at home, and uses my favorite color. The development of concrete operations permits the beginnings of stylistic comparison, and the recognition that a painting itself may have expressive qualities irreducible to its subject matter. Later stages are characterized by a heightened self-reflexiveness, evidenced by awareness that one's response is an interpretation, perhaps one among many that can be justified by reference to the comments of others, to various aspects of the pictorial medium, and to the original intentions of the artist within his or her social and historical context. Only at the fifth stage do viewers become reflexively aware that in the process of interpretation they both clarify they own feelings and ways of seeing the world in exploring the alternative manner of feeling and perceiving offered by the painting.

An interpretation that is adequate to the complexity of a work of art will locate that work of art appropriately in history and accept the challenge to engage feelingfully with the world in

FIGURE 10.1 *Anselm Kiefer,* Shulamite, *1983*

Source: Rosenthal (1987, 118), reproduced courtesy of the artist and Gagosian.

the way offered by that work; it will not reduce the work to a reflex of the viewer's own egocentric needs, or judge it according to moral evaluative criteria appropriate to other modes of action or expression. The capacity to produce such interpretations is a restricted one, particularly in relation to works of art produced in an autonomous art world and thus more directly oriented to art as such than to mundane contexts of practical interaction.

A good example of the different cognitive character of adequate and inadequate interpretations can be offered by critical responses to Anselm Kiefer's monumental oil-based paintings of the 1970s and 1980s, for example *Shulamite* (fig. 10.1). This painting is based on a 1939 design by Wilhelm Kreis, for the *Funeral Hall for the Great German Soldiers, in the Hall of Soldiers, Berlin* (fig. 10.2). Viewers and critics whose interpretations are based on single elements in the painting understand it in rather simple nationalistic terms. Some are shocked by the choice of Nazi monuments and symbols in the iconographic content, which they regard as a disturbing, because almost fascist, affirmation of some essential German identity. Others focus on the use of burnt materials as the medium for the painting, which they suggest symbolizes the cremation of a dead past (the Nazi era that can now be forgotten), from which the ashes of a new German painting can arise. More adequate criticism is able to integrate the discrete elements of such paintings with each other in a more systematic way, and to place them in the context both of history and the history of representation, as Andreas Huyssen (1989) has done. Huyssen shows how in *Shulamite* the monumental architecture of the Nazi past is transformed into a memorial for victims of the Holocaust: a ghastly brick oven, black from the smoke of cremation, lit at the end by a memorial candelabra with seven diminutive flames. Kiefer's painting not only transforms its antecedent but also questions the whole language of monumental memorialization, combining as it does monumental scale and central-vanishing-point perspective (avoided in modernism) with base and transitory materials (straw, ashes, burned wood). On the basis of this more adequate critical response, the very process of interpreting the painting involves the

FIGURE 10.2 *Wilhelm Kreis, Design for* Funeral Hall for the Great German Soldiers, in the Hall of the Soldiers, Berlin, *1939*

Source: Huyssen (1989, 42).

viewer in an exploration of the difficulty of constructing a way of constructing—a set of expressive forms—adequate to both the historical and the art-historical legacy of fascism. Exploring fascism in art involves feelings of fascinated attraction at the same time as horrified revulsion; aesthetics cannot sublimate the terror of the past, since it is partly constitutive of it.

The depth of the problem explored by Kiefer in terms of relationships to artistic materials, historical experience, and a whole range of representational means that were both internal to the experience of fascist terror and comprise a part of the representational tradition within which Kiefer found himself and which he sought to work through—all these could be articulated with each other to form a coherent expressive statement only by virtue of a highly abstract set of aesthetic operations. They require a correspondingly sophisticated set of transformational operations on the part of the critic, first to understand the painting and then to translate it into the simplified paraphrase that allows others without such competencies to see something of what Kiefer is doing and understand why it is so artistically powerful.

Critical competence and its use in the contexts of museums and galleries affords viewers the opportunity to explore the expressive-affective meaning of certain aspects of their social and cultural milieu and their experience of it in a highly individuated and autonomous way. Such viewing is much more individuated and autonomous than an act of worship involving religiously prescribed expressive acts, like the performance of a mass and ritual obeisance before an icon of Christ and Mary. In these cases, obligatory affective investments on the part of the viewer are evoked and reinforced. Abstraction of the practice of art interpretation from such concrete prescriptive norms permits a more individuated exploration on the part of a viewer of the potential significance of the expressive orientations objectified in a work of art, while the critical tools at his disposal permit a high level of reflexivity, both in observing his own response and in being self-consciously aware about exactly which dimensions of the work of art cause him to respond in particular ways.

The commitment to a "love of art" and the mandate for a feelingful response maximize the affective openness of the viewer to the potential expressive significance of the principles embodied in the work of art and encourage a deep exploration of them. Within an autonomous art world, the acceptance by the viewer of the expressive orientation offered by a particular work of art is not mandated by any authority external to the viewer. This contrasts with the strong expectation on the part of the church that the members of a congregation will express and feel the attitudes encoded in hymns or an altar-painting. Consequently, in an autonomous art world, each viewer is able to choose what individual combination of the expressive principles encountered within the gallery or museum to internalize as a basis of orientation within his own life-world—and whether or not to choose any. The abstraction of the expressive experience from the constraints implied within institutions or contexts of interaction where evaluative or religious-existential considerations have primacy makes it possible to explore feelings that might be difficult or emotionally disturbing within such contexts. Reflexive exploration and reconstruction of one's expressive orientations in the protected environment of the art museum conditions the development of increased affective autonomy and self-control.

Problems in the Institutionalization of the Modern Arts Complex

Both the varying intrinsic cognitive endowments of people and unequal opportunities to participate in high art at a sophisticated level because of the division of labor in complex societies mean that a relatively restricted number of people are able to interpret art on what would be in Piaget's terms a formal operational level. Furthermore, such an abstractly aesthetic orientation toward cultural representations is not relevant to every social context. Consequently the highly differentiated expressive orientations associated with high culture exist alongside less differentiated orientations, whether because of the different exigencies of different institutional contexts or the varying degree to which specific individuals have been socialized into such orientations.

This can be illustrated in a relatively concrete way by looking at the delicate balance between autonomy and dependence attending the commissioning of the Vietnam Memorial in Washington. The competition for the design of the memorial was organized through the Commission of Fine Arts, which chose Maya Lin's extremely interesting design (figure 10.3). Her abstract, ground-hugging, modernist monument in black granite eschews all the conventional features of a war memorial: figurative representation, white stone, verticality. It offers viewers the possibility of affectively thinking through and responding to deaths that could not be recuperated by traditional conceptions of sacrifice in a just cause. The design emphasizes the individuality of each of the dead as what they share with the mindful viewer, whose own face is reflected in the polished surface of the stone as he or she reads the names. As such the monument requires and encourages a sophisticated and individuated response, one that can accept and explore ambivalence and that places death in war on a more generalized level of meaning than traditional nationalist monuments. Perhaps not surprisingly, not everyone was capable of responding on that level; many condemned the monument as "something for New York intellectuals," as unpatriotic and unheroic. Changes to the proposed monument were demanded by the Department of the Interior, as a condition of the site for the memorial being made available. Both the artist and the Commission of Fine Arts insisted on retaining the integrity of the fundamentals of the design of the monument. Eventually a compromise was reached, in which Maya Lin's original concept remained substantially unchanged, but as an addition more traditional elements of a war memorial, a flag and some statues of soldiers, were installed nearby (Wagner-Pacifici and Schwartz 1991, 394–95; Berman 1992, 47–48).

Despite these controversies before the memorial was built, there is every reason to suppose that Lin's monument has contributed significantly to the process whereby survivors of the Vietnam War—veterans, their families, and also those who simply lived through the war—have been able

FIGURE 10.3 *Maya Lin,* Vietnam Veterans Memorial, *1982*

Source: Uncredited photograph, published in *Art Forum*, April 1983.

to affectively think through and come to terms with the trauma that the war inflicted on the whole society. The focus of the monument on the individual offers a means to transcend some of the social divisions and offered a vehicle for shared mourning, even for those who could in no way identify with the collective violence that may seem to be affirmed in more conventional war memorials, focused on soldiers as representatives of the nation-state. Similarly, in just looking, in taking crayon-rubbings of the engraved name of a friend or relative, or in leaving offerings—candles, flags, flowers, personal letters—viewers are able to mourn and remember in a way that is at once shared and highly individuated. In this respect, both the monument and expressive-aesthetic responses it arouses are an outstanding instance of the "institutionalized individualism" that Parsons regarded as one of the most progressive and most characteristic features of modern American society.[22]

Many of the debates over art and high culture that form such a large part of the journalistic discussion of the arts might obviously be seen in terms of the tensions or fragilities in the institutionalization of high culture and an autonomous or differentiated art world. Sociologists have been quite sensitive to these pressures toward dedifferentiation, largely because they seem to confirm that the most important issues in the art world are "really" social, rather than "aesthetic" (Dubin 1992). This is of course a classic instance of the fallacy of misplaced concreteness, since social interactions are conditioned by expressive-aesthetic considerations as much as vice versa. Certain aspects of postmodernist thought and analysis might be seen as the counterpart inflated aesthetic orientation, with roots in certain radical avant-garde movements, and giving primacy to aesthetic experience and expressive-authenticity at the expense of moral or cognitive claims of truth and validity (Featherstone 1989, 149).[23] Part of the problem is that sociologists of art have accepted the categories of "art" and "aesthetics" in a concrete way while simultaneously trying to deconstruct them, rather than reformulating the categories in a more analytical way. Paradoxically, they thus reinforce and perhaps exaggerate the boundedness of art from society that on another level they seek to deny. The attraction of Parsons's concept of expressive symbolism is that it does reformulate the concept art in an analytical way and implies that the very development of the concept of art as such is linked to the differentiation of an autonomous system of the arts. Conversely, it also implies that such an autonomous system needs to be integrated with other subsystems through processes of interchange parallel to those that sustain the autonomy of the university within a broader cognitive system.[24] Recognizing the functional specificity of the contribution of art to social processes and in particular how that operates in the context of high cultures or autonomous art systems enables us better to see the continuities between autonomous art and the more immediately practical products of the "expressive system" more broadly conceived that make possible and justify the autonomy of the high-cultural sector.

A full discussion of these issues would require a rather extended analysis, but I would like to conclude by sketching the shape that such analysis might assume, and the issues it could illuminate. First, like the university, institutions in the art world, especially museums, are heavily dependent on economic and political subsidy. Such resource dependency entails a risk that the aesthetic goals of the art world might be subordinated to those of other dimensional needs. New-style managers focus on profit centers, fundraising, and blockbuster exhibitions, which maximize attendance and revenue and encourage visitors to act as status-conscious consumers rather than critical-reflective viewers exploring their identity in more authentic ways through artistically challenging exhibitions. Although these are real pressures, other aspects of the institutional development of the art world suggest that these changes represent merely an adaptive upgrading of the arts complex, one that maintains the integrity of the core values which informed its development and thus establishes more secure differentiation. The new generation of managers, trained not in M.B.A. programs but in arts administration programs, are more aware of and oriented toward adaptive problems than their predecessors, but they are also more committed to values specific to the art world than ordinary business managers. In addition, the professionalization of both administrative and curator functions has led to the gradual replacement of curators who were members of the social elite, qualified only by leisure and personal interest, by university-trained art historians. This has both enhanced the independence of art museums from the elite status groups, like the Boston Brahmins, who had been their initial sponsors and has placed them in an environment shaped by new professional arts organizations such as the College Art Association and the Association of American Museums. This has created pressures to conform to art-oriented standards in the curation of exhibitions and the pursuit of research designed to make sophisticated art accessible to the public (DiMaggio 1991, 137–8).

Such relatively purely aesthetic-expressive outputs as exhibitions of art are supplemented by a whole series of more instrumental outputs of the art world that reciprocate its dependence on more conditional structures, and in which purely aesthetic-expressive criteria for the evaluation of artworks are moderated by relevance to the needs of specific clients. Artistic and aesthetic expertise is used in industrial and commercial design, in advertising, including political advertising, and in the creation of national communal symbols. One should also include here so-called "new cultural intermediaries," from advisers on interior decoration to style consultants, all of whom draw on aesthetic expertise of one kind or another to assist clients in finding appropriate means to articulate and express their personal identities in the home or to fashion identities expressively adequate to their public roles (Featherstone 1989, 184).

CONCLUSIONS

Interchange analysis offers a model for a much more abstract account of the interdependency of art with other dimensions of social and cultural order than is offered by the more concrete models of the social determination of art. The latter are more appropriate to eras before the development of a differentiated art world, when moral or religious concerns on a cultural level and political or social exigencies on a social-system-level—determined art production more directly—as was suggested in the accounts of Greek and early-modern European art in the first half of this paper. Interchange analysis complements the concept of expressive symbolism and Parsons's account of the seed-bed societies to offer a more fruitful set of conceptual tools for an analysis of the development, structure, and functioning of the modern art world than any currently competing framework.

I am grateful to the editors and two anonymous reviewers for comments, which greatly improved the final version of this chapter, as did the editorial assistance of Kate Scott at the Russell Sage Foundation. My thanks also to Geraldine Johnson for assistance with finding the picture of the Vietnam Veterans Memorial.

NOTES

1. On the educational revolution as a parallel on the general-action level to the Industrial Revolution on the social-system level, see Parsons and Gerald Platt (1973, 5–6).
2. In this respect my treatment differs from Erwin Panofsky's (1968) classic discussion empirically and theoretically. Panofsky (1924/1968, 11–32) makes an unsustainable claim for the development of a concept of the artist as creator in antiquity, partly on the basis of a Christianizing misreading of the Hellenistic Greek concept of "phantasia" (see Imbert [1980] for a current assessment). As a historian of ideas, he is also more concerned with the formulation of new concepts rather than with the ways such concepts become specified as norms regulating the organization of social relationships or the performance of specific cultural practices, which are crucial from a sociological point of view.
3. See Parsons (1971a, 1977, 309) for a comparison of classical antiquity with modernity in terms of the former's limited realization of the "institutionalized individualism" characteristic of the modern West.
4. See Rudolf Bultmann (1949/1956, 205) for one of the better comparisons of Judeo-Christian and Hellenic cultural orientations.
5. For a more developed version of this argument, with full discussion of the relevant primary evidence, see Jeremy Tanner (1999).
6. For references from Greek and Latin sources, the Oxford Classical Texts are followed; in cases where there is no Oxford Classical Text, the Loeb editions have been used. Translations follow the Loeb editions with adjustments.
7. Michael Baxandall is somewhat inconsistent in his account of the social construction of the artist's role. Here, for example, he adopts a broadly materialist perspective, seeing the artist's relationship to his work as primarily determined by economic relations of production, as specified in the contracts between artists and patrons. In his more theoretically explicit work (Baxandall 1985, especially 46–47), however, he adopts a more idealist definition of the artist's role, in terms of registering the artist's individuality in relationship to historical tradition.
8. I follow here the account of David Pears (1988, esp. 133–47) concentrating on the English case.
9. On the academic role as a fiduciary role and its associated freedoms from subjection to standard contractual arrangements, see Parsons and Platt (1973, 123, 125–32). On the adjustment of the bureaucratic work programs of the New Deal and after to assumptions about the special character of "creative" workers, see Steven Dubin (1987, 118). Of course, not all expressive workers were included in the category of "creative artist," and the extension of the privileges of an elite sometimes took place at the expense of depressing the status of others—see for example Gordon Fyfe (1986, 1988) on the vicissitudes of engravers and etchers in the context of the Royal Academy's attempts to protect the autonomy and enhance the status of painters and sculptors in

nineteenth-century Britain. Of course, many expressive workers (in design, advertising, and so forth) do not enjoy the moral rights of the "fine artists" recognized as "creative"; this does not mean, however, that we should ignore the structural innovation represented by the differentiation of an autonomous art world, and its social and cultural conditioning.

10. For an account of Beethoven that is attentive to the cultural and organizational frame within which his innovations were legitimated but somewhat underplays the radical character of those innovations and their cultural, social, and psychological conditioning, see Tia De Nora (1991). On the revolutionary character of Beethoven's innovations as an evolutionary advance within Western music, note also the interesting comments of Parsons (1961, 988).
11. Compare Robert Bellah's comments (1970, 94) on the limitations placed on "creative social innovation" in China by the "absence of a point of transcendent loyalty that could provide legitimation for it."
12. See Parsons (1971a, 1977, 306) on institutionalized individualism; Alexander (1983, 41) on the role of internalization in the presuppositional logic of Parsons's voluntarism and the possibility of an adequate theory of the modern "cult of the individual." Norbert Elias (1993, 47) also has an excellent discussion of the shift in balance between external and internal constraints with the displacement of direct patron-artist relationships by more distanced market relationships, and the greater psychic demands thus placed on the modern artist. It would be extremely interesting to compare this to the social restructuring and cultural reformulation of the artist's role during the modernization of Japan and China, which lack the Judeo-Christian legacy that so decisively shaped the structuring of the modern art world and artistic identity in the West.
13. Compare Bellah (1970, 42) on the symbolization of modern man as "a dynamic multidimensional self capable, within limits, of continual self-transformation and capable, again within limits, of remaking the world, including the very symbolic forms with which he deals with it."
14. See Tanner (2000) for a parallel account of the social structure of aesthetic judgment and response in the case of Greek civic portraiture.
15. For full analysis with references, see Tanner (2005).
16. See Wolfgang Ernst (1993) on the historicization of display.
17. The argument of this paragraph follows Colin Campbell (1987).
18. Contrast the hierarchical differentiation of high culture in the classical world, where art remained subordinate to religious culture, with the metaphysical ideals of reason: the nonlogical sensate aspects of art were correspondingly dispraised, and the aesthetic ethos in a (to our minds) rather paradoxical way was shaped in such a way as to minimize feelingful involvement such as might endanger rational self-possession. Correspondingly, notwithstanding its relatively high degree of autonomy, the high-cultural art experience was valued primarily in terms of its role in constructing a sensibility and expressive identity consistent with the high value placed on reason.
19. See Tomlinson (1997, 9–19) on the rethinking of art history that this entailed in countries with histories similar to that of Spain: there, because of the diverse political involvements of the Habsburgs, Italian and Flemish painters had probably determined the style and iconography of art more than their Spanish counterparts.
20. The English Royal Academy actually was founded relatively late (1768) and was established as a national institution. It was sponsored more by a social elite—a ruling class comprising the aristocracy and the new commercial elite—than the state as such. The nationalization of the academies in France and the German and Italian states—all originally founded as state institutions to serve the needs of absolutist monarchs and their courts—was a gradual process that took place during the eighteenth and nineteenth centuries.
21. In this respect, the obverse of the situation described by Baxandall (1972) in his classic study, *Painting and Experience in Fifteenth Century Italy*.
22. Something of the success of the monument as an expressive symbol can be gauged by the fact that it is the most visited outdoor monument in Washington, receiving as many as five million visitors in any one year. For the numbers of visitors, see Lopes (1987, 17). The book also contains excellent photographs showing exactly how the monument functions aesthetically, and the range of the forms of expressive attention, which it receives from its viewers.
23. Such orientations are of course quite unrealistic to the extent that they ignore the exigencies of any other demands on action than those of the purely expressive-aesthetic. It is doubtful whether even the demands of normal personality functioning—quite apart from social considerations—can be reconciled with such aesthetic

absolutism. As I have suggested, such an orientation is difficult to acquire and put to work even for cultural specialists with the appropriate supports offered in a relevant institutional context. Most of our expressive interaction and response operates at a much lower level of complexity This is particularly true insofar as our shared expressive culture is shaped by commercial television, for example, soap operas like *Family Ties* or *The Cosby Show,* that offer easy "kitsch" resolutions to the emotional dilemmas of racial and family relations.

24. See Alexander (1983, 103–8) for a succinct discussion of the analysis developed at length in Parsons and Platt (1973).

REFERENCES

Abrams, Meyer H. 1989a. "Art-as-Such: The Sociology of Modern Aesthetics." In *Doing Things with Texts: Essays in Criticism and Critical Theory,* edited by Michael Fischer. New York and London: Norton.

———. 1989b. "From Addison to Kant: Modern Aesthetics and the Exemplary in Art." In *Doing Things with Texts: Essays in Criticism and Critical Theory,* edited by Meyer H. Abrams and Michael Fischer. New York and London: Norton

Adler, Judith. 1975. "Innovative Art and Obsolescent Artists." *Social Research* 42(2): 359–78.

Alexander, Jeffrey C. 1983. *Theoretical Logic in Sociology.* Volume 4, *The Modern Reconstruction of Classical Thought—Talcott Parsons.* Berkeley: University of California Press.

Alexander, Jeffrey C., and Paul Colomy, eds. 1990. *Differentiation Theory and Social Change: Comparative and Historical Perspectives.* New York: Columbia University Press.

Antal, Frederick. 1948. *Florentine Painting and Its Social Background.* London: Kegan Paul.

Barasch, Moshe. 1985. *Theories of Art: From Plato to Winckelmann.* New York: New York University Press.

Bartman, Elizabeth. 1991. "Sculptural Collecting and Display in the Private Realm." In *Roman Art in the Private Sphere,* edited by Elaine K. Gazda. Ann Arbor: University of Michigan Press.

Baxandall, Michael. 1972. *Painting and Experience in Fifteenth Century Italy.* Oxford: Oxford University Press.

———. 1985. *Patterns of Intention: On the Historical Explanation of Pictures.* New Haven: Yale University Press.

Becker, Howard S. 1982. *Art Worlds.* Berkeley: University of California Press.

Bellah, Robert. 1970. *Beyond Belief: Essays on Religion in a Post-Traditional World.* New York: Harper & Row.

Berman, Marshall. 1992. "Why Modernism Still Matters." In *Modernity and Identity,* edited by Scott Lash and Jonathan Friedman. Oxford: Blackwell.

Blunt, Anthony. 1940. *Artistic Theory in Italy: 1450–1660.* Oxford: Oxford University Press.

Bourdieu, Pierre. 1967. "Systems of Education and Systems of Thought." In *Knowledge and Control: New Directions for the Sociology of Education,* edited by M. Young. London: Collier-Macmillan.

———. 1968. "Outline of a Sociological Theory of Art Perception." *International Social Science Journal* 20(4): 589–612.

———. 1984. *Distinction: A Social Critique of the Judgement of Taste.* Cambridge, Mass.: Harvard University Press.

Brilliant, Richard. 1984. "Pendants and the Mind's Eye." *Visual Narratives: Storytelling in Etruscan and Roman Art.* Ithaca: Cornell University Press.

Bultmann, Rudolf. 1949/1956. *Primitive Christianity in Its Contemporary Setting.* London: Thames & Hudson.

Bürger, Peter. 1982. "The Institution of Art as a Category of the Sociology of Literature." In *The Institutions of Art,* edited by Peter Bürger and Christina Bürger. Lincoln: University of Nebraska Press.

Campbell, Colin. 1987. *The Romantic Ethic and the Spirit of Modern Consumerism.* Oxford: Blackwell.

Cennini, Cennino d'Andrea. 1960. *The Craftsman's Handbook: "Il Libro dell'Arte" by Cennino d'Andrea Cennini,* translated and edited by Daniel V. Thompson, Jr. New York: Dover.

De Nora, Tia. 1991. "Musical patronage and social change in Beethoven's Vienna." *American Journal of Sociology* 97: 310–46.

DiMaggio, Paul. 1982. "Cultural Entrepreneurship in Nineteenth Century Boston: The Creation of an Organizational Base for High Culture in America; The Classification and Framing of American Art." Parts 1 and 2. *Media, Culture and Society* 4(1 and 2): 33–50, 303–22.

———. 1991. "Social Structure, Institutions and Cultural Goods: The Case of the United States." In *Social Theory for a Changing Society,* edited by Pierre Bourdieu and J. S. Coleman. New York: Russell Sage Foundation.

Dubin, Steven C. 1987. *Bureaucratizing the Muse: Public Funds and the Cultural Worker.* Chicago: University of Chicago Press.

———. 1992. *Arresting Images: Impolitic Art and Uncivil Action.* London: Routledge.

Duboff, Leonard O. 1984. *Art Law.* St. Paul, Minn.: West.

Eisenstadt, Shmuel N. 1990. "Modes of Structural Differentiation: Elite Structure and Cultural Visions." In *Differentiation Theory and Social Change: Comparative and Historical Perspectives,* edited by Jeffrey C. Alexander and Paul Colomy. New York: Columbia University Press.

Elias, Norbert. 1993. *Mozart: Portrait of a Genius.* Cambridge: Polity Press.

Ernst, Wolfgang. 1993. "Frames at Work: Museological Imagination and Historical Discourse in Neoclassical Britain." *Art Bulletin* 75: 481–98.

Featherstone, Mike. 1989. "Towards a Sociology of Postmodern Culture." In *Culture and Social Structure,* edited by H. Haferkamp. Berlin: Aldine de Gruyter.

Fyfe, Gordon J. 1986. "Art Exhibitions and Power During the Nineteenth Century." In *Power, Action and Belief: A New Sociology of Knowledge?* edited by John Law. Sociological Review monograph 32. London: Routledge & Kegan Paul.

———. 1988. "Art and Its Objects: William Ivins and the Reproduction of Art." In *Picturing Power: Visual Depiction and Social Relations,* edited by Gordon Fyfe and John Law. Sociological Review Monograph 35. London: Routledge.

Gibson-Wood, Carol. 1984. "Jonathan Richardson and the Rationalization of Connoisseurship." *Art History* 7(1): 38–56.

Hauser, Arnold. 1962. *The Social History of Art.* Volume 2, *Renaissance, Mannerism and Baroque.* London: Routledge & Kegan Paul.

Hawthorn, Geoffrey. 1991. *Plausible Worlds: Possibility and Understanding in History and the Social Sciences.* Cambridge: Cambridge University Press.

Huyssen, Andreas. 1989. "Anselm Kiefer: The Terror of History, the Temptation of Myth." *October* 48:25–46.

Imbert, Claude. 1980. "Stoic Logic and Alexandrian Poetics." In *Doubt and Dogmatism,* edited by Jonathan Barnes, Myles Burnyeat, and Malcolm Schofield. Cambridge: Cambridge University Press.

Kemp, Martin. 1989. "The 'Super-Artist' as Genius: The Sixteenth Century View." In *Genius: The History of an Idea,* edited by Penelope Murray. Oxford: Blackwell.

———. 1991. Introduction to *On Painting,* by Leon Battista Alberti. Harmondsworth, England: Penguin.

Kempers, Bram. 1987/1992. *Painting, Power and Patronage: The Rise of the Professional Artist in Renaissance Italy.* Harmondsworth, England: Penguin.

Kristeller, Paul O. 1990. *Renaissance Thought and the Arts.* Princeton: Princeton University Press.

Lidz, Charles W., and Victor M. Lidz. 1976. "Piaget's Psychology of the Intelligence and the Theory of Action." In *Explorations in General Theory in Social Science,* edited by Jan Loubser, Rainer C. Baum, Andrew Effrat, and Victor M. Lidz. Philadelphia: University of Pennsylvania Press.

Lopes, Sal. 1987. *The Wall: Images and Offerings from the Vietnam Veterans Memorial.* New York: Collins.

McClellan, Andrew. 1984. "The Politics and Aesthetics of Display: Museums in Paris 1750–1800." *Art History* 7: 439–64.

Moulin, Raymonde. 1967/1987. *The French Art Market: A Sociological View.* New Brunswick, N.J.: Rutgers University Press.

Mulkay, Michael, and Elizabeth Chaplin. 1982. "Aesthetics and the Artistic Career: A Study of Anomie in Fine Art Painting." *Sociological Quarterly* 23(2): 117–38.

Panofsky, Erwin. 1924/1968. *Idea: A Concept in Art Theory.* New York: Harper & Row.

Parsons, Michael J. 1987. *How We Understand Art: A Cognitive Developmental Approach.* Cambridge: Cambridge University Press.

Parsons, Talcott. 1951. "Expressive Symbols and the Social System: The Communication of Affect." *The Social System.* New York: Free Press.

———. 1961. "Culture and the Social System: An Introduction." In *Theories of Society,* edited by Talcott Parsons, Edward Shils, Kaspar D. Naegele, and Jesse R. Pitts. New York: Free Press.

———. 1966. *Societies—Evolutionary and Comparative Perspectives.* Englewood Cliffs, N.J.: Prentice-Hall.

———. 1971a. "Comparative Studies and Evolutionary Change." In *Comparative Methods in Sociology: Essays on Trends and Applications,* edited by Ivan Vallier. Berkeley: University of California Press.

———. 1971b. *The System of Modern Societies.* Englewood Cliffs, N.J.: Prentice-Hall.

———. 1977. *Social Systems and the Evolution of Action Theory.* New York: Free Press.

Parsons, Talcott, and Gerald Platt. 1973. *The American University.* Cambridge, Mass.: Harvard University Press.

Parsons, Talcott, and Winston White, 1961/1964. "The Link Between Character and Society." In *Social Structure and Personality,* edited by Talcott Parsons. New York: Free Press.

Pears, David. 1988. *The Discovery of Painting: The Growth of Interest in the Arts in England, 1680–1768*. New Haven: Yale University Press.

Perry, Gill, and Colin Cunningham. 1999. *Academies, Museums and Canons of Art*. London: Open University Press.

Potts, Alex D. 1982. "Wincklemann's Construction of History." *Art History* 5(4): 377–407.

———. 1994. *Flesh and the Ideal: Winckelmann and the Origins of Art History*. New Haven: Yale University Press.

Robbins, Derek. 1991. *The Work of Pierre Bourdieu: Recognizing Society*. Milton Keynes, England: Open University Press.

Rosenthal, M., ed. 1987. *Anselm Kiefer*. Exhibition catalogue. Philadelphia: Philadelphia Museum of Art.

Smelser, Neil J. 1973. "Epilogue: Social Structural Dimensions of Higher Education." In *The American University*, edited by Talcott Parsons and Gerald Platt. Cambridge, Mass.: Harvard University Press.

Summers, David. 1981. *Michelangelo and the Language of Art*. Princeton: Princeton University Press.

Tanner, Jeremy. 1999. "Culture, Social Structure and the Status of Visual Artists in Classical Greece." *Proceedings of the Cambridge Philological Society* 45: 136–75

———. 2000. "Social Structure, Cultural Rationalisation and Aesthetic Judgement in Classical Greece." In *Word and Image in Ancient Greece*, edited by N. Keith Rutter and Brian A. Sparkes. Edinburgh Leventis Studies 1. Edinburgh: Edinburgh University Press.

———. 2001. "Nature, Culture and the Body in Classical Greek Religious Art." *World Archaeology* 33: 257–76.

———. 2005. *The Invention of Art History in Ancient Greece: Religion, Society and Artistic Rationalisation*. Cambridge: Cambridge University Press.

Tomlinson, J. 1997. *From El Greco to Goya: Painting in Spain 1561–1828*. New York: Abrams.

Vernant, Jean-Pierre. 1983. "Work and Nature in Ancient Greece." *Myth and Thought among the Greeks*, by J-P Vernant. London: Routledge & Kegan Paul.

Wagner-Pacifici, Robin, and Barry Schwartz. "The Vietnam Veterans' Memorial: Commemorating a Difficult Past." *American Journal of Sociology* 97(2): 376–420.

Warnke, M. 1985. *The Court Artist: On the Ancestry of the Modern Artist*. Translated by David McLintock. Cambridge: Cambridge University Press.

Wittkower, R., and M. Wittkower. 1964. *The Divine Michelangelo: The Florentine Academy's Homage on his Death in 1564*. London: Phaidon.

Wolff, James. 1987. "The Ideology of Autonomous Art." In *Music and Society: The Politics of Composition, Performance and Reception*, edited by Richard Leppert and Susan McClary. Cambridge: Cambridge University Press.

Zolberg, Vear. 1990. *Constructing a Sociology of the Arts*. Cambridge: Cambridge University Press.

Chapter 11

The Weberian Talcott Parsons: Sociological Theory in Three Decades of American History

Uta Gerhardt

The relationship between Talcott Parsons's scholarship and Max Weber's classic thought has been debated in two recent contexts in American sociology. According to one viewpoint, Parsons's thought can be traced back to genuinely American intellectual origins, and was not, under Weber's influence, "made in Germany," incorporating the often-invoked Heidelberg myth in the 1920s—as some European disciples, including me, are said to assume (Camic, chapter 12, this volume). The other view stemmed from an anti-Parsonian impetus in the early 1970s, when three authors claimed to be preserving Weber's greatness as they attempted to "de-Parsonize Weber" (Cohen, Hazelrigg, and Pope 1975a).[1] To be sure, one of them, Whitney Pope (1973), had two years earlier attacked Parsons's interpretation of Émile Durkheim's theory in an attempt to refute Parsons's claim that his scholarship continued the tradition of the sociological classics.

The charge against Parsons was that, unlike Weber, he reduced action and authority to mere instruments of "the effective functioning and integration of collectivities" (Cohen, Hazelrigg, and Pope 1975a, 240). Jere Cohen, Lawrence E. Hazelrigg, and Whitney Pope thus replicated Dennis Wrong's allegations that Parsons promoted an "oversocialized conception of man" (Wrong 1961), oblivious of the fact that Parsons had decisively refuted that criticism (Parsons 1962) thirteen years earlier.

In his "Comment" in response to Cohen and his colleagues' criticism, Parsons stressed four issues on which these critics were wrong (Parsons 1975b). First, social theory, including Weber's and Parsons's own, was not a descriptive account of empirical reality, as Cohen, Hazelrigg, and Pope assumed.[2] Second, neither Weber nor Parsons had maintained, as Cohen, Hazelrigg, and Pope argued, that interests, let alone material interests, were the sole motivational force in economic action. Third, Parsons's own views on the relationship between the economy and society and between economics and sociology had undergone a major revision in the 1950s instead of remaining much the same as set forth in *The Structure of Social Action,* as Cohen, Hazelrigg, and Pope appeared to assume. Finally, Parsons charged, his critics had not attended to the argument of his 1964 address at the German Sociological Association's celebration in Heidelberg of the centenary of Weber's birth. There he had defended "objectivity" in Weberian terms, allowing for "Wertfreiheit" (value neutrality)—the absence of political partisanship in scientific analysis—and attacking politicization of the standards of proof endorsed by some contemporaries advocating humanistic social politics. All his life, he contended, "selective interest in a certain limited set of problems" had been his proper guide in choosing research areas. Accordingly, predominance of the knowledge interest had been his methodological credo, as it had been for Weber (Parsons 1975b, 668).

During his lifetime Parsons defended himself vigorously against charges that he could not legitimately call himself a Weberian. Today, Parsons needs to be defended vigorously against the charge that his sociology, presumably "made in Germany," nevertheless lacked his obvious Weberianism. In the context of his intellectual biography, the problem arises of what the relationship was between Parsonian scholarship and the Weberian legacy. Evidently, Parsons's scholarship was embedded in the politics and history (mainly of the United States) of the five decades between the 1930s and 1970s, the period when he wrote his sociological works (Gerhardt 2002). One can see that Parsons's action theory was closely related to changes in American social history from decade to decade. The consecutive changes in his conceptualizing of social action, its structures, and processes, I venture, document his understanding of the dynamics of modern society. As his oeuvre evolved, Weber's thought took on an ever new salience while remaining a source of continuous inspiration.

My aim is to contribute to an understanding of the development of action theory in the twentieth century by demonstrating that Parsons was a Weberian all his life, though he changed his reference to Weberian thought several times throughout his oeuvre. I will reconstruct the foundation of Weberian thinking in Parsons's work when I refuse to search for so-called roots from which grew a sociology "made in Germany."

Parsons's oeuvre spanned five decades, from the 1930s to the 1970s. The earliest articles, published in the late 1920s, were drawn from his Ph.D. dissertation on theories of capitalism and were precursors to his theory of the structure of social action, which he developed in the 1930s. His last major essay, "A Paradigm of the Human Condition," was written in the late 1970s. My essay concentrates on three decades when Weber's work was essential to Parsons's developing system theory, namely the 1930s, 1940s, and 1950s.

As an operational baseline I propose four tenets of what may be called Weberian sociology. These tenets derive from Weber's thought as expressed in the original German but also draws on some English-language secondary literature on his work (Bendix 1960, Bendix and Roth 1971, Alexander 1983, Sica 1988, Levine 1995).

The first Weberian presupposition I propose is voluntarism as contrasted with positivism and utilitarianism. Parsons knew from translating *The Protestant Ethic and the Spirit of Capitalism* that Weber had warned against contemporary "Fachmenschentum" and had endorsed instead the "spirit" of capitalism (Weber 1930/1976; Gerhardt, forthcoming). The orientation to "spirit" implied a voluntarism in the community of saints among Puritans, whose importance in the era of the doctrine of predestination Weber emphasized.[3] Parsons in turn made voluntarism a mainstay of his action theory in *The Structure of Social Action* and later works.

Another Weberian tenet is rationality in relation to reciprocity. Weber held that social action entails social relations. Rational action, in a social relation, entails reciprocity.[4] Parsons in turn established a rationality–reciprocity rationale for his theory of the structure of social action (Parsons 1937/1968, 101, 650; Gerhardt 2002, 47–48).

A third Weberian principle is "Wertfreiheit," value neutrality of scientific analysis. The refusal of social science in its schemas of proof (as distinct from specific applied studies) to serve political ends was fundamental for both Weber and Parsons (Weber 1904/1949a, 1917/1949b; Parsons 1964/1967). The guarantee of "Wertfreiheit," of the "objectivity" of sociological knowledge so as to protect scientific thought from ideology was a key theme in Weber's methodology—although it has frequently been misinterpreted in the secondary literature (Ringer 1997; Agevall 1999; Eliaeson 2002). Parsons affirmed the primacy of "Wertfreiheit" on many occasions, including his speech in honor of Weber at the Heidelberg Conference in 1964 (Parsons 1964/1967). This guarantee of objectivity must be considered a pivotal principle of methodology when one is assessing the continuity from Weber to Parsons (Gerhardt 2001).

The fourth Weberian tenet requires that the sociologist not emulate a politician. The personal way of life, the "Lebensführung," of the social scientist might make him a veritable zoon politikon, but his scholarly schemas must be free of political partisanship. Weber, until 1920, and Parsons, from the 1930s to the 1970s, were both politically active beyond their respective ivory towers, but both insisted on maintaining a separation between social science and social politics.[5]

I argue that as Parsons tackled various themes of sociological inquiry in the 1930s, 1940s, and 1950s, he honored these Weberian tenets. Weber remained a main source of scholarly inspiration all Parsons's life, and he related the many problems he studied throughout his oeuvre to Weber's theory. His sociological theory was grounded in an analysis of American society and democracy, and his attachment to Weber's legacy was woven into his discussions of many contemporary problems.

THE 1930s

Parsons's output of the decade of the thirties includes the German and English versions of his dissertation (written from 1926 to 1927), which focused mainly on Weber's conception of capitalism; "The Role of Ideas in Social Action," written in 1938, which was a rejection of ideological determinism; the essay on professionalism and economics, an afterthought to a prominent theme of his earliest writing, "The Motivation of Economic Activities," of 1939 (Parsons 1928, 1929, 1938a, 1939, 1940). The culmination of this first decade of his writings was *The Structure of Social Action* (Parsons 1937/1968). Its two major themes had been foreshadowed in the essay on ultimate values in connection with ethical neutrality (Parsons 1935/1991b) and a string of essays on the interface between economics and sociology, from "Wants and Activities in Marshall" (Parsons 1931) to "Certain Sociological Elements in Professor Taussig's Thought" (Parsons 1936).

Four Weberian Themes

Four Weberian themes in these works give a vivid picture of Parsons's understanding of American history and society in the 1930s. One theme concerned the relationship between the "spirit" of capitalism, including religious motivation for economic action, and modern capitalism. As he discussed the two conceptions of capitalism, he pointed out that Weber, in *The Protestant Ethic and the Spirit of Capitalism,* had been concerned with the difference between them. The earliest reference to this double nature of capitalism was in Parsons's review of a book by H. M. Robertson, a highly regarded British economic historian. Against Robertson, he cited "what Weber calls the element of 'rational bourgeois capitalism' as distinguished from 'capitalist adventurers.' It is this element, not the total concrete phenomenon of capitalism, that is the theme of the essay on *The Protestant Ethic*" (Parsons 1935/1991a, 62).

In *The Structure of Social Action,* Parsons insisted that Weber, in linking the religiously grounded "spirit" of capitalism with economic activity that, albeit unintentionally, engendered prosperity, had explained the rational structure of modern social action and authority. Legitimate, rational-legal authority involves disinterestedness and excludes unregulated "rugged" individualism. For Weber it was an order that stood for moral elements of the capitalist spirit, in opposition to the amoral or irrational utilitarianism of "adventurer capitalism." Regarding the legitimate order as a moral force, Parsons explained (1937/1968, 661):

> Legitimacy is for Weber a quality of an order, that is, of a system of norms governing conduct. . . . This quality is imputed to the order by those acting in relation to it. Doing so involves taking a given type of attitude toward the norms involved which

> may be characterized as one of disinterested acceptance. To put the matter somewhat differently, for one who holds an order to be legitimate, living up to its rules becomes, to this extent, a matter of moral obligation.

Parsons highlighted Weber's explanation that adventurer capitalism was not the origin of the modern socioeconomic structure. Weber distinguished sharply between economic action, which involves reciprocity in market-relations, and—as Parsons clarified—economic coercion, which relies on nonmarket relations. He quoted Weber's dictum that economic action is irreconcilable with coercion: "Das Pragma der Gewaltsamkeit ist dem Geist der Wirtschaft sehr stark [e]ntgegengesetzt" (Weber 1922/1956, 32; Parsons 1937/1968, 658).[6] Weber and Parsons both suggested that economic theory that idealizes the conditions of the market is unable to explain the reality of force and fraud that characterizes actual economic life.[7]

A second theme concerns political implications of economic liberalism. Two forms of liberalism had to be separated analytically. Utilitarian economics, Parsons knew, squared with so-called Manchester liberalism, which was also echoed in Social Darwinism (Gerhardt 2002, 27–32). In contradistinction, a liberal economy could also consist of market relations embedded in a democratic political culture. The latter could be anchored in the political philosophy of the Enlightenment, which had cultivated the liberty of the individual up to the point that one person's liberty had to allow for the liberty of others. In this context, Parsons postulated a fundamental need for restrictions on economic utilitarianism imposed by normative principles. He argued that the normative side of economic action, in Durkheimian terms, represented an essential backdrop to economic order, namely noncontractual conditions that regulate contractual relations (Durkheim 1933/1964, 206–19; Parsons 1937/1968, 313–19).

In drawing the distinction between two types of liberalism connected with different types of authority regimes he followed Weber closely. Weber, in *Economy and Society,* had argued that the most prosperous type of economic system is not connected with a "pure" type of authority. The type of authority that would best promote material welfare is different from ideal-typical rational-legal or charismatic regimes. In chapter 3 of *Economy and Society,* entitled "The Types of Legitimate Domination,"[8] Weber argued that there is a special subtype, which he discussed under the heading of "The Transformation of Charisma in a Democratic Direction." His idea was that an amalgamation of charismatic and plebiscitarian tendencies produces a regime that fosters democracy while also spurring a prosperous economy. Weber suggested (1968/1978, 269):

> The anti-authoritarian direction of the transformation of charisma normally leads into the path of rationality. If a ruler is dependent on recognition by plebiscite he will usually attempt to support his regime by an organization of officials which functions promptly and efficiently. He will attempt to consolidate the loyalty of those he governs either by winning glory and honor in war or by promoting their material welfare, or under certain circumstances, by attempting to combine both.

Weber saw this type of regime realized in the United States. When he visited the United States to attend the St. Louis World Fair in 1904, he observed the affluence and freedom enjoyed by Americans. As he remarked in *Economy and Society,* he found that "in such a big country even though millions of dollars were stolen or embezzled there was still plenty left for everybody" (Weber 1968/1978, 271).

Parsons followed Weber's lead when he perceived the America of the New Deal in the 1930s as a regime apt to combine democracy with economic freedom under a program of social welfare. He argued in *The Structure of Social Action* that economic growth depends on control of force and fraud, which in turn was a deliberate achievement of Roosevelt's policies.[9]

He also followed Weber when he analyzed National Socialism in Germany as the opposite of such a liberal structure. Weber had maintained that ideal-type charismatic rule is alien to economic rationality, calling it "spezifisch wirtschaftsfremd," literally "alien to the economy" (Parsons 1937/1968, 662), a term Parsons used in the original German when he analyzed the coercive system that he viewed as characterized by the triad of "Tradition—Affect—Wertrationalität" (Parsons 1937/1968, 661). On that background, he realized that force and fraud, exacerbated by charismatic rule, leads ultimately to a war of all against all—the opposite of social order and the kind of anomie that precipitated the coercion that characterized Nazi Germany.[10]

Another Weberian theme Parsons adopted was that empirical society is the subject matter of sociological theory. Weber, in *Economy and Society* and elsewhere, analyzed contemporary as well as historical societies, presupposing that social science had to explain empirical phenomena through Verstehen (systematic understanding). Weber aimed to explain "the unique individual character of cultural phenomena" by means of ideal-type concepts (Weber 1904/1949a, 101).

Parsons refrained from using ideal-type concepts, but followed Weber when he set out to explain empirical reality. *The Structure of Social Action* dealt with "four recent European writers" as empirical theorists. In the preface, Parsons informed his readers that his original intention was to explain modern capitalism, that is, to understand the empirical dynamics of the modern world and explain the empirical society in the first decades of the twentieth century. He recounted that as he had begun writing, he had been unaware of a deeper point, namely, that the four authors had contributed to "a single coherent theoretical system," and this now became the focus of his discussion (Parsons 1937/1968, xxii). In a version of the preface that he abandoned at the request of his publisher, he phrased it thus: "The basis on which the four writers were brought together for study was rather empirical," namely, their analysis of "the modern socio-economic order."[11] In the published preface he stressed that he sought to formulate a "single coherent theoretical system," yet he also mentioned that the subject matter was the modern economic order, described in terms of " 'capitalism,' 'free enterprise,' 'economic individualism' " (1937/1968, xxii).

Thus, empirical sociology clad in Weberian concepts supplemented by Durkheimian ideas underlay Parsons's two-pronged theoretical scheme of the structure(s) of social action. He juxtaposed anomie and integration as the opposite poles of empirical social systems in his day (Gerhardt 2002, 32–48). He had contemporary societies in mind when he contrasted the types of systems. He did not use ideal-type concepts but introduced the bipolar-action structure of systems of anomie and integration. As for the anomic society, he saw the closeness between ritual in Durkheim's sense and charismatic authority in Weber's sense, both merging in the Nazi dictatorship, which he viewed as the epitome of the War of All Against All. Integrated society was the opposite, characterized by a community pattern of structures of social action akin to Durkheim's organic solidarity but also to Weber's rational-legal authority transformed in the direction of democracy with the incorporation of a market economy.

A fourth Weberian theme in Parsons's writing of the 1930s was his emphasis on morality in the guise of ultimate values. Weber in 1917 had invoked the inability of social science to justify the politics of, say, Syndicalism. He had opposed the demagogic tendencies of Gesinnungsethik (ethics of convictions), including that of his former colleague and friend, Robert Michels, who had joined Benito Mussolini's Fascist movement in Italy. Weber insisted that the social scientist could not predict future developments nor prove from a social-science point of view that a particular world view was true. Although he personally endorsed the modern state's monopoly of power, Weber's reaction to the near dictatorship of the German military at the end of World War I was that the state should refrain from using its powers in dictatorial fashion. In any case, Weber stated (1917/1949b, 48–49), ultimate values were beyond the reach of scientific proof:

> The developments of the past few decades, and especially the unprecedented events to which we are now witness, have heightened the prestige of the state tremendously. . . . In the sphere of value-judgements, however, it is possible to defend quite meaningfully the view that . . . the state itself has no *intrinsic* value, that it is a purely technical instrument for the realization of other values from which alone it derives its value, and that it can retain this value only as long as it does not seek to transcend this merely auxiliary status.

In the middle 1930s Parsons felt that the problem of ultimate values that Weber had settled in 1917 needed further discussion. National Socialism had come to dominate state and society in Germany through officially promoted racism and militarism, and this raised anew the question of whether ultimate values were beyond sociological inquiry. Parsons distinguished between rational or intrinsic action, which was empirical and involved calculated expectations defining the means-end relationship that Weber had analyzed, and ritualistic, or symbolic, action, which was not susceptible to empirical proof or evaluation. He understood ritualistic action to be related to "the category of ultimate conditions" (Parsons 1935/1991b, 249). Ultimate conditions could in turn be "identified with the positivistic factors of heredity and environment" (250), quite distinct from ultimate values. This suggested "the view that . . . the 'end' in the strict sense . . . is . . . of the order of a value element and not a psychological drive" (250). He proposed that "it is in the form of the more diffuse value attitudes, rather than the more specific ultimate ends, that [value elements in our lives] can best be brought in." This suggested that for community life, "the diffuse value attitude is more relevant than the end" (255). If value elements were excluded from sociological analysis rather than being scrutinized for their implicit authoritarian or democratic potentials, he warned, this would mean inadvertently to "fall back on positivistic factors" in sociological explanation (255).

Like Weber, he discussed the state's monopoly of legitimate power in the context of value judgments. Echoing Weber, he stated that the modern nondictatorial state claimed legitimate authority; supplementing Weber, he noted that the state (as a modern accomplishment) regulated rather than merely represented power in the "general interest":

> The state is the focus of the political element because it is the association which attempts to regulate the power relationships of the community in the general interest, partly by its monopoly of the *legitimate* exercise of physical coercion. (Parsons 1935/1991b, 240, original emphasis).

His reference to the "general interest" was noteworthy as an invocation of the community of citizens as an indirect reference to American democracy. In the American setting, the citizen enjoyed freedom inasmuch as he respected the rights of others. In the academic culture, the community of scholars encouraged "free" scientific inquiry, governed solely by the responsibility of the scientist to analyze empirical phenomena using intersubjectively valid methods of proof. In the footsteps of Weber, Parsons warned that the sociologist had to keep the empirical world in mind and renounce grand schemes even as he conducted "ethically neutral" analysis. In the context of the 1930s, this statement had a double meaning. Parsons endorsed the kind of social science that would painstakingly honor empirical proof, but he despised the kind of social science that adopted grand schemes and claimed to encompass the entire empirical world, stating (1935/1991b, 257), "The scientist *starts* always from the empirical facts of a certain area of experience. . . . The philosopher goes directly to the whole. . . . I stand squarely on the platform of science."

To summarize his four Weberian themes in the 1930s: Two types of capitalism existed, one emulating the model of economic action steeped in the spirit of capitalism, and the other one (called by Weber adventurer capitalism) the system that allowed for economic coercion, the involuntary sequel to Manchester liberalism, and propelled utilitarian individualism.

Second, authoritarian regimes were typically "spezifisch wirtschaftsfremd," whereas modern Anglo-Saxon societies resembled Weber's type in which charisma is transformed in a democratic direction.

The third theme was that "the modern socio-economic order" as an empirical society (Parsons 1937/1968) was the subject matter of social theory, which was empirically oriented but not empiricist. Concepts needed an analytical frame of reference although they might not be ideal-type constructs.

Last but not least, the ethical neutrality of social science was imperative: in studying social structures and processes, the sociologist's concepts should be independent of social and political ideologies and no attempt to harmonize them should be made; sociologists had to renounce Gesinnungsethik, or "ethics of conviction," as Weber had demanded, and Parsons ventured that ultimate value attitudes should be grounded in empirical evidence, as science that claimed to deduce reality from "rational structures" was an anomalous and utterly deviant endeavor.

Society, Sociology, and American Democracy

These four elements of sociological thought emulated the theory and methodology of Weber. They could be used to analyze not only the society of the United States but also that of Nazi Germany. Two themes made this obvious in the 1930s.

One theme was the relationship of the economy to society. A second theme was the role of social science, including both economics and sociology, in the process of the democratization of twentieth-century society.

To recapitulate the economic situation in the late 1920s and 1930s: the collapse of the New York Stock Exchange in October 1929 triggered the Great Depression the following year (Schlesinger 1957; Bernstein 1989). In 1932, Franklin D. Roosevelt was elected president and soon introduced a series of measures designed to curtail fraud in financial markets, rescue agriculture and industry from bankruptcy through government loans, and conquer the effects of mass unemployment through welfare but also work programs—a program known as the New Deal (Brinkley 1989).[12] Writing in the 1950s, the historian Richard Hofstadter said (1955, 302) of the transition from Depression to New Deal,

> Once again the demand for reform became irresistible, and out of the chaotic and often mutually contradictory schemes for salvation that arose from all corners of the country the New Deal took form. In the years 1933–8 the New Deal sponsored a series of legislative changes that made the enactments of the Progressive era seem timid by comparison, changes that, in their totality, carried the politics and administration of the United States farther from the conditions of 1914 than those had been from the conditions of 1880.

The legislative measures introduced during the first three months after Roosevelt's inauguration included among others the Emergency Banking Act, the Economy Act, the Agricultural Adjustment Act, the Truth-in-Securities Act, the Tennessee Valley Authority Act, the National Industrial Recovery Act, the Glass-Steagall Banking Act, and the Farm Credit Act (Schlesinger 1958/1988, 20–21). These measures regulated the economy through legislation that called for the state to supplement but not replace the principles of the market and to enhance the self-determination and self-respect of American citizens.

Parsons was an ardent supporter of Roosevelt's New Deal in the 1930s. As a sociologist, he clad his liberalism in a critique of utilitarianism, the historian Howard Brick (1996) emphasizes. To Parsons, Brick stresses, utilitarianism posited a kind of economic system and also social science that denied freedom of choice to the individual and presupposed determinism in social life. Brick writes (1996, 378) of Parsons in the 1930s:

> Parsons described "the inherent instability of the utilitarian system" and showed how it "breaks down," devolving into a "mechanistic determinism" that explains human action solely in terms of "heredity and environment." To avoid that theoretical fate, Parsons urged a move in the "opposite direction"—away from biological reductionism to reaffirm the role of reason and the possibility of freedom—by "radically revising" the utilitarian system's "whole 'framework.' "

Parsons's concern was not only with American democracy in the economic crisis of the 1930s but also with the political fate of Germany in that period. In the year following publication of *The Structure of Social Action,* he gave several lectures in which he applied the conceptual tools of that major opus to a comparison of Nazi Germany and American democracy. In a lecture whose topic was "Limitations of Sociological Analysis," which he delivered at Yale University in March 1938, he used some of his analytical categories to characterize Germany under Nazi dictatorship. He saw Germany as an epitome of anomie and hypothesized that rapid social change had spurred the breakdown of its institutions. This anomic condition had in turn triggered aggressive nationalism and anti-Semitism. His lecture notes, which have been preserved in the Harvard University Archives (Parsons 1938b, 1–4), sketch these points:

> Anomie: Rapid industrialization. Changing class structure. Nationalism. Jews. Defeat + Humiliation. Goals + Means. Value-emotional-ideological side of Nazi Movement. Lack of firmness of liberal values. Seriousness of break in authoritarian structure. . . . Anomie—a breakdown of institutional integration: individualization, mobility—industrialization. Nationalism as obverse. Class structure—never entirely integrated. . . . Values—in Germany always more opposition to liberalism than elsewhere. Authoritarian structure much undermined but little to replace . . . Reintegration—questionable whether creative or not: Modern dictatorship largely a product of social disorganization.

As Nazi Germany menaced Europe and fascism and totalitarianism reigned supreme in Italy, Russia, and elsewhere, the international political situation in the 1930s was of grave concern to many American intellectuals (Mowrer 1933; Lasswell 1933, 1934; Schuman 1935). Writing a biographical reminiscence thirty-five years later, Parsons would explain that in the 1930s he had felt a strong urge not only to understand what was going on in Germany but also do something along the lines of political action (Parsons 1969, 60–61). As is known from archival materials, he helped persecuted Austrians and Germans such as the political scientist Eric Voegelin and the sociologist Hans Speier to enter the United States as refugee exiles. He also wrote letters to both senators for Massachusetts (one of whom was Henry Cabot Lodge, Jr.) to protest the Neutrality Act before it became law in November 1939.[13] He argued in these letters that the danger was that Nazi imperialism would eventually incite a world war unless the United States managed to overcome its isolationism and intervene in what was still a European war. In other words, emulating Weber when he followed his own sense of responsibility, as a social scientist Parsons juxtaposed two systems of political-economic structure, but as a citizen he endorsed the Anglo-Saxon system and openly challenged its Nazi German opposite.

The other theme he tackled was the question of how much social science could achieve in an era of political crisis. In "The Place of Ultimate Values in Sociological Theory" and elsewhere, he followed Weber's plea for "Wertfreiheit." He advocated methodologically grounded concept formation, thereby fulfilling the Weberian postulate. In this endeavor he tried to prove that sociology is a science in its own right and not a part of economics or political science. In a letter to the Chicago sociologist Louis Wirth, who in a book review of *The Structure of Social Action* had rejected Parsons's claim that sociology was an independent branch of the social sciences, Parsons positioned society alongside the economy and politics. He explained that inasmuch as each of these disciplines targets reality from a different angle using different conceptual schemes, sociology, like economics and political science, is scientific. All three social sciences use legitimate perspectives and none can grasp concrete empirical phenomena fully. He elucidated,

> By distinguishing politics from sociology, I do not mean to imply that concrete power relationships have no relation to values. The distinction is analytical and not a classification of concrete social structures. It is crucial to the methodological problem which I have followed through in terms of the status of economic theory that analytical systems such as economic theory or the corresponding type of sociology not only are not but cannot be adequate schemes for the analysis of classes of concrete phenomena for all purposes.[14]

In his defense of sociology as a science whose subject matter is society, Parsons followed Weber on "Wertfreiheit" in empirical analysis that resisted confusion between concepts and conviction. In *The Structure of Social Action,* he clarified to Wirth, empirical phenomena had been obvious to him in the theories of Durkheim and Weber. It was the convergence of their theories that had convinced him that there is a reality with its own intrinsic logic. Through Weber's and Durkheim's work he had discovered the empirical structure of (systems of) social action. He told Wirth,

> A theoretical system . . . is a complex set of relations between a considerable number of conceptual elements. That is why to me the convergence between Weber and Durkheim was such a tremendously impressive fact. In relation to religious ideas, institutional movements, charisma, ritual, symbolism and a variety of other categories a point for point correspondence not only in the categories and concepts and their definitions but in their specific relations as describing systems of action, is something which on grounds of probability simply could not happen fortuitously.

To summarize, the two themes in the 1930s that Parsons explored and that demonstrated his Weberian view were the relationship between economy and society in that decade of economic and political crisis, and the scientific nature of sociology. In this endeavor he embraced voluntarism, which he contrasted with positivism and utilitarianism, endorsing voluntarism through an image of man in modern, democratic society as an "active, creative, evaluative creature" (Parsons 1935/1991b, 231). To be sure, his Weberian circumspection made him endorse rationality in the guise of an intrinsic as opposed to a ritualistic orientation of social action. Rationality was structurally adequate only in a democratic, integrated society and was not structurally suited for a totalitarian, anomic one. The latter type society was contemporaneous in the charismatic regime of Nazi Germany, a system of ritualistic action patterns. Furthermore, he opted for "Wertfreiheit," which in *The Structure of Social Action* took the shape of adopting Alfred North Whitehead's philosophy of science as a framework safeguarding the "objectivity" of sociological inquiry (Parsons 1937/1968, 29–31).

As a political activist he went public with a verdict against National Socialism two weeks after the pogrom against Jews of November 1938 (Parsons 1938/1993a). In taking a position he was emulating Weber, who, concerned about a reactionary backlash in Germany in the event of a punitive peace treaty after World War I, had joined the German delegation at Versailles in 1919, when he had hoped to plead for conditions of the peace that would promise long-range stability to Germany's future democratic regime, the Weimar Republic (Mommsen 1994).

THE 1940s

Parsons wrote primarily articles, not books, in the 1940s, with two exceptions: a book he worked on with Edward Y. Hartshorne in 1941, which was never finished, and a project he worked on with John Riley from 1948 to 1950, a report for the Social Science Research Council, which also never became a book. In 1949, however, he brought out the first collection of his essays, of which eventually there would be six. In 1949 he also found a new publisher for the second edition of *The Structure of Social Action,* his first major opus; with this edition it was a success.

His main achievements of the decade were a number of essays and two memoranda that he wrote in 1940 and 1948 but that remained unpublished in his lifetime. (He revised the 1948 memorandum twice.).

Among the essays that were his major accomplishments in the decade, most dealt with contemporary problems. One, originally written in 1940, was devoted to anti-Semitism (1942/1993c). It was followed by two essays on Germany, originally drafts of chapters in the book planned with Hartshorne (1942/1993d, 1942/1993e). One was an analysis of Nazi Germany developed on the basis of Weberian categories (1942/1993d). A sequel outlined the structural changes necessary for Germany's democratization under the American military government after World War II (Parsons 1945/1993h). Another essay took up the problem of ressentiment, analyzing the dangers of racism and religious fundamentalism in a modern democracy (Parsons 1945/1993g). He discussed the topic further in an essay published in 1947 in which, using ideas developed during World War II, he explained the mundane sources of aggression in Western industrial societies, targeting the postwar period that also saw the beginning of the Cold War (1947/1993i).

In the second half of the decade, I find, much of his effort went into documenting the achievements of the social sciences during World War II (Parsons and Barber 1948), but also defending its undiminished importance for postwar planning (Parsons 1946, 1947). Furthermore, anticipating his accomplishments of the 1950s, he resumed his interest in general theory, which he had neglected since the late 1930s (Parsons 1945, 1948a).

The two memoranda that were among his major achievements in the decade were written in 1940 and 1948 respectively. The earlier one, undertaken for the Council for Democracy, an organization of scholars supporting the war effort, was a comparative analysis of Nazi German and American societies in the light of potential German aggression or subterfuge against the United States (Parsons 1940/1993b). The other memorandum, entitled "Social Science—A Basic National Resource," was written in 1948 for the Social Science Research Council, the most important agency for social science funding. In 1950, with John Riley, he revised it twice under the title "Social Science—A National Resource" (Parsons 1948b, Parsons and Riley 1950, Riley and Parsons 1950). The memorandum was written in the political context of the preparation for the establishment of the National Science Foundation, the federal agency set up to coordinate scientific research after World War II. In it Parsons pleaded that the legislation creating a national research organization should specify that funding sociological research be included in the foundation's activities.

Three Weberian Themes

In these works in the 1940s, three Weberian themes stand out. First was the question of religion. Weber dealt with religion in his analysis of the Protestant work ethic and capitalist spirit, and later in his studies of Hinduism, Taoism, and ancient Judaism. Parsons addressed himself to the problem of religion first in his analysis of anti-Semitism.[15] He observed that from antiquity on, Jews, "instead of being a people who *had* a religion, . . . came to be identified *with* their religion" (Parsons 1942/1993c, 132). In light of the antimarket economics of medieval Catholicism and early Protestantism, Jews had taken advantage of a loophole in the emergent city culture allowing for money lending and trade. In this situation, Jews had appeared to be personifications of universalism as it emerged with modern capitalism. In due course Jews were exposed to ressentiment from particularistic groups that opposed the changes in Western societies of the nineteenth and twentieth centuries. Thus, the Jews in the modern world came to be viewed as scapegoats for groups who found the accomplishments of modernity to be anathema:

> It so happens that the fields in which the Jews have met with remarkable success are precisely those that are highly valued by our society. . . . Moreover, the success of the Jews has been attained on the whole in fields which are the least closely integrated with the so-called *Gemeinschaft* patterns, as it is most conspicuous in trade and commerce, the professions, the arts, the theater, and the sciences. (Parsons 1942/1993c, 143)

Thus, he hypothesized that anti-Semitism was an indicator of social disorganization or anomie. It was an expression of deep-seated ressentiment on the part of groups of the population who rejected modernity. Such ressentiment would target free-market trade and commerce but also the arts and sciences. He explained how ressentiment turned into "free-floating aggression" (Parsons 1942/1993c, 143–44; 1942/1993f, 205), the seedbed of the phenomenon of anti-Semitism.[16]

As he was working on the manuscript analyzing anti-Semitism, he corresponded with Eric Voegelin, an emigré political scientist who was the author of a study titled *Political Religions* (1938), which analyzed the ostentatious antimodernity mentality and apparent theocracy in Nazi racism. In a five-page letter responding to one by Voegelin on the quasi-religious nature of Nazism and the Calvinist roots of Anglo-Saxon immunity to genocidal anti-Semitism, Parsons referred to Weber as a major source of his understanding of the Jewish plight. He began by thanking Voegelin for comments on the draft article,

> I am delighted that you liked the article on Anti-Semitism. There is very little that is original in it, I think, but it does perhaps bring together a number of different things in a way which is not as yet very familiar. Undoubtedly you will have recognized that the analysis of the historical elements of the Jewish tradition is overwhelmingly indebted to Max Weber. I have re-read his *Antike Judentum* three or four times and, I think, am more impressed with it each time. The historical and institutional side of it is, as you will remember, extremely complex and, I think, not particularly well presented from a literary point of view, so that ones [*sic*] first impression is of a confusion in which it is exceedingly difficult to discern any clear lines of analysis. On more careful study, however, it seems to me certain of these things stand out with beautiful clarity and throw a remarkable light on certain of the features even of the modern Jewish problem. My impressions from Weber have, however, been very strongly confirmed from other sources.[17]

A second theme concerned the social structure of Nazi Germany. Under Nazi rule, Germany waged war against and then exploited as it occupied one European country after another. Parsons devoted the entire first part of his seminal essay, "Max Weber and the Contemporary Political Crisis," to textual reconstruction of Weber's sociology of power and authority, and in the second part contrasted Western social structure with that of Nazi Germany. The first part, "The Sociological Analysis of Power and Authority Structures," recapitulated Weber's distinction between power and authority as sources of control in political systems. Weber's three types of legitimate authority were the rational, traditional, and charismatic, and Parsons ventured that the latter fitted Nazism. He commented on the dissolution of the boundaries between religious and political obedience as he characterized Weber's notion of charismatic rule as a tool for understanding the Nazi leadership:

> As Weber treats it, this [charismatic source of authority] focuses on the claim of an individual person, a "leader," to obedience from a group of followers. Though this is a personal claim, . . . it is a moral authority, which claims obedience as a duty. (Parsons 1942/1993d, 165)

Following up on a thought he had broached in *The Structure of Social Action,* he targeted the economy in the charismatic-type authority structure. Emulating Weber's characterization of such economy as "spezifisch wirtschaftsfremd," he emphasized that in Nazi Germany the economy functioned through coercion and force: "Routine provision is out of the question. There are two typical forms, free gifts, and 'booty,' that is, economically significant goods which are secured by coercion and force" (Parsons 1942/1993d, 165).

Contrasting the Western-type and Nazi societies, he made four points. First, the National Socialist German Workers' Party, the full name of the Hitler organization, was not a party but a movement destroying the party pluralism essential for democracy. Second, permanent consolidation of Nazi power would involve a return to an atavistic premodern feudalism based not on land but racist creed. Third, the outcome of the war—if the Nazis were to win—might involve authoritarian institutions establishing "fundamentalism" even in the then still democratic world, similar to what might have happened in ancient Greece had the Persians won the battles of Marathon and Salamis (a topic Weber had also addressed). The fourth point was that in order to fight that menace with all their might, the United States and its Allies needed to resort to an ethics of responsibility ("Verantwortungsethik"). Short of Gesinnungsethik, which, Weber felt, in its apolitical version involved only "a genuine Christian pacifism" and in its political version, Parsons stated, "degenerates into utopianism" (Parsons 1942/1993d, 183), the program definitely had to be one of Verantwortungsethik. In the United States, where isolationism had not yet completely disappeared, he felt, this meant that moral courage was essential for waging war, even incurring guilt in the service of safeguarding a future for Western democracy:

> "The adherence to *Gesinnungsethik* readily degenerates into utopianism. . . . To Weber this utopianism was an object of deep personal antipathy. . . . [T]he only honest procedure was that of *Verantwortungsethik,* which refused to judge any act, any means, any situation, as absolutely good or bad, which was as clear-headed as possible as to the complex ramifications of action, and which, above all, was not afraid to assume responsibility with its inevitable accompaniment of guilt, responsibility for being instrumental in bringing about things which, for their own sake, must without hesitation be judged to be evil." (Parsons 1942/1993d, 183)[18]

In this way, Weber's analysis of power and authority assisted Parsons in his analysis of Nazi Germany as an amalgamation of religion and force in a charismatic-type regime.

A third principle for following the thin Weberian line of scientific methodology was that "Wertfreiheit" was imperative. Weber's principle had been that political views and social science must remain separate, which means that an academic teacher must refrain from promoting his political credo as he explains the world to his students. In the two memoranda that he wrote for the Social Science Research Council, Parsons talked about "Wertfreiheit" as an issue concerning the value and use of social theory for understanding contemporary social problems. Posing the question as to what was scientific about the social sciences when they dealt with problems of importance to the ordinary citizen, he answered it by contrasting scientific and everyday concept formation. In *Social Science: A Basic National Resource* (originally dated July 1948) he emphasized that "theory" involved a special kind of knowledge. Theory meant knowledge grounded in conceptual schemes enabling "inference and prediction about hitherto unobserved situations" (Parsons 1948b, 4).[19] He spelled out the difference between commonsense and scientific knowledge (1948b, 4):

> All knowledge, no matter how close to the common sense level, involves conceptual schemes, though they are usually implicit rather than explicit. The transition to the scientific level consists of their greater logical clarity: the elimination of vagueness and ambiguity, increasing integration and consistency, the development of complex elaboration and interrelations which make inferences to new empirical insights possible.

He followed this up in the second version of the manuscript, now entitled *Social Science—A National Resource* and written with Riley. The nature of the social sciences was that they produced "verifiable knowledge, . . . to be distinguished from beliefs and dogmas, from myths and superstition, and from misinterpretations and guesswork" (Parsons and Riley 1950, I-1).[20] No doubt social-science research often appeared to seek answers to questions that common sense could answer, but the specific accomplishment of science was to approach these problems with rigorous methods and techniques of investigation:

> The criteria lie in the methods through which these subject matters are investigated, and the resulting established knowledge. It lies simply in the systematic search for objective knowledge and truth. (1950, I-2)

Under the heading "The Nature of the Social Sciences," Riley and Parsons in the second version of their manuscript endorsed Weber's principle of "Wertfreiheit," averring,

> From a substantive point of view, we shall use the term in this inquiry to denote the process of investigation and the resulting body of generalized knowledge relative to the behavior of human beings, with special reference to those forms of behavior involving relations of men to each other in social situations. (1950, 5)[21]

The outcome was that "theory-centered research" was a legitimate branch of empirical social science. In the chapter "Science and Common Sense," in the subchapter entitled "Theory-centered vs. Fact-centered Research," the manuscript maintained that "research [which] is primarily 'fact-finding' " was only one of two poles of scientific work. The other was "research [which] is predominantly theory-oriented" (Riley and Parsons 1950, 8–9). Theory-oriented research was the more fruitful approach, not only because it fulfilled requirements of concept formation dictated by the interest in creating knowledge, as Weber had outlined, but also in regard to analyzing contemporary political realities, which Riley and Parsons called "practical affairs":

> It is the interest in problems of basic or theory-oriented research in this sense which characteristically marks off the autonomy of science from other cognitive endeavors which are primarily aids to other interests. And it is out of the development of this type of autonomous interests that many of the most fruitful results of science in its application to practical affairs have come. (Riley and Parsons 1950, 8–10)

To summarize the three most significant Weberian foci in Parsons's work in the 1940s: For one, he analyzed anti-Semitism on the basis of Weber's sociology of religion, building on Weber's insights by examining racial and religious prejudices as exceedingly dangerous expressions of "free-floating aggression" merged with politico-religious "fundamentalism" (Parsons 1942/1993c, 1942/1993f, 1947/1993i). Second, he invoked Weber's sociology of types of legitimate authority in his analysis of National Socialism as an example of nearly pure charismatic authority, characterized by, among other things, abolition of the Rechtsstaat (constitutional democracy) and coercive exploitation in economic relationships (Parsons 1942/1993d). Third, he returned to the theme of "Wertfreiheit" as he documented the invaluable contribution of social science to winning World War II and to building the postwar world (Parsons 1948b, Parsons and Barber 1948, Parsons and Riley 1950). He and Riley invoked "theory-centered research" as the achievement of social science best suited to contributing to the nation's further advancement.

The Political-Historical Agenda

These three Weberian themes, I venture, had a vivid background in the history of the United States (and the world) during that decade. Two contemporary contexts stand out in this regard: National Socialism in Germany and World War II, in which the United States was a belligerent from December 1941 to VJ Day in 1945; and international politics in the age following the deployment of the atom bomb, which invoked a role for social science in modern society.

Two crucial events triggered the historical changes involved. On December 7, 1941, Japan destroyed the American fleet at Pearl Harbor, making the United States a belligerent in World War II (Ingersoll 1941; Handlin 1954, chapter 8). Days later, Germany declared war on the United States, a war that ended in the Allies' victory, in Europe in May and in the Pacific in August 1945.

Parsons responded to the outbreak of the war with Germany by elaborating on themes such as the sociology of religion in conjunction with authority and applying it to Nazi Germany in comparison to the United States (Parsons 1942/1993c). He capped this by writing on how to redemocratize Germany through "controlled institutional change" (Parsons 1945/1993h).[22]

When the Cold War broke out, triggered by deployment of the atom bomb on two Japanese cities on August 6 and 9, 1945, Parsons reacted to this challenge by analyzing the role of social science as a national resource that had helped preserve American democracy during World War II.[23] His alarmed response to the use of the atom bomb was a plea to incorporate the social sciences into the research program planned for the National Science Foundation (Gerhardt 2002, 149–67). He also warned of the threat to the survival of humankind inherent in the danger of suicidal blackmail by 'rogue states,' "since national states now command such destructive weapons that war between them is approaching suicidal significance" (Parsons 1947/1993i, 342). To make his standpoint known, he wrote a letter to the editor of the *New York Times* on August 8, 1945, in which he stressed the need for social-science analysis, anxious as he was about the fact that the danger of nuclear warfare had become an apocalyptic yet very concrete prospect:

> This leaves us with a glaring paradox. . . . The war had unleashed our energies and we have found that we can build battleships, aircraft carriers by the dozen and big bombers by the thousands. . . . We have realized that future strategic safety requires the vigorous encouragement of the sciences. . . . On the other hand we find the social sciences . . . not even mentioned among the necessary means to assure the world against the dangers of atomic bombs. Yet the idea that human brains must solve the human problems of world peace is not an unfamiliar one. President Roosevelt stated in the address which he prepared for the Jefferson Day dinner, "Today we are faced

> with the preeminent fact that, if civilization is to survive, we must cultivate the science of human relationships."[24]

To explain his conclusion that only social-science expertise and research could help expand understanding of the incipient problems of the nuclear age, he wrote, first alone and then with a coauthor, three book-length versions of the memorandum *Social Science—A [Basic] National Resource.* But he did more. He joined the Association of Atomic Scientists, among other important professional organizations concerned about nuclear warfare. One noteworthy result of his participation in discussions at meetings of the Association of Atomic Scientists was that he earned the respect of the atomic scientist J. Robert Oppenheimer.[25]

Thus, my interpretation of Parsons's work in the 1940s is that it embodied Weberian scholarship. His pivotal concern with voluntarism in his analysis of the totalitarian structure of Nazi Germany, a society antithetical to the democratic social system of Anglo-Saxon societies, made him recommend democracy for postwar Germany in his essay "The Problem of Controlled Institutional Change." Rationality coupled with reciprocity and opposed to the doctrines of instrumentalism and coercion inspired his idea of social science as a national resource—a resource worth preserving and even fighting for in the times when serious dangers threatened the democratic fabric of Western industrial societies. "Wertfreiheit," to be sure, required "theory-centered research"—a branch of the social sciences exceedingly valuable during World War II and still as important as "fact-finding research" in the era of the emerging Cold War. Last but not least, in the 1940s, Parsons openly engaged himself in political action, as he joined the Harvard American Defense chapter; taught at the Harvard School of Overseas Administration, where future military officers were trained; and advised the Foreign Economic Administration on the democratic principles for military government in Germany (Gerhardt 1996). Furthermore, after 1945 Parsons joined the Association of Atomic Scientists, became a member of the American Association for the Advancement of Science, and reactivated the Harvard chapter of the American Association of University Professors (AAUP), which became an invaluable bulwark against McCarthyism in the 1950s.[26] He was unsuccessful in his campaign on behalf of the social sciences as a resource for national achievement. Comparable to the Weber of 1918 to 1919, who had hoped to influence political life in the emergent Weimar Republic as he volunteered unsuccessfully to be nominated a candidate for the German Democratic Party preparing for elections for the Weimar national legislature (Reichstag) (Ay 2003), Parsons involved himself heavily in the debate as legislation concerning science was prepared, in which he recommended an equal status for the social sciences and the natural sciences. But his endeavors were utterly futile.

THE 1950s

Unlike the 1940s, the 1950s for Parsons were a period of a prolific production of books. Between 1951 and 1956 alone he published five books as sole author or major coauthor, and a wealth of articles (Parsons and Shils 1951; Parsons 1951/1964; Parsons, Shils, and Bales 1953; Parsons and Bales 1955; Parsons and Smelser 1956). The second edition of his first collection of essays appeared in 1954, and a new collection appeared in 1960, which contained essays of the 1950s analyzing contemporary American society (Parsons 1954, 1960a). A second feature of his work in the 1950s, though of lesser importance in the context of his contributions as a Weberian, was his open acknowledgment of the importance of Freudian psychoanalysis and his extensive publication on the relationship between psychology and sociology.[27]

His signal achievements of the fifties, in my opinion, were two systematic breakthroughs.

Improving Comparative Analysis

First, he developed four schemes for comparative analysis of social-action patterns. The first scheme was explained in his second major opus, *The Social System* (1951/1964), which presented a single comprehensive conceptual framework for analyzing modern industrial society. He named the scheme, which focused on value-orientation patterns in comparing modern and historical societies, "pattern variables." The idea was that five variables, each a bipolar dimension of normative orientation, defined institutional patterns. The sociologist could use the pattern variables to analyze, say, changes from traditional to rational-legal authority in Western society, or the difference between the mother-child and doctor-patient relationships. The action frame of reference, which is basic to system theory, could thereby be used for analysis of social structures.

The second scheme was first discussed in *Working Papers in the Theory of Action,* which adapted an analytical scheme developed by Robert Bales (1950), envisaging social action as a process of four stages. These stages were designated A-G-I-L, for *a*daptation, *g*oal attainment, *i*ntegration, and *l*atency.

Third, Parsons and his collaborators realized that socialization followed the same process pattern (as did therapy and social control), but in the reverse order of stages, L-I-G-A. That sequence, Parsons and his collaborators ventured, represented the dynamics characteristic of the therapeutic process and consisting likewise of the four stages: permissiveness, support, denial of reciprocity, and manipulation of rewards (Parsons and Fox 1952).

These three schemes helped social scientists to understand social action analytically. Together, the "pattern variables," the A-G-I-L, and the L-I-G-A schemes constituted a major breakthrough in Parsons's outline of sociological theory. He could now encompass analytically both social action and society, both of which formed social systems and could be analyzed as both structures and processes.

The fourth analytical scheme related to economic theory and involved application of the scheme of four functions to the social system as realized in its subsystems. As a visiting professor at Cambridge University from 1953 to 1954, he delivered the first series of the prestigious Alfred Marshall Lectures. To do justice to the theory of that eminent scholar, one of the four "European writers" whose work he had analyzed in *The Structure of Social Action,* he plunged into the enormous task of rereading the works of Marshall and other leading twentieth-century economists, also addressing the shortcomings of traditional economics over the previous fifty years. The outcome was *Economy and Society,* written with Neil Smelser, a work that was dedicated not only to Marshall but also to Weber (Parsons and Smelser 1956).

Welding together economics and sociology, this book laid the foundations for what was to become the revised analytical approach of Parsons in the 1960s and beyond. In the 1950s, he capped his reanalysis of economics by treating the economy as a subsystem of society.

Parsons also in the 1950s addressed the analysis of politics and especially the notion of power used in political sociology. In a critical review of C. Wright Mills's *The Power Elite* (Parsons 1957), and also an essay on the relationship between authority, legitimation, and political action (Parsons 1958/1960b), he ventured that power had a quality quite different from what political philosophy had focused on for centuries. He argued that power is lodged with collectivities rather than individuals and follows a logic that does not fit the usual "zero-sum" model. This argument became the basis for his first tentative conceptualization of political power as a medium of exchange. He elaborated this idea into an entirely new approach to system theory in the 1960s (Parsons 1963).

In his works of the 1950s, three themes stand out that transcended what he had already discovered in the previous decades and that demonstrate the Weberian heritage in his thought in that decade.

First, Weber's theory of social action became a definitive baseline for the analysis of the social system as such. *The Social System* made Weberian action theory the methodological foundation that underlay the entire analytical approach, systems analysis. The point was that "the *interaction* of individual actors," which as a process constituted "a system in the scientific sense," made up the "action frame of reference," the comprehensive analysis of which was the topic of the book (Parsons 1951/1964, 3). Of course, in its analytical approach *The Social System* had forerunners, one of them Weber (translated by Parsons): *Structure of Social Action; Essays in Sociological Theory;* and, Weber's *Theory of Social and Economic Organization* (Parsons 1951/1964, 4). In characterizing interaction as reciprocal rather than utilitarian, he adopted the frame of reference of Weberian action theory, which made the social relation an elementary unit, a methodological baseline for systems analysis.

Parsons clarified that reciprocity in social relations à la Weber was a sine qua non in understanding social action:

> The scheme, that is, relative to the units of action and interaction, is a *relational* scheme. It analyzes the structure and processes of the systems built up by the relations of such units to their situations, including other units. (Parsons 1951/1964, 4)

As Weber did in the "The Fundamental Concepts of Sociology" at the beginning of his *Economy and Society,* Parsons began *The Social System* by explicating basic properties and types of social action. Echoing Weber, who had stipulated, "Action is 'social' insofar as its subjective meaning takes account of the behavior of others and is thereby oriented in its course" (Weber 1968/1978, 4), Parsons defined social action as relational as well as governed by mutual construction of meaning. He stated, in the tradition of Weber, that the "frame of reference concerns the 'orientation' of one or more actors . . . to a situation that includes other actors" (Parsons 1951/1964, 4). From this Weberian baseline he derived the idea of an action system, which included symbols, in other words, culture:

> It is a fundamental property of action thus defined . . . that the actor develops a *system* of 'expectations' relative to the various objects of the situation. . . . [F]or present purposes . . . attention [can be] confined to systems of interaction of a plurality of individual actors oriented to a situation and where the system includes a commonly understood system of cultural symbols. (Parsons 1951/1964, 4–5).[28]

Going Beyond Weber

A second theme of Parsons's work in the fifties went far beyond making Weberian action theory a baseline for systems analysis. The 1950s were a decade when the assumption that anomie and integration were opposite structures of social action needed further clarification. Expertise in economics that Parsons had relied on sporadically since the 1930s was pivotal to understanding "the integration of economic and social theory," which was, indeed, the subtitle of *Economy and Society*. In adopting the same title as Weber's posthumously assembled major opus, *Economy and Society,* Parsons and Smelser reestablished the theoretical relevance of sociology to economics. They dedicated their book to Marshall and Weber as "great pioneers in the integration of economics and sociological theory."

Weber, Parsons and Smelser emphasized, had distinguished "between 'economic action' and 'economically relevant action,' the former belonging to the economy as a system, the latter not" (Parsons and Smelser 1956, 39). This distinction was to capture Weber's and equally Parsons's tenet that the economy as an action system depended on other systems, including the society as a whole, a comprehensive social system. For Weber, the difference between "economic action" and "economically relevant action" had meant, as Parsons and Smelser pointed out, that the "spirit" of capitalism was a main topic for sociological understanding of "economically relevant action." In contrast, "adventurer capitalism" or other forms of capitalist economy would be built on "economic action." "Economically relevant action," as Parsons and Smelser interpreted Weber, characterized capitalism that involved the notion of a "calling" or other similarly ethically grounded orientations, which had been Weber's concern in *The Protestant Ethic and the Spirit of Capitalism* (Parsons and Smelser 1956, 260).[29]

For Parsons and Smelser, the Weberian concepts provided a platform from which to criticize utilitarianism. They felt that the understanding of economics by Anglo-American theorists—with the possible exception of Alfred Marshall, John Maynard Keynes, and Joseph Schumpeter—had "been mainly blocked by the (often implicit) assumptions of utilitarian individualism" (Parsons and Smelser 1956, 39). They observed,

> We feel that the prominence of this 'individualistic' strain in the treatment of want-satisfaction and utility is a relic of the historical association of economic theory with utilitarian philosophy and psychology. If pushed to its extreme, it leads to a type of psychological and sociological atomism. (Parsons and Smelser 1956, 23)

To reach beyond this limitation they introduced the idea that the economy—considered a conglomerate of capital, labor, production, and entrepreneurship—was a subsystem of society as a system. That system, they proposed, involved functions, four in all, that required fulfillment: where collectivities were the reference entities, these were goal attainment and integration; where individual activities were the reference entities, these were adaptation and pattern maintenance or tension management. The economy, Parsons and Smelser stated, was not a collectivity, but a system. As a system, it fulfilled the adaptation (object manipulation) function for society as a whole. In the modern world, the economy, as subject matter of economics, could not be understood in terms of utility and cost, not even welfare, but needed to be understood in terms of analytic concepts based on reciprocity and targeting interchanges between various subsystems of the society. In this vein, the subject matter of economics, the economy, was a combination of "economic" and "economically relevant" action, in Weberian terms. A network of relational input-output interdependencies between societal subsystems had to be portrayed analytically, with the economy a pivotal subsystem. From this vantage point, the economy in empirical societies allowed for a sociological analysis of system integration as well as inter-system relationships.

As an analytical endeavor, Parsons and Smelser's *Economy and Society* was a model in interdisciplinary courage. Using Weber's distinction between "economic" action and "economically relevant" action as a baseline, they attempted nothing less than a redirection of modern economics. In *Economy and Society* they proposed that modern economics should change its conceptual approach to avoid the pitfalls they pointed out.

At the end of the book, having summarized eight decisive propositions as a plea for economics to link up with sociology, Parsons and Smelser restated their knowledge interest. They made it plain that their identity as sociologists led them to oppose utilitarianism:

> We have approached economics not as professional economists, but as sociologists; for this reason, perhaps, we have stressed certain difficulties and unresolved problems, and the need for supplementation of economic theory. (Parsons and Smelser 1956, 308)

They admonished colleagues in both disciplines to collaborate with each other to establish an empirically valid theory:

> The unfortunate fact remains that at present few economists and sociologists have even a modicum of interest or competence in the other's subject matter. It is our conviction that the trend of divergence between the interests in the respective fields must be reversed. . . . In short, neither the economist nor the "behavioural scientist" can afford to ignore what lies over the boundaries of his discipline. (Parsons and Smelser 1956, 309)

The third topic in a Weberian vein concerned the relationship between power and authority. Parsons's first tentative formulation, written for a conference in 1955 and published in 1958, was entitled "Authority, Legitimation, and Political Action" (Parsons 1958/1960b).[30] In it he argued that authority as originally analyzed by Weber was only one among a number of noteworthy power phenomena. Whereas Weber had concentrated on the aspect of legitimation as he focused on authority, Parsons proposed to cast a wider net. He redefined authority as "an institutionalized complex of norms . . . which on a general level define the conditions under which, in the given social structure, and in given statuses and situations within it, acts of others within the same collectivity *may* be prescribed, permitted, or prohibited" (Parsons 1958/1960b, 180). As an institution, and inasmuch as it was a central element in the polity, authority was not confined to the domination-obedience relationship on which Weber had concentrated. Parsons's definition of power abandoned the idea of "zero-sum," which had been self-evident to most previous writers, from Thomas Hobbes (1651/1949) to Weber to Harold Lasswell (1951). Weber's and Lasswell's theories were based on the assumption that wielding power meant that the person in power necessarily deprived others from wielding power—the sum total of all the power in a society, therefore, amounting to a "zero-sum." By contrast, he saw power as a phenomenon expressing consensus rather then conflict, lodged with a collectivity rather than individuals. He asserted, contra Weber as well as Lasswell,

> The concept which I am using here does not make opposition a criterion as such, though since I am talking about capacity to attain goals, it *includes* the overcoming of opposition. I thus consider the zero-sum concept to be a special case of the more general concept employed here. (Parsons 1958/1960b, 180)

Despite this partial departure from Weber, he held to one important tenet of Weber's as indispensable—the reference to meaning. Weber, in *Economy and Society,* had called action " 'social' insofar as its subjective meaning takes account of . . . others" (Weber 1922/1956, 4). This reference to meaning was essential to the notion of authority and invoked the sphere of meaning in the belief of the Puritan in his "calling," as Parsons explained when he saw legitimation of authority grounded in social values:

> On the level of belief the "justification" of values leads beyond empirical knowledge and roots in the realms of religion and philosophy. The existential propositions which men invoke to answer what Max Weber called the "problem of meaning," the more or less ultimate answers to questions on *why* they should live the way they do and influence others to do so, may thus be called the field of the *justification* of values. (Parsons 1958/1960b, 174–75)

In one specified area of his thinking Parsons went beyond Weber, although he derived it from "Weber's category of rational-legal authority" (Parsons 1958/1960b, 190). Parsons held that the authority of the law—or, rather, the relationship between law and institutions (including authority)—had to be clarified:

> My view is that law, or legal process, is a set of mechanisms which operate with respect to *all* categories of institutions in a society in which law itself is institutionalized.

> It is not, in terms of content, specific to any particular category of institutions. It does, however, have a special relation to the political function in the society since two essential functions of a legal system, the definition of the scope of jurisdiction, and the authorization and implementation of sanctions, inevitably involve political references. (Parsons 1958/1960b, 190)

To go beyond Weber meant that the law had to be included in the sociological discussion of authority. Both the "law-enforcement functions of political bodies," and the "legal frameworks . . . of political processes" were important (Parsons 1958/1960b, 192) to this extended discussion. Certainly, in "Authority, Legitimation, and Political Action," Parsons carefully, even tentatively, departed from Weber's sociology of authority as he interpreted it. His aim was to incorporate the law into the realm of authority while also placing the latter within the political process. The law was thus linked to power as it was tied to collectivities when power was not essentially a "zero-sum" phenomenon.

The Agenda of the 1950s

To recapitulate three important themes in Parsons's thinking in the 1950s: First, *The Social System* hinged on orientationally mediated social relations, a concept taken from Weber's *Economy and Society.* Second, Weber's distinction between "economic action" and "economically relevant action" called for analyzing the economy in conjunction with society, its enabling context, against the background of Keynesian economics, which had not existed in Weber's lifetime. Third, because legislation and jurisdiction had become important factors in the political process of modern Western societies, Weber's theory of authority needed to be extended, even superseded, by a theoretical approach addressing that non-"zero-sum" phenomenon.

Parsons's focus on these three topics, I suggest, was an intellectual response to the political situation and social problems of the 1950s. One characteristic of the 1950s history and society was McCarthyism. The House Committee on Un-American Activities, in the wake of World War II and particularly after the outbreak of the Korean War, examined the loyalty to the nation of citizens and organizations. Even Ivy League universities, the State Department, and the Army were targeted.

Parsons, an ardent critic of McCarthyism, published an analytical account of it only months after McCarthy's campaign began to subside (Parsons 1955). Although he was being targeted personally in 1954 and had to clear his name through a sworn affidavit (Gerhardt 2002, 180–82), his concern was how a campaign demanding exaggerated loyalty to the nation had been possible at all, endangering as it did the fabric of American democracy. To find an answer he went back to the end of World War II, when the United States had been thrown into a role of responsibility for world peace. After victory, most Americans might have preferred to return to isolationism, but the United States acquired a role of permanent world power. Particularly after the outbreak of the Korean War, he explained, the new international agenda overstretched traditional American patriotism. This scenario, evidently, created exaggerated demands for loyalty to the nation, and suddenly large segments of the law-abiding population, government agencies, and even of the military began to appear as potentially disloyal. Generalizing from his analysis of Germany's transformation from Weimar democracy to Nazi dictatorship in *The Social System,* he concluded that democratic culture could be threatened in any nation, even the United States. Modern democracy was never safe from lapsing into anomic tendencies.

In this account of McCarthyism he resumed his earlier analysis of ressentiment and emergent "fundamentalism." In the 1940s his discussion of these topics had been anchored in Weber's sociology of religion and sociology of authority. Now he supplemented that earlier discussion as he analyzed McCarthyism in terms of "pattern variables," specifically, the pattern-variable combination of universalism and ascription. He discerned the universalism ascription pattern, which, in *The Social System,* represented charismatic authority.

Another facet of American history in the 1950s was the Cold War (Gaddis 1987), accompanied by unprecedented economic growth during the boom that followed World War II (Galbraith 1958).[31]

The economic boom was the background for Parsons's reconsideration of the relationship between the economy and society. In the analysis he undertook with Smelser, he emphasized the embeddedness of economic processes in societal system structures. The unprecedented economic affluence of the United States in the postwar era signaled two different things. First, democracy combined with the market economy and welfare state became an arena for mass prosperity. Second, another aspect of the economy-society relationship was the world situation, which saw a world divided into two blocs. In the 1950s, highly affluent American capitalism was confronted with an ideological rival, the remarkably less affluent Soviet communism. The two types of economic and political systems made up the arena in which the Cold War emerged between two superpowers. Parsons understood, in *Economy and Society* (with Smelser), but also in his other writings in the 1950s, that both the United States and the Soviet Union were industrial societies. He saw that industrial society—whether Western or Eastern—promoted value orientations that promised a humane life-world for its citizens. The similarity was noteworthy despite the fact that the two regimes interpreted what constituted a democratic order in radically different ways: in Western society, as political pluralism; in the Eastern Bloc, as "people's democracy." Parsons's paper "Some Principal Characteristics of Industrial Societies," written in 1958 and published in 1960, attended to this problem. In comparing capitalism and communism from a sociological point of view, he argued that the two allegedly vastly different systems were not irreconcilable, because there were common value patterns. They were interpreted differently, but the difference could be overcome if communism would lose some of its dogmatic rigidity, and American capitalism would allow for equal participation of other nations in world trade. Interestingly, the paper was prepared originally for a Conference on Soviet Society, sponsored by Harvard's Joint Committee on Slavic Studies (Parsons 1958/1960c).

A third theme was desegregation. Blacks had been disenfranchised in the United States from the days of slavery, and the Civil War had failed to end political, economic, and social discrimination against them. In 1954, through the Supreme Court decision for the plaintiff in Brown v. Board of Education, a policy of desegregation was at last established (Patterson 2001). As whites refused to support desegregation, however, race riots broke out in southern cities such as in Little Rock, Arkansas, in 1958, when Governor Orville Faubus sided with the police who stood by as blacks were victimized. The events of the 1950s led to the civil rights movement, which eventually led to the Civil Rights Acts of 1964 and 1965.

Parsons welcomed the new action of the Supreme Court on civil rights. That legal institutions could serve as a leading sector in creating a new agenda for citizenship irrespective of race, religion, or gender became fully evident in the 1960s. In his essays in the 1950s, he tackled some aspects of the social change thus initiated (Parsons 1958/1960b, Parsons 1959/1960d). In his paper on legitimation and authority, he not only introduced the idea of the non-"zero-sum" nature of power but also made the analysis of the law a major realm for sociological inquiry.

Echoes of the Fifties

In the remaining two decades of his work Parsons emphasized that the law is of pivotal importance to the fabric of modern democracy. Particularly with regard to the integration of disenfranchised minorities such as blacks into American society, the law was indispensable. His realization in the 1950s of the importance of the legal system was connected to the problem of race relations. Even twenty years later, in an essay published in 1978, he complained that sociology had not yet fully appreciated the importance of legislation and judicial decision making for modern democracy. In the essay "Law as an Intellectual 'Stepchild' " (Parsons 1978), he listed reasons why sociology had not yet understood the enormous importance of the law for modern society and demanded that social theory recognize that importance. As proof of the fact that the law's role for democracy had been underrated, he referred to the issue of race relations.

In a draft for that essay, written presumably in 1974, he made it clear that he had never forgotten his insight from the 1950s. Race relations were a major arena for citizenship, and he cited a study "which seems to me a highly important harbinger of what I hope will become a major sociological trend" (Parsons 1974, 2). The study was the unpublished Ph.D. dissertation of Dr. John Akula (1973), who, as Parsons pointedly noted, was "one of the few who have combined full formal training in sociology and in law." Akula's dissertation, he averred,

> is a study of the effect of legal action in the United States on the status of Negro or as it is put now, Black people over a full century, broadly since just after the Civil War. He takes account both of legislation and of court decisions, and less so of administrative action, and very importantly studies both at the state as well as the Federal level. His broad conclusion is quite clear, that in the light of the historical evidence the action of governmental agencies through legal measures has, over the period, had a *major* effect in the clear direction of the strengthening of civil rights, as this is often put. (Parsons 1974, 2).

Thus, his stance in the 1970s was a sequel to his effort in the 1950s to stress the importance of legislation and judicial action as levers to improve race relations. He considered this to be a major accomplishment in social change. He welcomed legislation and judicial action as means of legitimate authority short of political action to improve the prospects for attaining full citizenship for black Americans.

McCarthyism, the Cold War (including the affluent society in the United States and relationships between economy and society in general), and authority involving legislation and judicial action were themes of Parsons's sociology in the 1950s. To be sure, *The Social System,* written at the beginning of the decade, concentrated on some topics that he had addressed in the 1930s and 1940s. These included discussions of Nazi Germany in terms of the value orientations of universalism and ascription (chapter 5), and the dilemma over secrecy in science that resulted when nuclear physics dominated military technology (chapter 8).

In the course of the decade, however, he became bolder in tackling themes that troubled the nation and the world. After he and Smelser had completed *Economy and Society,* Parsons shifted his attention more openly to the sociological understanding of the political structures of the contemporary world. Nevertheless, as he discussed McCarthyism, the Cold War (in the guise of analyzing relationships between economy and society), and the legislative practices of democratic authority structures, among others, he carefully observed the thin line between scientific analysis and political advocacy, as Weber had also done.

In the 1950s, no doubt, then, voluntarism was the frame of reference for systems theory, and Parsons's (and Smelser's) recommendation was, in *Economy and Society,* that positivism be overcome in yet another social science, economics. To be sure, although at the time he wrongly assumed that positivism was "dead," a judgment deriving from his dismissing Spencer in the beginning paragraph of *The Structure of Social Action,* he did not deviate from stressing the importance of meaning construction.[32]

Reciprocity, he felt, governed rationality in social relations, as it spurred four schemes of action theory that made meaning an indispensable element in social systems.

It is interesting that "Wertfreiheit" apparently was a postulate that Parsons reckoned needed little defense when it reigned supreme anyhow. (This was to change, however, in the 1960s, when Marxism as an element in the Critical Theory of the Frankfurt School became a bone of contention on the occasion of the Heidelberg Conference.)[33]

Was he a political activist in the 1950s? In the first half of the decade, it seems, he plunged into prolific academic work. But in the second half of the 1950s, in the aftermath of McCarthyism, when he became a member of Committee A of the American Association of University Professors, the committee investigating the cases of dismissal of university staff under investigation in the context of McCarthyism, he helped investigate every individual case of sanctions imposed on university personnel in the McCarthy era. (The AAUP compelled universities to reopen cases and take corrective action by university boards on behalf of faculty members treated unjustly.)[34] In this work, academic freedom, which allowed for science, was pivotal for Parsons as it had been for Weber, who had helped found the German Sociological Society in the interest of scientific sociology under the umbrella of "Wertfreiheit."

THE WEBERIAN PARSONS AND AMERICAN SOCIAL HISTORY, 1930s TO 1950s AND BEYOND

In this chapter I have undertaken to prove that Talcott Parsons was a Weberian. The effort of Cohen, Hazelrigg, and Pope (1975a) to "de-Parsonize Weber" was utterly futile, for they and other such critics face the dilemma that Parsons did not misunderstand Weber. To "de-Parsonize Weber" would require revealing mistakes in Weber's original thoughts, which Cohen, Hazelrigg, and Pope were neither able nor willing to do. Instead, they simplified and misread Parsons. Parsons, in his "Comment" in response to Cohen, Hazelrigg, and Pope (1975a) rightly defended his scholarship (Parsons 1975b). My point in this paper has been that he became fascinated with Weber's thought when he studied in Heidelberg in 1925 and 1926 and held on to this credo, though with some lessening in the degree of faithfulness, throughout the five decades of his oeuvre (of which I have analyzed three decades in some detail).

To prove him Weberian, I have used as a measuring rod four tenets of scholarship, traced in his oeuvre of three decades.

Voluntarism, as opposed to utilitarianism, derived from Weber's idea that voluntarism dominated the "calling" of the Puritan who acted in the spirit of capitalism. For Parsons, voluntarism in the 1930s stood against Spencer's utilitarianism, proclaimed "dead" at the beginning of *The Structure of Social Action*. In the 1940s, for Parsons voluntarism became the integrative force characteristic of democratic society, and was not present in dictatorial regimes such as National Socialism. In the 1950s, voluntarism represented the essence of action theory, and provided the frame of reference for social theory in *The Social System,* a monograph among several in which Parsons refined sociology's analytical endeavor.

The second tenet, rationality, linked reciprocity in social relations with means-end calculations. Weber's *Economy and Society* had made means-end rationality a basic reference point for sociology. In the 1930s, Parsons stressed this pivotal principle for democracy, lacking in anomic or authoritarian social structures. In the 1940s, rationality for him became the obverse of prejudice but also aggression, a type pattern normative and also moral, always and everywhere. In the 1950s, eventually rationality became a harbinger not only for society but also for the economy and politics, and equally important—apart from sociology—in economics and political science.

Third, "Wertfreiheit" in the 1930s and 1940s meant adoption of a conceptual scheme designed to accommodate the definition of facts in the social sciences, but also the distinction between "theory-centered" research and "fact-finding" research. In the 1950s, "Wertfreiheit" became to Parsons an antidote against McCarthyism.

The dual existence of the sociologist as a scientist and a citizen mattered to Parsons as it had to Weber. Weber, a veritable zoon politikon, vowed never to indoctrinate his students politically. Parsons, too, politically active from the end of the 1930s on, never involved his students in his activism. He fought National Socialism in the years until 1945 and subsequently campaigned for science legislation in the wake of the deployment of the atom bomb. In the 1950s he took part in the work of the AAUP, which led to a process of rehabilitation and reconciliation after the passing of McCarthyism. In all these activities Parsons did not stray far from academia. Unlike Weber in early-twentieth-century Germany, Parsons felt that in his role as a university professor, his convictions were best served when he used his expertise in the field where he was well equipped, namely, understanding problems of the society in the contemporary world.

The 1930s were the era of the Great Depression and the New Deal, and, in a wider context, the advent of National Socialism in Germany. Related themes in Parsons's works in this decade were the following:

- There are two types of capitalism, one emulating the "spirit" of capitalism and involving normative value orientations, the other, "adventurer" capitalism, involving force and fraud.
- Moral aspects of social action engendering community and suggesting integration are opposed to anomie, suggesting coercion.
- Modern capitalism, a structure of social action, was present in two types of systems, one involving democracy and the other dictatorship.
- The United States in the era of the New Deal came closest to Weber's type of transformation of charismatic authority in the direction of democracy, favoring pluralism and prosperity.

The 1940s comprised two eras. The Second World War, incited by National Socialism as an imperialist power and enemy of the United States that defeated it, was followed after victory in 1945 by the threat to survival of humankind through the possibility of nuclear warfare in the emergent Cold War. In this decade Parsons:

- analyzed anti-Semitism by means of Weber's sociology of religion in pursuit of elucidating "fundamentalism";
- analyzed National Socialism by means of Weber's charismatic-authority type to explain Germany's abolition of the Rechtsstaat and its being wirtschaftsfremd; and
- he invoked "Wertfreiheit," that is, absence of political partisanship in scientific analysis, to urge that social-science research be "theory-centered" instead of merely "fact finding."

In the 1950s, the issues were McCarthyism, American economic affluence in the world situation of Cold War, and desegregation through judicial action in the early years of the civil rights movement. Parsons:

- used Weberian action theory as the frame of reference for social-system theory;
- targeted the economy as a topic for analysis in conjunction with society analyzed against the background of Weber's *Economy and Society,* which also required recourse to Keynes and Schumpeter; and

- demanded that legislation and judicial action, which Weber analyzed in his sociology of law, needed urgent attention in sociology.

These themes were unequivocally Weberian. Indeed, throughout the decades, he frequently reread Weber. Whenever he addressed himself to a new topic, he returned to Weber, whom he treated as a baseline for what modern sociology could and should accomplish.

His lifelong admiration for that classic thinker did not, however, mean that he would not rethink Weberian formulae. And in fact, in his oeuvre in the 1960s and 1970s, he did eventually deviate to a certain extent from Weber's authoritative conceptualizations.

Starting around the end of the 1950s, Parsons began to transcend some classic formulations in the sociology of authority. Regarding the relationship between authority and legitimation, he came to examine the political authority of the law. This eventually made him abandon, to a certain extent, Weber's sociology of power and authority. His new idea was that political power was not a "zero-sum" phenomenon, as Weber had suggested.

In the 1960s and 1970s he would also reformulate the theory of international relations, thereby adapting Weber's nation-oriented perspective to the prospect of a global world where the division between a Western world and an Eastern bloc would eventually disappear. His revised theory addressed exigencies of the society of the 1960s and beyond, rendering Weber's thought a classic conceptualization of the world of the twentieth century and making the United States of the 1960s a forerunner of problems that would become prevalent worldwide only in the twenty-first century.

It is true that Parsons's first encounter with Weber's thought occurred in Germany, but his sociology should not therefore be labeled "made in Germany." Nor should it be denied that the beginning of much of Parsons's ingenious thought was when that eager American student sat in the Heidelberg University Library reading *The Protestant Ethic and the Spirit of Capitalism* with as much fascination as he would have felt reading a criminal novel.

All his life, apparently, he returned to reading Weber in the original German. In 1972 he wrote to Helmut Dahmer, who had sent him a letter in German, that he had never ceased reading in that language. Thanking Dahmer for a thoughtful letter, he acknowledged his debt to the language of Max Weber by saying, "I think it would be impossible to forget a language which one has used so much at any time in his mature life."[35]

NOTES

1. In the abstract of their article, Cohen, Hazelrigg, and Pope charged: "The crux of Parsons' misrepresentation is his overweening emphasis on the category of the normative. A confusion of 'factual regularities' with 'normative validity'—despite Weber's numerous warnings against such—led Parsons to an exaggeration of the importance Weber assigned to normative orientations of social action, legitimacy and collective integration, and, correspondingly, to a severe understatement of the importance of non-normative aspects of social action and structures of dominance" (Cohen, Hazelrigg, and Pope 1975a, 229). Shortly before the article "De-Parsonizing Weber" was published, both Cohen and Parsons had responded to an essay by Pope that had appeared two years earlier in which Pope had insisted that Parsons's comprehension of Durkheim was flawed. In his reply to both criticisms, Pope stressed non-normative elements of action even in Durkheim (Cohen 1975; Parsons 1975a; Pope 1975). Parsons, in commenting on Pope (1973), had defended his thesis that "Durkheim's theory is voluntaristic by virtue of its stress on the *moral* influences on action" (Parsons 1975a, 104).
2. He noticed that Cohen, Hazelrigg, and Pope thought that Weber had wished to render a descriptive account of the social world. This, he knew, would have been positivism. Yet in the eyes of Cohen, Hazelrigg, and Pope, Parsons failed at empiricism. They charged him with downplaying the non-normative elements in social action, which meant that they themselves highlighted the importance of the non-normative side of social action, including non-normative forces in the structures of dominance. The issue in the controversy was the role of

normative, or moral, elements in social action, a role that Parsons emphasized and that Cohen, Hazelrigg, and Pope minimized. In their "Reply to Parsons" they rejected his "Comment" (Parsons 1975b) and defended their view by saying that Parsons saw strong normative elements in, for example, traditional action. They argued that Weber had emphasized non-normative elements. They declared, "Parsons's quarrel is with Weber, not with us. Our original point was that Weber's category was not primarily normative. Parsons does not challenge us on this—the central issue" (Cohen, Hazelrigg, and Pope 1975b, 670). But if what they were saying about Weber was right, it would have made of him a theorist analyzing elements of anarchy instead of classifying types of the social order.

3. The idea of voluntarism was first introduced in Weber's *The Protestant Ethic and the Spirit of Capitalism* (*Die protestantische Ethik und der Geist des Kapitalismus*), originally published in 1904 and revised in 1920. In the original German text, Weber explained the impact of the Puritan idea of a "calling" for economic life ("die puritanische Berufsidee in ihrer Wirkung auf das *Erwerbs*leben"). He pointed at voluntaristic community formation: "Dass die Täuferbewegung . . . grundsätzlich 'Sekten' . . . schuf, kam . . . der Intensität ihrer Askese ebenso zustatten, wie dies . . . auch bei jenen calvinistischen . . . Gemeinschaften der Fall war, die *faktisch* auf die Bahn der voluntaristischen Gemeinschaftsbildung gedrängt wurden" (Weber 1904/1920, 162). Parsons translated the passage as follows: "That the Baptist movement everywhere and in principle founded sects and not Churches was certainly as favorable to their asceticism as was the case, to differing degrees, with those Calvinist, Methodist, and Pietist communities which were driven by their situations into the formation of voluntary groups" (Weber 1930/1976, 152–53).

4. Interestingly, the translations of Weber's type of means-end rationality in the two English-language versions of his "Fundamental Concepts of Sociology" from *Economy and Society* differ noticeably, although both presumably were Parsons's. In Parsons's translation of parts of *Economy and Society,* published in 1947, the passage about "zweckrationales Handeln" ran: "Social action, like other forms of action, may be classified in the following four types according to its mode of orientation: (1) in terms of rational orientation to a system of discrete individual ends (zweckrational), that is, through expectations as to the behaviour of objects in the external situation and of other human individuals, making use of these expectations as 'conditions' or 'means' for the attainment of the actor's own rationally chosen ends" (Weber 1947/1964, 115). But in the complete English-language edition of Weber's major opus that was published in 1968, which supposedly reused Parsons's earlier translation of the "Basic Sociological Terms," the same passage ran: "Social action, like all action, may be oriented in four ways. It may be: (1) instrumentally rational (zweckrational), that is, determined by expectations as to the behavior of objects in the environment and of other human beings; these expectations are used as 'conditions' or 'means' for the attainment of the actor's rationally pursued and calculated ends" (Weber 1968/1978, 24). The two translations were renditions of the following passage in Weber: "§ 2. Wie jedes Handeln kann auch das soziale Handeln bestimmt sein 1. *zweckrational:* durch Erwartungen des Verhaltens von Gegenständen der Aussenwelt und von anderen Menschen und unter Benutzung dieser Erwartungen als 'Bedingungen' oder als 'Mittel' für rational, als Erfolg, erstrebte und abgewogene eigenen Zwecke" (Weber 1922/1956, 12).

5. Weber was involved in politics all his life but nevertheless insisted that "politics as a vocation" was different from and should not be confounded with "science as a vocation." See Weber 1919/1948a, 1919/1948b.

6. Parsons translated this as: "The use of force is unquestionably very strongly opposed to the spirit of economic acquisition in the usual sense" (Weber 1968/1978, 64). This translation is taken from what presumably was Parsons's 1947 translation of large parts of Weber's *Economy and Society* (Weber 1968/1978).

7. In *The Structure of Social Action,* Parsons concluded that economic theory need not deal with all aspects of economic relations: "The exclusion of the noneconomic means from the position of variables in the system of *economic* theory seems clearly indicated" (Parsons 1937/1968, 658). The idea that economic theory was abstract and need not fit the bulk of observed economic relations might result from the influence of Joseph A. Schumpeter on Parsons's thought. Parsons had met Schumpeter at Harvard after his return from Heidelberg. Schumpeter had taught at Harvard briefly in 1927 and 1930 and became a professor in the Department of Economics in 1932. In various autobiographical accounts written after 1950, Parsons acknowledged his indebtedness to Schumpeter. For instance, he remembered in the late 1950s that Schumpeter had taught him the strictly theoretical perspective in economics (Parsons 1959, 6). The close relationship between Parsons and Schumpeter at Harvard is documented by Richard Swedberg (1991, 169, 279), who implies that one reason Parsons

was drawn to Schumpeter was because throughout the teens of the young century, the Austrian Schumpeter had been in close contact with Weber and had published in *Grundriss der Sozialökonomik* under Weber's editorship.

8. There is a controversy over the correct translation of the word "Herrschaft." Parsons translates Weber's "Herrschaft" as "authority," whereas Reinhard Bendix translates it as "dominance." Although Guenther Roth and Claus Wittich (Weber 1968/1978) in their complete edition of Weber's *Economy and Society* claim that they generally use Parsons's translations as they appeared in *The Theory of Social and Economic Organization,* they use the translation of "Herrschaft" chosen by Bendix, with whom Roth worked in the 1960s. As far as I know, the controversy over the translation of "Herrschaft" as used in Weber's *Economy and Society* has never been resolved. In the present paper, I use the two English terms, "dominance" and "authority," interchangeably.
9. On Parsons as a vigorous supporter of Roosevelt's New Deal in the 1930s and beyond, see further (p. 215, this volume).
10. For further discussion of Parsons's treatment of National Socialism as the epitome of anomic society in the 1930s, especially in *The Structure of Social Action,* see Gerhardt (1999, especially 136–57).
11. See the preface to *The Structure of Social Action,* preserved among the Parsons papers in the Harvard University Archives under the call number HUG(FP)—42.41, box 2.
12. As late as the middle 1950s, Parsons and Smelser, in their analysis of the relationship(s) between economy and society, returned to empirical work of the 1930s on unemployment, which was a major threat to the social order as well as individual identity, analyzed by, for example, E. W. Bakke (1940).
13. Letters to David I. Walsh and Henry Cabot Lodge Jr., dated September 28, 1939 (Papers of Talcott Parsons, HUG(FP) 42.8.2, box 3, Harvard University Archives).
14. Letter to Louis Wirth, dated October 6, 1939, p. 7; the next quote is from the same page (Papers of Talcott Parsons, HUG(FP) 42.8.2, box 2, Harvard University Archives).
15. Parsons's text, "The Sociology of Modern Antisemitism," was partly rewritten without his consent by Isaac Graeber, the senior editor of the book for which it was prepared, *Jews in a Gentile World.* For details of the controversy between Graeber and Parsons, who was furious, see Gerhardt (1993, 20–22). The text, reconstructed from Parsons's handwritten notes (preserved in the Harvard University Archives), has been published as Parsons (1942/1993c). Graeber's altering the manuscript is the obvious reason that Parsons did not include the essay on anti-Semitism in collections that he assembled in his lifetime.
16. He relied on Harold Lasswell (1933, 1934) to make the point about the relationship between "free-floating aggression" and anti-Semitic political racism (see also Gerhardt 2002, 47, 73–74, 95–97).
17. Talcott Parsons, letter to Eric Voegelin, September 27, 1940, p. 1 (Papers of Talcott Parsons, HUG(FP) 42.8.2, box 3, Harvard University Archives).
18. In the concluding part of "Max Weber and the Contemporary Political Crisis," Parsons used the German terms "Gesinnungsethik" and "Verantwortungsethik."
19. The report was published in the 1980s, in Samuel Z. Klausner and Victor M. Lidz (1986). I use the original because Klausner and Lidz edited Parsons's text to make it more readable. See also Gerhardt (2002, 155).
20. The chapters in the Parsons and Riley version of *Social Science—A National Resource* carried Roman numerals with each chapter paginated separately. This yielded page numbers such as, for instance, I-1, I-2, etc., or III-5, III-6.
21. In the revised version of the memorandum, Riley and Parsons—except for chapter I, from which this quote is taken—used Arabic numerals. They paginated each chapter separately yielding page numbers such as, 8–9 (page 9 of chapter 8).
22. He further contributed to postwar policy planning for Germany, consulting with the Foreign Economic Administration Enemy Branch (FEA) between March and October of 1945. For the FEA he wrote exceedingly detailed memoranda on Germany's past and future (Gerhardt 2002, 120–26). In 1948, he returned to the topic of German reeducation in a paper titled "The Social Environment of the Educational Process." He explored the "sociological analysis of educability" and discussed the "case of German re-education." Three years after the end of World War II, he warned: "Widespread ideas of re-educating the German people for Democracy by removing Fascist or Nazi influences from textbooks, press and radio and substituting democratic ideas illustrate neglect of dependence of education on the social system" (Parsons 1948c, 1).
23. In his analysis of sources and patterns of aggression in the social structure of Western societies, he warned against a danger that could make any nation a threat to humankind in an age of nuclear warfare. The danger

was imminent because the mundane worldview of contemporary Americans tended to judge disorder as prevalent wherever one looked: "The 'jungle philosophy'—which corresponds to a larger element in the real sentiments of all of us than can readily be admitted, even to ourselves—tends to be projected onto the relations of nation states at precisely the point where, under the technological and organizational situation of the modern world, it can do the most harm" (1947/1993i, 343).

24. *New York Times,* letter to the editor, August 8, 1945 (Papers of Talcott Parsons, HUG(FP) 42.8.4, box 19, Harvard University Archives).

25. In hearings held by the United States Senate, July 1 to 3, 1946, on the proposed establishment of the National Science Foundation, Oppenheimer used an argument that Parsons advanced in his own campaigning. Oppenheimer's argument was documented by George Lundberg (Lundberg 1947) in a report on the Senate hearings in *Scientific Monthly.* In regard to incorporating the social sciences into the proposed National Science Foundation, Oppenheimer said he was aware of the lack of rigorous criteria in the social sciences, but "we should recognize the great benefits which may come—I would like to say which will come—from attracting men and women of prominence to the study of these questions" (400).

26. Abundant materials preserved in the Harvard University Archives document this. See, for example, Parsons's own defense against the accusation of lack of loyalty, before the International Organizations Employees Loyalty Board (Papers of Talcott Parsons, HUG(FP) 42.8.4, box 13, Harvard University Archives), and evidence of his work as a member of Committee A of the AAUP, whose task was to investigate cases of wrongdoing when university teachers had been dismissed in the era of McCarthyism (Papers of Talcott Parsons, HUG(FP) 42.8.4, box 2, Harvard University Archives).

27. Evidently, the Freudian element in his thought merged with the Weberian element only twenty years later, in the 1970s.

28. It is my impression that Parsons here uses the term "system" in two different ways: to refer to an empirical phenomenon but also to its analytical representation in both a descriptive and a theoretical sense. On the one hand he speaks of empirical phenomena when he refers to "a commonly understood system of cultural symbols" or "systems of interaction of a plurality of individual actors." On the other hand he uses "system" as an analytical idea when he says that according to the concept of action, "The actor develops a system of 'expectations' relative to the various objects of the situation."

29. For further clarification, in addition to Weber's *The Protestant Ethic and the Spirit of Capitalism,* Parsons and Smelser referred to Marshall's *Principles of Economics* and Parsons's *The Structure of Social Action.* They especially cited chapter 4 of *The Structure of Social Action,* which dealt with Marshall, but they referenced also the entire book.

30. The paper was originally written for a conference on authority convened by a Harvard political scientist, Carl J. Friedrich. Parsons apparently discovered the new aspect of that topic as he tried to write a comprehensive account of what authority meant in the 1950s. (For discussion of the conference, see Gerhardt 2002, 233.)

31. In their textbook survey of American history, Mary Norton et al. (1999) discuss this period in the chapter titled "Postwar America: Cold War Politics, Civil Rights, and the Baby Boom." It is followed by "Reform and Conflict: A Turbulent Era, 1961–1974" and "The End of the Postwar Boom: Stagflation, Immigration, and the Resurgence of Conservatism, 1974–1989."

32. In the 1960s Parsons realized that positivism had returned with a vengeance. In particular, his Harvard colleague George Homans reintroduced utilitarian principles into a theory of social behavior, which was then taken up by Peter Blau in his exchange theory (Homans 1961, Blau 1964). For Parsons's reaction to the reintroduction of utilitarianism in the 1960s, see Gerhardt (2002, 220).

33. On the occasion of the Heidelberg Conference in 1964, the clash between Parsons and Theodor W. Adorno, then the president of the German Sociological Society, occurred over the question whether value-neutrality was imperative for scientific sociology (as Parsons maintained), or, on the contrary, endangered the claim of modern sociology to grasp the reality of late-capitalist society (as Adorno held).

34. For details see Ellen Schrecker (1986). For Parsons's work as a member of Committee A of the AAUP Committee on Special Freedom and Tenure Cases, see Papers of Talcott Parsons, HUG(FP) 42.8.4, box 2, Harvard University Archives.

35. Talcott Parsons, letter to Helmut Dahmer, February 8, 1972 (Papers of Talcott Parsons, HUG(FP) 42.8.8, box 10, Harvard University Archives).

REFERENCES

Agevall, Ola. 1999. *A Science of Unique Events: Max Weber's Methodology of the Cultural Sciences.* Uppsala, Sweden: Uppsala University, Department of Sociology.

Akula, John. 1973. "Law and the Development of Citizenship." Unpublished Ph.D. dissertation. Cambridge, Mass.: Department of Sociology, Harvard University.

Alexander, Jeffrey C. 1983. *The Classical Attempt at Synthesis: Max Weber.* Volume 3, *Theoretical Logic in Sociology.* Berkeley: University of California Press.

Ay, Karl-Ludwig. 2003. "Max Webers Nationenbegriff." In *Zeitperspektiven: Studien zu Kultur und Gesellschaft—Beiträge aus der Geschichte, Soziologie, Philosophie und Literaturwissenschaft,* edited by Uta Gerhardt. Stuttgart: Steiner.

Bakke, E. W. 1940. *The Unemployed Worker: An Empirical Study of Men in the Crisis of the Great Depression.* New Haven: Yale University Press.

Bales, Robert. 1950. *Interaction Process Analysis: A Method for the Study of Small Groups.* Cambridge: Addison-Wesley.

Bendix, Reinhard. 1960. *Max Weber: An Intellectual Portrait.* New York: Doubleday.

Bendix, Reinhard, and Guenther Roth. 1971. *Scholarship and Partisanship: Essays on Max Weber.* Berkeley: University of California Press.

Bernstein, Michael A. 1989. "Why the Great Depression Was Great: Toward a New Understanding of the Interwar Economic Crisis in the United States." In *The Rise and Fall of the New Deal Order, 1930–1980,* edited by Steve Fraser and Gary Gerstle. Princeton: Princeton University Press.

Blau, Peter. 1964. *Power and Exchange in Social Life.* New York: John Wiley.

Brick, Howard. 1996. "The Reformist Dimension of Talcott Parsons's Early Social Theory." In *The Culture of the Market: Historical Essays,* edited by Thomas L. Haskell and Richard F. Teichgraeber III. New York: Cambridge University Press.

Brinkley, Alan. 1989. "The New Deal and the Idea of the State." In *The Rise and Fall of the New Deal Order 1930–1980,* edited by Steve Fraser and Gary Gerstle. Princeton: Princeton University Press.

Cohen, Jere. 1975. "Moral Freedom Through Understanding in Durkheim. Comment on Pope, *ASR,* August, 1973." *American Sociological Review* 40(February): 104–6.

Cohen, Jere, Lawrence E. Hazelrigg, and Whitney Pope. 1975a. "De-Parsonizing Weber: A Critique of Parsons' Interpretation of Weber's Sociology." *American Sociological Review* 40(April): 229–41.

———. 1975b. "Reply to Parsons." *American Sociological Review* 40(October): 670–74.

Durkheim, Émile. 1933/1964. *The Division of Labor in Society.* Translated by George Simpson. New York: Free Press.

Eliaeson, Sven. 2002. *Max Weber's Methodologies.* Cambridge: Polity Press.

Gaddis, John Lewis. 1987. *The Long Peace: Inquiries into the History of the Cold War.* New York: Oxford University Press.

Galbraith, John Kenneth. 1958. *The Affluent Society.* Boston: Houghton Mifflin.

Gerhardt, Uta. 1993. "Parsons's Sociology of National Socialism." In *Talcott Parsons on National Socialism,* edited by Uta Gerhardt. New York: Aldine de Gruyter.

———. 1996. "Talcott Parsons and the Transformation of German Society at the End of World War II." *European Sociological Review* 12(3): 303–25.

———. 1999. "National Socialism and the Politics of *The Structure of Social Action.*" In *Agenda for Sociology: Classic Sources and Current Uses of Talcott Parsons's Work,* edited by Bernard Barber and Uta Gerhardt. Baden-Baden: Nomos.

———. 2001. *Idealtypus: Zur methodologischen Begründung der modernen Soziologie.* Frankfurt am Main: Suhrkamp.

———. 2002. *Talcott Parsons: An Intellectual Biography.* New York: Cambridge University Press.

———. Forthcoming. "Much More Than a Mere Translation: Talcott Parsons's Translation into English of Max Weber's *Die protestantische Ethik und der Geist des Kapitalismus.* An Essay in Intellectual History." *American Sociologist.*

Handlin, Oscar. 1954. *Chance or Destiny: Turning Points in American History.* Boston: Little, Brown.

Hobbes, Thomas. 1651/1949. *Leviathan, or the Matter, Forme, and Power of a Common-Wealth, Ecclesiasticall and Civill,* edited by Richard Tuck. Cambridge: Cambridge University Press.

Hofstadter, Richard. 1955. *The Age of Reform.* New York: Vintage Books.

Homans, George. 1961. *Social Behavior: Its Elementary Forms.* New York: Harcourt, Brace & World.

Ingersoll, Ralph. 1941. *America Is Worth Fighting For.* New York and Indianapolis: Bobbs-Merrill.

Klausner, Samuel Z., and Victor M. Lidz, eds. 1986. *The Nationalization of the Social Sciences.* Philadelphia: University of Pennsylvania Press.

Lasswell, Harold. 1933. "The Psychology of Hitlerism." *The Political Quarterly* 4(October): 373–84.

———. 1934. *World Politics and Personal Insecurity.* New York: Macmillan.

———. 1951. *Politics: Who Gets What, When, How?* Glencoe, Ill.: Free Press.

Levine, Donald. 1995. *Visions of the Sociological Tradition.* Chicago: University of Chicago Press.

Lundberg, George. 1947. "The Senate Ponders Social Science." *Scientific Monthly* 64(May): 397–411.

Mommsen, Wolfgang J. 1994. *Max Weber und die deutsche Revolution 1918–19.* Heidelberg: Stiftung Reichspräsident-Friedrich-Ebert-Gedenkstätte.

Mowrer, Edgar Allen. 1933. *Germany Is Putting the Clock Back.* New York: William Morrow.

Norton, Mary Beth, David M. Katzman, Paul D. Scott, Howard P. Chudacoff, Thomas G. Paterson, William M. Tuttle Jr., and William J. Brophy. 1999. *A People and a Nation: A History of the United States.* Volume B, *Since 1865.* 5th edition. Boston: Houghton Mifflin.

Parsons, Talcott. 1928. " 'Capitalism' in Recent German Literature: Sombart and Weber, I." *Journal of Political Economy* 36(6): 641–61.

———. 1929. " 'Capitalism' in Recent German Literature: Sombart and Weber, II." *Journal of Political Economy* 37(1): 31–51.

———. 1931. "Wants and Activities in Marshall." *Quarterly Journal of Economics* 46(2): 101–40.

———. 1936. "On Certain Elements in Professor Taussig's Thought." In *Explorations in Economics: Notes and Essays Contributed in Honor of F. W. Taussig,* edited by Jacob Viner. New York: McGraw Hill.

———. 1938a. "The Role of Ideas in Social Action." *American Sociological Review* 3(4): 653–64.

———. 1938b. "New Haven, March 1938. Limitations of soc. analysis." Handwritten lecture notes. Papers of Talcott Parsons, HUG(FP) 42.45.4, box 1, Harvard University Archives.

———. 1939. "The Professions and Social Structure." *Social Forces* 17(May): 457–67.

———. 1940. "Motivation of Economic Activities." *Canadian Journal of Economics and Political Science* 6(May): 187–203.

———. 1945. "The Present Position and Prospects of Systematic Theory in Sociology." In *Twentieth Century Sociology,* edited by George Gurvitch and Wilbert E. Moore. New York: Philosophical Library.

———. 1946. "The Science Legislation and the Role of the Social Sciences." *American Sociological Review* 11(December): 653–66.

———. 1947. "Science Legislation and the Social Sciences." *Political Sciences Quarterly* 62(2): 241–49.

———. 1948a. "The Position of Sociological Theory." *American Sociological Review* 13(April): 156–71.

———. 1948b. "Social Science—A Basic National Resource." Memorandum prepared for the Social Science Research Council. Papers of Talcott Parsons, HUG(FP) 42.41, Harvard University Archives.

———. 1948c. "The Social Environment of the Educational Process." Unpublished paper. Papers of Talcott Parsons, HUG(FP) 42.8.4, box 2, Harvard University Archives.

———. 1954. *Essays in Sociological Theory.* 2nd edition. New York: Free Press.

———. 1955. "McCarthyism and American Social Tension: A Sociologist's View." *Yale Review* 44(January): 226–55.

———. 1957. "The Distribution of Power in American Society." *World Politics* 10(October): 123–43.

———. 1959. "A Short Account of My Intellectual Development." *Alpha Kappa Deltan* 29(1): 3–11.

———. 1960a. *Structure and Process in Modern Society.* New York: Free Press.

———. 1958/1960b. "Authority, Legitimation, and Political Action." In *Structure and Process in Modern Societies.* New York: Free Press.

———. 1958/1960c. "Some Principal Characteristics of Industrial Societies." In *Structure and Process in Modern Societies.* New York: Free Press.

———. 1959/1960d. "The Principal Structures of Community." In *Structure and Process in Modern Societies.* New York: Free Press.

———. 1962. "Individual Autonomy and Social Pressure: An Answer to Dennis H. Wrong." *Psychoanalysis and Psychoanalytic Review* 49(summer): 70–79.

———. 1963. "On the Concept of Political Power." *Proceedings of the American Philosophical Society* 107: 232–62.

———. 1951/1964. *The Social System.* New York: Free Press.

———. 1964/1967. "Evaluation and Objectivity in the Social Sciences: An Interpretation of Max Weber's Contributions." In *Sociological Theory and Modern Society.* New York: Free Press.

———. 1937/1968. *The Structure of Social Action: A Study in Social Theory with Reference to Four Recent European Writers.* New York: Free Press.

———. 1969. *Politics and Social Structure.* New York: Free Press.

———. 1974. "Law as an Intellectual 'Stepchild.' " Unpublished paper. Papers of Talcott Parsons, HUG(FP), 42.45.4, box 7, Harvard University Archives.

———. 1975a. "Comment on 'Parsons' Interpretation of Durkheim' and on 'Moral Freedom Through Understanding of Durkheim.' " *American Sociological Review* 40(February): 106–11.

———. 1975b. "Comment on 'De-Parsonizing Weber.' " *American Sociological Review* 40(October): 666–70.

———. 1978. "Law as an Intellectual Stepchild." *Sociological Inquiry* 47(3–4): 11–58.

———. 1935/1991a. "H. M. Robertson on Max Weber and His School." In *Talcott Parsons: The Early Essays,* edited by Charles Camic. Chicago: University of Chicago Press.

———. 1935/1991b. "The Place of Ultimate Values in Sociological Theory." In *Talcott Parsons: The Early Essays,* edited by Charles Camic. Chicago: University of Chicago Press.

———. 1938/1993a. "Nazis Destroy Learning, Challenge Religion." In *Talcott Parsons on National Socialism,* edited by Uta Gerhardt. New York: Aldine de Gruyter.

———. 1940/1993b. "Memorandum: The Development of Groups and Organizations Amenable to Use Against American Institutions and Foreign Policy and Possible Measures of Prevention." In *Talcott Parsons on National Socialism.* New York: Aldine the Gruyter.

———. 1942/1993c. "The Sociology of Modern Anti-Semitism." In *Talcott Parsons on National Socialism*. New York: Aldine de Gruyter.

———. 1942/1993d. "Max Weber and the Contemporary Political Crisis." In *Talcott Parsons on National Socialism.* New York: Aldine de Gruyter.

———. 1942/1993e. "Democracy and Social Structure in Pre-Nazi Germany." In *Talcott Parsons on National Socialism.* New York: Aldine de Gruyter.

———. 1942/1993f. "Some Sociological Aspects of the Fascist Movements." In *Talcott Parsons on National Socialism.* New York: Aldine de Gruyter.

———. 1945/1993g. "Racial and Religious Differences as Factors in Group Tensions." In *Talcott Parsons on National Socialism*. New York: Aldine de Gruyter.

———. 1945/1993h. "The Problem of Controlled Institutional Change: An Essay in Applied Social Science." In *Talcott Parsons on National Socialism*. New York: Aldine de Gruyter.

———. 1947/1993i. "Certain Primary Sources and Patterns of Aggression in the Social Structure of the Western World." In *Talcott Parsons on National Socialism*. New York: Aldine de Gruyter.

Parsons, Talcott, and Robert Bales. 1955. *Family Socialization and Interaction Process.* London: Routledge & Kegan Paul.

Parsons, Talcott, and Bernard Barber. 1948. "Sociology, 1941–1946." *American Journal of Sociology* 53(January): 245–57.

Parsons, Talcott, and Renée Fox. 1952. "Illness, Therapy, and the Modern Urban American Family." *Journal of Social Issues* 8(1): 31–44.

Parsons, Talcott, and John Riley Jr. 1950. "Social Science: A National Resource." Memorandum for the Social Science Research Council. Papers of Talcott Parsons, HUG(FP) 15.70, box 2, Harvard University Archives.

Parsons, Talcott, and Edward Shils, eds. 1951. *Toward a General Theory of Action.* Cambridge, Mass.: Harvard University Press.

Parsons, Talcott, Edward Shils, and Robert Bales. 1953. *Working Papers in the Theory of Action.* New York: Free Press.

Parsons, Talcott, and Neil J. Smelser. 1956. *Economy and Society: A Study in the Integration of Economic and Social Theory.* London: Routledge & Kegan Paul.

Patterson, James T. 2001. *Brown vs. Board of Education: A Civil Rights Milestone and Its Troubled Legacy.* Cambridge, Mass.: Oxford University Press.

Pope, Whitney. 1973. "Classic on Classic: Parsons' Interpretation of Durkheim." *American Sociological Review* 38(August): 399–415.

———. 1975. "Parsons on Durkheim Revisited; Reply to Cohen and Parsons." *American Sociological Review* 40 (February): 111–15.

Riley, John W., Jr., and Talcott Parsons. 1950. "Social Science: A National Resource." Memorandum for the Social Science Research Council. Unpublished. Papers of Talcott Parsons, HUG(FP) 42.41, box 3, Harvard University Archives.

Ringer, Fritz. 1997. *Max Weber's Methodology: The Unification of the Cultural and Social Sciences.* Cambridge, Mass.: Harvard University Press.

Schlesinger, Arthur M., Jr. 1957. *The Age of Roosevelt: The Crisis of the Old Order.* Boston: Houghton Mifflin.

———. 1958/1988. *The Age of Roosevelt: The Coming of the New Deal.* Boston: Houghton Mifflin.

Schrecker, Ellen. 1986. *No Ivory Tower: McCarthyism and the Universities.* New York: Oxford University Press.

Schuman, Frederick L. 1935. *The Nazi Dictatorship: A Study in Social Pathology and the Politics of Fascism.* New York: Alfred A. Knopf.

Sica, Alan. 1988. *Weber, Irrationality, and Social Order.* Berkeley: University of California Press.

Swedberg, Richard. 1991. *Joseph A. Schumpeter: His Life and Work.* Cambridge: Polity Press.

Voegelin, Eric. 1938. *Die politischen Religionen.* Vienna: Bermann-Fischer.

Weber, Max. 1904/1920. "Die protestantische Ethik und der Geist des Kapitalismus." Volume 1, *Gesammelte Aufsätze zur Religionssoziologie.* Tübingen: J. C. B. Mohr.

———. 1919/1948a. "Politics as a Vocation." In *From Max Weber,* edited with an introduction by H. H. Gerth and C. Wright Mills. London: Routledge & Kegan Paul.

———. 1919/1948b. "Science as a Vocation." In *From Max Weber,* edited and with an introduction by H. H. Gerth and C. Wright Mills. London: Routledge & Kegan Paul.

———. 1904/1949a. " 'Objectivity' in Social Science and Social Politics." In *The Methodology of the Social Sciences: Max Weber.* Translated and edited by Edward A. Shils and Henry A. Finch. New York: Free Press.

———. 1917/1949b. "The Meaning of 'Ethical Neutrality' in Sociology and Economics." In *The Methodology of the Social Sciences: Max Weber,* translated and edited by Edward A. Shils and Henry A. Finch. New York: Free Press.

———. 1922/1956. *Wirtschaft und Gesellschaft: Grundriss der verstehenden Soziologie.* Tübingen: J. C. B. Mohr.

———. 1947/1964. *The Theory of Social and Economic Organization,* edited by Talcott Parsons. Translated by A. M. Henderson and Talcott Parsons. New York: Free Press.

———. 1930/1976. *The Protestant Ethic and the Spirit of Capitalism.* Translated by Talcott Parsons. London: Allen & Unwin.

———. 1968/1978. *Economy and Society: An Outline of Interpretive Sociology,* edited by Guenther Roth and Claus Wittich. Berkeley: University of California Press.

Wrong, Dennis. 1961. "The Oversocialized Conception of Man in Modern Sociology." *American Sociological Review* 26(April): 183–93.

Chapter 12

From Amherst to Heidelberg: On the Origins of Parsons's Conception of Culture

Charles Camic

The purpose of the chapter is threefold. The first is methodological: to call attention to the reductionist manner in which interpreters of Talcott Parsons typically connect the events of his life with the content of his ideas and to urge, instead, a more developmental—or life-course—approach. The second goal is to furnish a partial illustration of this approach through a brief intellectual-historical examination of the early phases in the development on Parsons's concept of culture. I take culture as the focus because, although it is one of the central concepts throughout Parsons's work, not only have Parsons scholars misunderstood its development, but the nature of this development was such that Parsons's own thought recapitulated early on a move between two polar approaches to culture whose contrast has continued to anchor social-scientific thinking about culture (see, for example, Geertz 1973; Griswold 1994; Swidler 1986, 2001). The third objective of the chapter is to use this intellectual-historical inquiry to shed critical light on Parsons's understanding of modern culture. In the course of this analysis, I will briefly introduce as evidence a translation of a previously unknown article that Parsons wrote near the start of his intellectual career.

BEYOND REDUCTIONISM IN THE STUDY OF PARSONS'S INTELLECTUAL BIOGRAPHY

Perhaps the least reductionist of major sociological theorists, Talcott Parsons bequeathed to those seeking to understand the development of his ideas a life the biographical reconstruction of which has tended to attract reductionist interpreters. The reductionist interpreter is one who believes that he or she has found the key: the decisive biographical moment, episode, or event through which the defining features of Parsons's thought were forged. As to where this watershed lay, commentators have proposed several different candidates, though in the last few years the scholarship has clustered mainly around two long-familiar contenders. One of these is the claim that Parsons was "made in the nursery," the other the argument that he was "made in Germany"; or, more precisely, that the essentials of Parsons's thinking emerged from the Protestant home in which he was raised or from his encounter, as a graduate student in Heidelberg, with the legacy of Max Weber.

The first of these interpretations builds on the known circumstances of Parsons's family of origin: namely, that his father, Edward S. Smith, began his own career as a Congregational minister and, after leaving the ministry for a series of academic positions, staunchly retained his commitment to spreading the reformist teachings of the "social gospel" movement that marked late-nineteenth- and early-twentieth-century American Protestantism. In the presumed impact of these teachings on his youngest son, Talcott, many interpreters see the biographical master key to the latter's subsequent theoretical position. In brief early statements of this view, William Buxton held that "the redemptive impulse of Parsons's liberal Calvinist commitments . . . guided the development of his thought" (1985, 12), while Jeffrey C. Alexander described Parsons's work as "a lifelong debate [with the] Christian inheritance" that derived from "Parsons' family roots" (1983, 131; see also Tiryakian 1975; Vidich and Lyman 1985). More recently, Jens Kaalhauge Nielson has elaborated such claims into the thesis that, "because of the influence of his father, Parsons's intellectual attitude was guided by religious ideas"; these infused his work within a pervasive "religious *Weltanschauung,*" anchored his major "intellectual ideas" within a "religious framework," and gave "a hidden meaning [to] everything he wrote" (2001, 213–14).

What makes such interpretations reductionist is that in assigning watershed status to the biographical moment in question (here, to Parsons's religious upbringing), they regard other episodes in Parsons's intellectual career as epiphenomenal, rather than as potentially formative experiences in their own right. Indeed, rather than probe the possible contribution to Parsons's intellectual development of these other experiences (to be sure, in interaction with his earlier experiences), reductionist interpretations either neglect such experiences altogether or present them as overshadowed by the determining effects of the prior watershed moment. It is in this manner that Nielson—to resume the above example—downplays Parsons's undergraduate education at Amherst College (1920–24). Commenting, for example, on the publication of two course papers that Parsons wrote during his junior year at Amherst, Nielson avers that these papers reveal "the basic ideas . . . that Parsons followed throughout his life"—in other words, "that the basic core of Parsons's theory was already in place in his Amherst papers," though *not* as a consequence of his Amherst education itself. To the contrary: According to Nielson, the system of ideas evident in the papers is so mature that it "could not possibly be the outcome of just four months of course work [during Parsons's junior year] or, for that matter, the previous two years at Amherst. Such a system must have originated long before Amherst, and the papers therefore point to Parsons's childhood upbringing, and especially to the influence of his father's philosophical and religious ideas" (Nielson 1996). Later I will suggest a less reductive view of Parsons's Amherst experiences.[1]

In contrast to the emphasis this first group of scholars places on Parsons's Protestant upbringing, a second line of interpretation accents the transformative impact of Parsons's sojourn in Heidelberg, Germany, in the period following his graduation from Amherst (and a one-year interlude at the London School of Economics from 1924 to 1925), particularly his encounter with the writings of Max Weber.[2] Representative of this position, which also has a long legacy (see, for example, Hamilton 1983; Turner 1996), is A. Javier Treviño's statement: "It was Max Weber who had the most persuasive influence on Parsons's intellectual development. Although Weber had died in 1920, his dominating presence was widespread at Heidelberg when Parsons matriculated there as a student. . . . It seems that everyone at the university was familiar with the work of Weber, and the young Parsons's imagination was fired by his first reading of *The Protestant Ethic and the Spirit of Capitalism*" (2001, xxi). Uta Gerhardt's work presents the apotheosis of this view; she claims that Parsons's "style of thought was adopted from the German when he read Weber . . . during his sojourn in Heidelberg" and thereafter constructed "his conceptual framework for sociology [by] emulating Weber, . . . remain[ing] a Weberian all his life," fixated on Weberian substantive and methodological topics throughout the subsequent stages of his career (2002, ix–x; see also chapter 11, this volume).[3]

To be sure, this second interpretation appears to have the imprimatur of Parsons himself who in later life recalled the Weberian world of Heidelberg as "an extraordinarily stimulating intellectual environment, participation in which was one of the most important factors in determining my whole intellectual and professional career" (1965/1967, 80), elsewhere characterizing "this study in Germany [as] a crucial experience in my life, in the first instance because of it bringing me into contact with the work of Max Weber" (1969, 59; see also Parsons 1959, 1970, 1980, and as quoted by Buxton and Rehorick 2001, 43). But statements of this type from Parsons must be used with caution: first, because, as intellectual historians and sociologists of sciences have shown, retrospective autobiographical statements (when not corroborated by more contemporaneous statements) typically are unreliable guides to a thinker's actual course of development; second, because Parsons himself goes no further than to call the Heidelberg experience "*one* of the most important factors" in his career, "*a* crucial experience"; and third, because even Parsons's own recollections point toward a factor that undermines reductive accounts of his encounter with Weber. This is the fact that "Max Weber" is not a radiant physical object impressing itself automatically on everything it contacts. That the twentieth century produced nearly as many "takes" on Max Weber as there were takers—readers of his work—serves as a reminder as to why "Max Weber" cannot be viewed as a determinant first cause of any reader's own course of intellectual development: "Max Weber" is an entity that exists through acts of interpretation—acts through which what the reader draws from (selected portions of) Weber's vast oeuvre is at least partly a function of what he or she brings to the task of reading Weber. That the young Parsons engaged in just such an interpretive process is suggested by his comment that Max Weber's "dominance in the intellectual atmosphere at Heidelberg was not without a great deal of opposition, [an] opposition [that] meant that there was an extremely lively controversy" under way in the 1920s about Weber's legacy (1959, 4). To reduce Parsons's intellectual development to the influence exerted upon him by Weber is to elide the prior influences that prompted Parsons, in this fluid situation, to ally with Weber and then to gravitate to some, rather than other, currents in Weber's work.[4]

In taking issue with reductionist interpretations of Parsons's intellectual development—of which "made in the nursery" and "made in Germany" are only the most prominent examples—scholarship of another type should also be acknowledged. The spate of reductionist interpretations is a fairly recent trend, most evident in studies that seek to use Parsons's intellectual biography as a means to explain the origins of his thought. For the most part, however, this explanatory agenda is absent in earlier works on Parsons's thought, many of which offer biographical sketches that are more catholic, following Parsons's life from birth through the multiple stages of his educational and professional career in a descriptive manner that can serve to correct reductionist accounts. Noteworthy here are the works of Bernard Barber (1949), Guy Rocher (1975), Martin Martel (1979), and Bruce Wearne (1989).

What is more, these works, while eschewing the explanatory agenda, hint at a possible way of advancing this agenda without lapsing into a reductionist account. Formulated in the terminology of contemporary sociological research, this alternative involves bringing a life-course perspective to bear on the study of the processes by which a thinker's ideas emerge, develop, and change.[5] Put briefly, a life-course perspective (as developed elsewhere in sociology): first, "defines the individual life as a . . . coherent entity in which there are *multiple* antecedent-consequent linkages that give it shape and substance" (Kerckhoff 1993, 3; emphasis added); second, holds that "the developmental impact of life events depends on their timing in life"; third, embeds "the individual life course . . . in historical time and place" (Crosnoe 2000, 383). Applied to the analysis of the intellectual career of Talcott Parsons, this approach suggests the need to examine the multiple episodes in Parsons's career, as contextualized "in historical time and place," beginning—because of the significance generally proven to attach to episodes timed relatively early in the life course—with his early experiences, and then following forward their diverse and protean intellectual consequences as Parsons underwent subsequent experiences.

In contextualizing such experiences historically, however, one must beware of returning to the approach of the traditional sociology of knowledge, with its tendency toward another form of reductionism, namely, the "explanation" of a thinker's ideas by appeal to the great macrolevel events of a period,[6] to the neglect of the mediating processes that incline different thinkers to respond differently to those events (for elaboration of this criticism, see Camic 1983). The aim of a life-course perspective, instead, is to include historical developments known to have impacted the thinkers of the age as a starting point, but then to take account of the biographical factors that led intellectual responses to these developments to vary from thinker to thinker, manifesting themselves unevenly across the different aspects of the thought of the same thinker.

This notion of potentially uneven effects bears special emphasis: analysis of the intellectual development of a complex figure like Talcott Parsons is generally well served when one resists viewing his work as a monolithic body of thought and, rather, carefully differentiates the relatively "discrete features" present in his writings—his concepts, methodological principles, explanatory logics, and so on (on these aspects, see Levine 1986)—since the developmental course of different features will often differ. Regrettably, interpreters of Parsons have tended not to follow this precept, a circumstance that perhaps explains why different interpreters nominate different episodes as the defining episode in the development of "his thought."

To circumvent this problem, this chapter focuses on a single aspect of Parsons's thought: his concept of culture. Moreover, it treats only a few early moments in the unfolding of this concept within his work, recognizing—in view of the centrality of culture in Parsons's writings throughout his career (Schmid 1992)—that this analysis could certainly go forward in time. The moments examined here, Parsons's experiences at Amherst and then in Heidelberg, are episodes that I have selected because Parsons, as he passed through them, left a paper trail that furnishes a window onto his ideas about culture during these moments. In considering these episodes I seek to call the two reductionist approaches discussed above in question as adequate accounts of the origins of Parsons's view of culture. While culture is not his exclusive focus, Nielson (1996), for example, includes Parsons's ideas about culture (about morals, values, and so on) as part of the "basic core" of the later theory that, in nascent form, allegedly was "already in place in his Amherst papers" as a result of Parsons's religious upbringing. And Gerhardt (chapter 11, this volume) identifies some of these same ideas, Parsons's approach to values, as part of his inheritance from Weber. Without undertaking a reconsideration of Parsons's religious roots (but see Camic 1991), I shall document that, while at Amherst, Parsons gave voice to a conception of culture that had only recently gained currency in American intellectual life. However, his conceptualization of culture was not fixed at this point. Rather, as I subsequently argue, Parsons's experiences in Heidelberg, interacting with those that came before, brought him to a very different conception of culture, one that corresponded closely to the German view of culture, albeit, as I shall describe, with a dissimilarity of critical consequence.

PARSONS AT AMHERST: INITIAL IDEAS ABOUT CULTURE

Belying its situation as a small educational establishment in an insular town in south-central Massachusetts, Amherst College in the 1920s was an institution that effectively deflected outward the sights of those among its students who were interested in the social sciences, forming for the young men in this group the porous inner layer of a sphere surrounded by several outer layers, three of them especially relevant in the present context.

The first and outermost of these layers was the wide world of contemporary American popular writing, the literature of serious journalism, of magazines carrying social and political commentary, and of books targeted to readers of weighty nonfiction. Describing this work during the 1920s and 1930s, the historian Warren Susman observes: "No fact is more significant than the general and even popular 'discovery' of the concept of culture, . . . [as] Americans then began thinking in terms of patterns of behavior and beliefs, values and lifestyles, symbols and meanings" (Susman 1984, 153–54). Prior to World War I, intellectuals of the Progressive era had begun the move in this direction when they decried America's "insane individualism" and "called for the development of a national culture . . .—a revolution in values and behavior—. . . that could heal the . . . divisions in American life" (Pells 1973, 6, 9). But these themes acquired greater salience and urgency in the United States of the 1920s, which historians characterize as an age when "cultural warfare was more intense than political combat. It was the era of contradictions—the decade at once of fundamentalists and flappers, prohibitionists and bootleggers, . . . disenchantment with war and enchantment with business, [as well as of the] basic cultural clash . . . between city and countryside, . . . cosmopolitans and nativists" (Schlesinger 2000, 47, 49).

Amid these conditions, an outpouring of writings appeared that concerned itself expressly with "culture," about what Americans took as the components of culture (values, lifestyles, and so on), and about "civilization," understood as the latest, and highly alarming, stage—the industrialized, machine-based stage—in the development of human cultures. In one of many books of the period with either "civilization" or "culture" in its title, *Civilization in the United States* (1922), Harold Stearns and others, aiming to provide a "critical examination of our civilization . . . in order to do our share in making a real civilization possible," adjudged that America was suffering "emotional and aesthetic starvation" because it lacked adequate "heritages and traditions to which to cling"—a stark assessment that reinforced growing anxieties about the disappearance of "community" and the breakdown of human communications into the morally hollow language of "stocks and bond quotations, football scores, [and] jazz music" (cited by Susman 1984, 115, 109). Such intellectual jeremiads fueled widespread contemporary fears that American civilization and culture were in "crisis" and, alongside these fears, a diffuse state of uncertainty over "what kind of culture would—and even more important what kind of culture could—emerge [in the] new machine-age civilization" (Susman 1984, 121, 191, 188; see also Pells 1973).

Gripped by this sense of crisis and looking to combat it, many popular writers sought counsel in an emerging academic literature where culture had recently surfaced as the subject of explicit treatment. This literature consisted of the writings of a group of American anthropologists clustered around the anthropologist Franz Boas. Their work forms the second, and somewhat nearer, of the outside layers that then enveloped Amherst College. Behind this Boasian literature lay one of the major developments in the American academy in the period from 1890 to 1920: the aggressive move by natural scientists to absorb the study of human beings and social conditions within the explanatory categories of the biological sciences (see Camic 1986). Committed to this cause, contemporary natural scientists opposed, in succession, the academic establishment of all the social sciences (except economics), but they took particular aim at the nascent field of anthropology, thereby calling forth, by the second decade of the twentieth century, a vigorous counterattack by Franz Boas at Columbia University and his students. The engine of this counterattack was "culture." Severing this term from its European roots and recasting it into a warrant for their discipline as an academic field independent of the natural sciences, the Boasians took the position that "culture operated autonomously from the determinants of the natural sciences" (Cravens 1978, 90). In the words of Robert Lowie, writing in 1917: "The ethnologist will do well to postulate the principle, *Omnis cultura ex cultura*"; "this means that he will account for a given cultural fact by demonstrating some other cultural fact, by merging it into a group of cultural facts, or by demonstrating some other cultural facts out of which it has developed" (cited by Cravens 1978, 89). By 1920, the Boasians had blanketed the social-scientific literature with this view, producing some fifty statements about the centrality of culture as an autonomous force (Cravens 1978, 89–120; see also Curti 1980).

Significant in itself, this development unleashed important ramifications at the third, and innermost, of the layers that surrounded the social sciences at Amherst in the 1920s. As the Boasian argument about the independence of culture from nature rippled through anthropology, it spread as well to neighboring academic disciplines and particularly into sociology, calling forth here a distinctive conceptualization of culture and a distinctive theory of the interrelationship among the elements of culture. Hamilton Cravens's (1978) research on the development of American sociology has shown that late-nineteenth-century American sociologists, because of their attraction to evolutionary theory, were generally slower than anthropologists to grasp the threat that the natural sciences posed to the academic autonomy of their discipline and to appreciate the "importance of the dictum *omnis cultura ex cultura*"; but that, "after 1920, American sociologists caught up with the Boasians," "recogniz[ed] the distinction between the biological and the cultural levels of human existence," and firmly aligned their discipline with the latter, as they too widely embraced "the culture idea" (Cravens 1978, 121–22, 147–48). This conversion is evident in the work of a diverse range of early-twentieth-century sociologists that included Charles Horton Cooley, Edward A. Ross, W. I. Thomas, Florian Znaniecki, Robert Park, Ellsworth Faris, Robert MacIver, and many others (Camic 1989, 43).

Most to the point, the spread of "the culture idea" brought with it a distinctive conception of culture, one well fitted to the battle that anthropologists and sociologists were waging against the natural scientists. This was a conception of culture that was at once omnibus and loose-knit: omnibus in that this conception encompassed all human products and activities that were not obviously reducible to nature; and loose-knit in that this conception viewed a group's cultural elements not organically—not in terms of their (varying degrees of) inner coherence and unity—but more discretely or atomistically.[7]

Representative of this conception were the definitions of "culture" reported in a contemporary survey by E. E. Eubank: "our attitudes, beliefs and ideas, our judgments and values; our institutions, political and legal, religious and economic; our ethical codes and codes of etiquette; our books and machines . . .—all of these things and many other things and beings, both in themselves and in their multiform interrelations" (Alexander Goldenweiser, anthropologist); "the sum total of all that is artificial—the complete outfit of tools, and habits of living, which are invented by man and then passed on from one generation to another" (Joseph Folsom, sociologist); the "totality of a people's products and activities, social and religious order, customs and beliefs which, in the case of the more advanced, we have been accustomed to call their civilization" (Roland Dixon, anthropologist); "all human institutions and human achievements make up the sum and substance of human culture" (Charles Ellwood, sociologist). From this conceptual standpoint, a society's culture, Eubank concluded from his survey, consisted of "thousands of separate items," forming a "list [comparable] to the catalog of a mail order house, each item of which may be likened to a separate [cultural] trait, the whole constituting the complete stock in trade. The sum total of its traits constitutes the culture of any people" (Eubank 1932, 338–39, 350).

Useful for wresting as much ground as possible away from natural sciences, this concept of culture also formed the basis of the period's most celebrated theory of culture, William Fielding Ogburn's "hypothesis of cultural lag." Ogburn's notion of culture followed that of his contemporaries: "The word culture properly includes [humans'] social heritage, both the material culture and also such parts of culture as knowledge, belief, morals, law, and custom, [as well as] social institutions or organizations. . . . To enumerate in detail the variegated subject matter of culture or the social heritage would include a very long list indeed" (1922, 4–5).

Employing this conception, Ogburn set about to address "a problem [that arises] only in modern times," a problem that results from "social change" or (equivalently) "cultural change." This is the "maladjustment" that occurs when "adaptive non-material culture"—that "portion" of culture consisting of customs, beliefs, and social institutions—"is slow to adjust to changed . . . material culture"—to the state of technology, machines, manufactured products, and other material objects (1922, 202, 264–65). And this condition of maladjustment was, according to Ogburn, the plight of American society in the 1920s: for, as a result of government inertia, habit, divisions across classes and other social groups, and related factors, "changes in adaptive culture do not synchronize exactly with the changes in material culture" (1922, 203, 257–64). A sociological museum piece on hindsight, this simple idea had great resonance in the context of the burgeoning popular and social-scientific literature on culture during the interwar period. Indeed, as Richard H. Pells notes, when "Ogburn offered his conception of 'cultural lag,' . . . the term quickly became an important part of the intellectual vocabulary," appearing to observers in and out of the academy not only "like a perfect description of America's own predicament" but as the diagnosis that opened the way for the deliberate building of a new culture (Pells 1973, 24–25).

In Parsons's years at Amherst, from 1920 and 1924, all of these surrounding layers of American thought broke through and penetrated the college. Alexander Meiklejohn, the school's reformist president (before his ouster in 1923), conceived liberal education as a lesson in "philosophy" in the largest sense: not the transmission of "specialized knowledge," but the acquisition of "the unified understanding which is insight," to which end, Meiklejohn held further, each educator and each student "must find a problem which seems to him real and must then let his reading and thinking develop from that" (Meiklejohn 1920, quoted by Gerhardt 1993, 4). Comporting with this view, a core of Amherst faculty members cast its sights widely (see Brick 1993), offering courses in step with intellectual trends elsewhere in the country. The young Parsons is on record as favoring this enlarged view of education, which he first encountered as a freshman in the college's signature course, "Social and Economic Institutions" (for fuller discussion, see Camic 1991, xiv–xv), a course he praised as "a solvent for that stock of preconceptions and prejudices which a freshman brings to college along with his other baggage" (Cutler and Parsons 1923/1991, 288).[8]

A contemporary syllabus from this course makes clear that all the intellectual currents described above were present on the Amherst campus, as students encountered generous selections from the popular literature about the crisis of industrial civilization, as well as from the writings of anthropologists battling for culture against nature and of sociologists and other proponents of the omnibus conception of culture. These works included Stearns's *Civilization in the United States* and books by Boas, Lowie, Goldenweiser, Thomas, Dixon, Ellwood, and a great number of other contemporary authors.[9] What was more, local Amherst figures themselves strongly reinforced many of the themes found in this literature. Walton Hamilton, the "institutionalist" economist who was arguably Parsons's most influential teacher while at Amherst (see Camic 1992), developed in these years the view that "modern industrialism is a peculiar *culture,*" one in the throes of "crisis" as a result of "incompatibilities between the advancing and stationary aspects of social development" (Hamilton 1925, 2, 10)—a diagnosis right out of Ogburn's cultural-lag theory. Elaborating this thesis, Hamilton described his age as a period that was undergoing "improvement . . . in the technique of production, the growth of business organization, and the expansion of the pecuniary system" without the requisite changes in "our legal arrangements, our fundamental institutions, or our ethical standards." On this basis, he voiced sympathy for contemporary demands for "a radical reconstruction of our whole scheme of life and values" (1925, 6, 12).[10]

In emphasizing the presence of these intellectual currents at Amherst, I do not claim that they were stand-alone forces, for they were not. As the young Parsons progressed through the college—gradually shifting his concentration from biology to economics and simultaneously taking seminars in German philosophy (on Parsons's course work, see Camic 1991)—he encountered a wide diversity of ideas of local, national, and international provenience. Some of these, and their implications for Parsons's later work, are treated elsewhere (Camic 1991, 1992; Brick 1993), while others remain for future excavation. In this chapter my focus falls on contemporary "cultural" currents because my present concern is with the development of Parsons's conception of culture.

Examined from this angle, Parsons's surviving course papers from his junior year (see p. 241 of this chapter) show how fully the early Parsons embraced contemporary American views. The papers in question—"The Theory of Human Behavior in Its Individual and Social Aspects" (1922) and "A Behavioristic Conception of the Nature of Morals" (1923)—are essays that Parsons wrote for a two-semester course that the philosopher and institutional economist Clarence Ayres taught under the title "The Moral Order." As course papers, their point of departure seems to reflect instructions from Ayres, who had apparently asked students to provide a critical assessment of evolutionary theories. Be this as it may, Parsons's essays situate him immediately in the contemporary debate over the role of nature versus culture, as they strongly argue the case for culture on strict Boasian grounds. Quoting "Mr. Lowie" and invoking the mantra "omnis cultura ex cultura," Parsons insists, against the claims of natural-scientific determinism, that "when we wish to explain the origin of any cultural phenomenon we [must] look very carefully for something closely related to it in the cultural condition that immediately preceded it" (1922, 9–11). Simultaneous with taking this stand, Parsons adopts the omnibus, loose-knit concept of culture that then dominated the American discussion of the subject. Under "culture" he includes "customs and usages" as well as "technology, etiquette, moral standards, institutional background, *and what not*" (1922, 16, 14; emphasis added), and he specifically warns against "assuming that a culture is . . . more of a unit than it really is" (1923, 20). As he puts it, cultures consist of relatively discrete "cultural elements" that groups borrow from one another and accumulate (much like items in Eubank's mail-order catalogue): "The essence of culture is the fact that its development is cumulative and any feature of it becomes the property of all succeeding generations" (1922, 15; 1923, 19). Accordingly, what differentiates "primitive civilizations" from "modern industrial civilizations" is chiefly "the introduction of machine technique" (1922, 7). Yet Parsons cautions against "assum[ing] that a culture advanced in technology is also advanced in morals, in institutions, in ritual, in all its aspects" (1923, 20)—an observation that then enables him to diagnose his own society explicitly in the cultural-lag language of contemporary thinkers like Ogburn and Hamilton. Parsons writes (1923, 20–21):

> In our civilization the great outstanding fact is the tremendous development of technology. Other aspects have developed, but there has never before been anything of the character of industrialism, and its advent has been out of all proportion to the contemporary change in morals, literature, philosophy, government, or religion. . . . Most of the mal-adaptations which industrialism has caused are due to the fact that this catching up of other aspects of civilization are [*sic*] so much slower than the rise of industrialism has been.

The thinness of the biographical record on Parsons's early life necessarily leaves open whether Parsons arrived at this set of ideas about culture by directly assimilating the contemporary literatures on culture and the views of his teachers; or by wrestling with the problems that engaged his contemporaries (the threat of the natural sciences, the march of the machine age) and independently formulating a similar intellectual response; or by bringing lessons his father taught him to bear in a new intellectual context; or by some combination of these processes. The package of ideas itself, however, so fully accords with the configuration of ideas present in American thought at precisely this period—yet still absent when Parsons was "in the nursery" and missing as well in his later work—that it furnishes evidence of a lost early phase in the development of his thinking. Considered from a life-course perspective, the question is then: With the Amherst years complete, how did Parsons's conception of culture subsequently develop?

A Note on the London School of Economics

Following his graduation from Amherst, Parsons accepted an offer that an uncle of his had extended to finance a year of study at the London School of Economics. With this support, Parsons attended the LSE as a nondegree student from October 1924 to June 1925, during which time he took courses offered by a distinguished group of social scientists (Camic 1991, xvii–xix). What impact this experience had on Parsons's thinking is difficult to determine, however, since, aside from a few routine letters, no manuscripts from this period in his life have yet come to light. Nonetheless, because one of Parsons's teachers at the LSE was the cultural anthropologist Bronislaw Malinowski, and because Parsons later recalled Malinowski's courses as important for his own understanding of culture (Parsons 1957/1977, 1959, 1970; Barber 1949; Martel 1979), it seems plausible that Malinowski may have been the figure who set Parsons's conception of culture on a new path.

In fact, however, different as he was from American anthropologists in some ways, Malinowski upheld a concept of culture that closely matched the omnibus idea of his American counterparts.[11] To the extent, then, that Malinowski's position did influence the young Parsons, the effect could only have been to reinforce the notion of culture that he already expressed in his Amherst papers. Malinowski wrote (1930, 621):

> Man varies in two respects; in physical form and in social heritage, or culture. [A jungle child], transported to France and brought up there, would differ profoundly from what he would have been if reared in the jungle. He would have been given a different social heritage; a different language, different habits, ideas and beliefs; he would have been incorporated into a different social organization and cultural setting. This social heritage is the key concept of cultural anthropology; . . . it is usually called culture. . . . The word culture is at times used synonymously with civilization, but it is better [to reserve] civilization for a special aspect of more advanced cultures. Culture comprises inherited artifacts, goods, technical processes, ideas, habits and values. [As well,] social organization cannot be really understood except as part of culture.

Interestingly, despite his admiration for Malinowski's work, Parsons subsequently denounced it specifically for its "encyclopedia conception of culture" (1957/1977, 97). According to Parsons's later statements, Malinowski's conception, useful as it was in its day for establishing "a clear distinction between man as a biological organism and man as the creator, bearer, and transmitter of culture," failed to differentiate social systems from cultural systems, wrongly combining "specifically cultural objects . . . in a narrow sense" with material artifacts and technologies, activities (such as custom), and social organization (1957/1977, 85, 87). Given that Parsons's own initial conception of culture was exactly the same as Malinowski's in this respect, however, courses with Malinowski at LSE would hardly have disabused Parsons of the position he adopted at Amherst.

PARSONS AT HEIDELBERG: NEW IDEAS ABOUT CULTURE

While at LSE, Parsons applied at the suggestion of one of his Amherst professors, Otto Manthey-Zorn, for a German exchange fellowship; when he received the award, his sponsors assigned him to the University of Heidelberg. To prepare for this, Parsons spent the summer of 1925 in Vienna taking a German-language course. He then spent the following academic year, commencing in October 1925, in Heidelberg. Afterward he went back to the United States for a one-year instructorship at Amherst. During the following summer, 1927, he returned to Heidelberg to take the oral exams required for the doctor of philosophy (D.Phil.) degree and to complete and defend his dissertation. Combined, the two semesters of study and the follow-up term of degree work constitute Parsons's celebrated "sojourn in Heidelberg" (for details, see Camic 1991, xix–xxiii).

Interpreters of Parsons who take this sojourn as the watershed in Parsons's intellectual development frequently overlook the brevity and interrupted character of the episode. Funded on a one-year fellowship, Parsons, once he decided to write a dissertation, felt the need to work fast, and within four months of his arrival he was already immersed in his thesis,[12] "Der Geist des Kapitalismus bei Sombart und Max Weber," a study that in many ways continued the central intellectual project of Amherst's institutionalist economists (Camic 1991, xxiii–xxx). Where Parsons soon departed from the lessons of Amherst, however, was in his approach to culture. While strongly primed by his college experiences to attend to the domain of culture, the manner in which Parsons conceptualized culture shifted dramatically from the omnibus, loose-knit view of the Americans to the delimited and organic view that surrounded him in Germany.

Educated Americans traveling abroad could hardly avoid contact with the German view even when they were not presensitized to the phenomenon of culture. Since the early nineteenth century, college graduates from the United States had been flocking to Europe for advanced degrees, and more than nine thousand young Americans had preceded Parsons to the universities of Germany, where the combination of state-of-the-art scholarship and easy entry and degree requirements offered strong enticement to American students (Herbst 1965, 1, 8–9). Substantial as it was, this migration paled in comparison with the influx that occurred in the 1920s, as "diplomatic and consular agents, military and naval attachés . . . social workers . . . artists, musicians, and singers . . . sales and financial agents . . . bedraggled fathers and cheery mothers . . . scholars, fellows, researchers [with] the money of foundations . . . [and] bespectacled students, male and female, thin and gaunt, long and short" unleashed what Charles Beard called the great "American invasion of Europe" (Beard 1928, 470; see also Rodgers 1998, 367–91). What was more, while Americans who were alarmed with the conditions of their own country came looking for fresh sources of enlightenment in Europe, many more came for narrowly economic reasons, glutting Central Europe and war-ravaged Germany in particular with American foods, movies, dime stores, machinery, loans, and much more (Rodgers 1998, 370–71, 380; see also Krutch 1928). In reaction to this American invasion, Continental writers responded with an outpouring of popular literature invidiously contrasting Europe and America as an opposition of "culture against mere machine civilization, spirit against materialism, higher against lower desires" (Rodgers 1998, 374; see also Beard 1928). In Weimar Germany, this culture discourse was especially ubiquitous—and by no means confined to the popular publications.

Indeed, according to Norbert Elias's famous analysis of social and philosophical thought in Germany in this era and in the period all the way back to the Enlightenment: "The word through which Germans interpret themselves, which more than any other expresses their pride in their own achievement and their own being, is *Kultur*" (1939/1978, 4). Of course Kultur[13] translates as "culture," but as Elias emphasized in Germany the word connoted a restricted realm contradistinguished from "civilization" (Zivilisation). That culture and civilization were hereby conceptualized in terms of a dichotomy highlights the distinctive German conception of culture in contrast to the view prevalent in the United States in the 1920s. The American omnibus, loose-knit notion of culture (which included "civilization") paralleled the German usage of "civilization"—with the difference that the German usage was not evaluatively neutral but was a way of dismissing the so-called "accomplishments" of the French and the British. Elias explained, the German "concept of 'civilization' refers to a wide variety of facts, . . . to political or economic, religious or technical, moral or social facts, . . . to the level of technology, to the type of manners, to the development of scientific knowledge, to religious ideas and customs" (1939/1978, 3–4). In contrast to this expansive view, "the concept of Kultur delimits," specifically demarcating "religious and philosophical systems," the realm of "intellectual, artistic, and religious facts"; at the same time Kultur organically unifies, comprehending these phenomena all as modalities "in which the individuality of a people expresses itself," its national spirit, its essential values (Elias 1939/1978, 4–5). *Der grosse Brockhaus,* the standard German encyclopedia in this period, captured this delimited, organic conception of culture when it defined Kultur in terms of the "development of [man's] ethical, artistic, and intellectual powers . . . [and] the products of such activity (cultural objects and values)"—adding that "civilization is to culture as the external is to the internal, the artificially constructed to the naturally developed, the mechanical to the organic" (cited by Ringer 1969, 89).

Nor was this conception of culture a viewpoint with low salience, relegated to obscure philological discussions and encyclopedias. To the contrary. As a result of a vast complex of factors, including major demographic, economic, and political changes within Weimar Germany, alterations to the German educational system at all levels, and felt threats from abroad by nefarious intellectual forces like "positivism" and "materialism" (not to mention the postwar invasion of foreign products and technologies), "by the early 1920's, [German academics] were convinced that they were living through a profound crisis, a 'crisis of culture,' of 'learning,' of 'values,' or of the 'spirit,' . . . a crisis of philosophy" (Ringer 1969, 3; Bambach 1995, 14; more generally, see Peukert 1987/1992). Certainly alarm over this situation dates back at least to the late nineteenth century, but by the post–World War I era it reached heightened intensity as members of the professoriate, the traditional cultivators and defenders of Kultur—of philosophy in the largest sense, of intellect and the arts, and of the ethical values that expressed their nation's spirit—came forth with tract after tract showcasing the German conception of culture by means of depictions of the cultural crisis, diagnoses of its causes, and diverse proposals to end the crisis by reinvigorating culture with a new Weltanschauung, an encompassing philosophical understanding, "a new set of values," "a reorientation of men's minds and hearts" (quoting from Ringer 1969, 402, 412; see also Bambach 1995; Kettler and Meja 1995; Loader and Kettler 2002; McClelland 1991; Muller 1987; Scaff 1989,1990, among many sources).

This dramatic movement enveloped all German universities of the 1920s, the University of Heidelberg among them (see Treiber and Sauerland 1995) and enlisted the active participation of all of Parsons's principal teachers at the University: the economists Edgar Salin (Parsons's thesis adviser) and Emil Lederer; the philosopher Karl Jaspers; the Privatdozent Karl Mannheim; and the economist-turned-sociologist Alfred Weber, Max Weber's now aging younger brother (see Ringer 1969; Marianne Weber 1948/1977).[14] Jaspers, for example, joining the debate about the future of culture, laid emphasis on a revival of "Geist"—of spirit "wanting-to-become-whole"—and on education as a process that imparted "ethical norms" and focused on "the inclusive, the whole" (Jaspers in 1923, quoted by Ringer 1969, 87, 395–96).

For his part, Alfred Weber—whose views merit particular note since he taught virtually every member of this group at some point—culture was the realm of symbols, "of the different cultural expressions (religion, philosophy, art)," which "exist as a totality in each historical organism" and embody "the specific quality of the soul that 'dwells' in the various historical organisms and constantly struggles for expression within the compass of their general destiny" (Weber 1921–22/1939, 9, 8, 60; see also Scaff 1990, 88–89). So understood, culture was "demarcate[d] sharply [from] the civilizational process," the sphere of material progress, whose advance was on the brink of imperiling cultural development: "Nothing is more problematic today," wrote Weber in 1923, "than . . . the nature and reality of the intellectual and spiritual fundament of Europe" (Weber 1921–22/1939, 13; and as quoted in Ringer 1969, 243).[15]

How much Parsons read of the works of any particular one of these teachers during his stay in Heidelberg is not known; rarely do his later writings reference their ideas. But it is clear that Parsons soon made their shared conception of culture—that is, the German idea of Kultur—his own. Indeed, so readily has Parsons embraced this conception by the time he returns from Germany that his first publications afterward (portions of his dissertation), much concerned though they are with cultural phenomena, present the delimited German view as so obviously correct that the meaning of "culture" is treated as a given and the term receives no formal definition.

Thus does Parsons slide, with no explanation, from the phrase "different cultural epochs" to the expression "differences between mental attitudes at different times and places" and onto statements about differences with respect to "particular set[s] of values," understood as "ethical values" of "religious origin" (Parsons 1928–29/1991, 3, 9, 27). And Parsons continues in this vein in the period immediately thereafter, not feeling a need to furnish more definitional specificity until, in an encyclopedia article a few years later, he inserts after a reference to "the elements of culture" the following clarification: "—scientific knowledge and techniques, religious, metaphysical, and ethical systems of ideas, and forms of artistic expression" (1934b/1991, 120). Apart from mention here of "scientific knowledge and techniques," this conception corresponds exactly with that of Alfred Weber (and of Elias, who was Alfred Weber's student), while the addition itself fits with other contemporary German formulations where science and technology were included within culture (see Herf 1984).

Elsewhere during this same stage in his career Parsons glosses the realm of culture simply as the "metaphysical theories, theologies, etc.," that ground "ultimate values" (1935b/1991, 238). And although he subjects this view of culture to considerable refinement and elaboration in *The Structure of Social Action,*[16] here, too, Parsons's tendency remains to equate "cultural" phenomena interchangeably with the domain "Geist" or "spirit," "a set of values" or religiously inspired "mental attitudes," and various "value elements" or "normative value ideas" with "close affinity [to] meaning systems such as religious and metaphysical ideas and artistic styles" (1937, 480–81, 511, 449, 487, 763–64). At all events, following his German experiences, Parsons was no longer the young author who, prior to his trip abroad, had accepted the omnibus American conception of culture as also encompassing "customs and usages," "etiquette," "institutional background, and what not." And never again would he return to this encyclopedic view.

Accompanying Parsons's turn to the delimited conception of culture, moreover, was his simultaneous shift away from a loose-knit view and toward an organic view of the relationship among the elements of culture. In the dissertation article that he wrote following his return from Germany, Parsons's awareness and appreciation of the organic alternative is immediately apparent. His discussion of Werner Sombart stresses that a "salient characteristic of [his] thought is his emphasis on the unity of a culture," his conviction that "our culture [is] a whole" (1928–29/1991, 13, 19). Most telling: Parsons expressly *concurs* with this view, save for remarking that Sombart "overshoots the mark" when he treats spiritual factors as rigidly determining patterns of social organization (1928–29/1991, 13, 18). Subsequently Parsons generalizes the point beyond Sombart, characterizing the entire "German historical school" in terms of its "emphasis . . . on the specific totality of a 'culture' and . . . the integration of its economic organization and activities with its religious and ethical values, or more vaguely 'Geist' or spirit" (1935b/1991, 188; see also 1937, 473–99), Moreover, aside from slight caveats that do not bear on the present discussion, Parsons embraces the organic view, writing, for example, that "it is unquestionably true . . . that an important and valid correction to [the atomistic economic theories] could be arrived at by viewing the phenomena concerned from the point of view of cultural totality" (1937, 480). Further, clarifying what he means by this notion, Parsons explains that a culture is a totality both in the sense that its elements cohere in a "system," "an harmonious whole" whose parts exhibit (in varying degrees) "logical fit" or "integration"; and in the sense that this system is (in varying degrees) "common to the members of a community" (1934a/1990, 332–33, 1935a/1991, 241–45; see also 1937, 481–87)—senses commonplace in the German literature on culture and at variance with Parsons's earlier view of a culture as made up of heterogeneous items that societies borrow from each other and accumulate.

CRITICAL REFLECTIONS

In Parsons's conversion to the German conception of culture lies one of the central paradoxes of his intellectual biography. What thrust the German conception so much to the fore at the time of Parsons's sojourn was the widespread conviction within the professoriate that German culture was in crisis. This belief was especially strong in the fields where Parsons's interest lay; as Fritz Ringer puts it, "German social scientists during the 1920s did their scholarly work in an atmosphere of extraordinary tension" and internal division, racked with a "sense of crisis [so] profound that it [reverberated even to discussions of] methods of analysis [and] research results" (1969, 22–28). When German social thinkers, situated in this context, characterized culture as organic and delimited, they were thus knowingly positing a counterfactual, asserting what they felt ought to be the case as a way of coming to intellectual terms with the contrary state of contemporary reality. For them, in other words, "culture" and "crisis" formed a single vocabulary.

But this is not so in any of Parsons's publications in the decade after his return from Germany.[17] Adopting the German notion of culture as delimited and organic, Parsons's writings sever this concept from the accompanying, overarching notion of culture in crisis. In other words, when the relevant German works are placed side by side with Parsons's early publications, the latter reveal a silent elision of a core cluster of ideas—an elision that Parsons nowhere explicitly remarks on or accounts for. Perhaps even more striking, the elided ideas figure centrally in the writings of one of Parsons's principal dissertation subjects, Max Weber himself. To be sure, Weber, who died in 1920, missed the height of the German cultural crisis. Nonetheless, it is useful to consider the views he expressed during earlier phases of the crisis, particularly given the importance that Parsons and his "made in Germany" interpreters assign to his encounter with Max Weber. Furthermore, this component of Weber's work is one that might be expected to have especially drawn notice from the young Parsons, since what attracted him about Weber's work, following his return from the land of Kultur, was (as he emphasized in his translation of *Die protestantische Ethik*) "Weber's grasp of cultural problems" and, indeed, of "*some of the most important aspects of modern culture*" (1930/1958, xi; emphasis added).

However, the hallmark of Weber's writings on culture was, as Lawrence A. Scaff has shown, the thesis that "modernity . . . does not tend toward a new unity" because "the world as we experience it is separated into different, even radically opposed 'orders of life' or 'spheres of value' " (2000, 103, 107). According to Weber, the result of this life experience is that "in the modern situation, [whatever an individual's values happen to be,] there are always other values equally compelling to others, and no single value-sphere that can be foundational [in the face of] an incommensurable and irresolvable battle among opposed ultimate value-standards and world-views" (Scaff 2000, 109). This stark characterization was the message of some of the pivotal sections of Weber's sociology of religion as well as of "Science as a Vocation," where Weber was explicit: "The different value spheres of the world stand in irreconcilable conflict with one another [as so many] different gods struggl[ing] with one another, *now and for all times for come*" (Max Weber 1918/1946, 147–48; emphasis added; for further discussion of this aspect of Weber's thought, see Brubaker 1984; Scaff 1989).

Yet of this central dimension of Weber's analysis of modern culture there is (so far as I have been able to determine) no echo in Parsons. To say this is not to rehearse the stock criticism that Parsons knows only of order, for that is true neither in his writings on society nor on culture (for a review of the various evidence against this stock criticism, see Camic 1989). Indeed, Parsons in his early work is careful to recognize that the system of values that is common to members of a society may call forth "different interpretations" and even "divergent formulations which, hardening into dogmas, become the basis of irreconcilable divisions in the social body, [as in] the religious wars of the post-Reformation period" (1934a/1990, 325–26; see also Camic 1989, 83–85, and the final paragraph). But such statements, few and far between, are always caveats; where Parsons offers them, he does so to qualify another, more basic line of argument (here, to explain what happens when regular institutional controls fail), not to describe inherent features of modern culture (note, Parsons's example pertains to the seventeenth century). Not by the most generous weighting do these statements suggest Parsons's endorsement of—or even his awareness of—Weber's belief in the "*priority* of value-conflict," that is, that it is "the 'fate of our culture,' fragmented and dispersed, [to manifest value-conflicts that] are no longer held in check by a single moral order, [and] instead . . . become more deeply entrenched and intractable" (Scaff 2000, 105, 110; emphasis added).

But insofar as Weber's claims here are empirically warranted—and Scaff (2000), among others, argues convincingly that the condition of contemporary societies powerfully bears out Weber's interpretation of modern culture—Parsons's German sojourn emerges in part as a missed intellectual opportunity.[18] Exposed firsthand to a society deep in the throes of a cultural crisis not only according to the general run of academic and popular opinion but according also to the stated views of his Heidelberg teachers (Alfred Weber, Karl Jaspers, and others), to the voices he would have encountered at gatherings of the local intelligentsia at Marianne Weber's celebrated salon (Weber 1948/1977),[19] and to Max Weber's own writings, Parsons takes from the Germans a conception of culture that theoretically defocalizes the crisis in culture and neglects either to enfold or even to engage some of the main tenets of Weber's acute analysis of this crisis of modern culture. To be clear: What makes this a missed intellectual opportunity is Parsons's own early avowed concern with the "main features" of the "modern" socioeconomic order and, hence, with using Weber as a guide to understanding "some of the most important aspects of modern culture" (Parsons 1937, xxii; 1930/1958, xi; see also Camic 1991). In this sense, then, this observation must be sharply distinguished from previous critiques that have faulted Parsons for overlooking Weber's comparative political sociology and various other features of his work; for Parsons's standard reply to these critiques was that his own intellectual "problem complex" naturally shaped his appropriation of Weber's work and these other features of the Weberian oeuvre fell outside this "problem complex" (on these critiques and Parsons's reply, see Camic 1989, 61–63). (This point is further evidence against the claim that Parsons was made by his reading of Max Weber's work, since it demonstrates that Parsons read selectively, with his own purposes in view.) Plainly, however, the same retort does not apply to Parsons's neglect of Weber's treatment of the crisis in culture because Parsons's early concerns specifically draw him directly toward Weber's work on modern culture.

At this juncture it is instructive to compare Parsons to another future sociologist who came to Germany during the Weimar era, Karl Mannheim. Slightly older, Mannheim arrived in Heidelberg just four years prior to Parsons, in 1921, having departed his native Budapest and embarked on a course of graduate study under the same scholars who would become Parsons's teachers, most notably Alfred Weber and Emil Lederer. Like Parsons, Mannheim participated in the intellectual circle that gathered around Marianne Weber; and, like Parsons, he was quickly attracted to the writings of Max Weber (Loader and Kettler 2002). Unlike Parsons, however, Mannheim reacted to these experiences by immediately registering and making salient the theme of cultural crisis. Indeed, this is the central motif of the letters Mannheim wrote soon after he arrived in Heidelberg in which he described the situation in Germany for a Hungarian audience: that in Heidelberg as throughout Germany, visitors (and permanent residents, too) confront a "confusing maelstrom of spiritual currents," a "crumbling . . . spiritual life," "chaos yawning in the depths of life and the soul," a "multiplicity" of sectarian cultural "isms," and a battle among "many local deities"—this last phrase recalling Weber's words about struggle among "different gods" (Mannheim 1921–22/2001, 87–95). From this depiction it was a short step to the vision of culture that Mannheim inscribed, a few years later, in *Ideology and Utopia,* which characterizes the modern age as a period of pervasive cultural "crisis"—a crisis seen in "the irreconcilability of conflicting conceptions of the world" and the "multiplicity of fundamentally divergent definitions" and "divergent opinions"—and places squarely on the sociological agenda the Weberian problem of the causes and consequences of this "breakdown of the unitary world-view with which the modern era was ushered in" (1929/1936, 33, 8, 6, 13).

That Mannheim's work focalizes and Parsons's defocalizes the pervasive sense of cultural crisis in the aftermath of their stays in Heidelberg in the intellectual thrall of Max Weber further attests to the need to substitute a life-course perspective for the reductionist practice of accenting single episodes when examining the development of a social thinker's ideas. For both Parsons and Mannheim, the formative "episode" is approximately equivalent, a period spent abroad studying the work of Max Weber in the Heidelberg milieu of the mid-1920s; yet the resulting conceptualization of culture differs, as do the intellectual experiences that come before (and after) in the lives of the two theorists.

Even so, when one extends this principle of the life-course perspective to Parsons and does consider what came before in his intellectual biography, doing so only increases the paradox of Parsons's neglect of the crisis thesis as he engaged Weber's work and otherwise appropriated the German concept of culture. This is so because, as shown, Parsons arrived in Germany following an education at Amherst that exposed him to currents of American thought that cast contemporary America as itself in far-reaching cultural crisis—a picture of the era that Parsons affirmed in his Amherst papers when he took up Ogburn's cultural-lag theory and wrote of the "mal-adaptations" present in his society owing to the failure of "morals, literature, philosophy, government, or religion" to keep pace with technological changes. One might anticipate that this American cultural-crisis discourse would have rendered Parsons particularly attuned to the German cultural-crisis discourse. That he seems instead to have tuned out the latter heightens still further the paradox of this phase in his intellectual biography.

What is more, one must rule out what would seem the obvious explanation of this riddle: namely, that once away from America and no longer in the grip of the omnibus, loose-knit American conception of culture, Parsons ceased as well to think of America in the crisis terms that were part and parcel of the American conception. On the contrary—and to ratchet up the paradox a final notch—Parsons remained gravely concerned about the state of American culture *even after his return from Germany*. Direct evidence for this comes from a short article, "Eindrücke eines amerikanischen Austausch-Studenten," previously unknown among Parsons scholars, that Parsons wrote in German shortly after his move to Harvard in the fall of 1927, for an invited collection published in Heidelberg in 1930 under the title *Der Student im Ausland*.[20] (This article, recently discovered by Hans Joas, is translated as a appendix to this chapter.)[21] The article presents a brief comparison of higher education in Germany and the United States and is most consequential for its last paragraph. Here, Parsons baldly lays down two cardinal points. The first is that "America's most pressing problem" is "to build a new culture"! The second is that, "in this regard, [Americans] can learn a lot from Germany," since "we Americans need more philosophy, more of an evaluation of existence as a whole, than we now have." This " 'philosophical interest' . . . is what the Germans have to an extraordinary degree[;] only through a deep struggle with philosophical problems is it possible to build a new culture. . . . And only in this way does a deeper community and communication between people become possible."

The passage is a striking amalgam of elements present both in the American and in the German contexts that Parsons had experienced by late 1927. The call for "deeper community and communication," the supposition that "a new culture" is something deliberately "to build," and, above all, the belief that "America's most pressing problem" is its need for this "new culture"—these were ideas heard over and over in the American popular and social-scientific literature of the 1920s. What is more, the notion that educated Americans "need more philosophy" harked back to the guiding principle of Amherst College in the Meiklejohn era, and it is noteworthy that this view of philosophy was reinforced for Parsons while in Europe in letters sent to him from Manthey-Zorn at Amherst.[22]

Finally, in Parsons's central claim, his assured conviction that the new culture would emerge from "philosophy"—in the expansive sense of the intellectual endeavor that addressed "the deepest questions of life and of science"—lies the German conception of culture. Indeed, the very notion that a new culture will spring forth from the work of those occupied with philosophy is an idea that is scarcely comprehensible if divorced from the contemporary German context, wherein engagement with "philosophical problems" and the development of a "Weltanschauung" were the essence of Kultur. For all this, however, there is in this 1927 passage the same unacknowledged elision: the failure to carry over from the German discussions the idea of culture in crisis, even as Parsons confronts the crisis in American culture. Instead, most ironically, at the historical moment when legions of Germans are decrying theirs as a culture in crisis (and a philosophy in crisis too), Parsons offers up Germany of the 1920s as the model to which contemporary Americans should turn to solve their own "most pressing problem."

At this point, unfortunately, this analysis must stop. Why Parsons took this position; why he missed the loud crisis refrain that was integral to the contemporary German conception of culture; why he saw the land of Kultur so differently than it appeared not only to members of the German professoriate but also to visitors like Mannheim: these are questions that must remain open until scholars learn more about this early phase of Parsons's intellectual career. Lacking answers, I would, however, tentatively offer one simple hypothesis, which future research may or may not support. This is the age-old tendency of the foreign traveler toward romantic totalizing, toward drawing a broad-stroke contrast between "the other," the site of the sojourn, and his or her native country, and then endowing "the other" with the positive evaluative traits that seem lacking at home. This tendency, common in everyday experience, is one that has also affected modern intellectuals, especially those who have gone abroad, as did the young Parsons, who are concerned with problems in their own societies but open to discovering solutions that they might then bring home and propagate (see Herbst 1965; Rodgers 1998). And among American intellectuals visiting Germany in the Weimar period, even those much more well traveled,

Parsons was by no means alone in his perception of the relative cultural condition of the two countries; as late as 1932, for example, Lewis Mumford wrote: "On any realistic scale of values, America is the poor country and Germany is the rich one" (Rodgers 1998, 398).

Add to this tendency certain particulars of Parsons's visit that may have muted his exposure to certain facets of the German discourse about culture: again, the brevity of his sojourn (a point he mentions in the 1927 article); his intense absorption in his dissertation project; his relative inexperience in the German language;[23] the concentration of his stay in a single location, Heidelberg, a scene of the cultural crisis but slightly less so that other intellectual centers in Germany (Steinberg 1973); and, finally, the specific timing of his visit, its occurrence entirely inside the historical window between 1924 to 1929, when economic and political changes in Weimar Germany produced "a short spell of relative calm" (Peukert 1987/1992, 75).[24] None of these particulars held for Karl Mannheim.

Another factor in Parsons's case were the missives of Manthey-Zorn, his main link between Amherst and Germany, warmly "envying" his great Heidelberg adventure and waxing to Parsons "sentimental as I picture you in those magnificent surroundings and in the company I am sure you will find there"[25]—a positive framing of the experience that would have reinforced the omnipresent popular literature which depicted the contrast of Germany versus America as "culture against civilization, spirit against materialism, higher against lower desires" (see p. 249, this volume [Rodgers's quote]). Against this backdrop, it does not surprise that Parsons, as he later put it (1969, 59–60), came "to love and respect" German culture and to view his sojourn as follows:

> At Heidelberg I came into contact with what most would regard as the very best of German culture in the early part of th[e twentieth] century, building on the great traditions of the German universities of the nineteenth century. This, combined with the evidence of German industrial achievement and the high level of general civilization, made a strong positive impression on a young American intellectual who, like many of his contemporaries, had reacted rather strongly against the pervasive and often crude American antipathy to things German that had developed during the war.

Written some thirty years after the event, this statement must be read cautiously, to be sure, although it does correspond closely with the idealized way that Parsons juxtaposed Germany and the United States in 1927, seemingly unaware at the time that, according to observers inside both countries, a cultural crisis existed not only at home but also deep within "the other." Rather than register this similarity, Parsons veers sharply in the opposite direction, as "the other"—represented, in a marked empirical inversion, with its cultural crisis removed—appears to become the living historical source that nourished for the young thinker, disturbed over the cultural maladaptations of his own society, the un-Weberian idea of the possibility of a (more or less) unified modern culture (for further discussion of this aspect of Parsons's thinking, see Schmid 1992).

That Parsons drew this paradoxical lesson from his Heidelberg sojourn in the aftermath of his years at Amherst does not mean that his thinking on this thicket of issues was fixed upon his return from Germany. Such fixity would be unusual from the perspective of a life-course approach, which would direct attention instead to the ways in which Parsons's ideas about culture continued to develop, albeit in interaction with the position he reached as a result of his encounter with the German conception of culture.

These later developments are a topic for future research, but in the meantime, two aspects of Parsons's work in the next phase of this career bear brief notice. First are his publications in the late 1930s and early 1940s on National Socialism, significant because Parsons here eschews his idealized view of Germany in favor of problematizing the country's "contemporary political crisis," in part by tracing it to social and cultural tensions in Weimar Germany (see especially

Parsons 1942a/1993, 1942b/1993, 1942c/1993; see, too, the other writings collected in Gerhardt 1993). In these publications Germany ceases to provide the model for America that Parsons took it for in 1927, a shift that represents a dramatic about-face in his judgment and indicates the need to revise Gerhardt's claim that the early Parsons was "always" engaged in the project to defend (democratic) American society over against the practices of such societies as (authoritarian) Germany (2002, especially 53, 64).[26]

Second, there are Parsons's unpublished writings from the 1930s, which, unlike his published work, explicitly treat the "crisis" of the period, partly in dialogue with yet another crisis discourse that lay still ahead on his path, the work of economists and political scientists at Harvard on the economic and political situation of the Depression (see Camic 1997). Yet, although sprinkled with occasional comments about recurring divisions in contemporary culture, even these writings provoke no turn to the Weberian vision of modern culture. Instead, in these writings, Parsons locates the solution to the societal crisis directly *inside* the realm of culture, as he had come to conceptualize culture while in Heidelberg, in other words, in shared ethical values of religious origins (see Camic forthcoming). In this fundamental respect, Parsons's thinking about culture continued to echo the missed opportunity his German experiences afforded to view modern culture through a different lens.

APPENDIX: "IMPRESSIONS OF AN AMERICAN EXCHANGE STUDENT" BY TALCOTT PARSONS

Written in German in the fall of 1927
Translated by Philip Gorski and Luisa Schwartzman

I was asked to say a little bit about my impressions as an American student in Heidelberg. Of course, at home one must do this verbally quite often, since not many in our "younger generation" have firsthand experience of German universities. But here, at home, where so few are in a position to contradict me, it is not so risky to talk about Germany. In contrast, saying something to the German audience after having spent only three semesters in Germany is somewhat more dubious. But I am writing about impressions, not research findings.

To begin with, I shall say some rudimentary things about the American university system, so as to make the contrast clearer. Some years ago I studied at a small college where there are only about five hundred students (none female) and where there is, for this reason, a communal life (*Gemeinschaftsleben*[27]) that is tighter-knit than that of the German universities. It is referred to as a "liberal college," and no specialized training is offered there. Boys go there when they are around eighteen years old and usually stay for four years, until they complete a bachelor's degree. Different subjects are studied, such as Latin and Greek, mathematics, literature, philosophy, history, macroeconomics (*Nationalökonomie*), natural sciences etc., all within a single faculty. The goal is not to prepare one for a specialized profession, but to acquire a general education (*Bildung*), in order to become an intelligent person and a good citizen. Anyone who wants to be a physician, a lawyer, a priest, or a scholar (and not a great percentage of students fall into this category) has to attend a special institution after college, a "graduate school," which is usually part of one of the large universities, where he will continue studying for at most three years and will receive his specialized education (*Fachbildung*). The organization of the secondary educational system is thus quite different than it is in Germany.

But this is by no means the only difference. In addition to one's actual studies other factors play a very big role: the so-called "outside activities." Sports are the most important of these activities. Each college has teams in several types of sports, which play against other colleges—in football, rowing, hockey, tennis, etc. There is also a newspaper that comes out twice a week and is produced solely by students, and clubs of the most different types, as well as a student government that oversees the financing of all these "activities" and also of various disciplinary issues. Having a position of leadership in any of these things imparts a considerable reputation in the eyes of one's fellow students. And it would be no exaggeration to say that the average student, especially in the early years, would much rather distinguish himself in football than in scholarship (*Wissenschaft*). This also obtains in colleges affiliated with large universities, such as Harvard or Columbia, for example.

In contrast, German university life is something completely different. Except within the fraternity system, college is, for the German student, a time for struggling with himself and with scientific work. He is very much wrapped up in himself, surrounded by a small circle of friends, and what everyone else does is of no concern to him. He has complete freedom until he is called to answer for himself in his doctoral examinations. At that point he must give an accounting for what he has done, unlike the American student, who is continually called to account through frequent exams.

This is the famous individualism of German university life. And it is worth noting that this individualism thrives in a country where economic and social individualism has never sunk roots. But the German student body is a social aristocracy, and these attitudes are only present within this circle. Studying is specifically for cultural (*geistige*) and academic purposes, and does not have much connection with real life (*das aüssere Leben*).

America, by contrast, is the country of societal individualism and atomism, at least in Europeans eyes. So where does this collectivism of the universities come from, where individuals' whole lives are thoroughly regulated and public opinion strongly impels each student to do everything that others do and to seek his rewards in the esteem of fellow students? No doubt, this socialization (*Bildung*) serves a very important purpose, that of cultivating the "communal" elements in our culture. The student community encourages the development (*Bildung*) of a gentlemanly type, who can eventually become part of a cultivated aristocracy (*Aristokratie der Bildung*)—cultivated more in the sense of how he interacts with others than of some specific technical knowledge (*Fachwissen*). The entire emphasis here is on community, including the smallest details of life, of clothing, manners, speech.

For those well acquainted with American history, it is not difficult to guess where this element of community comes from. In early colonial days, Puritanism was the dominant cultural phenomenon (*Kulturerscheinung*) in New England. And this culture (*Kultur*) consisted mainly of religious communities. The Puritans have always been very zealous pedagogues, and were the founders, and for a long time the heads, of most American colleges. And I believe that it is in this form that the communal feeling of the Puritans was absorbed into the broader American life. And one still senses a certain religious seriousness in this academic community.

The German universities have something similar to this, more than any other country in continental Europe, in their fraternity system. This is probably the reason why groups of American students who have visited German universities, under the guidance of the "German Students," got such a favorable and congenial impression of them. But the other German students, who play a much greater role in scholarship, lack this education in communal life, for interacting with people. This is probably why the typical American senses in Germans a certain brusqueness, formality of manner, and self-enclosedness. Such judgments are not to be taken too seriously, but I nevertheless believe that this state of affairs has deep causes in the difference between these two educational systems.

Where the role of science is concerned, one cannot directly compare a "liberal college" with a German university. Rather, one must also include "graduate school." Still, one can say that students in Germany generally attain a stronger interest in scientific matters earlier on, and especially when one takes the universities of the American West into account, one finds among the Germans a much larger proportion who display a real scientific interest.

One can obtain an excellent advanced education in the better American "graduate schools," where deeper interest is a prerequisite for entry. Otherwise one goes straight from the B.A. to practical life (usually business). But even in "graduate school" there is much more supervision than in German universities. One must attend more required courses and pass examinations.

But what American students most lack, even the most advanced ones, is the "philosophical interest," the desire to think about the deepest questions of life and of science and to attain a worldview (*Weltanschauung*) that is really one's own. And that is what the Germans have to an extraordinary degree. The downside of this is, perhaps, that the German becomes too immersed in himself; but we Americans need more philosophy, more of an evaluation of existence as a whole, than we have now. Because only through deep struggle with philosophical problems is it possible to build a new culture—America's most pressing problem. And only in this way does a deeper community and communication between people become possible. In this regard, I think that we can learn a lot from Germany, and that getting to know German university life through American students could be of the highest importance.

NOTES

1. Howard Brick (1993) also suggests a less reductive view of Parsons's Amherst experiences, tracing the interplay between the influences Parsons encountered at home and in college. But Brick then stops the developmental process, claiming that "in the rough, . . . Parsons's mature perspective was already apparent . . . in his college papers" (1993, 368). As I will show, this claim is incorrect with respect to Parsons's views on culture.
2. In a variation both on this and the "made in the nursery" interpretations, William Buxton and David Rehorick (2001) emphasize the importance of Parsons's encounter with Weber, but argue further that "Max Weber captured [Parsons's] interest by virtue of his spiritual orientation, an outlook that resonated with his own Calvinist background" (2001, 31; see also Buxton 1985).
3. Elsewhere, Uta Gerhardt (1993) inclines more to the view that Parsons's Amherst education exerted a "lifelong" influence on his ideas (1993, 4; see also Gerhardt 2002, 63–64). To my knowledge, she nowhere harmonizes this view with her Weber-centric one, nor attempts to integrate the two by means of a developmental perspective.
4. The reductive approach also overlooks the factors that subsequently *maintained* Parsons's interest in (certain aspects of) Weber's work. For some suggestive remarks on this issue, see Buxton and Rehorick (2001).
5. For an application of this perspective to understanding the thematic shifts in Parsons's early work, see Charles Camic (1991), a study that complements the present chapter. This previous study does not treat the development of Parsons's conceptualization of culture, just as the present study brackets the larger thematic shifts in his early work. A fuller analysis would, of course, combine the two focuses.
6. In the literature on Parsons, Alvin W. Gouldner's (1970) effort to explain the intellectual concerns of the early Parsons by reference to the economic and political situation of the United States during the Depression is the best-known among many accounts of this type.
7. Though atomistic in character, this conception nonetheless generally assumed the presence of a certain external compatibility among cultural elements that made contact with one another (see Eubank 1932, 350–54).
8. This statement contrasts with the claim that Parsons's views were formed "in the nursery."
9. Evidence for this statement is contained in the document "Syllabus of Topics and Readings for Course in Social and Economic Institutions in Amherst," from the Amherst College Archives.
10. In step with Meiklejohn, Hamilton decried his as an age of narrow intellectual specialization. Lecturing his contemporaries for "looking at things too narrowly," he lamented, "We manifested a contempt for philosophy and

general theory. We encouraged specialization, but overlooked the broad and general trying which should underlie it" (1925, 7).

11. In doing so, Malinowski no longer held, however, to the loose-knit view of the relation among the elements of culture, but emphasized instead their functional interrelation. This change of perspective is something that Parsons later identified as central to Malinowski's intellectual achievement, praising his principle of "the interconnectedness of all the element of a . . . culture" (1957/1977, 84). Insofar as Malinowski's teachings registered on Parsons in the same way during his time at LSE, they may well have moved him closer to the German position on the issue prior to his arrival in Heidelberg.
12. Letter of Otto Manthey-Zorn to Parsons, February 21, 1926. Talcott Parsons Papers, Harvard University Archives.
13. Hereafter, foreign words will not be italicized in this chapter as per Russell Sage Foundation house style.
14. The secondary literature is inconsistent on whether or not Parsons studied with Heinrich Rickert. The examining committee for Parsons's thesis consisted of Salin, Jaspers, Alfred Weber, and the historian Willy Andreas, so Rickert was not involved at this level. He was, however, still a member of the Heidelberg faculty, and on Parsons's copy of the Heidelberg Catalogue for 1925–26 he marked off Rickert's course "Weltanschauungslehre" (see copy of catalogue in Talcott Parsons Papers. Heidelberg catalogue, 1925–26. Box 2, HUG(FP) 42.8.2. Harvard University Archives). Parsons's later recollections of his Heidelberg years make no mention, however, of taking this course or otherwise studying with Rickert.
15. Discussions among this group of Heidelberg faculty members echoed among their students, the list of whom includes, during years that overlap Parsons's stay in Heidelberg, such future luminaries as Hannah Arendt, Norbert Elias, Erich Fromm, Hans Gerth, and Hans Speier (see Glucksmann 1977; Gerth 2002). Since multiple connections formed among these figures as they moved through many of the same formal and informal meeting places as Parsons did, it is easy to imagine how his path would have intersected theirs. That this actually occurred has yet to be established, however. (For an abstract comparison of Parsons and Elias, see Wearne 2001).
16. In *The Structure of Social Action* Parsons attempts to fold into the German view of culture Durkheimian ideas about norms and their regulatory effect on human conduct, on the one hand, and Alfred North Whitehead's notion of culture as the realm of "eternal objects," on the other hand (see Camic 1989).
17. Nor was this the case, with rare exceptions, at subsequent stages of his intellectual career, despite many later changes in his conceptualization of culture (see Schmid 1992).
18. I say "in part" here because in foccusing on Parsons's view of culture this chapter is dealing with only one facet of his thinking; with regard to other facets, there is much that he draws from his German sojourn (see Camic 1991; Gerhardt 1993; Buxton and Rehorick 2001).
19. On Parsons's attendance at Marianne Weber's salon, see Parsons (1965, 1980).
20. The full title of the collection was *Der Student im Ausland: Heidelberger Berichte zum Universitätsleben der Gegenwart,* edited by Henry Goverts and Elfriede Hober.
21. Although an undated typescript of the article has long existed in the Talcott Parsons Papers, Harvard University Archives, the discovery of the dated published version makes it possible to locate the paper in proper temporal relation to Parsons's other work. I am thankful to Hans Joas for finding the article in its German source, forwarding it to me, and allowing me to include it in this chapter. I am also grateful to Philip Gorski and Luisa Schwartzman for translating the article into English.
22. Letters of Otto Manthey-Zorn to Parsons, January 2, 1925, January 7, 1925, and February 21, 1926 (Talcott Parsons Papers, Harvard University Archives).
23. In this regard, the objections that manuscript reviewers raised a few years later to early versions of Parsons's translation from German to English of *The Protestant Ethic and the Spirit of Capitalism* bear notice (see Camic 1991, xxvii).
24. Detlev Peukert's fuller statement (1987/1992, 4) of the point is as follows:

> Although stability arrived in 1924, contemporaries were not prepared to regard it as more than "relative." Certainly, it is only in comparison with the several near-fatal crises of the early post-war period, and then with the world economic crisis at the end of the decade, that the years 1924–9 can be termed "stable." The cracks in the fabric of the [German] Republic remained fully visible, an outward sign of hidden weaknesses that might prove fatal when the structure was next subjected to severe strain.

25. Letter of Otto Manthey-Zorn to Parsons, September 27, 1925 (Talcott Parsons Papers, Harvard University Archives).
26. Indicated as well is the need to revise Brick's (1993, 369–73) account of Parsons's "agenda of 1927."
27. Foreign words only are italicized in the appendix of this chapter as it is a translation.

REFERENCES

Alexander, Jeffrey C. 1983. *Theoretical Logic in Sociology*. Volume 4, *The Modern Reconstruction of Classical Thought: Talcott Parsons.* Berkeley: University of California Press.

Bambach, Charles R. 1995. *Heidegger, Dilthey, and the Crisis of Historicism.* Ithaca: Cornell University Press.

Barber, Bernard. 1949. "Biographical Sketch." In *Essays in Sociological Theory, Pure and Applied,* by Talcott Parsons. Glencoe, Ill.: Free Press.

Beard, Charles A. 1928. "The American Invasion of Europe." *Harper's Monthly Magazine* 68: 470–79.

Brick, Howard. 1993. "The Reformist Dimension of Talcott Parsons's Early Social Theory." In *The Culture of the Market,* edited by Thomas L. Haskell and Richard F. Teichgraeber III. Cambridge: Cambridge University Press.

Brubaker, Rogers. 1984. *The Limits of Rationality.* London: Allen & Unwin.

Buxton, William. 1985. *Talcott Parsons and the Capitalist Nation State.* Toronto: University of Toronto Press.

Buxton, William J., and David Rehorick. 2001. "The Place of Max Weber in the Post-*Structure* Writings of Talcott Parsons." In *Talcott Parsons Today: His Theory and Legacy in Contemporary Sociology,* edited by A. Javier Treviño. Boulder: Rowman & Littlefield.

Camic, Charles. 1983. "The Enlightenment and Its Environment: A Cautionary Tale." *Knowledge and Society* 4: 143–72.

———. 1989. "*Structure* After 50 Years." *American Journal of Sociology* 95(1): 38–107.

———. 1991. "Talcott Parsons Before *The Structure of Social Action.*" In *Talcott Parsons: The Early Essays,* edited by Charles Camic. Chicago: University of Chicago Press.

———. 1992. "Reputation and Predecessor Selection: Parsons and the Institutionalists." *American Sociological Review* 57(4): 421–45.

———. 1997. "The Political Dimension of Parsons's Early Work." Paper presented at Conference on Talcott Parsons. Heidelberg (June).

———. Forthcoming. "Parsons as Political Thinker."

Cravens, Hamilton. 1978. *The Triumph of Evolution.* Philadelphia: University of Pennsylvania Press.

Crosnoe, Robert. 2000. "Friendships in Childhood and Adolescence: The Life Course and New Directions." *Social Psychology Quarterly* 63(4): 377–91.

Curti, Merle. 1980. *Human Nature in American Thought.* Madison: University of Wisconsin Press.

Cutler, Addison T., and Talcott Parsons. 1923/1991. In *Talcott Parsons: The Early Essays,* edited by Charles Camic. Chicago: University of Chicago Press.

Elias, Norbert. 1939/1978. *The Civilizing Process.* Oxford: Blackwell.

Eubank, Earle Edward. 1932. *The Concepts of Sociology.* Boston: D. C. Heath.

Geertz, Clifford. 1973. *The Interpretation of Cultures.* New York: Basic Books.

Gerhardt, Uta. 1993. "Talcott Parsons's Sociology of National Socialism." In *Talcott Parsons on National Socialism,* edited by Uta Gerhardt. New York: Aldine de Gruyter.

———. 2002. *Talcott Parsons: An Intellectual Biography.* Cambridge: Cambridge University Press.

Gerth, Nobuko. 2002. *"Between Two Worlds": Hans Gerth, eine Biografie, 1908–1978.* Opladen: Leske & Budrich.

Glucksmann, Alfred. 1977. "Norbert Elias on his Eightieth Birthday." In *Human Figurations,* edited by Peter R. Gleichmann, Johan Gouldblom, and Hermann Korte. Amsterdam: Amsterdams Sociologisch Tijdschrift.

Gouldner, Alvin W. 1970. *The Coming Crisis of Western Sociology.* New York: Basic Books.

Griswold, Wendy. 1994. *Cultures and Societies in a Changing World.* Thousand Oaks, Calif.: Pine Forge.

Hamilton, Peter. 1983. *Talcott Parsons.* London: Tavistock.

Hamilton, Walton H. 1925. *Current Economic Problems.* 3rd edition. Chicago: University of Chicago Press.

Herbst, Jürgen. 1965. *The German Historical School in American Scholarship.* Ithaca: Cornell University Press.

Herf, Jeffrey. 1984. *Reactionary Modernism: Technology, Culture, and Politics in Weimar and the Third Reich.* Cambridge: Cambridge University Press.

Kerckhoff, Alan C. 1993. *Diverging Pathways: Social Structure and Career Definitions.* New York: Cambridge University Press.

Kettler, David, and Volker Meja. 1995. *Karl Mannheim and the Crisis of Liberalism.* New Brunswick, N.J.: Transaction.

Krutch, Joseph Wood. 1928. "Berlin Goes American." *The Nation* 126: 564–66.

Levine, Donald N. 1986. "The Forms and Functions of Social Knowledge." In *Metatheory in Social Science,* edited by Donald W. Fiske and Richard A. Shweder. Chicago: University of Chicago Press.

Loader, Colin, and David Kettler. 2002. *Karl Mannheim's Sociology as Political Education.* New Brunswick, N.J.: Transaction.

Malinowski, Bronislaw. 1930. "Culture." In *Encyclopedia of the Social Sciences,* edited by Edwin Seligman. Volume 4. New York: Macmillan.

Mannheim, Karl. 1921–22/2001. "Heidelberg Letters: Soul and Culture in Germany." *Karl Mannheim: Sociology as Political Education.* New Brunswick, N.J.: Transaction.

———. 1929/1936. *Ideology and Utopia.* New York: Harcourt.

Martel, Martin U. 1979. "Parsons, Talcott." In *International Encyclopedia of the Social Sciences,* edited by David L. Sills. Volume 18, *Biographical Supplement.* New York: Macmillan.

McClelland, Charles E. 1991. *The German Experience of Professionalization.* Cambridge: Cambridge University Press.

Muller, Jerry Z. 1987. *The Other God That Failed: Hans Freyer and the Deradicalization of German Conservatism.* Princeton: Princeton University Press.

Nielson, Jens Kaalhauge. 1996. "Beyond the Myth of 'Radical Breaks' in Talcott Parsons's Theory: An Analysis of the Amherst Papers." *American Sociologist* 27(4): 48–61.

———. 2001. "Are There Cultural Limits to Inclusion? An Analysis of the Relation Between Culture and Social Evolution in Talcott Parsons's Theory." In *Parsons' "The Structure of Social Action" and Contemporary Debates,* edited by Gabriele Pollini and Giuseppe Sciortino. Trento: FrancoAngeli.

Ogburn, William Fielding. 1922. *Social Change, with Respect to Culture and Original Nature.* New York: B. W. Huebsch.

Parsons, Talcott. 1922. "The Theory of Human Behavior in Its Individual and Social Aspects." Talcott Parsons Papers. Parsons's Undergraduate Papers, ca. 1923. Box 2, HUG(FP) 42.8.2. Harvard University Archives.

———. 1923. "A Behavioristic Conception of the Nature of Morals." Talcott Parsons Papers. Box 2, HUG(FP) 42.8.2. Harvard University Archives.

———. 1928–29/1991. " 'Capitalism' in Recent German Literature: Sombart and Weber." In *Talcott Parsons: The Early Essays,* edited by Charles Camic. Chicago: University of Chicago Press.

———. 1930/1958. "Translator's Preface" to *The Protestant Ethic and the Spirit of Capitalism,* by Max Weber. Translated by Talcott Parsons. New York: Scribner's.

———. 1934a/1990. "Prolegomena to a Theory of Social Institutions." *American Sociological Review* 55(3): 319–33.

———. 1934b/1991. "Society." In *Talcott Parsons: The Early Essays,* edited by Charles Camic. Chicago: University of Chicago Press.

———. 1935a/1991. "The Place of Ultimate Values in Sociological Theory." In *Talcott Parsons: The Early Essays,* edited by Charles Camic. Chicago: University of Chicago Press.

———. 1935b/1991. "Sociological Elements in Economic Thought." In *Talcott Parsons: The Early Essays,* edited by Charles Camic. Chicago: University of Chicago Press.

———. 1937. *The Structure of Social Action.* New York: Free Press.

———. 1942a/1993. "Democracy and Social Structure in Pre-Nazi Germany." In *Talcott Parsons on National Socialism,* edited by Uta Gerhardt. New York: Aldine de Gruyter.

———. 1942b/1993. "Max Weber and the Contemporary Political Crisis." In *Talcott Parsons on National Socialism,* edited by Uta Gerhardt. New York: Aldine de Gruyter.

———. 1942c/1993. "National Socialism and the German People." In *Talcott Parsons on National Socialism,* edited by Uta Gerhardt. New York: Aldine de Gruyter.

———. 1957/1977. "Malinowski and the Theory of Social Systems." In *Social Systems and the Evolution of Action Theory,* by Talcott Parsons. New York: Free Press.

———. 1959. "A Short Account of My Intellectual Development." *Alpha Kappa Deltan* 29: 3–12.

———. 1965/1967. "Evaluation and Objectivity in Social Science: An Interpretation of Max Weber's Contribution." *Sociological Theory and Modern Society,* by Talcott Parsons. New York: Free Press.

———. 1969. "Author's Introduction" to *Politics and Social Structure,* by Talcott Parsons. New York: Free Press.

———. 1970. "On Building Social Systems Theory: A Personal History." *Daedalus* 99(4): 826–81.

———. 1980. "The Circumstances of My Encounter with Max Weber." In *Sociological Traditions from Generation to Generation,* edited by Robert K. Merton and Matilda White Riley. Norwood, N.J.: Ablex.

Pells, Richard H. 1973. *Radical Visions and American Dreams.* Middletown, Conn.: Wesleyan University Press.

Peukert, Detlev J. K. 1987/1992. *The Weimar Republic: The Crisis of Classical Modernity.* New York: Hill & Wang.

Ringer, Fritz K. 1969. *The Decline of the German Mandarins.* Cambridge, Mass.: Harvard University Press.

Rocher, Guy. 1975. *Talcott Parsons and American Sociology.* New York: Barnes & Noble.

Rodgers, Daniel T. 1998. *Atlantic Crossings: Social Politics in a Progressive Age.* Cambridge, Mass.: Harvard University Press.

Scaff, Lawrence A. 1989. *Fleeing the Iron Cage.* Berkeley: University of California Press.

———. 1990. "Modernity and the Tasks of a Sociology of Culture." *History of the Human Sciences* 3: 85–100.

———. 2000. "Weber on the Cultural Situation of the Modern Age." In *The Cambridge Companion to Weber,* edited by Steven Turner. Cambridge: Cambridge University Press.

Schlesinger, Arthur M., Jr. 2000. *A Life in the 20th Century.* Boston: Houghton Mifflin.

Schmid, Michael. 1992. "The Concept of Culture and Its Place within a Theory of Social Action: A Critique of Talcott Parsons's Theory of Culture." In *Theory of Culture,* edited by Richard Münch and Neil J. Smelser. Berkeley: University of California Press.

Steinberg, Michael Stephen. 1973. *Sabers and Brown Shirts: The German Students' Path to National Socialism, 1918–1935.* Chicago: University of Chicago Press.

Susman, Warren I. 1984. *Culture as History: The Transformation of American Society in the Twentieth Century.* New York: Pantheon.

Swidler, Ann. 1986. "Culture in Action: Symbols and Strategies." *American Sociological Review* 51(2): 273–86.

———. 2001. *Talk of Love: How Culture Matters.* Chicago: University of Chicago Press.

Tiryakian, Edward A. 1975. "Neither Marx nor Durkheim . . . Perhaps Weber." *American Journal of Sociology* 81(1): 1–33.

Treiber, Hubert, and Karol Sauerland, eds. 1995. *Heidelberg im Schnittpunkt intellektueller Kreise.* Opladen: Westdeutscher Verlag.

Treviño, A. Javier. 2001. "The Theory and Legacy of Talcott Parsons." Introduction to *Talcott Parsons Today: His Theory and Legacy in Contemporary Sociology,* edited by A. Javier Treviño. Boulder: Rowman & Littlefield.

Turner, Bryan S. 1996. "Talcott Parsons on Economic and Social Theory: The Relevance of the Amherst Term Papers." *American Sociologist* 27(4): 41–47.

Vidich, Arthur J., and Stanford M. Lyman. 1985. *American Sociology: Worldly Rejections of Religion and Their Directions.* New Haven: Yale University Press.

Wearne, Bruce C. 1989. *The Theory and Scholarship of Talcott Parsons to 1951.* Cambridge: Cambridge University Press.

———. 2001. "Elias and Parsons: Two Transformations of the Problem-Historical Method." In *Talcott Parsons Today: His Theory and Legacy in Contemporary Sociology,* edited by A. Javier Treviño. Boulder: Rowman & Littlefield.

Weber, Alfred. 1920–21/1939. *Fundamentals of Culture-Sociology.* New York: Works Progress Administration.

Weber, Marianne. 1948/1977. "Academic Conviviality." *Minerva* 15: 214–44.

Weber, Max. 1918/1946. "Science as a Vocation." In *From Max Weber: Essays in Sociology,* edited by Hans H. Gerth and C. Wright Mills. New York: Oxford University Press.

Part IV

The Human Condition

Chapter 13

Parsons and the Human Condition

Edward A. Tiryakian

> We conceive the human condition as a version of whatever universe may in some sense be knowable and which is quite specifically and self-consciously formulated and organized from the perspective of its significance to human beings and indeed relatively contemporary ones.
>
> —Talcott Parsons (1978a, 382–83), "A Paradigm of the Human Condition"

> It is little wonder that Parsons's oeuvre constitutes not only a general theory for sociology; it is, more accurately, a general theory for the social sciences and indeed, for the human condition.
>
> —A. Javier Treviño (2001, xxi), *Talcott Parsons Today: His Theory and Legacy in Contemporary Sociology*

"A Paradigm of the Human Condition" is an eighty-one-page essay that concludes the last volume of essays published by Talcott Parsons in his lifetime, *Action Theory and the Human Condition* (1978b).[1] One of the longest of the essays he published and the capstone of his theorizing ventures in the course of seven decades, it is also one of the least recognized and cited. This may stem from its complexity and the heterogeneity of its ingredients, or perhaps because the central theme smacks too much of "philosophy," which most sociological training leaves us unprepared to tackle. In any case, "A Paradigm of the Human Condition" has received very little attention from the larger sociological profession, both admirers and critics, certainly in comparison to the "early" essay collection *The Structure of Social Action,* or even the "middle" one, *The Social System,* or even the "later" ones, *The American University* and *The System of Modern Societies.* Outside of his Pennsylvania collaborators to whom he dedicated the volume *Action Theory and the Human Condition*—Harold Bershady, Willy de Craemer, Renée Fox, and Victor Lidz—the major theorist who has sat up to take serious but critical notice of "A Paradigm of the Human Condition" is Jürgen Habermas (1981/1989, 250–56); more "sympathetic" theorists such as Jeffrey C. Alexander (1983), Martin Martel (1979), and Richard Münch (1987, 1994) give the essay at best glancing attention.

The piece comes at the end of a long journey, and in some key respects retraces major steps taken in Parsons's theorizing about action systems. Yet it is also clear from both the preface to the volume as a whole and the essay's conclusion that it is intended less as a retrospective than as a prospective, pushing further the frontiers of theorizing "beyond even the general system of action to work out something at a still more general level—namely, that which is here called the human condition" (Parsons 1978b, x).

It is hard to gauge where Parsons might have gone in further elaboration of the paradigm, but as it stands, it is a work of great complexity, akin to the late quartets of Beethoven compared to the earlier ones. "A Paradigm of the Human Condition" should be treated not as a work in sociological theorizing (in the sense of theorizing about aspects of the social) but as a very distinct sort of metatheory.[2] At least that is how I view a piece elaborating a conceptual frame of reference that seeks to bring together the major structures and dimensions of the human condition in terms of a "big picture" that extends beyond the conventional boundaries of the behavioral sciences.

That is indeed a daunting task, even if or perhaps precisely because "the human condition" is such a generalized object of reflection cross-culturally and across the ages that at one level it would appear to be already suffused with "amateur" formulations, variations on the themes "Who are we? What are we doing here? What is the good life?" And few social scientists seem to have ventured beyond the confines of their disciplines to map explicitly a framework for studying the human condition that would be heuristic in linking different domains of inquiry.

Throughout his career Parsons was strongly motivated to integrate knowledge while advancing sociological theorizing. In the earlier *Structure of Social Action* (1937) he sought to integrate the theories of Alfred Marshall, Vilfredo Pareto, Émile Durkheim, and Max Weber in a broader analytical framework of social action. In his middle period in *Toward a General Theory of Action* (Parsons and Shils 1951/2001) he went further in the theoretical integration of analytical components of action systems: personality, culture, society. He continuously modified, refined, and added to his framework, linking it with what he saw as important relevant models such as cybernetics and modern genetics that added pieces to the overall cognitive puzzle.

At the core of his theorizing was the elaboration of the four-function paradigm into an elaborate taxonomy whose purpose was to answer the question of ordering: What are the basic processes involved in a democratic society that tend to maintain the identity and vitality of the system for its actors?[3] The paradigm had in preceding modifications evolved in a more differentiated form, with each sector or subsystem of the AGIL schema itself capable of being framed by the paradigm to provide greater functional specification of sixteen cells in all. Along the way, what had become integral to the analysis was formulating a *dynamic* aspect of the paradigm, viewing the sectors (and subsectors) of action as being interrelated and interdependent by symbolic media of interchange (Martel 1979; Lidz 2001). Prototypical of these media, Parsons posited, was money, which was based in the economy. For most observers, by the end of the 1960s the paradigm had apparently completed its mission, for better or worse, with perhaps some fine-tuning such as elaborating and changing the names of some of the sectors and processes. Even Parsons's subsequent writings on the evolution of modern societies (1966, 1971), which are important additions to modernization analysis and to the treatment of societal change, did not lead to new theorizing directions for the paradigm.[4] One might have thought that the presentation Parsons made at an important conference of theorists in 1968 (Parsons 1970) would turn out to be the terminus of his general theorizing.

Recall that at the beginning of the 1970s Parsons's public visibility in the sociological profession waned considerably, his functional analysis denounced as fatally flawed by critics on the left such as Alvin Gouldner and Immanuel Wallerstein and on the right such as George Homans and James Coleman. However, far from being the end, it would appear in retrospect that the last decade of his life spent in "exile" from Harvard was instead a sort of "latency stage" for a new vigorous formulation of the four-function paradigm, one that significantly amplified the dimensions of the scheme beyond dealing with action systems. This elaboration exhibited an important new feature, the conceptualization of the "telic system," which had emerged in the third part of the volume dealing with the sociology of religion and becomes more greatly elaborated in "A Paradigm of the Human Condition."

Throughout his career, Parsons had always sought and benefited from interaction with colleagues and students. During the 1970s he was involved with a faculty seminar organized at the

University of Pennsylvania that led to a new burst of collaborative activity, which for Parsons culminated in a revised draft of a theoretical statement published as "A Paradigm of the Human Condition."[5] To do justice to the human condition was, I would propose, an ultimate challenge for a general theorist who prided himself on formally linking major sectors and major intellectual influences in a broad cognitive tapestry. I cannot prove this but I do think that integrating fields of knowledge was indeed an important motivation for Parsons, perhaps in keeping with Comte's vision of "positive philosophy" providing an integrative evolutionary framework for the unity of knowledge.

Did he succeed? Judging by his last words in the essay, Parsons might well be the first to admit to the tentativeness of "A Paradigm of the Human Condition," despite the fact that he found the effort of metatheorizing quite promising.[6] It is not simple to pass judgment on what is ultimately an epistemological question of judging the fit between Parsons's paradigmatic representation of the human condition and the evidence he adduces. In the absence of a moot court to hear opinions on this matter, what I propose to do in this essay, standing truly on the shoulders of a giant, is threefold.

First, I outline a brief exposition of the main structures of "A Paradigm of the Human Condition," situating this magisterial essay in the development of Parsons's theorizing—it is, in a sense, the omega of his theory of action. A systematic exegesis and explication of this essay would require the same intense effort as, say, Norman Kemp Smith's masterful unpacking of Kant's *Critique of Pure Reason* (Smith 1930).[7] But such a labor of love might not have the optimal result intended by Parsons himself on this occasion. I see Parsons's intellectual restlessness as challenging us to situate and update his last testament.

Second, to gauge better its scope and thrust, it may be informative to compare it with a peer group of some other modern formulations of the human condition, whose authors are found predominantly in the ranks of social scientists. As an echo of the convergence among major theorists that Parsons noted in *The Structure of Social Action,* I attempt to link "A Paradigm of the Human Condition" with a major contemporary British theorist of the human condition, Margaret Archer, who herself seems unaware of Parsons's essay and of his late thinking on the subject.

Finally I venture some observations on taking the paradigm on another leg in its intellectual journey. This will be in the nature of two steps backward and one step forward, as I draw attention first to the original phenomenological status of action laid out quite clearly in *The Structure of Social Action* and then discuss how it was reactivated in some rather amazing passages in "A Paradigm of the Human Condition" which show that the early phenomenological stimulus Parsons received with Karl Jaspers at Heidelberg had not worn off half a century later.

THE STRUCTURE OF THE PARADIGM

"A Paradigm of the Human Condition" has seven sections. In the first Parsons outlines how the core interest of theorizing the human condition relates to previous materials he dealt with in analyzing what he termed the "general system of action." He begins by laying out the core concern of conceptualizing systematically how the system of action, central to his earlier stages of theorizing, relates to other systems of the human condition, two of which may be taken as internal, from an anthropocentric perspective, and two as external. The action subsystem, reflecting the decisive influence of Weber's definition of social action, had been of long-standing theoretical interest to Parsons and was at the base of the initial formulations of the AGIL paradigm as one of the two internal subsystems. Parsons brings in a first external system, which for this essay would be termed the "human organic system" (later he renamed it). The nexus of the organic to the social, he reminds us, was of equally long-standing interest to him, extending back to his participation in a famous Harvard faculty seminar led by the physiologist Lawrence J. Henderson, a figure he repeatedly cited in various essays, including the present one.[8] Living organisms do not function in a vacuum but in a physical world,[9] the other external system in the human condition. As noted earlier, Parsons takes our *empirical* knowledge to have three systems–the human organic, the action system (the system of social relationships and institutions), and the physical world. These can be known within a positivistic frame of reference. However, this does not exhaust the subjective experience we have of the world, for there is also a component of the human condition that is the "telic system." Understand by that what human beings have grasped to lie as real beyond empirical knowledge—the transcendental realm, which of course has cultural variations.

The action frame of reference would be developed, refined, and augmented by Parsons in the years and major works that followed.

But Parsons ventures an important second "internal" system, the "telic system." Where does this come from? It arises in part from numerous discussions with Robert Bellah, but Parsons also makes reference to the Harvard zoologist Ernst Mayr, who introduced the term "teleonymy" for the goal-striving property of organisms. I venture that Parsons used Mayr's "telic" to legitimate what he also considered a significant component of the human condition that a strictly empiricist standpoint would question, namely the transcendental, to which Kant had accorded a residual status as the "noumenal." Parsons unequivocally states (1978a, 356) that the telic has "especially to do with religion" and the "reality of the nonempirical world": "With full recognition of the philosophical difficulties of defining the nature of that reality we wish to affirm our sharing the age-old belief in its existence."[10]

In the second section Parsons outlines a new venture at hand, namely to interrelate the physical, the organic, the telic (or "transempirical") to the action system. The conceptualization of the telic is the springboard for conceptualizing the human condition; to do this he draws heavily on the familiar four-functional-categories framework, AGIL. Parsons's initial presentation of the general paradigm of the human condition is shown in figure 13.1.

Parsons reiterates that the paradigm presents categories of the human condition is terms of their *meanings* or, rather, the meanings of their referents to human beings. He is attempting the construction of scientific theory of a meaningful whole (1978a, 362). He elaborates the justifi-

FIGURE 13.1 *General Paradigm of the Human Condition*

	Instrumental	Consummatory
	L	I
Internal (to Human Condition)	Telic System	Action System
External	Physico-Chemical System	Human Organic System
	A	G

Source: Parsons (1978b, 361). *Action Theory and the Human Condition,* by Talcott Parsons.

cation for where in the basic paradigm each of the four systems is to be placed, and the justification for ordering these systems relative to one another in terms of a "cybernetic hierarchy"—derived from Norbert Wiener's categories of matter, energy, and information—which places systems high in information but relatively low in energy control over subsystems relatively low in information but high in energy.

Arranging the four systems in a cybernetic hierarchical order is problematic yet critical. On the one hand, this order is "the most important single axis of the directionality of evolution in the human condition at large" (Parsons 1978a, 366). On the other, from the human point of view, the phenomena of cybernetic ordering are limited by a finite conception of a "universe." Depending upon whether the universe is considered two-ended or one-ended, there is either two or one kind of limiting conception of order, and these limits are sources of inputs to the human condition relevant to some kinds of human experience (1978a, 367). Parsons acknowledges the very preliminary nature of the discussion of the "deep-ranging problems" involved here but shelves a more thorough-going discussion for later.

Parsons did not in this essay dwell longer on the problematic aspect of the ordering of the four systems and in particular that of the telic to the others. The relation of the organic to the human action system as an emergent level in the evolution of living systems receives a great deal of attention, with much discussion about Durkheim and Freud's contributions to the *symbolic* nature of cognitive knowledge in the human condition. The human action system, Parsons reiterates, is the primary point of reference, and symbolic meanings contribute an important aspect of a human personality that is not reducible to the organic or physico-chemical processes of the brain. But the human action system is not the sole ground of meaning, as Weber recognized when he referred to "problems of meaning" that cannot be yielded by causal explanations but by subjective understanding and beyond to the telic sphere of the transcendental. At that boundary of "ultimate concern," Parsons (1978a, 391) brings in Bellah's paradigmatic elaboration of the telic. This expansion can be seen in figure 13.2, which delineates the paradigm's broad coverage and shows the boundary interchanges between four subsystems of the human condition.

It is not necessary to further explicate the minutiae of the paradigm. I think Parsons felt that this mapping of the human condition and its attendant justification was nearly complete. Before reflecting on this, we need to consider alternative formulations of the human condition.

OTHER DEPICTIONS OF THE HUMAN CONDITION

To get a fuller appreciation of the overarching paradigm that Parsons sought to put together, it may be germane to consider other equally bold attempts in the twentieth century to come to grips with the human condition. Undoubtedly, this selection of a "peer group" of Parsons's program will appear arbitrary. I have chosen them because, even though not all my selections have the phrase "human condition" in their titles, I judge the contents to deal with fundamental aspects of the human condition and to be heuristic in broadening the discussion.

Émile Durkheim

Parsons readily acknowledged the influence of Durkheim in various critical respects beyond the early critique of utilitarianism: the notion of the internal environment of action systems (which Durkheim had in turn derived from the great physiologist Claude Bernard), the nexus of Durkheim and Kant regarding moral obligations linking the action and the telic systems (Parsons 1978a, 413), the very symbolic nature of social reality and its representations. Here I turn

FIGURE 13.2 *Structure of the Human Condition as System*

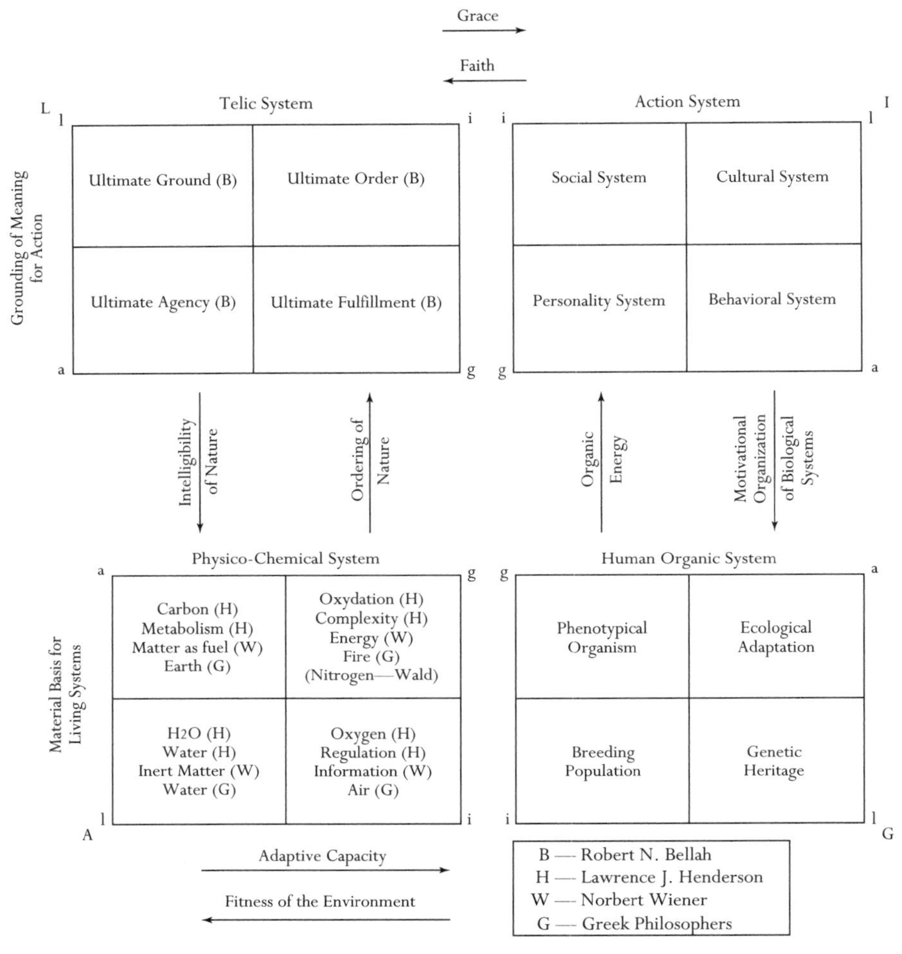

Source: Parsons (1978b, 382). *Action Theory and the Human Condition,* by Talcott Parsons. Copyright © 1978 by The Free Press, a Division of Simon & Schuster Adult Publishing Group. Reprinted with permission of the publisher.

to the last "academic" essay Durkheim wrote, on the eve of World War I, "The Dualism of Human Nature and Its Social Conditions" (Durkheim 1914/1960).

Like Parsons's essay, Durkheim's work begins with a look backward at what he had recently written, the controversial *Elementary Forms of Religious Life* (1912/1995). Durkheim chides his critics for missing the key principle on which his analysis rests, namely, the dualism of human nature. It is a universal aspect of human nature that humans have been aware of self as composed of two radically opposed elements, body and soul, the body being an integral part of the material universe, and the soul having an abode elsewhere and having a divine status not enjoyed by the former. Durkheim broadens his reflection regarding the validity of this age-old conception of Homo duplex, which, he says, gives our inner life a "double center of gravity" (1914/1960, 328). It is an aspect of the human condition that we cannot maximize one pole of our existence at the expense of the other; the inner contradiction is one of the characteristics of being human (1914/1960, 329). Durkheim does not seek to resolve this contradiction; he seeks to account for it sociologically.

Proceeding in typical Durkheimian fashion by first disposing of competing interpretations of the dualism of human nature, he argues that the two states of consciousness characteristic of human beings have a different origin and nature. One "merely expresses our organisms" and the objects connected to them; the states of consciousness here connect us only with ourselves as individuals. The other states of consciousness have a different source: originating in society, they connect us with "something that surpasses us" and turn us toward ends we hold in common with our fellow human beings (1914/1960, 337). For Durkheim, unlike for Parsons, beyond the sentience of the organism the transcendental is society; the other facet of our existence is nothing but an extension of society. And Durkheim makes clear the hierarchy of the dualism (which Parsons could easily incorporate in his cybernetic hierarchy) in arguing that passions and egoistic tendencies derive from our individual constitutions whereas the higher mental faculties, whether theoretical or practical, depend on social causes (1914/1960, 338).

Given that the needs of the organism and the needs of society, of the collective, have different requirements, there is a basic tension in our existence in the world. Society's sustenance—what we might here consider analogous to "pattern maintenance"—does not come free, but at the cost of "perpetual and costly sacrifices" (1914/1960, 338).[11] To live in society, to be a social actor, is to some degree to depart from our individual biological nature and thus to be in a state of more or less painful tension. Unlike the dream of the Romantics, there is no returning to a simpler, tension-free state of nature; the more history advances, Durkheim concludes, the more important the role of the social in our individual selves will become. Consequently, it is very unlikely that an age will come when human existence will lead an easier life, freer of tension: "To the contrary, all evidence compels us to expect our effort in the struggle between the two beings within us to increase with the growth of civilization" (1914/1960, 339).

Georges Gurvitch

The most influential French sociological theorist at the Sorbonne after World War II and until his death in 1965—and thus in a sense a French counterpart of Parsons—was Georges Gurvitch, who was as much of a social realist as Durkheim (whose chair in sociology he held). As with Parsons, a good deal of Gurvitch's theorizing was the elaboration of a typology relating the micro to the macro aspects of human existence, but there were major differences in the construction of their respective typologies. Gurvitch, reflecting different formative influences, from Marx to Mauss, privileged dialectics epistemologically and ontologically in what he came to term "dialectical hyperempiricism" (Gurvitch 1962, 1963, 489) in apparent contrast to the more systemic and structural approach of Parsons. Jacques Coenen-Huther (1989) has related Gurvitch to Parsons at length, so I will here restrict myself to pointing out that if the typology of social phenomena is methodologically central to both, there was little personal affinity between them. As far as I know, Parsons never took to Gurvitch's notion of "depth levels of social reality," nor to Gurvitch's critique of the alienation of technocratic society in favor of industrial production regulated by workers ("autogestion"). And Gurvitch on various occasions (see, for example, Gurvitch 1963, 464) showed disdain for Parsons, despite having coedited a volume in 1945 containing an important essay of Parsons that was in effect a research program of the latter's emergent structural-functional analysis (Parsons 1945).

That said, fifteen years before the appearance of "A Paradigm of the Human Condition," Gurvitch in *his* last major work, the revised edition of *La Vocation actuelle de la sociologie* (1963), made explicit remarks on "la condition humaine" in relating sociology to philosophy. Deploring the divorce of the new empirical sociological research from philosophy—a trend that had begun in the United States but had rapidly spread outward—Gurvitch saw the shirking of sociological theorizing as leading to noncumulative empirical data piling up behind loosely applied concepts.

Where is the nexus with philosophy, according to Gurvitch? Sociology, he affirmed, is the study of society in action, of collective and individual efforts and social conflicts by which groups generate and regenerate themselves and overcome obstacles. That, in a nutshell, is why sociology is the science of human freedom and of all constraints it meets and partially overcomes.[12] Dealing with individual and collective actions, with human freedom and consciousness, sociology and the other human sciences border directly on philosophical themes (Gurvitch 1963, 489). Moreover, Gurvitch adds, sociological and philosophical knowledge deal with totality.[13] The dynamic "total social phenomena" (as initially discussed by Marcel Mauss in his classic *The Gift* [1923–24/2000]) are constituted by types charged with a richness of meanings, of symbols, ideas, and values that relate to the human condition (Gurvitch 1963, 490). Gurvitch makes a point of reiterating: the reality that all social sciences study is the same: the human condition (490). Again in the conclusion, where he discusses the threshold common to philosophy and sociology, he mentions the human condition, as well as the realm of meanings, of symbols, of values, and mental acts (494). To deal with these complex phenomena that are subject to ideologies and dogmatization requires, says Gurvitch, the symbiotic relation of philosophy and sociological research.[14] But Gurvitch did not pursue this program further.

There are serious intellectual differences between Parsons and Gurvitch. Yet I also think there are important complementarities that await to be drawn out,[15] as Parsons boldly did in 1937 by indicating a certain theoretical convergence in the works of Weber and Durkheim, who probably had little personal affinity for one another.

Edward O. Wilson

In the same year that saw the publication of "A *Paradigm* of the Human Condition," a Harvard colleague of Parsons, the evolutionary biologist Edward O. Wilson, published a contrasting statement on the human condition. *On Human Nature* (1978) is a challenging endeavor to give a biological grounding not only to life but also to all the features of what might be taken as distinctive of humankind, including values and religion. His study is framed around discussion of two great "spiritual dilemmas": On the one hand, he affirms that no animal species, humankind included, "possesses a purpose beyond the imperatives created by its genetic history" (Wilson 1978, 2). On the other hand, since choice must be made from the ethical premises inherent in our biological nature, the question arises of "which of the censors and motivators should be obeyed, and which . . . curtailed or sublimated?" (1978, 2). To chart the future in a directed rather than automatic way, states Wilson, proper utilization of biological knowledge has to be put in place, with the study of human nature as part of the natural sciences. This entails "an explanation of mind as an epiphenomenon of the neuronal machinery of the brain," whereby "by a judicious extension of the methods and ideas of neurobiology, ethology and sociobiology a proper foundation can be laid for the social sciences" (1978, 195). In effect, Wilson argued in his treatise that the human condition can be reduced or explained in terms of organic evolution.

Although Parsons prepared his essay the year before Wilson's book appeared (Parsons 1978a, 360 n.18), he was well aware of Wilson's claims of dealing with human social problems from a sociobiological perspective. In a lengthy footnote in which he discusses Wilson's approach, Parsons noted that "he does not have a clearly articulated conception of a theory of action and its distinctively human relevance" (Parsons 1978a, 411 n.122). Apparently Wilson did not seek to enter into a dialogue with Parsons. Parsons, while highly aware of important linkages in action systems to the "organic system," rejected the deterministic view of human nature inherent in sociobiology, which he had essentially accounted for in the "genetic heritage" entry (G-l cell) of the "human organic system" of the Parsons paradigm (see figure 13.2).[16]

Hannah Arendt

In his introduction to the last part of *Action Theory and the Human Condition,* Parsons notes that the term "human condition" was already a widely used term, and he singles out as examples two works, André Malraux's novel *La Condition humaine* (1933) and Hannah Arendt's *The Human Condition.*[17] I will venture why he made no further reference to Arendt in his own essay, after outlining briefly her central points.

Philosophy has a central part in her depiction of the human condition viewed in broad historical terms. It is a rather pessimistic assessment of the unfolding of modernity as a process of depreciation away from the pre-Socratic philosophic seeking of truth as something given and disclosed in contemplation (the "vita contemplative"). The emphasis has turned to modernity's paramount concern with self, individual life replacing life in the body politic, the "vita activa" replacing the "vita contemplative," thought becoming the handmaiden of action, and "modernity's man" being Homo faber. While Arendt dutifully notes the significance of Weber's historical discovery of "innerworldly asceticism," the evaluation is not toward the "instrumental activism" that Parsons signaled but more toward having contributed to modernity's condition of alienation from earthly surroundings, with the motivation of modern man being "worry and care about the self" (Arendt 1958/1998, 254). Integral to the revolution of modernity, she argues, has been the dominance of historical consciousness in all spheres of knowledge, including, in the nineteenth century, the emergence of new disciplines: geology, or the history of earth; biology, or the history of life; anthropology, or the history of human life (1958/1998, 296). But Arendt makes no mention of sociology, despite her acknowledgment of Weber.

The portrayal of modernity, its emphasis on self and on a waste-based economy that rejects durability as an impediment to the turnover process, "whose constant gain in speed is the only constancy left," is a sober, rather pessimistic treatise on the human condition, one having affinity with the neo-Marxist critical theory approach of Max Horkheimer, Theodor Adorno, and Herbert Marcuse. Like Arendt, these thinkers were marked by the depressing influences of two world wars and living under a totalitarian regime in Germany. (The neo-Marxists mentioned here did not worry about Stalinism, only Nazism. Arendt had a more global view of totalitarianism, a perspective more fully validated by the revelations of Stalinism made in the 1960s by Khrushchev.) The core pessimism that underlies Arendt's *Human Condition* is quite at odds with Parsons's core optimism, manifest in various ways, including his depiction of the human condition.

Archer

The last work in this genre that deserves attention is a recent work by a British sociologist who is the first woman president of the International Sociological Association, Margaret Archer. Her *Being Human* (2000) is the most voluminous and complex of the writings on the human condition considered here, and the one that I find most compatible with Parsons's (whose "A Paradigm of the Human Condition" she, however, completely overlooks).

Her paramount concern is to give a richer account of the causal powers of human agency than is provided by two denatured composite models of mankind that seem to have taken hold in the social sciences in recent years. These she terms "modernity's man" and "society's being";

both can ultimately be traced back to the Enlightenment. The former was given in the paradigm of rationality, a paradigm that has continued to evolve in Homo economicus and rational-choice theory, purified of human emotions and passions, leaving "a less recognizable and an impoverished human being," (Archer 2000, 55). The polar model of "society's being" views the properties and powers of human beings, aside from the biogenetic legacy, as derived from, even "the gift of," society (2000, 86).[18] This general model takes human beings as passive social agents, determined by their roles or the interest groups to which they belong or, in a general Durkheimian perspective, to the society in which they are born. A handful of thinkers who have taken this microsociological tradition to its edge are aware of the dualism of inner and outer self (Mead's "I" and "me"), but, Archer states, taking Erving Goffman as an example, "they have erected a wall between them" (2000, 317): the self that is presented to others is shut off from the inner subject, from the sources of the inner subject.

Her textured endeavor to reconstruct agency, a revalorization of what it is to be a human being, entails a distancing not only from the Enlightenment concept of man but also from postmodernism's negation and dissolution of the human subject (Arendt might agree with this but without going further). Archer sees a continuous sense of self or consciousness that provides unity and integration to a variety of life experiences at various developmental stages as a distinctive aspect of our humanity. Social agency is more an end stage of the process, not the beginning; it is realized after encounters with three orders of reality: the natural order (which, I suggest, corresponds to what Parsons viewed as the physico-chemical system, the cell labeled "A" in the general paradigm of the human condition as shown in figure 13.1), the social order (broadly speaking, in Parsons's action system, figure 13.2, the I-i and the I-l subcells), and what she terms the practical order, the order of performance, acts, achievements, including the all-important achievement of language acquisition and utilization (broadly speaking, in the Parsonian schema, figure 13.2, the G-a and the I-g subcells). The human agent encounters these three orders with three forms of emergent and interactive knowledge: embodied knowledge of nature (things have real properties, for instance, fire can burn our skin), practical knowledge of material culture (we live in a world of artifacts), which has a higher cognitive content than embodied knowledge, and discursive knowledge, which is found in the sociocultural world. Archer's schema depicting the interrelations and interdependence of these orders of knowledge is shown in figure 13.3.

For Archer, there is a primacy of the inner life, one that evolves in situational contacts with nature, with practical activities, and with the sociocultural. These (which Parsons might see as conditions of action) do not arbitrarily place us as social agents; Archer, like Parsons, has a voluntaristic perspective of agency. It is not an idealistic perspective (she refers to her underlying approach as "analytical dualism") but an interactive one—inner interaction of conversation, interaction also with others and with the natural order as subject-object and subject-subject relations. Here Archer gives weight to Maurice Merleau-Ponty, the existential phenomenologist who drew attention to the significance of the body and its desires in our nexus to the environment and in intersubjectivity (Archer 2000, 133–36). Her developmental model of agency also gives importance to another component of the self that has been neglected by sociology: our emotions, which are among the main constituents of our inner lives and of our relation to the three orders of reality. Emotions are "commentaries on our concerns"; they are as such "anthropocentric perspectives on the situations in which we find ourselves and not dispassionate reviews" (Archer 2000, 207). Emotions have to do with sociality, but they also have to do with other concerns we have. How each works out a balance between the concerns we have in the three orders—we cannot attend to just one order, for the other two impinge on us—is not given

FIGURE 13.3 *Three Orders of Reality and Their Respective Forms of Knowledge*

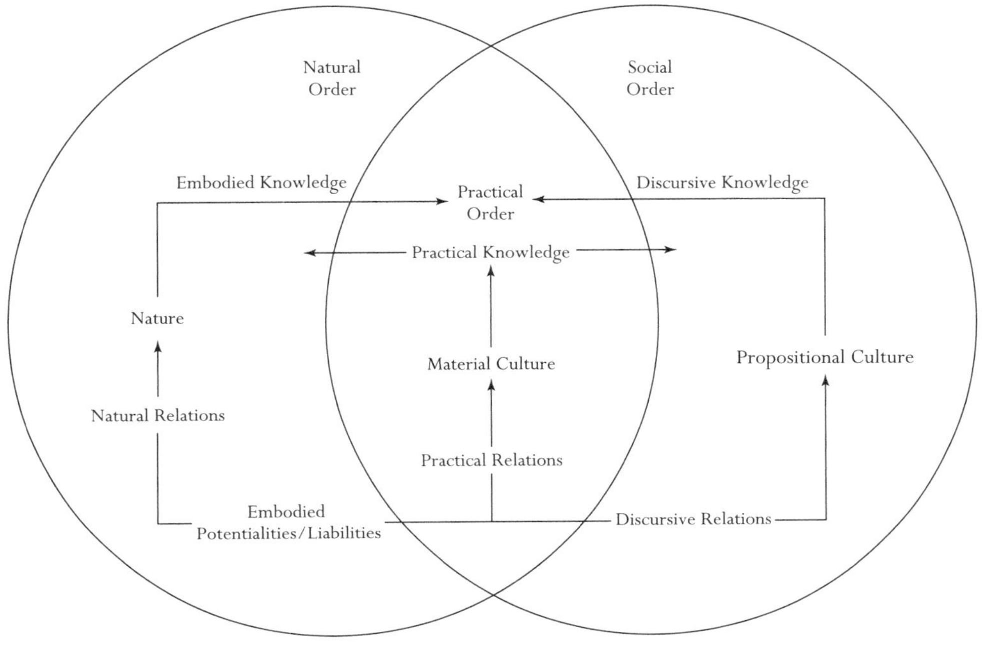

Source: Archer (2000, 162).

in socialization, it is not "the gift of society," but has to be worked out by "an active and reflective agent," by the active human subject with a personal identity.

The discussion of Archer has been given more space than the others, although it has been very cursory for the purpose at hand. I did want to indicate that I see in her approach an important compatibility with "A Paradigm of the Human Condition," one that needs a separate occasion for a fuller treatment. The basis of the compatibility, I would propose, is twofold. First, Parsons and Archer operate from a general voluntaristic perspective of the social actor, an active agent competent to make sense of her situation, to select, act, and interact in a nondeterministic way. Essentially, Parsons and Archer subscribe to a view of the world, including the social world, as being "an intrinsically open system" (Archer 2000, 221), one that allows, for example, a creative reflective response to unscripted circumstances.

The second basis of compatibility is more subtle. Archer's discussion of intersubjectivity, of the significance of Merleau-Ponty's phenomenology of lived consciousness and the body (Archer 2000, 127), of the basis of human agency is entirely intelligible within a broad philosophical underpinning of the human condition. Parsons in *The Structure of Social Action* acknowledged that phenomenological underpinning. It was less central in the middle of Parsons's career, when he gave paramount attention to the analysis of systems, but it reappears very much in his last new intellectual venture, "A Paradigm of the Human Condition." My conclusion points to a fruitful dialogue between Parsons and Archer.

A NEGLECTED GROUND OF ACTION THEORY

In the discussion of Gurvitch, his stress on the symbiotic relation of philosophy and social research and the ill effects for sociology of not encountering philosophy was noted. Although Parsons throughout his career sought interaction with other social scientists and with natural scientists more than with philosophers, he was by no means uninterested in philosophical concerns. Certainly he had sophisticated cognizance of Kant's epistemology, made extensive use of his reread of Kant in the essay titled "Death in the Western World," which immediately precedes "A Paradigm of the Human Condition," and again in the latter essay, as "an unreconstructed Kantian like myself," he takes a stand against Hume and Rousseau (1978a, 413). But I wish to draw attention not to the obvious link with Kant but to a link with modern, post-Kantian philosophical orientation, existential phenomenology, and particularly with one of its major interpreters, Karl Jaspers (1883–1969).[19]

However much attention has been given to *The Structure of Social Action,* only residual notice has been made of a key mention by Parsons in the very last chapter: "The action frame of reference may be said to have what many, following Husserl, have called a 'phenomenological' status" (Parsons 1937/1949, 733).

He elucidates that the action frame is not an empirical phenomenon but a framework within which we describe and think about the phenomena of action (what Husserl would take to be the noema constitutive of objects, that is, the structuring of the meanings of objects). And a few pages later Parsons reiterated this position when he first declared that a subjective reference is central to the means-end schema explanation of action: "It involves a real process in the mind of the actor, as well as external to it" (Parsons 1949, 750).[20] This, he acknowledged, insofar as it takes us into the question of "real subjective processes" of motivation, goes beyond Edmund Husserl's descriptive phenomenology into causal analysis, which might make psychology the synthesizing discipline of all sciences of action. And Parsons avoids the trap of psychological reductionism by affirming of the action schema, "Its phenomenological aspect, as a frame of reference, does not disappear; it remains implicit in any use of the action schema" (Parsons 1937/1949, 733–50).

In my first reading of *The Structure of Social Action,* I had noted this interesting underpinning without making much of a Parsons–Jaspers link. Somewhat later I became aware that Jaspers was on Parsons's dissertation committee at Heidelberg. While I thought Parsons might well have gotten introduced to Husserlian phenomenology by Jaspers (who, then in his forties, had become established as a major exponent of the new philosophy propounded by Edmund Husserl and Martin Heidegger), still, there is no entry for Jaspers in the index of *The Structure of Social Action,* and the one reference to him in the text is on page 790, where two of his studies of Max Weber are listed. If the action frame of reference was not dropped in the middle period of Parsons's career when he dealt more with institutions, systems, and symbolic media of interchanges, its phenomenological underpinning was very, very implicit.

However, without making it explicit, we can see that the phenomenological underpinning of "A Paradigm of the Human Condition" is manifested variously, keeping in mind the several references to the "anthropocentric point of view" in speaking of the human condition (Parsons 1978a, 361). It is indirectly suggested early in his essay, when Parsons distances himself from a positivistic position that only empirical science can provide valid understanding of the human condition (354). It is indicated more forcefully in the introductory section by the implication of multiples worlds: the organic world, the world of action, the physical world and the nonempirical (also later called the transempirical) telic world (357). "World" in a phenomenological perspective is not a material given, a constant "out-there"; worldliness is a structure of meanings experienced in perception (Merleau-Ponty 1962/1986). In the same bounded space are to be found multiple experienced worlds having different characteristics, yet which form a totality, *the* world. Parsons seemed very much to have a perspective consonant with this approach to the human condition, with the multiple worlds being interrelated vertically along the cybernetic hierarchy he derived from Wiener.

Section 4 of "A Paradigm of the Human Condition" contains a complex elaboration of the human condition with special emphasis on what it means organically speaking to say "I am human." Parsons makes extensive use of L. J. Henderson's *The Fitness of the Environment* to discuss features of the physico-chemical world for living systems, such as the importance of water and its chemical components (oxygen and hydrogen) as well as other elements of nature. After reference to Henderson and Wiener as respectable contemporary authorities, or "meta-scientists," Parsons then tacks on an intriguing transition to another authority, one that may risk eliciting "the accusation of wild speculation": pre-Socratic philosophy and its designation of the basic elements of nature: earth, air, fire, and water (Parsons 1978a, 387). Parsons immediately points out that the pre-Socratics were viewing things from a "human" point of view (387), and rounds out the discussion of assigning these pre-Socratic elements in the differentiated structures of the A cell of the paradigm, as shown in figure 13.2 (thus, earth in A-a, fire in A-g, air in A-I, and water in A-l).

This philosophical reference is yet another interesting convergence of Parsons with existential phenomenology, but this time not with Jaspers or Husserl but with Heidegger, surely one of the most influential philosophers of the last century. In his important interpretive study of the later thought of Heidegger, Vincent Vycinas (1961) brings out Heidegger's turning to a pre-Socratic philosophy that conceptualizes nature as physis understood in a dynamic sense. From the pre-Socratics Heidegger problematized the world as the interplay of the foursome ("Geviert"): earth, sky, gods, and mortals (Vycinas 1961, 224). Might there be a fit between these and the four-function paradigm? At least, one might make an initial venture that mortals may be understood as constituting the action system, and gods the telic system. Fitting the other two elements to the action system might present initial difficulty, but what appears intriguing is that Parsons and Heidegger would both find in pre-Socratic ontology important overlapping materials for theoretical analysis of the human condition.

I do not know of any personal linkage of Heidegger to Parsons, so perhaps the pre-Socratic philosophy nexus in the late works of both is just a coincidence. But a chance revisiting of a text opened up for me a new connection to Jaspers and phenomenology. The text in question is Camic's informative introduction to the early writings of Parsons—more specifically, to a footnote reference of "Parsons's view of Jaspers" (Camic 1991, xxi n.45). The referent turned out to be nothing less than a full biographical essay on Jaspers published the year Parsons died, which was a year after the publication of "A Paradigm of the Human Condition" (Parsons 1979). It is highly laudatory, as may be summarily judged by Parsons's reference to Jaspers as a "social scientist's philosopher" (1979, 345). It is also a comprehensive essay showing a thorough knowledge of the many contributions of Jaspers to "Existenzphilosophie" and to the intellectual situation of modernity, right down to one of the last works by Jaspers, published in 1968. The biographical essay of Parsons impresses one not only as a labor of love and respect but, even more, perhaps as a philosophical figure with whom Parsons shared a large universe of orientation to the human condition.

Some common denominators are readily apparent. Parsons begins with a brief biographical sketch of Jaspers, who began his career in medicine and psychiatry. Parsons himself had early thought of a career in medicine, and of course he retained an interest in medicine at various stages (as shown in the essays written with Renée Fox that appeared in part I of *Action Theory and the Human Condition*).[21] Another tie with Jaspers is indicated in viewing the latter's basic orientation as "Kantian" and his rejection of positivism and idealism as "closed systems of thought which squeeze out the element of freedom that was so essential to Kant" (Parsons 1979, 341).[22] Parsons approves of this position, retaining the centrality of the subject-object orientation as "essentially correct and exceedingly important" (342), although, Parsons argues, Jaspers may have overly identified positivism with "materialism" because there are nonmaterial scientific objects, like human organisms and action systems.

Yet another major tie was with Max Weber, the figure that so influenced Parsons at Heidelberg and whom Jaspers had personally known, admired, and written about on various occasions–including delivering the elegy of Weber at Heidelberg (Jaspers 1989). There are various references to Weber in the essay on Jaspers, foremost in the discussion of the subjective meanings of action that can be grasped only through the processes of Verstehen. Parsons extends the subject-object discussion beyond treating cultural objects by raising the question of levels of empirically existent reality, a hierarchical scheme of organization of the object world. Such a classification, Parsons asserts, would start with the world of physical objects and go on to the organic world. Weber, he indicates, had not worked out this hierarchy at the time of his death, but working out the hierarchical scheme of the organization of the object world in terms of "levels" was a common interest of Weber and Jaspers and, of course, of Parsons himself, since at this point he refers the reader to his own essay "A Paradigm of the Human Condition," with its cybernetic hierarchy. Parsons terminated the intellectual biographical essay of Jaspers by relating him anew to Weber. Jaspers's seminal analysis of subjective Existenz (worked out first in a three-volume study, *Existenzphilosophie,* and listed by Parsons in his references in the English translation of 1969 to 1971) may be seen as providing a philosophical grounding for Weber's methodology of Verstehen.

It would require an essay in itself to draw out fully the linkage—"elective affinity" might be more appropriate—between Parsons's explication of Jaspers's philosophy and "A Paradigm of the Human Condition," and perhaps, above all, a more rigorous demonstration of how this would be fruitful and heuristic for further development of the paradigm.[23] But there is one last connecting point that Parsons might have realized either when he was preparing "A Paradigm of the Human Condition" or else very shortly after, while preparing the essay on Jaspers. That connecting point is Jaspers's notion of transcendence as that lying beyond the limits of situations in which Existenz experiences the world(s). As Parsons carefully notes, "Jaspers introduces the concept of transcendence to denote the 'final' boundary in what can be called the 'telic' direction, which synthesizes the objective and the subjective. It is as the summit of whatever is conceived to be transcendentin this sense that Jaspers treats the concept of God" (1979, 343).

Earlier, Parsons had drawn attention to Jaspers's balanced analysis of rationality and the nonrational in *Existenz.* He noted that subjective experience of situated objects (outside or inside the conscious self) implies there are limits, or boundaries ("Grenzen") to the situation; the important theme of "boundary" implies "that what is beyond the limit is not simply 'nonbeing.' "[24] And Parsons closes this passage with an emphatic statement: "Jaspers' exploration of the implications of the limit and what can conceivably lie beyond it constitutes his most distinctive contribution" (Parsons 1979, 343).

I would propose that Parsons was "onto something" in bringing into his overarching frame of reference of the human condition the telic system, the component of the human condition that pertains to transcendence and to ultimate meanings. It appears that Parsons had received an important stimulus for this extension of the action frame from interaction with Bellah. If my interpretation is justified, Parsons also received an important philosophical justification for bringing in the telic from his renewed interest and awareness of the person who at Heidelberg had first brought phenomenology to his awareness and who had gone on to develop it in ways that Parsons found highly compatible in trying to conceptualize the human condition.

Parsons has given us in "A Paradigm of the Human Condition" a conceptualization as rich and suggestive as any other perspective of the major components of our human situation. And his interaction with Jaspers in the 1920s and, later, the 1970s provides action theory with an important philosophical grounding. The paradigm offered in this last essay is not the completion of an oeuvre but the progress report of one. Parsons was well aware of the significance of dealing with religious symbolism and linking it to the organic, action, and physico-chemical world—problems today, ranging from bioethics to eschatological motivations for war and terrorism that are very topical in our new century at various levels. To utilize, elaborate, and update the paradigm in the spirit of "relative and cautious optimism" with which he closed "A Paradigm of the Human Condition" is a most suitable way to recognize how much contemporary sociological theory owes to Talcott Parsons.

POSTSCRIPT

My major intention in this paper has been to provide the reader with an extended commentary on Parsons's attempt to come to grips with the human condition, as a more global context of his theory of action. My approach has thus been predominantly exegetical, with suggestions of how "A Paradigm of the Human Condition" connects with kindred approaches, in particular with that of Archer.

But "A Paradigm of the Human Condition" should not be treated solely with the respect given to a museum piece, albeit a deserving classic of modern theory. Rather, for a new generation of sociologists who may have never had contact with Parsons, its value will accrete as "A Paradigm of the Human Condition" is treated as a large blueprint—a prolegomenon in a larger and more metatheoretical sense—for conceptualizing the grounding of what humans experience in their perception of the world. If the major structures of that experience (see figure 13.2) are fundamental to the "life-world," what further aspects of our being-in-the-world need be incorporated in the paradigm? For the time being, I will limit myself to briefly inserting some addenda as a "postscript" to the Parsonian paradigm.

My remarks will gloss over another dimension of the human condition that is not in the original paradigm but is fundamental enough to be at least mentioned. It is that the human condition is a gendered condition. When Merleau-Ponty introduced an important dimension to social philosophy by pointing out that the self is incarnate ("I am my body"), he introduced an important corrective, but it need be taken another step. The she-he differentiation is not just a discursive one but, as Simone de Beauvoir brought out in her pioneering inquiry *The Second Sex* (1949/1989; Rodgers 1998), has an empirical referent in the male and female body differentiation. The world is experienced differently, proactively, and reactively, by men and women, and they have differential access to the public sphere.

Like most of those writing on the human condition, Parsons essentially took "man" as a generic term for humans. This has a certain validity, but because of the stimuli and critiques of feminist writings, we have to consider that a great deal of what is said about the "human condition" may or may not hold true for the condition of women. I refer not to the old misogynist or male chauvinist arguments about the superiority of men. I am referring to the fact that women's condition includes a great number of specific ordeals, from the biological ordeal of labor to the ordeals of women who are much more likely to be the victims of men than the other way around, not only in terms of physical, cultural, and economic violence but also in terms of legal sanctions. And even in relatively democratic societies, where women may enjoy relative demographic, political, and economic parity—a rather recent development in the course of human evolution—women are still subject to gross physical abuse. De Beauvoir tacitly opened up a searching but still partial critique of male-centered perspectives on the human condition in her pioneering postwar study (1949/1989). A more definitive analytical and comparative "upgrade" of the human condition paradigm is very much needed, one that would take into account the growing global consciousness of women, for example, in their coming together at the third and fourth World Conference on Women, held in Nairobi (1985) and Beijing (1995), respectively.

What I do wish to concentrate on is three phenomena—globalization, the collapse of the Soviet Empire, and 9/11—that have occurred in the quarter century since "A Paradigm of the Human Condition" appeared. These, of course, are of a different order of generality than the more abstract articulations of Parsons. But I think they add to the scheme in terms of the spatial-temporal frame. That is, the human condition is bounded in time and space, not the absolute and objective time and space of the natural sciences but the intersubjective societal time and space that provides meaning and structure to our experience of the world. The intersection of the spatial-temporal frame and the axes of the human condition what conveys historicity to the "life-world" of human beings. Let me specify this with reference to the phenomena I have cited.

First, the collapse of the Soviet empire in the late 1980s and early 1990s. This event (more properly a series of events) was unforeseen by nearly all, whether insiders or outsiders. It was a historical event, one that marks a dividing line between the world with a Soviet set of actors pitted against non-Soviets and the world without Soviet actors. It sets in motion a vast chain reaction. Part of its historicity lies in the fall being an implosion which, unlike the implosion of the czarist empire seventy years earlier, was not a by-product of a lost war but resulted from a combination of forces that took the stage from the autumn of 1989, with the resurfacing of East European nationalisms long thought buried, to the summer of 1991 and the removal of the threat of an internal counterrevolution.

The collapse was a historical global event for at least two reasons: one was that it was mediated, since the whole world was witness to the bravery of Boris Yeltsin confronting tanks in Moscow and the bravery of the periphery in unfurling their national flags. Second, on a longer time basis, it was a historical global event that reversed what 1919 had brought about, that is, the existence of a hard-core politically left presence with a geographical anchor that sought and was devoted to ending the world capitalist regime. Parsons's "A Paradigm of the Human Condition" does not have a political left-right component of action systems, nor, as far as I know, did Parsons make use of left-right as a basic societal or world structure formulated by one of Durkheim's prized students, Robert Hertz (1960). The antinomy of left-right has, one may argue, been a major motor of modernity, from the French Revolution to nearly the end of the last century. The modern left of the twentieth century was concerned with modernizing Marxist ideology in the service of the Soviet state and empire with Moscow as its metropole. That empire's demise in 1989 to 1990 was as unexpected as its arrival as a state power in 1919.

Fast-forward to another major historical event whose consequences are still unraveling, 9/11: its global import is shown by its being universally recognized without need to specify a calendar year. That between the fall of the Soviet Empire and September 2001 the United States was the undisputed global hegemon no one would dispute. But the unexpected and successful attacks by a nonstate on New York and Washington within minutes of each other on two powerful symbols of the hegemon—the money center in New York and the military defense in Washington—exposed at the collective, national level the contingency of existence, even that of the world's greatest superpower. At least, this has been the experience at the intersubjective level.

What the overwhelming majority of Americans in their quotidian lives had assumed to be their normative and physical "fortress"—one whose economic and political way of life had become after 1990 the tacit world standard—suddenly seemed imperiled. The possibility of further attacks by terrorists has been used to justify domestic and international preventive measures, including preemptive-first-strike policies, which have estranged the United States from popular sentiments abroad, including long-time allies who fume at aspersions cast on them for their unwillingness to join the United States' war in the Middle East. It would have seemed unimaginable even ten years ago that for a large section of the American public there is a greater terror of what may happen tomorrow than, say, what was experienced in 2000 with the advent of a "new millennium," much less the terror that some experienced (at least in retrospect) at the coming of the year 1000. Only future social historians will be able to put in perspective the consequences of 9/11, including the dark alleys that will be traversed in the quest for security. It will certainly mark a generation of Americans, particularly those living in metropolitan New York at the time of the event, as severely as the Great Depression marked an earlier generation (Elder 1974).

In fact, recent American history has been marked by crises that most of us have memories of: in the Kennedy era, for example, the Cuban missile crisis and Kennedy's assassination. Perhaps it was only national security that was perceived as jeopardized with these crises. But for four decades the real possibility existed of a thermonuclear war being set off by a contingent act of misreading the communication of "the Other." Perhaps what may differentiate the present uncertainty of the world from the previous state of the Cold War is that today we have no hot line with the terrorists, who have no state and therefore may be anywhere. Terrorists are perceived as nonrational enemies, unlike the Soviets who at least might be reached by phone to verify movements and intentions beyond public ideological statements. And this is not the first time in American history that we have faced a threat of terrorists who might seek to do away with the foundations of the American nation—the Red Scare at the beginning of the 1920s and the anarchists of the 1880s being also moments of collective fright. But, to reiterate, this may be the first time when a good deal of the population (perhaps half the electorate) are truly apprehensive that the United States might come to an end, unless vigorous measures of protection, including preemptive first strikes against nations suspected of harboring evil intentions and weaponries that might at some point be used against us, are taken irrespective of financial and civil costs.

This great fear is fueled by two further factors, which both bring in globalization. One is that the enemy is accepted to be a radical side of a universal religion, Islam. Since Islam is nearly ubiquitous globally, and radical members can be transported in global flows of migration, cross-border attacks can occur anywhere, anytime, from Manhattan to Madrid to a resort hotel in Bali or in the Sinai. What is perhaps harder for Americans to consider is that from the perspective of Islamic zealots, the evil forces of Judeo-American capitalism are equally ubiquitous and menacing. For both, the logic of the world is rendered by "who is not with us is against us." Hence, the world has in the past five years reverted to a bipolar ordering that seemed banished ten years ago, the bipolarity being at a general and somewhat caricatural level being between civilizations of the jihad (including here Judeo-Christian fundamentalism) and the civilization of modernity (Enlightenment secularism and commercialism).

Globalization is not simply a structure of the contemporary world of such "civilizational clashes." If, following Malcolm Waters (1995) we take globalization broadly to be a temporal compression of spaces via technology, resulting in very large flows of people, capital, goods, and communication and in the significant enlargement of cognitive global consciousness, the processes involved are not only far broader but also far older than the clash of two civilizations. However, these trends have tended to accelerate and to undergird our present life-world. Globalization, even without 9/11, introduces contingency at any local level: for example, a factory that provided occupation and meaning to the lives of hundreds of workers for two or more generations in a given community may be forced out of business overnight because of a competitor an ocean away who can ship goods to market much cheaper. A bank in existence since the eighteenth century (Baring's) is forced into bankruptcy because a rogue trader in a branch in South Asia has made huge trading losses. Globalization of communication, in a different vein, can bring communities together instantly via the Internet, and it can generate virtual communities that span oceans with or without physical contacts.

From these sketchy remarks I would suggest that globalization is making us aware that the human condition is very much a dynamic albeit fragile totality.[25] The contingency of the life-world is an aspect of this at the level of the human person, and certainly human societies have had some of this awareness in their respective conceptualization of what Parsons discreetly called "the telic." In the monotheistic traditions, as well as in other great religious traditions, the telic intervenes in human affairs. On occasions, individuals and collectivities seek to invoke that intervention. At the same time, the intervention, both expected and unexpected, also comes from other collectivities.

Relating globalization and 9/11 in one final manner leads us to a consideration of a core problem of the human condition: the antinomy of war and peace. Hans Joas has rightly chided sociological theory, including the modernization analysis associated with Parsons, for neglecting war as a central topic (Joas 2003). Since the United States has been at war most of the first decade of the twenty-first century, and the end is not in sight, it behooves us to reflect on the bearing of war on the human condition.

Human groups seem to be the only ones that both wage fierce war and also express a repulsion for it and seek, often after waging wars, to curtail this and ensure a reign of peace through various mechanisms (treaties, rituals, and the like). The Christian era has been marked by initiatives for peace which have failed, only to be succeeded by new initiatives. So, for example, Christianity introduced a strong normative thrust of this-worldly peace in the tenth and eleventh centuries with the introduction of the "peace of God" as periods and sanctuaries when and where wars would not be fought. Yet a few centuries later, Europe was torn asunder by wars of religion.

The peak of the Enlightenment vision of a rational civilization may arguably be the powerful statement for "perpetual peace" articulated by Kant (1795/2003), which continues to attract attention (Bohman and Lutz-Bachman 1997). Yet barely a century later, Europe plunged into the bloodiest war yet seen, and a generation later was again the fulcrum for yet another world war. In between the two wars, the Kellogg-Briand Pact of 1928 was adopted as a multilateral agreement to "outlaw war," and a new international organization, the League of Nations, was brought into being to ensure global peace. The search for lasting peace came to another end with World War II, which was another holocaust for the human species. And still another peace movement became institutionalized with the creation of the United Nations, which has been relatively successful in minimizing interstate conflicts but not so successful in preventing intrastate civil wars, particularly onerous for regions of the world that can least afford them, namely low-income countries badly lagging in development (Collier et al. 2003).

The United States has played and will continue to play a central role in the working out of this antinomy of the human condition. In terms of ideology, the country likes to define itself as the "peacekeeper of the world" and as advancing the conditions for the global societal community. Yet, sadly, the administration of George W. Bush seems a throwback to an earlier unilateral bellicose mode of foreign policy, having seized upon 9/11 to justify military action against nation-states that may allegedly attack us if we don't attack them first. Even more sadly, a large segment of the American public seems ready to accept the diagnosis and the prescription, regardless of costs to itself or to other nations.

How can the country that has taken the lead in peaceful initiatives of modernity in some many respects (the Peace Corps comes immediately to mind) be so prone to opt for war over peace? How can a country that suffered the anguish and turmoil of the Vietnam War a generation ago seem bent on repeating this path in a different Third World region today?

To conclude at a more metatheoretical level, how can sociological theory and the theory of action provide new directions not only to reflect on these and other facets of the human condition but also provide a forum for global integration? That, I think, is the ultimate charge of Parsons's "A Paradigm of the Human Condition."

NOTES

1. Parsons acknowledges at the onset that the piece was written in collaboration with Harold Bershady, Willy De Craemer, Renée Fox, and Victor Lidz, who organized a faculty seminar on the human condition at the University of Pennsylvania from 1974 to 1976.
2. The work in the sociological tradition that I would compare this to is Durkheim's *Elementary Forms of the Religious Life,* not only in its audacious explorations of the symbolic meanings of religion and society but also in its seeking a new grounding of basic philosophical concerns, especially those formulated by Kant. Parsons, needless to say, was much indebted to both Kant and Durkheim, as "A Paradigm of the Human Condition" demonstrates in many passages.
3. I justify including the qualifier "democratic" because I situate the question of "order," which frames the inquiry of *The Structure of Social Action* and its voluntaristic emphasis, as not only a theoretical but a political statement. In the decade of the 1930s, the action frame of reference was a clear negation of the collectivistic, authoritarian, and totalitarian regimes that were sweeping Europe. Parsons's later theorizing, whether on McCarthyism, race relations, or the inclusiveness of the societal community, continued to manifest the basic democratic approach to the question of social order and social control.
4. The nexus between Parsons's antecedent analyses of stages of societal evolution in a long-term historical process and the human condition paradigm is at the core of the illuminating essay by Victor Lidz in the present volume (" 'Social Evolution' in the Light of the Human-Condition Paradigm"). It should be noted that Lidz recognizes that social evolution, which might have provided Parsons with a more dynamic model, remains "an interesting residual category" in "A Paradigm of the Human Condition."
5. Parsons provides a brief account (1978a, 326) of what and who was involved in the development of the enriched paradigm. Lidz's introduction to his own essay in the present volume provides valuable information on the collaborative background of "A Paradigm of the Human Condition."
6. "On this note of relative and cautious intellectual optimism . . . it seems appropriate to bring this long and complicated . . . analysis to a close. The present close, however, is also the beginning of a new phase of exploration of these problems" (1978a, 433).
7. I am prompted to use this example because Kant was Parsons's favorite philosopher (1978a, 413), and Norman Kemp Smith gave his famous course on Kant's *Critique* of Pure Reason in Harvard's Emerson Hall, the same building where Parsons taught. Parsons in "A Paradigm of the Human Condition" makes extensive reference to Kant's epistemology as justifying the analytical filters of the human condition.
8. Henderson's *The Fitness of the Environment* (1913/1958) seemed particularly important for Parsons in treating the physico-chemical environment as a related component of the human condition, while avoiding a mechanistic or materialistic determinism (Parsons 1978a, 357–60). Henderson, co-founder of the Harvard Society of Fellows, pioneered interdisciplinary research in biochemistry and physics in opposition to the "mechanistic conception of life." Marking the ninetieth anniversary of his epochal work, a special two-day celebration was held at the Harvard-Smithsonian Center for Astrophysics in October 2003 (see www.templeton.org/biochemfinetuning/index.html [accessed May 3, 2005]).
9. I later draw attention to Parsons's use of "world" in this context for the German term "Umwelt," the natural environment, as phenomenologically different from the "Mitwelt," the world of social relationships. Both have real sets of objects.
10. Earlier I mentioned that Habermas is the one major theorist outside Parsons's immediate circle who has given a attentive albeit critical reading of "A Paradigm of the Human Condition." Much of what Parsons says about

action systems dovetails with Habermas's perspective, up to a point. His strong reservation enters with his noting that Parsons makes cursory reference to Kant's three critiques, then adds a fourth sphere of transcendental ordering to which Kant did not devote a special critique (besides the critique of pure reason, of practical reason, and of aesthetics): the sphere of religion. Habermas says that besides Parsons's religious needs and experiences, his system needs a fourth cell because "his systems-theoretical approach itself blocks any transcendental account of the human condition" (Habermas 1981/1989, 253).

Habermas, whom I read as a sophisticated secular humanist, cannot accept transcendence outside the spheres of nature, the organic and the social, that are ultimately known in the communicative (dialogical) action of the life-world. The telic system is not for Habermas a legitimate sphere of knowledge, but he acknowledges, "It is worth our effort to try and decode the transcendental version of Parsons' late philosophy in terms of the model of communicative action. This will lead to the discovery that behind the system of the basic conditions of human existence, behind the four subsystems of the 'human condition,' can be found the structures of the lifeworld complementary to communicative action—in a somewhat irritating version, to be sure" (Habermas 1981/1989, 254).

11. How costly those sacrifices could be would shortly be experienced by Durkheim and others: the conflict directly and indirectly took the lives of millions, including those of some of his most talented students and of his son. Ultimately he lost his own life. Durkheim died of prolonged grief at the disappearance of his son André in the expeditionary debacle of Galipoli.
12. The theme of freedom and constraint as an "antinomy of modernity" is one that Gurvitch obtained in a close reading of Pierre-Joseph Proudhon, the socialist rival of Marx (on Proudhon, see Gurvitch 1965).
13. On the theme of totality as central to Durkheim's theorizing, see Donald Nielsen (1999).
14. This calls to mind the classical essays of Robert Merton on the symbiotic relation of theory to research (1949).
15. For example, both Gurvitch and Parsons as graduate students in Europe in the 1920s were subject to the common influence of phenomenology in Germany (Gurvitch 1949), which is indicated in Gurvitch's conceptual framework of "depth levels" of social phenomena and Parsons's action frame of reference.
16. Parsons would have extended his critique to Wilson's later claim that sociobiology was paving the way for the integration and unification of knowledge (Wilson 1998), since Wilson makes short shrift of the social sciences (after a passing nod to economics). A more recent reduction of the human condition to the biogenetic dimension can be found in the provocative work of Francis Fukuyama, who asserts that "human nature is the sum of the behavior and characteristics that are typical of the human species, arising from genetic rather than environmental factors" (Fukuyama 2002).

In rejecting biogenetic reductionism, Parsons would have found an important ally in Claude Lévi-Strauss's more recent criticism (1983/1985) of Wilson in which he upholds the primacy of culture, which for Parsons is an irreducible component of action systems. However, Parsons would undoubtedly not have gone along with Lévi-Strauss's assertion that the problem of culture is "the problem of the human condition" (1983/1985, 35). Figure 13.2 suggests that for Parsons no subsystem can be privileged in describing the human condition.

17. First published in 1958, it has become a durable best- seller. Parsons's reference is to the 1970 edition; my references are to the 1998 edition.
18. That is encapsulated in the title of her chapter 3, "Society's Being: Humanity as the Gift of Society." Compare this with chapter 12 in *Action Theory and the Human Condition:* "The 'Gift of Life' and Its Reciprocation."
19. Years ago I argued that existential phenomenology was compatible with an important dimension of the sociological tradition (Tiryakian 1965). My recent awareness of Parsons's knowledge and deep interest in one of the major philosophical figures of this orientation has been serendipitous in the preparation of this chapter.
20. This is at the basis of what Parsons will term "analytical realism." The bridging of the subjective and the objective in the action frame of reference took the action frame of reference away from Hegelian idealism, on the one hand, and from material positivism, on the other. (Incidentally, Parsons's "analytical realism" is very compatible with Archer's "analytical dualism.")
21. He does note in connection with psychiatry that Jaspers was never attracted to Freud's ideas, but he does not extend the discussion as to what this might imply for his own perspective on human personality.
22. I have noted earlier that this theme of freedom was of equal importance to Gurvitch, not only because of his philosophical training but also as a result of the life experience of being threatened with incarceration and even execution for his opposition to Lenin's Bolshevik revolution (George Gurvitch, personal communication, October 1965).

23. An important link between Jaspers and Parsons is the notion of "situation." Martel points out that Parsons evolved his conceptual framework to "the more complex notion of an 'actor-orienting-to-a-situation' " (Martel 1979, 617), while Jaspers states "man's being consists primarily of his existence in economic, sociological, and political situations" (Jaspers 1932/1933, 24).
24. Mikel Dufrenne and Paul Ricoeur (1947, 173–94) provide a lucid explication of Jaspers's key notion of the boundedness of situations.
25. Drawing upon the writings of the sociologists Bryan Turner and Ulrich Beck, Jeremy Rifkin has recently emphasized that "in the global era, frailty and vulnerability become humanity's universal condition" (Rifkin 2004, 270).

REFERENCES

Alexander, Jeffrey. 1983. *Theoretical Logic in Sociology.* Volume 4, *The Modern Reconstruction of Classical Thought: Talcott Parsons.* Berkeley: University of California Press.

Archer, Margaret S. 2000. *Being Human: The Problem of Agency.* Cambridge: Cambridge University Press.

Arendt, Hannah. 1958/1998. *The Human Condition.* Chicago: University of Chicago Press.

Bohman, James, and Matthias Lutz-Bachman, eds. 1997. *Perpetual Peace: Essays on Kant's Cosmopolitan Ideal.* Cambridge, Mass.: MIT Press.

Camic, Charles. 1991. "Introduction" to *Talcott Parsons, the Early Essays,* edited by Charles Camic. Chicago: University of Chicago Press.

Coenen-Huther, Jacques. 1989. "Parsons et Gurvitch: exigence de totalité et réciprocité de perspectives." *Sociologie et sociétés* 21(April): 87–96.

Collier, Paul, V. L. Elliott, Harvard Hegre, Anke Heoffler, Marta Reynal-Querol, and Nicolas Sambanis. 2003. *Breaking the Conflict Trap: Civil War and Development Policy.* Washington, D.C.: World Bank and Oxford University Press.

De Beauvoir, Simone. 1949/1989. *The Second Sex.* New York: Vintage Books.

Dufrenne, Mikel, and Paul Ricoeur. 1947. *Karl Jaspers et la philosophie de l'existence.* Preface by Karl Jaspers. Paris: Seuil.

Durkheim, Émile. 1912/1995. *The Elementary Forms of Religious Life.* Translated and edited by Karen Fields. New York: Free Press.

———. 1914/1960. "The Dualism of Human Nature and Its Social Conditions." In *Émile Durkheim, 1858–1917,* edited by Kurt Wolff. Columbus: Ohio State University Press.

Elder, Glen H. 1974. *Children of the Great Depression: Social Change in Life Experience.* Chicago: University of Chicago Press.

Fukuyama, Francis. 2002. *Our Posthuman Future. Consequences of the Biotechnology Revolution.* New York: Farrar, Straus & Giroux.

Gurvitch, Georges. 1949. *Les Tendances actuelles de la philosophie allemande.* Paris: J. Vrin.

———. 1962. *Dialectique et Sociologie.* Paris: Flammarion.

———. 1963. *La Vocation Actuelle de la Sociologie.* 2nd ed. Revised. Paris: Presses Universitaires de France.

———. 1965. *Proudhon: sa vie, son oeuvre, avec un exposé de sa Philosophie.* Paris: Presses Universitaires de France.

Habermas, Jürgen. 1981/1989. *The Theory of Communicative Action.* Volume 2, *Lifeworld and System: Critique of Functionalist Reason.* Translated by Thomas McCarthy. Boston: Beacon Press.

Henderson, Lawrence J. 1913/1958. *The Fitness of the Environment: An Inquiry into the Biological Significance of the Properties of Matter.* Introduction by George Wald. Boston: Beacon Press.

Hertz, Robert. 1960. *Death and the Right Hand.* New York: Free Press.

Jaspers, Karl. 1932/1933. *Man in the Modern Age.* Translated by Eden Paul and Cedar Paul. New York: Henry Holt.

———. 1989. *Karl Jaspers on Max Weber.* Translated by Robert J. Whelan. New York: Paragon House.

Joas, Hans. 2003. *War and Modernity.* Translated by Rodney Livingstone. Cambridge: Polity Press.

Kant, Immanuel. 1795/2003. *To Perpetual Peace: A Philosophical Sketch.* Translated by Ted Humphrey. Indianapolis: Hackett.

Lévi-Strauss, Claude. 1983/1985. "The Anthropologist and the Human Condition." *The View from Afar.* New York: Basic Books.

Lidz, Victor. 2001. "Language and the 'Family' of Generalized Symbolic Media." In *Talcott Parsons Today: His Theory and Legacy in Contemporary Sociology,* edited by A. Javier Treviño. Lanham, Md.: Rowman & Littlefield.

Malraux, André. 1933. *La Condition humaine.* Paris: Gallimard.

Martel, Martin U. 1979. "Parsons, Talcott." In volume 18, *International Encyclopedia of the Social Sciences,* edited by David L. Sills. New York: Free Press/Macmillan.

Mauss, Marcel. 1923–24/2000. *The Gift: The Form and Reason for Exchange in Archaic Societies.* Translated by W. D. Halls. New York: W. W. Norton.

Merleau-Ponty, Maurice. 1963. *The Structure of Behavior.* Boston: Beacon Press.

———. 1962/1986. *The Phenomenology of Perception.* London: Routledge & Kegan Paul.

Merton, Robert K. 1949. "The Bearing of Sociological Theory on Empirical Research" and "The Bearing of Empirical Research on Sociological Theory." In *Social Theory and Social Structure.* New York: Free Press.

Münch, Richard. 1987. "Parsonian Theory Today." In *Social Theory Today,* edited by Anthony Giddens and Jonathan Turner. Palo Alto: Stanford University Press.

———. 1994. *Sociological Theory.* Volume 3, *Development Since the 1960s.* Chicago: Nelson-Hall.

Nielsen, Donald A. 1999. *Three Faces of God: Society, Religion, and the Category of Totality in the Philosophy of Émile Durkheim.* Albany: State University of New York Press.

Parsons, Talcott. 1945. "The Present Position and Prospects of Systematic Theory in Sociology." In *Twentieth Century Sociology,* edited by Georges Gurvitch and Wilbert E. Moore. New York: The Philosophical Library.

———. 1937/1949. *The Structure of Social Action: A Study in Social Theory with Special Reference to a Group of Recent European Writers.* New York: Free Press.

———. 1966. *Societies. Evolutionary and Comparative Perspectives.* Englewood Cliffs, N.J.: Prentice-Hall.

———. 1970. "Some Problems of General Theory in Sociology." In *Theoretical Sociology: Perspectives and Developments,* edited by John C. McKinney and Edward A. Tiryakian. New York: Appleton-Century-Crofts.

———. 1971. *The System of Modern Societies.* Englewood Cliffs, N.J.: Prentice-Hall.

———. 1978a. "A Paradigm of the Human Condition." *Action Theory and the Human Condition.* New York: Free Press.

———. 1978b. *Action Theory of the Human Condition.* New York: Free Press.

———. 1979. "Jaspers, Karl." In *International Encyclopedia of the Social Sciences,* volume 18. New York: Free Press/Macmillan.

Parsons, Talcott, and Edward Shils, eds. 1951/2001. *Toward a General Theory of Action,* with a new introduction by Neil J. Smelser. New Brunswick, N.J.: Transaction Publishers.

Rifkin, Jeremy. 2004. *The European Dream.* New York: Jeremy P. Tarcher/Penguin.

Rodgers, Catherine. 1998. *Le Deuxième sese de Simone Beauvoir: un héritage admiré et contesté.* Paris: L'Harmattan.

Smith, Norman Kemp. 1930. *A Commentary to Kant's "Critique of Pure Reason."* London: Macmillan.

Tiryakian, Edward A. 1965. "Existential Phenomenology and the Sociological Tradition." *American Sociological Review* 30(5): 674–88.

Treviño, A. Javier, ed. 2001. *Talcott Parsons Today: His Theory and Legacy in Contemporary Sociology.* Lanham, Md.: Rowman & Littefield.

Vycinas, Vincent. 1961. *Earth and Gods: An Introduction to the Philosophy of Martin Heidegger.* The Hague: Martinus Nijhoff.

Waters, Malcolm. 1995. *Globalization.* London and New York: Routledge.

Wilson, Edward O. 1978. *On Human Nature.* Cambridge, Mass.: Harvard University Press.

———. 1998. *Consilience: The Unity of Knowledge.* New York: Alfred A. Knopf.

Chapter 14

What Do American Bioethics and Médecins Sans Frontières Have in Common? The Relevance of Talcott Parsons's Theory of Universalism, Particularism, and Modernity

Renée C. Fox

During the past ten years I have been involved in two major research projects. One of them is a study of the emergence of the young field of bioethics in the United States—its origins, ethos, and progressive institutionalization, and its civic as well as medical import in American society.[1] The other is a still-ongoing examination of medical humanitarian and human rights witnessing action—its underlying ideology and value commitments, the moral dilemmas it entails, and its (unintended as well as intended) consequences. This is being done chiefly through the medium of a sociological case study of Médecins Sans Frontières (MSF)—also known as Doctors Without Borders—the international, nongovernmental, medically oriented humanitarian organization that was awarded the Nobel Prize for Peace in 1999.[2]

In many explicit and implicit ways, these investigations have been influenced by the theoretical framework that Talcott Parsons developed over the course of his intellectual lifetime: by the conceptual and empirical insights that it has generated, and by my own internalization, as his abiding student, of Parsons's way of thought and angle of vision (Fox 1997). His perspective on the importance of health, illness, and medicine to the functioning of a society, their cultural meaning, their relationship to proximate, ultimate, and transcendental values, beliefs, and ends, and their intrinsic connection to the human life cycle and the human condition have heightened my awareness and enlarged my understanding of the macrosignificance of the ethical and humanitarian issues that these research ventures involve, and motivated me to undertake and pursue them. It contributed to my awareness of distinctively American attributes in the ethos and world view of U.S. bioethics, and to my critical concern about its "cultural nearsightedness" and "provincialism" (Fox and Swazey 1984, 337, 359–60). And it emboldened me to tackle the cross-cultural challenge of studying an organization such as MSF, which is conducting some 400 projects in more than eighty societies. There is a latent link, too, between Parsons's view of social action as a complex, interrelational process that continuously confronts its participants with dilemmas of choice, and the fact that the themes around which my research on Médecins Sans Frontières has crystallized are a series of dilemmas intrinsic to humanitarian action that are closely associated with the ethical intricacies and practical difficulties of achieving purposive good. This is not a coincidence. Rather, it exemplifies Parsons's convictions about the indispensable role that theory plays in social research, through the focus that it provides in the collection of empirical data, and as a guiding referent in the analysis and interpretation of those data (Parsons 1938).

Within this general framework and these specific contexts, in this paper I would like to explore a set of dilemmas that have assumed special importance in my research on both bioethics and humanitarian action. In the setting and parlance of bioethics, the dilemma-ridden issues involved turn around the bearing of questions of "cultural diversity," "cultural relativity," "ethical relativism," and "ethical imperialism" on the committed search for overarching, "universal," "common morality" precepts. In the milieu of humanitarianism, the kindred dilemmas encountered center on what the former president of the Czech Republic Václav Havel (1994) has called the central task of this century: "the creation of a new model of coexistence" that enables us to be "global and at the same time multicultural." In their internal and public discourse about these issues, bioethicists and those engaged in humanitarian action commonly refer to human rights as embodiments of a "set of universal principles" that "belong to all people," and that "are (or ought to be) binding on [them] . . . wherever they may dwell and whatever may be the political system or the cultural traditions of their country or region of the world" (Macklin 1999, 243).

As I pondered these matters, one of Talcott Parsons's pairs of "pattern variables"—"universalism-particularism"—seen in relationship to several of the other "alternative pairs" he formulated, and to certain aspects of his theory of societal evolution and of modernity, seemed especially pertinent to the value-orientation dilemmas, and the dilemmas of action that are involved. In this connection I found it interesting that although he did not attribute them to Parsons, the philosopher Daniel Callahan, a founder of American bioethics, used the concepts of "universalism" and "particularism" to frame and entitle an essay that he wrote about one of the major questions associated with these dilemmas, "Universalism and Particularism: Fighting to a Draw" (Callahan 2000, 37), where he asks: "How are we [bioethicists] as a community, dedicated to pluralism, to find room for the different values and moral perspectives of different people and different groups" and also "find a way to transcend these differences in order to reach consensus on some matters of common human welfare?"

As the foregoing suggests, I did not superimpose these Parsonian concepts on my research. Rather, they emerged inductively from reflection on the data I was collecting, and once they did, it became apparent that comparably patterned dilemmas, structured around the axes of universalism and particularism, were phenomenologically present in the intellectual and social worlds of both bioethics and humanitarianism and in the collective experiences of their members.

What do the concepts of universalism and particularism—their definition, and the place that they occupy in Parsons's theoretical framework—contribute to understanding this complex of dilemmas with which bioethicists and humanitarian workers are confronted? In turn, what do the information and insights about the way they are perceived and experienced in bioethical and humanitarian milieux that I have gathered through my research suggest about how the Parsonian formulation of universalism-particularism might be modified or enriched? (Parsons would have attached as much importance to the second question as to the first. For not only did he view "analytical theory [as] a crucially important guide to the direction of fruitful research" [Parsons 1938, 20] but he also regarded empirical research as essential to the development of theory. In what he referred to as "the intimate co-operation of empirical and theoretical work," which he saw as a two-way process, he was "very hopeful for the future of sociological science" [Parsons 1938, 20].) As a prelude to addressing these two questions, I will first describe the forms that these dilemmas and responses to them take in bioethical and humanitarian contexts.

AMERICAN BIOETHICS

Bioethics is a multidisciplinary area of inquiry and action that made its appearance on the American scene toward the end of the 1960s. From its beginnings, this new field has concentrated its attention on certain advances in biology and medicine and on the actual and potential questions and quandaries to which these scientific, technological, and clinical developments, and the means of achieving and deploying them, have contributed. Assisted modes of reproduction, genetic screening, manipulation, and therapy, organ replacement (through organ transplantation and artificial organs), the application of the life-support and life-sustaining paraphernalia of modern medicine, euthanasia, and the involvement of human subjects in medical research have been the most constant empirical centers of bioethical interest and engagement. Cross-cutting and interconnecting these biomedical focuses have been the more latent but persistent metathemes of U.S. bioethics: on the one hand, the beliefs and values basic to American society, its cultural tradition, and its collective conscience with which U.S. bioethics is interlaced and on the other, human-condition questions—above all, issues concerning life and death and human personhood, their definition and meaning, beginning and end—that are integral to health, illness, and medicine and their existential significance (Fox and Swazey 1984, 336; Fox 1999, 7). The recognition of what Parsons would call these "telic" themes in American bioethics has been curtailed and, to a certain extent, delegitimized by the kind of analysis and discourse that has been characteristic of U.S. bioethics. Nevertheless, they are persistently—perhaps even indwellingly—present.

The overarching conceptual framework within which American bioethics has evolved was brought to the field and made prominent within it by philosophers, who rapidly became the most predominant, intellectually influential subgroup of bioethicists (among physicians, biologists, jurists, theologians, religionists, and relatively few social scientists). Most of them were trained in the Anglo-American tradition of analytic philosophy, the prevailing approach of American university philosophy departments. They "arrived on the bioethics scene" with a "turn toward normative ethics in their field, and [a] drive to ground ethics in good theory" (Callahan 2000, 40), which would enable them to deal with moral questions, decisions, and actions logically, rationally, and objectively, with rigor, and in a universalizable way. The framework that they forged for doing so, which has been labeled "principlism," was authoritatively codified in what has become the canonical text of the field, *Principles of Biomedical Ethics,* by Tom L. Beauchamp and James F. Childress, which has been published in five successive editions since its original publication in 1979 (Beauchamp and Childress 1979/2001), and has been translated into numerous languages. Principlism is based on a "relatively small set of concepts" (Gustafson 1990, 127): the "principles of respect for autonomy, nonmaleficence, beneficence (including utility or proportionality), and justice, along with the derivative principles or rules of veracity, fidelity, privacy, and confidentiality" (Childress 1994, 79). It is to the principle of autonomy—conceived of as a highly individualistic and self-determining form of individualism and individual rights—that bioethics has accorded primacy. To a degree, greater importance has been attached to individual than to common good, and in a way that has overshadowed the social values of relatedness, reciprocity, and solidarity.

Although these four clusters of principles are not viewed as exhaustively coterminous with morality, they are regarded as the constituents of a "single, universal, common morality." Beauchamp and Childress (Beauchamp and Childress 1979/2001, 3–4, 403) state that "no norms are more basic in the moral life." They are a "set of norms that all morally serious persons share as *the common morality*" (italics in original), and that "bind all persons in all places" in a way that is "morally authoritative for [their] conduct." Further, Beauchamp has emphatically stated,

> The common morality is not merely *a* morality that differs from *other* moralities. . . . All human conduct is rightly judged by its standards. The norms of the common morality . . . are necessary to *ameliorate or counteract the tendency for the quality of people's lives to worsen or for social relationships to disintegrate.* In every well-functioning society norms are in place to prohibit lying, breaking promises, causing bodily harm, stealing, fraud, the taking of life, the neglect of children, and failures to keep contracts. These norms are what they are and not some other set of norms, because they have proven that they successfully achieve the objectives of morality . . . those of promoting human flourishing. . . . [It is] preposterous to hold that . . . norms qualify for inclusion in the *common* morality because they are rooted in custom or consensus. . . . Any given society's customary or consensus position may be a distorted outlook that functions to block awareness of common morality requirements. (Beauchamp 2003, 260–61; italics in original)

In this perspective, and in the outlook of American bioethics more generally, these normative principles of common morality "transcend" "community-specific," "local" moral norms, "customs and attitudes" that "spring from particular cultural, religious, and institutional sources." The existence of "significant cultural differences" in moral precepts is acknowledged, but they are considered to be subsidiary to universal concepts—not only secondary to them in importance but also potential sources of "amoral, immoral, and selectively moral" (Beauchamp 2003, 265) beliefs and behaviors that are not acceptable to the "persons in all cultures" . . . *serious about moral conduct,* who subscribe to and "accept the demands of the common [universal] morality" (Beauchamp and Childress 1979/2001, 3–4; italics in original).

Throughout the relatively short intellectual, clinical, and public policy history of bioethics, as can be seen, a consistent tension has existed between what Callahan calls "universalist and particularist perspectives" (Callahan 1999, 290). The "central dilemma," he has stated, is that "an overriding effort to devise universal principles neglects the complexity of individual moral lives and social circumstances, while an indiscriminate immersion in their particularity allows no room for ethical distinctions and prudential judgments." Callahan has taken the position that "no decisive choice should be made between universalism and particularism. Each will have its place in different situations and each will ordinarily have to be influenced and informed by the other" (Callahan 2000, 41). Nevertheless, the overall skew of American bioethics has been tipped in the direction of an intellectual and moral preference for universalism in the form of commitment to the notion of culture-transcending ethical principles, accompanied by wariness about "simply respecting" other societies and cultures, and succumbing to "local meanings" in a way that eventuates in "cultural and ethical relativism." An "against-relativism" stance, anchored in "general principles," the philosopher-bioethicist Ruth Macklin has forcibly argued (Macklin 1999), is essential to one of the most crucial roles of ethics—the development and application of "a systematic way to [make and] justify ethical judgments" about values, beliefs, and practices "across cultures" as well as within them. For Beauchamp, a "profoundly important feature of the common morality is its provision of cross-cultural standards," which endows it with "the capacity to criticize and evaluate existing groups of communities whose viewpoints are morally deficient" (Beauchamp 2003, 272). Although he frames and phrases it somewhat differently, Callahan also considers this to be a major function and obligatory purpose of bioethics. "Bioethics does not well serve society simply by promoting a respect for other cultures," he has written. If it "is to be of any value at all, that value will come from its effort to help devise responsible ways of making justifiable moral judgments . . . [about] which practices and values should be accepted and affirmed, which simply tolerated, and which rejected" (Callahan 2000, 44). "Here we need to think not merely in terms of what universally has been the case," Beauchamp adds, "but in terms of what universally ought to be the case" (Beauchamp 2003, 272).

The strong commitment of U.S. bioethics to its conception of ethical universality has had several consequences. It has contributed to a tendency for bioethicists to devalue social and cultural differences on the one hand by minimizing their importance and on the other by characteristically associating such differences with cultural beliefs and practices that they consider morally problematic. In this latter regard, they have paid considerable attention to practices that they view as emanations of the oppression and discrimination to which women are subject in many "foreign," traditional societies, focusing, for example, on female genital cutting as an especially abominable custom that "mutilates" women. Within the sphere of American society, the downplaying of cultural differences to which bioethicists have been prone has played a part in the notable degree to which they have been inclined to overlook the exceptional cultural diversity and pluralism of the United States.

U.S. bioethicists' moral preference for universalism, their penchant for distrusting particularism, and their aversion to relativism have also played a significant role in the difficulties they have had in recognizing and acknowledging the ways in which their approach to ethics and their mode of reasoning about moral questions have been influenced by Western, and specifically American, culture patterns. As Henk ten Have, a Dutch physician and philosopher, wrote in his "European Criticism of U.S. Bioethics" (1994, 104, 106), "The dominant conception of bioethics has developed within a particular cultural context":

> The fundamental ethos of applied bioethics, its analytical framework, methodology, and language, its concerns and emphases, and its very institutionalization have been shaped by beliefs, values, and modes of thinking grounded in specific social and cultural traditions. Nowadays, the bioethics literature serves as one of the powerful means by which to express and articulate these traditions. The literature, however, only rarely attends to or reflects upon the sociocultural value system within and through which it operates. Scholars usually assume that its principles, theories, and moral views are transcultural.

In effect, American bioethics has exhibited a tendency toward what the French sociologist Pierre Bourdieu has termed "*the imperialism of the universal* [italics in original] . . . universalizing its own . . . particular characteristics by tacitly establishing them in a universal model" (Bourdieu 2001, 3). And it has been prone to underestimate the complexities of what Václav Havel (Havel 2002) considers central to the "foundations of . . . coexistence in this globally connected world": the urgent and intricate task of seeking and finding "the values or basic moral imperatives [that] . . . the various spheres of civilization, culture, nations, or continents . . . have in common."

During the 1990s, as U.S. bioethicists became more involved, intellectually and institutionally, in international and global bioethics, and their contacts with colleagues, organizations, and ethical questions became less exclusively American, their social and cultural perspectives broadened. Nevertheless, they have entered this more international era of their engagement with a deficiency in what the philosopher-classicist Martha C. Nussbaum (1997, 147), in another connection, calls "a Socratic knowledge of their own ignorance—both of other world cultures and, to a great extent, of [their] own." To use a phrase coined by William LaFleur (2002), a historian of Japan, American bioethics has become "more international without becoming internationalized" at an historical juncture when its predominant paradigm is being exported all over the world.

MÉDECINS SANS FRONTIÈRES (DOCTORS WITHOUT BORDERS)

Médecins Sans Frontières—Doctors Without Borders—was founded on December 20, 1971, by two groups of young French physicians who found their concerns converging. In the context of the civil war in Nigeria, under the joint aegis of the French and the International Red Cross, the first group of doctors had served as volunteers in Biafra, doing medical relief work among the Ibo from 1968 to 1970. The second group had volunteered in 1970 to treat the victims of a tidal wave in eastern Pakistan (which later became Bangladesh). Galvanized by their field experiences and by the charismatic leadership of Dr. Bernard Kouchner, these physicians came together to create MSF. Their collective intent was to change the way that they had seen humanitarian aid delivered in times of crisis, by providing more medical assistance more rapidly, with less deference to national boundaries and the political will of individual nation states, and by "witnessing" and advocating on behalf of the imperiled populations whom they serve. Between 1981 and 1986, Belgian, Swiss, Dutch, Spanish, and Luxembourgian sections were consecutively added to MSF's founding French section.

As its name Médecins Sans Frontières testifies, MSF emanates from a globally transnational, humanitarian vision. It conceives of itself as a movement and as a "solidarity"-based "association" militantly though pacifically dedicated to alleviating the suffering of people urgently in need of medical care and succor, regardless of their nationality, gender, race, ethnicity, social class, religion, or ideology, wherever on the face of the earth such suffering and need occur, and whatever its cause—be it warfare between or within nation-states, epidemics, poverty, disenfranchisement, oppression, persecution, torture, terror, exile, exodus, or "natural" disasters such as earthquakes, droughts, and floods. Its medical humanitarian action is grounded in an "impartial" belief in the equality of all victims, guided by a principle of "proportionality" that accords the highest priority to assisting persons undergoing the greatest suffering and danger. This is accompanied by MSF's witnessing and advocacy: by the exercising of what it regards as its ethical responsibility to communicate information about the predicament of the individuals and populations to whom it provides assistance, and about what could and should be done to improve their situation and, where there are serious violations of human rights, to publicly condemn those abuses in a nonpolitical way. Its combined medical humanitarian and human rights action is carried out within the framework of its resolute dedication to "independence" from all governmental, political, religious, economic, or financial organizations and powers, and to the maintenance of a critical attitude toward all systems, including "the humanitarian system." The persons recruited by MSF who work under its auspices—even those who receive remuneration for their activities—are defined as "volunteers" who are motivated by an "independent, selfless," and nonmaterialistic spirit. Such "voluntary service" is considered essential to the integrity of MSFers' individual and collective commitment and, as one member put it, to the constant renewal of "freely using one's liberty to making the world a more bearable and better place."

In everyday and in front-lines situations, what I have termed the "nonideological ideology" of MSF, the structure within which it functions, and the nature of the work that it does continuously confront its members with the complexities of reconciling the multiform local and national, social, and cultural differences that they encounter in the field and inside their organization with their international, transnational, and universalistic outlook. To begin with, MSF's projects bring it into direct contact with a large number of societies, cultures, and subcultures, and with the significant, historically rooted, and tenacious ways that they diverge from one another—their shared humanity notwithstanding. The "without borders" orientation of MSF does not exempt its volunteers from the pragmatic necessity of recognizing, understanding, and dealing with the distinctive social and cultural values, beliefs, and practices that they face in each of the milieux where they carry out their humanitarian action. And in certain respects, their universalistic convictions may even enhance the difficulties they experience when they come into contact with cultural attitudes and conduct that not only differ from their own but that violate what they define as basic human rights—for example, with regard to the status and treatment of women, the conceptions of social deviance and of justice, and the modes of punishment in many of the societies in which they work. Furthermore, the missions that MSF undertakes entail operating in many settings where feuds and violent strife between clans, subclans, tribes, ethnic and religious groups occur and recur, accompanied by "terror, vengeance, and retribution that in numerous instances have eventuated in massacres of genocidal proportions, grave danger to the institutions of the society and their capacity to function, and the [forced] massive displacement of whole sectors of their populations" (Fox 2002). Under these circumstances, where it is difficult to distinguish the "victims" from the "victimizers," and the aid given may enable persons who have harmed or killed others to do so again, MSF faces painful questions about how to adhere in action to its principle of responding impartially to all people in need.

Within MSF, tensions surrounding its transnational calling and its multinational structure and composition also exist. MSF's five "operational" sections, based in France, Belgium, Holland, Spain, and Switzerland, directly control field projects by deciding when, where, and what medical aid is necessary, and when to close programs. The fact that all of these sections are situated in Western European countries is an organizational indicator of the importance that MSF's European origins continue to play in its culture, decision making, and governance. In addition there are thirteen "partner" sections located in a spectrum of countries that are not confined to continental Europe, including Australia, Canada, Hong Kong Special Administrative Region of China, Japan, the United Kingdom, and the United States, and, in continental Europe, Austria, Denmark, Germany, Italy, Luxembourg (partnered with MSF-Belgium), Norway, and Sweden. Their primary functions are to recruit an active pool of volunteers for placement with an operational section, raise funds for field projects, and conduct public outreach and education projects. In 2001, MSF's field personnel comprised 2,989 persons, referred to as "expatriates," who undertook missions in countries other than their own (an average of 1,567 such persons are serving in field posts at any one time in the course of the year), and an estimated 13,100 so-called "national" staff members who worked in their countries of origin. Both of these groups included doctors, nurses, various other health professionals, logistics experts, water and sanitation engineers, project and financial coordinators, and humanitarian affairs officers.

Although they are philosophically united by their "sans frontières," "without borders" vision, and are interconnected by an international office, the various sections of MSF are often involved in debate and negotiation with one another over the differences in perspectives, approaches, opinions, and reactions that exist between them, which their own national subcultures influence. For example, in the ongoing relations between MSF's three most important operational sections, the "French-ness" of MSF-France, the "Belgian-ness" of MSF-Belgium, and the "Dutch-ness" of MSF-Holland enter into the recurrence of certain patterned differences in the ways that they see and respond to issues. And there has even been one instance, in 1999, when the organization expelled a partner section, MSF-Greece, for the allegedly non-neutral, nationalistic manner in which it initiated and conducted a mission to the Serbs at the height of the Kosovo crisis. The internal functioning of MSF in countries where it has projects and missions also requires the reconciliation of diverse viewpoints, disagreements, and strains that may arise in relations between "national" and "expatriate" staff, and among staff members from the same country who belong to different tribal, ethnic, or religious groups. (MSF's International Council—composed of representatives chosen by every section, the president and the executive director of each section, and the secretary of the international office—which meets four times a year, constitutes an organizational forum in which such issues can be deliberated in a suprasectional, policy-relevant context.)

For MSF, as for American bioethics, the concept of universal human rights, especially as articulated in the Universal Declaration of Human Rights of 1948, occupies a central position of high moral importance in its system of values and its binding commitments. It is the core reference for MSF's witnessing activities, and their fulcrum. Like U.S. bioethics, MSF tends to deemphasize the persistent questions about the universality of these rights, which have been debated for more than fifty years—questions about the degree to which this doctrine of human rights originates in, expresses, and imposes Western individualism on the many societies in the world that have more "communitarian" cultures, and about its overall compatibility with the respectful acknowledgment of cultural diversity and pluralism.

Nevertheless, in the field, on a global scale, MSF works in a multitude of societies in which accepting as well as recognizing certain cultural differences may be pragmatically necessary if its presence and interventions are to be tolerated and effective in those settings. In some of these contexts, where traditional cultural attitudes and conduct run counter to supposedly universal human rights and are actively as well as passively assented to by a critical mass of MSF members, MSF is faced with hard choices between what it regards as conflicting practical and moral courses of action.

Just as numerous are the societies in which MSF conducts programs where, in the face of the poverty, illiteracy, violence, anarchy, or the pervasive breakdown of institutions that reign, it would be unrealistic and, beyond that, utopian to suppose that conditions exist for the realization of these human rights, or for effective human rights activism. In the face of these latter circumstances, MSF is inclined to cleave to the ideal of universal human rights and to advocate for them—though not without chagrin about their imperfect fulfillment or moral indignation sometimes approaching despair in situations where their violation results in collective tragedy.

A PARSONIAN PERSPECTIVE: PATTERN VARIABLES

What bearing does a Parsonian perspective have on this synoptic, comparative account of the ways in which American bioethics and Médecins Sans Frontières are interlaced with the themes of universalism and particularism? What light does Parsons's theoretical system—especially his core conception of normative order in social life—shed on the specific and on the more general meaning and import of universalism and particularism in these contexts, and on the questions and challenges that they pose? To begin with, Parsons regards the variables of universalism and particularism as fundamental, structural, cultural, and motivational axes of social life that are "patterns of cultural value-orientation" which "become integrated both in personalities and in social systems" (Parsons and Shils 1951, 79). In his view, along with the four other pattern-variable pairs, they are intrinsic to all social action and interaction, and to their meaning "through a microscopic-macroscopic range of action systems" (Parsons, Bales, and Shils 1953, 12). Furthermore, albeit in different permutations and combinations, they are dynamically present in societies in every stage of development, be they "primitive," "archaic," or modern. As Parsons phrased it, the primary issue to which universalism and particularism pertain concerns whether in their social orientation, roles, and relations, and also in their ideas, actors as individuals or in groups give primacy to particularistic norms and values that are integral to their own social attributes and those of the persons with whom they are involved, or whether they accord priority to more general, universalistic norms and values that transcend any specific relational system to which they and the persons with whom they are in interaction belong. This entails what Parsons considers a "major dilemma of orientation"—a crucial set of choices in a "series of choices that the actor [or actors] must make before the situation will have a determinate meaning" (Parsons and Shils 1951, 76). In his original conception of universalism-particularism, and the four other pairs of pattern variables as well, Parsons conceived of them as "dichotomies, and not continua." "Each concept," he declared, "sets up a polarity, a true dilemma" (Parsons and Shils 1951, 91).

Reviewing and reflecting upon the place that Parsons accorded to universalism-particularism as one of the basic sets of variables around which social action is oriented and organized in all social systems, "from the microscopic to the macroscopic" (Parsons, Bales and Shils 1953, 106), has augmented my appreciation and understanding of the importance that they have for MSF and bioethics, both internally and in relation to the societies in which they function and with which they are concerned. Furthermore, Parsons's characterization of these variables as foci of key dilemmas of choice that must be made not only for decisive individual and collective action to take place but also to endow that action with meaning has furthered my insight into what he would term their "expressive symbolism" for bioethicists and MSFers (Parsons 1951, 384–427; Parsons, Bales, and Shils 1953, 58–62, 69–85). In this connection, Parsons's "breakthrough" formulation that "every symbol has *both* [italics in original] expressive and cognitive meaning-references, and that every overt act or performance of an actor is in one aspect an expressive symbol" (Parsons, Bales, and Shils 1953, 80) is revelatory. It enabled him to see the pattern variables less dichotomously than he had originally. It also contributed to his exploration of their interconnections and to his identification of a systematic array of different combinations between universalism and particularism, ascription and achievement (quality-performance), specificity and diffuseness, affectivity and affective neutrality, and self-orientation and collectivity orientation. Parsons reached a point in his continually unfolding theory where he envisaged the possibility of interplay between universalism and particularism and of their co-institutionalization in a structured variety of ways, with each other as well as with other pattern variables. In contrast, both MSF and U.S. bioethics are inclined to polarize the principles of universalism and particularism, to regard them as inflexible antitheses, and to imbue their commitment to universalism, as opposed to particularism, with especially strong symbolic, emotional, and moral import.

This comparison with the trajectory of Parsons's thought about universalism-particularism has led me to consider the ways in which American bioethics and MSF could be viewed as social movements whose beliefs, values and goals, bases of collective identity, and patterns of solidarity are ideologically as well as intellectually shaped. My underlying assumptions about what constitutes an ideology are drawn from Parsons's conception of it as "a system of ideas held in common by the members of a collectivity . . . including a movement," that are not only "cognitive in nature," but also include "evaluative beliefs" about "the empirical nature of the collectivity and of the situation in which it is placed, the processes by which it has developed to its given state, the goals to which its members are collectively oriented" and to which they are empirically, symbolically, and affectively committed, and "the relation of these goals" to "the future course of events" (Parsons 1951, 349).

MSF would not consider it erroneous to be depicted as a movement. Quite to the contrary, as stated previously, it explicitly refers to itself as such, and as "a place . . . and a culture . . . of deeply convicted . . . ideas in debate . . . where ideas matter for action."[3] Nor has MSF objected to my portrayal of the core principles of its charter as a "nonideological ideology." Rather, it is being called an "organization" to which MSF is inclined to react negatively, because its members associate the term with the ever-present danger of becoming such a large, structured, hierarchical, bureaucratic, and impersonal entity that its founding "flame" would be dimmed and, to use Max Weber's language, its "charisma" would be "routinized."

In contradistinction, most bioethicists would be loathe to concede that their value preference for universalism, their cautiousness—bordering on mistrust—of particularism and of yielding to cultural differences, and the ardent quality of their espousal of the precepts of "principlism" contain elements of ideology. Their collective commitment to an ethical outlook, mode of thought, and purpose that are based on and dedicated to an olympian kind of rational intellectuality ideologically incline them to believe that their perspective, their intent, and their policy emphases and recommendations are ideology-free. However, in a recent publication, Daniel Callahan has challenged this assumption. "I call . . . the almost complete triumph of liberal individualism in bioethics . . . an ideology rather than a moral theory," he declares (Callahan 2003, 498), because

> . . . it is a set of essentially political and social values brought into bioethics, not as a formal theory but as a vital background constellation of values. If it does not function as a moral theory as philosophers have understood this concept, it is clearly present and pervasive as a litmus test of the acceptability of certain ideas and ways of framing issues. As a familiar constellation it encompasses a high place for autonomy, for biomedical progress with few constraints, for procedural rather than substantive solutions to controverted ethical problems, and for a strong antipathy to comprehensive notions of the common good.

PARSONS'S THEORY OF SOCIETAL EVOLUTION AND MODERNITY

Universalism and particularism are also pivotal variables in the analysis of the evolutionary unfolding of modern society that Parsons developed. His evolutionary perspective on modernity and its core attributes, the process of institutionalization that modernization entails, and the challenges that it poses provide a larger sociohistorical context for considering the value orientations of U.S. bioethics and of MSF and for understanding the tensions that exist between their ideals and the social and cultural characteristics of the situations in which they operate and to which they respond.

Parsons's analytic account of the evolution of modern societies revolves around four basic processes of interacting structural change that he termed "differentiation," "adaptive upgrading," "inclusion," and "value generalization" (Parsons 1961; 1966, 21–24; 1971, 26–30). As a society becomes increasingly modern, he postulated, it develops a more elaborate and complex division of labor with a multiplicity of new, specialized roles and a greater amount of "role-pluralism"—"the involvement of the same persons in several collectivities" (1971, 12). Key to what Parsons referred to as "the emergence of societies from primitiveness" is the development of a system of social stratification that involves a break with kinship-based ascription on the one hand and on the other, a kind of "cultural legitimization" that is sufficiently independent of kinship and of a diffuse, undifferentiated religious tradition to provide a society with an inclusive definition of itself as distinct from and in relationship to other societies.

According to Parsons, once these social-stratification and cultural-legitimization propellants have moved a society past the primitive stage, four other "features" or "complexes" that are "fundamental to the structure of modern societies" develop and become progressively institutionalized, "each with varying degrees of completeness and relative importance." These are bureaucratic organization, money and markets, "generalized, universalistic legal systems," and "the democratic association," with elective leadership and a fully enfranchised citizenry. In addition, Parsons identified "certain cultural developments" as events of special importance to the process of modernization, and to the viability of a modern society (Parsons 1964; Parsons 1971; Parsons 1977). These developments were the "philosophical breakthroughs" that produced what Robert Bellah has called the "world" religions (and Shmuel N. Eisenstadt, the "axial" religions), the "level of institutionalization" that science and technology reached in the course of the twentieth century, and "the continuous extension of the education of the population."

In overview, then, underlying these "structural foundations" of modernity and "tying them together," as Parsons saw it, are the broadening of a society's "emancipation from ascription"; its increasing differentiation, complexity, pluralism, and egalitarianism; the greater autonomy of its "subunits" (Parsons 1964, 312, 325); and the grounding of its collective identity, cultural legitimation, and conception of morality in a system of general, universalistic norms and values that transcend particular individual and group relationships (Parsons 1977, 113–14). Furthermore, he contended that this movement away from ascriptive particularism toward inclusive universalism was creating a "new kind of societal community" that is "not peculiar to . . . one society but permeate[s] the whole modern—and 'modernizing'—system." Partly as a consequence of the industrial revolution, the democratic revolution, and, more recently, the educational revolution, he observed, virtually all contemporary societies were not only becoming more modern, but also more similar to one another as they incrementally moved in the direction of forming "one modern culture" (Parsons 1977, 229).

Although Parsons regarded the combination of social- organizational and cultural attributes that he associated with modernity as "evolutionary universals" fundamental to the process of modernization in whatever society it occurs and as conducive to a global "convergence of sociocultural development" (Parsons, 1977, 229), he recognized and wrote extensively about the origins and rootedness of modern societies in Western European culture and history. He also insisted that the contemporaneous trend toward modernization in an increasingly interdependent world did not mean that societies were "carbon copies of one another." Rather, he said, they "remain differentiated from one another," especially with regard to the roles they play in the still-evolving modern world system; and, he predicted that "variations within the modern type of society will probably turn out to be great" (Parsons 1977, 215, 228–29). In this connection he "paid special attention" to American society. This was not, he averred, because of his "parochial loyalties" or chauvinistic tendencies (Parsons 1977, 215). Rather, he said, without implying that evolution connoted "moral superiority," he viewed the United States as a "lead society" and exemplar of the new type of modern societal community that was emerging—one that had gone further in institutionalizing the value patterns of "instrumental activism," individualism, "differentiatedness," "associational pluralism," egalitarianism, decentralization, and a wide range of freedoms, than any other comparable large-scale contemporaneous society (Parsons, 1971, 86–121; 1977, 215; Parsons and Platt 1975, 223).

Seen from a broad, evolutionary vantage point, Parsons claimed, these developments brought with them an increase in the collective performance of a society and the greater possibility and likelihood that individuals and groups within it would have freer access to a more extensive range of resources—including knowledge and skill—that would augment their opportunities, productivity, creativity, and achievement. In this connection, he did not deal with an eventuality that has in fact come to pass in numerous postcolonial African, Asian, Middle Eastern, and South American societies—namely, that through both the corrupt and the legitimate exercise of influence and power, the resources and opportunities that the process of modernization has opened up have been appropriated by a small, self-interested group in the society at the expense of the population at large, who are subject to great deprivation.

Nevertheless, Parsons was mindful of the fact that these concomitants of modernity did not eliminate societal problems of inequality, social justice, and poverty, and might even enhance the tension surrounding them. In addition, he was keenly aware of the critical issues of integration that modern societies faced. Their chief locus, he said—their "storm center"—lay "not in the economy, the polity, or the value system . . . [but] in the societal community," because the process of modernization "undermin[es]" the legitimacy of such older, more particularistic, ascriptive bases of membership as "ethnic affiliation, region or locality, and hereditary position." Consequently, "the motivational bases of social solidarity" and generalized trust within a "large-scale," "extensive," "pluralistic" modern society can be problematic (Parsons 1977, 119, 121, 143).

Parsons identified "fundamentalism" as one of the more serious difficulties that the major social and cultural changes effected by modernization could engender—especially through the ways that the "process of rationalization" modernism entails, disrupts, and dynamically alters "the primary symbolic systems which help to integrate the life of a society" and "the structure of the situations in which a large part of the population must carry on their activities" (Parsons 1954c, 315). In his view, it was the most traditionally oriented groups of persons in a society who were the most likely to be acutely "threatened" by these at once ramifying and deep-structure changes and to respond to them with a "fundamentalist reaction" that "exaggerated" and might also "distort" traditional values. The values around which such fundamentalism tended to "cluster," he stated, were "those particularly important in the constitution and symbolization of informal group solidarities—those of families, social class, socioreligious groups, ethnic groups, and nations"—that, he remarked, were "seriously in conflict with the explicit values of the Western world which largely stem from the rationalistic traditions of the Enlightenment" (316–17). He also pointed out that in addition, modernizing changes could trigger a "reverse" kind of fundamentalist reaction—an equally exaggerated and aggressive assertion of "emancipated values" that branded traditional values as " 'stupid,' reactionary, [and] unenlightened" and thereby helped to create a "vicious circle of mounting antagonism" within a society (317).

Parsons cited a wide array of ideological forms in which fundamentalist patterns of reaction could occur, including the religious and societal conservatism of Dutch Calvinists in South Africa during the era of apartheid, the "Fascist movements of the twentieth century," and the "fundamentalism of the extreme left, from certain phases of various Communist parties to the . . . New Left" (Parsons 1977, 194–95). However, he directed most of his attention to fundamentalist patterns in twentieth-century Fascism, particularly in Europe, with special concentration on Nazi Germany and on nationalism as the "readiest channel" into which both "traditional" and "emancipated" forms of fundamentalism could mutually "flow" (Parsons 1954a; 1954b, 138).

PARSONS'S THEORY AND THE MODERN SOCIOHISTORICAL CONTEXT OF U.S. BIOETHICS AND MSF

Parsons's treatment of the evolutionary development of modern society helps to historically and sociologically situate the value systems of U.S. bioethics and MSF, the issues of universalism and particularism they have encountered, and the ways they have dealt with them. His theory has heightened my awareness of the extent to which the history of bioethics and of MSF is integrally connected with the unfolding scenario of modernization during the second half of the twentieth century. It might even be said that, to a significant degree since their inception and during the more than thirty years of their existence, through their intellectual analysis and ethical testimony, their public policy involvements and pronouncements, and (in the case of MSF) their humanitarian action, American bioethics and Médecins Sans Frontières have been consistently concerned with the fulfillment, implementation, and extension of what Parsons considered some of the most important fruits of modern society. At the same time they have also played an actively watchful and admonitory role with regard to what Jürgen Habermas (2002, 61) has referred to as "the Janus-like face of modernism" and the (often unintended) adverse effects that the process of modernization can bring, and has brought, in its wake. In this latter respect, they (most particularly MSF) have been more impressed than Parsons by the ramifying disparities and forms of harm to which the repercussions of modernity have contributed, nationally and globally. (I will return to this last observation.)

It is pertinent to note that bioethics emerged in the United States, and MSF originated in France in the late 1960s and early 1970s during a time of reverberating social protest in both societies, spearheaded by the so-called "student revolution," and a cascade of "liberation" and "rights" movements, including women's, antiwar, and human rights movements, the civil rights movement in the United States, and in Europe, especially in France, "tiers-mondisme," or "third-worldism" (Judt 1992, 284–86), precipitated by the widespread occurrence of anticolonialist movements in Africa, Asia, and Latin America. A significant number of the founder-leaders and the first-generation members of MSF and American bioethics had been intensively involved in these movements. They brought to the new realms of humanitarian and bioethical activity the ardent commitment to the modern Western ethos of egalitarian and individualistic universalism on which their previous engagements were based. From the outset, both MSF and bioethics have been strongly inclined to consider the Universal Declaration of Human Rights (first set forth in the Charter of the General Assembly of the United Nations on December 10, 1948) a touchstone statement of the major universalistic principles they espouse. They have not been as disposed to examine whether the fact that it is a proclamation emanating from Western tradition and historical experience makes it less culturally universal than they have assumed. MSF's very name—"sans frontières," "without borders"—expresses the encompassing transnational, simultaneously European and worldwide vision of universalism on which it was founded.

U.S. bioethics' universalistic outlook has been more abstractly and apolitically confined to the four sets of what it considers to be its "common morality" principles in which, especially during the 1970s and 1980s, a very Western, and distinctively American, emphasis on an autonomous, self-determining form of individualism predominated. There are elements of paradox in the ways that particularistic, Western, cultural assumptions have contributed to the importance that MSF and U.S. bioethics mutually attach to universalism.

The development, application, and institutionalization of advanced modern science and technology—especially their relationship to medicine—have also been core focuses of the ethos and action of bioethics and of MSF. As the neologism "bioethics" was intended to connote, since its inception, this field has concentrated its attention on "a particular cluster of [modern] scientific, technological, and clinical advances in biology and medicine, and on the . . . [moral] questions and quandaries to which these . . . developments, and the means of achieving them have contributed" (Fox 1999, 7).

The raison d'être of Doctors Without Borders is fundamentally medical. Although the personnel of MSF is not confined to physicians or exclusively to health professionals, its basic humanitarian mission is to bring universalistically delivered medical assistance and care to victims of natural and human-made disasters, and to those who lack care as a result of social, economic, or political exclusion. Their action involves far-reaching efforts to make available to the populations they serve a pharmacopoeia of the most pertinent and needed modern drugs and the logistical and technological skills of water and sanitation specialists and other public health experts, along with hands-on medical care.

Increasingly the medical and public health aid that MSF provides has come to center on what is euphemistically referred to in medical parlance as the "emergence and reemergence" of infectious diseases. This is in response to the fact that the incidence of "old" and "new" infectious diseases of epidemic and pandemic proportions has become the most serious world health problem. The most devastating of an estimated twenty-five or more new infectious diseases that have made their appearance in the past twenty-seven years is HIV/AIDS. Among the old infectious diseases that have recrudesced, the most significant in their scope and serious adverse implications are multi-drug-resistant tuberculosis (often associated with HIV/AIDS), malaria, and measles. There is irony in this state of affairs, not only because MSF came into being in a post–World War II medical era of hubristic triumphalism, when it was assumed, and even proclaimed, that modern Western medicine had "conquered" infectious disease and its pathogenic agents, but also because among the many factors that have contributed to the current epidemics are the iatrogenic consequences of the extensive, often overextensive, use of certain modern so-called "wonder" drugs, such as antibiotics, in human and veterinary medicine and in agriculture and aquaculture as well. This has led to the development of strains of microbes that have become resistant to a substantial proportion of these drugs. In addition, the impact of still other modern and modernizing conditions has played a role in the outbreak and spread of epidemics. Increasing population density in cities, the extension of global travel, and, most notably, the ways the expansion of free-market capitalism has progressively widened the gap between rich and poor countries—especially during the 1990s—have worsened the situation of the world's poor and made them more vulnerable to infectious disease.

The issues U.S. bioethics and MSF deal with and the values they espouse bring them into close contact with the modern pharmaceutical and biotechnology industry. In the case of bioethics, this contact is largely associated with bioethics' historic involvement in the ethics of human experimentation and of clinical trials and with its research and policy reflection on ethical issues in genetics—including genomic and genetic engineering, the patenting and licensing of genetic tests, gene therapy, stem-cell research, cloning, genetically modified organisms and foods, and the use of DNA data bases. Some of the bioethical inquiries undertaken in these areas receive funding from for-profit drug and biotechnology companies that are involved and invested in the very activities that bioethicists are examining. This has raised conflict-of-interest-related ethical questions and generated increasingly heated debate about them within the bioethics community.

The relationship of MSF to the pharmaceutical industry has been more challenging and disputatious. MSF has played a catalytic and a leadership role in showing that life-saving medicines are not available or affordable to people in many of the countries where they work. Using the money that they received in 1999 when they were awarded the Nobel Prize for Peace, they launched an ongoing Campaign for Access to Essential Medicines. A key focus of their advocacy has entailed demonstrating and speaking out about the part that drug companies have played in this "lack of access" through their profit-oriented, exorbitant pricing of drugs; their blockage of the distribution of less expensive generic drugs by the self-protective maintenance of patents on drugs that they manufacture; their reluctance to produce, sell, or try to develop effective drugs for diseases, such as tuberculosis and malaria, that primarily affect the poor and are the most common killers in developing countries, as against their emphasis on tapping into more lucrative drug markets by developing drugs for conditions such as heart disease, obesity, and impotence. MSF also organized and convened the Drugs for Neglected Diseases Initiative, a framework for experts from around the world to tackle these matters. This working group's analysis held not only the pharmaceutical industry responsible for the access to essential medicines, neglected diseases, and "orphaned drug" problems but also the public sector for failing to set up "solidarity mechanisms" to counter this crisis. In 2002, at the annual "National Assemblies" held by their operational sections, MSF took an unprecedented further step when it voted to become a fully participating member in the Drugs for Neglected Diseases Initiative by using part of its financial resources to help support research and development for drugs for neglected diseases undertaken by academic, public, nongovernmental, and private research groups, including pharmaceutical and biotechnology companies. Involvement in this initiative "will entail certain changes in MSF's mission and activities," an internal MSF document states. But it "responds to field-based, medical problems we have been raising for many years" (Pécoul 2002).

As previously indicated, in a striking number of the societies where MSF is present to render care and witness, particularistic "wars of all against all" are being waged that seem to belie Parsons's analytic account of a progressively modernizing world in which the values of a universalistic "solidarity among strangers" (Jürgen Habermas 2002, 61) and an autonomous individuality are becoming more widely embraced and institutionalized. On the continents of Europe, Africa, and Asia and in South America and the Middle East, MSF's humanitarian activities take place in many settings where such ferocious primordial conflict has been occurring for years between primary ascriptive groups. Furthermore, in several of the countries where MSF is at work, fundamentalist Islamic governments are in power that autocratically and militantly enforce neotraditional thought, structures, and behavior on the basis of religion, gender, kinship, and tribal and ethnic affiliation. These traditional strictures include severe restrictions on the conduct of women both inside and outside the home. Much of MSF's work must be viewed in the context of the European Union (EU), the transnational, legally established, and democratically conceived economic and political community that was formed after World War II. A number of MSF's projects involve tackling some of the medical, economic, and social repercussions of nationalistic responses triggered by the EU's challenge to the nation-state, national sovereignty, and national culture, and of exclusionary and xenophobic reactions to the massive influx of immigrants and refugees to Western European countries that has taken place in recent years. In addition, in various European settings, as elsewhere, MSF grapples with particularistic strains and conflicts within its own organization that occur partly because of and partly in spite of its "sans-frontièrisme."

THEORETICAL IMPLICATIONS

What implications does this cursory examination of the relationship of MSF and of U.S. bioethics to some of the concomitants of modernization have for Parsons's theory of social evolution and modern society, especially with regard to his concepts of universalism, particularism, and societal community?

On one level, it seems to substantiate Parsons's depiction of the major attributes of modernity, and of the pervasive impact of the process of modernization on societies throughout the contemporary world. At the same time, in spite of his theoretical emphasis on the "pattern-maintenance" properties of values and beliefs, statuses, role relationships, and affiliations and their anchoring and integrative functions in a society, and despite his insistence on the "many factors of continuity with the past" that can be discerned in the "major changes . . . in process" (Parsons 1971, 142–43), Parsons appears to have underestimated the tenacity of ascriptive particularism and its manifestations in the face of modernizing forces. Furthermore, although he identified the problems of "integrating the consequences" of modernization with "the exigencies" of the new kind of societal community that it has brought in its wake, and though he expressed his "conviction" that these problems would not be "solved without a great deal of conflict" (1971, 143), he did not realize the extent to which this would prove to be the case even in those societies that he characterized as "the more 'privileged' societies of the later twentieth century [that] to an impressive degree [had] successfully institutionalized the more 'liberal' and 'progressive' values of that time" (1971, 115).

More striking still was Parsons's failure to imagine that in the midst of what he portrayed as a continuing world evolution toward a "culminating phase of modern development" that he hoped might move toward "completion" over the course of the twenty-first century, many societies of diverse cultural traditions located on every continent of the globe would be rent by internecine conflict between the kind of ascribed, particularistic groups that are characteristic of a more primitive, kin-centered and kin-organized society. Among the factors contributing to this strife and also to the installation of fundamentalist Islamic regimes in South Asia, the Middle East, and Africa is the perturbation caused by the social and cultural influences of modernity and the neotraditional reaction formation that they have engendered. In this rather perverse way, it could be said that these developments support Parsons's contention that although it originated in the West, modernization has become a powerful global force. However, Parsons was impressed by what he referred to as the "significance of the nation-state" as a "dominant power unit" and by the "strong pressure to internal unity" and "ultimate loyalty to one's government" that existed within each nation. This led him to suppose that the main targets of societal "aggression" in the modern world would not be inward ones; rather, he assumed that, sparked by nationalism, this aggression would be projected outwardly and expressed mainly through enmity, confrontation, and war between national societies (1954c, 318–19). A scenario that he did not envision is that of a nation-state being brought "to the brink of extinction" by strife *within* the society, or by the convergence of conflict between warring parties both from within and from outside the society—a situation that currently exists in a number of countries (Mutua 2002).

We have seen that Parsons did anticipate a considerable degree of "deflation" of commitment to modern values in the form of "fundamentalism" and that he regarded the social and cultural phenomena associated with it as dangerous. Nonetheless, he was outspokenly critical of what he called the "widespread . . . ideological pessimism over the viability of modern societ[ies] . . . and their moral right to survive without the most radical changes," which he felt was "especially [prevalent] among intellectuals" (Parsons 1971, 142). And he did not foresee the magnitude and scope of reactive despotism, xenophobia, violence, and terrorism that modernity—often perceived as "exported from the West," especially from the United States—would unleash during the last decades of the twentieth century and the early years of the twenty-first. Perhaps this was due in part to the fact that in the 1970s, the historical period when Parsons was elaborating his theory of social evolution and modern society—which was also the last decade of his life—the Cold War and the titanic politico-ideological struggle that it entailed between Communism, especially in its Soviet Union and People's Republic of China models, and the democratic capitalist West still occupied the center of the world stage. As a consequence, the threat of violence about which he was mainly concerned and on which he centered his attention was the danger that under these circumstances a head-on collision between nation-states might eventuate in nuclear destruction.

As Leon Mayhew has pointed out (1982, 54–55), Parsons's "solidly grounded," intellectually "sophisticated" theory of modernity was undergirded by his "faith in modern society in general and the American version in particular." His own value commitments in this regard may account in part for the relatively minor conceptual and empirical attention that he paid to the sorts of unfavorable consequences of modernization and modernity with which MSF and U.S. bioethics, each in its own way, dedicatedly deal. I think it important to reiterate here that the values embraced and upheld by MSF and U.S. bioethics—especially their conceptions of universalism, individualism, equality, and justice—have roots in modern as well as Western cultural tradition and that, as mentioned earlier, their universalistic convictions notwithstanding, the guiding ethos of MSF continues to be discernibly European, and the principles and outlook of U.S. bioethics identifiably American. Because they would consider it a sign of defective universalism, neither bioethicists nor members of MSF would be easily inclined to acknowledge this, and they would no doubt be startled to hear that they share with Talcott Parsons a strong belief and hope in the worth and worthiness of modern society.

CODA

At the inception of the twenty-first century, both U.S. bioethics and MSF are confronting new, politicized forms of particularism that constitute serious threats to their universalistic commitments. Inside the American bioethics community, particularism is manifesting itself in the form of escalating ideological and political animosity between so-called "liberal" and "conservative" bioethicists:

> The rancorousness has been most conspicuous in statements made by bioethicists in professional publications and in the media about stem cell research, human cloning, genetic enhancement, the use of fetal tissues and embryos more generally, the place of religious thought and belief in ethical analysis, and about the potential dangers and harms, as well as benefits that advances in medical science and technology can bring in their wake. . . . There is a sense in which the divisiveness that has developed inside of bioethics mirrors the passion-accompanied divisions between liberals and conservatives about "moral values" in American society that the U.S. presidential election of 2004 brought flamboyantly to the surface (Fox and Swazey, forthcoming).

In Afghanistan and Iraq, where MSF and other non-governmental humanitarian organizations attempt to bring assistance to civilian populations, their aid workers have become targets of life-endangering attacks that have caused them—with expressions of "deep sadness and regret"—to leave these countries (Gillies and Buissonnière 2005). Rowan Gillies (2004), president of the MSF International Council, delivered a speech in Amman in November 2004, upon accepting the King Hussein Humanitarian Leadership Prize that was awarded to the organization. In this speech, he attributed the "assaults against humanitarian organizations" in large measure to the "increasing attempt by Western governments to co-opt the humanitarian act by presenting combat tactics and political strategies as humanitarian operations. . . . We are told," he declared, " 'be with us or against us,' " and "warned against a clash of cultures [that denies] the universal nature of both humanitarian action and medical ethics. . . . Being humanitarian," he asserted with universalistic fervor, is:

> - NOT about winning the hearts and minds of the people,
> - It is NOT about imposing a political system, good or bad,
> - And it is NOT about winning wars, or even building peace.
>
> It IS a visceral and practical response of one human being to the suffering of another. It is an apolitical act and by definition a civilian act (Gillies 2004, emphasis in original).

Although these present-day historical developments extend beyond Parsons's life span, they are illumined by his conceptions of universalism, particularism, and the unfolding of modern society. At the same time, as he would have quickly recognized, they raise important questions about how his theory might need to be altered to account for their occurrence and to analytically interpret their significance and meaning. I believe that he would have been troubled, even alarmed, by the societal and global implications of the kinds of menaces to universalism that U.S. bioethics and MSF are now facing.

NOTES

1. Judith P. Swazey and I were the principal investigators of this "Bioethics in American Society" project, which we conducted with the assistance of Carla M. Messikomer. The project was supported by grants from the Greenwall Foundation, the National Library of Medicine (RO 1 LMO6893), and the National Science Foundation's Program on Societal Dimensions of Engineering, Science, and Technology (SBR-910579). The views about bioethics expressed in this paper are those of the author.
2. I am the sole investigator involved in this research undertaking, which has been supported by grants from Medicine in the Public Interest, the Acadia Institute, the Nuffield Foundation, and the Andrew W. Mellon Foundation.
3. James Orbinski, letter, personal communication (April 11, 2002).

REFERENCES

Beauchamp, Tom L. 2003. "A Defense of the Common Morality." *Kennedy Institute of Ethics Journal* 13(3): 259–74.

Beauchamp, Tom L., and James F. Childress. 1979/2001. *Principles of Biomedical Ethics.* 5th edition. New York: Oxford University Press.

Bourdieu, Pierre. 2001. "Uniting to Better Dominate." *Items and Issues* (Social Sciences Research Council) 2(3–4): 1–6.

Callahan, Daniel. 1999. "The Social Sciences and the Task of Bioethics." *Daedalus* 128(4): 275–94.

———. 2000. "Universalism and Particularism: Fighting to a Draw." *Hastings Center Report* 30(1): 37–44.

———. 2003. "Individual Good and Common Good: A Communitarian Approach to Bioethics." *Perspectives in Biology and Medicine* 46(4): 496–507.

Childress, James F. 1994. "Principles-Oriented Bioethics: An Analysis and Assessment from Within." In *A Matter of Principles? Ferment in U.S. Bioethics,* edited by Edwin R. DuBose, Ronald P. Hamel, and Laurence O'Connell. Valley Forge, Pa.: Trinity Press.

Fox, Renée C. 1997. "Talcott Parsons, My Teacher." *American Scholar* 66(3): 395–410.

———. 1999. "Is Medical Education Asking Too Much of Bioethics?" *Daedalus* 128(4): 1–25.

———. 2002. "A Proposal to Convene a Planning Group to Organize a Conference on Unanticipated and Unintended Consequences and Moral Dilemmas of Medical Humanitarian Action." Unpublished paper.

Fox, Renée C., and Judith P. Swazey. 1984. "Medical Morality Is Not Bioethics—Medical Ethics in China and the United States." *Perspectives in Biology and Medicine* 27(3): 336–60.

———. Forthcoming. "Examining American Bioethics: Its Problems and Prospects." *Cambridge Quarterly of Healthcare Ethics.*

Gillies, Rowan. 2004. "The King Hussein Humanitarian Leadership Speech." MSF Press Release, posted on the MSF Website on November 11. Available at: www.msf.org (accessed November 24, 2004).

Gillies, Rowan, and Marine Buissonnière. 2005. *The Year 2004 in Review.* Available at: www.msf.org (accessed January 5, 2005).

Gustafson, James F. 1990. "Moral Disclosure About Medicine: A Variety of Forms." *Journal of Medicine and Philosophy* 15: 125–42.

Habermas, Jürgen. 2002. "Toward a European Political Community." *Society* 39(5): 58–61.

Havel, Václav. 1994. Address on receiving the Liberty Medal at Independence Hall. Philadelphia (July 4, 1994). Transcript. *The Philadelphia Inquirer.*

———. 2002. "A Farewell to Politics." *New York Review of Books* October 24, 4.

Judt, Tony. 1992. *Past Imperfect: French Intellectuals, 1944–1956.* Los Angeles: University of California Press.

LaFleur, William R. 2002. "Finding the Breaks: Japanese Critics of America's Biotech Juggernaut." Book proposal sent to author.

Macklin, Ruth. 1999. *Against Relativism: Cultural Diversity and the Search for Ethical Universals in Medicine.* New York: Oxford University Press.

Mayhew, Leon H., ed. 1982. *Talcott Parsons: On Institutions and Social Evolution.* Chicago: University of Chicago Press.

Mutua, Makau 2002. "Struggling to End Africa's World War." *New York Times,* August 8, 2002, A21.

Nussbaum, Martha C. 1997. *Cultivating Humanity: A Classical Defense of Reform in Liberal Education.* Cambridge, Mass.: Harvard University Press.

Parsons, Talcott 1938. "The Role of Theory in Social Research." *American Sociological Review* 3(1): 13–20.

———. 1951. *The Social System.* Glencoe, Ill.: Free Press.

———. 1954a. "Democracy and Social Structure in Pre-Nazi Germany." *Essays in Sociological Theory.* Revised edition. Glencoe, Ill.: Free Press.

———. 1954b. "Some Sociological Aspects of Fascist Movements." *Essays in Sociological Theory.* Revised edition. Glencoe, Ill.: Free Press.

———. 1954c. "Certain Primary Sources and Patterns of Aggression in the Social Structure of the Western World." *Essays in Sociological Theory.* Revised edition. Glencoe, Ill.: Free Press.

———. 1961. "Some Considerations on the Theory of Social Change." *Rural Sociology* 26: 219–39.

———. 1964. "Evolutionary Universals in Society." *American Sociological Review* 29(3): 339–457.

———. 1966. *Societies: Evolutionary and Comparative Perspectives.* Englewood Cliffs, N.J.: Prentice-Hall.

———. 1971. *The System of Modern Societies.* Englewood Cliffs, N.J.: Prentice-Hall.

———. 1977. *The Evolution of Societies,* edited and with an introduction by Jackson Toby. Englewood Cliffs, N.J.: Prentice-Hall.

Parsons Talcott, Robert F. Bales, and Edward A. Shils. 1953. *Working Papers in the Theory of Action.* Glencoe, Ill.: Free Press.

Parsons, Talcott, and Gerald M. Platt. 1975. *The American University.* Cambridge, Mass.: Harvard University Press.

Parsons, Talcott, and Edward A. Shils, eds. 1951. *Toward a General Theory of Action.* Cambridge, Mass.: Harvard University Press.

Pécoul, Bernard. 2002. "Frequently Asked Questions on MSF Involvement in the DNdi." Unpublished report. Paris: MSF.

ten Have, Henk 1994. "Principlism: A Western European Appraisal." In *A Matter of Principles? Ferment in U.S. Bioethics,* edited by Edwin R. DuBose, Ronald P. Hamel, and Laurence J. O'Connell. Valley Forge, Pa.: Trinity Press.

Chapter 15

"Social Evolution" in the Light of the Human-Condition Paradigm

Victor M. Lidz

Talcott Parsons's method of developing theory involved repeated revision of even basic concepts (Lidz 2000). His conception of the action frame of reference, for example, first formulated in *The Structure of Social Action* (Parsons 1937), was revised in the manuscript *Actor, Situation and Normative Pattern* two years later (Parsons 1939), and again in *Toward a General Theory of Action* (Parsons and Shils 1951), resulting in the now familiar triad of the cognitive, cathectic, and moral-evaluative dimensions of action. The 1951 formulation was in turn revised with the introduction of the four-function paradigm in the *Working Papers in the Theory of Action* (Parsons, Bales, and Shils 1953). Further modifications were proposed in the "General Introduction" to *Theories of Society* (Parsons 1961a) and the essay "Some Problems of General Theory in Sociology" (Parsons 1970), and in the theoretical sections of *The American University* (Parsons and Platt 1973). Similarly, the pattern variables first proposed in *Toward a General Theory of Action* and *The Social System* (Parsons 1951) were reformulated two years later in *Working Papers in the Theory of Action* in light of the four-function paradigm. Several years later, when abstract implications of the four-function paradigm had been clarified, Parsons attempted to reframe the pattern variables again in the essay "Pattern Variables Revisited" (Parsons 1967, chapter 7).

The same type of reworking occurred in Parsons's treatment of less abstract, more substantively focused topics. His analysis of social stratification in the first essay of 1941 (Parsons 1949, chapter 7), the wartime essays on the emergence of Nazism in Germany (reprinted in Gerhardt 1993), the early four-function essay on stratification (Parsons 1953, chapter 19), the two books on social evolution, *Societies: Evolutionary and Comparative Perspectives* (Parsons 1966) and *The System of Modern Societies* (Parsons 1971), and finally in an unpublished manuscript, "*The American Societal Community,*" (Parsons 1979) shows a progressive reworking of core insights in terms of an increasingly refined understanding of strata formation in complex societies.

In this chapter I undertake a process of reconsidering Parsons's schema of social evolution, which was developed during the 1960s and early 1970s, in light of the human-condition paradigm, which was presented in Parsons's last major essay (Parsons 1978, chapter 15), but had been under development from the summer of 1974. I try to engage the basic implications of the human-condition paradigm for understanding human evolution. As will become apparent, this undertaking is complicated and raises questions about formulations at many levels of the theory of action. I try to suggest the conceptual richness of the basic dimensions of the human-condition paradigm and the problems it raises for understanding human evolution. Although it will not be possible to resolve all of the issues, I hope to stimulate continuing discussion.

Parsons taught courses titled "Comparative Institutional Analysis" from the 1930s nearly until his retirement from Harvard University in 1973. The courses usually followed the plan of Max Weber's comparative studies in religion and civilization. In the early 1960s, however, Parsons began to introduce his course with the assertion that it was time to reclaim the theory of social evolution from the disrepute that had resulted from decades of cultural relativism, particularly in anthropology. An "evolutionary" theme of growing complexity of social institutions then served as the integrating principle for wide-ranging analyses of comparative materials in his lectures. Course readings and Parsons's lectures in the 1960s and 1970s discussed materials as diverse as W. Lloyd Warner's *A Black Civilization* (Warner 1937) on an Australian aboriginal people, Henri Frankfort's writings on ancient Egyptian religion and society (Frankfort 1948), selections from Max Weber's studies of world religions and the civilizations they generated, works on medieval and Reformation Europe, Perry Miller's writings on Puritan society in colonial New England (Miller 1933, 1961, 1965), historians' analyses of modernizing social change in Europe and America, and social-scientific works on economic and political modernization in non-Western societies. Parsons outlined four-function paradigms for analyzing whole societies as well as specific institutional complexes.

The theme of social evolution penetrated Parsons's more technical graduate seminars as well as his lecture courses. In the early 1960s, his seminar "Topics in the Theory of Social Systems" focused on the theory of generalized symbolic media but included presentations on evolutionary changes in the media. In the spring of 1963, Parsons taught a seminar "Social Evolution" with Robert N. Bellah and Shmuel N. Eisenstadt. Parsons's own presentation discussed considerations in favor of an evolutionary analysis of economic institutions. The seminar read *Political Systems of Empires* (Eisenstadt 1963), then in page proofs, and Eisenstadt discussed processes of the growth and decline of empires with diverse historical illustrations. Bellah presented on religious evolution, outlining a specific theory of stages, later published in his article "Religious Evolution" (Bellah 1970, chapter 2). Bellah's presentation marked a turning point in the seminar. After his talk, the seminar members gave priority to outlining parallel stages for other institutional domains of society, including political systems, law, and social stratification. Parsons picked up the stage theory himself, closing the seminar with a discussion of evolutionary stages in the development of economic institutions.

The following summer Parsons began to write the manuscripts that years later in third drafts became *Societies: Evolutionary and Comparative Perspectives* (Parsons 1966) and *The System of Modern Societies* (Parsons 1971). His draft materials show that in the course of writing these works he studied a considerable body of materials on many societies, historical epochs, and institutional complexes, produced many provisional analyses of particular societies, stages of evolution, and processes of social change, and revised his more general evolutionary formulations several times. As his student and research assistant in this period, I became a convinced social evolutionist and framed much of my own thought, teaching, and writing in evolutionary terms. Among my early publications were brief essays schematically introducing sections of the *Readings on Premodern Societies* (Lidz and Parsons 1972), essays in which I offered some refinements of the evolutionary scheme of stages that he had developed.

In the early 1970s, Parsons convened two conferences at the American Academy of Arts and Sciences on relations between biological and social theory (discussed in Parsons 1977, chapter 5). His goal for the conferences was to demonstrate a convergence between elements of biological and sociological theory. Although that goal was more frustrated than fulfilled in the exchanges between biologists and social scientists, Parsons revitalized his interests in homeostatic theory and hierarchies of control in complex systems while preparing for the conferences. These interests had led him to fruitful insights at least as far back as his first formulations in functional theory, influenced in part by Walter B. Cannon's *Wisdom of the Body* (Cannon 1932/1963); Lawrence J. Henderson's writings in physiology (Barber 1970), and, later, Norbert Wiener's cybernetic concepts (Wiener 1948). At the time of the conferences, Parsons updated his biological interests by reading James D. Watson's *Molecular Biology of the Gene* (Watson 1965). I attended both conferences and at the second one presented a paper comparing the role of language as a medium of the general action system providing means of circulating information to all subsystems of action, to the role of blood as a circulating medium of the human body (Lidz 1981).

In the summer of 1974, Parsons prepared a memorandum for a number of his collaborators that first outlined the human condition paradigm. The memorandum was in part a response to a reformulation of the boundary between the action system and the human organism proposed in a manuscript by Charles W. Lidz and me (Lidz and Lidz 1976). As Parsons was then teaching at the University of Pennsylvania, Renée Fox organized an informal seminar to discuss the human-condition paradigm and its implications, both theoretical and empirical. The seminar continued to meet occasionally over a period of several years. Although the seminar never produced a volume of essays as it had planned to do, Parsons did publish an essay exploring implications of the paradigm, "A Paradigm of the Human Condition" (Parsons 1978, chapter 15), which incorporated material from its deliberations. The present chapter grew out of an assignment Parsons gave Harold Bershady and me for the planned volume: to compare principles of explanation for adequate theories of physico-chemical, biological, and action systems.

In thinking about the theoretical issues basic to that assignment, I have come to the view that true evolutionary theories apply only to systems based on processes of genetic variation and natural selection, hence strictly to biological systems. Change in sociocultural systems, including their growth in complexity in the course of human existence, seems to require explanation framed in terms of categories of the action frame of reference, even though they are undoubtedly conditioned, in Parsons's sense of the cybernetic hierarchy of controlling and conditioning factors (Parsons 1961a, 1966), by biological processes subject to natural selection and thus evolution. A parallel argument concerns the conceptual status of change in physico-chemical systems. They, too, have grown in complexity from the time of the Big Bang, when particles organized at the atomic level first came into existence, but they have not "evolved" in the sense of Darwinian biology.

PARSONS'S CONCEPTION OF SOCIAL EVOLUTION

Parsons's writings on social evolution (Parsons 1966, 1971) present an integrated overview of human social change from early paleontological and archaeological records to present times. The schema underlying these works is integrated in four senses. First, it attempts to encompass all human societies, to the extent that we have knowledge of them, within one comprehensive account of human experience. It also outlines an integration of historical knowledge of many civilizations and epochs that has developed in many academic disciplines, including sociology, anthropology, archaeology, religious studies, specialized fields in history, classical studies, and studies of specific civilizations. Second, it applies general themes of analytic theory—for example, the cybernetic hierarchy of control and the four-function analysis of societies into subsystems—to all societies and civilizations. With this approach, it avoids the materialistic or economistic reductionism that has predominated in portrayals of long-term social change or evolution, for example, by the archaeologist V. Gordon Childe (1951); the anthropologists Leslie White (1949, 1959), Julian Steward (1953), and Marvin Harris (1974); by Marxian theorists; or in more qualified ways by the sociologists Gerhard Lenski (1987) and Jonathan Turner (2003). Third, it avoids the difficulties of so-called unilinear theories of evolution, for example, as proposed by

White, that project one line of development on all of human experience. Yet it also avoids the trait atomism of evolutionary theories that focus on specific convergences in development across societies, but ignore the general institutional structures of the societies, as in Robert Carneiro's (2003) work. Fourth, the theory elaborates basic themes in classic macrosociology: the development from Gemeinschaft to Gesellschaft, from predominance of mechanical to predominance of organic solidarity, and the decisive significance of the axial age and the emergence of world religions with transcendentally grounded ethics.

The core of Parsons's theory of evolution consists of a scheme of stages of evolutionary development of human societies. Parsons (1966, 1971) distinguished stages of elementary "primitive," or preliterate; "advanced primitive," more complex, yet still preliterate; archaic; historic; early modern; and advanced modern. He was skeptical about whether a postmodern stage was yet emerging (Parsons 1971, 143) but clearly indicated that new stages could emerge in the future. The criticism that his analysis of modern societies (Parsons 1971, chapters 4–7) centered too much on his own society, the United States, has justification, but claims that he viewed the United States as the culmination of human history are incorrect and unfair.

The elementary stage of preliterate societies (Parsons, 1966, chapter 3) is exemplified by small populations, often without fixed settlement and with indefinite boundaries of solidarity and community membership vis-à-vis other societies. The systems of religious belief permit members of the community to participate directly in the sacred through periodic rituals, changes in which at times of social stress may initiate basic institutional changes. Ties of social solidarity are structured mainly in terms of kinship status and social statuses are stratified principally in terms of gender, age, and personal qualities of trust, leadership, and skill. Hence there is an absence of social class differences and hierarchies in these societies. Political leadership is highly traditionalized and based on the personal qualities of individuals. The circulation of resources is almost entirely through diffuse relations of repeated gift exchanges and without market-mediated exchange.

The advanced stage of preliterate societies (Parsons 1966, 42–50) involves religious belief systems with more complexly articulated conceptions of the sacred, including greater distance between the human and sacred orders. Only select individuals acting under special circumstances are able to move beyond the human order to participate in the sacred. There are larger and more diverse cycles of myths and multiple local cults with differentiated ritual relations to the sacred order. Communities are generally settled and maintain interlocal solidarity that ties a number of settlements into a bounded society. A simple class system concentrates control of resources in a kinship-based upper class. There are courts associated with institutions of chiefdom or kingship that enable a small kinship group within the upper class to exercise political leadership and make authoritative decisions over an extended domain. The economy incorporates settled horticulture complemented by a number of specialized crafts with skills conveyed from generation to generation in traditional, often heritable, social roles. There are elementary institutions of taxation and local produce markets to complement gift exchange as means of saving and circulating resources.

Archaic societies (Parsons 1966, chapter 4) emerge after the development of "craft literacy," or the literacy of specially trained status groups, which are typically chief bearers of a religion-centered high culture. Craft literacy generally develops first among priests attached to cult centers with the written language becoming a means of codifying rites, myths, and, over time, theology attached to the cults. The priests develop concepts of gods and other sacred beings that rule a cosmic order reflected in and thus legitimating the social order of the society. The cosmic order is conceived in terms that emphasize its vastness—the eons and eons over which it has existed, the world-encompassing order it establishes, the monumental size of its visible symbols, as in the Egyptian pyramids. Central cults become associated with privileged classes and kinship groups, chief political authorities, and concentrations of wealth. Archaic societies incorporate a number of previously independent communities, either by acculturation or conquest, or by combinations of the two. Class and status systems grow more highly differentiated, often with several classes being distinguished and gaining explicit privileges or obligations in law. Privileged classes may cultivate styles of life that emphasize luxury and control of substantial human and material resources. Laws become codified with the creation of centralized courts, the compilation of authoritative cases, and their promulgation as "official" grounds of decision making, dispute resolution, and imposition of punishment. Institutions of rulership or kingship are elaborated into hierarchies of patrimonial authority, reaching from a central to a number of regional courts. Staffs of patrimonial "officials" emerge to implement policies of the courts. Patrimonial authorities may also maintain armies of trained warriors under their command. With taxation and corvee labor having developed out of asymmetric institutions of gift exchange, patrimonial authorities are able to coordinate major work projects and stockpile food, clothing, tools, arms, and other resources. Trade in food, wine or beer, textiles, tools, cult or art objects, and various luxury items may be organized by patrimonial courts, major cults, or even merchant status groups between communities and even between societies. Local markets may emerge for peasants to exchange food, wood, or other raw materials for clothing and craft products in villages or small towns.

Parsons (1966, chapter 5) followed Eisenstadt (1963) in using the term "historic civilizations" for the societies that developed during and after what Karl Jaspers (1957/1962) called the "axial age" of the emergence of the "world religions." World religions are distinguished from archaic religions in having developed transcendental conceptions of the sacred and the sources of ethical obligation in social life, thereby breaking through the cosmological or cosmogonic frameworks of archaic cultures. The transcendental conceptions of the sacred have provided a philosophic capacity to address the "problems of meaning" intrinsic to human life and thought. As Weber (1922/1963) demonstrated, the world religions have promoted ethics based on rejection of the "world" and have attracted followers to higher, transcendentally defined principles and ends. They have all attracted followings among peoples of diverse ethnic and cultural backgrounds. All have gained institutionalization in very large-scale societies with ethnically and culturally diverse populations. Each has been institutionalized only after radical transformation of previous societies. In each case, the transformation has been led by a status group of specially educated, qualified, and prestigious adherents of the religious ethic, for example, Hindu Brahmins, Buddhist monks, Confucian mandarins, Catholic priests.

In all of the historic civilizations, complex and changing class and status orders emerged that were based on the contributions of different groups as evaluated in terms of the established religious ethics. All of the status systems have centered on the privileged bearers ("Träger") of the religious ethics, but have also accommodated other socially diverse groups: merchants, warriors, officials, craftsmen, peasants, and so forth. All of the historic civilizations developed systems of law codified in terms of the principles of their respective religious ethics, such as Confucian law in China, Brahmin-interpreted law in India, or Stoic-influenced law in the Roman Empire. All of the historic civilizations developed large-scale patrimonial structures of authority and maintained complex balances of centralizing and decentralizing political forces over extended periods of time. Typically, the ethically privileged status groups, Mandarins in China, Brahmin jati in India, or Stoics and other philosophically trained thinkers in Rome, played essential and transformative but not politically dominant roles in the patrimonial structures.

All of the historic civilizations also developed highly differentiated economies capable of producing considerable wealth and concentrating it in the hands of the courts and privileged status groups. All of them developed agricultural institutions and means of transporting food capable of supplying cities with many thousands of residents, courts that maintained large circles of wealthy patrimonial retainers, and status groups that were sufficiently freed from the need to produce food and other necessities of life that they could cultivate highly skilled techniques for producing luxury goods. Historic economies typically included many kinds of skilled craftspeople producing a wide variety of goods through well-structured social roles. All developed extensive market institutions to circulate produced goods, mechanisms of taxation to secure centralized control of resources, and abilities to coordinate large-scale work projects, as in the Roman roads, aqueducts, and other public works or the Chinese system of water control and irrigation.

Parsons (1971) followed Weber in viewing Western modernity as a distinctive social formation of universal significance. Like Weber, he (Parsons 1971, chapters 3 and 4) traced its origins to the dynamic combination of urban, feudal, and Church-related universalistic institutions that emerged in Western Europe in the medieval and Renaissance periods and, more immediately, to the Protestant Reformation, which gave rise to a religious ethic of inner-worldly asceticism and, later, a newly disciplined spirit of capitalism. The resulting emergence of an entrepreneurial middle class, first in Britain, next in areas of Western Europe, and then most aggressively in the United States, led by late in the nineteenth century to the growth of large-scale industrial capitalism and the institutionalization of continuous improvement in efficiency of production (Parsons 1971, chapters 5 and 6).

Other factors also contributed to the rise of capitalism: universalistic law, administered with a reasonable degree of impartiality; a class and status system that permitted an entrepreneurial middle class to concentrate the productive resources needed for economic innovation; effective private and civil administrative apparatuses, including "bureaucratic" roles separated from the personal statuses of officials; an ethically disciplined and eventually educated labor force; and market systems that extended to labor, capital, credit, and producer goods and services.

Over time, Parsons argued, the institutions of industrial capitalism were complemented by changes in class and status orders that displaced aristocratic groups and promoted a more inclusive and diverse middle class with overlapping groups of professionals, educated public officials and corporate employees, owners of large and small enterprises, and skilled workmen. Rigid class lines between peasants or farmers, workers, and the middle class disappeared as farming became capital-intensive and businesslike, corporate employment entailed a broader range of social statuses, and wider ranges of skills became essential to production. The expansion of educational institutions also transformed class and status systems, first with "universal" elementary education and literacy, then establishment of secondary education as a common standard of qualification for skilled working and lower-middle-class economic roles, and later the institutionalization of higher education as a qualification for most middle-class roles and of advanced education for professional roles. In the political domain, democratic institutions, centering on the franchise and competitive election of public officials, transformed public authority and strengthened the social position of middle-class groups. Democratization of political processes also legitimated ideals of service to constituents and accordingly expanded the policy goals of the state. As a result, civil administrative apparatuses grew in size and effectiveness.

Parsons suggested that an "advanced modern" type of society began to emerge in the decades following World War II (Parsons 1971, chapters 6 to 8). Increased cultural differentiation provided the main impetus, as nonreligious components of culture responded to the long-established predominance of inner-worldly asceticism. The vast growth in the sciences, the other intellectual disciplines, and the learned professions, fostered by the large contemporary university systems, has played a key role. The arts have become increasingly prominent, and they address increasingly diverse expressive interests and concerns associated with specific generational, ethnic, political, regional, national, and religio-moral groups and strata. The analysis of and deliberation on public issues has come to be framed increasingly in terms of secular ideologies and moral-evaluative thought. These cultural frameworks, though rooted historically in the Enlightenment, have spread internationally and now affect a worldwide system of modern societies (Lidz 1979). In their wake have come ever higher standards of education, the growth of a variety of educationally specialized and qualified status groups within the broad middle class, and the expansion of economic and political roles based on trained technical competence. Processes of law and legal regulation, administrative procedure in public and private organizations, and allocation of economic resources among processes of production have all become vastly more rationalized and complex than in the "early-modern" period. Particularly conspicuous has been the international or global reach of economic production. Not only markets and the buying and selling of consumer and producer goods, but also corporate operations routinely span the globe and involve many nations and peoples. Many corporations are now "empires" on which the sun never sets—perhaps more so than the nineteenth-century British Empire, although as more highly specialized institutions.

Parsons also noted the emergence of "postindustrial" economies in which work grows ever more concentrated in professional, entrepreneurial, administrative, and other office-based, paper-intensive roles, while industrial production moves to regions of the world with lower labor costs.

Robert Bellah (1970 and personal communication) has asked whether "advanced modernity" is truly independent of the modernity that began with the Protestant Reformation. He argues that if modernity represents a social revolution comparable to the axial age in scope and consequences, it presumably takes many centuries to play itself out. He also maintains that the changes Parsons identified as "advanced modern" appear still to follow from the religious ethics of inner-worldly asceticism. While I agree with Parsons that growth in the secular domains of culture has been a major impetus to trends of social change in recent phases of modernity, I agree with Bellah that all phases of Western modernization since the Reformation are in their fundamentals unitary. Advanced modernity may be a historical subtype, not a full and independent stage of human development.

Parsons's basic "evolutionary" typology of societies can be refined. He noted two ancillary types himself. One is the "seedbed" type (Parsons 1966, chapter 6). He discussed two seedbed societies, ancient Israel and ancient Greek or Hellenic societies. Smaller in scale than the historic civilizations and more closely tied to ethnic identity, they remained archaic in many of their institutional forms. However, during the axial age they originated religious and philosophic ideas that were later integrated into Christian theology and religious ethics as well as Western republican thought. Western understandings about the historical purpose and destiny of society, the nature of human community, and citizenship have derived from traditions they established. They have thus had significant effects on Western civilization in both its medieval "historic" and modern phases.

The second ancillary type is feudal (Parsons 1971, chapter 3). Following Weber (1920/1947; 1930/1976, section 4) and Eisenstadt (1963), Parsons noted that the decline of historic civilizations precipitates processes of infeudation. Scarcity of resources leads to recrudescence of local and personal structures, breakdown of trust among communities and strata, loss of confidence in cultural and political institutions essential to more inclusive social integration, and growing conflict. Feudal societies in this sense sustain features of historic civilizations, but collapse back to archaic structures—particularistic relationships among persons, such as the fief, that are embedded in diffuse kinship and locality-based ties.

We may note a third ancillary type or complex of types: border societies, which are close to and have exchanges with historic or modern civilizations and are often transformed by the contacts. For example, the Celtic and Germanic peoples who occupied much of Europe during the ascendance of the Roman Empire adapted to its predominance in many ways (Hubert 1934/1972). The Roman influence made them something different from simply advanced primitive tribes in the process of establishing archaic institutions. Much of world history over the past several centuries has been shaped by the adaptation of other peoples and civilizations to the dynamics of expansive—originally Western—modernity. Colonial structures in which traditional societies of various types—preliterate, archaic, and historic—have been dominated politically and culturally constitute variants of this general type of border society.

THE PARADIGM OF CHANGE

Parsons explained specific processes of social change in terms of a well-known four-function paradigm that he had developed shortly before beginning his project on social evolution (Parsons 1961b). This paradigm analyzes processes that result in increased complexity and adaptive capacity of an institution, sector of society, or whole society in terms of four dimensions: structural differentiation, adaptive upgrading, inclusion, and value generalization. Parsons's argument was that an institution under stress may devise ways of dividing its operations into two or more sets, each of which then functions in a more specialized and effective manner. The instance Parsons originally analyzed, following Neil J. Smelser's treatment in *Social Change in the Industrial Revolution* (1959), was the differentiation between household and manufactory as a focus of institutional innovation during the Industrial Revolution.

Consolidation of the more highly differentiated structures, Parsons argued, requires three additional changes. First, new types and quantities of resources must be developed and allocated to the differentiated units, so that each becomes capable of sustaining its distinctive operations. As compared with the more diffuse needs of household workshops, a factory will need larger quantities of raw materials. It will not need the same kind of personal affection that is a crucial resource for a family, but families whose members spend much of the day working in factories will likely need a new intensity of affection within the home in order to maintain household solidarity during the short hours they are together. Of course, families that do not produce in the household will not need the quantities of raw materials that home workshops require.

Second, both types of units—large-scale manufactories and nonproducing families—must gain inclusion within the solidary structures of the community, a process that generally entails change in the normative order, often the law. Inclusion also entails the earning of trust by both of the new types of units, so that other entities in the community will accord them positive social statuses. Ever since the start of the Industrial Revolution, modern societies have experienced controversies about the normative standards that factories and more broadly business firms and working families must meet. Third, the applicable value complexes of the society must become more generalized, so that each of the new, more differentiated types of social units can legitimate itself within them. The "Halevy thesis" (developed by Elie Halevy) about the role of Methodism in keeping the oppressions of the British class structure from precipitating a political revolution of the French type (Halevy 1924/1987), and E. P. Thompson's (1963) related study of how the Methodist movement transformed the culture of the British working class, both address aspects of value generalization in the Industrial Revolution and its aftermath.

In its later uses, the paradigm of change was not limited to instances of change toward increasing complexity, as was its original formulation. In his later analyses, Parsons treated the four elements of change as independent dynamic factors that must be kept in balance with one another for a society or institutional complex to maintain homeostasis (Parsons 1971, 1979). Pressures toward devolution or loss of differentiation, as in Weber's analysis of the "fall" of the Roman Empire (1930/1976, section 4) or Shmuel Eisenstadt's (1963) treatment of processes of infeudation in the decline of other historic empires, result when resources needed by one or another type of institution become extremely scarce, when key units of a society lose the trust of other elements of the community, or when "fundamentalist" changes in the moral culture undermine the legitimacy of basic institutions. In a more general construction, the paradigm of change may be seen as addressing in dynamic terms the dimensions of an institution's overall adaptation to its surrounding community or society.

Processes of change, whether toward greater or lesser complexity, do not always begin with differentiation or loss of differentiation among operative units of a society (Smelser 1963). Responses to stress may start with the other elements of the change process, for example, with extension or contraction in the level of generalization of values. Major long-term trends of change in civilizations, as in the axial age or the Reformation, have been generated by cultural reorientation focused on value systems. The civil rights movement in the United States has involved change primarily in the norms of inclusion affecting citizenship roles and the societal community, secondarily in resource allocations among citizens.

Parsons claimed that the paradigm of change, more generally construed, is directly parallel to the processes of natural selection in biological evolution (Parsons 1966, chapter 2; 1971, chapter 2). His paradigm deals with the conditions in which a new variant of an institution becomes stabilized in a community or society or fails to become stabilized and undergoes further change before a new equilibrium is attained. However, the question for us is: Are the processes of change sufficiently similar to those of genetic variation and natural selection to warrant use of the term "evolution"?

To answer this question, we must note that the paradigm of change can be used only with at least implicit articulation with the typology of stages and the functional analysis of subsystems of society. To assess a change in level of differentiation, upgrading of resources, inclusion, and value generalization, one must first develop a baseline analysis of the affected institutional order. To do so one must analyze the principal institutions of the time in degree of complexity or institutional development and in their functional contributions to the broader society. Parsons proceeded in this way when he took Smelser's (1959) analysis of the preindustrial British home spinning and weaving industry as the baseline for his treatment of the differentiation between manufactory and household. In a less formal treatment, I (Lidz 1989) described the earlier relationship between institutions of political leadership and social strata formation as a baseline for an analysis of how the emergence of a competitive political party system changed institutions of social integration in the United States during the first decades of the nineteenth century.

The typology of stages and the paradigm of change, although highly abstract in general formulation, are dynamic schemas. They pertain not simply to abstract relationships among sets of institutions, but focus analysis upon the complex interdependence among actual institutions. They address practical ramifications of specific changes in the fields of interdependence. My critique of the stage typology below does not presume that Parsons's concepts are static, as typologies are sometimes claimed to be. On the contrary, it is based on recognition of the dynamic character of the typology. I argue that its dynamic properties, designed to capture the qualities of action systems, cannot be contained within the framework of evolutionary theory, that is, genetic variation and natural selection.

THE HUMAN-CONDITION PARADIGM

Social evolution is discussed only in passing in Parsons's essay "A Paradigm of the Human Condition" (Parsons 1978, chapter 15). In the years before writing the essay, Parsons had, as observed above, devoted substantial thought to continuities between biological and social theory, emphasizing concepts of control and cybernetic ordering, system, function, and equilibrium, interchange of resources among differentiated subsystems, and generalized mechanisms of mediation of systemic processes (Parsons 1969, 1977, 1978; Parsons and Platt 1973). He highlighted, for example, parallels between biologists' treatment of the roles of DNA and messenger RNA in controlling protein synthesis and his own emphasis on the special regulatory functions of value systems. He also discussed a parallel between the biological functions of hormones in regulating rates of metabolic processes and the social functions of the generalized symbolic media of interchange, money, power, influence, and commitments. He had examined evolution as an area of continuity or convergence as well, highlighting a parallel between population biology's conception of a breeding population and sociology's conception of a society, both of which he noted were analytic, not concrete.

Given the importance of biological and social evolution in Parsons's prior work, it is striking that "A Paradigm of the Human Condition" says little about social evolution. Social evolution is thus an interesting residual category in his discussion of the human condition. As Parsons himself taught, from *The Structure of Social Action* (1937, chapter 1) to the end of his life, residual categories are strategic points to probe in advancing theory. What I will now explore is the conceptual status in which the human condition paradigm places social evolution.

Parsons organized his discussion of the human condition paradigm in terms of three overlapping theoretical issues. First is the functional differentiation and specialization of the four subsystems of the human condition, namely, the telic or transcendental ground of order (pattern-maintaining), the system of human social action (integrative), human organic system (goal attaining), and physico-chemical systems (adaptive). Second is the structural interpenetration of the four distinct subsystems with one another. And third is the processual interchanges among the four subsystems. For present purposes, it is crucial to review the first two of these issues, although the discussion of structural interpenetration will address somewhat different aspects than Parsons's own account.

The discussion of structural differentiation emphasizes that each of the four subsystems is made up of a distinct class of objects and accordingly requires its own explanatory principles and schemata. The physical-chemical world is made up of subatomic particles, atoms, and compounds, energies, and forces. Parsons emphasizes the transcendental element in the conceptual schemes needed to explain physical-chemical phenomena and quotes Gerald Holton, a physicist and historian of science, as saying, "The basic achievement of Einstein's theory was . . . [that] it gave us a new unity in the understanding of nature" (Parsons 1978, 359n). Parsons understood that the conception of a unitary physical-chemical "world" independent of the worlds of life, human action, or the telic-transcendental is a result of modern culture and knowledge. By contrast, the human condition of ancient or nonliterate peoples entails a more diffuse adaptation to physical-chemical realities. Yet the realities do set conditions to which all peoples must adapt. Peoples who have not known of the theory of gravity and who have attributed life, human motives, or even "magical" powers to everyday objects have nevertheless expected such objects, when unsupported, to fall, and they have known the regularity of the days and seasons, the heat of the summer sun and the cold of the winter wind.

The human organic "world" consists in the first instance of living human organisms, but includes, as Parsons makes clear, their ecological adaptation to all of the biosphere. However, it concerns the specific adaptations of human life within the biosphere. Parsons contrasted the human condition to the "fish condition," which would involve ordering the elements of the biosphere and physical-chemical world in terms of adaptive, ecological salience to the lives of fish. From time immemorial, peoples have had some understanding of the human organism's needs for air to breathe, food to eat, a safe or guarded place to sleep, shelter from extremes of weather, and so forth. Our modern understanding of the organism involves refined conceptions of such functions as metabolism and reproduction, and the many life processes that serve them. For nearly one hundred fifty years, we have had an overview of biology based on the principles of genetic variation and natural selection. Our understanding of the entire world of living beings, all phenomena of life, follows from the Darwinian conception of natural selection. Evolution is the conceptual framework that provides unity and integrity to our understanding of organisms and the biosphere, including human organisms, as an aspect or dimension of the human condition.

Action systems are characterized by symbolic process and meaning.[1] Cultural systems, social systems, personalities, and behavioral systems (or minds, in a sense derived from George Herbert Mead's conception, in which mind is differentiated from self or personality) are all different modalities of organizing symbolic process (Parsons 1964, 1970; Parsons and Platt 1973; Lidz 1976; Mead 1934). They all create and process meaning. Yet they are not reducible to symbolic process and meaning, because they all add other "value" to symbolic processes. Cultural systems order symbols in terms of meaning in the context of extensive belief systems, religious, moral, expressive, or cognitive or scientific. Social systems order symbols by their implications for social relationships, for example, as indicative of normative expectations or as representative of the lifestyle of a status group. All action systems have symbols and meanings as constituents. Symbols and signs (symbols with conventionally established meanings) may be shared among subsystems of action, as when a mind understands a culturally organized symbolic relationship or process, a personality cathects and internalizes it in terms of affective meaning, or a social system institutionalizes it in a particular kind of social relationship.

Our modern understanding of action systems is thus organized in terms of conceptions of meaningful symbolic process, as differentiated from physical-chemical or life processes. As noted, before modern times, understanding of events in the human condition often projected symbolic significance into the physical-chemical and life orders—projections we now consider "magical" thought. The integrity of understanding of action phenomena in our era rests on differentiating them from the physical and biological orders. This is an accomplishment of the action frame of reference, synthesized from the works of figures—Émile Durkheim (1915) on collective representations and social solidarity, Max Weber (1922/1963) on belief and problems of meaning, Sigmund Freud (1938) on the motivational and affective meaning of symbols, Jean Piaget (Flavell 1963) on the organization of cognition—who clarified the chief dimensions of our understanding of symbolic process and meaning.

In sum, the human-condition paradigm suggests that categories of understanding for systems of action must capture the symbolic character of the phenomena of social action. With symbolic character, we should now add, beyond Parsons's analysis, that all basic mechanisms of action systems have a capacity to generate indefinitely many new, creative, and yet interpretable combinations of signs (Lidz 2001). This quality of generativity has been studied extensively as an essential property of human languages since the publication of Noam Chomsky's *Syntactic Structures* (1957) nearly forty years ago. Generativity is a product of an ability to follow a set or structure of rules which can be applied recursively in the creation of a sequence of situated actions (Chomsky 1968, 1980). It appears to be a quality of rule-governed social action generally, and human actors attribute to one another the ability both to create new sequences of action and to interpret and adapt to others' newly created sequences of action (Lidz 1976, 1981, 2001). Generativity is thus embedded in the exchanges of everyday interaction and is also basic to the operation of fundamental institutions, such as the law of contract, which enables economic actors to create ever new contractual relationships by reference to a limited body of laws.

The generativity of human uses of symbols is a dynamic character of human social action that should be distinguished from the relationship between genetic heritage and phenotype in biological systems. It is part of the "Lamarckian" quality of human action systems in which cultural heritage changes during the lives of individuals and is passed on, with the changes, to succeeding generations. This "Lamarckian" quality of action violates the principles of natural selection in biological systems. It is a key *empirical* basis for questioning the applicability of the category of evolution to the understanding of change in human social systems. Parenthetically, the problematic status of evolutionary concepts highlighted here emerges as more complicated but not basically different if we consider all four of the premises regarding the essential nature of social action.[2]

Finally, the telic system provides the latent pattern-maintenance anchorage for the human condition. Understanding of the physical-chemical, biologic, and action systems as mundane orders of phenomena in the sense of our modern understanding presupposes a discipline of not seeking transcendental significance in events within them. Yet our modern intellectual understanding depends on transcendental categories that refer to the telic. As Parsons conceived it, the telic order does not act or organize action, but is an open manifold of potential ultimate groundings. Its import for the human condition is that actors seek to apprehend ultimate groundings and use the resulting transcendental concepts, categories, or principles to organize their thought and action. As Durkheim argued in the *Elementary Forms of the Religious Life* (1915), preliterate beliefs about the sacred and in particular their formative categories, primordial efforts to apprehend the telic, provided the origins for all ordered understanding of the human condition. Since the axial age, truly transcendental apprehensions of the telic have been fateful factors in guiding human experience. In modern times, thinkers have sought more differentiated and highly disciplined apprehensions of the telic. As Kant demonstrated, the Newtonian grounding of mechanics was a first frame of reference to bring transcendental categories to bear specifically on scientific understanding. Einstein's theories of relativity achieved the new unity of understanding, to which Holton referred (cited by Parsons 1978, chapter 15), by establishing a substitute transcendental frame of reference, although in generality it fell short of the unified field theory to which Einstein aspired. As I understand it, contemporary physics still seeks a deeper, more general theoretical grounding. In social science, the action frame of reference may be the closest we have to a transcendental grounding, although all of our specific formulations appear far from adequate. In moral theory, the early-modern natural law theorists took the goal of establishing transcendental grounding most seriously, even if their Western-centric understandings are glaringly apparent to the comparative social scientist. Contemporary theology seems to struggle with adapting its traditional transcendental categories to cultural settings in which other disciplines lay claim to autonomous and in certain contexts contradictory groundings and understandings.

INTERPENETRATION OF THE ACTION SYSTEM AND BIOSPHERE

As Parsons emphasized, the subsystems of the human condition interpenetrate or share content that is differently organized in each system. Within action systems, he illustrated the principle of interpenetration by noting that the same normative content—for example, standards of how a physician should treat patients—may be institutionalized in a social system and internalized in personality systems (Parsons 1951, chapter 10). In the human-condition system there are basic interpenetrations between the physical-chemical order, the biosphere, and human social action.

Parsons discussed the interpenetration of the physical and life worlds by citing arguments of Lawrence J. Henderson (1913/1958) in *The Fitness of the Environment,* notably, the argument that the complex organic molecules essential to life are made up principally of carbon, oxygen, and hydrogen, to which Parsons, citing the authority of George Wald, a Harvard biologist, added nitrogen (Parsons 1978, 388). Life could evolve only in physical environments with sufficient concentrations of these elements, which we now understand took eons to emerge after the Big Bang, and then occurred only in, as far as we know, a special microenvironment of the cosmos. However, there are other dimensions to penetration of the physical environment into living systems. For example, the frame of space and time sets conditions for all of life and action. Living and acting systems incorporate limitations of space and time by virtue of existing at specific times and places. All types of biological processes have time parameters, whether the nanoseconds of the oxygenation of hemoglobin, the variable (within limits) pacing of beats of the human heart, the hours (but not weeks or months) that humans take to digest a meal, or the quarter to a third of a day that adult humans ordinarily sleep. Some of these time parameters, such as the periodic need for meals and time for sleeping, penetrate into action systems as well as biological systems. They affect cognitive orientation to the day, changing personal motives for immediate action, and institutionalized patterns of eating and sleeping, although differently from culture to culture. Similarly, living and acting systems exist only within certain parameters of radiant energies, forces of gravity, and rates of acceleration and deceleration relative to immediate environments.

The human-condition paradigm shifts the frame of reference regarding physical and biological conditions of action from ones that have been customary among sociologists and anthropologists for a number of decades. As a strategy of resisting reductionism, social scientists have generally abstracted beyond such factors unless they have been seen as irreducibly salient to the understanding of specific problems, as when Erving Goffman, in *Stigma: Notes on the Management of Spoiled Identity* (1963), focused attention on anomalies of individual human organisms. With the human-condition paradigm we can study physical and biological factors of social action by examining their modes of interpenetration with action systems while not conceding a field of understanding to reductionism. Thus, causes and effects, even in the symbolic sphere of human action, can occur only in the physical sequence of time. Human societies have developed calendars and ways of marking time within calendars, ranging from observation of the sun and stars to sundials and watches, to coordinate social activities within the passage of time (Zerubavel 1981). In our society, many institutional activities—religious rituals, sporting contests, university classes, court proceedings, family celebrations, political elections—are physical events that require the cooperation of many individuals and are coordinated in terms of calculable regularities in time by use of widely shared calendars and timepieces. Similarly, human communication must occur within physical media. Speech is limited by the constraints of sound and its travel, although today it can be amplified, recorded, and replayed, even at great distance from the original events. Written language must be recorded on physical media, whether of pen on paper or bytes on hard drive.

Human activity penetrates into the physical order as well. Many of the physical settings within which we live and work have been created by human construction and engineering. In modern metropolitan areas, humans have vastly reshaped natural environments to serve the complex needs of large, highly differentiated communities. Many areas within a metropolis are microenvironments created in terms of highly specific standards: the antiseptic surgery suite, the dust-free electronics factory, the scientific laboratory, the control room of the nuclear power plant, the courtroom, the church, the control tower of the airport, the home kitchen or bathroom, and so forth. In these places, highly specialized activities can occur only because quite specific physical conditions have been created.

The foregoing are only some instances of the ways human action alters the physical-chemical environment, and with it the biosphere, through agriculture, construction, and manufacturing. Economically developed societies, especially those of the past century and a half, have changed the environment far more radically than earlier societies, leading to such present concerns as global warming, the loss of wilderness, and the disappearance of many species. European landscape paintings of the sixteenth to eighteenth centuries portray a mode of life—with mud roads curving along streams and around old trees, small thatched houses nestled into natural features of the land, and farms with small fields, few cattle, and free-ranging chickens—that adapted to nature while changing the environment far less aggressively.

The biosphere and human action systems also interpenetrate. Human individuals are living organisms as well as social actors. As living organisms, they share much of the biology of other mammals and must meet such functional needs as respiration, nutrition, metabolism, and reproduction just as they must meet functional needs of action systems. In everyday life, action systems accommodate to the needs of members of society as organisms, with time taken for eating, sleeping, exercise, rest, and so forth. The concept of "stress" addresses in one aspect the ways social expectations on role performance of individuals fail to allow adequately for biological needs of the same individuals. Societies differ in the ways they accommodate the organismic needs of members, however, as we can see in comparing Northern European practices with Mediterranean institutions of the late evening meal, a shorter period of overnight sleep, and midday break and siesta. Societies also change over time, as indicated by present concerns in the United States over lifestyle regimens of little exercise and diets of large caloric intake, leading to a population that has become heavier and more vulnerable to hypertension, diabetes, renal failure, and cardiovascular disease.

Human action also rests on substrata within the organism that become habituated to the standards of conduct and expectations of particular societies, communities, and status groups. The substrata are themselves complexly organized and include independent components that, through interpenetration, are coordinated with one another at the level of the organism as well as the action system. One set of strata are the language centers in the brain, which learn particular languages, including their phonological, syntactic, and semantic elements, in support of action-level uses of language (Pinker 1994). Another set involves the pleasure centers of the brain (Damasio 1999). Through experience (psychologists often say "conditioning"), they become attached to the rewarding features of customary patterns of action, such as tastes of food, comforts of rest and sleep, or satisfactions of sexual relationships. They also interact with the motivational mechanisms of the personality such that attainment of goals in which an individual has been highly invested, for example, an achievement at work, brings pleasure at the level of the organism.

Another complex set of strata are perceptual. The eyes and ears become sensitive to perceiving events in the environment that have particular significance to cognitive schemata of the mind. The "ear" of the musician or lover of music, meaning the auditory centers of his or her brain, becomes highly trained in the service of a cognitive understanding and aesthetic appreciation. The "eye" of the painter, sculptor, or person who appreciates art becomes similarly trained. Finally, the centers of the brain that coordinate sensory-motor behavior become skilled in implementing complex sequences of behavior that, as Piaget's work demonstrates, are controlled by intricate mental schemas (Piaget 1952; Flavell 1963). Driving a car, throwing a football, or managing a piece of laboratory equipment has a substratum of skilled behavior without which action-level processes cannot be implemented. In sum, this is the significance of the organism's goal-attainment status in the human condition paradigm.

The interpenetration between the action system and the organism is in many respects structural. On the side of the action system, the cognitive schemas and personality motivations, typically supported by social institutions and cultural patterns, become stable and effective dispositions of the individual. On the side of the organism, the neurons in various brain centers are changed by experiences, such as the ones discussed, that create enduring behavioral dispositions of many kinds. One index of the strength of such neurological dispositions is the difficulty of learning to hear and articulate the appropriate sounds when learning a language radically different from one's native tongue, as when an English speaker learns Navajo or Chinese.

The complexity of these processes and structures make it important to review the line of differentiation between the organism and the action system. The organism consists of cells, tissues, organs, and bodily fluids, including the neurochemicals of the brain. Changes in the organism that result from experience are principally changes in neurons, synapses, and the circulation at many centers in the brain of a number of neurochemicals. The action system consists of mental schemas, personality motives and dispositions, social interests, expectations, and institutions and cultural representations, signs, and beliefs—all modalities of the organization of symbols and meanings and all characterized by generativity. The action system changes just noted concern principally schemata of the mind and motives of the personality, but with institutional and cultural factors in the background (Lidz and Lidz 1976; Lidz 2001). Although the foregoing discussion concerns mutual accommodations between action system and organism, it does not imply a lack of fundamental difference in makeup and substance between the two.

EVOLUTION AND THE INTERPENETRATION OF BIOLOGICAL AND ACTION SYSTEMS

The emergence of the species Homo sapiens through evolution involved close mutual dependence between organisms and action systems. Human organisms are not self-sufficient on the biological level but require integration into systems of action. Human cognition, emotion and affect, and normative and moral judgment have an indirect biological reality through the human organism's dependence on them. They are aspects of a universal heritage of the human species in that all societies must provide cognitive, affective, and normative orders for human populations to survive. If societies fail to provide them, as in cases of extreme anomie, human life becomes truncated and its reproduction insecure. Local populations may come under intense adaptive pressure and may even disappear, as has occurred not infrequently in human history and presumably prehistory.

We do not know the details of how this mutual dependence between organisms and action systems first evolved, but it certainly required a long developmental process. The growth of the language centers and other symbol-processing areas of the brain suggests that the evolutionary process was complex (Pinker 1994). It likely involved a sequence of developments through which symbolic communication gradually became better consolidated, imparting selective advantage to individuals whose brains were better adapted to processing symbols.

Robert N. Bellah has suggested that Durkheim's analysis of the effervescence of the Australian corroboree festival may provide a model of the prehistoric emergence of central collective representations (Bellah 2003). However helpful this approach may be, another aspect of the problem involves the emergence of structures of rules or normative orders. A primordial structure of rules is embedded in all human languages, namely, the complex rules we call grammar, which are a specialized normative order. For a generation, linguists have been demonstrating with analytic precision that there are universal elements embedded in the diverse grammars of human languages (see, for an early and basic example, Chomsky 1968).

Noam Chomsky has long argued that recursive rules are an important formal property of the universals of grammar and therefore of the ability of speech communities to share understandings of linguistic communication (Chomsky 1968, 1980). He has recently proposed that a formal capacity to use abstract rules in a recursive manner was the crucial biological advance that led to the evolution of human cognitive capacities and mind. He has hypothesized that an ability to use rules recursively, imparted first through one discrete genetic change in brain structure, gave a selective advantage to a particular population of protohumans (Hauser, Chomsky, and Fitch

2002). The population's subsequent evolution consolidated and generalized that crucial capacity and the advantages it brought in natural selection. We may further hypothesize that early language, emerging from less thoroughly regulated modes of symbolization through the addition of recursive rules, provided a primordial core of normative order. A "speech community" likely comprised the first normatively ordered community as distinct from a coresident breeding population—the point at which a sociological "society" evolved from a biological breeding population. Over time, rules then developed regarding pragmatic uses and interpretations of speech and gradually grew into the comprehensive normative orders that characterize every human society of which we have any record.[3]

The key role of language in the development of the human species appears to be marked in the anatomy of the human brain (Pinker 1994). Human brains have distinct speech centers that are not found in the brains of other species. They also have distinct neuronal projections that connect the speech centers to other centers of thought and emotion, transforming the ways in which these centers function as compared with similar anatomical structures in the brains of mammals and primates. By contrast with the speech centers and projections, areas of the brain involved in or underlying human motivational, perceptual, and even some cognitive mechanisms are modest expansions and restructurings of areas characteristic of other primates—and mammals generally. It is for this reason that neuroscience is able to use so-called animal models to understand many aspects of the functioning of the human brain. The functions of neurochemicals such as dopamine, serotonin, norepinephrine, GABA, and glutamate, their binding to specific anatomical sites, their movement by so-called transporters, their agonists, partial agonists, and antagonists have been studied largely with animal models (Damasio 1999). However, linguistic communication cannot be studied with animal models (Hauser, Chomsky, and Fitch 2002). Even when higher primates such as chimpanzees are trained to sign and use lists of symbols, linguists do not agree that they are mastering the basics of significant communication (Pinker 1994). Similarly, sociologists are not persuaded, despite claims of some observers to have seen elements of culture in primate communities, that normative order has ever been observed outside of human societies. Indeed, normative order appears to exist only where members of a community can, using language, cite instances of its rules and expectations.

As these considerations suggest, the interpenetration of human organisms with actors, of human breeding populations with communities, is deeply rooted in human evolution. Human life has never existed without social action, just as social action has never existed aside from the presence of human organisms. Human life could not have evolved except in mutual dependence with rudimentary systems of social action. Humans as organisms are entirely dependent on functioning systems of social action to live and reproduce. Natural selection has produced a species in which organisms are capable of self-sufficiency as breeding populations only because they are also communities of social actors. In its necessary role as a complement to a breeding population, human society is profoundly implicated in evolution.

Social formations also affect the ability of populations to reproduce and, thus, the processes of natural selection. To cite obvious examples, the size, stability, and continuity of human populations have grown as societies have become more complex in institutional makeup. Each of Parsons's stages from advanced primitive to modern has entailed expansion in populations and generally increases in demographic stability as compared with simpler forms of society. So-called "natural increase" of populations is actually driven by sociological changes toward larger, more diverse societies with greater institutional complexity. The emergence of world religions in the axial age has probably been the greatest force in human history for uniting larger societal communities and providing greater, though far from complete, security for demographic expansion (Eisenstadt 1963).

In the contemporary world, modern market economies and systems of public health and sanitation have resulted in further increases in the size and density of populations. While dense populations are more vulnerable to wars and "natural" disasters, to which hundreds of millions of lives have been lost during the twentieth and twenty-first centuries, the probabilities that particular individuals will live to reproduce have never been greater than in societies of Parsons's modern type. These societies secure a historically exceptional level of "fitness" for their members.

Conceptually, fitness, though to a large degree secured by social institutions, is a quality of breeding populations (Mayr 1963). Natural selection is a process of the biosphere, even if affected by the interpenetration of structures of social action. The continuing roles of infectious disease, lifestyle effects, and genetic vulnerabilities in mortality make the biological character of natural selection clear. Yet the many-staged progression from preliterate to modern societies has had a greater impact on "fitness" (in the sense of probability that individuals will pass their genes on to succeeding generations) than any genetic changes in specific breeding populations of humans. In this respect, given the interpenetration between action and biological systems, the long-term trends of social change toward larger-scale, more complex, more highly stable societies have had fateful consequences for human biological evolution. These massive effects and their causes have been overlooked by the school of evolutionary biology emphasizing the "selfish gene." David Sloan Wilson, however, is an evolutionary biologist who has analyzed community effects on human evolution (Wilson 2002). His treatment of the adaptive significance of religio-moral beliefs for religious groups and communities partly converges with the foregoing discussion.

EVOLUTION AND "SOCIAL EVOLUTION"

With this background, we can consider whether it is conceptually justified to characterize the progression of societies through the stages of development as a process of evolution.

Biologists have long traced the evolving heritage of life in the form of branching trees (Simpson 1949, 1953; Mayr 1963). The "logic" of the branching tree is based on the principle that all species on a single branch share common ancestors, while species on separate branches do not. When we speak of broad categories of life forms—vertebrates, mammals, or primates—we are referring to shared structural patterns *and* common ancestry. The link between shared form and shared ancestry is, of course, shared genes, common DNA. In the link between shared form and shared ancestry through common DNA, we see the workings of natural selection on a large scale and over the long term. The link between form and genetic ancestry lies at the core of the evolutionary process. Grasping that linkage was Darwin's fundamental insight. It remains down to our time a foundation of all biology, as basic to molecular biology as to paleontology and comparative anatomy.

To be sure, there are instances of the independent evolution of specific adaptive mechanisms. Bipedal walking emerged independently in birds and in primates among species ancestral to Homo sapiens. Australopithecus was an early bipedal primate, although not directly ancestral to Homo sapiens. Parsons (1966 chapter 2; 1967, chapter 15) cited George Wald as identifying at least three independent origins of the same biochemical processes involved in vision. These examples show that similar phenotypic characteristics do not necessarily indicate common genetic pattern and ancestry. To understand the course of evolution, comparisons of DNA sequences are needed and patterns of shared and divergent genes must be related to phenotypic characteristics.

Parsons (1967, chapter 15) devised the important concept of "evolutionary universals" in part by analogy to Wald's discoveries in the biochemistry of vision and in part by considering the changing functional needs of societies at each of his stages of social evolution. Evolutionary universals characterize in general terms the key institutions that societies have needed as they changed from preliterate to archaic to historic to modern, although Parsons's discussion focused on institutions basic to modern societies, such as differentiated cultural systems, universalistic law, flexible class and status systems, formal organization, and markets for the factors of production. The concept of evolutionary universals generalizes across many societies at each stage of social evolution, abstracting beyond wide variations within each stage, as Parsons acknowledged.

Attention to variation within each stage of social evolution is a strength of Parsons's comparative sociology (Parsons 1966), but it also exposes the fact that his typology of stages has a different conceptual status than taxonomies used to group and compare species in evolutionary biology. As we have seen, the categories of vertebrates, mammals, and primates designate groups of species that share ancestors and genetic heritages. By contrast, the categories of archaic, historic, and modern civilizations includes societies that attained comparable levels of institutional complexity from different historical backgrounds and traditions. Parsons's analysis of historic civilizations contrasted the ways in which they emerged from earlier traditions and highlighted differences among their institutions, including kinship, education, law, status groups, political authority, and economic production (Parsons 1966, chapter 5). The study of variation is equally essential for biologists, as when they trace out the sequences by which species of dinosaurs, brontosaurs, tyrannosaurs, triceratops, and so forth evolved from a common ancestry. Creating the type of historic civilization by comparing convergent developments among civilizations with independent origins, as in China, India, and the Roman Empire, is a basically different conceptual undertaking.

These considerations lead to the conclusion that Parsons's stage concepts have a different theoretical status than the concepts for analyzing speciation in evolutionary biology. The treatment of variations within type also has a different conceptual status. Variations do not always represent departures from a common origin, as in comparisons of mammalian species, but often different paths toward given levels of societal complexity and adaptive capacity, whether archaic, historic, or modern. Parsons's key analytic procedures thus reverse the logic of evolutionary biology. His scheme of levels or stages of societal complexity can be characterized as evolutionary only by abandoning the conceptual status of the term in biology.

That Parsons's taxonomy of stages follows a different method from the one used in evolutionary biology does not mean that it is faulty, however. Its logic may differ from evolutionary biology's precisely because it captures characteristics of societies and action systems that set them apart from biological systems.

Parsons often cited (for instance, 1966, chapter 2; 1971, chapter 2; 1978, chapter 10) a formula he adopted from the biologist Alfred Emerson (1956): in human evolution, the symbol has replaced the gene. Leaving aside the consideration that in this usage "symbol" is a vague term, we can say that Emerson's formula leads to a key insight into the human condition. Natural selection is a slow process. Homo sapiens emerged from earlier primates over a period of roughly three million years. By comparison, the processes of fundamental sociocultural change are relatively efficient and rapid. From the earliest horizons of archaic civilizations to the present stage of modern society, no more than 9,000 to 11,000 years have passed. From the start of the axial age to the present is approximately 3,000 years. From the start of modernity to the present is approximately 500 years. When the symbol joined the gene in regulating human change (it did not truly replace the gene, as human populations continue to evolve genetically), a process that likely entered its crucial phase some 200,000 years ago and culminated perhaps only 30,000 to 50,000 years ago (Hauser, Chomsky, and Fitch 2002), the human condition in the present sense first emerged. It then gained an ability to develop rapidly.

Emerson's essential point was that the symbol (or shared cultural belief), with the property of generativity, we may add, changes more rapidly and comprehensively than the human genetic heritage. Genomes change slowly and in limited ways during reproduction—by substitution of one base for another along the strand of DNA, by displacement of a segment of DNA during replication, or, most frequently, by new combinations of established variants. In certain key epochs in history, however, entire domains of cultures have changed in the course of a social movement, as in the several generations of ancient Hebrew prophets, the early development of Islam through Mohammed's prophecy and the leadership of his immediate followers, the Reformation, the Enlightenment, or the rise of modern science. The organization of culture involves hierarchies that give specific complexes of belief strategic importance throughout large domains. Changes in superordinate components, for example, the constitutive beliefs of a religion or the principles of a secular moral-evaluative culture may have system-transforming effects on an entire society or civilization. Changes of this kind have more sweeping effects on action systems than genetic changes can have on organisms.

Moreover, the symbol or cultural belief is not intrinsically tied to a particular population, as is the gene or shared DNA. Symbols, culture, and institutions are not limited to the societies or epochs of their origin in the respect that genes are limited to related populations. (At least, this is true aside from the special gene therapies and transspecific implants that have been developed in recent decades for agricultural plants and animals and that for humans are now emerging on the horizon of laboratory studies.) From the axial age to the present, the sharing of cultural elements across societies has been a major force in social change. All of the world religions have converted peoples from many previous cultural backgrounds. When communities undergo conversions, the controlling elements of their cultural orientations are changed, usually with consequences for a wide range of social institutions. In the modern era, not only have religious movements gained adherents across the boundaries of civilizations, but secular belief systems of Western origin have also gained nearly global adherence. Scientific knowledge, methodology, and research procedures have become fundamentally intersocietal, although, to be sure, not understood or accepted in all cultures. Democratic ideals have also developed a broad intercivilizational appeal, again with variants and again with highly uneven levels of reception and institutionalization. The spirit of capitalism, in a number of variants, not all closely resembling Weber's description of the original Puritan-influenced type but generally complemented by beliefs legitimating economic innovation and market systems, has spread to many non-Western societies. Thus, core elements of modern civilization, despite cultural origins in a limited set of Western societies, have gained worldwide appeal, and their reception has often been significantly independent of previous cultural heritage. Biological evolution shows no parallel to this pattern of mobility of cultural elements across civilizations.

As a consequence of the intercivilizational mobility of cultural complexes, particular historic or modern civilizations have lacked unity of cultural heritage and experienced stress in attempting to create cultural traditions that can unify diverse populations. The Roman Empire underwent an extreme degree of such stress, and many contemporary societies also struggle with multiple currents of culture. In replacing the gene as a controlling factor in development, the symbol has imparted mobility and flexibility to cultural combinations that, whatever the adaptive advantages, also bring stress. This flexibility and consequent stress are now features of the human condition that contrast with processes of biological evolution.

It is said that a chicken is an egg's way of making another egg—of reproducing its genetic material. By contrast, society, because of the "Lamarckian" nature of symbol systems, is more than a symbol or culture's way of reproducing itself. Although there are strong tendencies toward maintenance of culture, societies produce new cultural patterns and pass them on to succeeding generations indefinite in number. Action is less conservative than biology, and sociocultural change is not limited to mechanisms of natural selection. In the context of the human-condition paradigm, we see that the human organism, given its dependence on and interpenetration with an action system, is adapted for change to a degree not true of other species.

DARWINIAN EVOLUTION AND THE THEORY OF SOCIAL CHANGE

Ernst Mayr has explained that confusions over the nature of evolutionary theory have origins in the complexity of Darwin's argument (Mayr 1991). He suggests (36–37) that Darwin proposed not a unitary theory but a "conceptual framework" within which five independent theoretical elements can be distinguished:

1. Evolution itself, or the theory that life is not constant or cycling, but steadily changing and very ancient in origin
2. Common descent, or the theory that all life forms, despite their great diversity, are descended from "a single origin of life on earth"
3. Multiplication of species, or the theory that species divide into "daughter species" or bud off into "geographically isolated founder populations that evolve into new species"
4. Gradualism, or the theory that species evolve into new species through "gradual change of populations," not by sudden appearances of new types of individuals
5. Natural selection, or the theory that evolutionary change occurs through abundant variation in genetic makeup of individuals and that only the individuals with "a particularly well-adapted combination of inheritable characters give rise to the next generation"

Mayr goes on to argue that it is the element of natural selection that truly distinguishes Darwin's conceptual scheme from the theories of Jean-Baptiste Lamarck, Herbert Spencer, Ernst Haeckel, Thomas H. Huxley, Thomas Hunt Morgan, and other influential biologists who struggled to understand the variety of species but did not achieve an authentically evolutionary understanding. Natural selection was also the central conceptual element around which the mid-twentieth-century neo-Darwinian synthesis was developed by George Gaylord Simpson (1949, 1953), Theodosius Dobzhansky (1962), and Mayr himself (1963). It provides the dynamic connection between the "central dogma" of molecular biology, namely, that DNA and RNA direct protein synthesis, but proteins and the information they carry "are not translated back into nucleic acids" (Mayr 1991, 150), and recent evolutionary theory. Natural selection is the summary account of the dynamic processes by which genetic variation is shaped into the branching of life forms that we call speciation.

Parsons was familiar with key writings of Simpson, Dobzhansky, and Mayr, and he cited them. He understood the centrality of natural selection to modern evolutionary biology. Yet his writings on social evolution concentrated on developing a broad taxonomy of societies based, as we have seen, on a conception of stages. His attention to variation within stages acknowledged the sociological equivalent of multiplication of species, but, as we have noted, the logical relationship between stages and variation in his scheme differs from that in evolutionary biology. He defined his stages not by tracing specific paths of societal formation, comparable to speciation, but by making broad generalizations about societies with multiple historical origins. Where the evolutionary biologist analyzes the branching of a given species into two or more through changes in a particular genetic heritage, Parsons analyzes parallel institutional developments across multiple societies within a stage type or in transformations from one stage type to another.

We must now ask, does Parsons's treatment of development *in particular societies* follow the model of evolutionary theory? Perhaps by looking beyond the stage types we can find a more direct parallel to biological evolution in his analysis of particular societies. Here, we examine processes of change within or transformation of the institutional order of a particular society, which may be a different matter than speciation as treated in biology. When Parsons (1971) discusses the change brought about in eighteenth- and nineteenth-century British society by the Industrial Revolution, for example, he addresses a massive process of social change, one central to an "evolutionary" advance in the terms of his stage schema. However, it was a type of change different in form from the emergence of, say, a new species of primate. The extent to which a particular society in a particular stage can change at the level of institutional order without becoming a distinct society may be a marker of differences between action and biological systems, and hence of the inapplicability of evolutionary theory, strictly construed, to societal change.

We may also ask whether there is an essential parallel between Parsons's paradigm of the four dimensions of social change and the processes of natural selection? The paradigm of social change addresses the ways in which change in specific institutions affects the overall "adaptedness" of an institutional order or society, as illustrated, again, by Parsons's analysis of the differentiation between household and manufactory in the Industrial Revolution. However, this analysis, too, differs from natural selection in structure of explanation. Explanation of change through natural selection begins with a range of genetic variation and then examines the resulting changes in the phenotypic characters of individuals that, within given environments, may lead to greater or lesser rates of survival to reproduction. Parsons's analysis of change starts with an action system's general analogue of genetic variation, emergence of new values, only in certain cases (see Smelser 1963; Gould 1987), such as the broad change precipitated by the Reformation. More frequently, change is initiated by efforts to modify much more specific institutions. Stabilizing the change generally follows improved functioning on the part of the newly formed institution and thus firmer maintenance of the broader social structure. However, Parsons's paradigm addresses changes in institutions as components of social systems. It does not directly address characters of individuals or their "fitness." The social changes are treated as direct effects on social systems, not, as with changes in species, indirect effects of different rates of reproduction in a larger population among individuals with different characters.

Finally, the basic consideration is that dynamic processes of action systems cannot be analyzed in the terms of a conceptual scheme designed to address biological realities. To be sure, there are certain broad continuities between biological and action systems, and it is appropriate for social science to adapt concepts that have proved valuable in biology. Concepts of complex systems, homeostasis, function, cybernetic control, teleonomic mechanisms, and feedback processes are ideas that Parsons used and that have useful applications in sociology as in biology (Parsons 1977, chapter 5). Yet Parsons adapted such concepts from biology and other sciences in highly flexible ways that articulate with insights of previous sociological thought. His treatment of the cybernetic properties of action systems, for example, was simultaneously true to Wiener's (1948) basic insight, Max Weber's comparative sociology, and his own previous treatments of normative regulation of the give and take of practical interests. Similarly, his use of the concept of evolution drew not only on biology but, more directly, on his own previous analyses of change in social systems. His evolutionary theory continued to emphasize characteristics of social life, including meaning, voluntaristic decision making, goal-oriented action, and the motivational energy expended in action, that cannot be accommodated in biological theory. These characteristics are, as Parsons's later paradigm of the human condition emphasized, emergent properties of action systems that set them apart from the domain of phenomena addressed by biology, including evolutionary theory. His analyses of social evolution take account of the "Lamarckian" features of social action that set it apart from biological systems and prevent a theory of natural selection from capturing its essential dynamics.

Evolutionary biology applies to the human condition, as does the theory of action. What is only now beginning to emerge is an evolutionary biology that includes an open conceptual boundary where it can articulate with social-scientific analyses of action systems, thus contributing to a more comprehensive understanding of humankind. Works such as David Sloan Wilson's *Darwin's Cathedral* (2002) have just opened that boundary of evolutionary thought. However, the social science with which a future evolutionary biology will articulate must, as Parsons's work has done, represent essential qualities of action systems, not reduce them to biological phenomena, as did Edward O. Wilson in his *Sociobiology* (1975), a work that disappointed Parsons (see his critical comment in Parsons 1978, 411 n. 122). To assume their proper role in interdisciplinary exchange, sociologists should follow the substance of Parsons's comparative institutional sociology, but avoid conflating its concepts with those of evolutionary biology, which are not suited to the phenomena of social action.

CONCLUSION

In his writings on social evolution, Parsons challenged a relativism common to the social sciences in the decades following World War II, a relativism based on an insistence, as he used to phrase the premise, that all societies have been created equal. Parsons demonstrated the fundamental importance of the growth of institutional complexity and greater adaptive capacity in human social history. By using the term "evolution," he emphasized broad continuities between biological and social development. In the background was his long-term commitment to adapting functional concepts from biology to the needs of sociological theory. As I have tried to underscore, his typology for analyzing long-term macrosocial trends toward greater institutional complexity represents a major synthesis in comparative sociology. The integration of stage concepts with a common framework, rooted in the four-function paradigm, for analyzing institutional orders across levels of societal complexity is the crux of this achievement. After thirty years, the stage schema remains, I believe, a vital starting point for research in comparative macrosocial analysis.

As the human-condition paradigm leads us to expect, human biology and human social action are closely related. The interpenetration of mind and brain is one example of the many ways in which the human condition is an outgrowth of biological evolution. Just as fundamentally, all human populations require institutionally ordered social organization to sustain life and achieve reproduction. Moreover, macrosocial change affects the evolution of human populations. Growth in scale, complexity, and demographic density of societies changes the workings of natural selection in shaping human populations. The rise of larger-scale civilizations after the axial age initiated biological as well as social adaptations, including relationships with other living species, from domesticated animals to cultivated plants to infectious microbes.

Despite these examples of the interdependence between social and biological factors in the human condition, Parsons's theory of "social evolution" addressed different issues. His typology of stages and paradigm of social change were intended, together, to provide an encompassing causal analysis of the major qualitative changes in the institutional organization and functioning of human societies throughout history. I have tried to show that the form and logic of his analysis are not consistent with the conceptual framework of evolution in Darwinian biology.

My critique has focused on Parsons's claim that the stage concepts constitute a scheme of social evolution. I have argued that the paradigm of the human condition enables us to discern in principle a number of difficulties with his claim. First, the claim to a degree overrides the distinction between action systems and biological systems, a distinction that is basic to the human-condition paradigm. The two classes of system are distinct in constitution and accordingly require differently framed explanatory theories. That both systems can be analyzed with concepts of function should not obscure the fundamental distinction between living and acting, organic-metabolic and symbolic-generative, systems, especially as the ideas of function used in biology and in sociology are different.

Second, Parsons's theory of the dynamics of social change differs in several ways from the Darwinian theory of genetic variation and natural selection. In describing the four dimensions of change, Parsons outlined a process that appears more flexible and highly varied than the dynamics of natural selection. Future work should amplify our understanding of this process, not seek to constrain its analysis toward the simpler dynamic of natural selection.

Third, Parsons's stage concepts have a fundamentally different empirical status than the categories biologists use to group species. They are synthetic categories created by drawing together careful analyses of levels of institutional complexity among societies that in essential cases are unrelated in their histories and traditions, for example, the Egyptian, early Indus, and Mayan archaic civilizations. The category of archaic civilizations does *not* represent a set of societies that have evolved out of a common heritage, as is true in biology of such categories as reptiles, dinosaurs, or mammals. In this literal respect, it is a comparative, not an evolutionary, concept. The same consideration applies to all of Parsons's stage concepts.

How, then, should we refer to studies that analyze societies in terms of levels or stages of complexity and explore transitions between levels or stages? I suggest there are two answers to the question. Studies that detail the development of a particular society or culture over time should be characterized as social or cultural history, perhaps institutional history, when they focus on sectors such as religion, law, or the polity. They focus on continuities, changes, and adaptations or redirections of particular traditions and require grounding in "historicist" understanding of particular cultural and institutional frames. Studies that are comparative and cross-societal, cross-civilizational, or cross-epochal in focus should be characterized as developmental. They, too, require that the scholar command understanding of the cultural frames of particular "historical individuals," but the focus of analysis shifts to abstraction of developmental schemata from sets of particular cases. The crux of the analysis concerns definition of such matters as *levels* of development and differentiation, upgrading of resources, inclusion, and value generalization as dimensions of development. In these terms, it is to developmental analysis that Parsons made fundamental theoretical contributions in his writings under the rubric of "social evolution."

NOTES

1. In a recent paper, Harold J. Bershady and I (Lidz and Bershady 2005) argue that there are four essential premises regarding qualities of social action underlying Parsons's action frame of reference: that action has symbolic meaning; is voluntaristic; involves relations of ends to means and thus is goal-oriented; and entails expenditures of energy and motivation. Here, I simplify by focusing on the element of meaning with its more concrete indicator, symbolic process.
2. See previous note.
3. In a recent essay (Lidz 2001), I have argued that language should be treated as the common matrix from which developed all of the generalized symbolic media that Parsons identified. I also sought to demonstrate that uses of all of the media in social relationships and interaction remain in contemporary societies closely linked to uses of language.

REFERENCES

Barber, Bernard, ed. 1970. *L. J. Henderson on the Social System.* Chicago: University of Chicago Press.

Bellah, Robert N. 1970. *Beyond Belief: Essays on Religion in a Post-Traditional World.* New York: Harper & Row.

———. 2003. "The Ritual Roots of Society and Culture." In *Handbook for the Sociology of Religion,* edited by Michelle Dillon. New York: Cambridge University Press.

———. 2005. "Durkheim and Ritual." In *The Cambridge Companion to Durkheim,* edited by Jeffrey C. Alexander and Philip Smith. New York: Cambridge University Press.

Cannon, Walter B. 1932/1963. *The Wisdom of the Body.* New York: Norton.

Carneiro, Robert L. 2003. *Evolutionism in Cultural Anthropology; A Critical History.* New York: Perseus.

Childe, V. Gordon. 1951. *Social Evolution.* London: H. Schuman.

Chomsky, Noam. 1957. *Syntactic Structures.* The Hague: Mouton.

———. 1968. *Language and Mind.* New York: Harcourt Brace Jovanovich.

———. 1980. *Rules and Representations.* New York: Columbia University Press.

Damasio, Antonio. 1999. *The Feeling of What Happens: Body and Emotion in the Making of Consciousness.* New York: Harcourt Brace.

Dobzhansky, Theodosius. 1962. *Mankind Evolving: The Evolution of the Human Species.* New Haven: Yale University Press.

Durkheim, Émile. 1915. *The Elementary Forms of the Religious Life.* London: George Allen & Unwin.

Eisenstadt, Shmuel N. 1963. *The Political Systems of Empires.* New York: Free Press.

Emerson, Alfred E. 1956. "Homeostasis and Comparison of Systems." In *Toward a Unified Theory of Human Behavior: An Introduction to General Systems Theory,* edited by Roy Grinker. New York: Basic Books.

Flavell, John H. 1963. *The Developmental Psychology of Jean Piaget.* Princeton: Van Nostrand.

Frankfort, Henri. 1948. *Kingship and the Gods.* Chicago: University of Chicago Press.

Freud, Sigmund. 1938. *The Basic Writings of Sigmund Freud.* New York: Modern Library.

Gerhardt, Uta, ed. 1993. *Talcott Parsons on National Socialism.* New York: Aldine de Gruyter.

Goffman, Erving. 1963. *Stigma: Notes on the Management of Spoiled Identity.* Englewood Cliffs, N.J.: Prentice-Hall.

Gould, Mark. 1987. *Revolution in the Development of Capitalism: The Coming of the English Revolution.* Berkeley: University of California Press.

Halevy, Elie. 1924/1987. *A History of the English People in 1815.* London: Routledge & Kegan Paul.

Harris, Marvin. 1974. *Cows, Pigs, Wars, and Witches.* New York: Vintage.

Hauser, Marc D., Noam Chomsky, and W. Tecumseh Fitch. 2002. "The Faculty of Language: What Is It, Who Had It, and How Did It Evolve?" *Science* 298: 1569–79.

Henderson, Lawrence J. 1913/1958. *The Fitness of the Environment.* Boston: Beacon Press.

Hubert, Henri. 1934/1972. *The Greatness and Decline of the Celts.* New York: Benjamin Blom.

Jaspers, Karl. 1957/1962. "Socrates, Buddha, Confucius, Jesus." In *The Great Philosophers. Volume 1.* New York: Harcourt Brace & World.

Lenski, Gerhard. 1987. *Human Societies: An Introduction to Macrosociology.* 5th ed. New York: McGraw-Hill.

Lidz, Charles W., and Victor Lidz. 1976. "Piaget's Psychology of Intelligence and the Theory of Action." In *Explorations in General Theory in Social Science,* edited by Jan J. Loubser, Rainer C. Baum, Andrew Effrat, and Victor M. Lidz. New York: Free Press.

Lidz, Victor. 1976. "Introduction to part 2, General Action Analysis." In *Explorations in General Theory in Social Science,* edited by Jan Loubser, Rainer C. Baum, Andrew Effrat, and Victor M. Lidz. New York: Free Press.

———. 1979. "Secularization, Ethical Life, and Religion in Modern Societies." In *Religious Change and Continuity,* edited by H. M. Johnson. San Francisco: Jossey-Bass.

———. 1981. "Transformational Theory and the Internal Environment of Action Systems." In *Advances in Social Theory and Methodology,* edited by Karin Knorr-Cetina and Aaron V. Cicourel. London: Routledge & Kegan Paul.

———. 1989. "Founding Fathers and Party Leaders: America's Transition to the Democratic Social Condition." In *Social Class and Democratic Leadership: Essays in Honor of E. Digby Baltzell,* edited by Harold J. Bershady. Philadelphia: University of Pennsylvania Press.

———. 2000. "Talcott Parsons." In *The Blackwell Companion to Major Social Theorists,* edited by George Ritzer. Oxford: Blackwell.

———. 2001. "Language and the 'Family' of Generalized Symbolic Media." In *Talcott Parsons Today: His Theory and Legacy in Contemporary Sociology,* edited by A. Javier Treviño. New York: Rowman & Littlefield.

Lidz, Victor, and Harold J. Bershady. 2005. "Parsons's Tacit Metatheory." In *Action Theory: Methodological Studies,* edited by Helmut Staubmann. Münster: LIT Verlag.

Lidz, Victor, and Talcott Parsons, eds. 1972. *Readings on Premodern Societies.* Englewood Cliffs, N.J.: Prentice-Hall.

Mayr, Ernst. 1963. *Animal Species and Evolution.* Cambridge, Mass.: Harvard University Press.

———. 1991. *One Long Argument: Charles Darwin and the Genesis of Modern Evolutionary Thought.* Cambridge, Mass.: Harvard University Press.

Mead, G. H. 1934. *Mind, Self and Society.* Chicago: University of Chicago Press.

Miller, Perry. 1933. *Orthodoxy in Massachusetts.* Cambridge, Mass.: Harvard University Press.

———. 1961. *Errand into the Wilderness.* New York: Harper TorchBooks.

———. 1965. *Life of the Mind in America.* New York: Harcourt Brace Jovanovich.

Parsons, Talcott. 1937. *The Structure of Social Action.* New York: McGraw-Hill.

———. 1939 "Actor, Situation, and Normative Pattern." Unpublished paper. Papers of Talcott Parsons, Manuscripts of Articles and Essays, 1937–c. 1970. Box 1: Miscellaneous Manuscripts, 1937–38, HUG(FP) 42.45.4. Harvard University Archives. Published in German as *Aktor, Situation und normative Muster: Ein Essay zur Theorie sozialen Handelns,* Translated and edited by Harald Wenzel. 1986. Frankfurt: Suhrkamp.

———. 1949. *Essays in Sociological Theory: Pure and Applied.* New York: Free Press.

———. 1951. *The Social System.* New York: Free Press, 1951.

———. 1953. *Essays in Sociological Theory.* Revised edition. New York. Free Press.

———. 1961a. "General Introduction" to *Theories of Society,* edited by Talcott Parsons, Edward A. Shils, Kaspar D. Naegele, and Jesse R. Pitts. New York: Free Press.

———. 1961b. "Some Considerations on the Theory of Social Change." *Rural Sociology* 26(3): 219–39.

———. 1964. *Social Structure and Personality.* New York: Free Press.

———. 1966. *Societies: Evolutionary and Comparative Perspectives.* Englewood Cliffs, N.J.: Prentice-Hall.

———. 1967. *Sociological Theory and Modern Society.* New York: Free Press.

———. 1969. *Politics and Social Structure.* New York: Free Press.

———. 1970. "Some Problems of General Theory in Sociology." In *Theoretical Sociology: Perspectives and Developments,* edited by John C. McKinney and Edward A. Tiryakian. New York: Appleton-Century-Crofts.

———. 1971. *The System of Modern Societies.* Englewood Cliffs, N.J.: Prentice-Hall.

———. 1977. *Social Systems and the Evolution of Action Theory.* New York: Free Press.

———. 1978. *Action Theory and the Human Condition.* New York: Free Press.

———. 1979. "The American Societal Community." Unpublished manuscript. Papers of Talcott Parsons, Toward an American Societal Community. Boxes 1 and 2, HUG(FP) 42.45.1, HUG(FP) 42.45.2. Harvard University Archives.

———. 1953/1986. *The Marshall Lectures: The Integration of Economic and Sociological Theory,* edited by Richard Swedberg. Department of Sociology Research Reports. Uppsala, Sweden: Uppsala University, Department of Sociology.

———. 1991. *The Early Essays,* edited by Charles Camic. Chicago: University of Chicago Press.

Parsons, Talcott, and Robert F. Bales. 1955. *Family, Socialization and Interaction Process.* New York: Free Press.

Parsons, Talcott, Robert F. Bales, and Edward A. Shils. 1953. *Working Papers in the Theory of Action.* New York: Free Press.

Parsons, Talcott, and Gerald M. Platt. 1973. *The American University.* Cambridge, Mass.: Harvard University Press.

Parsons, Talcott, and Edward A. Shils, eds. 1951. *Toward a General Theory of Action.* Cambridge, Mass.: Harvard University Press.

Parsons, Talcott, Edward A. Shils, Kaspar D. Naegele, and Jesse R. Pitts, eds. 1961. *Theories of Society.* New York: Free Press.

Parsons, Talcott, and Neil J. Smelser. 1956. *Economy and Society.* New York: Free Press.

Piaget, Jean. 1952. *The Origins of Intelligence in the Child.* New York: International Universities Press.

Pinker, Stephen. 1994. *The Language Instinct: How the Mind Creates Language.* New York: Morrow.

Simpson, G. G. 1949. *The Meaning of Evolution.* New Haven: Yale University Press.

———. 1953. *The Major Features of Evolution.* New York: Columbia University Press.

Smelser, Neil J. 1959. *Social Change in the Industrial Revolution.* Chicago: University of Chicago Press.

———. 1963. *The Theory of Collective Behavior.* New York: Free Press.

Steward, Julian H. 1953. "Evolution and Process." In *Anthropology Today,* edited by Alfred A. Kroeber. Chicago: University of Chicago Press.

Thompson, E. P. 1963. *The Making of the English Working Class.* New York: Random House.

Turner, Jonathan H. 2003. *Human Institutions: A Theory of Societal Evolution.* New York: Rowman & Littlefield.

Warner, W. Lloyd. 1937. *A Black Civilization.* New York: Harper.

Watson, James D. 1965. *Molecular Biology of the Gene.* New York: Benjamin.

Weber, Max. 1930/1958. *The Protestant Ethic and the Spirit of Capitalism.* Translated by Talcott Parsons. London: Allen and Unwin; New York: Scribner's.

———. 1920/1947. *The Theory of Economic and Social Organization.* Oxford: Oxford University Press.

———. 1922/1963. *The Sociology of Religion.* Boston: Beacon Press.

———. 1930/1976. *The Agrarian Sociology of Ancient Civilizations.* London: NLB.

White, Leslie A. 1949. *The Science of Culture: A Study of Man and Civilization.* New York: Grove Press.

———. 1959. *The Evolution of Culture: The Development of Civilization to the Fall of Rome.* New York: McGraw-Hill.

Wiener, Norbert. 1948. *Cybernetics, or Control and Communication in the Animal and the Machine.* New York: John Wiley.

Wilson, David Sloan. 2002. *Darwin's Cathedral: Evolution, Religion, and the Nature of Society.* Chicago: University of Chicago Press.

Wilson, Edward O. 1975. *Sociobiology: The New Synthesis.* Cambridge, Mass.: Harvard University Press.

Zerubavel, Eviatar. 1981. *Hidden Rhythms: Schedules and Calendars in Social Life.* Chicago: University of Chicago Press.

Index

Boldface numbers refer to figures and tables.